HISTORY OF MANKIND

CULTURAL AND SCIENTIFIC DEVELOPMENT

VOLUME IV

By LOUIS GOTTSCHALK

LOREN C. MacKINNEY and EARL H. PRITCHARD

THE FOUNDATIONS OF THE MODERN WORLD

PART ONE

INTRODUCTION; THE POLITICAL, ECONOMIC
AND SOCIAL BACKGROUND—MAJOR RELIGIOUS
EVENTS—SOCIAL AND POLITICAL THOUGHT

*Prepared under the auspices and
with Financial Assistance of the
United Nations Educational Scientific and
Cultural Organization*

Editorial Consultants

Professor Roland Mousnier (Sorbonne), with the collaboration
of Professors Georges Canguilhem (Sorbonne), André Chastel
(Sorbonne), Alphonse Dupront (Sorbonne), Olivier Lacombe
(Sorbonne), Pierre Le Gentil (Sorbonne), Raymond Picard
(Sorbonne), Raymond Polin (Sorbonne) and Bertrand Gille
(University of Clermont-Ferrand).

PRINTED IN GREAT BRITAIN
in 11-pt. Plantin type
BY UNWIN BROTHERS LIMITED
WOKING AND LONDON

INTERNATIONAL COMMISSION
FOR A HISTORY OF THE SCIENTIFIC AND
CULTURAL DEVELOPMENT OF MANKIND

CORRESPONDING MEMBERS

Argentina
Dr R. Frondizi

Australia
Professor R. M. Crawford

Austria
Dr Karl Jettmar

Belgium
Professor Marcel Florkin
Professor Charles Manneback

Brazil
Professor Fernando de Azevedo
Professor Gilberto Freyre
Professor Sergio Buarque de Hollanda
Dr José Honorio Rodrigues

Burma
Dr Htin Aung

Canada
Professor Wilfred Cantwell Smith

Chile
Dr Ricardo Donoso

China
H.E. M. Ching Chi-yun

Colombia
Professor German Arciniegas
Professor Luis Martinez Delgado

Cuba
H.E. Dr J. Remos y Rubio
Dr. Sergio Aguirre Carreras
Dr. Julio Le Riverend Brussone

Denmark
Dr Kaj Birket-Smith

Egypt
Professor Aziz S. Atiya

France
Professor Julien Cain
Professor J. B. Duroselle
Professor C. Lévi-Strauss

Federal Republic of Germany
Dr Georg Eckert
Dr Hermann Heimpel

Honduras
H.E. Prof. Rafael Heliodoro Valle

India
Professor J. N. Banerjea
Dr Humayun Kabir
H.E. Sir Sarvepalli Radhakrishnan
Professor K. A. Nilakanta Sastri

Indonesia
Dr S. T. Alisjahbana
Professor M. Sardjito

Iran
Professor Ali-Asghar Hekmat

Iraq
Dr Abdul Aziz al-Duri

Israel
Professor B. Mazar

Italy
Professor Domenico Demarco
Professor Giacomo Devoto
R. P. Antonia Messineo

Japan
Professor Shigeki Kaizuka
Professor Suketoshi Yajima
Dr Seiichi Iwao
Professor Daisetz Suzuki

Lebanon
Emir Maurice Chehab
H.E. Dr Charles Malik

Mexico
Dr Alfonso Caso
Professor Samuel Ramos
Professor Daniel Cosio Villegas

Nepal
Professor Gókal Chand

Netherlands
Professor Dr R. Hooykaas
Dr Maria Rooseboom

New Zealand
Dr J. C. Beaglehole

Pakistan
Dr A. Halim
Dr I. H. Qureshi

Philippines
Professor Gabriel Bernardo

Senegal
H.E. M. L. S. Senghor

South Africa
Professor A. N. Pelzer

Spain
Professor Claudio Sanchez Albornoz
Professor Antonio Garcia Bellido
M. Ciriaco Pérez Bustamante
M. F. Cantera
Professor Emilio Garcia Gomez
Duke of Maura

Sweden
Professor Axel Boëthius

Switzerland
Dr Werner Kaegi
Professor Jean Piaget

Syria
H.E. Khalil Mardam Bey

Thailand
Prince Dhani Nivat

Turkey
H.E. Mehmed Fouad Köprülü

Union of Soviet Socialist Republics
Professor A. V. Artikhovski
Professor B. Kedrov
Professor Guber
Professor N. A. Figourovsky
Professor D. V. Sarabianov
Professor V. P. Zoubov
Professor N. A. Sidorova

United Kingdom
Dr Joseph Needham
Earl Russell

United States of America
Professor Eugene Anderson
Professor Salo W. Baron
Professor Norman Brown
Professor J. K. Fairbank
Professor Harold Fisher
Professor R. H. Gabriel
Professor Oscar Halecki
Dr C. W. de Kiewiet
Professor Martin R. P. McGuire
Professor H. W. Schneider
Professor Richard Shryock
Professor John Wilson

Uruguay
Professor Carlos M. Rama

HISTORY OF MANKIND
CULTURAL AND SCIENTIFIC DEVELOPMENT

AUTHORS' PREFACE

THE 'plan' of the *History of Mankind* adopted by the International Commission for a History of the Scientific and Cultural Development of Mankind, provided a blueprint for each volume[1] which was based upon the premise that, no matter how distinct the several cultures of the world might have been and may remain, they show a perceptible tendency to interchange one with another, so that in the course of time they will appear—to borrow a physiographical analogy—like a river system, each tributary rising from its own sources and running more or less independently for shorter or longer stretches but eventually (perhaps, if the world survives, only after centuries) merging to form a main stream, though without necessarily losing its own identity.

It was hoped that such a history of the scientific and cultural development of mankind would serve as a supplement to, perhaps even a substitute for, the so-called 'universal' histories which have appeared in considerable number, particularly since the eighteenth century—'so-called' because they were in fact, when not nationally oriented, histories of the world from a European or an American point of view.[2]

Volume IV was planned to trace the theme that the world's cultures developed from a stage around 1300 where mankind was largely dominated by a variety of religions in relatively isolated regions to a stage around 1775 where it was dominated largely by secular interests in increasingly interrelated regions. No significant contribution to culture, even if limited to a given time or area, was, so far as space and competence permitted, to go unmentioned and those contributions which had entered or might enter into the global diffusion of cultural achievements were to be given special consideration. Authors with such a purpose would be expected to avoid giving nearly all their space to European cultural developments and to give special attention to the lesser known achievements of non-European peoples that met the test.

The actual writing of Volume IV was entrusted to a team consisting of an author-editor, two associate author-editors, and six collaborators. The author-editor hoped at first to gather this team from all over the world, but practical considerations obliged him to limit the choice to specialists available in the author-editor's country. In the course of the work, and thanks to the procedures adopted by the International Commission, several hundred specialists scattered all over the globe have had a chance to read and criticize the several typescripts of this volume, and over sixty separate critics in fact did so.

Wherever the authors thought a criticism justified, they tried to meet it either by correcting or modifying their text, and wherever they thought they could not accept it, they informed the Secretariat of the International Commission why they could not, with a view toward having such disagreements mentioned at the disputed points in footnotes especially prepared to indicate the gist of such disputes.

In addition to the criticisms from all over the world the authors were able to exploit a series of articles published in the *Journal of World History*,[3] sometimes planned especially for their needs upon their solicitation and written by specialists from the culture under consideration.

In consequence of this international cooperation the typescript which was submitted to the French scholars who acted as the final editorial consultants for Volume IV was the product of at least four revisions and, for some parts, as many as seven. The helpfulness of this cooperation of scores of historians from all parts of the world was greater than the reader perhaps will detect, for a number of the errors and debatable statements they caught were corrected, leaving no need to mention the critic's comments in the footnotes. Those footnotes which survived were allowed to stand because they were regarded as sufficiently important supplementation, correction, or variant interpretation of the relevant text to justify the space required. In a few instances the authors felt constrained to reply to the consultant's observations and so affixed a rejoinder. They did so mostly where the critic had over-emphasized—in their opinion—the importance of his own specialty, coloured (as specialties tend to be) by focussing upon limited considerations, chrono-logical, departmental, ideological, national, regional, or denominational or combinations thereof. The critic who is a specialist in the history of music, for example, asks for more space for music and less for art; the specialist in Turkish art wants Turkish art to get more, and more favourable, attention; the economic determinist thinks too much emphasis is given to religious motivation; the Catholic critic believes the authors to be too positivistic or too Protestant, and vice-versa; the Asian historian contends that Europe has received far too much and Asia far too little wordage, and vice-versa; the historian of early science demands more pages for his centuries even at the expense of later centuries; the English critic complains that while we give too much detail about Henry the Navigator, we fail to mention that his mother was English; and so on. In cases like these, if we have responded at all, we have indicated that, no matter how justifiable the criticism, the purpose of the authors, in keeping with the philosophy which prompted the Inter-national Commission and which they subscribe to, was, so far as their competence permitted, to write a history of *mankind's* scientific and cultural development within a prescribed period (which, incidentally, everyone concerned recognized must in some regards be quite arbitrary) with special attention to the relative significance of developments and with special effort to lean over backward against their own regional, ideological, departmental, and other preferences. If we have knowingly sinned in any regard (if that be a sin), it is in our studied effort to render to the reader some account of the achievements of all known cultures in their contribution to the cultural and scientific development of mankind between the fourteenth century and 1775.

*   *   *

The authors' indebtedness to those who have provided texts, documents, ideas, corrigenda, and addenda is indicated elsewhere. Here we wish to express our gratitude also to the late Professor Ralph E. Turner and to Dr Guy S. Métraux. We owe to Professor Turner the original blue print of this volume. If we have departed from it to a considerable extent, it nevertheless served as our point of departure and as a criterion of the degree to which we were fulfilling the Commission's purpose. We are in debt to Dr Métraux and his staff not merely for the usual services of a secretariat but in addition for his assistance as an editor and critic of our text, as gatherer and editor of the illustrations in the volume, as editor (at least in part) of the articles in the *Journal of World History* which we have mined, and as editor of the footnotes which, having survived the process described above, are now at the end of each chapter of this volume.

Several foundations and libraries have also placed the author-editor in their debt. The Fulbright Commission, the Center for the Advanced Study of the Behavioral Sciences, the American Council of Learned Societies, and the Social Science Research Committee of the University of Chicago were among those that have at various times helped to provide the time, money, and assistance needed for his share in the writing and editing of Volume IV of the *History of Mankind*. The libraries of the University of Chicago, the University of Wisconsin, Cornell University, Kent State University, and Stanford University were among those whose resources he has exploited. To the staffs of these foundations and these libraries and to those that have aided the work of his associate author-editors and collaborators he wishes to present his apologies and thanks.

LOUIS GOTTSCHALK

NOTES

1. 'Plan of a History of the Scientific and Cultural Development of Mankind', *Journal of World History*, I, i (1953), pp. 223–38.

2. See *inter alia* Jean-Pierre Aguet, 'De quelques "Grands ensembles" historiques récents: Essai d'analyse historiographique', *Journal of World History*, VIII, iii (1964), pp. 395–425, and Louis Gottschalk, 'Projects and Concepts of World History in the Twentieth Century', International Committee of the Historical Sciences *Rapports*, IV (Vienna, 1965), pp. 5–19.

3. The *Journal of World History*, I–   (1953–   ), published by Les Editions de la Baconnière, Boudry-Neuchâtel, Switzerland, for the International Commission for a History of the Scientific and Cultural Development of Mankind, under the auspices of Unesco.

NOTE ON THE PREPARATION AND EDITORIAL TREATMENT OF VOLUME IV OF THE *HISTORY OF MANKIND*

THE original typescript of Volume IV of the *History of Mankind: Cultural and Scientific Development*, prepared by Professor Louis Gottschalk and his collaborators, was submitted in 1958 to the members of the International Commission for a History of the Scientific and Cultural Development of Mankind, to a group of specialists appointed by the President of the International Commission, and to the National Commissions for Unesco in the Member States of the Organization.

The International Commission received from these sources a considerable number of comments and suggestions about this text. The author-editor and his collaborators undertook to analyze these materials and, in so far as possible, to integrate them into the original typescript. The revised text was again submitted to a group of selected scholars whose comments enabled the preparation of the final version of Volume IV of the *History of Mankind: The Foundations of the Modern World, 1300–1775*.

★   ★   ★

The author-editor, Professor Louis Gottschalk, and his two associates, the late Professor Loren C. MacKinney, Kennan Professor of Medieval History, The University of North Carolina, and Professor Earl H. Pritchard, Professor of History and Chairman of Oriental Studies, The University of Arizona, benefited from the cooperation of various specialists in preparing the original manuscript of this Volume. The author-editor and the International Commission would like to acknowledge gratefully the collaboration of the following scholars:

George A. Foote, Associate Professor of History, Goucher College, Towson, Md., who wrote the first draft of many passages dealing with the history of Western science and technology.

The late Marshall G. S. Hodgson, Professor of History and Chairman of the Committee on Social Thought, University of Chicago, who prepared the materials on Islamic culture.

Samson B. Knoll, Dean of the Graduate Division and Head of the Department of History, Monterey Institute of Foreign Studies, Monterey, Calif., who was responsible for the preliminary drafts of the section on the development of religion and religious history in the West after 1500.

Earl E. Rosenthal, Associate Professor of Art, University of Chicago, who wrote most of the chapters on the development of art in Europe.

Karl J. Weintraub, Associate Professor of History and Chairman of the Committee on the History of Culture, University of Chicago, who prepared the pages concerning Western literary history, and collaborated in the elaboration of Chapter I and the Conclusion (Chapter XVII).

J. A. B. van Buitenen, Professor of South Asian Languages and Civilizations, University of Chicago, who aided the authors in the preparation of the passages on India and the Indian cultures.

Margit Varro, sometime Lecturer at Roosevelt University and the Illinois Institute of Technology, Chicago, who wrote on the history of music in Europe.

In addition, the Spanish National Commission for Unesco and the Institute of History of the Academy of Sciences of the Union of Soviet Socialist Republics provided for this volume original memoranda on certain questions. Professor

Gottschalk and his associates availed themselves freely of this valuable contribution, for which the International Commission would like to express its gratitude.

*   *   *

In revising the manuscript, the author-editor and his associates utilized the comments and suggestions of the following scholars:

Members of the International Commission for a History of the Scientific and Cultural Development of Mankind
> The late Professor E. J. Dijksterhuis (The Netherlands).
> Sir Julian Huxley, FRS (United Kingdom).
> Professor Erik Lönnroth (Sweden).
> Professor R. C. Majumdar (India).
> Professor Mario Praz (Italy).
> Professor C. K. Zurayk (Syria).

Corresponding Members of the International Commission
> Professor Oscar Halecki, Fordham University, New York.
> Professor R. Hooykaas, The Free University, Amsterdam.
> Dr Maria Rooseboom, National Museum of the History of Science, Leiden.
> Professor Nilakanta Sastri, Institute of Traditional Cultures, Madras.

Scholars Consulted by the International Commission
> Dr T. Althin, Technical Museum, Stockholm.
> Professor J. Bonfante, University of Turin.
> Professor Fernand Brunner, Université de Neuchatel.
> Professor Hermann Heimpel, Director, Max-Planck Institut für Geschichte, Goettingen (also Corresponding Member of the International Commission).
> Mr Eric E. Hirschler, Brooklyn College, New York.
> Professor Angulo Iñiguez, Director, Instituto 'Diego Velasquez', Madrid.
> Professor Hubert Jedin, University of Bonn.
> Professor F. H. Lawson, formerly of Oxford University.
> The late Professor J. M. Romein, Co-author, *History of Mankind*, Volume VI University of Amsterdam.
> Professor Raymond de Roover, Brooklyn College, New York.
> Mr Claude Secrétan, Université de Lausanne.
> Mr A. Stowers, Science Museum, London.
> Professor René Wellek, Yale University, New Haven, Connecticut.

Scholars Consulted by the National Commissions for UNESCO

Austria:	Professor Erna Patzelt, Institute of Cultural and Economic History, Vienna.
Czechoslovakia:	Professor J. Polišenský, Charles University, Prague.
	Dr František Kavka, Charles University, Prague.
France:	Professor Roland Mousnier, Faculté des Lettres (Sorbonne), Paris.
German Federal Republic:	Professor J. Derbolav, Institute of Education of the University of Bonn.
	Professor Friedrich Blume, Bonn.
	Dr Hans Schimank, University of Hamburg.
Hungary:	Professor László Makkai, Institute of History, Academy of Sciences of Hungary, Budapest.

Professor György Márkus, Institute of Philosophy, Budapest.
Professor Imre Révész, Academy of Sciences of Hungary, Budapest.
Dr Anna Zádor, Institute of the History of Art, Budapest.
Dr Jolán Zemplén, Technical University, Budapest.

Israel: Professor I. Katz, Kaplan School of Economics and Social Sciences, Hebrew University, Jerusalem.

Japan: Professor Suketoshi Yajima, Tokyo College of Sciences (also Corresponding Member of the International Commission).
Professor Naofusa Hirai, Kokugakuin University, Tokyo.

Lebanon: Professor David C. Gordon, American University, Beirut.

Norway: Dr Andreas Holmsen, University of Oslo.

Spain: Professor Emilio Lorenzo, University of Madrid.
Professor Luís Diéz del Corral, University of Madrid.
Professor Fernando Chueca Goitia, Madrid.

Turkey: Professor S. Kemal Yetkin, University of Ankara.
Professor Aydin Sayili, University of Ankara.
Professor Abidin Itil, University of Ankara.

*Union of
Soviet Socialist
Republics:*   Dr E. A. Belaiev, Institute of Oriental Studies, Moscow.
Professor I. U. Budovnits,
Professor A. N. Chistozvonov,
Dr N. M. Goldberg.
Professor A. N. Kuznetsov,
Dr E. V. Paevskaya,
Professor V. P. Zoubov (also Corresponding Member of the International Commission).

Viet-Nam: Dr Nguyen Dình Hoà, Faculty of Letters, University of Saigon.
Professor Truöng Búu Lâm, Saigon.

In addition, critical materials were made available by the Ministry of Education, Ceylon, the Indian National Commission for UNESCO, the United Kingdom National Commission for UNESCO, as well as by the Academy of Sciences of Bulgaria and the Polish National Commission for UNESCO.

The final text of Volume IV of the *History of Mankind* was submitted in 1966 to a group of scholars at the University of Paris (Sorbonne) for the preparation of editorial notes on various aspects of the text of the author-editors. Professor Roland Mousnier, Chairman of the Centre de Recherches sur la Civilisation de l'Europe moderne, presided over a panel which included Professor Georges Canguilhem, Professor André Chastel, Professor Alphonse Dupront, Professor Olivier Lacombe, Professor Pierre Le Gentil, Professor Raymond Picard, Professor Raymond Polin, and Professor Bertrand Gille (University of Clermont-Ferrand).

The editorial notes constitute an important addition to the volume; in some cases they complement sections of the text, in others they expand the point of view of the authors or provide a variant interpretation. In each instance, it will be seen, the authorship of the notes has been clearly indicated; these notes were prepared quite independently of the work of the authors and reflect the opinions of the critics. On certain questions, however, the author-editor and his colleagues have written rejoinders in which they explain their position. The editorial matter prepared by the author-editor has been printed in italics to distinguish it from the critics' comments. This material was edited by the Secretary-General of the International Commission.

* * *

Several of the French scholars who examined the text of Volume IV before publication have expressed some doubt whether the authors have employed the best possible arrangement for achieving a synthesis of the main cultural and scientific developments of the period under consideration, a period which marks the inception of modern cultural and scientific developments, achievements, institutions, and conventions. In order to illustrate their point of view (and before we present the authors'), we quote at length the comments of Professor Roland Mousnier on this subject:

'Concerning the composition of the book, we find an analytic plan in which each subject is studied in and of itself (e.g. mines, wood, hunting, fishing, trade) so that the subdivisions of each chapter look like a juxtaposition of descriptive passages, a series of dictionary articles. This is good as a means of ensuring that nothing is forgotten. But the links between the facts studied in each case and those considered in other categories are rarely shown clearly enough or even not shown at all. There is lacking a general view of all these human activities, their reciprocal actions and reactions, their relationships as variables and functions. Yet it is precisely the links between these activities which are the essential material of history and the aim of monographs.

'This failure to consider things as a whole has made it impossible, on the one hand, to distinguish types—types of societies, types of civilizations, types of states—and, on the other hand, to distinguish periods characterized by the predominance of certain types. The period from 1300 to 1775 is too often regarded as a whole with little difference from beginning to end. The movement and flow of time is too often lacking in this study of history. Would it not be possible, at any rate for Europe and possibly for the world as a whole, to single out a period from 1300 to 1450 (in which Europe was moving towards a scientific and technological capitalist civilization which created the axle rudder with hinged stern-post, borrowed the magnetic needle from the Chinese, disseminated the bill of exchange and capitalism, invented the system of crank-shaft, launched the caravel—a ship suited for long ocean voyages—improved rural tools and the tools of craftsmen and, with the great nominalists, inspired by William of Ockham, Jean Buridan, Albert of Saxony, Nicolas Oresme, began the great intellectual mutation of mankind, the creation of mathematical physics), a renaissance period from 1450 to 1650, and an Age of Enlightenment from 1650 to 1775? At the very least, an effort should have been made to determine a period, or periods, allowing for all the factors and all the aspects of civilizations.

'Finally the absence of any synthesis has made it impossible to establish hierarchies between civilizations, between peoples, and between states. These hierarchies could be established according to several very different criteria: the rôle played during a given period in the general movement of history, scientific creations and inventions, the intensity and quality of religious spirituality, etc. But it would seem to be the duty of the historian to establish such hierarchies, to constitute within orders of human activity various series of growing intensity and to distribute human groups at different levels. The authors of the book undoubtedly rejected any hierarchic structure because they confused the establishment of such series with value judgments and were reluctant to call into question the dignity of a given people or state. But nobody could take offence at such observations and, in any case, all civilizations, all regions of the globe, all peoples, all states have contributed in turn to the general advancement of mankind. Could anyone have felt injured if the authors had emphasized the preponderant rôle played by Europe in the constitution of modern science, in the religious, philosophic and political movement ? Such observations are also part of the historians' profession.'

Professor Louis Gottschalk and his associates, having considered Professor Roland Mousnier's strictures, wrote the following comment:

'Without denying the validity of Professor Mousnier's comments as one historian's approach to world history, the authors of Volume IV claim that, in part at least, they have conformed to his specifications and that in so far as they have departed from them, they did so in keeping with another equally justifiable concept of global history.

'Professor Mousnier, they take it, does not mean to imply that the names, developments, and periods he gives by way of illustration of his approach are not contained in their text; rather he means that individual regions, periods, etc., do not receive sufficient evaluation and characterization, and that the main interrelations among developments are not clearly enough delineated.

'On the matter of evaluation and characterization, the authors think they have assigned as much space and prominence as the chronological and geographical dimensions of their subject and physical manufacturing limitations of their book would permit to the cultural and scientific achievements which they judged worthy of selection. Of course, another team of authors would probably have made a different selection in some regards and with different relative emphasis, but that another selection might have been as good or perhaps better is debatable and, in any event, does not render theirs untenable.

'If their presentation sometimes leaves the interrelations between cultural developments obscure, as Professor Mousnier claims, it is probably because such is a more or less inevitable result of the topical arrangement which they, fully conscious of the risk, have nevertheless chosen for their presentation. They, and the International Commission as a whole, believed that the topical arrangement for a history of the cultural and scientific development of mankind, if it was not to centre upon a preferred continent, region, or culture, was preferable to a strictly chronological or geographical arrangement, since it would permit laying emphasis upon developments within the separate departments of culture and science, subordinating biographical, chronological, and geographical details to their place inside the larger subjects of the chapters. It is true that, thus the work of the same personality (Pascal, for example) may be discussed in several different contexts—as a physicist, a mathematician, a philosopher, a theologian, a man of letters, etc.—but they have tried to counterbalance this sort of vivesection by frequent cross-references and by numerous reminders that developments in a given field of endeavour depend upon developments in others, whether antecedent or concurrent.'

GUY S. MÉTRAUX
Secretary-General

CONTENTS
PART ONE

LIST OF MAPS

CHAPTER I

THE POLITICAL, ECONOMIC, AND SOCIAL BACKGROUND

NATIONAL DEVELOPMENTS (1300–1775)

THE political geography of the world of 1775 would have appeared relatively familiar to modern viewers of the generations before World War I. It revealed a few more or less extensive states in Eurasia roughly like those known in 1914—the Japanese, Chinese, Russian, Ottoman, and Habsburg empires. It showed vast colonial realms dominated by the Dutch, the Spanish, the Portuguese, and the British in southern and southeastern Asia, parts of Africa, and the Americas. It suggested in western Europe the national consolidation of Spain, Portugal, France, Great Britain, Holland, Denmark, and Sweden. The fragmentation of Germany and Italy might still have reminded the modern viewer of the confusing political systems of the Middle Ages, but even there feudal relationships had virtually broken down, and on their ruins more powerful and centralized states or consolidated dynastic realms had arisen. Although in 1775 borders frequently were vaguely defined, unsurveyed, or in dispute, the political affiliations of many areas were fairly discernible. Several different kinds of political entities existed. Among them were to be found sprawling but contiguous empires and Western colonial empires, ethnically unified states and kingdoms that bound ethnically divergent groups together by dynastic ties, crowded city states and tiny principalities, and tight or loose tribal organizations, while some peoples formed parts of greater states without having lost their sense of being separate nations, though temporarily suppressed or frustrated.

Compare that relative clarity of 1775 with the geographical situation in 1300. For one thing, in regions remote from the more advanced civilizations the tribal structure was probably a more prevalent type of political organization at the earlier date. In general, the tribe was a loosely organized unit in which the obligations of kinship were usually more important than governmental authority. The numerical strength of the tribes was comparatively small, and the areas in which they lived were sparsely populated—e.g. the semi-deserts of north central and south central Africa or central Asia, the prairies of central North America, the steppes of Siberia, the jungles of central Africa and southern America, and the island world of the Pacific Ocean. Often the demarcations of their holdings were provided by some protective topographical feature such as a wide river, a high mountain range, or a thick forest. In general, very little is known about the political history of these tribal peoples in 1300 except where they came into contact with more urban, literate, or civilized peoples such as the Aztecs and Incas, the Chinese and Hindus, or the Muslims and Christians, or where more recently anthropologists have provided some knowledge about their culture.

*   *   *

Tribal Peoples

At times some of these nomadic peoples played an important part in the political history of the higher civilizations. Such was the role of a semi-nomadic people, the Mongols of inner Asia, who, under the leadership of great chieftains like Kublai Khan (d. 1294), founded a new dynasty in China (the Yüan dynasty, 1260–1368). In its day the Mongolian Empire was the largest relatively consolidated realm of the world. It stretched from the Yellow to the Black Sea and from Mongolia to Vietnam (Annam). At its height it included not only Mongolia, Turkistan, and other central Asian areas, where the Mongols had originated, but also Tibet and China, which they now considered their major seat; and it nominally had the allegiance of Korea, the Tatar Empire of the Golden Horde, which included the areas around Moscow and Kiev, and the enormous Persian Empire of the Ilkhans, which reached between India and the Byzantine Empire. The Mongol Empire was not destined, however, to last many decades beyond 1300.

No political achievement comparable to the formation of the enormous Mongol realm was performed by tribal peoples during our period. Timur (the fabled Tamerlane) revived the Chagatai Mongol power at Samarqand in the last decades of the fourteenth century and created an ephemeral empire from Anatolia and the Sea of Azov to northern India in imitation of the original Mongols, but, except for his beautifying of Samarqand, his role was chiefly destructive. Between the end of the fourteenth and the beginning of the sixteenth century the Turkoman tribes of the Black Sheep and the White Sheep played a significant part in Persia's history, mostly by supplanting one another in control and by becoming enmeshed in military entanglements with the successors of Timur (the Timurids). And Tai and Shan tribes were involved in Siam and Burma during the early phases of our period. But Asia's history was not to centre on tribal peoples.

Of sub-Saharan Africa knowledge even for the greater realms of our period is derived chiefly from the incomplete accounts of Muslim and other travellers. Between 1300 and 1775 some of these lands had an arresting political history. In the Sudan region, exposed to Islamic penetration from the north, lived Negro tribal peoples that had developed a high culture, now generally called Sudanic. One of the Sudanic peoples that inhabited the upper valley of the Niger was sometimes called Mandingo, from the name of its area, Mandé. This people built up a Mandingo empire[1] (1238–1488) which by any criteria was huge and which reached its peak during the fourteenth century. This empire was known to Arab geographers as that of the Mali and its people as Malinké. Their most illustrious ruler, Mansa ('king') Musa (1307–32), won the submission of the neighbouring land of Songhai and its inhabitants, the Soninké, a Negro people to their north who had already made Timbuktu a great commercial centre and Gao an impressive capital. Amid these cities of grass huts Mansa Musa's architect Es-Saheli built enduring buildings of sundried brick. Musa made a pilgrimage to Mecca in 1324 with a vast retinue and established a probably deserved reputation for piety and charity.

In the fifteenth century the Mali empire was partly conquered and superseded by a Songhai empire (1488–1591), and with the rise of the Mande-speaking Bambara kingdoms on the Niger in the seventeenth century, the Mandingo empire of the Mali lost nearly all of its remaining power. The Songhai rulers meanwhile made Jenne their commercial capital and Timbuktu a renowned Islamic cultural centre with its own university and library. Mohammed Ture (d. 1528), the most famous of the Songhai kings, is sometimes called 'the Great'. He took the dynastic name of *Askia*, which seems to apply to his unacceptability ('he is not' or 'he shall not be') to his predecessors, and founded a line of Askias. He caught the attention of the entire Islamic world by his imposing retinue and generous alms upon a pilgrimage to Mecca. The prosperity of cities like Gao, Jenne, and Timbuktu attracted raiders—twice, for example, the Mossi of the Volta valley (1333 and 1477)—and they were conquered by the Muslims of Morocco in 1591–92. Although Timbuktu achieved independence again in the 1660's, their prosperity vanished.

Farther inland, among the Hausa people in the Lake Chad region, Kano, another Islamic city, then became the metropolis of the trans-Sahara trade. Even during the lifetime of Askia Mohammed, a confederation of city kingdoms of the Hausa tribe had begun to displace the Songhai dominion in its eastern reaches. At the end of the sixteenth century King Idris Alooma (1571–1603) of Bornu conquered Kano and most of the nearby areas and, provided with firearms by the Turks, founded the Kanem-Bornu empire. Invaded in its turn by its neighbours, this empire began to crumble by the end of the eighteenth century. The Bagirmi and Wadai kingdoms were foremost among its threatening neighbours.

Other African kingdoms burgeoned at different times during our period and continued beyond it. The absolute monarchs of Dahomey won notoriety for their human sacrifices and their Amazon warriors. A powerful Ashanti federation flourished in the early eighteenth century under King Osai Tutu. In the region now called Nigeria, the Yoruba empire and the Benin kingdom developed a non-Islamic culture that won the admiration of European explorers and flourished until the nineteenth century (see Chapter XII).

These sub-Saharan kingdoms and empires were generally Negroid in race and often Muslim in religion (see Chapter II). Their chief articles of commerce were salt, gold, ivory, and slaves. Some of them suffered greatly from Berber raids and conquests as well as from wars with one another. During our period, movement among the African peoples was particularly marked. Southward migrations and invasions of Hamitic-speaking Muslim peoples (including Tuaregs and Kabyles) took place in central Africa and west Sudan, while the Arabs pushed down the East African coast. In the southern half of the African continent peoples of Bantu origin (including Zulus and Kafirs), spreading for centuries from their original homeland in the Cameroons, reached from the mouth of the Congo east to Lake Tanganyika and from the vicinity of the Cape north to the Ogoue River and today occupy approximately a third or more of Africa. They built huge empires: the realm of the *Mwenemutapa* (or Monomotapa, as the ruler at the 'royal village', the Great Zimbabwe, was called by the Portuguese) flourished from the thirteenth to the eighteenth century in the Zambesi valley; their neighbours, the dynasty of the Changa-miras, created a rival stone-building culture within a state whose zenith came in the late sixteenth and early seventeenth century; the power of the Xosa-Kafirs rose to a high point under King Palo (d. 1775); and kings with the dynastic title of Mwata Yamwo founded a Luba-Linda kingdom that in the middle of the seventeenth century dominated the Angola–Congo region and remained strong until the close of the nineteenth century.

In the east central part of the African continent lay the ancient Ethiopian monarchy. Still retaining its Coptic Christian traditions, it was sometimes identified with the fabled land of Prester John. It constituted the most durable and cohesive state of sub-Saharan Africa. For a short while during the six-teenth century it established contact with the Portuguese, only to expel them as soon as differences developed over religious policies.

Contact with Europeans was generally more disastrous for tribal peoples than the continuing contact with other civilized peoples such as the Arabs. Conflict with Europeans usually ended in the subjugation, at times the eradication, of the tribes or in their gradual dispersion to the less habitable regions. Beginning in the sixteenth century, the Spanish subjugated the Philippines and the Marianas, the Portuguese and the Dutch some of the Malaysian archipelago. After 1450 much of sub-Saharan Africa's coastal regions passed step by step under the political and especially the commercial control of the Portuguese, Spanish, Dutch, British, and French. With the introduction of the plantation system in the Americas, Negro tribes of west Africa were with increasing frequency sought by slave-traders, and large numbers of Negroes, some already slaves and purchased, others brazenly kidnapped, were packed off to bondage in the New World. In our period, however, Europeans in Africa and Asia rarely went beyond their widely scattered coastal settlements. Russian expansion into central Asia and Siberia after the fifteenth century, since it went overland, was an exception to the general rule, and it was perhaps even more effective therefore in putting an end to the political, though not always the cultural, independence of many of the tribes encountered.

In America sensational, and often tragic, conflicts occurred between Europeans and Americans. The Spanish and the Portuguese established dominion not only over the highly civilized Incas, Chibchas, and Aztecs but also over many primitive Indian peoples. The Iberian rulers regarded the Indians as subjects. In the centuries that followed the initial conquests a number of tribes, especially those in *reducciones* (separated settlements) or in areas protected by missions, preserved their racial purity, but through inter-marriage with and economic dependence upon Whites, others were largely absorbed in a Latin-American melting-pot of peoples, and a few, especially in the Caribbean islands, were exterminated by war or disease.

The North American Indians of the Atlantic and Great Lakes region had a somewhat different fate. In the beginning these Indian tribes were regarded as sovereign states. In the areas of French domination they enjoyed a relatively peaceful co-existence with their new neighbours, chiefly because of the sparseness of French colonization and the French settler's readiness to make alliances with them. The British, Dutch, and Swedish settlers, however, with a driving hunger for land and a marked reluctance to mingle directly with the Indians, became embroiled in frequent and embittered wilderness warfare, in the course of which whole tribes were either extirpated or pushed farther and farther inland. Attempts at peaceful cooperation (such as those of Roger Williams in Connecticut and William Penn in Pennsylvania), though con-spicuous, were rare. The eastern coast of North America became largely a white man's country, while the displacement of the Indian and the Negro created problems that have remained thorny ones down to our own times.

*   *   *

Asian Empires

Before our period began, some regions had been organized at least nominally into states of vast dimensions. In the Far East the dominant political unit was the huge realm of China. Around this core were loosely grouped the more or less unified states of the Japanese Empire, the kingdoms of Korea and Vietnam, and to the north and northwest the tribal organizations of Manchu, Mongols, and Uighurs. The kingdoms of Burma, Cambodia, and Siam and the great island world of southeast Asia, all of which looked to India for cultural leadership, were united under the Javanese state of Singhasari. Several Muslim and Hindu kingdoms, some of them of enormous area, shared the Indian subcontinent. The Islamic states of the Middle East and the northern coast of Africa, though for a long time ruled by independent dynasties, had until 1258 owed a shadowy homage to the 'universal' caliphate of the Baghdad 'Abbāsids. In eastern Europe the Byzantine Empire was a direct descendant of imperial Rome, and in the West the myth of a Christendom united in a Holy Roman Empire was still a potent though troublesome factor, especially in the German lands. In the Americas the Aztecs, Chibchas, and Incas had also built great empires.

During the century roughly centring in the year 1300 some of these huge realms underwent tremendous turmoil and change. In Asia the great Mongol khans upset the established dynasties by imposing their vast dominion upon China and its empire. In the Malay island world the Javanese empire fell to pieces. The Muslims extended their sway almost throughout the Indian subcontinent but then broke up into several, though still strong, Islamic kingdoms. In the Middle East the existing political order was overthrown by other Mongol conquerors, and the 'Abbāsid caliphate disappeared. In western Europe intermittent fights for the allegiance of Christendom between emperor and pope reduced the theory of the universal theocratic empire to impotence.

These turbulent events in Eurasia brought a period of readjustment during which much of the state system familiar to moderns evolved. Some of the great empires revived while others were superseded by governments of a different structure. On the ruins of some arose ethnically cohesive states, while in others strong dynasties managed to hold together divergent peoples. Sometimes previously insignificant states developed into powerful ones. Some of these states, in the main on Europe's Atlantic seacoast, created great colonial empires. Some European peoples, however, not strong enough to cope with more powerful neighbours, failed to achieve independent status.

The most interesting, and in some respects the most significant, political development in Europe between 1300 and 1775 was the growth of the national state—that is to say, a country centred on a more or less unified linguistic group, a culturally homogeneous population, or a largely accepted government. Sometimes a people was or thought it was relatively 'pure' ethnically (e.g. the Great Russians of the early Muscovite realm, the Swedes, or the Portuguese) so that it could easily be formed into a cohesive state. Sometimes a common historical background or a common cultural tradition in religion, education, literature, customs, and institutions exercised such a persuasive power that peoples within its reach could readily feel as one on current issues and anticipate a common destiny. At other times geographic compactness and common interests of commerce and defence held together culturally divergent peoples, as for instance in Spain, Switzerland, or Great Britain. Yet compactness was not always decisive: Italy, though relatively compact geographically and kindred culturally, failed to form a unified state. Dynastic policies and leadership helped to achieve political cohesion in certain instances where divergent traditions might otherwise have proved obstacles to union—e.g. France (united by Valois and Bourbon), Burgundy (itself destined to disappear but part of which was to be the precursor of the Low Countries), and Russia (in the course of its expansion after c. 1400). During our period, when popular government, and hence the feeling of personal identification with national affairs, was at best nascent and in most places unknown, the decisive factor in creating patriotism and a sense of national cohesion usually was a transcendent loyalty to the ruling dynasty.

The Chinese people had the oldest continuous sense of political solidarity. Over the centuries it had developed a cohesive civilization that was able either to absorb or to expel invading conquerors, so that it never ceased to exist as a relatively homogeneous state. The Mongols, though failing to make China the core of a lasting Mongol empire, did succeed in establishing a branch of Chingiz Khan's family as a new dynasty on the Chinese throne (the Yüan dynasty, 1260–1368). In the course of time this dynasty became partly sinified and in any case put its dynastic interests ahead of those of the Mongols. The realm grew more unified than before, with some increase in territory to the north and southeast. The native Ming dynasty replaced the Mongol Yüan dynasty in 1368 but succumbed in turn (1644) to internal revolts and the invading Manchus from the north. Under the Manchus the realm remained a unified state and for a century and a half enjoyed prosperity. The Manchu dynasty continued to rule until the Chinese Revolution of 1911–12. It increased the empire by the inclusion of Manchuria (the Manchu homeland), the Amur area, Sinkiang, and Formosa (taken from the grandson of the pirate king Koxinga in 1683) and placed Tibet and Mongolia under China's supervision.

For many centuries before 1300 the Japanese had formed in their islands a nation with its own institutions, traditions, and culture, though it borrowed heavily from those of China. Notwithstanding internal divisions and devastating civil wars, the Japanese Empire had preserved its independence from Mongol attack (1274 and 1281). In the last quarter of the sixteenth century the great military leader Hideyoshi, with the help of Tokugawa Ieyasu, brought the internal wars to a conclusion. The Japanese then embarked on a programme of expansion. In 1592 and 1597 large-scale expeditions succeeded in seizing much of Korea, but the death of Hideyoshi and the drainage of resources induced the Japanese to give way before Korean naval power and the large Chinese armies that came in from the north. Ieyasu in 1603 founded the Tokugawa shogunate, a highly centralized regime which was to rule Japan in effect while the emperors remained nominal heads. Under Ieyasu Japanese traders ranged throughout eastern Asia and Japanese shipping rivalled Muslim and Christian in Chinese waters and the Indian Ocean. In the 1630's the shoguns, fearing Christianity and desiring to insure the stability of their regime, secluded Japan from other peoples, particularly Westerners, who in the sixteenth century had established footholds for trade and missions in the islands. After 1641 a small Dutch trading settlement on the closely guarded artificial island of Deshima near Nagasaki constituted the only contact with the Western world. Chinese traders also were permitted a limited access.

In addition to Japan, several states on the fringe of the Chinese colossus achieved a considerable degree of political unity. Korea, Vietnam, and the Tai kingdom of Siam (which arose in the fourteenth century) enjoyed local cohesion and virtual independence although sometimes recognizing a tributary relationship to the Chinese Empire. From the middle of the fourteenth to the middle of the sixteenth century, the Vijayanagar Empire of India remained a powerful Hindu state despite the conquest of north India by Muslim invaders. The Delhi sultanate, for all its ups and downs, was one of the most lasting states in Islamic annals. After 1500 the Muslim rulers at Delhi fashioned a strong, centrally administered state.

Another perdurable state of Asia was the Persian Empire. The cohesiveness of the ancient Persian culture had made that country a distinguishable area even during the centuries in which it had been part of the 'Abbāsid Caliphate. Since it was situated across the routes taken by the central Asiatic invaders on their way to the Near East, Persia suffered greatly for several centuries from a constant change of rulers. Various Turkish and Turkoman tribes, the Mongol Ilkhans, Kurds, Afghans, and the Timurids ruled Persia or parts of Persia at various times. When a greater measure of political stability returned to the Islamic world towards the end of the fifteenth century, a new dynasty, the Ṣafavids, succeeded, with the aid of a fresh combination of Turkish tribes, in establishing a new Persian Empire. The great Persian shahs of our period were 'Abbās the Great (1571–1629) and Nādir (1688–1747). The Persian Empire also became embroiled in religious conflicts resulting from the ancient division of Islam into Shi'ites and Sunnites; the Persians for the most part remained loyal Shī'ites (see Chapter II). The Persians' pride in their language (though some of them did not speak Persian), the glory of their cities (especially Isfahan, 'half the world'), their preferred version of the Islamic religion, their age-old cultural traditions, and their successful maintenance of political independence enabled them to attain a cohesive loyalty and political unity during our period, despite the rivalries of clans and tribes, the succession of dynasties, and the frequency of war with their neighbours.

To the northwest of Persia arose a state that was destined to become one of the greatest powers of modern history. Until the fifteenth century most of the area now known as Russia lay under the domination of a mixed Asian people led by Mongols and generally called Tatars. Beginning in the thirteenth century the Tatars invaded Russia in two waves—first the Golden Horde and then the White Horde. Their government was the Kipchak Khanate. In the fourteenth century the princes of Moscow began the lengthy process of shaking off Tatar suzerainty. In 1380 on the Kulikovo Plain the Russian princes, united behind Dimitri Donskoi (1350–89), grand prince of Moscow, defeated the Golden Horde in a battle sometimes said to have had no fewer than 300,000 participants. Thereafter, though Moscow was again threatened, the Tatar yoke grew weaker. Towards the end of the fifteenth century the suzerainty of the Golden Horde was ended, leaving small and disunited Tatar lands on the periphery of Russia.

East Europe

Meanwhile the princes of Moscow had initiated a systematic expansion to the north and west towards the Novgorod Republic, the Lithuanians, and the Poles and to the east towards Tatar Kazan. After the end of the Byzantine Caesars (see below), Ivan III (the Great) claimed, and Ivan IV (the Terrible) actually assumed, the title of *czar*, or *tsar*. The conquests of these two rulers extended Russia by 1580 approximately to the Dnieper Valley and the Gulf of Finland in the west, the White Sea in the north, the Ural Mountains and the Ural River in the east, and the Caspian Sea and the lands bordering on the Black Sea in the south. In the early decades of the seventeenth century Russia endured a period of serious internal strife occasioned by boyar rivalries and aggravated by peasant wars and foreign interventions ('the Time of Troubles'). The country recovered quickly, however, and throughout the century energetically settled the steppes of southern Russia and explored Siberia (see Chapter XIV). Peter the Great (1672–1725) continued the work of expansion, particularly to the northwest, and in a prolonged struggle known as the Great Northern War (1700–21) with the adventurous Swedish king Charles XII (1682–1718), Peter obtained an outlet to the Baltic Sea, founded St Petersburg, and made it his capital. He also sent armies to the south against the Ottoman Empire to gain an outlet to the Black Sea, but that aim was definitely accomplished only under Catherine the Great (1729–96). Before the close of her reign, Catherine reached much farther still in both directions, at the expense of the Polish kingdom and the Turks.

While the early expansion of the Moscovite state had meant a unification of the Great Russian peoples, the conquests of the tsars brought other ethnic groups into the empire. In some instances, these were (like the White Russians and Ukrainians) closely related to the Great Russians or other Slavic peoples (like the Poles), but they also included some Europeans (like Esthonians, Livonians, and Lithuanians) who were not Slavs, as well as Asians (like Tatars, Kazaks, Kalmuks, Bashkirs, and Siberian nomads). Russians moved into the newly won lands as explorers, farmers, land owners, administrators, and soldiers. Certain 'russifying' policies were pursued by the tsars, and institutions closely associated with the rulers, such as the Russian Orthodox Church, formed a cohesive force making the vast polyglot empire a more or less united country.

To the west of the growing Russian colossus lay the largest nominally united European country of the day—the union of Poles and Lithuanians. Both peoples had been separately subjected to the *Drang nach Osten*, the eastward push of Germans during the Middle Ages, but each finally succeeded in putting a halt to inroads by the Teutonic Knights, who had been particularly active in the German expansion along the Baltic Sea. At the same time, the Poles helped to stem the Mongol advances into Europe from the east. Until the fourteenth century Lithuania and Poland formed separate and loosely organized countries, in which the power of the duke of Lithuania and

B*

the king of Poland was seldom stronger than that of the great magnates, towns, or tribal chieftains. Yet the ruling classes were ardent patriots, particularly in Poland, and their patriotic spirit grew stronger as their neighbours became more threatening.

Early in our period the two peoples were politically federated. The Lithuanian state was much larger and at first tended to be the stronger partner, but later Polish power completely overshadowed a rapidly disintegrating Lithuania. Lithuania and Poland formed a personal union when Duke Jagiello of Lithuania married Queen Jadwiga of Poland (1386). The territories of this united realm extended deep into White Russia and the Ukraine and at its southern end reached close to the shores of the Black Sea. Military successes against the Teutonic Knights, particularly the crushing Battle of Tannenberg (1410), ended the *Drang nach Osten* and helped to establish the union's closer control over the shores of the Baltic. The conversion to Catholicism of the Lithuanians, the last European people to adopt Christianity, also promoted the unity of the state.

For all its bigness, the Polish–Lithuanian kingdom was weak. The monarch was elective, and so no strong dynasty was established. The nobles who elected him frequently manoeuvred with foreign powers and candidates. Moreover, each Polish noble acquired the power to veto legislation in the Polish diet (Sejm) by the right known as *liberum veto*, and so the centrifugal tendencies continued in Poland at the very time that centralization had begun to enhance dynastic strength in neighbouring lands.

Thus the very size of the Polish–Lithuanian union was a source of weakness rather than of strength. When Russia seriously began its westward expansion and the newly founded Ottoman Empire (see pp. 17–18) pushed beyond the Black Sea regions, the union's territory shrank. After 1500 the Poles encountered on their borders a host of new powers that were interested in taking Polish lands. The consolidating Habsburg empire prevented further Polish expansion immediately to the south. To the west and northwest the growing state of Brandenburg-Prussia threatened expansion eastward at the cost of Poland. To the north and northwest the Swedish kingdom during the seventeenth century established a dominant position on the Baltic coasts and frequently clashed with Poland over trade, territory, and dynastic issues. Moments of greatness, exhibited in such feats as the daring Polish expedition into Russia (1607–09) and the valiant service rendered to western Christendom by King John Sobieski's rescue of Vienna (1683), did not suffice to save Poland from the encroachment of its neighbours. By the end of the seventeenth century Poland had become internally weak, and the Polish crown during the subsequent century became a pawn of various European powers. Although the map of Europe in 1772 still showed Poland as one of the largest continental states, it had not much longer to survive as such. That year it became the victim of its three most powerful neighbours, Russia, Prussia, and Austria. Despite Polish resistance, they took large parts of Poland's territories in the first of three partitions whereby, before the end of the eighteenth century, Poland became chiefly an historical memory and a patriotic cause.

Northern Europe

In northernmost Europe lived the Danes, Norwegians, and Swedes, whose similar languages, customs, and ethnical character might have served to unite them into one Scandinavian state. By 1300, however, they had been separate and independent kingdoms for nearly three hundred years. Dynastic inter-marriage gave Denmark and Norway in 1375 a joint ruler, and in 1389 Queen Margaret, already regent of Denmark and Norway, succeeded in ousting an unpopular German ruler from Sweden. In 1397 at Kalmar she proclaimed her nearest kinsman, Eric, king of all three realms. This so-called Union of Kalmar lasted nominally for well over a century, though punctuated by long periods of Swedish independence. In 1520 Sweden and Denmark–Norway separated definitively (see pp. 262–63). Finland, whose people were Swedish and Finnish, remained part of the Swedish kingdom.

Meanwhile, in 1450, Denmark had concluded 'a perpetual union' with Norway, which was to last actually only until 1814. Denmark–Norway engaged in several important political conflicts during our period. Among them were the struggle by which the joint kingdom freed itself from the economic control of the North German Hansa (a remarkable economic league of towns about which more will be said later), the intervention under Christian IV on behalf of the German Protestants during the Thirty Years' War, and a series of wars with Sweden over control of the Sound, the main gateway from the North Sea to the Baltic. These conflicts assured Denmark–Norway of its independence.

Sweden, despite its very sparse population, was destined to be one of Europe's greatest powers during the seventeenth century. After consolidating its home territory, the Swedish house of Vasa began to expand along the shores of the Baltic. By 1617 Sweden had wrested Karelia, Ingria, Esthonia, and Livonia from the Russian Empire. Shortly afterwards, Swedish armies under King Gustavus Adolphus played a heroic role in the Thirty Years' War, marching hither and thither in Germany to aid the German Protestant cause. From this war Sweden emerged as the greatest of the northern powers, having acquired both an enviable military reputation and new Baltic posses-sions in Pomerania and at the mouth of the Elbe River. It was able to maintain and even to promote its Baltic domination against powers like Denmark and Poland, but at the beginning of the eighteenth century the rising states of Brandenburg–Prussia and Russia began to chip away its possessions. By military victories and diplomatic skill Brandenburg–Prussia annexed part of Pomerania, while Russia moved into the northeastern Baltic area. The defensive–offensive exploits of Sweden's young king Charles XII during the long Northern War (1700–21) took Swedish armies on romantic invasions deep into Poland and Russia, but they exhausted the home country. At the war's end Sweden lost nearly all its possessions south of Finland and thenceforth played only a minor role in European political affairs.

*   *   *

Western Europe

The most notable examples of the rising national state during our period were provided by three large western European countries (Britain, France, and Spain) and three small ones (Portugal, the Netherlands, and Switzerland). Except for the Netherlands, unification began in all these countries before 1300. Four (Britain, France, Spain, and Portugal) were created by strong dynasties.

Since the time of the Angevin kings the English monarch had been accumulating power in the British Isles. By 1300 England had an uncertain claim to most of eastern Ireland and a temporary suzerainty over Scotland. In 1301 an English prince for the first time took the title of prince of Wales, though Wales was not incorporated with England until 1536. Scotland regained its independence in 1314 at the Battle of Bannockburn and preserved it by a series of wars, usually in alliance with France, until final union with England through the accession of the house of Stuart to the English throne in 1603. A formal Act of Union in 1707, by uniting the parliaments of England and Scotland, created the United Kingdom of Great Britain. A pretender's rebellion in the middle of the eighteenth century was the United Kingdom's last serious domestic war outside Ireland; it ended in failure. English dominion over Ireland, though challenged on several occasions, was not firmly established until the eighteenth century, but the British Isles nevertheless remained a single strong state. It was essentially the United Kingdom of Great Britain and Ireland, although that name did not become official until the Act of Union with Ireland in 1801.

During this time England had not been exclusively an island power. From the times of its Norman and Angevin rulers it had inherited claims to large areas of western France and in 1300 still controlled the southwestern lands of Guyenne and Gascony. In a prolonged series of wars with France, the so-called Hundred Years' War (1337–1453), the English kings attempted to exert and even to expand their continental claims. On the death of their warrior-king Henry V, the English were actually in control of the northern half of France and still retained portions of the southwest. Joan of Arc's feats at Orleans, however, turned the tide in favour of the French (1428–29), and the English began to retreat. By 1453 they retained only a narrow strip opposite Dover, and even that remnant was surrendered in 1559. England thus lost its continental empire, but about the time that it was reduced to an island realm in Europe, its seamen set out to conquer one of the greatest colonial empires of all time.

The rise of France was interwoven with England's continental losses. It was in part the outcome of the long struggle of the Capetian monarchs to establish control over every vassal and province of the land. Their progress was impeded by English conquests during the Hundred Years' War but was resumed under Joan of Arc's leadership. In subsequent centuries the forces threatening to disrupt national unity were broken. The Duchy of Burgundy, which we shall encounter again and again as one of the richest, strongest, and most cultured states of Europe during the fifteenth century, was brought down by the machinations of the French king Louis XI (1461–83) and the ambitions of its own last duke, Charles the Bold. Thereafter France's principal source of danger, which felt in turn endangered by French advances, was the Austrian Habsburg dynasty, which not only ruled in the Austrian duchies, Bohemia, and Hungary but also regularly held the imperial title in the Holy Roman Empire and, until 1700, could count on a family alliance with Spain. France's northeastern border was consistently pushed farther towards the Rhine at the expense of the Habsburgs and the Holy Roman Empire; in a series of wars that continued until 1713 some important Flemish towns and fortresses passed into French hands. Meanwhile the particularism of the Huguenot (French Protestant) towns and the prouder nobles was ended, though only after serious religious and civil conflict. By the final decades of the seventeenth century France had become a unified and centralized state in which, despite continuing regional differences, all acknowledged allegiance to the same Bourbon dynasty.

Almost as soon as it had rid itself of its English conquerors, France asserted itself as a great power in international affairs and began to strive for what later came to be called its 'natural boundaries'. In the seventeenth century, guided by able kings or statesmen like Henry IV, Richelieu, Mazarin, and Louis XIV, it acquired important border territories in drawn-out conflicts. Beyond the threshold of its 'natural frontiers', however, France frequently ran into stolid opposition and had less success. In its Italian ventures it encountered the effective resistance of the Habsburgs, both Spanish and Austrian. The same foes, supported by the Dutch and the English, thwarted France's encroachments on the Spanish Netherlands (now Belgium) and the Rhineland. A bold attempt under Louis XIV to gain control of Spain through something resembling a personal union failed because of the coalition of Europe's great powers in the War of the Spanish Succession (1701–13).

If France's more ambitious projects of expansion came to naught, its statesmen, by an effective system of alliances, succeeded in preventing inroads on French territories. Against the encircling Habsburgs, France could always bring a Turkish, Polish, Prussian, or Swedish ally into the field, but when Prussia became a common danger to them both, the Bourbons and the Habsburgs contrived a 'diplomatic revolution' by becoming allies. Against England, Scotland and Spain served France as ready assistants. And, until the nineteenth century, by playing the many states within Germany and Italy against one another, France prevented the rise of strong united powers on its eastern and southeastern frontiers.

Until the thirteenth century the Iberian peninsula had been dominated by the Moors. Only in the more rugged, mountainous areas of the north did the Christian states of Portugal, Leon, Castile, Navarre, and Aragon succeed in preserving their independence. By 1300, led by the kingdoms of Castile and Aragon and the duchy of Portugal, they had succeeded in breaking the Muslim power, now confined to a section in the south around Granada. Portugal had become a united state, incorporating all the territory it was ever destined to hold in Europe. In the Battle of Aljubarrota (1385) the Portuguese decisively upheld their independence against the Castillians and, with the exception of a sixty-year period (1580–1640) in which Portugal was bound to Spain by a personal union, remained independent. Until the Napoleonic era Portugal's status as a unified nation was not again threatened. Meanwhile its tremendous colonial exploits carried Europe's influence to several other continents.

In the country that is now called Spain the founding of a unified nation was more gradual. After the Muslim possessions were reduced, the rest of the country remained a congeries of rival Christian kingdoms, but, as frequently happened elsewhere, dynastic alliances finally provided the answer to their disunity. Leon had already been merged with Castile in this way in the thirteenth century. In 1469 the heiress of the Castillian throne, Isabella, married Ferdinand, the heir of Aragon, and as the 'Catholic Kings', this royal couple laid the foundations of a unified Spain. They tied the country together by a stern programme of administrative and ecclesiastical reforms, conquered Granada, the only remaining Moorish state on Spanish soil, and by supporting Columbus's venture (see Chapter XIII) began a vast overseas empire. The Spain that they left to their successors retained its unity thereafter, though troubled at times by particularist tendencies. Jews and Moors, although they had lived in Spain for centuries, were eliminated by mass expulsions.

By the beginning of the sixteenth century, the calculated policy of Spain's rulers had made it a powerful and homogeneous state. Through further marriage alliances they gained possession also of two of Europe's richest areas, the Low Countries and northern Italy. In 1519 the man among whose many glittering titles was that of King of Spain as Charles I (1516–56), became also Emperor Charles V of the Holy Roman Empire. For a century thereafter Spanish forces not only dominated large parts of Europe but also protected it, standing off the Turks on land and sea. Spain managed to preserve its preponderance in Italy until the eighteenth century, but in northern Europe, where it served as the great protagonist of Catholicism, it was less successful. Despite its stubbornness in a war that lasted, on and off, for eighty years (1568–1648), it failed to subdue the insurgents of the northern Netherlands, aided at times by England. The failure to reimpose control upon the Dutch and to establish superiority over the English on the seas hastened the decline of Spain's political prestige. After 1700 it was generally considered a second-rate power, save for a brief resurgence under Charles III (1759–88).

Through the very struggle that marked Spain's decline the Dutch were forged into an independent, federated republic. Before some of them declared their independence from Spain (1581), the collection of 'provinces' known as the Netherlands or Low Countries had formed no united state, for their political allegiance was divided in most complicated ways. Nominally at least they were a part of the Holy Roman Empire, although certain provinces had stronger political ties with France. Furthermore, the various provinces were engaged in feuds with one another—Flanders and Holland over the possession of Zeeland; Holland, Friesland, and Utrecht over control of the Zuider Zee. In 1363 an event occurred that ultimately was to have significant consequences for the Low Countries. King John the Good of France conferred the Duchy of Burgundy on his son Philip the Bold, who subsequently, like many other medieval dynasts, increased the size of his realm by war, diplomacy, and marriage. Philip got possession of most of the Netherland provinces by marrying Margaret of Flanders. In the ensuing century the Burgundian possessions (now including the Low Countries) developed into one of the richest and most powerful realms of western Europe. But for the rash ambitions of Duke Charles the Bold of Burgundy (1433–77) it might have become an enduring Rhineland kingdom. Charles's overreaching was foiled, however, by his Swiss, French, and German rivals, and all that remained to the immediate heir of his once far-flung holdings was the Low Countries. Nevertheless, Charles's successors continued to make illustrious matches, and thus in 1515 one of them not only inherited the Habsburg domains of Austria as well as the Low Countries but also became King Charles I of Spain. This was the young man who, as already indicated, four years later was elected to the throne of the Holy Roman Empire. He was thenceforth generally known as Emperor Charles V.

Upon Charles's voluntary abdication, the Low Countries passed (1555) to his son Philip. Philip II, unlike his father, considered himself primarily a Spaniard. He soon had a major revolt on his hands, for he disregarded local privileges and customs, tried to suppress the Protestant heresy, and sought to confine the Low Countries within the Spanish orbit. In the Eighty Years' War already mentioned the Spanish managed to keep only the southern provinces (essentially present-day Belgium), while the northern provinces succeeded in winning their independence. They thus, along with the earlier examples of Switzerland and Bohemia, provided a modern precedent of successful revolt—in this case, largely middle-class—against a disowned monarchy.

Out of these northern provinces grew a remarkable little state. Notwithstanding its loose federal structure and diversity of interests, it became one of the most prosperous and powerful nations of seventeenth-century Europe. The new United Provinces, or Dutch Republic, had a hereditary 'semi-royal' stadholder who, when an effective leader, did much to hold the divergent provinces together. The Dutch Republic became a rich country, especially after its navigators discovered and claimed a vast colonial empire. It was perhaps the greatest naval power of the seventeenth century until it lost out to the English, although by that time the Dutch stadholder, William III, had become the king of England. Gradually thereafter its status as a world power declined. Yet, despite internal crises, it continued to provide a conspicuous example of how areas with diversified backgrounds and interests but with a common memory of a common fight for a common cause might form a strong national union.

Another remarkable example of a nation composed of almost autonomous units with greatly divergent interests was the Swiss Confederation. The sharp decline of the power of the Holy Roman Empire during the thirteenth century gave some of the Swiss cantons (originally only Uri, Schwyz, and Unterwalden) a chance to begin a long fight for independence and self-determination. By successful battles over three centuries they shook off the authority of the Habsburgs, Burgundy, and Savoy, and resisted the attempts of German emperors and French kings to control their mountain passes, which formed the main avenues between Italy and northern Europe. In the course of these wars, in which the Swiss won an impressive reputation for military prowess, other cantons joined the original three in a loose federation. A federal diet guaranteed a certain unity among them against foreign powers but left the major participating cantons with their different ethnic and linguistic populations almost completely autonomous. Despite numerous inter-cantonal wars, which increased in bitterness during the Reformation, when the country divided into Protestant and Catholic cantons, the federation held together.

* * *

Heterogeneous Empires

Dynastic centralization, though often resisted by feudal nobles and imposed upon unwilling populations, yet served as a major stage on the road to modern popular nationalism. In an era of relatively primitive methods of communication and transportation, the great empires, though also created and dominated by ambitious dynasts, were, by their very size and heterogeneity, generally less effective than the more compact realms in this nationalizing process.

The Mogul Empire of India was one of these overgrown dynastic creations. At the beginning of our period the vast sub-continent of India, approximately as large in area as western and central Europe combined and probably larger in population, had been inhabited by peoples (as we shall see in the chapters below that discuss religions and languages) that were no less varied than Europeans and no less divided among conflicting states. In 1300, the northern states were more or less controlled by the Muslim sultan of Delhi, Muslims were engaged in conquering the Deccan, and Muslim conquest of the

Dravidian Hindu far-south bade fair to succeed also until (*c.* 1335) it was stopped by the formation of the Vijayanagar kingdom. At the end of the fourteenth century, the Delhi empire lost its more southerly provinces to independent Muslim dynasties and then was shattered by Timur's thrust. Thereupon several rival sultans arose in north India. At the beginning of the sixteenth century, a descendant of Timur, Bābur, king of Ferghana, conqueror of Kabul, and thereby ruler of Afghanistan, began the conquest of India. From about 1525 to about 1750 the Mogul Empire, thus founded, united great bodies of Hindus and Muslims under the rule of one powerful house. The early Mogul princes Bābur and Akbar established their sway over a host of previously disunited principalities, and Mogul dominion reached its greatest extension with the incorporation of the southern parts of the Deccan into the empire by Aurangzīb, the last great ruler (1658–1707). The empire, tied together for over two centuries by effective military relations and a sound administration, was characterized at times by an extraordinarily tolerant religious policy, which permitted Hindus and Muslims to live peaceably together (see pp. 340–42). Its eventual collapse was due to a combination of circumstances, prominent among which were the reversal by Aurangzīb of the policy of tolerance, the ineffectiveness of the later Mogul rulers, invasions of the northern areas by Afghans and Persians, the independence movements of the Sikhs, the Marathas, and some of the southern states, and the development of an Indian commercial class in the great ports.

European activities were peripheral to Indian history for most of our period but had accumulating significance as time went on. The rivalry of the Portuguese, Dutch, French, and British for territorial and commercial advantages in India began in the seventeenth century and turned decisively in favour of the British when Robert Clive, at the head of the British East India Company's sepoy and European forces, routed a larger but disaffected Bengali army at Plassey in 1757. By that time, however, the Mogul Empire had already become a mere shadow of its earlier greatness. Indian nationalism was to develop only slowly in the ensuing centuries.

Two other great dynastic realms, the Habsburg and Turkish empires, were also far-flung, multinational states. Though they lasted as powerful international forces until the beginning of the twentieth century, their contribution to the growth of modern nationalism was different from India's, for they served as irritants and obstacles against which their minorities reacted.

For some time before 1300 a small Turkish state in northwestern Anatolia had served as a kind of frontier garrison at the border between the Seljuk Empire and the declining Byzantine realm. When the Seljuk Empire collapsed under the Mongol onslaught, these Turks began to expand westward. Under Ertogrul and his son Osman (1281–1326) they embarked upon a series of conquests that was to last for about three hundred years, resulting in an immense Osmanli (or Ottoman) Empire. The first conquests, chiefly at the expense of the Byzantine Empire, reached the Aegean shortly after 1300, and in 1354 the Turks made their first permanent settlement on the western side of the Dardanelles. Despite fierce resistance, they gained possession of Bulgaria and defeated the Serbians in the storied Battle of Kossovo (1389)— permitting them, however, until 1459 to preserve a semblance of sovereignty. By 1453, of all the once great Byzantine Empire, only the metropolis of Constantinople still withstood them, but that year it too succumbed.

After the besieging forces of Sultan Mehmet II (1451–81) conquered the city, it became the centre of the ever-expanding Ottoman realm. The conqueror now added to his empire not only Serbia but also Bosnia, Albania, Greece, Wallachia, and the land of the Crim Tatars, as well as the eastern parts of Anatolia. For a while the advances in Europe were halted and efforts were concentrated on the conquest of Upper Mesopotamia and the Mamlūk (Mameluke) realm in Egypt and Syria. For about two and three quarters centuries (1250–1517) the Mamlūks had ruled in Egypt, forcing the Crusaders out of Syria, withstanding the Mongols and Timur, and making Egypt one of Islam's most highly developed countries and Cairo one of its most beautiful cities. In 1517 Cairo surrendered to the Turks, and by 1520 the eastern Mediterranean was under Turkish rule.

That year the greatest of all Ottoman sultans, Sulaimān the Lawgiver, known in the West as 'the Magnificent' (1494–1566), came to the throne. Under him the empire was practically doubled. Most of the northern coast of Africa was either directly conquered or submitted to Ottoman suzerainty. Armenia and Mesopotamia to the Persian Gulf became Turkish provinces, and European Christendom had good reasons to grow apprehensive of the Turkish peril when Sulaimān's troops conquered Hungary (including Transylvania and Moldavia) and laid siege to Vienna.

Europe had not known such a vast contiguous empire since the great days of Rome, and gradually awakening to the danger, it began a counter-offensive. In 1571 a Christian league badly defeated the Turkish fleet at Lepanto in the greatest naval battle since Actium, but with relatively small results. Though control over the western Mediterranean stayed with the Spanish Habsburgs and their Italian allies, the Barbary States of the Maghrib (Tripoli, Tunis, Algeria, Morocco) made much of the sea unsafe until the eighteenth century. On the European continent also the Ottoman Empire reached the peak of its power. Its last great effort to push into the heart of the continent came to naught when in 1683 combined European armies, particularly the Poles under Sobieski, relieved the Turkish siege of Vienna. After that, the steady advances of Russian and Habsburg power systematically reduced the size of the Ottoman realm. By the end of the eighteenth century it was still an enormous empire but weakened internally by nationalist movements among its conquered peoples. The concessions made to Russia by the Treaty of Kuchuk Kainarja in 1774 foreshadowed that Turkey's decline would soon constitute the delicate international problem that came to be known as 'the Near East Question'.

The proud dynasty that held together the great Christian multinational state of our period originated in the modest Swiss castle of Habsburg. Count Rudolf of Habsburg (1218–91) started his family's aggrandizement by acquiring Austria, Styria, and Carniola and by establishing the precedent for choosing the Habsburg ruler as Holy Roman emperor. The Habsburgs first expanded westward, but, as we have seen, early lost control of the Swiss cantons. Until 1500 their realm was primarily an upper Danubian state. Through a fortunate series of marriages (already outlined) the House of Habsburg allied itself to Burgundy and Spain. Thus it happened that Charles of Burgundy became the ruler of the Netherlands when his father died, of Spain with its Italian and colonial possessions when his maternal grandfather died, and of Austria when his paternal grandfather died, and in 1519 he was elected emperor.

A few years before his death, Charles, baffled by the complications of ruling so vast a realm, abdicated and divided it between his son Philip and his brother Ferdinand. Ferdinand inherited the Austrian dominions and the family claim to the imperial title. Through this title, which remained in their hands until 1806 (with a brief interruption in 1742–45), the eastern branch of the Habsburgs exercised considerable control over central Europe. Their real power, however, rested upon their vast territories in the Danubian area. Back in 1526 when the king of Bohemia and Hungary, Louis II, perished in battle with the Turks at Mohacs, Ferdinand, his brother-in-law, had been elected king of Bohemia and had advanced a claim to the throne of Hungary that was disputed by both Turks and local rivals. After almost two centuries of warfare with the Turks over the rich plain of Hungary and Transylvania, the Habsburgs finally achieved (1718) complete domination of the middle Danube and its principal tributaries up to the borders of present-day Rumania. About the same time, in the partition that ended the War of the Spanish Succession, Austria acquired most of the formerly Spanish possessions in Italy and the Low Countries but soon lost all her Italian lands except Milan. Silesia, part of the Bohemian kingdom, was seized by Frederick II of Prussia in 1740, but by way of compensation the Habsburg realm was rounded out to the northeast by the acquisition of Galicia in the first Partition of Poland in 1772. Thus, by 1775 the Habsburg dynasty ruled over not only German-speaking Austria but also a vast realm of Czech, Slovak, Polish, Hungarian, Croat, Serbian, Rumanian, Italian, and Belgian peoples.[2]

*   *   *

Colonial Expansion

The type of political organization that consisted of a mother country and overseas settlements—i.e. the colonial empire—was not unknown before 1300, and with the global expansion of Europe's Atlantic nations after 1500, such empires became a familiar part of the international pattern. The forms of colonial possession varied a good deal. Some colonies consisted of areas in the Americas or Africa that were settled by Europeans themselves, as, for example, the Spanish in Mexico and the Rio de la Plata region, the Portuguese in Brazil, the Dutch in the Cape Colony, the French in the St Lawrence River valley, the English, the Dutch, and the Swedes along the Atlantic seaboard of North America, or the Spanish, the French, the English, the Dutch, and the Danes in the West Indies. In other instances, a small number of European conquerors imposed their rule upon a large indigenous population, gradually interbred with it, and thus eventually formed a new 'nation'. Interbreeding of this sort happened with the Spanish colonization of Mexico, Central and South America, and the Philippine Islands, and with the Portuguese colonization of Brazil and the Azores. In still other instances European traders, often employees of great, government-protected trading companies, gained within more or less civilized and sovereign states control over specified areas, to whose inhabitants they left a varying degree of autonomy so long as their own trading interests remained unaffected. Such control was established by the Portuguese in parts of India and the Indonesian archipelago, by the Dutch on Ceylon and in Malaysia (where they succeeded in largely eliminating Portuguese and British competition), and by the British in India (where they superseded without totally replacing the Portuguese and the French). (Map I.)

The Portuguese and Spanish monarchies were the first great modern colonizing powers. Seafarers in their service early understood oceanic explorations (see Chapter XIII) and staked out claims for their masters in the lands they discovered. In order to forestall fruitless competition on the American continents, the two Iberian countries twice (1493 and 1494) submitted their rival claims to papal arbitration. Accordingly, by the Treaty of Tordesillas (1494), the Spanish laid claim to all of America from the Gulf of Mexico to Cape Horn with the exception of Brazil, which was claimed by the Portuguese. Spanish conquerors, at times with amazingly small armies, overran the great realms of the Aztecs, the Chibchas, and the Incas, and won fabulously rich lands for the Spanish crown, reaching well into the areas that now form the south and southwest of the United States. In the Pacific Spanish conquests were limited to the Philippine Islands and other scattered archipelagoes. The Portuguese empire extended westward to the Azores and Brazil, southward to some coastal areas of west and east Africa, and thence to scattered trading settlements on the coast of India and to the Moluccas in southeastern Asia. These empires lasted, with some modifications, throughout our period.

If the papal division of the world could have been effectively upheld, other European powers might never have acquired new colonies. France, the United Provinces, and England, however, were at times engaged in war with Spain (which for a time, as already mentioned, included Portugal). Moreover, as Protestant countries, the United Provinces and England, paid little attention to papal lines of demarcation. Even before the English and Dutch defeat of

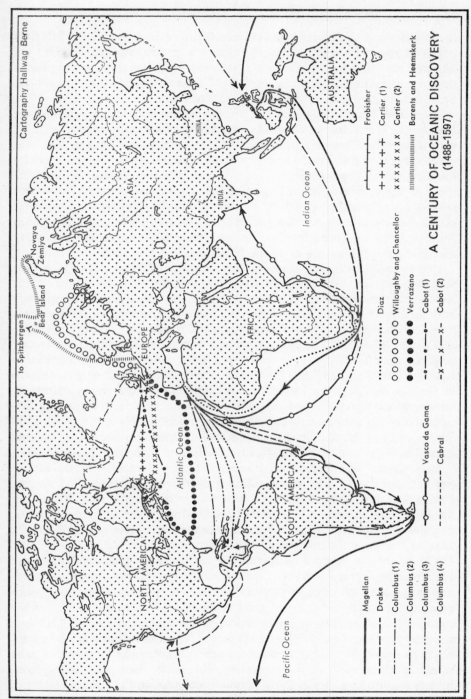

A CENTURY OF OCEANIC DISCOVERY
(1488-1597)

Magellan
Drake
Columbus (1)
Columbus (2)
Columbus (3)
Columbus (4)

Diaz
Willoughby and Chancellor
Verrazano
Cabot (1)
Cabot (2)

Vasco da Gama
Cabral

Frobisher
Cartier (1)
Cartier (2)
Barents and Heemskerk

Cartography Hallwag Berne

MAP I

Spain's 'Invincible Armada' in 1588, ships under French and English flags began to roam the seas looking for loot and empire, and the Dutch soon followed suit, obliging the Spanish to take extraordinary measures to protect their treasure fleets. In some instances, Spain's rivals made inroads on Spanish and Portuguese land possessions. (Map I.)

Thus the Dutch East India Company succeeded in supplanting the Portuguese in the Indian Ocean and founding a fabulously wealthy empire, with its centre at Batavia, in the East Indies, Ceylon, and Malaya. This was predominantly a commercial empire with less explicit political power than, for instance, that of the Spanish colonies. As a stopover on the long sea route to the East the Dutch acquired Cape Colony in 1652, the only major overseas area which Dutchmen settled extensively. In the Western Hemisphere they established themselves permanently in Dutch Guinea and some of the Lesser Antilles (Curaçao, Aruba, etc.), and for a while during the seventeenth century they had a flourishing colony in the Hudson valley.

France likewise engaged in several major colonizing enterprises. During the sixteenth century her explorers staked out claims to land on the North American continent. French settlers, missionaries, and garrisons gradually built an empire on both sides of the St Lawrence River system. They penetrated westward to the Great Lakes region and finally came to the wide rivers that run to the south. The Mississippi and its tributaries served as an avenue between their Canadian possessions and their semi-tropical settlement in Louisiana. In South America the French encroached upon Portuguese claims in Guiana. In the West Indies they managed to wrest some economically important islands from Spanish control. In the Eastern Hemisphere farsighted French seamen and military commanders established a foothold in Senegal, and by the middle of the eighteenth century they had begun to build an empire in the southeastern part of the Indian sub-continent. In a long series of wars, sometimes referred to as the Second Hundred Years' War, the French concentrated upon the European rather than the overseas issues, and by 1763 France lost her North American possessions to Britain and Spain. But Senegal, the islands in the West Indies and the Indian Ocean, French Guiana, and a few settlements in India remained to form the bases of a new French colonial empire in the nineteenth century.

The power that profited most from the decline of the Spanish, Dutch, and French colonial empires was the United Kingdom. Its first attempts at overseas expansion took place shortly before 1600 on the North American continent, and this was the scene of most of its efforts before the middle of the eighteenth century. Unlike the Spanish and the French, the English, though also making wide claims, followed a policy of 'effective settlement'. By means of patents granted to chartered companies and individual proprietors, who subsequently settled their territories with north European immigrants, Britain acquired a series of fairly populous colonies on the Atlantic seaboard of North America. Nearby enemy settlements, like those of the Dutch in New

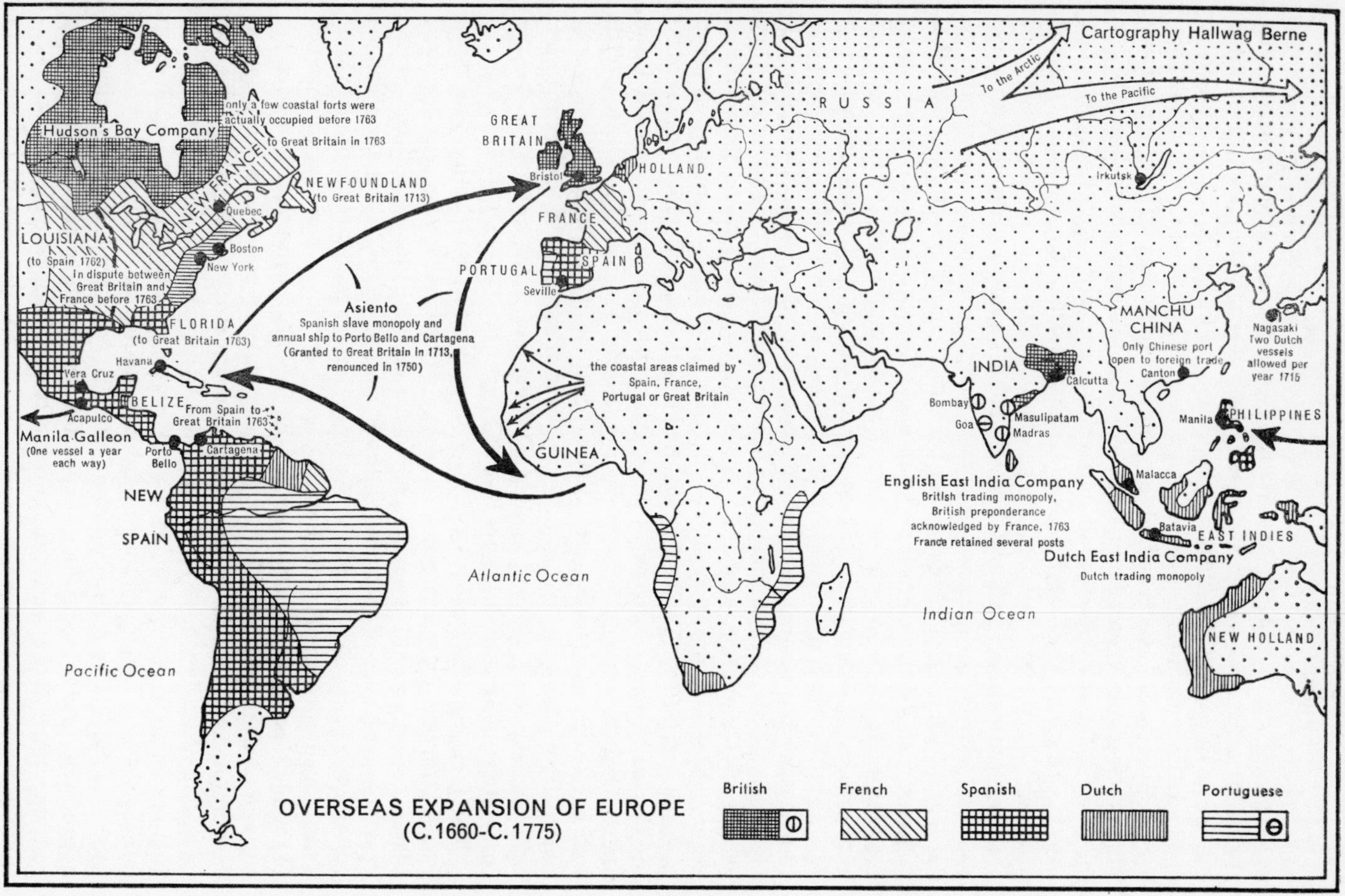

OVERSEAS EXPANSION OF EUROPE
(C. 1660–C. 1775)

MAP II

Cartography Hallwag Berne

Legend:

British | French | Spanish | Dutch | Portuguese

Hudson's Bay Company

NEWFOUNDLAND (to Great Britain 1713)

only a few coastal forts were actually occupied before 1763

GREAT BRITAIN

Bristol

LOUISIANA (to Spain 1762) In dispute between Great Britain and France before 1763

FRANCE before 1763

Quebec
Boston
New York

FLORIDA (to Great Britain 1763)

Havana

BELIZE From Spain to Great Britain 1763

NEW SPAIN

Vera Cruz
Acapulco
Porto Bello
Cartagena

Manila Galleon (One vessel a year each way)

Pacific Ocean

Asiento
Spanish slave monopoly and annual ship to Porto Bello and Cartagena (Granted to Great Britain in 1713, renounced in 1750)

FRANCE
PORTUGAL
SPAIN
Seville

the coastal areas claimed by Spain, France, Portugal or Great Britain

GUINEA

Atlantic Ocean

RUSSIA

To the Pacific

HOLLAND

Irkutsk

To the Pacific

MANCHU CHINA

Nagasaki Two Dutch vessels allowed per year 1715

Only Chinese port open to foreign trade Canton

PHILIPPINES

Manila

INDIA
Calcutta
Masulipatam
Madras
Bombay
Goa

Malacca

Batavia EAST INDIES

English East India Company
British trading monopoly, British preponderance acknowledged by France, 1763. France retained several posts

Dutch East India Company
Dutch trading monopoly

Indian Ocean

NEW HOLLAND

Amsterdam (now New York) and the French in Acadia (now Nova Scotia), were early brought under British control. A more serious obstacle in the path of further expansion was encountered in the French colonies to the north and northwest, but the British, supported by their American colonials, finally defeated the French. In campaigns between 1754 and 1763, the British became masters of Canada and all the continent to the east of the Mississippi. When their empire seemed safe, however, their own American colonies began the first great anti-colonial revolt in modern times, firing the shot that, if not then 'heard round the world', was to be heeded eventually by other colonial peoples.

In the East, the British and French colonial conflict centred upon their political jockeying in India. In the 1750's the British, primarily represented by the British East India Company, undertook a concerted effort to establish themselves on the sub-continent. Their major advance was in the north along the Ganges valley, where the decline of the Mogul power and the rivalry of local princes and officials played into their hands, but they also opposed and defeated the French effort to dominate the region known as the Deccan (south India). After the elimination of their major European foe, their meddling in the affairs of the Indian states was less impeded, and in the 1760's they became the dominant economic power among the Europeans in India. Malfeasance and mismanagement in the East India Company became notorious and in 1773 Parliament passed a Regulating Act, which proved to be the first in a series of measures designed to place British interests in India under the direction of the crown. By the close of our period the British were well ensconced in several provinces and had started on the road that was eventually to lead them to political control of that vast land, which, together with Canada, was, after the collapse of her American empire, to be the cornerstone of an immense new British Empire.

The great colonial powers of Europe were of necessity also its great naval powers, for the colonies consisted mostly of coastal regions and scattered islands. Specks on the map like St Helena or Mauritius constituted prized possessions because of their usefulness as marine stations in an era when sea voyages were long and hazardous. At times the powers quarrelled more about a little sugar-producing, slave-buying Caribbean island than about thousands of then less profitable square miles on the American continent. In Africa the rush for lands did not begin before 1870, and colonial possessions were limited to very narrow coastal strips. European settlements in India, with the exception of England's as yet quite tenuous push into the Ganges valley and France's temporary penetration of the Deccan, were during our period all in coastal towns. The Dutch penetration into the interior of the huge islands of their vast Malaysian realm also came later. Only where Europeans settled in appreciable numbers and then inched forward in the everlasting search for resources did colonies stretch into the hinterland. This kind of inland exploration was particularly characteristic of the colonies in the New World, and they proved the ones least amenable to the control of the mother-country and quickest to acquire national independence.

★   ★   ★

Local and Particularist Tendencies

During our period, several peoples of the world, for one reason or another, failed to achieve either dynastic cohesion or national independence. The most glaring examples of European peoples of this type were those of Italy and Germany. Both had once constituted powerful states and were destined to do so again; both made significant cultural contributions to the history of our period; yet until the nineteenth century, both remained divided into a number of little countries.

Some of the Italian states (for example, Venice, the Papal States, and Savoy) were of great antiquity, wealth, power, or spiritual importance. None of them seemed willing to relinquish any part of its sovereignty in favour of a unification of Italy, and their reluctance to unite was reinforced by foreign powers, like Spain, France, and Austria, which coveted or already had possession of some parts of the peninsula or were dynastically allied with some Italian prince. These powers proposed to prevent the rise of a united Italy that they might not be able to manipulate, and papal interests also tended to discourage the attainment of Italian unity under secular leadership.

Germany was even more thoroughly disunited. The number of German states was immense; in 1775 several hundred German principalities, ecclesiastical states, knighthoods, and towns were still more or less independent of each other. In theory at least, they constituted, all together, the Holy Roman Empire, but in fact the emperor was nearly powerless as such, and the Imperial Diet was an ineffective body. For all practical purposes, such as internal administration, taxation, and the conduct of foreign affairs, every prince of a large state was a sovereign, and the lesser princes likewise strove, usually with success, to be sovereign. With great difficulty an emperor might obtain military aid from some states for a campaign against a foreign foe like Turkey or France, but in general the brunt of these wars was borne by the emperor's own people, the Austrians, whose attention was frequently drawn away to Turkey, Italy, Poland, and other non-German areas. As a result of the Reformation, which failed to make Germany wholly Protestant, and of the Counter-Reformation, which failed to make it wholly Catholic, the division of the country was deepened. A series of civil conflicts aimed at creating greater religious unity, the Thirty Years' War (1618–48), brought foreign powers like Denmark, Spain, Sweden, and France into the country and left it exhausted, possibly retarding the development of nationalist sentiment for a century or more. In the eighteenth century, on foundations laid by the Great Elector of Brandenburg-Prussia, Frederick William (1620–88), and by King Frederick William I of Prussia (1688–1740), a strong, essentially German nation arose. The latter's son, Frederick II (1712–86), generally known as 'the Great', left Prussia a world power, whose interest would eventually point in the direction of German unity.

The peoples of India were divided, like those of Europe, by language, religion, and political loyalties, and, more than those of Europe, by a multiplicity of castes. In addition, foreign invasions were frequent, and neighbouring rulers, especially those of Afghanistan, encouraged intrigues and warfare among India's rival dynasties and states. Even after the Mogul conquest, unity, as we have seen, was precarious. Gujarat, for instance, was not conquered by Akbar until 1573. Bengal was taken from its Afghan princes only in 1576, and in 1765 it passed under the jurisdiction of the British East India Company. In 1674 the Marathas established a strong and independent state under Sivājī Raja (1627–80). Though it fell apart under his successor, who was captured by Aurangzīb, it survived to form the basis of the Mahratta States. In the eighteenth century the Marathas seemed ready to create a strong northern nation but were crushed by the Afghans and Persians under Ahmad Shah Durani in the Battle of Panipat (1761). Meanwhile, the Sikhs of the Punjab had developed from a religious community (c. 1500) into a militant people under their guru Govind Singh (1666–1708) and during the Mogul-Afghan wars of the eighteenth century succeeded in establishing a semi-independence of both Delhi and Kabul. In south India a vast Muslim realm, the Bahmani kingdom, vied through most of the fourteenth and fifteenth centuries with a vast Hindu realm, the Vijayanagar kingdom. At the end of the fifteenth century the Bahmani kingdom broke up into several independent viceroyalties, but they eventually combined, destroyed the capital city of Vijayanagar (1565), and liquidated its empire. The Bahmani successor states themselves finally were conquered in the seventeenth century by Aurangzīb. In the disruption which followed that emperor's death, the nizam of Hyderabad became the dominant ruler in the Deccan, but disputes among the nizam's successors gave the British and the French a chance to take opposing sides, with the results already suggested. Several Indian nationalities, like some European nationalities, were able to achieve a lasting political unity with a highly conscious cultural tradition. Thus, until divided by the British in the twentieth century, Bengal, even when part of larger empires, maintained its distinctive political personality. For all that, in India over-all unity among the conflicting nations appeared at times more attainable than in Europe because of the preponderant strength of a single ruler.

In Europe, several populations that once had formed or were in the course of time to form separate nations or peoples were after 1300 incorporated in the dynastic states. The Habsburgs and the Ottomans were masters, sometimes alternatively, of the countries of the Balkans and southeast Europe—Serbia (which for a time in the fourteenth century was itself a great independent empire), Bulgaria, Greece, Albania, Croatia, Rumania, Hungary (a powerful sovereign state until the Battle of Mohacs), and Bohemia (which, as Chapter

III will explain, until the 1430's successfully defied the German Catholic crusades that sought to crush her Hussite heresy). Castillians ruled over Catalonians and Andalusians; Frenchmen over Provençals and (later) Alsatians; Englishmen over Welsh and Irish. The Belgians changed masters about every hundred years. Norwegians were ruled by Danes, and Finns by Swedes. The big Russian realm swallowed up numerous ethnic groups distinctly separate from the Great Russians—among them Estonians, Letts, Tatars, and various Siberian tribes. In Spain, Moors were forcibly converted. Jews were unwanted wherever they went in their centuries-long history of suppression, segregation, and expulsion, mitigated by a limited toleration only toward the end of our era. Everywhere, and particularly in Rumania and Hungary, the Gypsies carried on their nomadic tradition apparently without desire to create a united Gypsy nation.

THE CENTRALIZATION OF POLITICAL POWER

The proper balance of central and local interests is a major political problem for all societies at all times. Of the few states that by 1300 had found a lasting answer to this problem, China, though one of the world's largest empires, was most conspicuous. It had established a fairly centralized bureaucratic government long before 1300, and the subsequent changes of dynasty hardly affected the traditional domestic structure. With the coming of the Manchus, government offices were reshuffled, but the general organization of the empire was maintained with provinces, prefectures, and districts headed by governors, prefects, and magistrates, who, in theory at least but not always in practice, acted upon directives from Peking and supervised the actions of officials subordinate to themselves. This system presupposed a well-selected and well-controlled class of administrators, which, when it functioned efficiently, was the envy and model of other rulers. In Egypt and Syria the Mamlūks had in the thirteenth century inherited a fairly well developed administrative machinery. In Europe the Byzantine Empire, heir to the Roman emperor Diocletian's regimented administration, could boast a some-what similar civil service, which, despite civil wars and the inroads of Serbs, Bulgars, Turks, Venetians, and Genoese, remained effective until the Empire's demise in the fifteenth century. At the beginning of the fourteenth century peculiar circumstances had permitted certain relatively small areas also to achieve a fair degree of governmental centralization. Norway, for example, was a quite centralized monarchy, largely because its aristocracy was reduced by economic decline to a few families, while its mountainous terrain made the heavily armoured feudal horseman ineffective. The England of Edward I (1239–1307) was well on the way toward royal administrative control, largely because of its insularity.

The idea of centralizing Europe as a whole into a Christian empire had recurred from time to time but had never been more than a dream. Even within the separate European states the process was a complex one. In Poland, for instance, for a number of reasons an elective kingship never achieved enough power and prestige to dominate the feudal lords, and the king was hardly ever able to persuade them to participate in a united effort, particularly after the middle of the seventeenth century, when the *liberum veto* became the rule. The centrifugal tendency thus illustrated was not political alone. The Polish peasant economically as well as politically was in the main dependent on, and felt responsible to, his local lord and not his king. The same held true largely for the peasants of Hungary and of the numerous principalities of Germany. The Russian serf, the Prussian peasant, and the French, English, or Spanish tenant farmer (to give but a few examples) continued to live in subservience to local landlords.[3] Feudal services and payments were exacted from large sections of the agricultural population by local lords until the nineteenth century.

*   *   *

The Rise of the Middle Class

In those countries that were able to establish a strong government, the population was subjected to the central regime as well as, and sometimes more than, to the local lords. Even before 1300 military allegiance was shifting from local lords to sovereign governments, and certain taxes tended to drift into the king's treasury rather than the lord's. Regulation of trade was passing into the hands of the central authority, and jurisdiction over many kinds of behaviour and obligation once left to the lord's court was passing to the king's courts.

The processes by which feudal powers were gradually transferred to the central government varied. In some instances the political complications of feudalism diminished as a single feudal family rose to prominence. Japan provided an instance of this phenomenon. The imperial power had seriously declined since the twelfth century, and at times two competing courts demanded allegiance. During the first three centuries of our period the Japanese suffered prolonged civil wars among various feudal factions, but from this exhausting civil strife emerged one dominant feudal family, the Tokugawas. By means of the shogunate, a kind of *major palatii* with extensive centralized powers exercised nominally in the emperor's name, they managed to hold the empire together.

Unlike the Tokugawas, the Tudors, the Bourbons, and some of the other dynasties of Europe that likewise rose to dominance over the prostrate bodies of rivals assumed the regal title. In some western European states, royal power had been ascendant long before 1300, and the processes, whether peaceful or warlike, by which this ascent had been achieved were still being successfully applied. Some kings strengthened their hands by exploiting the ecclesiastic domains within their realms, as when Philip the Fair (d. 1314) contrived to get possession of the French properties of the military order of the Knights Templars (see Chapter III), and this procedure became particularly enticing after the decline of papal power in the fourteenth century. The Protestant Revolt gave to Protestant kings an especially good opportunity to confiscate church properties, and to Catholic kings a good reason or pretext to confiscate the properties of Protestant nobles, and to keep them or reassign them to royal supporters. Occasionally a European sovereign was sufficiently strong to dominate powerful nobles without civil war and to sequester the domains of contumacious vassals, a procedure favoured by the French rulers after the Bourbon Henry's accession (1598). In general a strong king could take advantage of whatever winds might blow. Concerted opposition of the nobles could generally be averted by fostering rivalries among them.

In Europe effective support for the monarchs in their centralizing efforts often came from the cities and their middle-class populations. Urbanization was fairly well advanced in western Europe even before 1300. Urban population until the nineteenth century constituted, to be sure, only a small portion of the total, and society everywhere remained basically agricultural, but the political and social influence of city-dwellers was greater than their numbers alone would have warranted. The walled city, with its burgher militia, its guilds, and its income from trade and industry, frequently became independent of the feudal lord or, if it remained subject to him, was generally autonomous and might even be hostile to him. It sometimes gave asylum to serfs who wanted to escape from his rule, for, as an old medieval proverb declared, 'City air makes free', and its market, which stimulated the development of cash crops, frequently enabled a peasant to substitute money payments for degrading servile dues and thus to buy higher status and a freer disposal of his time.

Urbanization, therefore, was seriously undermining the power of the feudal barons at the same time that royal centralization was also working towards the same end. To promote this common objective effectively a town would sometimes frankly ally itself with the royal power. Although some towns were merely bureaucratic or ecclesiastical capitals or sites of agricultural fairs rather than true commercial or industrial centres, urban society was predominantly commercial and industrial, and as such it was interested in the creation of a strong central power that might further trade by eliminating tolls and provincial customs-barriers, suppressing local disorders, highwaymen, and robber barons, building roads and canals, dredging rivers and ports, granting monopolies, charters, and privileges, and providing the protection of arms and tariffs against outside competition. The monarch, for his part, found in the commercial activities of this new class a source of revenue, mostly in the form of cash, wherewith he could build his own administrative and military systems, independent of the more cumbersome and less reliable feudal contributions of a stiff-necked aristocracy. In times of emergency the merchants and city banking circles could be approached for loans to be repaid in coin or commercial concessions rather than in lands and political privileges, which were the usual methods of compensation for feudal vassals.

At times, however, the considerations impelling king and town to ally against their common enemy, the nobility, did not counterbalance the burghers' fear of autocracy or their desire for political power of their own, and in such instances the centralizing power encountered solid opposition from the towns. The political ambitions of the Flemish cities, for example, were a serious obstacle for the French kings during the early centuries of our period. Emperor Charles V was at times more dependent on the support of the cities of his realm than was compatible with his political plans, and the support of Paris and of London had to be purchased dearly by their respective French and English rulers and sometimes could not be obtained at all. The revolt of an important city could be crucial for a ruler, as was exemplified by the role of London in the constitutional crisis of seventeenth-century England. When cities were controlled by forces at odds with the central government, as was the case of the Huguenot towns in France before Richelieu's day, they constituted a seriously disruptive element in the body politic. Despite the price, however, the allegiance of the towns was always a desideratum—in times of war or revolution, since they were usually strategically located and fortified, and in times of peace, since the wealth and influence of the middle class often was decisive in political manoeuvring.

So sovereigns in a number of countries came to look to the middle class for support. Louis XI of France counted heavily upon the help of a strong urban population. Henry VIII, Elizabeth I, and other Tudor rulers of England sought the aid of the country gentry as well as of urban middle-class advisers. In Russia, Ivan IV acquired the assistance not only of the gentry in his service but also of the Moscow townsfolk (*posad*), and Peter the Great frankly courted the middle class, promoting commerce, industry, and other bourgeois interests.

*   *   *

The Decline of the Feudal Nobility

Some of the struggles between Europe's kings and feudal lords were long and fluctuating. France, England, and Spain during the fourteenth and fifteenth centuries were at times close to a state of complete political anarchy in which rival noble families battled as they pleased for superiority without being curbed by monarchical rule. In the 'Time of Troubles' (1604–13) after Ivan IV the newly consolidated Russian realm was rent asunder by the resurgence of the great nobles. About the middle of the same century the grand French magnates, having been deprived only recently of many of their powers by the late Cardinal Richelieu, staged a major but futile attempt—the so-called 'Fronde'—to regain their previous position at the expense of the monarchy.

Hardly anywhere (England was a notable exception) was the feudal power of the nobility totally eliminated before the close of our period. Thus, centralized rule did not generally bring the tightly totalitarian form of government which modern technology and politico-economic practices have made possible. Conditions in that day rendered so high a degree of centralization difficult if not inconceivable. Centralization then meant not so much the concentration of power in the hands of a central authority as a *modus vivendi* whereby the national ruler and the various particularist forces could cooperate towards a well-ordered state and the prevention of feudal chaos. It meant absolutism rather than totalitarianism, the king being regarded as the head but not the whole of government. His power, to be sure, was checked or balanced only by tradition, local custom, corporate rights, grants, capitulations, and charters rather than by countervailing force. Such checks, however, were ordinarily respected. Since the kingly power was hereditary, the obligation to observe these traditional or historical limitations was also inherited, and it was not easily disregarded. Hereditary absolutism was thus more restrained than revolutionary totalitarianism. In the states that developed into coherent units, the disruptive aspects of feudalism were curbed, but the great nobility, though bereft of the powers that the ruler thought he needed to monopolize for the conduct of royal policy, was nonetheless still able, as a strong, privileged, and honoured order, to influence the conduct of affairs.

Naturally, in some countries the nobles were more powerful than in others. In the great dynastic states of the Turks and the Habsburgs, the magnates, and to a certain extent the smaller landowners (such as the Hungarian gentry), actually ruled their provinces in much the same way as in medieval times, though with a greater readiness to accept the guidance of the sovereign dynasty. Even in some of the more thoroughly centralized states like France, Prussia, and Russia the great landlords retained a fair amount of their feudal privileges and local power. Moreover, their social standing, their still great economic power, and their still considerable political and military prestige enabled them to continue to play a significant role in public affairs. Up to the very end of our period important levelling programmes (such as proportional taxation, free access to certain professions, or an even chance for the common-born to reach the higher ranks of church or army) could be successfully advanced almost nowhere, except perhaps in Britain, because of opposition from aristocratic interests. The so-called absolute monarchs of the late seventeenth and eighteenth centuries, therefore, had predominant but not unlimited political power within their realms. Their power was checked, to some extent at least, not only by the nobility but also by various other influential groups such as the church, the chartered cities, the guilds, and the privileged provinces, as well as by the rising middle class.

In the process of centralization the rulers strove to obtain control of the most important governmental functions. Where they succeeded, command of the military, which is likely to be the *ultima ratio* of all effective political power, passed into their hands. The system of feudal levies, by which the sovereign was dependent on the cooperation of his vassals, was replaced by a system of standing (frequently mercenary) armies, made possible by the monarch's new sources of income, whose rank and file were His Majesty's soldiers and ultimately subject only to his command. Wherever feasible, private forces of great lords were altogether eliminated or became privately raised and more or less proprietary regiments in the royal army. A statesman bent on centralization, like Henry IV or Richelieu, nullified even the defensive power of the magnates by destroying castles and fortresses and transforming them into peaceable chateaux. By the eighteenth century the primary vestige of the feudal lords' once unquestioned military eminence was that the highest ranks in the army were as a general rule reserved for nobles. In other words, feudal independence in this as in most other regards had been converted into aristocratic privilege.

*   *   *

The Rise of Royal Legal Systems

Another significant increase of power for the central government resulted from the consolidation of judicial functions in the hands of the rulers. The development of a royal judicial system was well on the way before 1300. Yet local courts with jurisdiction over only local affairs, adjudicating cases by the application of local custom and of laws differing from region to region, still created confusion. In Europe, until about 1500, the process of creating a unified system of courts and law codes and of providing a more rigid super-vision of justice was retarded by the disintegrating effects of the Black Death, a plague that spread from India to Europe in the fourteenth century, and by frequent wars, invasions, and baronial conflicts. After 1500 the process was considerably accelerated. The justice dispensed at the king's court by the king's judges came in general to be looked upon as superior, not only because the king usually could employ men of greater talent but also because it stemmed from the actually or potentially best source of law enforcement in the land. The appellate function of royal justice was thus greatly strengthened. For certain types of cases, such as those involving taxation or tariff, military affairs, constitutional questions, and more serious criminal offences, juris-diction came to rest with the royal rather than the seigniorial courts. Besides, after 1500, in Christian countries, the partition of legal authority between the secular power and the church, with its separate ecclesiastical courts and canon law, became less sharp, for the independence of the church from the crown was considerably weakened. Although, until the French Revolution and beyond, the church retained jurisdiction over marriage, divorce, inheritance, and similar civil-law issues, and in cases involving clergymen, it too became more and more an instrument of the crown.

The judicial systems that resulted in most countries from the centralizing efforts of the monarchy were mixed systems, since the royal courts did not replace the old courts but rather took places beside them. The courts of the church continued to function. The seigniorial courts retained a certain, though diminished jurisdiction over feudal obligations and other relations of lord with tenant. Since, except in the United Kingdom, serfdom still survived and in some countries had even been intensified by the end of our period (as, for instance, in Prussia, Russia, Poland, and parts of the Habsburg realm), these feudal courts remained a significant force in rural society. In urban society many issues involving artisans and workers continued to be adjudicated in the courts of the guilds. As the guild structure gradually collapsed, its judicial functions were absorbed by royal courts. Mercantile law after 1300 was generally enforced by the merchants themselves (either through guild courts or through municipal courts, which they controlled), but it tended to become a province of royal jurisdiction in the last century or so of our period, most notably in England. In almost none of these fields of law, however, was a clear-cut distinction made between the royal and the other forms of justice. Jurisdictional disputes were frequent between the royal courts and local or church courts but were resolved more and more in a fashion that enhanced the royal power.

In due course the king's courts came to be looked upon as higher courts. Some of them were ambulatory, travelling through assigned districts with the express purpose of holding appellate jurisdiction over the local courts. In England, for instance, itinerant royal judges heard indictments brought before local justices of the peace, who were themselves royally appointed, although they continued to be chosen from the local gentry. In France a similar system of legal appeal developed, for the king was likewise regarded as the source of justice, but there the highest courts of the land were the parlements. Until the fifteenth century the Parlement of Paris had been the single highest court of the land, but then various provincial parlements were created, and in the eighteenth century there were thirteen (at one time fourteen). Because of their claim on the right to 'verify' constitutional changes, frequently they came into opposition with the crown. The king, however, as the fount of law and justice was able to dominate the parlements except in instances when public feeling ran high in their favour. In addition to the regularly constituted courts, royal administrative appointees in towns or provinces on occasion exercised appellate function. The trend towards taking the administration of justice away from church, local, or private authority and placing it under the central government was general and persistent during our period.

In Europe, and its spheres of influence across the seas, the movement towards a centralized system of justice was greatly furthered by the influence of Roman law in the west and of Roman–Byzantine law in the east. By 1700 Roman law had largely replaced customary feudal law or at least had greatly modified the customary law everywhere in western Europe except in England, Scandinavia, and Switzerland. We shall return to the legal consequences of the Reception of Roman law in Chapter VIII. The political consequences were also significant. Justinian's *Corpus Juris*, in particular the *Digest*, became a common meeting-ground for all lawyers, a sort of common domain of juris-

prudence. The principles of Roman law greatly influenced the royal administration of justice. It appealed especially to monarchs because it emphasized the
powers of the ruler. Aided by lawyers trained in Roman law (the so-called
civilians), they applied its principles increasingly in jurisdictional disputes.

Another factor in the process of judicial centralization was the tendency
towards codification of the laws. In Europe codification had been common to a
certain degree before 1300. The rise of the middle class gave impetus to the
movement towards clear and uniform law, and the most remarkable secular
codes between 1300 and approximately 1500 were of laws merchant, or
commercial laws, which we shall examine in Chapters VIII and IX. Yet the
codification of the laws of the respective nations proceeded rather slowly, and
indeed was notably successful only after our period. No European monarchy
entirely succeeded before 1775 in creating either a uniform legal system or a
truly centralized administration, for the monarchs could not entirely eliminate
particularism and feudal vestiges. Local custom and tradition persisted and
did not readily yield to national legal concepts, whether of written or common
law. Everywhere a mixture of the old and the new continued, although the
trend towards the new was evident.

*   *   *

The Rise of Bureaucracy

The gradual centralization of royal government brought with it a bureaucratic system and the rise of a bureaucratic 'class'. The courts of even the least
practical sovereigns were becoming more and more dependent upon a trained
and experienced personnel dedicated to administrative affairs—in royal
councils, chancelleries, tribunals, and exchequers as well as armies. By 1300
most sovereigns had at their command at least a core personnel out of which a
central bureaucracy might arise and with which the local government
machinery had to cope. At the beginning of our period the most highly
developed administrative systems were to be found in the states with the
greatest centralization, the Chinese, the Mamlūk, and the Byzantine empires.
The Chinese civil service with its selective examinations seems to have
engaged the interest, at least during the later centuries of our period, of those
who contemplated a similar system in central Europe.

Royal administrative policies varied with the intensity of centralization.
Countries that retained a large part of the feudal system, as did Russia and the
Ottoman Empire, inevitably also retained a number of local administrative
agencies and left governmental functions in the hands of the feudal lords or
military leaders of the provinces. An important new element, however, was
introduced into this arrangement: the nobles serving as district and provincial
governors were gradually deprived of freedom to act on their own discretion
and were made more responsive to the basic decisions of their sovereigns. In
Russia, to be sure, where the boyars, at first mostly high-born servants of the

tsars, were being displaced by hereditary landlords, especially in the eighteenth century, this tendency seemed to be reversed, since the landowner steadily acquired greater control over his serfs and sometimes exercised considerable independence of the tsar. Yet in most states, Russia included, in the course of time the central governments developed media through which they could supervise and check the conduct of feudal administrators. Imperial and royal officials periodically inspected the work of the district governors. Royal fiscal agents checked their books and tax records; itinerant judges provided royal courts of appeal with power to correct the injustices of local judges; military inspectors kept watch on the district commanders and their commands. Though many of the provincial posts were still hereditary in the local noble families, rulers steadily increased their hold upon them by insisting upon formal appointment, by designating officers of their own with parallel or overlapping powers, and by occasional dismissals and replacements. The resulting administrative patterns in such instances were a composite of feudal and royal—the ruler, however, emerging, with growing frequency, as the dominant figure.

Wherever feasible, the central government sought to place its own appointees in local administrative posts or to replace agencies of long-standing particularist interests with new ones that owed allegiance to the crown alone. In that fashion, the French provinces were, after Richelieu's reforms, governed by royal *intendants* as well as by members of the great noble houses, and the once autonomous towns of Spain increasingly lost their independence to royal agents such as the *corregidores*. In military affairs lines of command came to reach more directly from the monarch down to the newest recruit, and since centralization at times depended on the army as the means of preventing rebellion and disobedience, civil administrative functions were often united with the military in a district commander (e.g. the beys and pashas in the Ottoman Empire and the military commanders in the Mogul realm). Fiscal administration was usually centralized at the top but frequently the actual collection of taxes and excises was in the hands of local tax collectors if not of semi-private 'tax farmers' who bought their posts. Administrative and judicial posts could sometimes also be bought from the king (as, for example, certain magistracies in France) and thereby become a hereditary property.

In medieval Europe, because learning had been restricted for the most part to ecclesiastical circles, the clergy had been dominant in royal administration. With the increase in lay education, the development of universities, and in particular the availability of laymen trained in civil law, many positions came to be filled by members of the legal profession. Nevertheless, the king's highest advisers, his governors, and the regional representatives of the crown still were frequently drawn from the most eminent aristocratic families, whether or not trained as clergy or lawyers. Even after the Reformation, certain positions—in the universities, for example—continued to be regarded as the special prerogative of clergy. Members of the bourgeoisie who managed to rise to high governmental positions were sometimes promoted to an aristocratic status by the granting of a title or, as in France, came to form a separate 'aristocratic' administrative class (the nobility of the robe). While the trained members of the middle class were most often employed in the central bureaucracy (i.e. the royal councils, the bureaus of the capital, etc.), others were used in municipal governments, as they came increasingly under royal control, or were put in charge of local offices dealing with the crown's economic or fiscal affairs. Many middle-class persons found employment also as scribes, clerks, and minor officials in the royal service. The interest and participation of 'the third estate' in the nation's government was thus both cause and effect of the bourgeois stake in the centralization of royal authority.

With the help of its administrative machinery the central government widened its control of the people's activities. As we shall note in more detail in Chapters II–V, administrative centralization helped to establish the supremacy of the state over the church. In the countries where Greek Orthodox Christianity prevailed, no pope had achieved independence of the emperor, and the church had been subjected to state domination for ages. The Russian tsar, especially after the Turkish capture of Constantinople and still more so with Peter's church reforms, was the chief authority for all Orthodox Christians in his realm. In Roman Catholic Europe monarchs exploited the weakness of the papacy after 1300 to arrogate powers that had previously resided in the church hierarchy. They established close supervision over ecclesiastical appointments and fiscal affairs, and curtailed the foreign activities of the clergy. Papal relations with a national church were subjected to the approval of the crown. Church institutions (the Inquisition in Spain, for instance) were used by the monarchs as instruments of state. Even in Catholic countries after the Reformation, the church tended to become a national institution, and like other subjects, ecclesiastics tended to become loyal subjects first and faithful members of the Roman Catholic hierachy afterwards. In Protestant countries rulers usually were more than nominal heads of their state churches; the clergy were appointed by them and subject to their control. Many of the administrative functions that had previously resulted from the clergy's feudal status as landowners were eliminated when the state 'nationalized' church lands. In a sense, therefore, the ecclesiastical hierarchy became the branch of the civil service in charge of the religious, and sometimes the educational and welfare functions of the state.

In political affairs the royal councils and officers in charge of judicial, fiscal, military, and economic administration became the highest governmental agencies. In the course of time these councils were divided into various 'ministries', which were sometimes under the general supervision of a high administrative official (e.g. the Turkish viziers and the eighteenth-century English 'prime' ministers). At other times they were coordinated only through the monarch (as in Spain under Philip II and in France under Louis XIV). The councils maintained contact with the regional officials of the crown and its plenipotentaries abroad, mostly through a system of correspondence and written accountings, thereby laying the foundations of the modern 'paper bureaucracy'.

★   ★   ★

Distance usually dictated that the administration of colonial enterprises be divided between the crown and local authorities. Colonial administration was in certain instances in the hands of chartered companies, like the various East India companies, rather than directly under royal officials. Where, however, it actually was a function of the home government, it manifested in a striking fashion the characteristics of the centralized system; for in establishing governmental agencies for newly acquired lands, colonizing monarchs rarely had to cope with obsolescent feudal or ecclesiastical institutions and interests. One of the most impressive of such colonial systems was devised by the Spanish. Under direct control of the king, a Council of the Indies, responsible for formulating laws and policies for the colonies, studiously scrutinized the conduct of colonial officials, who were its appointees. High officials like viceroys, governors, and captains-general were usually assigned to their posts for a relatively short time, in order to keep them from acquiring too much personal power. During their terms of office they were subject to inspection by visiting officials (*visitadores*), and at the conclusion of his service each was expected to render a careful accounting of his administration. Over the centuries, further checks and regulations were inserted in this highly centralized system until the machinery became so cumbersome as to raise doubts regarding its effectiveness.

As Spanish colonial experience illustrates, the high degree of centralization that absolutism entailed carried with it the seed of its own destruction. It alienated first the class that had been the king's allies—the nobles—causing him to seek allies among the commoners; and sometimes it alienated also the class that had helped him to build up his absolutism—the middle class—but not until centralization had served its major purpose, which was to counteract the centrifugal forces of feudalism. The middle class was an uncertain ally at best. Even while it fought beside the king in the common fight against decentralization, it was aware that the fight was a three-cornered one.

THE QUEST FOR LIBERTY AND SOCIAL JUSTICE

In Europe the erection of safeguards against absolute royal power was largely (but not exclusively) the work of the rising bourgeoisie. At first, members of this class had usually been eager to exchange the tyranny of the few (the feudal lords) for the rule of one (the prince who might make common cause with them against the lords). Ultimately, however, the bourgeoisie did much, occasionally in conjunction with rival classes, to foster the growth of institutions and ideas that helped to secure individual freedom and responsible government, neither of which was always welcome to princes.

Before 1300 the nobles and the churchmen of a realm were on occasion summoned by their king to advise and approve some policy or to function in some other special capacity. Around 1300 such assemblies began to be more representative, including deputies from the cities and the higher strata of the common or *roturier* (i.e. neither noble nor ecclesiastic) class. With the addition of bourgeoisie, gentry, and smaller landowners, these assemblies of the 'estates' (or orders of society) developed rapidly as parliamentary bodies and began to assume an important position in their countries' affairs. The Cortes of the various Spanish kingdoms, the Estates General in France, the Parliament of England, the Riksdag of Sweden, the Sejm of Poland, and, to a much more limited extent, the Diet of the Holy Roman Empire and the Staende in the Habsburg realm acquired certain concessions in return for financial or other aid to their princes. Among these concessions, in addition to the right to be convoked periodically for consultation and to be heard on fiscal matters affecting the whole realm, was the right to petition for redress of grievances. By coupling the granting of finances with petitions for redress, parliamentary bodies fashioned a powerful weapon against monarchs in need. They acquired a certain degree of legislative power, thus foreshadowing their main later function. On occasion, kings had to change their policies because of the unwillingness of the estates to grant the necessary finances, and a balking parliament might delay or entirely prevent an accretion of royal powers. In some countries in which the monarchs established firmly centralized rule (e.g. Spain, France, and Denmark) representative bodies declined during the period of absolutism and enlightened despotism; in others, however, they remained as at least a slight check on otherwise absolutist rule (e.g. Hungary, the Belgian Netherlands, and other realms of the Habsburgs).[4]

The English Parliament eventually became the outstanding example of a representative assembly in a monarchy. It had developed out of the great councils of the English kings, and by the beginning of our period was on its way to becoming more generally representative through the inclusion of the lower feudal order (the knights of the shires) and the burghers. Soon these elements of the population began to meet as a separate body and became the House of Commons. Parliament was an extension of the king's council, summoned to give its approval to great acts of state and appearing most frequently when the monarch had most need of public support. The real basis of Parliament's power resided in its ability to grant or withhold needed revenues. The rule of the impoverished Lancastrian kings was characterized by frequent Parliaments, but the first Tudor, Henry VII (d. 1509), as soon as his independent revenues were sufficient, summoned Parliament no more. The decisive change in the status of Parliament occurred in the reign of his successor, Henry VIII, who was compelled to invoke a representative legislature to sever connections with the Roman communion (see Chapter IV). In each of the next three reigns Parliament was called to legislate on fundamental changes in the nation's religious creed and establishment.

The effect of the Reformation in England was initially to increase the power and wealth of the monarchy and of the classes represented in Parliament. But the Reformation also divided opinion. The Parliaments contained groups that opposed the policies of the successive monarchs. As the wealth of the classes represented in the House of Commons increased and that of the crown declined by comparison, the position of the monarch weakened. Queen Elizabeth I (1533–1603) successfully withstood most attempts of the Commons to meddle with state policy, but under the Stuart kings, James I (1566–1625) and Charles I (1600–49), Parliament (and particularly the House of Commons) continued to enlarge its claims to initiate policy and control the government. Numerous conflicts now arose between the crown and the House of Commons over several issues of royal prerogative. These issues, coupled with the religious conflict of Puritans and episcopalians, finally resulted in the Civil War, in which the monarchy was overthrown, and England was for a time (1649–53) governed as a republic (the Commonwealth) by a surviving faction of the House of Commons.

On the whole, this pseudo-parliamentary government proved to be unstable and ineffectual. For one thing, it could not control the army, where the more radical of the puritan factions (the Independents and other sectaries) predominated and demanded church disestablishment and toleration. Nor could it compose the differences between this army and the Presbyterian party, which had once dominated the House of Commons and had hoped to acquire an exclusive control over both the monarchy and the established church. Parliamentary rule without a strong executive was discredited, and the vacuum was now filled by a written constitution that provided a strong executive, subject to parliamentary safeguards (the Protectorate). An able protector was found in Oliver Cromwell, leader of the army, who quarrelled with his Parliament, dissolved it, and was driven to secure a modification of the constitution after a brief period of military rule. The regime did not long survive his death, and in 1660 the Stuart dynasty was restored to the throne, on condition of ruling with Parliament. Many of the old political and religious issues, however, revived in somewhat different forms. The new king, Charles II (1630–85), improved his position by skilful manoeuvres and was able to rule without Parliament for the closing years of his reign. His successor, James II, was emboldened to advance further, and led on by initial success, he gave mortal offence to the Anglican Church by his preference for Roman Catholics, which also lost him the support of non-Anglican Protestants. These Protestants eventually joined the bulk of Anglican England and Presbyterian Scotland in welcoming William of Orange as a deliverer in the 'Glorious Revolution' of 1688.

Subsequently Parliament assumed greater and greater responsibilities. Various areas of conflict remained, but on the whole the crown and Parliament learned how to cooperate, forming a system that preserved many of the good features of centralized rule without jeopardizing the rights of the governed. Representation in Parliament, and corresponding political influence, was restricted to the nobility, the gentry, and the wealthy burgher class, but the idea of representative government and of limited monarchy had been established as a working principle. Unlike the French aristocracy, the British aristocracy was not privileged in taxation, and movement into the higher civil and military offices was easier for the poor and low-born in Britain than in France. On the whole, the people in Britain who made policy also carried it out and paid a fair share of its cost. The machinery for representative processes developed to such an extent that the nineteenth-century transition from limited to mass suffrage would take place in England without extensive civil strife.

If the Puritan Revolution failed to create a Puritan commonwealth, it nevertheless demonstrated that even strong monarchs could not always with impunity dispense with the consent of the governed. Revolution or the threat of revolution (as we shall see in Chapters VIII and IX, where we shall analyse the political thought of our period) thus became a more effective check than ever before upon the exercise of arbitrary power.

★   ★   ★

Republicanism

The contemporary instances of republicanism provided examples of another political force that might be employed to counteract the trend towards royal absolutism. Republicanism (i.e. government by some sort of representative body), which had been a vital and characteristic element of the culture of Antiquity, reasserted itself during our era, particularly in the cities. For the most part European cities were run by oligarchies working through guild organizations. The major exceptions to this general rule were to be found in those Italian Renaissance cities that were ruled by hereditary autocratic despots. Even before 1300 the Visconti dynasts (and later the Sforzas) in Milan, the house of Este in Ferrara, the Malatestas in Rimini, and other Italian ruling families had created highly developed absolutist systems. Occasionally during one period certain Italian republics also fell under the sway of a single ruling family, as Mantua under the Gonzagas and Florence under the Medici. The intense political rivalry within and among the Italian city-states, complicated by the frequent interventions of Spanish, Austrians, and French, was not conducive to the maintenance of the balanced political leadership always desirable for and frequently characteristic of republics. Continual strife usually left them with governments too weak for effective defence or conduct of foreign affairs. Nevertheless, the republican form of government prevailed in some Italian cities, such as Siena, Genoa, and Venice, which for centuries was the most successful of all republican states. Even Medici-dominated Florence retained at least the outward forms of republicanism. The cities of western and northern Europe, especially in the regions with limited centralization of government such as Germany and the Low Countries, were usually republican in form, even though they owed allegiance to the emperor or a local prince.

Originally many city governments had derived their power from their guilds as well as from the local aristocracy. But with 'the commercial revolution' of the thirteenth and fourteenth centuries the richest merchants came to dominate municipal government. For reasons to be taken up when we come to deal with economic matters, the guild system eventually weakened under the impact of early industrialization and concurrent changes in commercial and financial practices, and between 1300 and 1450 the lesser workers of some areas attempted by violence to gain a share of power. Occasionally these attempts were lower-class uprisings, like that of the Ciompi (wool-carders), who in 1378 took over temporary control of the government of Florence, but usually the only lasting success of such uprisings was to gain some representation on the town councils. They were not able to eliminate the overwhelming political, social, and economic influence of the great merchant families. For the most part, the plutocrats continued to dominate the councils and, in consequence, the entire city administration. Often in the civil strife between a town's rich and poor, help from a neighbouring feudal lord or monarch was obtained by one of the opposing factions. Many cities thus lost their autonomy to a nearby potentate.

Nevertheless, the republican spirit remained alive. The humanist movement, which was strong among the patricians of Renaissance Italy, tended to do honour to the old republican virtues of Rome as well as to its caesarism. Brutus and Cicero, prototypes of the true republican, were glorified, and tyrannicide, the assassination of political oppressors, was sometimes openly defended in principle. By deference to a different set of models, the republican ideal found favour among the religious radicals of the fourteenth century, the Lollards of England and the extreme Hussites (Taborites) of Bohemia; they harked back to the democracy of government and the community of property among the primitive Christians (see Chapter III). During the Reformation, the religious thought of some of the great reformers—Zwingli, Calvin, and especially the Anabaptists and Levellers (see Chapter IV)—was likewise compatible with republican institutions. Zürich, Strasbourg, and Geneva were outstanding both as city republics and as early centres of Reformed or Calvinistic activities. Later this Protestant movement became prominent also in the urbanized areas of southwestern Germany and the Netherlands. Calvinism in France, too, was concentrated in the cities, and some of them (as mentioned above) became independent enough to threaten to become little *imperia in imperio*. Moreover, each of the sects, whether old or new, in the communities which it did not itself control was dependent upon the exercise of religious toleration by others for its very survival. Hence they

c*

all kept up a lively interest in safeguards against religious and political oppression where they were weak (even though they might ruthlessly persecute dissidents where they themselves were strong). We shall deal with such political views in Chapters IV and IX.

By 1700 republics were few, and republican institutions seemed to be giving way completely to the monarchical form of government. Small states like the provinces of the Netherlands and the cantons of Switzerland were able to retain republican or semi-republican constitutions only, according to Montesquieu and some other eighteenth-century observers, because they had joined together into confederations for mutual protection. Venice and Genoa were still strong states but had long passed the peak of their glory. The German free cities managed to preserve their republican institutions against princely encroachments, but sometimes only with difficulty. London remained a semi-independent commune. Most of the other European towns, however, had lost whatever republican structure they might once have had. In so far as the Polish monarchy and the Holy Roman Empire might be considered republics by virtue of having elective rulers, they lent little prestige to the republican tradition. Few principles and lessons derived from the history of ancient and contemporary republics seemed relevant to the philosophy (see Chapters VIII and IX) of those concerned with the limitation of governmental authority in Europe.

*   *   *

Federalism

The story of federalism is closely associated with that of republicanism. Most of the federations of our period were leagues of small republics, each of which retained some degree of control over its internal affairs while otherwise submitting to a central authority. Usually federations arose out of the need for united effort against an actual or potential enemy. During the Middle Ages towns banded together for defence of their local independence and the preservation of their privileges against strong rulers or feudal magnates. The resulting leagues as a rule were loosley organized, but they had been strong in northern Italy. After 1300, stronger ones emerged in the German Empire, where the central government was steadily losing power. The German leagues had predominantly political aims, seeking to obtain more influence in the imperial Diets and the general affairs of the realm by presenting a united front. Among them were a league of the Swabian cities, a league of the important Rhenish towns, a short-lived league of the Westphalian towns, and, by far the most eminent, the Hanseatic league of northern Germany and the Baltic areas.

In the final decades of the thirteenth century, a number of north German towns had crowned their earlier cooperative enterprises by forming a league called the Hansa or the Hanseatic League, primarily for commercial purposes. With Lübeck as its centre this union, which may have included at times as many as seventy or eighty members, adopted a common legal code (the Sea Laws of Lübeck), sought to standardize its trading activities, offered military and naval protection to its members, and tried to procure and safeguard monopolies in the areas which it controlled. It never developed into a strong political federation, since member cities were not only independent in their internal affairs but also free to withdraw. From time to time delegates from participating towns met to deal with urgent political, military, and commercial matters. The League's common foreign policy was to protect and further its commercial position in the Baltic and the North Sea, where for decades it encountered opposition especially from the Danish kingdom. It negotiated with the important princes of northern Europe for trading privileges, established *kontors* ('trading settlements') abroad, improved port facilities, and policed piracy. During much of the fourteenth and fifteenth centuries the Hansa dominated north European trade and also exercised considerable political power. Then the strengthening monarchies began seriously to curtail its trading privileges; the League, unable to compete effectively with the state-protected trade of the Dutch and the English, declined and in the seventeenth century, though it never formally dissolved, ceased to have significance. Nevertheless, the mercantile achievement and the civic independence of this remarkable commercial–political federation engendered a pride that is still discernible in former league cities like Hamburg, Lübeck, and Bremen.

Only three European countries (if we exclude states united only by virtue of a personal union under the same ruler) had governmental structures that were based upon the application of federal principles to a group of contiguous areas. They were Switzerland, the United Provinces, and the Holy Roman Empire. We have already seen that Switzerland began as a federation. Each of its cantons was practically independent in the conduct of its internal affairs and jealous of its independence, since the population differed widely from canton to canton in language and economic interests, and after the Reformation also in religion. Some of them were only 'allied' to the Confederation or to some of its members; others, along with some areas now outside Switzerland, were 'protected' cantons; and some (twenty about the year 1600) were territories 'subject' to one or more cantons. All of them were bound by a series of treaties promising mutual defensive aid against attacking powers. Foreign and other common affairs were handled by a diet chosen by a complicated representational system. By the Treaty of Westphalia of 1648 the Swiss Confederation was finally recognized as independent of Austria (thereupon passing under the political influence of France). Although the practically complete autonomy of the cantons resulted in several civil wars, the Swiss showed that divergent areas could cooperate to achieve a joint strength that could be reconciled with a high degree of local autonomy.

When the seven northern provinces of the Netherlands united in 1579 to form the Dutch Republic or United Provinces a federal structure was indicated for their union. The provinces were left autonomous. They elected representatives to a States General, which, with its executive Council of State, acted as a government for the entire land. This body, however, could make no major policy decisions without instructions and directives from the provincial estates, which were dependent on the nobility in the eastern provinces, where agriculture was the major pursuit, and on the municipal councils in the provinces of Holland and Zeeland, where financial and commercial interests prevailed. In time of peace this complex arrangement made the formulation of a generally acceptable federal policy extremely hard.

Two forces, nevertheless gave great cohesion to the union. One was the predominance of the province of Holland and its chief executive official, the grand pensionary. Holland was the most populous and economically as well as culturally the most eminent area of the Netherlands, and its agents were so frequent and prominent abroad that foreigners often assumed 'Holland' to be identical with 'The Dutch Netherlands'. Under the leadership of strong men like Jan van Oldenbarneveldt (1547–1619) and Jan De Witt (1625–72) it tended to dominate federal politics. The other cohesive force was the House of Orange. As the great opponent of the bourgeois Democratic Party of Holland, it was the rallying-point of an Orangist movement. The Orangists sought greater national centralization under the leadership of the stadholders, who were at first elective in the separate provinces but were so regularly taken from the House of Orange that the office became practically hereditary before 1747 and then became officially hereditary. Despite republican opposition, the stadholder was elected by the provincial estates also as captain-general and admiral-general of the realm in times of war and so played a most important role in cases of national emergency such as the wars of liberation and the conflict with Louis XIV. The stadholder's office steadily accumulated responsibilities, but because of the strong republican tradition, especially in Holland, the Netherlands were not turned into a monarchical country until the Napoleonic era. Although before the later decades of the seventeenth century the United Provinces began to lose their powerful international position, this decline was not due primarily to the weaknesses of their federal structure and resultant domestic disputes. The provinces generally held together firmly as a federation in times of foreign invasion, and the union was envied and respected for its peacetime achievements. In many ways the Dutch Netherlands, despite religious and political dissensions, were an example of good government, in which a large degree of freedom was available to the individual within the provinces and to the provinces within the union.

The Holy Roman Empire may in a way be considered an aristocratic federation. Its numerous separate states, particularly after the Treaty of Westphalia formally gave them *Landeshoheit* ('domestic sovereignty'), governed their own domestic affairs. Yet they also acknowledged a certain allegiance to the central authority, feeble though it was, of the emperor, who was elected by those German princes who had the title of 'elector'; they all were represented somehow in one of the three houses of the Imperial Diet; and they all looked upon the Golden Bull of Charles IV (1356), which set forth the fundamental law of the Empire, as more or less constitutionally binding. Though the Treaty of Westphalia modified the provisions of the Golden Bull considerably, weakening the emperor's position still further and giving the member states freedom in foreign affairs, it still required them to make no alliances against the emperor or the Empire. If, however, the Holy Roman Empire was a federation, it was a weak one at best.

*   *   *

Government and Individual Rights

Conflict over the distribution of domestic power—like that of the Swiss with Austria, the Dutch with Spain, and the English with the Stuarts—and opposition to the menace of a foreign master state or ruler helped to reinforce old concepts and institutions or to evolve new ones that became fundamental in the development of Europe's liberal principles. In Britain, the seventeenth-century revolutionary movement brought or reconfirmed certain 'rights', protecting the individual from arbitrary arrest, star-chamber proceedings, and torture to elicit testimony and assuring him of *habeas corpus* and trial by jury. In Chapter IX we shall find political philosophers assuming, largely on the basis of the English experience, that a systematic division of governmental powers was necessary if tyranny was to be avoided and advancing the need of intercedent bodies between the potentially despotic ruler and the potentially suppressed people. Though for different reasons, both the bourgeoisie and the privileged classes subscribed to these principles.

Certain arguments essential to the case for the strong nation-state, by a strange irony, contributed to the growth of the philosophy (of which more will be said in Chapters VIII and IX) upon which the egalitarian democracies of later eras were based. The theory of divine-right monarchy stressed the assumptions that government was instituted for the benefit and welfare of the whole community and that God held the monarch responsible for it. Louis XIV's comment on his place in the state (which has been reduced by legend to the succinct '*L'état c'est moi*') implied responsibility proportionate to power. In the Enlightenment notion of benevolent despotism, this sense of responsibility received greater emphasis, and the ruler was considered the 'first servant' of his people, as one ruler, Prussia's Frederick II, liked to put it. The true monarch, in other words, was expected to be either God-fearing or paternalistic or both. Coupled with this expectation went the concept that there existed a 'social contract' between the governors and the governed which was binding on both parties. Even though apologists for monarchy stressed the obligations incumbent upon the governed, they held to the age-old principle that the individual possessed certain basic 'natural' rights that were superior to man-made laws and that no ruler ought to disregard. In general, monarch and people were thought to be engaged in a common quest for good government. Although this quest often led to the centralization and hence the strengthening of the monarchical state, the people at least insisted on 'just' government and the fulfilment of the 'contract' by the ruler. They were frequently disappointed to find that power corrupts.

The idea of a social contract carried the implication that men under given circumstances had the right, and perhaps even the duty, to revolt against oppression. If a ruler neglected the obligations imposed upon him by the contract, his subjects were freed of their obligation to give him loyalty and obedience; or if he so carried out his obligations as to infringe on the natural rights of groups and individuals, they were entitled to resist and, if they succeeded, to overturn his government. If the major premises were granted, the theory worked with even greater logic in the field of religion, where in fact it was applied earlier (see Chapter IV). Radical religious sects nearly always felt that they must obey God rather than man, and that in case of conflict between the things that were God's and the things that were Caesar's they must prefer God and, if necessary, resist Caesar, at least passively. This philosophy was eventually elaborated to justify the efforts of the Dutch to gain political independence by the use of force or of the Catholics in England and the Huguenots in France to resist their rulers in church matters.

On occasion the assassins of tyrants claimed to have acted in the name of a higher justice. Tyrannicide, we said above, was familiar to the humanist scholar from his study of Roman history; it was no less familiar as an actual event in the turbulent atmosphere of Renaissance Italy. In northern Europe of the sixteenth century and after, assassination was scarcely less common, but there it often was associated also with religious controversy. Thus ended the lives of eminent men like William the Silent, the Duc de Guise, Henry III and Henry IV of France, and Wallenstein; Charles I of England was condemned to death after a civil war by perhaps legal but certainly revolutionary procedures; and Louis XV of France barely escaped assassination by a religious fanatic.

⋆   ⋆   ⋆

Social and Political Revolt

Popular uprisings against the prevailing order, particularly prominent in the earlier centuries of our period, often followed a similar pattern. They tended to burst forth suddenly and for a while sweep everything before them, only to subside just as suddenly. Frequently they were based on economic and social grievances, taking the form of a bourgeois repudiation of patrician claims, a peasant revolt against noble or ecclesiastical landlords, an uprising of the urban proletariat against the dominant bourgeoisie, or a complex of these and other socio-economic conflicts. The fourteenth century, the era of the recurrent Black Death, witnessed several violent uprisings of a proletarian nature. We have already mentioned the Ciompi of Florence. In the same century, the Flemish cities, in one of the most densely populated, urbanized, and industrial regions of Europe, suffered violent insurrections. Departing from the usual pattern, they began as revolts of powerful bourgeois and urban artisans, chiefly weavers, against patrician domination but quickly took on wider significance because of the related political claims and interests of French and English kings and Flemish counts. In Italy the civic disorders time and again appeared to be mere struggles among conflicting factions of the leading families. Perhaps the most spectacular, though probably not the most important, was that led by Cola di Rienzi (1313–54), who believed himself called to restore the old Roman Republic in the city of the absent popes. Though encouraged by no less a personage than Petrarch, Rienzi's fantastic experiment lasted but a few months. A revolt led by Etienne Marcel (d. 1358), who aimed to put the government of France under the control of the Estates General rather than the king, was similarly vain (see Chapter VIII). Many of the subsequent urban uprisings in Europe were not so much social conflicts between the rich and the poor as political protest against a sovereign's curtailment of municipal liberties and privileges. Thus, for instance, Ghent revolted against Charles V, Paris refused to pay allegiance to Henry IV until he had gone over to Catholicism, and Amsterdam resisted Maurice and William II of Orange.

These revolts were for the most part urban in origin and ran their course inside the confines of cities. Unrest among Europe's peasantry likewise resulted in open rebellions that failed to achieve their objectives. As a rule failure was due to inadequate formulation of objectives and lack of effective leadership but also to the abiding strength of the conservative forces. Many insurrections were directed against practices and conditions, which we shall shortly analyse, that the peasants (and others) felt to be unjust but for which solution would be forthcoming only with a thorough overhaul of the economic and social structure for which society was not yet ripe. At times peasant outbursts were fuelled by religious fervour and supported by clerics. Pious expectations and longing for a better world in which each would have his needs fulfilled, where justice, equality, and, for some devotees, a communistic type of economy would prevail, took the place of a reasoned revolutionary programme. The revolts usually started rather suddenly, quickly assumed dangerous proportions, and were brutally suppressed. Among the most famous were the 'Jacqueries' of the fourteenth century in France (interwoven in a complex pattern with the merchants' uprising in Paris under Marcel), the great Peasants' Revolt of 1381 in England under the leadership of Wat Tyler and John Ball, the German Peasants' War of 1524–25, and the peasant rebellions in Russia led by Ivan Bolotnikov in 1606–07, Stepan Timofeevich Razin in 1667–71, and Yemelyan Pugachev in 1773–75. Their achievements were small, but their frequency and intensity gave easily credible testimony that even the lowest layers of European society were not always cowed by authority and might yet share in the search for a better world.

Philosophical justification of resistance to the point of tyrannicide and lower-class protests to the point of revolt thus contributed substantially to a revolutionary tradition (to use a term that in itself may be a contradiction). But a more effective carry-over came from political revolutions. The most significant before 1775 have already been mentioned and will be mentioned again—the Hussite wars of Bohemia, the Dutch War of Independence, and the civil strife in England that culminated in the Puritan Revolution and the Glorious Revolution of 1688. These were insurrections of peoples against their sovereigns with the aim of protecting or obtaining what they considered their rights. In their course arose many of the important issues concerning the reciprocal rights and duties of kings and subjects. The Hussite wars broke out largely over the questions of liberty of conscience that were to loom over a much greater area during the Reformation. The Dutch Revolution, we have seen, created a new federal republic that long served as a model of toleration and freedom in a Europe where such attitudes were rare. The Puritan Revolution failed for many complex reasons, but its impact on the future of political developments in England was tremendous, and the Glorious Revolution finally confirmed the principle of parliamentary participation in government, setting prescribed limits to royal prerogative and giving precise privileges to Parliament.

Roughly contemporaneously with the Puritan Revolution a wave of less important revolts swept over several continental countries. Two of them reflected the on-going contest between the forces favouring the centralizing dynasties, real or potential, and those favouring local and particularist rights, privileges, and tendencies. William II of Orange, stadholder of the Netherlands, faced with stalwart opposition from the town of Amsterdam, was foiled in an attempt to convert the Dutch Republic into a centralized monarchy. More serious was the insurrection known as the 'Fronde' in France, where dissatisfied nobles, threatened by the centralization engineered by Cardinals Richelieu and Mazarin, rebelled and, with the aid of various dissatisfied elements of the population which sought to defend their local liberties and privileges, threw the country headlong into fruitless turmoil, which lasted a number of years. Several other contemporaneous movements were based upon a more popular type of protest—a people desiring greater autonomy or independence and rising up against a sovereign whom it did not consider a good or a rightful ruler. Examples of such protests were the outbreaks in Catalonia, which had a hoary tradition of opposition to Castilian rule, and in Naples, which had not had a truly Neapolitan dynasty for centuries. Both failed. The contemporary insurrection in Portugal, however, was a successful attempt to regain national independence, which had been lost—and lost for decades (1580-1640)—when Philip II brought the country into a personal union with Spain.

Some observers have maintained that the most influential single political development of the period before the great revolutions of the eighteenth century was 'the new Leviathan'—the dynastic state. The evolution of cohesive states, characterized by a steadily increasing centralization of administration, a growing tendency of government to intervene in religious, economic, cultural, and social affairs, a perhaps greater insistence upon uniformity of law, legal codes, and legal systems, and mounting demands upon the allegiance of subject or citizen, must have left very few men and women unaffected and unconcerned. Not least among those affected were the ones who, either because they had lost (or feared to lose) power to Leviathan or because they had gained (or hoped to gain) power along with Leviathan, were concerned about institutions and opinion hostile to the strong, centralized state. Those who had lost most were the privileged orders; and those who had gained most were the urban middle class. The latter thus was faced with a dilemma, of which some who stopped to think were conscious: the middle class was highly instrumental in a long-run process of furthering both strong government on the one hand and protection of the individual from the all-encompassing state on the other; in consequence, at times middle-class sympathy lay with the kings against the privileged classes, at other times with the privileged classes against the kings. To be sure, the voices of Anabaptists, Levellers, and other radical revolutionary or millennial groups proclaimed that the fight was more than three-cornered, that the complex grouping which might be called a 'fourth estate' was also involved. But for the most part the middle class, sometimes in paradoxical alliance with the privileged orders, was as yet the chief standard-bearer of liberty, since liberty still meant to most men freedom from dynastic absolutism on the one hand and from the claims of feudal, corporate, or constituted authorities on the other. The time when it would mean to many economic and social equality, too, was not far distant.

Concepts of liberty and social justice, we shall point out in Chapters VIII and IX and elsewhere, were not peculiar to Europe. To cite only outstanding examples, in Confucian China 'the mandate of Heaven' was thought to depart from rulers who became 'bad emperors', and in Anglo-America a set of institutions and an ideology were taking shape that in 1775 was to light 'the spark that changed thought into action'.[5] In Europe, however, natural rights first became a political creed widely accepted and nurtured as a tradition and championed (as well as by others) by a full-grown Third Estate, politically conscious, able, strong, and energetic. The identification of that powerful class with that liberal creed was one of the important factors in the West's departure from the feudal, privileged, and patrician or dynastic political structure which until 1300 had been fairly common throughout the world.

ECONOMIC CHANGES AND THEIR POLITICAL IMPORT

The economic and social changes, too, of the period from 1300 to 1775 ultimately led to a markedly altered life for much of mankind. In Europe and its growing dominions overseas an economic system arose that differed considerably from the predominantly peasant societies which had previously been common to all cultures. Of the several forces that interacted to remould Europe's socio–economic structure, three call for special emphasis: the growing significance of the city, the expanding intercourse between Europe, Asia, and America, and the increasing tendency to apply scientific knowledge to industry, trade, and agriculture.

Change in social life and in the direction of economic developments generally tends to be set by the urban communities. The growth of cities helped to break up the old feudal and manorial order, to substitute a money economy for one of barter and payment in service, and to cause a marked increase in agricultural specialization, the number of free tenant farmers, and the rural standard of living. The art of trading was improved immeasurably by refinements in the methods of payment, in the transfer of goods and money, and in the safeguarding of accumulated wealth. Banks and financial corporations, characteristic of a capitalistic society, began to flourish. Religious opposition to a philosophy of life whose major end is material gain diminished, and the acquisition of wealth became an approved social practice. 'Conspicuous consumption' and the use of luxuries greatly increased.

The era of the Black Death and the Hundred Years' War, which came close upon the heels of the 'commercial revolution' mentioned above, was marked by economic setbacks. Until the end of the fifteenth century recovery was slow. After that, however, the long-run trend was almost uninterruptedly upward toward prosperity. Despite rising prices and resulting hardship for wage earners, the general material standards of the ordinary man also rose because of cheaper and more accessible goods (textiles, hardware, fuel, etc.), richer harvests, better methods of animal husbandry, and, above all, the introduction of new crops from overseas that yielded not only luxuries such as sugar, tobacco, tea, and coffee, but also cheaper staples such as potatoes and maize, not to mention new fowl, fruits, and vegetables.

Colonialization cooperated with urbanization to effect economic change. For those who were economically or otherwise bold or desperate, the overseas colonies beckoned, promising rewards from the exploitation of new lands, resources, and markets. At the same time emigration somewhat relieved the congestion in Europe. The virgin soil of the New World held the promise of a larger agricultural yield, and the vastly expanded possibilities for trade in exotic goods provided new sources of wealth for those who dared to invest labour or money in producing or marketing them. More and more of those who stayed at home found employment in slowly evolving industries, which, though a far cry from the large-scale factories of our time, nonetheless provided a greater industrial potential than could the small shops of the Middle Ages.

With the multiplying changes in political, religious, and cultural life came changes in the professions. Lawyers, soldiers, doctors, engineers, artists, ministers, and teachers were among the professional men whose special interests and skills reshaped and were reshaped by the new tendencies. Pressure to apply the growing technological and scientific knowledge (see Chapters XIII–XV) gave rise to new professional and technological procedures. They were particularly productive in industrial pursuits, and towards the end of our period a large-scale 'industrial revolution' was in the making in England, France, and Belgium. In 1776 Adam Smith was to publish his famous *Wealth of Nations*, which advanced the arguments basic to most subsequent economic theorists of the *laisser-faire* school. The readiness of some of the nascent political parties to accept the new economic philosophy was to a large degree a result, and at the same time a crystallization, of a conviction (see Chapters VIII and IX) that the hitherto prevalent theory and practice of government regulation (mercantilism) was not adaptable to an expanding world market.

Agriculture

These economic and social effects of urban, colonial, and other developments came only slowly. As before 1300, agriculture continued to be the primary mode of production; for the great majority of mankind the traditional agricultural systems underwent very little modification until recent times. In Japan, China, southeast Asia, India, and the Islamic world, as well as in most of the tribal societies, the system of landholding, the methods of planting, cultivating, and harvesting crops, the theory and practice of animal husbandry, the types of crops grown, and the preparation of meals remained more or less what they had been for centuries. In some of the advanced civilizations, where imposing cities already existed, urban influences attained no greater comparative prominence after 1300 than they had earlier. By the beginning of our period, therefore, the economy of those civilizations was already fairly well balanced between urban and rural interests, and it changed but little until the nineteenth century. This kind of stability was particularly prevalent outside of Europe, in societies that did not undergo a scientific or ideological 'revolution' and whose rate of agricultural productivity and consumption varied appreciably only with the incidence of war, drought, flood, and similar acts of God or man.

In Europe, however, urbanization had advanced so far that as early as the thirteenth century its effects upon the social structure were easily discernible. The manor or village community that under an almost autonomous landlord was able to provide its own material and spiritual needs had already been widely replaced by a village structure that permitted more frequent economic and social relations with the growing population centres. Whether commercial and industrial compounds, garrisons or fortresses, bureaucratic, ecclesiastical, or university centres, or large villages whose population still earned a living by agriculture (a type that could be found particularly in southern Europe), towns were dependent upon the surrounding countryside for their food supply, and the country folk in turn relied on the town markets for the disposal of their cash crops. Agriculture, therefore, had to adapt itself to the needs of the nearby urban population. This urban demand extended not only to food but also to the raw materials required for industrial processes.

What happened in the Flemish textile industry at the beginning of our period well illustrates the growing economic interdependence. That mushrooming industry demanded ever greater amounts of woad for dye and of wool and flax for yarn and thread. Thus the cities of Flanders stimulated both the growth of woad and flax in neighbouring Picardy and the conversion of crop fields to pasture in England, which, climatically suited for the production of a superior type of wool, soon began to compete with Flanders in textile manufacture. The consequence was a considerable degree of regional specialization in agriculture. With the intensification of agricultural specialization, the neighbouring countryside became incapable by itself of provisioning the Flemish cities, and so foodstuffs and textile materials, sometimes cheaper and frequently better, had to be imported by sea from far-off regions. A considerable amount of the grain used in Flanders came from the Baltic countries, of the raw wool used in England from Spain and Germany, and of the wool yarn used in Italy from England, while Normandy and Provence helped to provide the needs of the urban areas of Spain and Italy.

Cash crops gave peasants the means to substitute money payments for the obligations in kind or services that they owed their lords. In this way the feudal and manorial order in western Europe was gradually transformed into a tenant system. The tenant system often meant considerably higher living standards for the peasant and a rise in their self-esteem. It also brought greatly increased social mobility. Being no longer necessarily tied to the soil, more and more farmers worked for their own profit rather than in subjection to the programmes of their lords. Many peasants actually moved into cities and thus relieved the pressure upon the land that from about 1100 to about 1350 resulted from the general increase in western Europe's population.

In fact, the increase in population at times outstripped the ability of the land to provide food. Seriously unbalanced situations resulted that were responsible for some of the dreadful famines of the late thirteenth and fourteenth centuries. These famines explain in part why certain areas contemporaneously experienced a sudden reversal in the demographic trend. During the second half of the fourteenth century the appalling epidemics known as Black Death inflicted additional losses upon Italy, Spain, France, England, Germany, and Norway. Plague combined with famine and the general economic depression already mentioned to cause a general decline in Europe's population after 1350—in some countries a decline of 40 per cent or more. The ravages of war also at times decimated the peasant population, particularly in France during the Hundred Years' War (1337–1453) and in Germany during the Thirty Years' War (1618–48). Yet such catastrophies, horrifying and spectacular though they were, did not mean a permanent setback to the population growth of the smitten areas. By the sixteenth century population figures were again at their earlier levels except in Norway, where losses seem not to have been overcome for at least another century. Thereafter Europe's population rose steadily. In 1650 it was about 100,000,000, while Asia's was about 250,000,000. In 1750 the respective figures were about 140,000,000 and 406,000,000. By 1800 they had risen to about 187,000,000 and 522,000,000 respectively. The world's population had meanwhile grown from 465,000,000 to 660,000,000 and then to 836,000,000. China's alone rose from about 60,000,000 in 1368 to 583,000,000 in 1953.[6]

The demand for food and space grew correspondingly. New land was constantly exploited for agricultural purposes both through territorial expansion to the east of Europe and through cultivation of fields that had previously lain fallow. Forests diminished in number and size on the Continent, and even more in the British Isles, where profit from the raising of sheep increased the demand for pasture even at the sacrifice of tilled fields. Morasses and swamps were drained, and the Dutch developed amazing proficiency in reclaiming land from the sea and rivers. In 1600 the Low Countries were able to put a much larger area under cultivation than three hundred years earlier. On the other hand, China, Ceylon, India, Mesopotamia, Egypt, North Africa, Italy, Spain, and other regions clamouring for water had long made use of irrigation and were thus able to turn arid stretches into fertile fields. The New World and south Africa also provided virgin lands for Europe's relatively dense agricultural population to exploit.

A more intensive exploitation of the available soil was simultaneously under way. China, Japan, and southeast Asia, nearly always congested, had made a transition to the intensive farming of rice at an early stage of their development. In Europe soil conservation by field rotation had become traditional before our period, but in the seventeenth century a change from field to crop rotation and therefore from extensive to intensive cultivation began; and in the eighteenth century came the 'industrial revolution' described in more detail in Chapter XV. Improved agricultural tools and techniques saved labour, enlarged the scope of a day's work, and considerably furthered the use of fertilizer and fodder crops. New staples like maize and potatoes had meanwhile entered from America into the European agricultural system, providing a highly satisfying yield and considerably increasing the food supply of the poorer classes. At the same time, horticulture, one of the most intensive forms of agriculture, developed all over Europe, especially in the Low Countries, and some farmers prospered by concentrating on the production of fruit trees, vegetables, flowers, and ornamental shrubs in orchards, suburban gardens, and even the parks of patricians. The techniques of animal husbandry, which together with farming was the major source of rural wealth, also made great strides. In short, between 1300 and 1775 the average yield per acre, and, therefore, the average income to the farmer, was greatly enhanced, with benefit to the population as a whole.

*   *   *

Agricultural Labour

These developments worked toward the economic emancipation of the smaller farmers. To be sure, by 1775 serfdom was far from extinct in western Europe and indeed had probably grown worse east of the Elbe, and even the free peasant anywhere was often miserable. Nevertheless, a large number of peasants whose ancestors had been serfs during medieval times had become either independent or tenant farmers, with a greater degree of freedom in running both their farms and their personal affairs. On the less fertile soils many had become *métayers* ('sharecroppers'), and though their lot as such was also wretched, it tended to improve. The size of these more emancipated groups was especially impressive in western Europe. Although emancipation often meant no more than membership in a landless rural class that made a living only by hiring out as agricultural labour, a number of peasants acquired their own land and livestock. Some leased lands for a money rental, most frequently on long-term arrangements, from a lord who left them free as long as they paid the still surviving dues and respected his seigniorial rights. Even where they were still dependent on the local lord or still responsible for *corvées* to the government (often no more than a few days' labour *per* year on roads and bridges), the freeholders and tenant-farmers of 1775 were considerably better off than serfs and sharecroppers. If the lord remained a dominant figure in rural affairs, he was no longer the undisputed master of the local peasantry. Independent or partly independent farmers could now grow what they wanted, sell their harvests where they could get the most for them, marry off their daughters without seigniorial consent, appeal to royal administrators when they felt unjustly treated, and move away if they preferred. The increased productivity of agriculture and the rising prices for his produce induced the peasant to seek more land and greater freedom from his remaining servile obligations. For similar reasons, the landlords sought to retain feudal dues, cheap labour, and good lands. Thus the peasant's 'land hunger' in some places collided with the lord's 'feudal reaction'. Even though much of the peasant's servile heritage remained a burden when, in the 1780's, the revolutionary era began in western Europe, he had already taken some meaningful steps towards economic emancipation in the more advanced areas.

In eastern Europe agrarian conditions were less promising. During the *Drang nach Osten* the new settlers had in general formed the freest and most emancipated peasantry of Europe. This enviable situation lasted for a few centuries after 1300. Towards the close of our period, however, the increasing demand for agricultural products in the more rapidly urbanizing countries made the stabilizing of the labour supply more desirable for eastern landowners, and the great lords of eastern Germany, Austria, Bohemia, Poland, the Baltic areas, and Russia managed to stabilize theirs so well that serfdom of a highly restrictive kind ensued. As land ownership passed more and more into private hands, more peasants became permanently tied to the soil and passed completely under seigniorial or church jurisdiction. The Russian church was one of the worst exploiters of serf labour, the Troitse-Sergiev Monastery alone, according to one estimate, owning over 106,000 male serfs in the 1760's, when the largest noble landowner had fewer than 5,000.[7] The serfdom that ultimately developed in the eastern countries lacked some of the mitigating features of western serfdom. The lord was virtually absolute. He determined the hours of labour; he fixed the taxes; he meted out punishment; he decided who was allowed to marry whom; and he had the right to recapture any runaway serf. At times it was not easy to distinguish this type of serfdom from outright slavery. Occasionally a more enlightened monarch attempted to alleviate the peasants' lot, but the results of such attempts usually proved only temporary. Peasant revolts were frequent.

Under such conditions the general level of agricultural production in eastern Europe failed to rise. Although Russian peasants brought vast areas in northeastern Russia, the southern steppes, and Siberia under cultivation and initiated the peoples of Siberia into the knowledge of agriculture, Russian agricultural methods and tools remained relatively primitive. Animal breeding in eastern Europe never reached the point attained in the west, and of the new crops only the potato played a major role, though as fodder more than as food in our period. Some rulers like Peter the Great in Russia or the Great Elector and Frederick II in Prussia made serious attempts to introduce some of the refinements of western European agriculture but seldom were able to advance beyond the experimental stages. A splendid model farm established at Oranienburg did little to ameliorate the traditional methods and squalor of the vast multitude of Prussian peasants. For the peasant masses east of the Elbe notable improvement of personal and economic status did not come before the nineteenth century.

Rural social conditions in the New World were a strange mixture of what was good and advanced with what was bad and backward in European agriculture. Besides independent settlers, numerous indentured servants and *engagés* (bound by contract, written or understood, for a definite period) went as colonists to the English and the French colonies of North America. Whether their engagements were involuntary (for example, to escape imprisonment for debt) or voluntary, these servants and *engagés* joined the ranks of independent settlers, once their contracts were fulfilled. Such settlers, as well as many Spanish and Portuguese farmers in Central and South America, were probably among the freest farmers in the world. Each had his own land (often plenty of it), houses, tools, and livestock. He could move almost whenever it suited him and carve out a new holding in the immense stretches of unclaimed wilderness. He was more or less subject to officials who derived their power ultimately from the home country, but in the distant new lands governmental authority was generally very little felt. Most of these settlers, having possessed no land or having been only small holders in the Old World, had improved their lot tremendously.

In some areas, however (especially in the southernmost English colonies on the north Atlantic seaboard, in Mexico, and in large sections of Central and South America, as well as on the islands of the Caribbean), while Europeans enjoyed an enviable position, the non-European agricultural labourers were either serfs or slaves. The pre-Columbian Indian population in the Spanish colonies of America has been estimated at 14,579,500. By 1570 it had dropped to 9,253,850. By 1650 it had begun to climb (10,359,000), and by 1825 it was up to 15,814,000.[8] In the Spanish colonies with a large Indian population an institution known as the 'encomienda' flourished. The encomienda was a later-day version of a medieval fief. It was usually the right to exploit (along with the obligation to care for) the native population in an assigned area granted (without outright title to the land) to a European conqueror or governor by the Spanish crown. It might include several native communities, whose inhabitants were obliged to pay tribute and render services to the 'encomendero' (proprietor of an encomienda). The encomienda gave way later in the sixteenth century to a more thoroughly organized, state-controlled labour system called the 'repartimiento', which in the seventeenth century was in its turn largely displaced by the privately owned plantation, or 'hacienda'.

The hacienda was often a latifundium in which not only the land but also the labour of the Indian farmers residing on it belonged to the European colonist. The home government and the church had intended that the Indians should be free and should be converted to Christianity. Notwithstanding the efforts of some humanitarian reformers, these intentions were seldom put into practice. Instead, the natives, subject to tribute in encomienda or reparti-miento if they remained in their own communities, went off to the haciendas. There they usually acquired greater indebtedness than they could pay off and so became peons. The peon was legally free but economically a kind of serf. He was either a paid labourer or a tenant farmer on a big estate, but in either case for all practical purposes he remained perpetually indebted to the landlord and thus bound to him. Even where native village communities persisted, they were frequently subject to the neighbouring 'haciendado', or proprietor of a hacienda. The Spanish conquests thus superimposed a few rich and powerful European colonists upon vast masses of Indians, who were reduced to the status of peons.

In Brazil the Portuguese crown at first attempted to create a feudal system. It divided the country among fifteen 'donatorios' with powers limited only by the rights reserved for the crown. But from the start this system did not work well. A governor-general took over the donatorios' political powers after a few years, and in the eighteenth century the crown also took over their land grants. Meanwhile, a few thousand white settlers had been importing Negro slaves and enslaving Indians except where the Jesuits were able to settle Indians in *aldeas* ('missions'). The Marquis de Pombal, the Portuguese minister who expelled the Jesuits from Brazil (1759), also made Indians equal to white men in the eyes of the law.

Another agricultural institution, the plantation system, came into special prominence in what is now the southern part of the United States, the West Indies (whether Spanish, English, French, Dutch, or Danish), and Brazil. These were areas where the European landowner found the climate too uncomfortable for hard manual labour but very favourable for the cultivation of cash crops such as tobacco, cotton, and sugar cane. The answer to his dilemma proved to be the plantation (large farm) worked by indentured or slave labour, which enabled him to secure both comfort and profit. The plantation was much like the European manor or, though generally less extensive, like the Spanish–American hacienda.

The labour force for the plantation consisted primarily of Negro slaves, most of whom were imported from the west coast of Africa, and the trade in slaves became a most profitable enterprise for the merchants of the seafaring nations. Originally the right to import slaves into the Spanish colonies—the *asiento*—was limited, having to be purchased from the Spanish crown. By the Treaty of Utrecht in 1713, the British gained this right as a prize of war. A country's slave trade was, however, much too profitable to remain a monopoly; it attracted so many merchants of other lands that it was never easy to protect it against slave runners. The actual capture of slaves was usually the enterprise of West African chiefs. European shippers bought them cheap and transported them to America under conditions so abominable that appalling numbers died during the ocean voyage. This traffic brought to the American shores thousands upon thousands of unfortunate chattels whose descendants created a thorny political and social problem that abides to this day. Their labours, however, made the land productive, and thus they were an important factor in shaping the culture of the tropical and subtropical regions of North and South America.

One of the arguments advanced to justify Negro slavery was similar to that used (by the sixteenth-century historian Juan Genés de Sepúlveda, for example) to excuse the reduction of the Indian populations to the status of forced labourers in the encomiendas: according to Aristotle, part of mankind was set aside by nature to be slaves, and through slavery pagans could be introduced to civilization and Christianity. Some representatives of the Catholic Church—Bartolomé de Las Casas foremost among them—felt responsible for preventing the exploitation of the natives on this basis, and wherever they succeeded in exercising influence, the position of the Indians was relatively improved. At Valladolid in 1550 Sepúlveda and Las Casas presented their respective arguments before an illustrious gathering of officials, clergy, and lawyers. After several papal and royal protests and prohibitions, the sale of Indians into slavery in the Spanish colonies gradually came to an end (with exceptions in regions where nomadic warfare continued), but Negroes replaced them in the slave markets. On the whole, the lot of Negro slaves in the Spanish and Portuguese colonies was less harsh than in the English colonies of North America. By virtue of certain precedents in Roman civil law, Spanish and Portuguese slaves were manumitted more readily and were better protected in property and family affairs than slaves, for instance, in Virginia or the Carolinas, where the common law was silent on slavery and so left them subject to the mercy of their masters. Since civil law recognized marriage with slaves as binding, intermarriage further helped to improve the lot of the Negro in Spanish and especially Portuguese areas. To a large extent the more humane attitude of the Iberian governments is attributable also to the intervention of the crown and to the abolitionist efforts of such churchmen as Las Casas and Alonso de Montúfar in the sixteenth century. Toward the end of our period some Protestants—the American Quaker John Woolman (1720–72) and the English philanthropist Granville Sharp (1735–1813), for instance—campaigned against the institution of slavery with equal fervour, and eighteenth-century *philosophes* and humanitarians made abolition one of their numerous reform causes.

The use of slave labour on immense tropical and semi-tropical plantations made possible the production of lucrative crops of sugar, tobacco, indigo, and rice, which would have been less economically produced on small-scale farms. Cotton also was grown but, before the patenting of the cotton gin (1794), in quantities too small to compete with Eastern sources. The plantation provided large-scale, specialized farming, very different from the subsistence farming of most other agricultural areas, and it flourished as long as European and North American markets demanded tropical products. Between the lands in which the plantation system prevailed and the older countries a simple trading pattern emerged. The planters had to export their specialized crops and to import other agricultural necessities as well as much of the labour and equipment they required. At first, dependence on the mother country's economy was natural and convenient, a fact that made it easier for the mother country to retain a monopolistic position even after the colonies might otherwise have preferred independence.

*   *   *

Relative Stability in the East

While the conditions and methods of the agricultural classes were undergoing these marked changes in the West, only few variations took place in the agricultural methods of Asia, Africa, and the Islamic world. In China the two-crop-per-year system spread in the south, and the sweet potato and Indian corn were introduced from America via Manila, contributing to a remarkable growth of population in the eighteenth century. Where Islam established itself in India, it brought about the rise of some new Hindu sects and some new attitudes towards caste, labour, and Muslim–Hindu relations (Chapters II, III, and V), but it left the village structure essentially unchanged. Emperor Akbar (1542–1605) allowed Hindu rajahs to rule in some states and Muslim nawwābs in others, contenting himself with fairly heavy but systematic taxation, and his successors retained his system with certain modifications.9 In Japan, once the Tokugawas ended the feudal warfare of the Ashikaga period and inaugurated their own centralized regime, considerable new land was brought under cultivation, and by the 1720's the population increased to about 30,000,000. It long remained at that figure because no new agricultural techniques were introduced. Meanwhile, the gradual expansion of commerce promoted the growth of towns, undermined the feudal system, and further impoverished the peasants, many of whom lost their rights in their land to money-lenders, either of merchant or of peasant origin. Many peasants also, despite prohibitions, moved into the towns.

★   ★   ★

Industry

Modern industry was born long before James Watt meditated upon his tea-kettle. The impressive speeding-up of industrial methods in the eighteenth century was preceded by a long and important evolution in which various complex technological and interrelated factors had prepared the ground (see Chapters XIII–XV).

Despite the cumulative impact of the new forms of production, some medieval industrial practices persisted. The small artisan's shop, protected to some degree by guild organization or caste rules, continued in all countries to provide many of the manufactured articles that are now generally produced by large-scale industrial processes. Articles were seldom ready-made. If a coat was needed, one ordinarily turned to the local tailor; for a pair of shoes the local shoemaker was engaged; what furniture was not inherited and could not be made at home was provided by the local carpenter or, for finer work, by the cabinet-maker. In some localities tailors, potters, or weavers were not needed, since the farming population was quite capable of manufacturing many of its own necessities. Shopkeepers were craftsmen when they sat at their workbenches and merchants when they stepped to the sales counters. Except for man-made regulations they could in most instances ply their trade wherever they decided to set up shop, for ordinarily they were not dependent on ready access to raw materials and markets or to running water and other sources of energy. The things they required could generally be provided by the town market, the surrounding countryside, and itinerant merchants.

Even in medieval times, however, certain trades were dependent upon special conditions. Some industrial processes required a fast flow of water or steady winds, for water and wind were, next to humans and animals, the primary sources of power for mills before the development of the steam engine. At times enterprises remained localized because their raw materials were bulky or otherwise uneconomical for distant transportation. Thus, some specialization of production was necessitated by simple facts of nature—the availability, for example, of running water, forests (for charcoal), clay, or stone quarries. But since such natural features were abundant, such industries could grow up in many regions. Intensive specialization began only when differences in the quality and supply of raw materials and, above all, in the costs of their manufacture became significant considerations in fixing prices in a competitive market.

Even before 1300 physiographical features along with local craftsmanship and other factors had worked toward a regional specialization of production. The wool yarn and cloth produced in Spain, England, and the Low Countries was found to be superior to most other wool. The silk grown in the warm climates of Italy, Spain, and southern France proved superior to that produced farther north, and the best silk was produced in China. The flax of Ireland, Flanders, and Holland surpassed that used for linen in other regions. Kaolin made much finer pottery than common clays, and the finest porcelains acquired the generic name of 'chinaware' in tribute to their place of origin. The best cotton goods, as their names indicated—calico (from Calicut), chintz (from a Sanskrit word meaning *spotted*), and even muslin (though probably first made in Mosul)—came from India. Muslim craftsmen had long exhibited extraordinary skill with steel as armourers and cutlers, and extraordinary taste as well as skill in silk weaving, carpet making, and embroidery. Some Spanish towns in close contact with the Moors had learned Moorish methods of production of armour and blades, and some Italian towns, by their contact with the Levant, had learned how to manufacture most beautiful brocades. Venetians and Bohemians knew how to blow exceptionally beautiful glass. The finest rugs came from Persia. After 1300 other than regional factors combined to intensify the specialization of industry (see Chapter XV).

*   *   *

Beginnings of Capitalism

Between 1300 and 1775 the development of industry was speeded up, for one thing, by extraordinary improvements in the techniques of finance and commerce. One of the most patent drawbacks to industrial progress around 1300 was the lack of adequate capital for the creation of bigger workshops, the acquisition of new tools and machinery, the purchase of larger quantities of raw materials, the better financing of long-term sales, and larger reserves to weather the fluctuations of the market. If a town's artisans, united as they were in a guild, had massed their capital in a cooperative enterprise, the necessary expansion of money and credit might have been achieved. But the general attitude of guild members was that their guild's purpose was protective—to restrict production, prices, and labour conditions—and by such monopolistic policies to guarantee for themselves a certain standard of living and of production without free competition. With all its corporative features the guild system worked against the abandonment of the small independent craftshop for the large-scale corporative factory.

Industrial capital had to come from other sources. In Florence and other towns of Italy increasing urbanization made investments in land a good basis for further profits. Furthermore, the expansion of Italy's trade made possible the accumulation of capital by commercial activities. Gradually this accumulated capital was invested in industrial processes, and some merchants became both traders and industrial entrepreneurs. Investments in industry earned additional money, which could be reinvested in the further expansion of realty, commercial, and industrial establishments. The interplay of land, commerce, and industry made for an effective interaction of financiers with landlords, merchants, and manufacturers. Simply stated (but we shall have to consider many complications later), it produced marketable articles which, when sold by the merchant, brought profits, which, when deposited with banker or broker, were reinvested in the production of additional marketable articles. Capitalism, or the investment of accumulated wealth for purposes of further gain, became a much more familiar process in the world's economy after the fourteenth century than it had been before.

Industry first developed on a large scale in Europe in the manufacture of textiles, especially wool and linen cloth, in some of the towns of Lombardy and Tuscany and, above all, Flanders. Flemish entrepreneurs found it profitable to import the superior wools of England and Spain in great amounts and 'put it out' to Flemish farmers for spinning and weaving. In this way they avoided the regulations of the guilds, which usually dominated the manufacture of cloth in the towns. Since the farmers and their families could give them only their spare time, they found that they had to employ fairly large numbers of workers. They were thus using many hands to work numerous but individually small quantities of raw material into large quantities of finished goods—the basis of large-scale manufacture. In this way extensive capitalistic enterprises either grew up beyond the reach of the guilds or, where bold entrepreneurs chose to make a stand against guild restrictions, were eventually constrained to try to break the power of the guilds.

The 'putting-out' or 'domestic' system was cumbersome, and a natural urge developed to concentrate manufacturing processes in one location or 'factory' and under the entrepreneur's immediate direction. In the textile industry specialized labour had long been the rule and a large number of employees in separate operations washed, combed, dyed, carded, and spun raw wool into yarn for weavers to make into cloth. Innovation here took the form of combining some of these operations under the same roof and under the financial and managerial supervision of the same entrepreneur. As specialization of production set in, compensation for skill in the various steps of the manufacturing process fell while that for speed in one of the diversified operations rose. Workers might find prolonged repetition of the same process monotonous, but output was tremendously increased by such division of labour and unification of management, and the goods thus produced, though not necessarily better, were generally cheaper, especially where labour-saving devices and improved tools were employed (see Chapter XV).

Because industry characterized by technical and regional specialization proved able to supply existing demands most economically, it expanded steadily, especially in England in the eighteenth century, but not without tremendous social opposition. The ever growing centres of these specialized industries, the factories, brought smoke and slums, and some of the opposition was on aesthetic and humanitarian grounds. The loudest and most constant denunciation of the capitalistic entrepreneur, however, came from the guilds, and in some countries they were successful in delaying the rise of large-scale industries. In the long run they succumbed before the capitalist's economic strength. The small craftshop was in no position to compete with the new-comer's greater output and cheaper prices. By 1775 the guild system was moribund, and the small artisan was being driven to the wall by the large-scale producer. Nevertheless, he was to outlast his guilds and to survive until our own day as a craftsman.

The development of large-scale industries gave a new impetus to the growth of the urban proletariat, already under way because of the increasing need for labour in small-scale industry and in commercial enterprises. A mounting number of workers ceased to be skilled journeymen with relatively secure social positions and became semi-skilled or unskilled labourers owning no part of the tools of production and enjoying no guild protection. Even where the guilds managed to maintain themselves, the medieval system of graduation from apprentice to journeyman to master became limited to fewer and fewer aspirants, for the new competition induced the masters to keep down the number of journeymen. In consequence, apprenticeship was prolonged, and many a journeyman was forced to remain a journeyman for his entire life. Thus social conflict was intensified in two different ways: between journeymen and masters in the guild structure, and between entrepreneur and proletarian in the capitalist system. As we have seen, these conflicts sometimes assumed a violent character, and the towns experienced serious unrest, especially during the early centuries of our period, when the capitalist system was slowly establishing itself more effectively. Since strikes were illegal and were frequently accompanied by violence and political tension, they often merged with or developed into revolt. Once the larger industries were firmly founded and enjoyed the protection of the governments, which could effectively meet violence, this type of social disorder became less frequent. By 1775 such workers' 'insurrections' were rare, but the intrinsic tension persisted, to break out more widely and more successfully in the nineteenth century. Meanwhile they served, in a day when other channels of public opinion hardly existed, as a means, though usually latent, of pressure upon governments.

*   *   *

Mechanization and Mining

After 1700, industrialism began to be characterized by rapid mechanization. This development was based on a series of technological innovations to be described in Chapter XV. The especially striking changes in industry during the eighteenth century are sometimes called 'the Industrial Revolution', with the same justification and with the same inaccuracy as in the case of 'the Scientific Revolution'. While some of its palpable effects seemed sudden and startling, it was the result of a process that was long and slow and has been continuous ever since. When James Watt finally patented a steam engine which was really usable (1769 and 1775), a type of industrial expansion that was destined to bring a thorough change in man's productive methods got under way. England, especially in textile manufacture, laid the foundations of its later industrial superiority in the last decades of our period. France and Belgium at first unsuccessfully tried to keep pace, but the revolutions and wars of the succeeding decades impeded them, and they fell considerably behind.

As Chapter XV will show in greater detail, only when machinery became relatively familiar did mining gain substantially in safety against its numerous hazards and therefore in productivity. After 1500, technological devices like fans, rails, and, above all, pumps were installed in some European and American mines, and they became more common after 1700. The improvement in mining operations, by making 'precious metals' less precious helped to cause an inflation of prices, already discernible at the close of the fifteenth century. In the sixteenth century a number of factors—among them a strike of silver in Bohemia, Portuguese importations of gold from Africa, and the discovery of the 'patio' process of producing silver, which made Mexico and Peru the source of abundant Spanish treasure—aggravated this so-called 'price revolution'. Although Europe's and Peru's output of silver diminished as lucrative mines were depleted, Mexico's grew, and the discovery of gold in Brazil at the close of the seventeenth century brought a gold rush to the wilderness. The rise in prices, except for a downward trend from about 1660 to about 1745, continued. Conservative calculations indicate that the prices of a number of staples almost tripled in Europe between 1500 and 1800. This increase, however, was due not alone to the abundance of precious metals but also to government manipulations like debasing the coinage.

The output of iron, copper, and tin also mounted sharply, but perhaps the most remarkable mining development of the age was the steady expansion of the production of common coal, especially in England. With the invention of the coking process in 1735, coal rapidly became an indispensable component of the British metallurgical industry, and coal mining became a leading source of goods, wages, and profits.

*   *   *

Wood, Game, and Fish

The coal mine gradually replaced the forest as the chief source of fuel. Wood, however, was not only an important fuel; it was also indispensable for buildings, shorings, vehicles, furniture, and ships. In the fourteenth century the supply of wood was sufficient nearly everywhere for fuel, timber, veneers, and similar needs. With the increasing deforestation and the growth of industry and ship-building, the traffic in wood spread and the areas of Europe around the Baltic (Russia and Scandinavia, in particular) profited greatly because of the superiority of their timber. Some of the more far-sighted monarchs of Europe awakened to the dangers of deforestation and attempted to stem it. Relatively late in our period a scientific approach to forestry manifested itself in the development of silviculture.

Hunting, which in the earlier centuries of our era was still an important source of meat, was associated with forestry. Since in many regions it formed one of the most cherished privileges of royalty and nobility, the biggest and best forests were generally the possessions of kings and aristocrats, and hunting rights were jealously guarded. Popular resentment against these privileges was outspoken and persistent. With the growth of animal husbandry, hunting lost some of its economic significance, which passed to the rancher. Cattle were important not only as a source of meat and hides but also as an incentive in the settlement of the New World, where the *bandeirantes* of Brazil, the *vaqueros* of Spanish America, and the cowboys of North America were often pioneers. Edible game was practically wiped out in England before the eighteenth century, and in civilized lands, hunting became more of a sport for gentlemen with leisure than a way of procuring food. To the peasant it also represented a nuisance, since, if the game he might not freely shoot or trap did not eat his crop, the hunter might trample it.

Fish, unlike game, never lost its importance as part of the staple diet of civilized man, and for many island peoples, primitive or advanced, sea food continued to be the major article of diet. In Europe fish had gained special significance because the church considered it permissible for meals on fast days. At first the only ways of preserving fish were to dry it or to smoke it (a process which was known to some people from time immemorial and to Europeans by the fourteenth century). A Dutchman named William Beukelszoon devised an improved process of gutting and salting herring (c. 1375). From then on fishing developed into a large-scale industry, and the countries located around the North Sea grew rich on it; Amsterdam is sometimes said to have been 'built on herring bones'. In the seventeenth and eighteenth centuries the fishing banks near Newfoundland were so profitable that their possession became a factor in international diplomacy from the Treaty of Utrecht (1713) on. As a source of oil, spermaceti (important in making candles and cosmetics), and whalebone, whaling was a special branch of fishing, producing huge profits at great risk by filling needs now generally supplied by petroleum, plastics, and steel. Spitsbergen was the centre of 'the Greenland fishery', which slaughtered whales by the thousands.

*　　　*　　　*

Expansion of Trade

The increasing productivity of seas, soil, and mines might well have been only of localized benefit had it not been for a concomitant development in the ways of distributing goods and services. The expansion of trade was a natural result of the expansion of geographical knowledge during the centuries between 1300 and 1775.

Before 1300 Europeans had been outclassed in trade and finance by the great trading nations of other regions. Japanese shipping went out into much of the world, rivalling Muslim and Christian traders as far west as the Indian Ocean. The Chinese also had long distinguished themselves as merchants. Their powerfully developed guild system protected their common interests and regulated many aspects of their trade and competition. Chinese merchants knew of bookkeeping, paper credit instruments, trading associations, complicated methods of payment for transactions between distant points, and other refinements for facilitating the exchange of goods long before such practices became common in the West. Much of Chinese trade was domestic and independent of export and import, since the vast regions comprising China were relatively self-sufficient, and until the nineteenth century the Chinese professed only limited interest in relations with European traders. Even so, Genoese and Venetian merchantmen could be seen in Chinese waters in the fourteenth century, the Portuguese established a prosperous post at Macao in 1557, and the annual visit of the Spanish galleon from Acapulco brought Chinese junks in droves to Manila to exchange their wares for those of Europe and America.

Still more spectacular perhaps than the trading activities of the Chinese were those of the Muslims, particularly the Arabs. The central position of Islam in the Afro-Eurasian land mass had long made the Muslims the natural middlemen for the flow of goods among the several regions. Their caravans travelled to far-off places; their ships roamed the seas southward to East Africa, westward all over the Mediterranean, and eastward to Ceylon, the Malay Archipelago, and the China coast. In Asiatic waters Muslim traders had built a commercial empire centring upon Malacca, and Arab dhows competed successfully with Chinese, Japanese, Javanese, Persian, and Indian junks and sampans before the end of the fifteenth century, and after that with Portuguese and other European caravels as well. Merchants held a respected position in Muslim society and literature, and the acquisition of money by hard work and trade carried no social disapproval such as was expressed in certain quarters of contemporary Europe.

On foundations laid in the eleventh, twelfth, and thirteenth centuries, the economic system that we have already identified as capitalism grew up in western Europe. In this system an essential role is assigned to the investment of money and to the drive to accumulate more money—for a higher standard of living and for the expansion of economic enterprises as well as for the satisfaction of basic material needs. In the capitalist system economic rationalization (i.e. careful calculation of the most efficient means of exploiting the various sources of wealth) is cultivated, a clear social differentiation may and frequently does separate the owners (whether of factory, trading establishment, or bank) from those who work for them, manufacturing and selling ordinarily occur on a grand scale, production does not take place upon order but rather on the basis of anticipated demand or even of studied creation of new demand, and motivation, frankly based upon the incentive of profit in an autonomous, competitive market, at times eludes the restraints of custom or religious precept.

The growth of capitalism during our period took place in the face of many obstacles but also under the protection of the dynastic state. Although significant in agriculture and industry too, between 1300 and 1500 its effects were most notable in the development of commerce and finance. The merchant guilds were gradually replaced by independent merchants, many of whom became veritable 'merchant-princes' (such as Jacques Coeur of Bourges, the Medici family of Florence, and the Fuggers of Augsburg) or by group organizations (such as partnerships, trading companies, and commercial leagues like the Hansa). The guild, emphasizing local control and regulation, was not adaptable to the rapid expansion of trade; it could not readily reach out geographically or lend itself to quick manipulations, as could the more ambitious entrepreneurs. Independent commercial groupings were easily initiated and in general gave greater leeway to their members, thus facilitating commerce over vast areas and taking advantage of special opportunities. The new businessmen did not always advocate unrestricted competition and freedom of enterprise; on the contrary, they frequently sought monopolistic rights and privileged status from their sovereigns. Independence from government regulation and freedom of trade became the businessman's objectives only later, when the new master, the powerful state (especially if a foreign state), became an obstacle to capitalistic enterprise.

Some of the richest traders were strong enough to go their individual ways without partners. The biggest among them had their own quarters and offices, tended by stewards or minor partners, in scattered trading centres such as Venice, Florence, Bruges, Augsburg, Nuremberg, or London, and later Antwerp or Amsterdam. They had their own pack trains or, if they engaged in maritime trade, their own ships. The ambitious Jacques Coeur actually had a whole fleet for his Levantine trade and branch offices in the major towns of France and Italy. Only the really wealthy or venturesome merchants dared run the risks of trading as lone entrepreneurs, for ships and pack trains were too frequently destroyed by natural disasters, piracy, and highway robbery, and markets were often undependable. For the more cautious, the mutual sharing of profit and loss through some kind of short-term (*commenda*) or long-term (*compagnia*) partnership constituted a safer arrangement. In addition, marine and commercial insurance was inaugurated in Italy before 1300 and spread to other regions in the fifteenth century, though only toward the end of our period was it widely employed. Occasionally partnerships involved unfamiliar legal complications, but they were gradually regularized in a separate branch of civil law based on Roman practices.

The development of trans-oceanic trade after 1500 stimulated the rise of the trading company with numerous partners. Such a company frequently included individuals who merely made a contribution toward the purchase of 'stock' in return for a share in the expected profits without being actively engaged in the trading activities. Some of these 'joint-stock' companies, such as the British and the Dutch East India Company, founded respectively in 1600 and 1602, grew so powerful that they controlled vast colonial empires, each with a standing army of 10,000 or more and with a huge administrative personnel. Most of these associative forms of commerce (as noted also in connection with manufacturing) found a powerful protector in the state. Rulers were interested in safeguarding the welfare of the companies they chartered and granted them protective tariffs and subsidies in addition to privileges and monopolies, in the expectation that the royal treasury would profit as the companies' revenues increased. When the dynastic states grew strong enough, they sometimes took over the role of protector-exploiter that had been filled earlier by great commercial leagues. In the course of time merchant and monarch seemed to become ever more closely linked by a chain of gold.

★   ★   ★

Transportation and Travel

During the Middle Ages long-distance trade was particularly profitable in luxury goods. Because of the general self-sufficiency of the manorial system and because of transportation difficulties, bulk goods constituted but a small part of Europe's trade. Although trade in luxury goods remained important after 1300, the character of the principal commodities changed as specialization by region became more pronounced in industry and money economy gradually superseded manorial and feudal economy. Bulk goods like textiles, grains, wine, fish, and lumber became more common as articles of commerce. Regular fleets, first annually and then at more frequent intervals, went from Italy to carry luxury goods to the north and to bring Flemish cloth from Bruges. Other ships brought Baltic grain and wood to Flanders and England. Wine was shipped from Gascony and Portugal to England. Swedish ores went to northwestern Europe. From Novgorod the Western countries imported furs and candle wax. Where possible, bulk goods were moved by important inland water routes such as the Rhine, Loire, Seine, or Danube. Even overland traffic increased, though on a much smaller scale, profiting from new types of wagons, better methods of harnessing horses, and improved roads. The separate parts of Europe gradually learned to depend upon various other regions for varied goods. (Map III.)

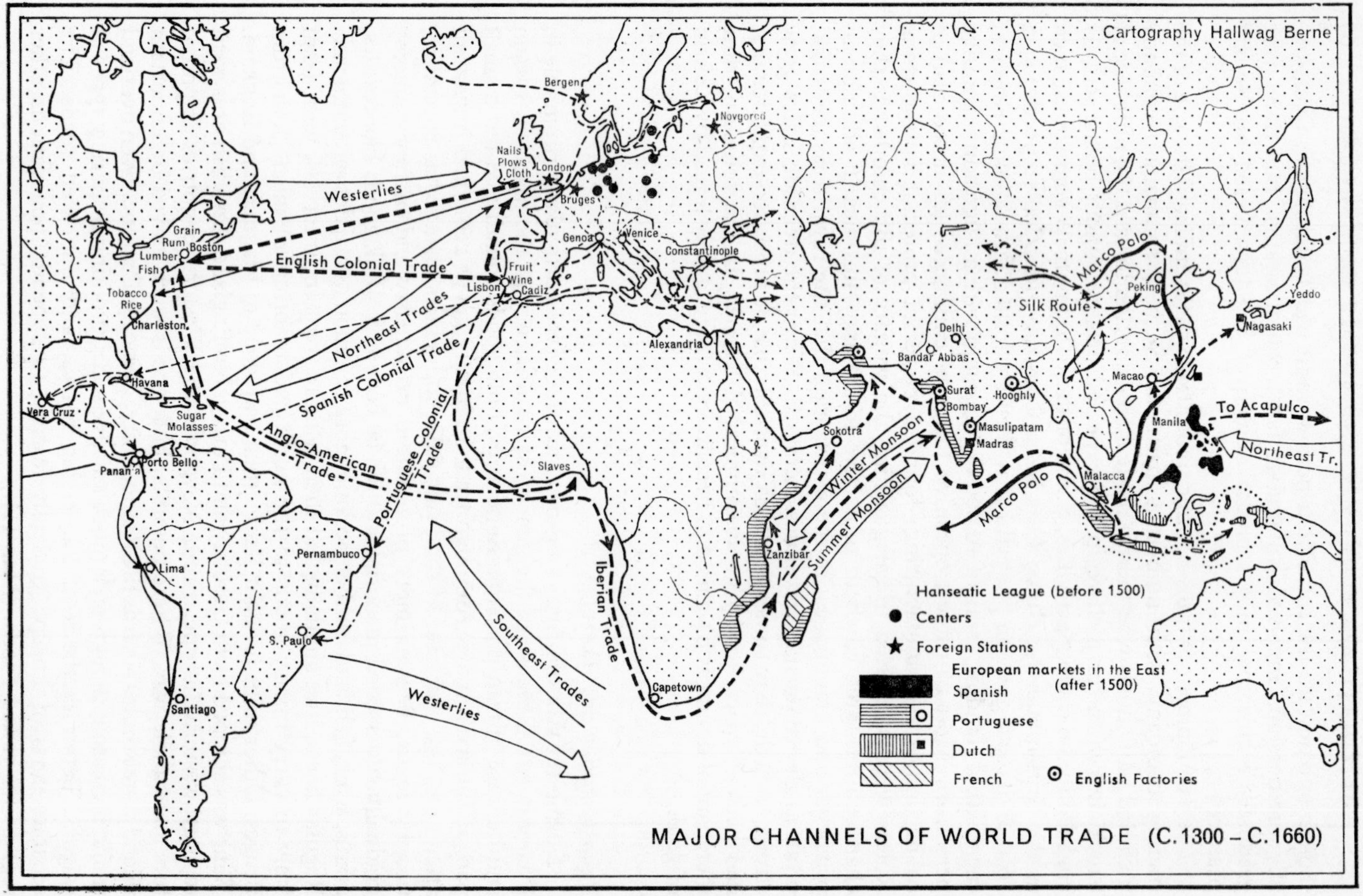

MAP III

MAJOR CHANNELS OF WORLD TRADE (C. 1300 – C. 1660)

Cartography Hallwag Berne

Hanseatic League (before 1500)
Centers ●
Foreign Stations ★
European markets in the East
Spanish
Portuguese
Dutch
French
English Factories

To Acapulco
Northeast Tr.
Yeddo
Nagasaki
Marco Polo
Peking
Macao
Manila
Silk Route
Malacca
Marco Polo
Delhi
Bandar Abbas
Surat
Hooghly
Bombay
Masulipatam
Madras
Socotra
Winter Monsoon
Summer Monsoon
Zanzibar
Capetown
Iberian Trade
Southeast Trades
Westerlies
Novgorod
Bergen
Venice
Constantinople
Genoa
Alexandria
Nails
Plows
London
Cloth
Bruges
Fruit
Lisbon
Wine
Cadiz
Slaves
Portuguese Colonial Trade
English Colonial Trade
Northeast Trades
Spanish Colonial Trade
Anglo-American Trade
Westerlies
Grain
Rum
Lumber
Boston
Fish
Charleston
Tobacco
Rice
Havana
Sugar
Molasses
Panama
Porto Bello
Vera Cruz
Lima
Santiago
Pernambuco
S. Paulo

The greatest increase in trade came when European sailors, with improved ships, marine instruments, and navigational methods, found their way to the great productive centres of Asia and the almost untouched resources of the New World. After 1500 the products of the Orient that previously had trickled to Europe by long, broken overland stages could arrive directly oversea and *en masse*. A shipload of spices or cottons or chinaware, for example, might bring immense profits in regions that had developed a taste for things like those, which helped make life pleasanter. The Asian civilizations had little demand for European goods and generally preferred payment in precious metals, thus causing a flight of gold and silver from Europe to India and China.

Europe's colonies in the New World, in compensation, constituted an expanding market for European manufactures and a source of precious metals. As long as the overseas dominions could be prevented from creating industries to meet their own needs, they were dependent upon the homeland for manufactured goods like hardware and cloth, for which they paid with colonial products (gold, silver, sugar, rum, timber, tobacco, pelts, hides, etc.). But this trading pattern, particularly favourable to England, encountered serious disruption when the colonies began to produce their own textiles and metal goods. The Anglo-American settlers also built excellent ships, and their merchant fleets rivalled the home country's. Besides, they participated in smuggling on a wide scale, thereby further undermining the British mercantilist system. Despite French, British, and other pirates and smugglers, the Spanish and the Portuguese proved more successful in controlling the trade of their colonies, and the exchange of colonial raw materials for Iberian goods and African slaves was not seriously interrupted. Hence the Latin-American colonies, unlike the Anglo-American ones, failed to develop their own industries (except gold and silver mining).

Trading activities increased in large part because of the improvement of transportation. The advances in science and technology that helped to bring about that improvement will be considered in Chapter XV. Ships were built that made sea voyages more economical and safer. First, the less manoeuvrable but more profitable carrack replaced the galley, and about the same time came the small pioneering caravel of the Portuguese and Spanish; then the big, lumbering galleon; later, the speedier merchantmen of the Dutch and British; and, finally for our period, the fast American vessel, ancestor of the clipper. Considerable numbers of Europeans became skilful sailors provided with ever-improving nautical instruments, maps, and techniques with which to conquer the vast spans separating their homelands from the rest of the world. The seas also became better highways, to the distinct commercial and strategic advantage of the thalassocratic countries. Port facilities improved as wharves, docks, repair shops, and supply depots were built. Better and more abundant markers, lighthouses, and buoys helped the sailor find his way more safely. Piracy remained a serious problem (especially as it was condoned by other nations as a means of harming the commerce of rivals). The Barbary corsairs, the terror of the Mediterranean, roamed as far as Iceland. Towards the end of our period European governments began to cooperate to reduce piracy.

Better transportation developed simultaneously on land. Carts with increased capacities, stronger draft animals, and better harness made possible bigger loads. The road net of Europe slowly expanded, and the French and other governments required a special *corvée* for work on road surfaces. Inns and rest places grew up on all highways for the ever-growing number of travellers, who were thus no longer dependent on monastic hospices and mission houses. Regular postal systems (longer known and better developed in some of the eastern civilizations) were introduced into several European countries. Additional bridges and ferries were installed. Highway robbery remained a scourge, and attempts to counter the danger led to better policing and severer penalties. In general, until the end of our period, roads were bad, and since shipping was cheaper than land transportation, the seas, rivers, and canals carried the bulk of trade. On the whole, transportation facilities, especially by sea, kept pace with the expanding needs of merchants and in many cases made possible trade achievements that might well have astonished former generations.

*   *   *

Banking and Finance

With the expansion of trade, the exchange of coin grew more common, and the transportation of bullion became a serious problem. For a while shipments, especially those to Rome, were entrusted to the knightly orders (Templars in particular), but as the quantities became larger and more cumbersome, other methods were sought. Italian money-lenders, particularly Lombards and Genoese, had learned, despite church scruples, to make a profitable business out of exchanging one coinage for another, and many of them were engaged in collecting papal revenue from all over Europe. In transactions with some of the Italian merchants travelling to northern European fairs, they gradually developed customs and institutions from which the modern banking system has evolved (see Chapter VIII).

Instead of transporting money throughout the Continent and actually handling vast cash sums in large transactions, merchants came to deposit cash in 'banks' in some of the important trading centres of Europe. Originally such institutions were 'exchange banks', where it was possible to exchange one coinage for another, a process which contributed only slightly to solving the problem of money transportation. Realizing that business could be conducted in a much more efficient way by a system of credit that would eliminate the necessity of transporting large sums of hard money, Italian bankers established branches all over Europe at which merchants could complete transactions without actually having to handle coin. In this way a note, or 'bill of exchange', issued by the agent of an Italian banker in England might be redeemable in cash in Milan, Florence, Venice, Genoa, or Siena; and instead of hauling Florentine coins to Bruges to pay for cloth bought there, the Bruges agents of the bankers, whether Bardi, Peruzzi, or Medici, would draw on their Florentine deposits there.

Some such method of branch agencies whereby ownership of money might shift by means of notes, bills of exchange, or other banking paper had been known to the ancient Sumerians and to the Arabs, Jews, Chinese, and Japanese at various times before 1300. In Europe, however, it developed into a banking system. From the private banks established by the Italian dynasties of money-changers eventually evolved state banks such as San Giorgio in Genoa and Rialto in Venice. The steps at first were simple. International loans were floated by groups of private bankers, a noteworthy example being the 'consortium' (partnership) of several Florentine families to provide Edward III of England (1312–77) with funds for an invasion of France at the outset of the Hundred Years' War. The handling of papal revenues and the proceeds of the English wool trade came to be dominated by Florentines and other Italians. The giro-bank, or deposit and transfer bank, in which one could deposit money and transfer it to others for business payments, appeared about 1300 and gradually became more ambitious and complex.

Only, however, with the development of double-entry bookkeeping during the fourteenth and fifteenth centuries could banks become more than simple institutions. Double-entry bookkeeping made possible a better understanding of assets and liabilities, profits and losses, and thus enabled banker and customer to have a complete financial statement and accounting at any stage. It was used by the great trading companies as well as the banks of the day, and it is hard to see how big business could be conducted without it. Some of the greatest exchange banks such as the Amsterdamsche Wisselbank, the Bank of Hamburg, and Venice's Banco del Giro were founded or acquired importance only after 1600.

These exchange institutions at first did not perform a function which is essential to the development of the modern bank: in general, they made no loans from bank deposits. Church scruples against certain kinds of interest restricted the ways in which such transactions could be made profitable. But with increasing accumulations of cash and growing needs of merchants for capital, loans of bank deposits became an accepted feature of economic life. The early loan offices of the Flemish cities (*tables de prêt*), often set up temporarily at fairs, made loans in forms which resemble modern promissory notes. Italian and Catalonian bankers often united in city-wide associations (such as the Genoese, Barcelonian, or Florentine deposit banks). German merchant families like the Fuggers and the Welsers began to refine the system by using cash deposits, funded debts, and even notarized contracts of business transactions for making loans, on which they collected interest according to varied and rather complicated principles. Subsequently, bankers in the Low

Countries developed a system of negotiable commercial paper (much like cheques), which were backed by deposits in their banks. About 1650, acceptance of such negotiable credit papers became general. Still later national banks such as the Bank of England were established and issued national currencies.

In the beginning many banking enterprises were closely associated with political activities. Sometimes such association brought disaster. The Italian houses of the Bardi and the Peruzzi were ruined when Edward III repudiated his Hundred Years' War loans. The financial wizard Jacques Coeur went bankrupt because of the machinations of numerous enemies at the French court. On the other hand, bankers could exert tremendous political pressure. Some became international powers, as the Medici and the Fuggers.

As commerce developed, it became more and more dependent upon an improved monetary system. While some primitive societies continued to use shells and glass beads as a means of exchange, the more advanced cultures depended on metallic coinage, usually of gold, silver, and copper. The need for reliable standards and close supervision of coinage grew as trade on an international basis prospered and coins of various types had to be interchanged. It became essential that coinage be kept constant in weight and alloy. Paper money began to be acceptable as a substitute for precious metals in the seventeenth century in some European countries. The population could be expected to accept such paper promises only if assured that they were backed by adequate deposits of bullion. The minting process therefore became more than ever the concern of monarchs and municipalities that coined their own money. The confidence in the money of Florence was so general that after the thirteenth century its monetary unit, the 'florin', was the most commonly acceptable coin in Europe, a sort of international monetary standard, comparable to the 'pound sterling' of later centuries. Although the mints at first were in the hands of privileged semi-private entrepreneurs, they came to be more thoroughly regulated by law and supervised by government fiscal agents. By gradually nationalizing mints governments reduced the profusion of coinage so that only a few remained in international circulation and national currencies moved towards uniformity.

Governments were not always above dubious practices such as debasing their coinage. They soon found, however, that they were not really at liberty to manipulate finances at will but were subject to certain laws of economics. Populations refused to accept paper that was not backed by sufficient confidence or by precious metal, as the English and the French discovered in the booms of the late-seventeenth and early-eighteenth centuries. Neither could rulers improve the wealth and living standards of their countries by merely accumulating precious metals without concurrent expansion of production through industry and commerce. This lesson became painfully manifest with 'the price revolution' already mentioned. Inflation benefited only a few elements of the population, particularly the trading classes, which could count on resulting rises in prices, while those with fixed or slowly rising incomes suffered. Prices soared especially in Spain, which neglected to build its own industries since it could afford to purchase abroad whatever it needed.

*   *   *

Government and Business

Between 1300 and 1775 governmental intervention in economic affairs both by direct intent and by the indirect effects of governmental processes tended to become more frequent. Princes recognized that the international relations of their countries were an important factor of domestic economic strength. War, of course, was generally assumed to be potentially either detrimental or beneficial to the total economy of a country. The circumstances that might render it detrimental were obvious. Agriculture might suffer from the impact of battles and a looting soldiery, especially since this was an era of mercenary armies. Warfare might also mean heavy taxes, levied primarily upon the commercial classes, and a serious disruption of trade. Long and intense fighting, indeed, might altogether paralyze trade and gravely retard the development of industry.

On the other hand, a war might sometimes be profitable. Armies rarely numbered more than 50,000 men before the French Revolution and were not so serious a drain on blood and treasure as in subsequent eras. On the other hand, they brought business to the suppliers of munitions (the manufacture of which tended to become nationalized), horses, food, and, when uniforms became common, cloth and clothing. War also furthered the aims of the mercantile classes in less direct ways. For example, when a ruler needed taxes, he might have to make political concessions to those whom he taxed, thereby fortifying the bourgeoisie in particular. Furthermore, victory in battle or diplomacy frequently benefited a country's commerce, winning strategic territory, eliminating customs lines, forcing trade concessions, and consolidating newly acquired markets and resources with the old. The Hansa trade in the eastern Baltic would in all likelihood have been less feasible without the pacification of that area by the Teutonic Knights; the Mongol conquests enabled a considerable amount of goods to flow from east to west directly; British trade gained explicit advantages from the War of the Spanish Succession; and the Dutch might never have acquired a colonial realm if they had not been fighting Spain during the late-sixteenth and early-seventeenth centuries. State-supported piracy, as practised by English and Dutch marauders on the Spanish Main and by the Barbary *reises*, was a lucrative business. The moral issue of war was not lost on contemporaries like Hugo Grotius (1583–1645) and the Quakers (see Chapter IX), and some questioned whether commercial advantages could not better be procured by peaceful means. Nevertheless, since military action could generally be localized, *raison d'état*, the overriding interest of the state, was regarded as well served by the
D*

triumphant sword, and so the threat of war and war itself were regular instruments of diplomacy and persuasion.

Yet political decisions, if based on considerations of power or national unity alone, might have significant economic consequences. Political motives took precedence over economic ones in the expulsion of Jews and Moors from Spain and of Huguenots from France. The granting of monopolies and other mercantilist practices, and certain taxes (for example, ship money), were sometimes justifiable by the logic of politics rather than of economics. Invasions commonly meant some degree of destruction for the fortified cities in the invader's path. Merchants tried to find protection against political arbitrariness or miscalculation through mercantile leagues, commercial codes, guilds, municipal charters, and royal grants of special privilege. When necessary, they did not hesitate to take part in open revolt against their sovereigns and, as indicated earlier, were conspicuously involved in some of the great rebellions and civil wars of the period.

At certain times and places the hazards of domestic competition were kept somewhat under control through guild supervision of production, markets, prices, weights, measures, and the training and accrediting of the labour force. In some areas the interests of the state and of the mercantile classes were more or less identical (as in Venice, Holland, and Geneva). In the rising dynastic states, however, the overall concern was less for the protection of guild interests than for the safeguard and advance of the economic and political power of the total state. Whereas guilds generally looked after their members only and often worked at cross-purposes with one another, a ruler usually identified himself with his realm as a whole and manifested concern for its economic welfare. For this reason and others already discussed, the guilds steadily lost their importance, and various of their functions were taken over by the political authorities. The tightening grasp of the state through state supervision of markets, state protection of trade, and state support of commercial and industrial enterprises hastened the decline of the guilds perhaps more rapidly than exclusively economic factors.

The deliberate, vigorous participation of the state in economic life during our period is known as 'the mercantilist system', a term made common by the system's major critic, Adam Smith (see Chapter IX). This system was dominant during the latter half of our period. It was the reflection in the economic sphere of the growing political importance of the national state. The basic unit of mercantilistic concern was not the single individual, a *homo economicus*, or any special group of producers or consumers but rather the state as such, the national wealth as seen from the rulers' point of view and as expressed in terms translatable into money. In broadest terms the mercantilist system aimed at creating a strong economic foundation for a strong political state by regulating private economic interest and making the state as far as possible autarkic, or self-sufficient. The policy was regarded as working satisfactorily if the state exported more than it imported in commodities and imported more than it exported in bullion (i.e. if it had what was called a 'favourable balance of trade'), for then it was held to be using its own resources beneficially, to be independent economically of its neighbours, and to be in some way indispensable to the countries with which it maintained a trade balance in its favour.

With these aims in view, governments did other things than regulate trade. They did their best also, for example, to build and control overseas colonies and to gain commercial advantages by diplomacy and war. At home they sought to improve agricultural self-sufficiency so that foodstuffs would not have to be purchased abroad, permitting the export of grain in case of surplus. They encouraged new products and methods that might yield richer harvests. Model farms and agricultural societies were subsidized by state funds in order to present to farmers improved ways of using the soil. New tools and crops would often be introduced on royal estates, stimulating imitation elsewhere. A decision between conflicting systems of agriculture sometimes depended on the preference of the ruler (as in the case of the victory for enclosures and sheep farming in England). Agriculture ceased to be an activity merely of landlords and farmers and became in addition an area of interference by the state for reasons and by means other than taxation.

The concern of governments for industry was perhaps still more serious. Colbert, Louis XIV's 'economic tsar', provided a pat example of a mercantilist statesman. He subsidized and otherwise promoted new industries in France in order to make her independent of imports and capable of earning additional bullion by exports. He encouraged skilled foreign workmen to settle in France (without being able, however, to prevent a flight of skilled workers when his master revoked the Edict of Nantes, which had until then granted toleration to Huguenots). He tried to stimulate shipping and shipbuilding (but had trouble finding sailors to man the ships). Like many other statesmen before and after, he attempted to regulate the flow of goods out of and into France by decree and by the manipulation of tariffs and excises. Like other mercantilists he considered colonies important in this policy and therefore exerted himself to found new ones and to exploit existing ones more efficiently, counting on them to provide raw materials for manufacture in France, markets for the manufactured goods of the home country, and outlets for France's surplus population.

Mercantilism and Cameralism

Mercantilism's basic tenet—government control of economic life for the sake of fortifying the power of the state—aimed also at the advance of the general welfare and thus corresponded closely with the political doctrines by which absolute monarchs sought to justify their position. When some of the eighteenth-century *philosophes* cast the prince in a paternalistic role and made of the 'enlightened monarch' an ideal (see Chapter IX), they gave particular emphasis to his responsibility for his subjects' material welfare. In Teutonic countries mercantilism was frequently equated with *cameralism*, a term derived from the systematic study of state management in the Prussian schools that provided training for government office (*camera*). Impressive examples of rulers who raised their countries' economic level by mercantilist methods were Frederick William I (1713–40) and Frederick II (1740–86) of Prussia. Frederick II went so far as to discourage subjects from indulging in exotic beverages like coffee when the need existed for guns, ploughs, and seed-grains. Mercantilism was a guiding principle of the reforming tsars Alexis (1645–76) and Peter the Great (1682–1725). Charles III of Spain (1759–88) and Joseph I of Portugal (1750–77) extended their paternalism also to their empires in America and the East.

Although mercantilism and cameralism remained the prevalent politico–economic philosophies of this era, they incurred a good deal of criticism, too. Traders and manufacturers naturally were satisfied with government interference if it took the form of protecting their own monopolies and privileges, but if state control interfered with their business or if they did not belong to the groups that benefited from the privileges, they were likely to be resentful. The more advanced colonies began to object to their home governments' regulation of their industries and commerce. When, for example, England changed the long-standing policy of 'salutary neglect' of her navigation acts to one of stricter enforcement, bitterness grew among the colonists who had engaged in illegal (though hitherto rarely policed) industrial and commercial operations. In addition, mercantilism suffered in practice through inevitable loopholes and exceptions. In order to enforce regulations a numerous personnel was needed, and its cost went far to wipe out the profits that theoretically ought to have accumulated. As will become more apparent in Chapter IX, criticism of mercantilism found expression also among certain economic theorists of the late-seventeenth and the eighteenth centuries, particularly in the writings of the Physiocrats, who taught that rulers might improve the economic welfare of their lands by taxing land, relaxing commercial and industrial regulations, and permitting an autonomous market. Finally, in 1776 appeared Adam Smith's *The Wealth of Nations*, which laid the theoretical foundations of the free-enterprise economy of subsequent generations. It was no mere chance that the American Declaration of Independence, the classical statement of anti-colonialism and self-determination of nations, was also promulgated that very year. Absolutism, mercantilism, and colonialism followed hard upon one another and so encountered antagonists about the same time.

SOCIAL CHANGES AND THEIR POLITICAL IMPORT[10]

Before the revolutions of the eighteenth and nineteenth centuries all peoples with the possible exception of certain primitive ones, were divided into readily recognizable strata. Between these strata frequently existed rigid legal barriers and nearly always an appreciable difference in political, economic, and cultural status. Men of different strata were rarely considered by the law equal either in rights or in opportunities, and they derived their standing in society as a rule from the stratum in which (often unalterably) they belonged. One's professional training and social function thus depended upon the social structure of one's culture rather than upon personal aptitude, preference, or achievement. Women suffered or benefited not only from these social classifications but also from special considerations appertaining to their sex.

For a large part of Asia the social structure had become stabilized on foundations laid before 1300. Hindu society had numerous castes, sharing some of the features of the clan, the social class, and the guild. Allegedly derived from the four traditional castes (described in Vol. II, pp. 190–91), they were in our period based more upon birth, geographical location, and modes of employment. While the formation of a group into a new caste was always possible, custom made it hard for an individual to change his caste.[11] In the northern parts of the Indian peninsula the Muslim way of life had flourished since about AD 1000 and became even more dominant under the Mogul Empire (1526–1857). In general, despite periods of Muslim persecution of Hindus (see Chapter V), the newer Muslim culture adjusted in some ways to the Hindu culture, while remaining distinct. Where Muslims had established themselves, either a mixed society had grown up in which Hindu and Muslim lived more or less amicably together or, more frequently, where the Muslims had come as conquerors, they formed a separate stratum that considered itself superior to the Hindu population. In China the general social order was scarcely changed by the several invasions of foreign peoples. The central Asian peoples (Mongols, Tatars, Mamlūks, etc.) remained basically nomadic, even though they had become better acquainted with more advanced civilizations (Chinese, Islamic, and Russian) and had learned new techniques from them.

In some areas of the Pacific, on the other hand, significant cultural change took place during our period. In the Malay Archipelago (particularly Sumatra and Java, its most populous and civilized islands), after 1400, a majority of the people gradually and voluntarily substituted Islamic beliefs and patterns of behaviour for their earlier Hindu–Buddhist ones. In Japan internal upheavals during the later Heian period (see Volume III) had led to the rise of a new class, and with it new social ideals. In the resulting feudal society the *daimyos*, or feudal lords, and their retainers, the *samurai*, emerged with their own specific code of behaviour and with substantial economic and legal privileges. During our period this class further entrenched itself and rose far above the Japanese farmers; and the leading daimyo, the shogun, particularly after the beginning of the seventeenth century, followed an earlier precedent of ruling in fact, though in the name of the mikado. The ideals of the samurai—their faithfulness to duty, their obedience to higher authority, their low regard for life itself (especially if it meant life without honour), and their martial spirit—

were to help shape *Bushido*, the strict though unwritten Japanese code of chivalry (see Chapter III).

In the Islamic world the stratification of society underwent a variety of changes. In India, new governors (nawwābs) were appointed to administer newly conquered areas. The Ottoman Turks, like many other Muslim regimes that controlled large populations of different stock and religion, made efforts to absorb at least those who belonged to the upper social layer. This process was supplemented by a unique system of assimilation: Christian children who showed aptitude were taken from their parents, raised in the Islamic faith, and turned into loyal and carefully trained slaves of the sultanate. The crack troops of the Porte, the Janissaries, were recruited in this fashion, to the exclusion, at least at first, of the free-born Ottoman aristocracy. So were some of the best civil administrators. This system achieved its purpose—complete devotion to the sultan—until the Janissary corps was opened to free Muslims (*c.* 1600), when discipline gave way to competition for advantage.

Until Ottoman rule was firmly established, the Turks ravaged Bulgaria, Serbia, and other countries that resisted, deporting or forcibly converting stubborn Christians. Once submissive, however, conquered peoples generally received, except for the tribute in children, a considerable measure of economic freedom and religious tolerance. For some important functions, especially in commercial and financial affairs, the Turks made direct and open use of the skill of their Greek-Orthodox, Armenian, and Jewish subjects. Yet—aside from the Bogomils, a heretical Christian sect that, though persecuted since its origin in the tenth century, still survived in Bulgaria, Serbia, and especially Bosnia (see Chapter II)—Turkey's Christians did not voluntarily turn Muslim in large numbers, and their desire for religious and political independence remained strong.

The Structure of European Society

During the centuries between 1300 and 1775 (except in England, where class lines tended to lose some of their distinctness) European society as a general rule was divided into three basic social classes—nobility, bourgeoisie, and peasantry. These classes, however, did not grow in quite the same way in the several regions of the Continent over the centuries. The social configuration of the eastern countries (Poland, the eastern Baltic regions, and the huge Russian realm) differed from that of the western countries in at least one significant respect: eastern European society seemed, in contrast with western society, to be divided into landowners and peasants alone, with relatively negligible middle classes. To be sure, the eastern countries had a well-to-do bourgeoisie in the cities and some more or less free farmers in the country districts, but towards the close of our period these middle classes, primarily because of their failure to keep pace in commerce and industry, did not achieve an influence comparable with that of their counterparts in western Europe. Stratification essentially into two classes—servile and ruling—had a profound effect on the culture of the eastern populations. A rich folk-culture survived among the lower classes and was particularly varied and impressive in tales, fables, song, dance, and handicrafts. It was fortified and encouraged by the churches—Orthodox in Russia, and Catholic and Uniate in Poland. The upper classes, however, largely imported their culture from western Europe (particularly France, but also Germany and Italy). They adopted western fashions, ideologies, and speech, along with western art, architecture, and literary standards, to an extent that their nineteenth-century nationalists were to consider unforgiveable.

Social cleavage was likewise intensified in the central European area (Austria, Hungary, Bohemia, and eastern Germany, for instance). Even more than in France, the nobility tended to move toward the court and away from the farms, and in so doing they moved in spirit away from the farming population. In post-Reformation Hungary, religion confirmed the gap between the great landlords (the magnates), most of whom were Catholic, and the lesser nobles, many of whom adopted, for a time at least, the Calvinist or Lutheran faiths. Two factors, however, distinguished the social pattern of central Europe from that of Russia and Poland. In the first place, although the majority of central as well as eastern European peasants were either tenants or serfs, there was also in central Europe, especially in the mountainous areas, a type of farmer that was relatively free from, or merely nominally subject to, a landlord. Perhaps more important, the urban middle class of central Europe, despite the weakening of the Hansa, did not lag so far behind western European standards as did the middle class of eastern Europe. The German middle class was prominent especially in Saxony, Bohemia, and such Hansa towns as still throve, and it was sufficiently effectual to help assure a measure of commercial and industrial advance and a significant cultural development. By the eighteenth century, if not earlier, many of the trends and purposes characteristic of the western European middle class were to be found among the bourgeois inhabitants of Vienna, Budapest, Prague, Leipzig, Dresden, Munich, Nuremberg, Augsburg, and Berlin. Though to a degree that was not so regularly attained as it was farther west, an urban middle class flourished even in Moscow, St Petersburg, or Warsaw (which owed their prominence, however, chiefly to being royal or ecclesiastical capitals and bureaucratic centres rather than commercial and industrial metropoles).

In western Europe seigniorial society was obviously declining, even if still very much alive, foreshadowing a future in which middle-class sentiments, with a strong penchant for anti-aristocratic, if not egalitarian, philosophies, would ultimately prevail. As already explained, the middle class arose among the citizens of the towns, the bourgeois. By the eighteenth century the terms *bourgeoisie* and *middle class* were generally, if somewhat inaccurately, interchangeable. Members of the middle class penetrated the ranks of the nobility to an ever-increasing degree through marriage, elevation to nobility by sovereign decree, or appointment to certain ennobling functions. Although many bourgeois gentlemen doubtless tried to adapt themselves to the outlook and conduct of the highest social class, they also gave a bourgeois cast to aristocratic social standards. By a similar process middle-class norms and preferences were accepted in turn as ideals by those lower social groups that sought to be identified with the bourgeoisie. Unlike the nobility, the middle class was 'open' at both bottom and top, and, unlike the peasantry, it enjoyed some social prestige. Since advancement into and out of it was legally permissible and relatively feasible, it became accountable for a good measure of social mobility. The scion of a peasant or urban workman might become a merchant and accumulate wealth. He might invest again in land in the hope that future generations of his family might enter the nobility with a good place-name. Some added place-names to their family names without titles of nobility. The possibility of *anoblissement* often provided an incentive for a bourgeois capitalist who aimed to rise above his status. The *philosophe* Montesquieu suggested ennoblement as a regular device for recruiting the ablest bourgeois for the nobility (provided they left their bourgeois activities behind). Largely because of the mobility of the bourgeoisie, despite its support of institutions (like guilds) and principles (like property qualifications for voting) which tended to make it a closed and privileged cast, society was not 'frozen' and the push-and-pull toward social advancement became a powerful political force. In Britain, where primogeniture deprived younger sons of titles and estates and often forced them into trade or commerce, and where the lines between yeoman and gentry and between gentry and nobles were indistinct, social mobility was more pronounced than in other monarchies.

The professions also provided a good avenue towards social advancement. As previously remarked, before our period specialization of labour was rarely found in Europe in any field of endeavour. A feudal lord might be judge, administrator, soldier, and landlord. A barber was very likely also a surgeon. An artist might well be also an engineer, an architect, or a craftsman in a variety of crafts. And a churchman might combine several functions, such as social worker, teacher, writer, councillor, and librarian, with that of spiritual leader. In the well-developed civilizations of the Far and the Near East, as in Classical Antiquity, specialization of labour had been more common than in medieval Europe. After 1300, even in Europe, the trained and specialized professional man assumed an ever greater significance in society. As education and specialization became more common (see Chapter XVI), the rapidly maturing professions gradually displaced the clergy from some of its activities. Lawyers were often named to political offices previously held normally by high clerics. With the spread of learning among laymen, it was less often necessary to call upon clergymen for work that required an ability to read, write, and cipher or some fuller measure of education. Secular artisans and artists developed techniques and arts that had previously been largely monopolized by monks.

Conspicuous changes in the importance of the cleric as professional factotum came with the Renaissance and the Reformation. Wherever teaching was influenced by humanists, many teachers were not clergy at all or were so only in name. At the higher social levels private tutors became more common, and in keeping with humanist educational ideals, they tried to equip their pupils with the secular knowledge and skills required of ladies and gentlemen as well as with Christian doctrine. The arts and sciences were with growing frequency pursued by laymen, and for purposes unconnected with the church. After the Reformation, although the political power of the clergy did not vanish in either Catholic or Protestant lands, its hold upon government offices was greatly diminished. The Jesuits until their temporary suppression in 1773 and other teaching orders rebuilt the church's educational influence in Catholic countries, but there were no Protestant charitable and teaching orders or, for that matter, monastic farms, wineries, commercial enterprises, or convent hospitals and almshouses. Although the clergy still engaged in numerous activities not directly religious in character, even Catholic church-men became concerned with religious affairs more exclusively than before, while the state took over other functions they had previously performed. Some of the more radical sects held that a true Christian life could be led altogether without the help of an organized priesthood (see Chapter IV), but they nowhere gained control long enough to abolish the church entirely. In fact, even in Protestant countries the churchman remained an influential figure in society and politics, whose presence was practically indispensable at baptisms and funerals and highly desirable at weddings, if the participating parishioners wished to be considered Christians, and he was frequently consulted on ethical problems. Yet most of the clergy, once Europe's most ubiquitous and versatile professional group, tended towards the close of our era to wander less frequently outside the field of religion and theology. The national church organization had become, so to speak, that part of the bureaucracy which handled the spiritual needs of the community, although its subordination to the government was rarely complete even in Protestant countries.

The lay professions acquired importance as the clergy lost it. The trend towards specialization in such fields as medicine and law had already set in before 1300. Ancient Greek medicine was well known among the Arabs and, when spread in Europe, brought more specialized medical training from the twelfth century on. Advances in physiology, anatomy, and drugs during the Renaissance and after made more obvious the need for specialization within the curative arts. Although the medieval physician had always been held superior to the surgeon and the pharmacist, the reason had been the method of his work (speculative as opposed to manual) rather than its subject matter. Great surgeons and pharmacists (see Chapters XIII–XV) dotted the genera-tions before the Royal College of Surgeons was founded in London (1800). As their arts became more refined and effective, and as manual labour acquired dignity, the surgeon and later the pharmacist, but rarely the dentist, became esteemed members of society, although they (and the physician, too, but less so) remained the butt of satire in art and literature. The healing professions in general attempted, with the aid of governments, to exclude quacks from their ranks, to increase their never-ending accumulation of knowledge, and to raise their standards.

The expansion of legal knowledge and the demand of the developing nation-state for minds trained in law resulted in the evolution of a profession that became one of the most powerful and respected in Western society. We have already alluded to the lawyers' significance in political and administrative service to their governments. Their training (see Chapter XVI) and interests tended to make them the spokesmen of the middle class, and they were found in large numbers in middle-class representative bodies. They became judges and chancellors, and as such they were in a very real sense the repository of the law, and hence the protectors of society against arbitrary power. Although they were in general faithful servants of their rulers, they did on occasion oppose the royal policies, as the frequent friction between French kings and parlements demonstrates. The British justices of the peace, who were generally unpaid members of the gentry commissioned by the crown to administer justice in the counties, received an excellent training in law and administration without necessarily being professional lawyers. Since the legal profession had articulate rational and secular principles, derived from Roman law and the concept of natural right, its influence on the development of a rational and secular approach to the problem of justice will call for closer examination (see Chapters VIII and IX).

Relevant chapters below (X and XVI) will deal with the developments by which the artist and the technical expert became distinct from the artisan classes to which they had previously belonged. Until the thirteenth century, although Far Eastern painters were personally recognized and esteemed as artists, a European artist rarely signed his work. After 1300 Europe's painters, musicians, and sculptors worked less often in anonymity, becoming instead proud lions of a society that prized their individual talents. We know the names of only few architects of the Gothic cathedrals, but eventually engineering and architecture became so individualized that designing was entrusted to reputed experts, trained in the sciences, draughtsmanship, and mathematics, whose names became bywords. No longer restrained by guild regulations, such experts could aspire to a prestige and remuneration inaccessible to the mere artisan.

Military duty had been one of the obligatory services of the feudal lord and his vassals during the Middle Ages. Although this feature of the feudal system continued in several countries after 1300, in general it gave way, with the advent of new methods of warfare and with the decline of feudalism, to reliance upon specialized, professional soldiers. In place of feudal levies, rulers preferred to raise standing armies, sometimes of mercenary soldiers. Mercenaries were an expensive commodity, and often they were hired only for specific campaigns, passing from one employer to another. For Italian *condottieri* or German and Swiss *Landsknechte* the hiring-out of veterans was a profitable business. Mercenary captains were in general competent officers with expert knowledge of the new firearms and the latest defence and siege tactics. Their men were long-term regulars (sometimes enlisted for life) who hoped to amass small fortunes from their pay and loot. They normally showed greater loyalty to their leaders than to their employers. They were frequently capable of highly specialized services (see Chapter XV).

Mercenary armies remained a fairly familiar military institution until the French Revolutionary era. Although eventually replaced by national standing armies, they persist, after a fashion, in such corps as the French Foreign Legion and the Papal Swiss Guard. The professional officer and the soldier of fortune did not disappear *pari passu*; and some of the great military leaders of the eighteenth century served countries in which they were foreigners (e.g. Prince Eugene of Savoy and Marshal de Saxe), giving their loyalty to appreciative sovereigns rather than to their native countries. Many noblemen of ancient lineage still considered the officer's profession their chief and most fitting field of activity, but they were no longer complete masters of their own troops (even when, as was still permissible, they commanded contingents regarded as proprietary), for they were now subordinate to the king's service. They remained, however, a privileged military class (except in England, where army commissions were easily bought), since non-nobles could advance to the higher ranks only with difficulty and in certain units not at all. The common soldier or sailor was to an ever-increasing extent drawn from the native population. Military life might be tough, but soldiers and sailors were not generally hard to get in times of peace, since soldiering presented a considerable economic and social advancement for the poorer classes. In times of war conscription and impressment sometimes were resorted to. The practice of sentencing prisoners to the galley oars of the French navy persisted until 1748.

Professional specialization helped to change Europe's social structure by enhancing the opportunities for economic reward and social advancement through recognition of individual worth rather than of family status. Modern culture would be inconceivable without the specialized services of many different kinds of experts commanding various degrees of pecuniary compensation and prestige. Though professional distinction was not unknown in the earlier Middle Ages, in large part the modern elite in so far as it is a professional elite arose during our period.

* * *

The Status of Women

Before the nineteenth century women occupied an inferior position in most cultures. Although some polite circles accorded highborn women great respect and even chivalric gallantry, in nearly all civilized societies wives were considered both by law and by social usage subject to their husbands. While a woman might own property in her own right, a European woman of property would rarely remain a spinster or a widow outside a nunnery for long. Even in Protestant countries single women of good family might enter Protestant nunneries. Women might do the larger share of physical labour or contribute significantly to cultural life and yet not enjoy the rights and privileges of men. Variations in the legal and social standing of women were numerous. Their rights in a monogamous society differed from those in a polygamous one. Their position in rural communities was not the same as in the cities. Different religious cults regarded them differently. In addition, caste and class divisions inside the same culture made for differences in the roles assigned to them. In general, except in some primitive matriarchal societies, the master of the household had ultimate control over property, wife, and children, and was the arbiter of everyday decisions.

The European attitude toward women had been subtly changing since at least the twelfth century. Woman was becoming something more than a drudge or a plaything between breeding periods. For one thing, she began to be economically more independent. The church provided one avenue of economic emancipation. Women from all walks of life had always been permitted to join the religious orders, and in a society that had a high esteem for such institutions the nun's or sister's habit brought security and public admiration. Nuns took 'solemn vows' (including poverty); lay sisters took 'simple vows', permitting them to retain property. The number of orders of sisters in hospital and school work increased during our period, giving to a large number of women a chance for useful and dignified occupation without male interference.

The rising economic importance of the bourgeoisie provided another means of raising the economic status of women. The marriage of daughters of merchants to scions of the nobility often meant economic advantage for the latter and social advantage for the former. Land, the primary source of wealth in a feudal society, lost none of its value when it passed to a daughter (in those societies where land could be inherited through the female line), but possession of land had been largely limited to the nobility before the rise of the bourgeois class. The new wealth, readily transferable, played havoc with such class distinctions. It easily became part of a rich dowry, whether the bride or groom was noble or ignoble, since feudal practices and obligations did not apply to it. A wife with a good negotiable dowry was not so easily disregarded as a wife with entailed and enfeoffed land, dependent on her husband for the performance of her feudal services.

Meanwhile the intellectual standing of women was also improving. We shall from time to time below encounter women who played a significant part in the politics and letters of India. In Europe, Renaissance artists and writers portrayed women, sacred and profane, as possessed of wit as well as beauty and grace. Renaissance women of the higher classes often were well educated, and in the eighteenth century quite a number achieved fame as writers, actresses, and artists; witness Madame de Lafayette, Madame de Sévigné, Mrs Siddons, Vigée Le Brun, and Angelica Kauffmann. The hostesses of the famous salons of the eighteenth century added to the spirit of the Enlightenment. Learned men of the Enlightenment like Fontenelle and Voltaire dedicated books to women who had helped them in their scholarly work. Writers and teachers throughout our period concerned themselves with the education of girls, and special girls' schools were founded, of which Louis XIV's St Cyr and Catherine the Great's Smolny were outstanding examples (see Chapter XVI).

Of course, women, as always, played an important part in politics. When not themselves generals or rulers, they were the mothers, wives, sisters, mistresses, or friends of generals and rulers. Lucretia Borgia as a useful pawn in the designs of her brother Caesar was one of several women active in Renaissance governments. The political destiny of France lay at times in the hands of women—Joan of Arc, Anne of Brittany, Catherine de Medici, and Madame de Pompadour. Isabella of Castile and Leon helped shape the course of the Spanish Empire. England has good reason to regard the reign of Elizabeth I as one of her periods of highest glory. Catherine the Great was among Russia's most capable rulers. The Habsburg realm was preserved from disintegration by the vigour of Maria Theresa. St Catherine of Siena and St Theresa of Avila in different ways, helped to determine church policies (see Chapters III and IV). Such an array of gifted and influential 'petticoats' (to use Frederick the Great's term) could come only in an age that had begun to regard merit as no less important than either rank or sex. Even though women were not granted equal political rights, the new attitude prepared the ground for their future political equality.

Altogether the structure of European society during our period was gaining a fluidity that made for changing social ideas. Power, wealth, leisure, education, and cultural achievement became less of a monopoly of one stratum of society or of one sex. Together with a liberal political ideology and a rationalist notion of unlimited human perfectibility, these ideals helped to prepare the ground for the belief in a future where all human beings, enjoying equal rights, would be able by sufficient effort to raise themselves to the level of free gentlemen.

THE GROWING INTERDEPENDENCE OF PEOPLES

The cultures of Eurasia, the Americas, and sub-Saharan Africa had been largely detached from each other before 1300. Communication between Europe and Asia, however, had long been feasible and profitable to both sides, although contact between Europe and the Far East was infrequent and mostly indirect. In the era centring upon 1300, the Mongol conquests broadened Europe's direct communication with the Far East and India.

Interrelations among Eurasian civilizations were altered in a fundamental way from the fifteenth century on, and not alone because of the recession of Mongol power. Land bridges from east to west began to lose their importance, with the exception of the Siberian routes, which were continually being opened wider by the Russians. The Middle East and the Syrian coast ceased to be the great entrepot for traffic between the Indian Ocean and the Mediterranean. The Levant trade of the Italian cities (especially Venice and Genoa) gave way as the main channel for eastern goods destined for consumption in Europe. And Arab ships from the ports of the Red Sea and the Persian Gulf yielded their leading place as the chief carriers in the Indian Ocean. In contrast, the Atlantic seacoast, on the outermost western edge of the enormous Eurasian continent, became the centre of a new web that meshed the world together—and it was now an expanding world.

A lengthy series of advances in physiographical knowledge and navigational techniques had made possible a number of geographical explorations, which in turn helped to bring about this fifteenth-century geographical revolution. That story will be told in detail in Chapters XIII–XV. The land explorations of greatest consequence for Europeans before 1775 were limited to America and Asia, for the interior of Africa remained relatively untouched until the nineteenth century. In America, Europeans gradually took possession, and the vast northern steppes and forests of Siberia underwent a similar gradual occupation. The more civilized regions of Asia, however (with the exception of parts of India towards the very end of our period), resisted European penetration.

Iberian Explorations and Conquests

The first centuries of exploration of the Orient by Spanish, Portuguese, Dutch, French, and English resulted in little more than the establishment of trade relations and the founding in the coastal areas of entrepots and missionary settlements. European penetration of India and Malaysia became vigorous only about the 1750's and was not carried out on an effective scale before the nineteenth century. For a while it seemed that ardent and able missionaries might drive Christian wedges into the resisting Chinese, Japanese, and Indian cultures, but a reaction against Christianity set in. Resistance was rather early and thorough in Japan, later and far from thorough in China, and casual in India. On the whole, because of a tendency on the part of Asians and Europeans to feel culturally superior to each other, the accumulating knowledge in Europe of the great Asian civilizations (and vice versa) brought less cultural than political and economic consequences during our period. But (as we shall have occasion to observe in several contexts) the cultural consequences were also considerable.

For our period (1300–1775) the occupation and penetration of the American continents by Europeans had the most immediate and decisive cultural consequences. Other areas of the world that came into contact with the West retained their indigenous culture practically intact until the fuller development of Western technology became a major determinant of their ways. But in South and North America, either immense stretches were only sparsely inhabited by nomadic peoples or, where fixed cultures had developed, they could not match the Europeans' technology. Hence the Amerindians, unable to place great obstacles for long in the path of European encroachments, were overwhelmed with relative ease, though not without partly transforming the culture of their conquerors in the process.

Until 1518 the interest of the Spanish explorers had been largely absorbed by the West Indies and the neighbouring coastal areas of the mainland. In that year, however, the first of the great *conquistadores*, Hernando Cortes, set out with a company of 600 men, 17 horses, and 10 cannon to conquer new lands for the Spanish crown in the interior of Central America. After landing north of Yucatan and founding a settlement near the modern city of Vera Cruz, he advanced inland and was the first European to come into contact with the Aztecs.

These people, who were part of the large language group of the Nahua, had conquered the Toltec Indians and had absorbed a good part of the ancient Toltec-Mayan civilization. As the Toltec-Mayan empire declined, the Aztecs began to dominate the area around what is now Mexico City (*c.* 1325), rapidly expanding their rule over an estimated 5,000,000 subjects. They reached a high level of culture, with a fairly accurate calendar, a complex system of writing, and a well-developed sense of history, mathematics, and astronomy. They could boast some admirable achievements in various arts and engineering; they used metals for implements and ornament; their religion was far from primitive (see Chapter II). Without knowledge of the wheel or beasts of burden, they built impressive monuments, temples, and pyramids (see Chapter XII). The Aztec realm was the first advanced civilization with which the Spanish conquerors came into contact in the New World. As is clear from the reports of Cortes and his followers, the splendour of the capital Tenochtitlan, the country's apparent wealth, and the size of the population filled the invading Spaniards with amazement.

Yet at the time of Cortes' invasion the Aztec civilization, along with the others of Central America, seems actually to have begun to decline. The Aztecs had established a sort of league or confederation of subject or allied towns and a fairly centralized government based largely on a powerful army. Its aristocracy was engaged in the process of replacing the clan community of property by a system of private and hereditary property. The position of 'emperor', though nominally elective, had come to be hereditary by the regular choice of the war leader and principal spokesman from the same family. Apparently strong resentment had arisen against tribute, serfdom, slavery, conscription, human sacrifice, and the stern rule of the 'emperor', for the invading Spaniards easily found tribes that were willing to side with them against their Aztec overlords. Cortes' force, despite its paucity, conquered the land in an incredibly short time, for it had the advantages of small-arms, cannon, horses (none of which the natives had ever before encountered), and the Aztecs' expectation of a white deliverer. When they subsequently revolted, Cortes cruelly repressed them, and Spain came into full possession of her first major colony on the American continent. From there Spanish explorers, missionaries, and settlers advanced northward into California and the area of the Pueblo Indians, and southward into other regions of Central America.

South of the Isthmus of Panama, in the area of present-day Colombia and Venezuela, existed another Indian realm, the Chibcha Empire, with a sound political structure and a lively trade with the civilizations to the north and south. The Chibchas used a pictographical script, which was not, however, quite so far developed as the writing of the Toltecs and Aztecs, and they had a good calendar and system of counting. Their engineering skill was not equal to that of the Aztecs to the north or the Incas to the south, but they perhaps excelled all other American Indians in the art of working gold. The conquest of their land began on behalf of the Welsers of Augsburg, to whom Emperor Charles V, to discharge a heavy indebtedness, had given huge concessions within his Spanish overseas realm. The Welsers' exploitation of the Indians soon evoked considerable complaint and, for that and other reasons, the crown deprived them of their concession. Spanish subjects subsequently conquered the remainder of the vast Chibcha territory, and eventually it became the Viceroyalty of New Granada.

Soon after the conquest of Mexico the Spaniards learned about the great empire of the Incas located, south of the Chibchas, on the Pacific coast in the high Andes. The Inca civilization had reached the peak of its territorial expansion during the fourteenth century. It stretched along the Pacific coast roughly from south of what is now Valparaiso in Chile to what is now Quito in Ecuador, centring in Peru and Bolivia. The ruler—the Sapa (only) Inca—governed an estimated population of 8,000,000 Indians by means of a highly centralized and in many ways oppressive administrative machinery and a strictly stratified society. He was an all-powerful despot but was expected paternalistically to look after the needs of his subjects. His army was of considerable size and had an excellent road and messenger system at its disposal. While the Incas were inferior to the Chibchas, Mayas, and Aztecs in science, their textiles, gold-work, and ceramics were at times superior. They had not learned to write, but trained initiates could send and interpret messages by *quipus*, or knotted threads of different colours. They carried on a limited trade, especially in coastal vessels. Their music and poetry, though unrecorded, were fairly well developed; and their stone-work, architecture, and engineering (particularly in irrigation and water works) still excite admiration.

Between 1524 and 1528 Francisco Pizarro, one of a family whose ruthlessness gave a bad reputation to all *conquistadores*, undertook an expedition that took him as far south as modern Ecuador. There he learned directly of the

Inca realm farther south. In 1531 he returned with 180 men, 16 horses, and only two cannon, and began the conquest of the most powerful American Indian empire. In a fashion similar to Cortes's conquest of Mexico, the large Inca realm was overrun, and subsequent revolts failed to expel the intruders. Spain thus acquired another rich colony, one that contained the most productive silver mine (Potosi) of all America. From Peru her soldiers and missionaries advanced during the next decade into the region which now forms the state of Chile, and by 1600 the whole length of South America along the Pacific coast was hers.

On the Atlantic side of South America, with the exception of the Rio de la Plata region, the interior remained for the most part unoccupied by white men until the nineteenth century. The Portuguese settled only on the coastal fringe of Brazil and did not penetrate inland until later. The Spanish, however, founded several settlements along the Parana and Salado tributaries of the Rio de la Plata as early as the sixteenth century. The Jesuits established a colony in Paraguay in 1607 and converted the Indians to Christianity and communal life in a theocratic state which prospered as a most interesting political and economic phenomenon until the expulsion of the Jesuits. By 1775, with the exception of Patagonia and the immense valley of the Amazon and its tributaries, Europeans had claims, superficially at least, upon all the South American continent.

The American realms of Portugal and Spain underwent population changes that differed considerably from those of other European colonies. In Asia the colonizing powers encountered peoples with long-established civilizations, some of whom bowed to the Westerners' military might but were not yet deeply affected by their mode of life. Even where Europeans succeeded in establishing trading posts, garrisons, or supply depots, they left the local populations, which vastly outnumbered them, more or less to themselves. The Dutch and the English did very little to convert the Asians who fell under their military and economic control. The only place in the East where a colonizing power succeeded in making conversions on a large scale was the Philippine Islands, where the rival missionary efforts of Spanish Dominicans, Franciscans, and Jesuits produced appreciable results. In the African coastal settlements, handfuls of Europeans domineered and segregated the surrounding Negroes—except in the Portuguese colonies, where Europeans and natives mixed on a limited scale. In North America, where the native tribes were, with few exceptions, nomadic and spread rather thinly over vast areas, the European immigrants usually expelled the Indians from their lands and pushed them into the interior, massacring and being massacred in the process. In the West Indies, French and English settlers exterminated or deported the warlike Caribs, from whose name the word *cannibal* is derived. In French Canada the trappers commonly lived among the Indians, but before 1775 only a small fraction of the population was half-breed (*métis*).

In contrast, Iberian America became a great 'melting pot'. Social prejudices, to be sure, tended to keep the races apart, especially in aristocratic circles, which prided themselves on their Castilian lineage. Since, however, the civil law of the Portuguese and Spanish and the attitude of the Roman Catholic Church countenanced intermarriage, children of mixed parentage were born in increasing numbers. The mixed population included *Mestizoes* (White and Indian), *Mulattoes* (White and Negro), and *Zambos*, or *Sambos* (Indian and Negro). Eventually the basic population of the West Indies islands as well as some of the continental areas was mixed.

Nevertheless, social discrimination persisted. Colonial officials, mostly Spaniards born in Spain, though fewest in numbers, formed the highest social stratum. Next was a larger stratum of Whites born in America (Creoles). Then came the part of the population that was partly white (Mestizoes and Mulattoes). Last came the Indians, Negroes, and Zambos. Most of the wealth of the colonies was in the hands of the white strata, and they also held the most important church posts, as well as a dominant position in government, letters, education, and the arts. The increase of the mixed populations, however, tended to break down the barriers between strata, and by the time of the Wars of Liberation in the early nineteenth century the Mestizo had become a significant political and social force. Although the unmixed Indian was generally regarded as inferior and the mixed Latin American populations took centuries to win a dignified status in society, they might well have been worse off if the races had been rigidly separated from the beginning.

The Spanish and the Portuguese succeeded in creating a relatively strong cultural unity out of their colonial realms by providing all strata of society with common bonds such as church and language. From the start the religious orders (Franciscans, Dominicans, Mercedarians, Jesuits, Augustinians, and Capuchins) undertook a vigorous missionary programme by which most of the natives were converted to Catholicism. By these conversions the Catholic Church perhaps gained more adherents than it lost to the Protestants in Europe, although the Indian's devotion was often a confusion of Catholic and pagan beliefs and practices. The church in Latin America played the role of protector and educator of the native population. Largely through ecclesiastical efforts the Indians were introduced to European languages, agricultural and industrial methods, learning, pastimes, and social customs. Universities (modelled after Salamanca), Baroque architecture, and Spanish law were introduced into America rather early and exercised a deep influence. The European settlers in turn adapted themselves to certain customs and uses of the Indians, such as rubber, quinine, and various foods and dyes (see Chapter XV). Out of the symbiosis of the several races grew a mixed culture which, though basically European, yet was different. The peoples of this new culture gradually came to look upon themselves as distinct and identified their interests with the lands they inhabited rather than with the countries of their ancestry. The more enterprising among them began to feel and act as

Mexicans, Peruvians, or Brazilians rather than as Spanish or Portuguese, Inca or Aztec, Negro or White, and the time was not distant when they would become independent peoples responsible for their own destiny.

★   ★   ★

North America

After the sixteenth century the foundations were laid also for the present-day nations of the North American continent. At first the discoveries and explorations of French, Dutch, Swedish, and English led to no substantial colonization, largely because of preoccupation with religious controversy at home and with civil and international wars. After 1600 the north European powers began to found settlements, build forts, and create companies to further overseas enterprises. With the re-exploration of the St Lawrence River and several of its tributaries by Samuel de Champlain (1567–1635), French colonies along their banks began to prosper. In 1608 Quebec, and in 1642 Montreal, were founded and in subsequent decades French missionaries and soldiers (e.g. Father Marquette, Joliet, and La Salle) explored the Great Lakes region and the rivers south of it that led to the Mississippi. Shortly thereafter the French advanced along that river and founded the Louisiana colony. A great chain of rivers (with some difficult portages) linked their sparsely settled Canadian and Mississippi empires (see Map II).

During the same century English adventurers and dissenters, both Protestant and Catholic, undertook to colonize the Atlantic seacoast between the areas that are now Maine and South Carolina. Subsequently the Dutch and the Swedes entered into rivalry with them. By 1700 Europeans from other lands than Spain and Portugal occupied the New England region, the Hudson and Delaware valleys, the Chesapeake Bay area, and the coast of the Carolinas. The English predominated among them in numbers and political strength. Seventy-five years later the lowland east of the Appalachians had a population of about 2,500,000, of whom the more restless, daring, or desperate had begun to push westward across the mountains. The Indian tribes had been driven out of the coastal territory, decimated in intermittent wars, or, in rare instances, absorbed into the white population. This extermination contrasted with the fate of the Indians in Canada, where a much smaller French population had learned to co-exist with the natives.

The civilization that grew up in the English colonies was, therefore, almost entirely European. Yet these colonists had learned much that was new from the Indians, such as the use of potatoes, maize, snowshoes, canoes, tobacco, and certain methods of fighting and trapping, and they had adapted the patterns of the 'old countries' to conditions imposed by wilderness, extremes of climate, and strange surroundings. The demands of frontier life thus left an indelible imprint on the Anglo-Americans,[12] which, however, was different from that left on the 'mixed' cultures of Latin America with their majorities of non-Europeans. The Anglo-Americans also developed into a new people, one that began to feel American rather than British, particularly after the danger of the French in Canada and Louisiana was removed by British success in the Second Hundred Years' War. All thirteen English colonies had interests that differed from, and sometimes conflicted with, those of the British Isles. They had originated from a country where the individual was already fairly mobile physically and socially. The self-reliance taught by conquering a wilderness, the distance from and disputes with the mother country, and sometimes from and with each other, had led some of them to entertain relatively new ideas and try relatively new institutions—a citizen army, separation of church and state, legislative defiance of royal governors, written compacts, charters, and patents that set forth the fundamental principles of their government. They also grew rapidly in power and self-sufficiency. As the young Turgot, as early as 1750, and other observers foresaw, it was but a question of time until they would demand self-determination and independence. Their fight for those rights, the first successful anti-colonial movement of modern times, not only altered Europe's colonial practices and shifted its major colonial endeavours to other scenes but also inaugurated a series of almost continuous political revolutions that took their inspiration from 'the laws of Nature and of Nature's God'.

★   ★   ★

Migrations

Between 1300 and 1775 a considerable movement of peoples took place inside Europe and its vicinity. The Mongols, pushing far and wide over the immense Eurasian continent, settled in parts of eastern Europe. The Ottoman Turks found a permanent home in Asia Minor and the Balkan Peninsula, and some systematic transfer of other peoples occurred under their rule. The Russians moved farther and farther eastward. The Jews were expelled from England in 1290, from France in 1394, and from various parts of the Holy Roman Empire in the fourteenth and fifteenth centuries, and took refuge in Poland for the most part. In 1492, Spain's rulers expelled the Jews, and in 1609 the Moriscos (nominally Christianized Moors), from the Iberian peninsula. Most of the Moors crossed the Straits of Gibraltar into North Africa. The Spanish Jews and Marranos (nominally Christianized Jews) sought refuge in southern France, the Netherlands, and the Ottoman Empire. Less fortunate Jews found temporary or more permanent but still uneasy abode in various ghettoes without being welcome anywhere. During and after the Reformation religious preferences or intolerance caused population shifts of Christian minorities as well. Radical groups (Anabaptists, Moravian Brethren, Mennonites, and Socinians) were regarded with dislike by the more conservative Protestants, and some of them had a social philosophy that was unbending toward outsiders. Since they found it difficult to live with their fellow countrymen, they migrated, some to the Netherlands, some to the Bohemian mountains, Poland, and Transylvania, and some to Pennsylvania. Catholics left Protestant-dominated regions in considerable numbers, as in the Irish exodus to France in the seventeenth century. A diaspora of French Huguenots took place after 1685, when His Most Christian Majesty revoked the edict which had granted them toleration. More than 50,000 families, including many of France's learned men, industrialists, merchants, and skilled workers, left the country and found asylum in England, Scotland, Holland, and Brandenburg, as well as overseas, particularly in Dutch South Africa and the English Carolinas. France's loss thereby thus was the gain of several states that were her actual or potential enemies. During the Age of Enlightenment, as rulers began to realize the possible disadvantages to a state from religious intolerance, religiously motivated mass migrations came to an end (except for the Jews).

The migration that eventually involved the highest numbers and the widest spread was Europe's overseas expansion. It went east, west, north, and south over a period of centuries. The movement to the Orient was numerically less impressive than that to America. Missionaries, traders, adventurers, sailors, and soldiers went east in goodly numbers, but comparatively few settled there permanently. The death-rate among them was exceptionally high, but those who returned home after completion of their journeys were often enriched not only in material ways but also in experience unavailable in their homelands. They helped spread the knowledge of other civilizations and stimulated two-way cultural diffusion.

To the western half of the world flowed an ever-increasing stream of European emigrants. Spanish and Portuguese went to South America, Central America, the West Indies, and the areas that are now the Southwest and the Gulf region of the United States. Frenchmen went to Canada, Louisiana, Guiana, the West Indies, and the Carolinas. The Dutch settled in the Caribbean, Guiana, and the Hudson valley. The British constituted the major part of the white population of the wilderness bounded by Florida, Louisiana, and Canada as well as some of the West Indies and parts of Central and South America. Scotch–Irish and Germans settled in western Pennsylvania and the Appalachian valleys. Swedes and Danes also went to various parts of the western hemisphere. Other migrations were of French and Dutch to Cape Colony, of Spanish to the Philippines, and of Africans to all parts of the Americas. Wherever Europeans settled they usually exterminated, displaced, segregated, or subordinated the natives, but sometimes, especially where Roman and canon law set the precedent, they interbred to an appreciable extent.

Entire populations were not involved in these moves. Only individuals or segments of peoples left home. Some of them sought only adventure, but others were induced to undertake perilous voyages by the desire to find greater freedom, well-being, or wealth, and still others were impelled by force or missionary zeal. Peasants and artisans in debt looked upon indentured service in the lands across the oceans as a means of paying for passage away from landlords and creditors. Devout people who were not willing to bow to the religious preferences of rulers or whose religious convictions made it impossible for them to continue to live in the communities where they had been born crossed the Atlantic to build new communities more to their liking. Spanish, Portuguese, and English authorities sentenced to transportation tens of thousands of felons, paupers, and political prisoners. Black men were forced to move to America by slavetraders, white men to Africa and America by intolerant rulers, black and red men to remoter areas of Africa and America respectively by white intruders who did not want to live among independent men of colour. Thousands of monks and other missionaries took upon themselves the hardships of emigration in order to spread the Gospel and at times to protect the natives from the exploitation of fellow Europeans. Wherever settlers, traders, and missionaries went, garrisons were also likely to go.

Whatever their motives, these emigrants to the new continents ran grave risks. The means of transportation were, by our standards, primitive; the seas were dangerous; the climate of the new countries frequently was harsher than Europe's; the wilderness was often trackless and unexplored; and the natives generally were hostile. Those who ventured forth left behind the culture in which they had grown up, and probably also friends and kin. Thousands died for the lack of medical care, police protection, and defending armies. Not all of them were rewarded by economic gain or greater liberty in the new lands. Collectively, however, they contributed to mankind the concept of a new life in a new world. They brought whole continents, hitherto essentially isolated from one another, into the orbit of a potentially global civilization. They made useful to all mankind parts of the earth which before had lain fallow or had been known only to a few. As subsequent chapters will show, they spread ideas and beliefs, techniques and arts, as well as material goods from which a greater number of men could profit. They committed injustices and crimes, to be sure, and in some places they exhausted the resources of forests, mines, and soil, with consequences that were sometimes serious for future generations and disastrous for some peoples. At the same time, they performed a prodigious amount of hard work in building new cities and exploiting new resources and showed great ingenuity in solving unfamiliar problems and in achieving workable governments. Despite their own intolerance on some occasions, they passed on to future generations an abiding love of that freedom for which they had made great sacrifices. These migrants, transplanting their cultures to new lands, modifying them as pioneer conditions required, borrowing from and lending to the cultures they encountered, basically widened the outlook of man. They developed two kinds of 'new worlds'. Before their time most men knew of only a small part of mankind, but by 1775 the concept of 'humanity' comprised distant regions and strange peoples all over the planet Earth. Furthermore, the concept of 'new world' was no longer a religious concept alone; a 'new world' seemed possible also on the terrestrial globe, a promised land easier of access than the one in the heavenly spheres. And all this went on at the same time (see Chapter XV) that astronomers also were discovering new worlds in the skies.

*　　　*　　　*

Wars and Cultural Diffusion

Conflict and war as well as trade and exploration have meant new contacts among peoples. We shall have several occasions to note how initial contacts, as of Europeans with China and Japan, sometimes led to suspicion and aloofness. Nevertheless, as we have already found, even hostile contacts such as war or the fear of war may promote the interchange of culture. Military campaigns took soldiers to other countries and acquainted them with different civilizations (as was particularly true of the Crusades). Sometimes military conquest necessitated a reorientation either for the conqueror (as in the case of the Mongols in China) or for the conquered (as in the case of the Spanish in the Philippines), and at other times it brought something of a mutual acculturation to both conqueror and conquered (as in the Muslim subjection of India). Occasionally wars built bridges between peoples (e.g. between Europeans and Asians because of the Mongol invasions) or penetrated the seclusion behind which remarkable cultures were hidden from the rest of the world (e.g. the conquest of Mexico, Peru, and some of the African kingdoms).

For better or worse, warfare was a factor of significance in the exchange of cultural influences during the centuries covered in this volume. Some wars were negligible as instruments of intercultural exchange—mere skirmishes for the possession of fortresses or strips of land, or civil wars that frequently resulted in bitter fighting and fearful atrocities but no interchange of peoples and their ways. Some were waged between small states or neighbouring towns, adding little to their previous knowledge of each other. Sometimes, however, coalitions of great states involved whole continents in their clashes, carrying their conflicts far overseas and working important changes among distant peoples. Fought in the name of religion and with all the viciousness man is capable of, warfare on occasion altered the religious concepts of those involved. A few wars were conducted like games according to unwritten but traditionally respected gentlemen's rules, but when nations battled for their very existence or for ideals they cherished, they usually fought bitterly and ruthlessly. Some wars were practically over before they started; others, though perhaps intermittent, lasted so long that they became known by the length of time they had endured—the Hundred Years' War, the Eighty Years' War, the Thirty Years' War, the Seven Years' War.

Between 1300 and 1775 marked changes in technique, tactics, and strategy widened the area, incidence, and consequences of warfare. Warships, equipped with new firearms, became veritable floating fortresses and highly effective instruments of battle (see Chapter XV), and a country with a redoubtable fleet was a formidable power even if it had no great land forces. For the European nations engaged in overseas ventures naval power assumed an unprecedented importance, and the minister of the navy often was minister for the colonies as well. Eventually the great naval and colonial powers of the Atlantic superseded Venice and Genoa in the Mediterranean also. Small feudal cavalry armies (where generally man fought man) disappeared in Europe, though they survived in Japan and China and though in the Middle East huge armies on horseback, equipped with firearms, bows, and swords, were among the best soldiers of the period.

The introduction of firearms hastened the rise of standing armies under the control of a central government (see Chapter XV). Soldiering became a trained and regular profession from which the vast multitude was excluded, providing instead the taxes for the upkeep of the military establishment. Only for special occasions, such as defence against an invader or during a siege, did the whole population of a region or town take to arms. In general, the civil populations were innocent bystanders or unfortunate victims while the professional fighters clashed, looted, and ravaged, until, with the French Revolutionary wars, came the principle of 'the nation in arms' and popular mass armies.

Unquestionably, war wrought senseless destruction, blind havoc, and immeasurable misery. Certain states—Russia under the Tatars and Germany after the Thirty Years' War provide good examples—suffered for generations after contending armies had ravaged their cities and countryside. Ambitious conquerors wasted manpower and economic resources in fantastic and ephemeral projects of expansion, as did Tamerlane (c. 1336–1405) and Charles XII of Sweden (1682–1718). As in all ages, some of the most ruinous belligerent acts were performed by men, like Philip II of Spain (1527–98) and Aurangzīb, who professed high religious ideals and great respect for civilization.

Wars nevertheless produced results now and then that seemed worth the sacrifice entailed. Political freedom, national independence, or the right to worship with a free conscience was gained on occasion (e.g. by the Vijayanagar and the Dutch wars of independence) by means of arms. Sometimes unbearable or anarchical political situations were remedied by the use of force (e.g. the Russians' expulsion of the Tatars and the French Wars of Religion). Once in a while military conflict encouraged cultural contact between peoples that otherwise might have remained mutually aloof (e.g. Christians and Turks). From time to time invading soldiers carried home, along with disease and loot, fruitful ideas, laudable customs, or new crafts, as did those of the French king Charles VIII from Renaissance Italy. Religious faiths and aesthetic impulses spread similarly. Frequently the pressure of war stimulated or hastened economic, scientific, and technological developments at home (see

Chapter XV). Thus, warfare, man's most destructive activity, has at times proved to be a channel of cultural change.

One of the natural consequences of war is the reaction to its horror, with consequent efforts to restore peace and to regulate future relations among nations by pacific means. Philosophers, theologians, and humanists whom we shall encounter in several chapters (see especially VI–IX) were deeply concerned about the warlike proclivities of man, which they considered out of keeping with God's laws, the nobler side of human nature, and the principles of civilized international conduct. Outright pacifism and non-resistance to force were preached by certain religious sects and given serious consideration by influential thinkers. Several political treatises were written expressly to promote an international structure assuring all men undisturbed peace in their pursuit of higher values or to lay down an international law that would promote peaceful relations and diminish the horrors of war. These efforts, though they remained largely without effect during our period, contributed to a growing consensus that man must somehow achieve enduring international peace. Despite the contemporaneous maturing of nationalism and the continued reliance of statesman on force as the *ultima ratio*—and, in a way, because of nationalism and the reliance on force—the yearning spread for some kind of collective organization to preserve peace.

More concrete contributions to the civilized coexistence of nations were made by developments in the conduct of diplomacy. In order to win concessions or to negotiate differences and avoid armed conflict, rulers had always been accustomed to send *ad hoc* representatives to one another's capitals. At the beginning of our period the Italian city-states, Venice in particular, adopted the policy of requiring a diplomatic agent to stay in a given capital continuously. Other nations soon followed suit, and so began the international practice of exchanging permanent embassies. Notwithstanding the intrigue and secrecy that standing diplomatic missions tended to create, they formed a sounder basis for international relations than occasional ones. A regular international exchange of information and opinion on day-by-day affairs made possible better mutual understanding and readier negotiation of differences.

Another diplomatic amelioration of the day was the appearance of great international congresses. Perhaps the most illustrious was that of Westphalia (Münster-Osnabrück), which lasted about four years and finally in 1648 brought the Thirty Years' War to a close. Meetings of the representatives of belligerent countries for the purpose of arranging a peace were common enough before the Congress of Westphalia, but never before had deputations from so many governments negotiated a peace settlement touching so many areas of the world. Despite their exorbitant attention to trivia such as diplomatic precedence, these early congresses made at least a beginning toward the establishment of a 'Concert of Europe'. Congresses were called even in times of peace (notably that of Cambrai-Soissons in 1724–28) to forestall potential causes of a new war. But those and other schemes, we shall have to record again and again, failed to bring international peace. If anything, during our period increasing contacts among nations and peoples seemed to bring more rather than less armed conflict at the same time that they brought more cultural interchange.

NOTES TO CHAPTER I

1. For African names we have usually followed Basil Davidson, *The Lost Cities of Africa* (Boston, 1959), which is the same book as *Old Africa Discovered* (London, 1959). See also Diedrich Westermann, *Geschichte Afrikas, Staatenbildungen südlich der Sahara* (Köln, 1952); Denise Paulme, 'L'Afrique noire jusqu'au XIVe siècle (deuxième partie)', *Journal of World History*, III (1957), pp. 561–88; and Roland Oliver and J. D. Fage, *A Short History of Africa* (Harmondsworth, 1962).

2. Professor Roland Mousnier feels that certain terms should have been handled with more precision. In particular: Can the Mongol 'Empire' a victorious army occupying a conquered country, be compared to the Germanic Holy Roman Empire of Charles V or, better still, the 'Empire' formed by all the possessions of Charles V, a sort of federation of peoples united by the person of the sovereign on the basis of the principles of legitimacy and respect for the laws and customs of each political unit?

   The same applies as regards the absolute monarchy. The monarch of Dahomey was certainly not absolute in the sense that Louis XIV was, even allowing for the dictatorial nature of the latter's war-time government. The concept of representation is not sufficiently clarified and the fundamental distinction between the *major pars*, the plurality, and the *sanior pars*, the best and healthiest part of the population, which should out-weigh the *major pars*, is not clarified. In most cases, it was, in law or in fact, a group of privileged individuals, mostly a small minority, who sent representatives to an assembly. For us, therefore, this assembly had no representative value but, on the other hand, it had a considerable value for contemporaries who would doubtless have despised our system of universal suffrage and regarded those elected under that system as being representative to only a very limited degree. In most cases, the assembly was made up of individuals whose interests were so closely tied to general prosperity that they fully expressed the inmost wishes of all and did so even better than those directly concerned could have done; alternatively, the assembly was made up of those who, by reason of their position as royal officers, were the deputies and interpreters of all, the very mirror of justice, ideal proxies for both governors and governed. In France in the eighteenth century, and in England in the seventeenth century, men made the transition from the Society of Orders to the Society of Classes on the basis of the domination of a sort of middle class, a class derived from wealth and ability, embodying sovereignty, with another type of representativity, the plurality or majority, to use a term deriving from Anglo-Saxon usage, the law of number replacing the *sanior pars* but the majority deriving from a sort of *sanior pars* designated roughly by its resources. This new *sanior pars* took a materialistic form. On this question see: L. Moulin, 'Sanior et major pars', *Revue historique de droit français et étranger* (1958, 4° série, 36, pp. 368–491); *Revue historique de droit comparé*, (1955); *Revue française de science politique* (1952); *Revue internationale d'histoire politique* (1953); *Revue internationale des sciences administratives* (1951 et 1955); *Cahiers de Bruges*, 6, (1956).

   Frequent reference is made to a republic but without sufficiently demonstrating that republic here is not equivalent to democracy unless we consider as democratic any government which is not an absolute monarchy or a dictatorship. But the republics of the Low Countries, Switzerland, and Venice were oligarchies or aristocracies with no genuinely democratic element involved. The power was not in the hands of the greatest number nor were the greatest number represented. Small groups comprising the wealthy, the well to do or those of noble birth were the only ones to participate in the exercise of political power at its various levels.

The authors were aware of these strictures. The word empire *was used in a sense which it frequently bears in English 'an extensive territory ruled over by an emperor or a sovereign state'. Absolute monarchy was used with the following connotation: 'unlimited (as opposed to limited) monarchy'. In this Introduction an attempt was made to provide a generalized summary of world-wide socio–politico–economic developments over nearly five centuries, so far as possible without undue violence to the known historical particulars: a process which demands a deliberate effort to employ judiciously flexible terminologies and classifications. In later Chapters the terminology will be found sufficiently distinctive. (See also Note 10.)*

3. Professor R. Mousnier believes that the tremendous differences between the English landholder and the French 'censitaire' and between the latter and the Russian serf would seem to exclude any possibility of grouping them in the same category.

In England as early as the fifteenth century, the precarious tenure of the peasants was widely accepted. The peasant could be dispossessed virtually at the whim of the feudal lord. In this way, enclosures were facilitated and the peasants became, so to speak, proletarians or tenant farmers. In France, on the other hand, the distinction between the 'direct' seigneury of the feudal lord and the 'useful' seigneury of the peasant became more marked as from the fifteenth century. The peasant, a free man in the majority of cases, became a genuine owner with the right to make use of his produce and to dispose of the land through sale or bequest. Where the 'Coutume de Paris' prevailed, the peasant owner was almost exactly the same as he became in the nineteenth century after the Revolution. See also F. Olivier-Martin, *Histoire de la coutume de la Prévosté et Vicomté de Paris*, (1928–31), 3 vols. In Germany, east of the Elbe, beginning in the sixteenth century, the feudal lord tended to exploit vast areas of land himself, to subjugate the peasants, and to transform them into forced labourers at his pleasure. When serfdom was paramount in Russia in the second half of the seventeenth century, the serf was virtually no more than a thing in the eyes of the lord and Russian serfdom was in fact little different from slavery.

The authors, however, feel that the generalization they made is valid in the broad context of world development.

4. Professor R. Mousnier, by way of addition writes: 'To speak of representative bodies for Spain, France, Denmark, etc. would at the very least call for some explanation as to the concept of representation. Contemporaries considered that an aristocratic or oligarchic minority very adequately represented the whole populace. They were the *sanior pars*, if not the *major pars*. In the French estates of Languedoc, membership of a body of representatives was a privilege deriving from ownership. Twenty-two barons occupied positions in the estates by virtue of a right attached to the baronies they held but four quarterings were required on both the paternal and maternal side. As far as the clergy were concerned, the archbishops and the bishops had a place in the estates by right of their position. The Third Estate was represented by the consuls of certain towns by virtue of their position: for each diocese the episcopal town, the main town which sent deputies every year; sometimes a few towns of lesser importance, which sent deputies in turn. The representivity of such an assembly seemed incontestable. The three types of deputies were regarded as an 'epitome of the provinces and the peoples' proxies'. They were the 'Fathers of the Homeland', doubtless because as great landowners or representatives of great landowners their interests were closely linked to the prosperity of all. (See also R. Mousnier, 'La participation des gouvernés à l'activité des gouvernants dans la France du XVII et XVIIIe siècles'. *Recueils de la Société Jean Bodin pour l'histoire comparative des institutions*, Vol. XXIV, pp. 246 et 256.

5. J. E. E. Dalberg-Acton, *Lectures on the French Revolution* (London 1910), p. 20.

6. R. R. Kuczynski, 'Population', *Encyclopedia of the Social Sciences*, XII (New York, 1937), p. 241; Ping-ti Ho, *Studies on the Population of China, 1368–1953* (Cambridge 1959).

7. Figures taken from 'Additional Material in Connection with the Remarks of Soviet Scientists on the Plan of Volume IV . . .' (MS, 1957), p. 105.

8. R. Barón Castro, 'El desarollo de la población hispano–americana (1492–1950)', *Journal of World History*, V (1959), pp. 325–43. For a closely similar estimate see Silvio Zavala, *The Colonial Period in the History of the New World* (Mexico City, 1962), pp. 162–63. See,

however, Woodrow Borah and S. F. Cook, *The Aboriginal Population of Central Mexico on the Eve of the Spanish Conquest* (Berkeley, 1963), which implies a much higher figure for 1519 and a much lower one for 1570. See also C. Gibson, 'The Transformation of the Indian Community in New Spain, 1500–1810', *Journal of World History*, II (1955), pp. 581–607, and Richard M. Morse, 'Some Characteristics of Latin American Urban History', *American Historical Review*, LXVII (1962), pp. 317–18.

9. Professor R. Mousnier points out that, ultimately, Akbar's successors, Jahāngīr (1605–27), Shāh-Jehān (1628–57), and Aurangzib (1659–1707), did not understand his policy and disorganized the Hindu administration. They abandoned payment of their officials by salary and reverted to payment by *jaghir* a sort of 'living', a group of villages which the official administered as his own property and from which he derived an arbitrary salary. In respect of the tax on land, the emperors abandoned Akbar's system, which involved an estimate of the areas and yields and adopted something approaching a quota tax while they also allowed the officials to divide the tax between the villages without regard to the position of individual farmers. The rulers sold the charges of governor, which often became hereditary, and exploited the peasants mercilessly. The peasantry was crushed. Agriculture and industry declined. India grew impoverished.

10. Professor R. Mousnier believes that the authors should have given more stress to the analysis of social structure, which, in his opinion, constitutes perhaps the essential phenomenon in history, more important than the economic element, which it frequently determines. As far back as Hesiod and Plato men observed the behaviour of their contemporaries and devised a mental picture of the society in which they lived as if it were composed of groups forming social levels or strata superimposed in hierarchical order. They generally called these strata *classes*. The authors follow this example and use the word *classes* at every turn. But, at the very least, a distinction must be drawn between stratification into *castes* as typified by Hindu stratification; stratification into *orders* (Stände, Estates), which is so frequent and in which social groups are placed in hierarchical levels not, in principle, according to the wealth of the members and their consumption capacity, not according to their role in the production of material goods, but according to the respect, honour, and dignity attached by society to social functions which may have no relationship with the production of material goods—the profession of arms in France from the thirteenth to the seventeenth century, the scholar with an inclination for public office in China of the Ming and Ch'ing periods, etc.; finally, stratification into *classes* when, in a market economy, it is the role played in the production of material goods and the money earned by fulfilment of this role which places the individual in the various levels of the social hierarchy. A class, then, is formed by those who have the same source of income, fortunes or income of comparable extent, a similar type of life, common interests. A class is perfect if it also recognizes everything which is held in common together with a common action. The authors have not distinguished these three types (nor several others). Similarly, they have not studied the types of family, corps, and colleges existing within each social stratum or cutting across social strata. They have not sufficiently described the territorial units, villages and communities, towns or provinces. They have not studied the relations and the balance of all these social groups between each other, i.e. the social structures. They have obviously only indirectly touched on the vast movement which in France, for example, led from a society of orders based on the pre-eminence of the warrior in the fifteenth and sixteenth centuries to a society of orders based on the magistrate in the seventeenth and eighteenth centuries and to a society of classes based on the pre-eminence of the bourgeoisie, financiers, dealers in products or producers of material goods at the end of the eighteenth century. For Professor Mousnier this is a serious shortcoming since social history while it is no more the driving force of history than economic history (man as a whole is the driving force of history) is nevertheless the most fundamental part of history for the understanding of civilizations. What is the history of technology, sciences, literature, the arts, religion, if it is impossible to relate the inventors, the engineers, the artists, the writers, the connoisseurs, the publics, the clergy, the saints, the unbelievers to specific social groups? (See R. Mousnier, J. P. Labatut, and Y. Durand, *Problèmes de stratification sociale, deux cahiers de la noblesse, 1649–51* (Paris, 1965).

In the opinion of the authors this classification is helpful and, in the chapters that follow, have they used these various terms within the proper context; however, they cannot wholly accept Professor Mousnier's refined distinctions among caste, order *and* class *since for various purposes an hereditary aristocracy, for example (or a trained clergy or landowning merchants) might even by his definitions belong in more than one of the three categories at the same time.*

11. In the opinion of Professor R. Mousnier the essential feature of the social stratification by castes is the fact that it is based on the degree of hereditary religious purity, a feature which in regard to castes outweighs all the others.

12. For a discussion of the literature on this subject, see Robert E. Riegel, 'American Frontier Theory', *Journal of World History*, III (1956), pp. 356–80.

CHAPTER II

THE MAJOR RELIGIONS (*c.* 1300)

GENERAL REMARKS

CHAPTERS II–V will deal with questions of ecclesiastical establishments and with the creeds and events that, at least in part, centred upon them rather than with questions of theology as a branch of abstract thought. Theology and related disciplines will be dealt with in Chapters VI and VII. From time to time Chapters II–V will also refer again to the political, social, and economic events that have been sketched in the preceding chapter, for church developments and conflicts cannot be well comprehended except as influenced by, as well as influencing, contemporary affairs of a secular nature. Nevertheless, a deliberate effort will be made in Chapters II–V to concentrate attention upon religious organization in order to depict the largely ecclesiastical orientation of the intellectual atmosphere of 1300 and its persistence until 1775. Subsequent chapters will describe other aspects of culture and the modifications of the prevalent intellectual atmosphere.

In a fashion and to a degree that no longer is common, reverence or fear of God, gods, or other supernatural beings was prominent in daily life at the opening of our period. The supernatural was immanent for Christians in Europe and beyond, for Moslems in Africa, the Middle East, and India, for Hindus, Buddhists, Taoists, Confucianists, or Shintoists in India, China, Japan, and other parts of southeastern Asia and the Far East, for Jews scattered through Europe, the Near East, and elsewhere, and for the various animist and polytheistic creeds that were to be found in those areas of Africa, Eurasia, Australia, and the Americas that had not yet been reached by or, if reached, not yet converted to Moslem, Christian, Buddhist, or other proselytizing religions. God (or the gods) and the Devil (or devils), demons and witches, the souls and ghosts of the departed, saints and revered ancestors were present everywhere and took an active part in life and thought. To speak to them, to demand guidance of them, to propitiate or worship them, whether by set rituals or by spontaneous acts of devotion, was no less a part of the day's activities than intercourse with one's other neighbours and generally was considered more important for lasting welfare.[1] (Map IV.)

In general, the several religions tended to centre upon a given local structure. The priest might be only a witch doctor revered by a thinly populated tribe and under the jurisdiction of no prelate, or he might be a parish curé responsible to a hierarchy headed by a pope regarded by some as responsible only to God. He might feel that his gods and demons were responsive to his prayers and his rites effective only so far as the recognized

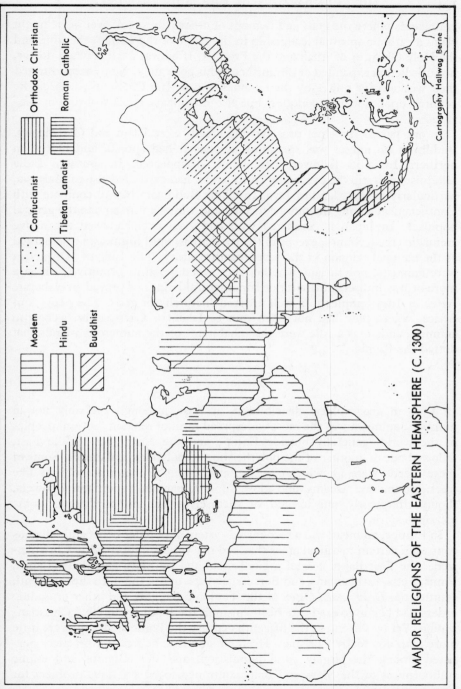

MAP IV

MAJOR RELIGIONS OF THE EASTERN HEMISPHERE (C.1300)

Moslem

Hindu

Buddhist

Confucianist

Tibetan Lamaist

Orthodox Christian

Roman Catholic

Cartography Hallwag Berne

boundaries where the gods and demons of other tribes took over or he might claim a catholic spiritual leadership in the name of the Father, the Son, and the Holy Ghost or of Allah and the Prophet. If he was a tribal witch doctor, his jurisdiction expanded or diminished as his gods and demons demonstrated their weakness or power by the fortunes of war. If a Christian patriarch, he counted upon not only conquest but also missionary effort to bring in converts.

In our period the chief proselytizing creeds were Islam and Christianity. Buddhism no longer was spreading as once it had spread, and indeed in northern India its followers had almost disappeared. In southern India Hinduism was still the prevailing creed, and it had expanded also to Malaysia, particularly to the island of Java. In China Buddhism had to compete with Confucianism among the more educated and with Taoism among the general populace. In Japan it competed with and even overshadowed the native animistic creed, Shinto, except in the rural areas, until Shintoism re-emerged as the national religion in the seventeenth century. The Indians of America were animistic polytheists, whether they worshipped in primitive fashion a more or less indiscriminate set of supernatural beings or prayed in elaborate Aztec or Inca temples to a well ordered hierarchy of gods. The peoples of Africa, where they had not been won to Islam or Christianity, were also animists, and so as a rule were the inhabitants of the numerous islands that dotted the Pacific.

ANIMISM

In 1300 in geographical distribution, at least, although probably not in numbers, animism was the most widespread form of religion. Several peoples of the world, generally outside Europe and the Near and Middle East, followed one or another of the polytheistic and polydemonial creeds. Some of these creeds were likewise animistic, attributing to inanimate objects like trees, mountains, streams, and idols, superhuman and supernatural powers, though frequently not in and of themselves but rather through some vicarious spirit.

In Europe, animism was a recognized system of popular belief and religious control in certain marginal areas that had not yet been thoroughly Christianized. The East-Baltic coastal region, inhabited by Slavs and Balts (Lapps, Finns, Letts, Lithuanians, and Borrussians) was one of them. In the thirteenth century the *Drang nach Osten* of the Teutonic Knights and other crusading orders had begun to eradicate heathenism in the Baltic by forcible Christianization. Yet by the end of the fifteenth century the Baltic lands still were little more than nominally Christian. Heathen animistic beliefs and practices persisted among the largely rural population, and the religious and ethnic stubbornness of the Slavs and Balts continued to be a serious problem for Christian rulers.

In the broadest sense of the term, including demonology and various sorts of kindred occultisms, animism also survived to a certain extent in many rural sections of Christendom. For example, Celtic animism hung on tenaciously among the more primitive of Irish clans, both in folklore and in upper-class literature. Animistic ideas persevered to a surprising degree even in highly civilized centres. Though a keen-minded cynic in other regards, Machiavelli believed that the air was peopled with spirits; Ficino actually defended demonology as well as astrology. The Catholic Church formally condemned witchcraft, demon worship, and pagan incantations of all kinds, and overt acts involving such heathen practices were punished. Shortly before 1300 the Inquisition began to burn witches at the stake. Despite the public stand of the church, individuals among the clergy defended, with quotations from Holy Scripture, occult practices such as palmistry, haruspices, and especially astrology. Some astrologers claimed that even the events of Jesus' life had been horoscopically predictable, since in his mortal form he had been 'under the stars'.

In a similar fashion, in the other major civilizations earlier animistic traditions survived amid more advanced religions. In areas where the great religions associated with urban cultures had not yet penetrated, animistic beliefs prevailed and in great variety—from the totemism of the Australian aborigines to the pre-animistic belief of Polynesia and Melanesia in a ubiquitous impersonal supernatural power (*mana*). These faiths revolved around special persons—medicine men, sorcerers, shamans—and practices by which the spirits could be exorcized, propitiated, controlled, or enlisted. Animistic practices ranged from offerings of flowers, liquids, foods, animals, and human sacrifice through various forms of magic, formulas, chants, and spells to very elaborate rituals. They had become engrafted on or fused with some of the higher religions to such an extent that in many cases it was impossible to indicate precisely where animism ended and a higher form of religion began. About 1300 the animistic elements in the religious practices of many areas were, it appears, of more immediate importance to the masses of the people than were higher religious concepts, which were only a veneer over the underlying culture of the masses.

Perhaps the most common and fundamental features of the religious practices of southern and eastern Asia were some form or other of nature worship and ancestor worship. In India the worship or propitiation of a host of demons and spirits, both evil and benign, was practised as an integral part of Hinduism along with the worship of higher gods. Some of the demons were the creation of higher gods; others were the spirits of departed humans. Cremation and other elaborate death ceremonies were regarded as necessary to assure that the departed would become benign rather than evil; ancestral spirits were fed and worshipped to help them in the spirit world and to preserve their friendly disposition toward the living. Male progeny was considered important as a guarantee of the continuation of ancestral worship.[2]

E*

Persons who died sudden or violent deaths under conditions that prevented proper cremation and funeral ceremonies became spirits that roamed about with malevolent proclivities. Crimes and sins lived after their perpetrators in the form of malign demons (*bhūta* and *preta*) searching for victims who could be instigated to commit similar crimes; disease and death resulted from the acts of such spirits. These *bhūta* and *preta* were propitiated or exorcized by offerings of food, by incantations or formulas, and by the services of sorcerers. Village and household spirits were given honour to win their friendly disposition and prevent them from taking vengeance. Heroes, saints, various natural forces, trees, rivers, and animals—especially cows, snakes, and monkeys—or their spirits were invoked to confer benefit or prevent disaster.

Spiritism and ancestor cults were prominent also throughout southeastern Asia. In Burma spirits (*nats*) were thought to inhabit houses, villages, bodies of water, trees, persons, and other abodes. Most of them were considered malevolent but propitiable by offerings and ceremonials. *Nat* shrines were found outside most villages and often near homes. Siam had especially malevolent ghosts (*phi*), and the spirits of women who had died in childbirth or with unborn children were particularly dreadful. Violent spirits were sometimes provided for the defence of forts or city walls, while they were being constructed, by driving posts through a living victim, who had been well fed beforehand. In Vietnam the ancestral cult was especially strong, and the spirits of the earth, trees, animals, the heavens, the air, and the patrons of particular trades were especially important. The tiger cult was prominent on the edge of forests. The spirits of girls who had died before marriage were believed to seize upon young men to satisfy their desire for children. Most villages had temples or altars dedicated to the Fire Dame, who might prevent or diminish the destructiveness of fire in the bamboo villages. In the Philippines, certain high gods shared veneration with lesser gods and goddesses and a host of good and evil spirits (*anitos* or *diwatas*); the spirits of one's own ancestors were generally good, while those of one's enemies were bad. For the Malay-speaking peoples of Indonesia both good and evil spirits (*yang*) came from the dead and from swamps, creeks, and great trees. The Negritos of the Andaman Islands believed that various spirits of the dead might cause or cure sickness and bring death and might impart some of their supernatural powers to mortals during dreams or serious illnesses. Some Negritos believed in a superior spirit, Biliku (apparently the northeast monsoon), who insisted upon a number of ritualistic taboos. He ate, drank, slept, and reproduced like a human, and the natives would threaten him with the bite of a mythical snake if he allowed too much rain. Throughout southeastern Asia sorcerers or medicine men were commonly employed to deal with spirits, but for most purposes specialists were not indispensable, and so no dominating priesthood arose.

In Australia there existed religious totemic groups that possessed a secret mythology and ritual associated with the ancestral hero represented by the totem. This ancestor was believed to have created most of the spirits in a mythological age and to have placed unborn spirits in centres from which, when needed, they could be incarnated into human, animal, or material forms and to which they returned after death. The groups' ceremonies were regarded as essential to these incarnations; unborn spirits could be found in dreams or placed in the womb by the totemic hero. The ceremonial included the re-enactment of the appropriate part of the mythology at sacred places and the anointment of a sacred stone with blood from the arm or genitals. Serious illnesses were attributed to sorcery or the spirits and could be cured by the ministrations, partly magical, partly practical, of medicine men.

Among the Polynesians the spirits of natural forces and of reptile-like ancestors were worshipped. The Polynesians believed also in *mana* and *tapu* (from which the word *taboo* is derived). *Mana* was an inward power that might be transferred to things (weapons in particular) or persons under appropriate circumstances; *tapu* connoted the quality of being set aside for private use. The gods and spirits, certain individuals and things, and strange, mysterious phenomena possessed *mana*. A woman was *tapu* for (reserved to) her husband after marriage; the remains of a meal of a chief were *tapu* to an inferior on pain of a sore throat or other ill. A long list of taboos affected the whole range of life. Dreams were a means by which ancestors or spirits foretold coming events or guided the destinies of the living. Bloody sacrifices were common. Fingers were amputated to secure the recovery of a superior; frequently pigs and domestic animals, and occasionally humans, were immolated; in New Zealand a Maori chief might offer up a favourite child at the ceremony marking the foundation of a building.

The Ainus of Hokkaido, Japan, worshipped natural forces and objects— sometimes directly, sometimes as spirits—especially the sea, the bear, fire, and millet. Ceremonials were generally not elaborate. Millet was worshipped by cooking it and reciting a simple phrase: 'O Millet, thou hast grown well for us; we thank thee; we eat thee', and the bear by slaying a specially raised cub during a ceremonial dance and tasting its blood. Ainu practices had no doubt been influenced by long contact with the Japanese, and certain elements of Japanese nature worship, in turn, were probably derived from the partial amalgamation of the two peoples.

Although the native religion of the Japanese had been largely replaced at the top by Buddhism, indigenous animistic beliefs and practices continued among the masses. At heart this folk religion centred around the worship of natural forces or their spirits, although human beings were also deified and worshipped. *Kami*, a term usually translated as *god* or *spirit*, means *something superior, sacred, or miraculous*. The greatest of the *kami*—among a host of others, some national, most of them regional or local—was the Sun Goddess, ancestress of the imperial family. There were *kami* of the earth, soil, rivers, rain, wind, rice, mountains, waterfalls, war, learning, good luck, and clans. A simple stone resembling a phallus might be the *kami* of a field, insuring its fertility. Although the Japanese had their share of demons, their attitude towards the spirits was generally one of appreciation, love, and gratitude rather than fear. Worship was usually simple, consisting of offerings of food and liquor, bowings, clapping of the hands, and the stating of simple requests; ritualistic purity, obtained through washing, fasting, and the like, was stressed. Ancestor worship, possibly introduced from China, was almost universal by 1300. Vague elements of earlier religious practice such as shamanism, fetishism, phallicism, and perhaps totemism survived in popular religious practices. State Shintoism was distinguishable from the folk religion and will be considered separately below.

Among the Tibetans and the Mongols, Tunguses, and Koreans of northeast Asia, shamanism was widespread. Basically it was a cult of ancestral ghosts or spirits. Spirits on and above the earth were generally benign; those below were evil. Some might be approached only directly, others through mediating ancestral spirits with the aid of a shaman. A shaman was one who was capable of ecstatic spells during which he was thought to be possessed by ancestral spirits and through them to be able to communicate with, influence, and even control other spirits. This power was considered inherent in certain families. The shaman also arranged sacrifices, purified homes, drove out evil spirits, and acted as physician, prophet, and soothsayer. Popular Korean religious beliefs were a mixture of ancient shamanistic practices, ancestor worship, and the worship of various deities either borrowed from or profoundly influenced by Chinese archetypes. *Pansus* (*diviners*), who were generally blind, and *mutangs* (*sorceresses*) performed the functions of the shaman.

In China popular religious beliefs and practices contained animistic elements. The cult of ancestors formed the heart of China's religious and social structure. Although by 1300 many of the educated members of the cult may no longer have believed in its purely animistic elements, for the masses ancestral spirits seem still to have been very real. Most Chinese were practical and a bit sceptical, but they were also tradition-bound and superstitious and dared not disregard the possibility that spirits, ancestral, natural, or abstract, might really harm or help. If upon proper appeal the spirits failed to end a drought or other disaster, they might be punished but they could not be ignored. The power of heaven might be impersonal, but the spirits of the earth and soil seemed far less remote. Every village had its tutelary deity; every craft had its patron spirit; and rivers, mountains, marshes, lakes, trees, and deified heroes were worshipped. Good spirits were known as *shen*, and evil spirits as *kuei*. *Kuei* could cause death, disease, and other evils, and by committing suicide a man could cause his *kuei* to hound his enemy. At the lower levels of society *Wu* priests were employed to communicate with spirits, exorcise them, and cure disease; on a higher level Taoist and Buddhist priests (as we shall soon see) performed similar functions. In addition, local natural forces might act upon buildings, graves, and other structures to advantage or disadvantage, and *feng-shui* (*wind and water*) specialists were consulted to discover advantageous sites. Man, nature, and the spirits were thus associated in an inseparable unity.

The North American Indians, as was to be expected of peoples so widely and thinly scattered and so diverse in culture, differed in their religious practices and beliefs. The more primitive tribes believed in many kinds of spirits—of mountains, rivers, and forests, of sun, moon, and stars, of animals and departed people. Ghosts and ancestral spirits were propitiated with sometimes intricate rites, which included songs and dances and the ministrations of magicians and medicine men. Nearly all tribes worshipped a hierarchy of holy beings, ranging from mythical heroes through ogres and dwarfs to a Great Spirit, whose good will had to be courted if disease was to be cured, crops were to multiply, and battles were to be won. The North American Indians sometimes buried their dead in carefully selected mounds, although funeral rites were generally simple. Spirits were frequently represented in totems; and the totem pole as a common object of worship was a symbol of clan or tribal unity.

The more civilized Amerindians in Central and South America developed a concept of the Great Spirit that came close to monotheism. The Zapotecs of south Mexico worshipped a Creator who was himself 'uncreated, without beginning or end'.3 He was not, however, alone in his divinity but shared it with less powerful gods and spirits, who inhabited caves, rocks, trees, and other abodes. These gods were worshipped in cave temples by a hierarchy of priests, of whom the high priest was the guardian of the sacred city Mitla ('city of the dead'), whose ruins still reveal the remnants of temples, pyramids, huge stones inscribed with hieroglyphs, and other vestiges that mark it as a burial place for the mighty. Mitla apparently began to fall in ruins only late in the fifteenth century, after the Aztecs conquered the Zapotecs. The Mayans worshipped a chief god whom they called Hunab-Ku, 'the one divine existence'.4 Although he was invisible and remote from the daily life of the people, he contributed to the later Aztec concepts of divinity. The Aztecs had a well-respected priestly order, hieroglyphic records (kept on a paper that they had learned to manufacture before the Europeans knew paper), a calendar (with a surprisingly exact calculation of the year's length) probably based upon priestly knowledge, and temples that roused the admiration of the Europeans who saw them. At the head of a host of gods was Teotl, invisible and remote like Hunab-Ku of the Mayans. Teotl himself, however, owed his origin to 'a single dual principle, male and female, which had engendered gods, the world and men'5—a single Cause. The Incas also had a remote supreme god who was 'Creator of the Universe'.

The Indians generally believed in a life after death. Surviving ruins of mounds and pyramids testify to their respect for the dead; the Incas mummified their dead; the Mayans sometimes cremated their nobles. Heroic warriors went to a just reward, but dreadful hells awaited those whom the gods did not favour. Spiders were sacred to the Chibchas because they were the companions of the dead in the hereafter. Appeasement of the numerous gods was indispensable if hell was to be avoided after death, and some gods were not content with offerings of food alone; they had to be propitiated with animal and sometimes with human sacrifice; the Chibcha and the Aztec gods were particularly severe. Great numbers of captives, criminals, and even children were sacrificed to the demanding deities on terraced and truncated pyramids.

The best beloved of the Aztec gods was Quetzalcoatl. This legendary Feathered Serpent, or White God, had been the Aztecs' great teacher. His story reflects the high cultures that flourished in the area now known as Mexico and Guatemala. Originally a Toltec hero, he became identified with the hero-god Kukulcan of the Mayas when the Toltec civilization collapsed (c. 1200), and survived as an Aztec god after civil war, disease, and migration brought, in turn, the collapse of the glorious Mayan Second Empire (c. 1437). He was believed to have taught the Aztecs how to plant maize, make metals, read, and weave, and to have given them their laws, institutions, and calendar; and some day as a white, bearded leader he would return from the east to lead them again. The white men who came from the east, however, carried by large birds with great wings of canvas, were not Aztec gods but Spanish conquerors.

Priesthood and government were closely bound together in the higher Amerindian cultures. The Aztec rulers were also high priests, for the gods had given the art of government to them. Class distinctions existed in the Aztec heaven (and so were presumably still more justifiable upon earth). Human sacrifice made a religious sacrament out of the destruction of war prisoners. The Incas especially emphasized the religious sanction of their government, each tribe having its own sacred ancestor, symbolized by some bird or animal, probably with totem significance; and the Sapa Inca was considered to be a direct descendant of the Sun-God. The peoples whom the Incas conquered were forcibly converted to the Inca religion, which became in its later stages a species of sun worship, outshining but not necessarily displacing the local religions. Some elements of these Amerindian cults were to lend themselves easily to adaptation to the Christian faith and organization.

HINDUISM AND JAINISM

In 1300 Hinduism was confined mainly to the Indian peninsula and Ceylon. A form of Hinduism mixed with Buddhism was also practised in official quarters in east Java, and the rising Javanese empire of Majapahit was to expand the influence of this cult in the East Indies. It was perhaps still the formal official cult in the Khmer empire of Kāmbuja (now Cambodia) at Angkor and in Champa (southern Indo-China), but Hīnayāna Buddhism (see below) was fast becoming the dominant religion in Cambodia, and the Hindu priestly caste (Brahmans), though still employed by the rulers of the Indo-Chinese peninsula, were losing its religious influence.

In India itself Hinduism was undergoing an ordeal. As we shall soon see, Buddhism and Jainism flourished also in some parts of India; communities of Nestorian (Syrian) Christians and of Jews continued in Cochin on the Malabar coast, and a group of Persian Zoroastrians, known as Parsi (Parsee), survived in Gujarat. (In the seventeenth century the Parsis moved into the Bombay area.) Besides these old competitors Hinduism faced a newer and more militant faith—Islam. Although Islam had been known in Sind and in several mercantile cities for some time, not until Muslim conquerors established themselves in north India and the Deccan in the thirteenth and fourteenth centuries respectively did the full force of this new faith make itself felt in India. The invaders destroyed Hindu temples and seats of learning and instituted various forms of persecution but were unable to destroy the popular faith or the influence of the Brahman caste, and in the end Hinduism emerged, if not unscathed, at least unconquered. The modern Islamic state of Pakistan in the Punjab and Bengal, along with a numerous Muslim minority in the Indian Union, bears testimony to the extent of the lasting inroads of Islam into Hinduism.

Hinduism was the traditional religion of India, but in a larger sense it was the way of life, the *dharma* (law, custom, and duty—social, religious, and cosmic), of the Hindus. It was not primarily a proselytizing faith; one either was born into the faith or entered it as a member of a group that through time had accommodated itself to Hindu ways, had become a caste, and had found a Brahman to be its spiritual leader. Since freedom of religious speculation was unlimited, Hinduism developed elaborate but very diverse theological or philosophic systems. A tolerant polytheistic creed, it permitted many varieties of religious experience. Beliefs ranged from animistic magic to the absolute principle of *brahman* (or *atman*), 'eternal, unbound by time, space, and causality, consisting of pure existence, consciousness, and bliss'.[6] Practices varied from sex rites to puritanical morality; rituals from the worship of demons, spirits, and godlings to abstract monotheistic ceremonies;[7] and theology from essentially atheistic to devout theistic concepts. Among the basic requirements of the creed were (1) acceptance of the Vedas as revelation and (2) deference to the Brahmans as spiritual leaders, together with (3) the caste system associated with Brahman leadership. Exceptions, however, could be found even to these requirements.

In 1300 Hinduism was already divided into sects, generally devoted to one of the three principal divinities—Shiva the destroyer, Vishnu the preserver, and the Great Goddess Shākti. All sects, however, shared at least some of the following tenets: (1) faith in a world soul (*brahman*) or supreme being from which everything comes and to which everything returns, and in the union of the soul or self (*atman*) with this universal soul or supreme being; (2) the doctrine of metempsychosis—i.e. the rebirth, reincarnation, or transmigration (*samsāra*) of the soul from one existence to another; (3) the concept of *karma*, or the belief that the sum-total of good and bad deeds in this and all past

existences determines the condition of the next rebirth; (4) the hope of salvation, or escape (*moksha*) from the chain of rebirths, attainable through
knowledge, good works, asceticism, devotion (*bhakti*), or some combination
of them; (5) conviction of the efficacy of ritualism and hence of sacrifices,
pilgrimages, ceremonials, invocations of the deity, and the use of chants, spells,
and charms (*mantras*); (6) adherence to a rather elaborate ethical system,
which was so intimately tied up with the rules of caste and other externals
and with the aim of self-mastery as a step towards individual liberation that it
sometimes lost much of its moral tone (so that the gods were not constrained
by common standards, and temple prostitution was not considered evil if
sanctioned by caste rules or connected with the worship of some deity);
(7) respect for the contemplative ascetic (*sannyāsī*, or '*renouncer*'), who was
held up as the ideal to pursue after one's duties as husbandman and householder had been discharged; (8) acceptance of the unity and sacredness of all
life with the consequent ideal of non-injury (*ahimsā*) to all living things,
especially the cow; and (9) worship of the reproductive forces, expressed in
ways such as phallic symbols, adoration of female deities, and erotic religious
literature.

The literature still sacred to Hinduism in 1300 was voluminous. It was
divided into works of three general categories: *shruti* (revelation), *smriti*
(sacred tradition), and the so-called 'later works'. The *shruti* consisted of the
four Vedas, which, despite their divine origin, were of much less importance
in our period than the other two categories.

The *smriti* for the most part consisted of certain compendia of highly
compressed aphorisms (*sūtras*), two great epics, certain legal books (*dharma-
shāstras*), and the versified works known as *purānas*. The oldest of these were
the prose *sūtras*, of which two call for specific attention: the *Brahma-sūtra* (or
Vedānta-sūtra), which epitomized the doctrine of monistic idealism, and the
Bhakti-sūtra, which set forth the idea of loving devotion to a personal god.
The two epics presented much of Hindu mythology: the *Mahābhārata* was
significant to most Hindu sects, and the *Rāmāyana* was of special interest for
the worship of Vishnu (Vishnuism or Vaishnavism). The *Bhāgavad-gītā* ('Song
of the Adorable'), one of the late sections of the *Mahābhārata*, was also
principally a Vishnuite work. The *dharmashāstras* dealt with civil and religious
obligations, the *Mānava Dharmashāstra*, or '*Laws of Manu*', being particularly
respected. The more than sixty *purānas* were the real scriptures of sectarian
Hinduism; the eighteen principal ones had been written before 1300, but
some were written later.

The 'later works' (some of which, however, were older than some of the
purānas) fell into three groups. The first, comprised of many and diverse
semi-secret sectarian manuals usually in Sanskrit, were generally known as
tantras or *agamas*. Some were composed after 1300, but their general concepts
were as old as Hinduism itself. They dealt with mythology, philosophy, the
dharma ('duty') of householders, and primarily the ceremonials and ways of

communicating with or controlling the supernatural. They expounded a system of initiation rites, drink, foods, spells, chants, charms, formulas, mystic diagrams, physical and psychic training, meditation, yoga practices, and sexual passion designed to bring the individual stage by stage to unity with *brahman*. A teacher was regarded as necessary for learning this system properly. Some of these practices were functionally analogous to Christian sacraments, but others were not.

A second group of the 'later works' comprised the poetic devotional and philosophical literature of south India written in Tamil. The *Nālāyira Prabandham*, a collection of lyrical hymns, was Vishnuite. A similar group of devotional poetry relating to Shivaism (the worship of Shiva) was collected in the *Tirumurai*, or *Drāvida-shruti* (Tamil Veda), to which, in the thirteenth and fourteenth centuries, was added a group of theological and instructional treatises known as the *Siddhānta-shāstras* or *Shaiva Siddhānta*.

A third group of 'later works' was the writings of the *āchāryas* ('systematic teachers'). These works were usually in the form of commentaries on older scriptures by leading theologians and sectarian leaders (see Chapters VI and VII). Among the most important commentaries clearly composed before 1300 (see Volume III and below) were those by Shankara, which were non-sectarian; those by Rāmānuja and Madhva, which were Vishnuite; those by Shrīkantha (Nīlakantha), which were Shivaite; and the *Gīta Govinda* ('*Song of Krishna*') by Jayadeva (*c.* 1170), which narrated the courtship by Krishna (an incarnation of Vishnu) of Rādhā, his beloved.

No ecclesiastical organization of the Western fashion united Hinduism's holy places and holy men. Nor did any of its three great cults—Vishnuism, Shivaism, and Shāktism—have an over-all hierarchical system. Only the sects and mendicant orders into which the great cults were subdivided were organized, and they, like some of the later Protestant sects of Christianity, were as a rule more or less loosely organized. Sub-sects had arisen that were generally independent of the parent body or autonomous. Many temples, shrines, and monasteries were completely independent, counting upon their own endowments and earning capacity. Others belonged to one or another sect, monastic order, or school and were under the general supervision of its head. Despite this loose organization Hinduism had a remarkably cohesive power, probably attributable to the Hindu social system, which tied religion, family, and caste intimately together and accepted the social, religious, and philosophical leadership of the Brahmans. Throughout the centuries the Brahmans maintained their claim to intellectual and religious leadership over the warrior and lower castes, but in the process they admitted into Hinduism almost every sort of religious or philosophical belief and practice that would accept Brahman supremacy.

If religious organization was weak, religious leadership was not. The Brahmans were the religious leaders; yet all Brahmans were not priests in the technical sense, nor were all priests Brahmans. Priests (*pūjārīs*) officiated in the temples, but these priests were not always held in the highest esteem, and their posts were often filled by low-grade Brahmans or by non-Brahmans. Some important public religious ceremonials outside the temples and many others connected with family observances could be performed only with the aid of Brahmans. In north India, generally speaking, any Brahman could perform such functions, but in most of south India only certain Brahmans would suffice. Most villages and well-to-do families and all Hindu princes had a domestic chaplain (*purohita*) to administer the necessary domestic ritual, and these *purohitas* were Brahmans. Hindu custom also required that neophites have a guru, or religious teacher or sponsor, and gurus were also to be found in most villages and attached to well-to-do families. Gurus were not all Brahmans. Gurus, like the *purohitas*, were greatly reverenced, although the amount of guidance one received from them might vary from the most perfunctory instruction to long years of intimate teaching.

Ascetics also were nearly universally admired as holy men (*sādhus*) and were held up as models. Long before 1300 Hinduism had borrowed from Buddhism the idea of the organized monastic group. Many monastic orders were open to all, regardless of caste. While nearly every sect had its special monastic orders, numerous orders had no connection with any sect. The sectarian orders were more systematically supervised and generally had monastic centres (*maths*) from which the monks set out on their pilgrimages. Most of the non-sectarian orders revered Shiva as the great ascetic, although some sought only the philosophical idea of *brahman*. Begging, contemplation, renunciation, wandering, and various other austerities (*tapas*) were common to nearly all groups, but celibacy was not universal. Some ascetics practised yoga, while others wrote theological or philosophical treatises. Some were ignorant, while others were learned. Some went naked, while others wore simple clothing. Some practised moderate austerities, while others went to such lengths as holding their hands above their heads until they could no longer be moved. The ultimate objective of all true ascetics was *moksha* (escape or salvation) through enlightenment or union with the divine.

★   ★   ★

Smārta and Bhakti Cults

All of the important Hindu cults and many major sects of later times were already in existence by 1300. They may be classified into three divisions: (*a*) the Smārtas, or traditionalists, (*b*) the theistic cults, which believed in salvation through *bhakti* (devotion), and (*c*) miscellaneous folk and local cults (not counting the non-Hindu tribal cults and the cults that had dissociated themselves from Hinduism). Perhaps the majority of Hindus were not specifically associated with any of the several major cults but practised an ancestral and household worship and adored one or several folk or local deities, while also paying respect to Shiva, Vishnu, or Shākti as they chose.

The Smārtas accepted and attempted to follow the Vedas and the great body of sacred tradition (*smriti*). Intellectual descendants of ancient Brahmanism, they were essentially polytheists who accepted the monistic pantheism of Vedānta philosophy (see Chapter VI). They were probably more numerous then than now, and their core then as now probably consisted of the Smārta Brahmans, centred in the Sringeri Monastery of Mysore, founded by Shankara. In domestic life and public ceremonials they aimed to follow *smriti* ritual and practice. Animal or pseudo-animal sacrifices were performed in open places without the use of images. Although a majority of the Smārtas perhaps considered Shiva their favourite deity, they regarded Brahmā, Vishnu, and Shiva alike as mere manifestations, not themselves eternal, of the impersonal, omnipotent, absolute, eternal *brahman*. For the Smārtas, *moksha* was attainable through proper ceremonial asceticism and knowledge, and not through emotional surrender to the divine. Their monastic adherents were celibate, as were their great teachers.

The theistic cults, the Bhakti, were the most numerous. Their acceptance by ancient Brahmanism betokened concessions to popular needs and to the competition of Buddhism and Jainism. They offered a simpler, a less philosophical and ritualistic approach to religion and an easier route to salvation than did the Smārtas. Emotional faith in the saving grace of a particular deity was the chief article of their credo. Their separate deities possessed all the qualities of the absolute *brahman* but were more personal. A Bhakti cult did not deny the existence of competing deities but explained or accepted the competitors as mere manifestations of its own omnipotent deity. The principal Bhakti cults were those of Shiva, Vishnu, and Shākti.

*   *   *

Shivaite Sects

Shivaism was the worship of Shiva as the supreme lord of the universe, the power that destroys and recreates, and of his wife, Pārvatī or Umā. Both took other forms and names as well. Shiva was known also as Mahādeva (the great lord), Bhairava (the terrible one), and Pashupati (lord of cattle—i.e. souls), and was depicted in different forms—as a seated thinker, an ascetic smeared with ashes, or an ecstatic dancer, often with three eyes or five faces and four arms. He was generally represented and worshipped in the form of a *linga* (a stone pillar, originally having phallic connotations), often combined with a *yoni* (symbol of the female). He lived in the Himalayas and presided over a heaven where his faithful worshippers, safe from transmigration, dwelt with him in bliss. Shivaites were generally vegetarian. The theology of the major sects of Shivaism was found in the writings of various northern teachers and the *Siddhānta-shāstras* of south India (see Chapter V).

By 1300 practically all of the sects of Shivaism were already in existence. The cult may be divided into northern and southern branches. Northern Shivaism, the older, was essentially unorganized, consisting of local Shivaite temple groups that adhered to common doctrines and practices. Its scriptures were in Sanskrit. By 1300 it was already subjected to persecution and competition from Islamic invaders. Southern Shivaism, or the Siddhānta school, on the other hand, was by 1300 in the process of developing an effective organization and formulating a specific theology. Its canon, the *Shaiva Siddhānta*, was in Tamil; otherwise its doctrines and practices were not essentially different from those of Northern Shivaism. In 1300 it was engaged in a vigorous if essentially peaceful effort to win over the Jains and Buddhists of the south.

The Vīrashaivas were one of the offshoots of Shivaism. Heretical Shivaites, they were in revolt against the caste and ritual system, and hence the authority, of the orthodox Brahmans. Brahmans as well as lower castes took part in this revolt. The moderate among the heretics were known as the Ārādhyas, and the radicals as the Lingāyats ('*Linga* Wearers'). The Lingāyats are sometimes supposed to have completely broken with the orthodox Brahmans in the twelfth century, but more likely the schism was a gradual process extending into the fourteenth century. Although in theory the Lingāyats accepted the Vedas while rejecting later Brahmanic literature, two *purānas* in Karanese, bearing the names of their reputed founders (Bāsava and his nephew Channabāsava), became their chief scriptures. They rejected caste, repudiated sacrifice and other orthodox rites, allowed widows to remarry, did not insist on child marriage, and denied that birth, death, and menstruation defiled or that prayers for the dead were necessary. They were, after a fashion, puritans, since they forbade the eating of meat or the drinking of spirits and insisted on a rigid moral code. They rejected the use of images but worshipped Shiva in the form of a *linga*, which they always carried, generally around the neck. Theologically they took a position of qualified monism (see Chapter VI). They were divided into *jangams* or *āchāryas* (priests), laity, and followers. The married *jangams* served as ordinary priests, while the celibate lived as monks in *maths*, from which they went out as itinerant ascetics. The sect, centring in Kalyan in the Deccan, had a close-knit organization.

The Pāshupatas, another of the lesser sects of Shivaism, were the remnant of an ancient north Indian sect that had spread to the south. Their theology was more distinctly dualistic than was general among the Shivaites. As their name indicates, they emphasized both *pati* ('lord'), the lord Shiva as direct, universal, and absolute cause, and *pashu* ('cattle'), the souls or things caused by and entirely dependent upon the lord. They held that the individual soul was effective only in so far as it acted in conformity with the predetermination of Shiva and that, once saved, it remained essentially distinct from Shiva. The sect's practices included singing, dancing, gesticulation, and ecstatic acts.

Two other lesser sects of Shivaism, known as the Kashmir sect, seem to have been confined almost entirely to monastic pundits.[8] They were the Spanda and the Pratyabhijna, each founded by a different leader but not much different otherwise. Essentially philosophic in tone, they consisted of monistic idealists, for whom Shiva was the only reality, all else being unreal apart from him. The individual soul as part of Shiva was real, but its reality was obscured by *māyā* ('illusion'). Meditation helped the soul to realize its true identity with Shiva.

Numerous other orders engaged in begging and ascetic practices of varying severity. Most of them operated from some monastic headquarters. They wore either a distinctive garb or no clothes at all, carried distinguishing marks or symbols, practised special initiation rites, and buried rather than cremated their dead. The most moderate, best regulated, and most intellectual of the orders were the Sannyāsīs ('Renouncers') and the Dandīs ('Staff Bearers'), who traced their origin to Shankara and considered themselves followers of his monistic philosophy. Although they were generally attached to Shiva, some were Vishnuites. Some of the Sannyāsī groups accepted members from all castes, but the Dandīs were restricted to Brahmans. The professional Sannyāsī should be distinguished from the ordinary Brahman householder *sannyāsī* (mentioned above), who renounced the world late in life. Likewise, some Yogis were organized in Shivaite orders (although the term *yoga*, properly speaking, applied to a widespread system of self-control and meditation and not alone to a specific ascetic order). The Kāpālikas and the Kālāmukhas were ancient sects, whose extreme practices had been denounced by Shankara. They worshipped Bhairava the terrible one. The Kāpālikas used human skulls as eating dishes and ate the flesh or ashes of corpses.

*   *   *

Vishnuite Sects

If Shiva was a terrible god of power and force, Vishnu in contrast was a benevolent preserver. Vishnuism was the worship not only of Vishnu and two of his *avatāras* ('incarnations'),[9] Krishna and Rāma, but also of his beautiful and benevolent wives Lakshmī (or Shrī) and Rukminī. Vishnu was the adorable lord (Bhagavān), creator, destroyer, and preserver of the universe. He had been a minor solar deity in the *Rig Veda*, while Krishna and Rāma were deified heroes. Krishna, although in an older form a heroic warrior, appeared besides as a youthful cowherd beloved by the neighbouring milk-maids, especially Rādhā, who in time rose to divine equality with her lover, their ardour symbolizing the soul's passion for God. Rāma was the personification of chivalry, and his wife Sītā of chastity. In 1300, specific Rāma and Rādhā cults had not yet become widely popular. In some quarters Buddha too was regarded as an incarnation of Vishnu—a clear attempt to attract Buddhists to Vishnu. Vishnu, Krishna, and Rāma each presided over his own heaven. Vishnuites were strict vegetarians.

The Vishnuite sects had all developed out of an earlier Vishnuism, which had originated in north India and then spread to the south. Of the earlier Vishnuites, the Bhāgavatas, who worshipped Vishnu as their adorable lord (Bhagavān) under the names of Vāsudeva (son of Surya the sun) and Nārāyana (mover in the water), were perhaps the most important. In 1300 many little-organized Bhāgavata groups and some earlier sects still survived, and the four main sects (*sampradāyas*) of present-day Vishnuism were perhaps already in existence. These four were (1) the Shrī-Vishnuite sect or Rāmānujas, (2) the Brāhma sect or Mādhvas, (3) the Shanākadi sect or Nimāvats, and (4) the Rudra sect.

The Vishnuism of these sects was a theistic reaction to the Vedānta ('completion of the Veda') philosophy systematized and popularized by the ninth-century philosopher Shankara. The Vedānta philosophy was based on the *Upanishads*, the philosophical treatises that come at the end of the Vedas. Shankara taught an absolute monistic doctrine known as *advaita* (see Chapters VI and VII): nothing exists except *brahman*, which is identical with the individual self or soul, and our phenomenal world is only *māyā* (illusion, a world of appearances), created in sport and without purpose by *brahman*. This philosophy left little place for a warmer theism, for homage to a personal God who saved individual souls.

The first effective champion of the theistic groups was Rāmānuja (*c.* 1100), who developed a qualified monism (*Vishistādvaita*), which made room for the eternal individual soul and a personal god while remaining within the framework of the Vedānta philosophy. For most Vishnuites, *brahman* was in some way identified with God (Vishnu), from whom the universe, souls, and matter came into being. Thus the Vishnuite sects were imperfectly monotheistic, reaching from pantheism at one extreme to polytheism at the other. All worshipped the Supreme Being (Vishnu) under various names. All rejected the sacrificialism of traditional Brahmanism as the basis of salvation and substituted in its stead knowledge and meditation accompanied by *bhakti* (or emotional homage) to a personal God, who repaid devotion with help and loving grace.

The Shrī-Vishnuite sect (Rāmānujas), established by Rāmānuja, was the first of the four great systematically organized popular sects of modern Vishnuism. It was based on his qualified monist philosophy, but its ritual and ceremony were less emotional than those of some later Vishnuite sects. Rāmānuja is said to have founded seven hundred maths (colleges or religious centres) and eighty-nine hereditary abbotships (since members of his order were allowed to marry). The sect accepted Hindu institutions, including the caste system, as part of the tradition supposedly revealed to it by Shrī, consort of Vishnu. It revered Vishnu most often under the old names of Nārāyana and Vāsudeva. A fuller account of its theology will be given in Chapter VI. By 1300 the sect was in the process of dividing into two branches.

The Brāhma sect (Mādhvas), founded by Madhva during the thirteenth century, spread especially in south India. Its doctrines were supposed to have been revealed by Brahmā. Madhva developed a dualistic philosophy (*dvaita*) based upon the *Upanishads* and so remained within the Vedānta system, but he was continuously in conflict with the monistic followers of Shankara. The

Mādhvas generally called God Vishnu or Nārāyana; Brahmā, the creator, and Vāyu, wind or spirit, were his sons. Salvation was believed impossible except through Vāyu, one of whose incarnations was Madhva. Members of the sect honoured Vishnu by taking his names, by being branded with his discus and conch shell, and by worshipping him with their voices, their bodies (giving alms), and their hearts (showing love, faith, and mercy).

The Shanākadi sect (Nimāvats) was devoted to the worship of Vishnu in the form of Krishna. It was founded by the *āchārya* Nimbārka, who is generally placed in the twelfth century but more probably lived in the fourteenth, for the later dating of the rise of the Nimāvats fits better into the general history of the Krishna-Rādhā worship.[10] According to Nimāvat doctrines those who felt their helplessness and completely surrendered in faith and devotion to Krishna received his saving grace.

The Rudra sect worshipped Vishnu in the form of Krishna, although its revelation was believed to have come originally not from Vishnu but from Rudra (i.e. Shiva). The *āchārya* Vishnusvāmī is generally said to have been the founder of the sect. According to one tradition, he lived in the thirteenth century, but another would seem to fit Indian religious development better. It places the founding of the Rudra sect in the fifteenth century, when Vishnusvāmī allegedly moved from south India to the Gujarat area and began to preach; the father of a later religious leader, Vallabha (see Chapter V) is supposed to have migrated north with Vishnusvāmī, and Vishnusvāmī's philosophic position is conceded to have been similar to Vallabha's pure monism (*shuddhādvaita*). Vallabha would thus appear to have been at least the moulder, if not the actual founder, of the sect.

*   *   *

Shāktism

Another of the great Bhakti cults was Shāktism, or goddess worship. *Shakti* connotes, among other things, the power of the universe as represented in the consort (*shakti*) of a god. It was identified also with *prakriti* (nature), *māyā* (the illusory world of the senses), and the energy, coexistent with *brahman*, that creates and destroys. Goddesses (Shaktis) were sometimes beneficent, but most often were awe-inspiring, demanding bloody sacrifices, especially of human males, and sexual rites. The most popular Shaktis were the consorts of Shiva—in such terrible forms as Kālī the black destroyer, Durgā the inaccessible slayer of demons, and Bhairavī the terrible. For this reason, Shāktism has sometimes been considered a part of Shivaism, but it is actually a separate cult. By 1300, goddess worship was found in all parts of India, but its centres were Bengal, Bihar, and Assam.

The rise of Shāktism was associated with the increase of Tantrism (see below) and the decline of Buddhism. Shāktism represented the amalgamation of numerous local goddess cults, brought about by time and the ingenious speculations of Brahmans presented in the *Tantras*, the sacred literature of

Shāktism. The amalgamation, however, was imperfect; Shāktism lacked formal organization, and its adherents (Shāktas) worshipped at local shrines dedicated to particular goddesses or groups of goddesses. The village mother goddesses of south India, the mothers of Gujarat, and the *Shaktis* of Vishnuism were but imperfectly integrated into the system. No single deity dominated the cult as in Vishnuism and Shivaism.

The *Tantras* represented for Shāktism the only road to salvation. They prescribed rituals, ceremonials, formulas, and practices aimed at propitiating, beseeching, and compelling the goddess. Goats and other animals were sacrificed publicly; one's own blood might be offered; but most pleasing to the goddess was a willing human male. Ritualistic uses included domestic worship of the nude image of a goddess or of a nude woman, and under certain conditions the sex act formed part of the ritual. Other uses were of mystic diagrams (*yantras*), combinations of words and sounds believed to have magical power (*mantras*), certain gestures, actions, and patterns of touch (*mudrās*), amulets, meditation, and yoga. Some of the yoga, intended to bring about union with Shakti, was perhaps based on influencing the vagus nerve and hence affecting the nervous system and bodily controls. Sometimes the ritual called for such practices as the manipulation of a corpse in a graveyard at night.

The *Tantras* held up Shāktism as a higher stage of religious development than Vedaism, Vishnuism, or Shivaism. Only after the aspirant had passed these lower stages did he enter the first real Shākta stage of development, called *dakshina* ('right-hand'). In that stage, through meditation and certain rituals and practices, including animal sacrifices, he might begin to understand the nature of the goddess. The next stage, called *vāma* ('left-hand'), was secret and required special initiation and the guidance of a guru. Here passion was directed 'upwards and inwards' and transformed into power. The fetters of ignorance, fear, caste, and ordinary conventions were cut away by the five-elements ritual (*pañcatattva*) and by certain yoga and other esoteric practices. The *pañcatattva* involved the ritualistic partaking of wine, meat, fish, and parched grain and of sexual intercourse at midnight. Several other stages followed, until the adept reached the *kaula* stage, where he became a *divya*, a divine being united with the goddess—an all-seeing, all-knowing *brahman*, who retained merely the outward form of a man.

The ultimate objective of these practices was liberation through the attainment of union with the goddess, but lesser objectives were also sought. Most of the sacrifices, and perhaps some of the sexual rituals, seem to have been primarily propitiatory, aimed at inducing the goddess to be kind and helpful rather than cruel and dangerous. This emphasis on the Shakti's terrible nature no doubt reflected a realistic appraisal of the tragic conditions of life, and Shāktism apparently flourished best in times of greatest trouble. Another objective seems to have been to gain the Shakti's aid in the destruction of one's enemies. The sexual practices, while undoubtedly reflecting older fertility rites, appear to have had an escapist component. The cult's minimization of caste, its generally favourable attitude towards women, and its emotion-packed public festivals appealed to the oppressed. The Shāktas usually were well-to-do householders, only a few adept being ascetics. Most Shāktas seem to have been guided by their local gurus and affiliated with particular temples honouring particular goddesses.

*　　　*　　　*

Folk and Local Cults

Alongside the major cults flourished a number of folk and local cults. They centred around mother goddesses, rivers, mountains, other geographical phenomena, disease, heroes, animals, and the patron gods of villages and particular professions. Some of these local deities had been more or less identified with Shiva, Vishnu, or a Shakti, but perhaps the majority had not. Several local cults of Bengal were particularly noteworthy. They were folk cults associated with sex, magic, and agriculture, and with goddess, snake, and animal worship, mingled with elements of Tantric Buddhism. Their amalgamation with Vishnuism, Shivaism, and Shāktism continued throughout the period of our study. Local deities were held in great respect by most Hindus, even adherents of the great cults. Although the majority of Hindus paid deference to the principal deities, the local cults provided a religious outlet second in importance only to the domestic rituals.

Hinduism was elastic and thus able to absorb a considerable variety of creeds. Nevertheless, several creeds of India remained independent, and today millions of Indians are still classified as tribals—that is, belonging to tribal groups not yet integrated either in the Hindu caste system or in the international religions. Each of these tribals had its own gods and religious practices. In 1300 they must have had as adherents a greater proportion of the population than today.

*　　　*　　　*

Jainism

Except for Buddhism, among the native religions that had dissociated themselves from Hinduism Jainism was the only one of importance. In 1300 although suffering from Mohammedan persecution and vigorous Hindu competition, numerous Jain communities continued in northeastern India, Gujarat, the Maratha country, and in the Deccan, and in the fourteenth century they were well treated in the Vijayanagar Empire. Jainism was atheistic in that it denied the existence of a supreme being and regarded gods as other living beings subject to transmigration and *karma*. The Jain world, self-existent and eternal, was composed of souls, matter, and other separate and eternal substances. Souls occurred in all animate and inanimate matter and were basically free, but through a tendency to action and passion they followed false ways and acquired bad *karma*. The way to salvation (*nirvāna*) was to end the accumulation of bad *karma* and annihilate what had accumulated. This goal was reached by right faith, right knowledge, and right conduct. Right conduct involved the five vows (not to kill, not to speak untruths, not to take anything that was not given, not to be unchaste, and not to take pleasure in external objects) and asceticism (repentance, humility, meditation, the suppression of desire, self-denial, and self-mortification). Asceticism might culminate in death by voluntary starvation, which, if properly achieved, destroyed *karma* and led to *nirvāna*, a realm above the heavens of the greatest gods, where freed souls resided in happiness beyond compare.

The Jains were divided into laity and ascetics (both male and female). Modifications of the rigid rules were allowed for the laity, who supported the ascetics. The ascetics spent most of their time on pilgrimages and took extreme precautions to avoid injury to life other than their own. Since agriculture and other professions that might involve injury to living things were considered unbecoming though necessary, laymen were chiefly merchants.

The Jains were divided into two major sects: the Digambara, who believed in nudity for its ascetics, and the Shvetāmbara, who wore white clothes and believed women might attain *nirvāna*. Each sect had a separate canon (*Siddhānta*). The Jains had well-ordered animal hospitals, schools, rest-houses for their ascetics, and temples adorned with figures of their saints. Worship was simple, consisting of offerings to the saints of flowers, incense, lights, and praise. A long line of patriarchs had succeeded Mahāvīra, the probable founder of the religion, a contemporary of Buddha, but sacerdotalism was not strong, and the real strength of the group resided in the tight organization of the laity.

*   *   *

Hindu Ritual

Hindu worship differed materially from that of the Western creeds, but in 1300 the difference was probably not so great as now, since Protestant congregationalism has emphasized the worshippers' participation.[11] Hindu congregational participation was definitely subordinate to the service performed by the priest. There was no temple preaching, but preaching by wandering ascetics and revivalists was common. Public worship comprised regular temple ceremonies, festivals, pilgrimages, and the adoration of certain animals and rivers. The gods and their attendants were worshipped in the form of consecrated images or symbols housed in an inner sanctuary of the temple. Worship (*pūjā*) normally took place daily in the temples. The simplest form of priestly ritual was practised in Shivaite temples; leaves or flowers were placed on the *linga*, and holy water was poured over it to the accompaniment of chants or readings from sacred books. A common ritual treated the god in his image as an honoured human. He was awakened, bathed, dressed, fed, allowed to nap at the usual hours, otherwise waited upon, and finally put to bed at night; all this activity was accompanied by appropriate gestures, lights, chants, *mantras*, and scripture readings. In many south Indian temples the ritual included dances and songs by temple dancing girls. In Shākta temples animal sacrifice was normal and in Shivaite temples occasional but in Vishnuite temples unknown. Cows, monkeys, and snakes were especially holy and were not to be molested or injured. Cowdung was used for many ceremonial purposes.

The god held court at certain times, which were the most appropriate for individual worshippers to pay homage. The devout usually entered the shrine individually, rang a bell, washed his hands, bowed or prostrated himself, presented his offering, recited a prayer or incantation, made a personal petition, and backed away. In some temples daily, in others at less regular intervals, and particularly in Vishnuite and Shākta temples, a type of worship took place in which priest and congregation took part. Such congregational participation involved offerings, music of gongs and drums, hymns, prayers and incantations, flaming lights, dancing and singing by the temple dancers, acts of homage, the distribution or eating of consecrated food, and ablutions in the sacred tank or pond. In Vishnuite and Shivaite temples offerings usually consisted of flowers, leaves, rice, oil, perfume, water, and money. Wine and sandalwood as well as animals and the devotee's own blood were favourite offerings to the Shaktis.

Numerous festivals and holy days provided occasions for special ceremonies and rejoicing. The gods were taken in processions through the streets or into the countryside and received offerings and adoration as they went. Special religious ceremonials open to all were performed by the priests on the premises of some wealthy worshipper. Sectarian lines were largely disregarded on festival occasions, and spectators thronged the temples. During the ten-day Durgā (Shakti) festival in September great crowds witnessed the decapitation of large numbers of goats in the goddess's temples. Pilgrimages were an integral part of Hindu religious life. Holy places like Benares and Puri were continually crowded by pilgrims with offerings. To bathe in or drink the waters of holy rivers like the Ganges was deemed particularly efficacious for washing away sin or effecting cures.

Public religious observances were of much less importance than those performed in the home. Domestic rites consisted of (1) traditional ceremonies associated with caste and obligatory for all caste Hindus, (2) special household obligations for those who belonged to certain sects, and (3) ancestor worship. In a sense, all caste rules were religious obligations, but some of them had a more explicit religious bearing than others.

Every family that could afford it had a private chapel or domestic shrine, where the gods—Brahmā, Vishnu, Shiva, and others special to the household —were worshipped. Prayers, food, and flowers were offered to the gods before meals. Specific rituals were prescribed for rising, cleaning the teeth, bathing, greeting the sun, preparing the hair, putting on sacred marks, meditating, reading sacred books, eating, and other daily acts, each accompanied by appropriate gestures and prayers or incantation. Fasts were required twice a month as well as on special occasions. Twelve household sacraments were provided in the ancient Manu code, but undoubtedly by 1300 many observed some of these only loosely. The more important ones related to birth, name-giving, food-giving, tonsure, betrothal, initiation (when a boy began his education), marriage, and death. All required the service of a private domestic chaplain (*purohita*) or the village Brahman. These household requirements varied in some details from caste to caste. Since their full performance needed four or five hours daily and was very costly, their abbreviation was necessary for many Brahmans, to say nothing of the poorer castes.

For the separate sectarians special rites replaced some of the above cere-monies. Shivaites adored a small stone *linga*, Vishnuites a stone *sālagrāma* (a black ammonite with spirals) or a *tulsī* plant, and Shāktas a diagrammatic *yoni*. Some rites in the private worship of the goddess were very elaborate, including breath control and burnt offerings.

Ancestor worship was a fundamental part of the Hindu religion. Elaborate funerals included cremation and the offering of enough food for the ten days considered necessary to transform the departed soul from a dangerous ghost into a proper ancestral spirit. After these obsequies, which were regarded as inauspicious, came the auspicious *shrāddha*, or act-of-faith ceremonies. The male relatives of a head of a household for three generations before and three generations after him were called his *sapindas*, and all surviving *sapindas* of the head of the deceased's household normally took part in the *shrāddha*, together with Brahmans, friends, and local notables. The central feature of the *shrāddha* was the offering of food to all the deceased within the *sapinda* circle. The ceremony was repeated monthly for a year and thereafter annually, and a feast regularly followed. Rites like these were deemed essential to the well-being of one's ancestors and hence of the living, because ancestors, if properly treated, would give aid and protection. The ceremonial of ancestor worship solidified and strengthened the family but usually was costly and helped to impoverish many.

BUDDHISM

The movement traditionally ascribed to Gautama (the Buddha) in the sixth century BC was a reaction against contemporary religious practices in India. It rejected the pretensions of the Brahmans, sacrificial rites, and extreme forms of asceticism in favour of a 'middle way'. It preached a high standard of moral conduct and laid special emphasis on gentleness, impersonal love and kind-ness, and the sanctity of life. Its approach to salvation was essentially personal; salvation could be attained here and now through individual initiative and effort by anyone who had the stamina, courage, and capacity to follow and understand the programme of conduct and training outlined by the

'Awakened', the Enlightened One, the Buddha. It accepted the ideas of transmigration and *karma*, *karma* being portrayed as a universal principle of
causality by which any action inevitably caused an appropriate effect. It also
denied the existence of the immutable soul or self (*atman*), i.e. of the soul as a
permanent, unitary entity that would be reborn, and advanced instead the
idea of *anatta* (non-soul or non-self), in which existence or consciousness was
conceived as a constantly changing combination of material and mental
qualities (*skandhas*),[12] which were reconstituted in another form after death as
determined by its *karma*, much as one wave of the ocean grows out of another
in a varying but endless process.

The Buddha had proclaimed the Four Noble Truths. They were (1) that
existence was suffering, (2) that suffering originated in desire and the thirst for
life, its wants and ambitions, all of which, by *karma*, led to rebirth, (3) that
suffering ceased with the cessation of desire, and (4) that the Eight-Fold
Path—the middle path between indulgence and austerity—led to the cessation
of desire. The Eight-Fold Path consisted of right belief, right resolve, right
speech, right behaviour, right occupation, right effort, right contemplation or
mindfulness, and right concentration or rapture. The last involved mental
application and yoga practices. The continuation of desire and of rebirth
could be ended, and enlightenment (*nirvāna*)[13] attained, only by properly
following the Four Noble Truths. *Nirvāna* thus meant the extinction of desire
and the attainment of an infinite state of calm joy and inner peace. The
understanding *arhat* (disciple of Buddha) might personally attain *nirvāna* by a
rigorous following of the Eight-Fold Path, and the way to pursue the Eight-
Fold Path was to become a member of the *sangha* (Buddhist monastic order).

As time went on, Gautama's doctrines were elaborated by accretions from
Hindu and Far Eastern practices and by the speculations of fertile Indian
minds, and were organized into elaborate religious systems. The three main
systems, Hīnayāna, Mahāyāna, and Tantric, despite their wide divergencies,
shared some basic tenets and practices. The most important were (1) belief in
Buddha and enlightened beings (Buddhas) who are superior to all deities and
from time to time appear on earth to teach *dharma*, the eternal law or way; (2)
the idea of transmigration; (3) the concept of *karma*; (4) the doctrine of *anatta*
(non-soul), although the distinction made between soul (self) and consciousness (existence) was such as to render *anatta* of no practical significance in
ordinary life; (5) the conviction that the aim of life was to escape re-birth and
attain *nirvāna*; (6) a highly ethical code, which often, however, became
corrupted in peculiar ways; (7) gentleness, kindness, helpfulness, and respect
for the sanctity of all life, although the sacredness of human life in certain local
practices was almost forgotten; (8) emphasis on monastic life to an extent
that made monastic groups the centre of Buddhism; (9) lay participation in the
Buddhist ideal, which varied greatly from country to country but everywhere
failed to integrate the laity effectively; (10) a democratic and equalitarian
attitude, which helped to promote Buddhism's popularity; and (11) tolerance

towards and readiness to adopt local practices and ideas, which facilitated Buddhism's spread to many lands.

*   *   *

Main Systems of Buddhism

Around 1300 Buddhism was still divided into three main systems. Hīnayāna (Little Vehicle) Buddhism, also called Pali or Southern Buddhism, was the oldest and simplest of them. It emphasized self-centred discipline and knowledge, epitomized in the ideal of the *arhat*, who aimed at personal salvation and enlightenment (*nirvāna*) by means of monastic life. Mahāyāna (Great Vehicle) Buddhism, also called Northern Buddhism, was a later form; it was more theistic and devotional. It held up as the ideal the *bodhisattva*,[14] who aspires to salvation through many incarnations devoted to the salvation of others. Tantric Buddhism was a late form of the Mahāyāna, best represented by the Lamaism of Tibet. Emphasizing the esoteric and demoniac elements of Tantrism, it aimed at identification with or control of the deities through magic and self-hypnosis.

Hīnayāna Buddhism was found in south and southeast Asia, for the most part outside of India. It was predominant in southern Ceylon (the Sinhalese-speaking areas), Burma, Siam, Cambodia, and Laos, and some remnants still survived in south India, Java, and Sumatra. In these areas it had adopted certain native ideas and practices or was in the process of doing so; in some parts of Cambodia at least, it was also in competition with a still surviving Mahāyānaism assimilated with Shivaism. It was known but no longer actively practised in China, Korea, and Japan. Although it showed no great originality, it exhibited considerable ability to assimilate and expand, and remained vigorous if not creative.

China, Korea, and Japan were the major centres of the Mahāyāna. Although it had originated in north India and perhaps central Asia, China became its foster home, from which it spread to Korea, Japan, and Vietnam. In China Mahāyāna ideas had been supplemented and modified, and still further adaptations took place in Korea and Japan, but the essential characteristics of Indian Mahāyāna were preserved wherever it went. Although it never displaced native religious practices and had to compete with Confucianism and Taoism, it became a strong force in China; and in Japan for a time it bade fair (as we shall see) to absorb Shintoism. By 1300, however, the Mahāyāna, except in Japan, had lost its appeal and creative power, and in China it had definitely begun to decline before the assaults of a revived Confucianism (Neo-Confucianism). In central Asia, except at Turfan and perhaps other points, Buddhism had given way before the Muslim conquest.

Certain Tantric elements were to be found in the Mahāyāna, but as Buddhism lost ground in the land of its birth to Hinduism, the Tantric practices which affected both religions came to dominate Indian Buddhism's remaining centres. These were Bihar, Bengal, and Orissa. From these centres

Tantric Buddhism was transmitted to the East Indies, Nepal, and Tibet, where it assimilated various native practices. Tibetan Buddhism, or Lamaism, developing a missionary zeal, established centres in Mongol China, was accepted by Kublai Khan in 1261, and was thus enabled to expand among the Mongols. In southeast Asia a Tantric form of the Mahāyāna, apparently largely assimilated to Hinduism (principally Shivaism) and to native practices, was dominant in Malaya, Champa (Cochin-China), Sumatra, and Java and had centres of influence in other East Indian islands. Indian Buddhism barely survived the destruction of its centres by the Muslims, and after 1300 the more or less leaderless Tantrics of eastern India gradually degenerated, to be absorbed ultimately by Hinduism or converted to Islam.

Each of the major divisions of Buddhism had a canon of sacred literature, called *Tripitaka* (*Three Baskets*). The Hīnayāna *Tripitaka* was written in Pali, probably the literary language of Magadha, the scene of much of Gautama's activity, and it unquestionably constituted the oldest surviving Buddhists teachings. Its three sections or *pitakas* (baskets) were the *Vinaya* (rul es of the monastic order), the *Suttas* (largely sayings or dialogues attributed to the Buddha or his disciples), and the *Abhidhamma* (metaphysical and philosophical treatises), which were certainly later than the other parts. The Pali canon was accepted in Ceylon, Burma, Siam, and Cambodia.

Mahāyānaist literature, arising in north India and central Asia, was originally written in Sanskrit. No specifically Mahāyānaist canon probably ever was defined. Both Mahāyānaist and Hīnayānaist works in Sanskrit tended to disappear as Buddhism died out in India, and they have survived only partly in Nepal and central Asia, and in Chinese and Tibetan translations. The Chinese *Tripitaka* (*San Tsang*), which also served Japan, Vietnam, and Korea, was a collection of 1662 works of Hīnayānaist, Mahāyānaist, and Chinese genesis, in which the Mahāyāna texts predominated. Although the original scriptures were of Sanskrit derivation, in 1300 the Chinese collection was the basic canon of Mahāyāna Buddhism.

The scriptures of Tantric Buddhism were preserved in Tibetan in the *Kanjur*, or Tibetan canon, supplemented by the *Tanjur*, a thesaurus of exegetical literature. The two collections together were considerably larger than the Chinese canon. They contained most of the originally Sanskrit texts found in the Chinese canon and had many more *Tantras* besides. Translated between the seventh and thirteenth centuries, they formed the sacred literature of the late Tantric Buddhism of Bihar and Bengal also.

*   *   *

Buddhist Organization and Practices

Although a world religion, Buddhism never has had a world organization. By 1300 India, once the well-spring of the faith, was no longer its source of inspiration. Ceylon had come to be the seat of authority for Hīnayāna (Pali) Buddhism, and China for the Mahāyāna, while Tibet had replaced Bihar and Bengal as the centre of Tantric Buddhism. None of the three creeds as yet had a unified structure, but Tantric Buddhism was to develop one as the grand lama of Tibet became a sort of pope.

From the very beginning the core of Buddhism was its monastic system, and consequently the various monastic orders became the bases of Buddhist organization. A Buddhist sect consisted of a group of monasteries and their lay adherents, who accepted a common body of beliefs centring upon particular scriptures and a certain degree of supervision from a head or patriarch. Since the *sangha* (monastic order) cultivated a distinct sense of carrying on a sacred institution founded by the Buddha, considerable attention was paid to ordination. Hence sects founded in new lands or whose purity of descent had come into question tried to get started or restarted through properly ordained monks from older centres. China originally depended on India and central Asia, and Korea, Japan, and Vietnam in turn on China; Burma and Siam at times sent to Ceylon for authentic monks, and Ceylon later had to call on Siam and Burma; Tibet originally counted upon India. Once proper succession was established, a monastery might carry on under its own abbots with a minimum of supervision from a sectarian head.

Buddhist organization tended to develop along national lines, as in Japan, Burma, Siam, and Tibet, although it might vary from country to country and from time to time in the same country. No country except Tibet, however, developed a theocracy or close identification of church and state of the Christian or Islamic type.[15] Rulers often patronized, regulated, or in various ways interfered with the Buddhists, and at intervals Buddhism occupied the position of a state religion, but the state seldom, except in Tibet, became an agency for enforcing religious orthodoxy.

Buddhism's inadequate provision for lay participation probably accounted for its failure to develop a strong organization outside the monastic sects. Despite its emphasis upon kindliness and compassion, for a long time the only road that led to *nirvāna* was a life of monastic asceticism; and although the Mahāyāna developed easy and popular routes to salvation, monastic life remained the ideal, thereby discouraging the establishment of churches for the laity. Men who were prepared to practise a prescribed though less rigorous discipline than the monks were nevertheless admitted to the monastic groups as a sort of lay brotherhood. And the laity in general was encouraged to follow as much of the Buddhist doctrine and moral discipline as their knowledge and condition would permit; they were in particular encouraged to adhere to the Five Precepts (not to take life, drink intoxicants, lie, steal, or be unchaste), to honour the Three Jewels (Buddha, *dharma*, and *sangha*), and to support the monasteries. Merit was also to be won by avoiding garlands and perfume, sleeping on mats, not eating after midday, practising such social virtues as pleasant speech, kindness, and helpfulness, going on pilgrimages, listening to the reading of the *sūtras*, having the *sūtras* copied, engaging in religious conversations, giving alms, endowing monasteries .building temples, preserving respect for the law, and performing the mutual obligations of parent or child, pupil or teacher, husband or wife, friend or befriended, master or servant, and layman or cleric. The laity might win merit too by visiting temples and shrines to offer gifts, perform acts of respect or worship, make supplications, observe ceremonials performed by the monks, and listen to the preaching or the reading of scriptures on certain days of the month.

In early Buddhism and subsequently in Hīnayānaism these good deeds could do no more than improve one's *karma*. Mahāyāna, however, held out the possibility of redemption through *bodhisattvas* and through faith in Amitābha (one of the Buddhas), and thus opened an easier way to salvation for layman and ascetic alike. Still, except to a limited extent in Japan and to a lesser extent in China, no effective lay-oriented sects developed. The monastic life was arduous, permissible lay participation was basically passive, and, above all, no secular clergy were provided to organize and promote the *dharma* among the laity. As a result, only where Buddhism became a sort of national religion did the monks take on the functions of a secular clergy sufficiently to develop large and close-knit followings.

Monastic practices in 1300 differed considerably from country to country and from sect to sect. The early ideal of the wandering mendicant had declined outside India, and most monks now resided permanently in a monastic establishment, although they engaged in pilgrimages and itinerant activities. Major differences distinguished Hīnayāna from Mahāyāna monasticism. The life of a Hīnayāna monk, whose ideal was the *arhat* and whose purpose was personal salvation, tended to be somewhat more strictly ascetic than that of the Mahāyāna monk, whose ideal was that of the *bodhisattva* who accumulated merits for the benefit of mankind. Monastic vows were generally revocable. Poverty was the established rule for Hīnayāna monks but seems not to have been universally demanded of Mahāyāna monks, and in neither group did it apply to the monastic foundation. One of the important functions of the abbot and the administrative staff of a monastery was to husband its properties, and some monasteries became extremely wealthy. Celibacy was the general rule in both Hīnayāna and Mahāyāna monasticism, except in Japan, where some sects abandoned it and many monks became essentially secular, marrying and living among the laymen they served. Among Tantric Buddhists of this period celibacy seems to have been largely abandoned. Vegetarianism was also the general rule except among the Tantrics. An alms bowl, certain vestments, a staff, a razor, a toothpick, and a water-strainer (to avoid taking insect life) were standard equipment for monks.

Most monastic recruits seem to have been young boys, pledged to monkhood by their parents. They were trained either at monastic schools or within the monastery prior to taking their first vows (see Chapter XVI). Monastic orders for nuns existed, but they seldom had wide appeal and were generally under the control of the male orders.

The daily routine in most Buddhist monasteries was similar. It included

F *History of Mankind*

morning and evening devotional services, reading and memorization of sacred texts, worship of the Buddhist images, meditation, and domestic work. In Hīnayāna lands the monks usually ate only at noon, and begging was a daily occupation, but in Mahāyāna countries three meals were normal, begging was rare, and the monks appear to have lived in greater ease and comfort. Certain days of the month were fast days, and on the bi-monthly Uposatha fast-and-confessional days the monks in congregation recited the Prātimoksha, a catalogue of 250 vows or prescriptions concerning conduct.

Monks performed a large variety of public services. They instructed the young (especially those destined for monkhood), read the scriptures aloud on certain days each month, occasionally preached and lectured, distributed food (often obtained by begging), and chanted *sūtras* and other formulas in connection with public festivals, holidays, sickness, death, and the exorcism of evil spirits. In Tibet Tantric charms and formulas were considered especially efficacious in the general war on demons. The average level of learning and piety seems not to have been very high in most of the monastic orders, and standards in Tantric Buddhism often seem low. In Japan some of the orders maintained troops and engaged in conflict with the feudal lords. Most of the orders in Japan, Korea, and Tibet engaged in politics.

⋆　　⋆　　⋆

Southern Buddhism

Hīnayāna Buddhism corresponded more nearly to early Buddhism than did the Mahāyāna. In a way the Hīnayāna was more a rationalist ethical system than a religion; it held out no promise of salvation through faith, and it called for individual self-reliance and discipline. It paid devotion to only one Buddha, the terrestrial Shākyamuni, although it also recognized previous Buddhas and the *bodhisattva* Maitreya, who would come to preach the law sometime in the future. Strictly speaking and for the learned few, the Buddha was not a god but a superman superior to all gods. Out of compassion for mankind he had come and shown the way to salvation; he had then passed on to *nirvāna* and was beyond the reach of prayers or supplications;[16] only his *dharma*, his teaching of the way to salvation, remained. In the popular mind, however, he was in practice a supreme deity who could answer prayers and petitions. In the minds of learned and untutored alike, the important purpose of human existence was the improvement of one's *karma* by appropriate acts and a meritorious life. The idea of a series of universes, heavens, and hells had also grown up, along with a group of supernatural beings ranging from ghosts and tempters through saints to *devas*, or gods. In popular thought rebirth in one of the hells was greatly dreaded. Native animistic beliefs had been grafted to Buddhism in all Hīnayāna countries, and charms, spells, images, relics, and pilgrimages to holy places remained Hīnayāna practices.

In Ceylon the Hīnayānaism of the large Mahāvihāra Monastery, which had preserved the Pali canon, had won out over Mahāyānaist ideas. Sinhalese

Buddhism, having accommodated ancient animistic beliefs, was in the process of accepting also a group of *devatas* as attendants of the Buddha. These attendant deities, often appealed to for personal help, included Brahmā and especially Vishnu. A type of Hīnayānaism similar to that of Ceylon survived in various localities of south India too.

In Burma the Talaing school of Buddhism long was dominant. The collapse (*c.* 1298) of Pagan as the political centre of Upper Burma appears to have left Thaton, in the Talaing country of Pegu, the leading Buddhist centre. Nevertheless, before 1300 each of several groups of Burmese monks, having been ordained at the Mahāvihāra Monastery in Ceylon and having established monasteries in Burma and Pegu, claimed to represent the only proper descent by ordination. The old Talaing and five new Sinhalese schools thus competed for control in the fourteenth century. The Pali canon of Burma contained some works that were not recognized in the Sinhalese canon. Otherwise Talaing Buddhism was essentially the same as that of Ceylon (except perhaps for a few Mahāyānaist elements). It, too, had to adapt itself to the popular worship of native spirits (*nats*), some of which were accepted as attendants to Buddha or as guardian spirits.

By 1300 the Thai kingdom of Sukhothai and the Khmer Empire were essentially Hīnayānaist. Pali Buddhism was a well-organized state religion in Sukhothai, probably having come from Pegu and Burma. The worship of native spirits (*phis*), ancestors, and natural forces had to be accommodated, as in Ceylon and Burma, along with certain Mahāyāna elements, such as the belief in *bodhisattvas* and merits, which had probably come from the Khmer Empire of Cambodia. In Cambodia itself, however, Hīnayānaism was in the process of displacing that combination of Hinduism and Mahāyānaism which was mentioned above as perhaps the official cult. When the Chinese traveller Chou Ta-kuan visited Angkor, the capital of the Khmer Empire, in 1296, Hīnayāna Buddhism was already becoming its dominant religion.

*   *   *

Northern Buddhism

Just as Hīnayāna Buddhism moved southeastward, so Mahāyāna Buddhism moved northeastward. Although transformed, as it moved, by Persian, central Asian, Greek, and local adaptations, Mahāyāna had developed logically from early Buddhism. Prominent among its distinctive features were the belief in *bodhisattvas* and the idea that their merit could be transferred. A *bodhisattva* was a sort of saviour, a potential Buddha, who, out of compassion for mankind, had renounced Buddhahood and laboured through countless ages to accumulate merits (something like Christian 'good works') which could be transferred to the use of ordinary people. Gautama was believed to have been such a being prior to attaining *nirvāna*. Seven *bodhisattvas* became especially prominent. Among them Avalokita, saviour and personification of divine mercy, transformed into a goddess of mercy (Kuan-yin in China, Kwannon in

Japan), became the most important, and Maitreya (Mi-lo or Miroku) remained significant as the future Buddha. Heavenly *bodhisattvas* who had never been on earth also laboured constantly for the salvation of mankind. The idea developed that anyone might become a *bodhisattva*, and the final stage of monkhood was initiation as a *bodhisattva*.

Another prominent idea of Mahāyāna Buddhism comprised a sort of composite of polytheism and trinitarianism. Buddhas were regarded as innumerable and distributed through infinite space and time, but they were conceived of also as forming a kind of trinity. This idea was set forth in the doctrine of *trikāya* and *dharma-kāya* and in the concept of Ādi-Buddha (see below) in essentially the same way though in different forms. *Trikāya* was the concept of the three bodies or personalities of the Buddha. The highest form of this trinity was the *dharma-kāya* (literally, 'the body of the law'). It was the essence of all Buddhas—in fact, the essence of all things; it was true knowledge, the ultimate reality underlying phenomena; it was the norm of being or the principle of the universe; and it was personified, capable of willing and reflecting. In other words, the first form of the trinity was a personalized, omnipresent, absolute, and supreme being. The second was the blissful heavenly Buddhas in their paradises. The third was that of the Buddhas who had appeared on earth as humans.

The figure of Ādi-Buddha arose in late Indian Buddhism (and, as we shall soon point out, remained especially important in Tantric Buddhism). Ādi-Buddha was the original essence, the basic stuff from which all Buddhas came. Ādi-Buddha by contemplation created five *dhyāni* (contemplational or heavenly Buddhas), who in turn created human Buddhas, *bodhisattvas*, and other sacred beings. Out of the multiplicity of Buddhas that were thus conceived, six stood out. Foremost among them were Shākyamuni (known as Shih-chia-mu-ni in Chinese or Shaka in Japanese), who was Gautama, and Amitābha (O-mi-to in Chinese, Amida in Japanese), who was the Buddha of measureless light and infinite compassion. Shākyamuni was the human Buddha, and Amitābha was one of the *dhyāni*. Amitābha had a great treasury of merits that he could dispense to those who in true faith called upon him. The invocation of Amitābha's name might thus assure the supplicant rebirth in the Blessed Land, or Western Paradise.

The Mahāyāna developed a distinctive system of metaphysics that anticipated but was basically very similar to the monistic Vedānta (see Chapter VI). The concept of the *dharma-kāya* was essentially the same as that of the Hindu *brahman*. Different philosophical absolutes arose among several Mahāyāna schools, but they were all identified with the *dharma-kāya*, which in turn was identified with *nirvāna*. Philosophical *nirvāna*, or enlightenment, thus came to mean the realization that the Buddha essence was everywhere, that hence it was within oneself, and that we are all one with the *dharma-kāya*.

The Mahāyāna also developed an elaborate system of universes, heavens, hells, and spiritual beings (many of them evil). Among the host of attendants of the Buddhas were the Four Kings of Hīnayānaism, the Sixteen *Arhats* (Eighteen *Lohans* in China), the Five Hundred *Lohans*, and the twenty-four tutelary deities (including Brahma, Confucius, and Kuan-ti, the Chinese god of war). This complicated system of heavenly and hellish hosts gave to Mahāyāna Buddhism another of its distinguishing features, a complex ritual involving the use of numerous formulas and charms with an elaborate iconography and art.

* * *

Sects of Mahāyāna Buddhism

A number of Mahāyānaist sects flourished in 1300. Some of them were either ascetic or philosophic in character (such as the Lü or Vinaya, the Fa-hsiang or Yogācārya, and the Hua-yen or Avatamsaka) and did not attract a great following. Other sects or schools were more influential. The Pure Land or Lotus sect (Chinese, Ching-t'u; Japanese, Jōdō), infused with much Taoist language and imagery, expounded the ideas of salvation through faith in Amitābha. Its special scriptures were the three *Pure Land Sūtras*, which portrayed the Western Paradise. Its doctrine of simple salvation had affected all the sects in China, and it had spread rapidly in Japan, where the *nembutsu* (the formula *Namu Amida Butsu*, 'home to Amida Buddha') became the popular route to salvation. It divided into many sub-sects in Japan.

The Shin or Ikko sect of Japan was a logical extension of the Pure Land doctrine. It held that faith in Amida was all important, that one sincere *nembutsu* was adequate, that while penance, fasting, pilgrimages, and celebacy were useless, prayer and purity were desirable. The successors of its founder married, becoming a hereditary clergy living among the people. It was numerous and met in congregations for worship and preaching. It denounced other sects, arousing keen opposition, which kindled into physical conflict as the Buddhist sects became feudalized (see Chapter III).

Hardly less popular, and in some ways more important, was the Meditative (*Ch'an; Zen*) or Sudden Enlightenment sect. It seems to have been the outcome of a long evolution, in the course of which it unquestionably was profoundly influenced by Taoist ideas. It emphasized that the only reality was the Buddha quality in every man, that prayer, asceticism, good works, and learning were of no real importance to salvation or enlightenment, but that through meditation, self-study, and introspection enlightenment might come in an intuitive flash. It honoured no scriptures beyond the lives of the Ch'an (Zen) saints, gave little regard to systematic doctrine or instruction, and recommended occasionally slapping or kicking neophytes to help bring on the flash of enlightenment. Great lovers of nature and solitude, the Ch'an (Zen) monks located their monasteries in out-of-the-way scenic spots and developed important schools of poetry and landscape painting in both China and Japan. The simplicity, austerity, and self-discipline of the Zen sect appealed to the Japanese, especially the military class.

Among the popular sects the T'ien-t'ai (Tendai), which took its name from a monastery near Ningpo, was the one most given to intellectual pursuits. Rejecting the Ch'an's disregard of instruction, it became a many-sided school that advocated learning as well as meditation, discipline, and ecstasy. It endeavoured to harmonize Buddhist ideas by suggesting that the Buddha had set forth different levels of teaching during his lifetime—first the doctrine of heavenly beings of the *Avatamsaka-sūtra* (which expounded the *dharma-kāya* doctrine), then the Hīnayāna ideal of the *arhat*, then the Mahāyāna ideal of the *bodhisattva*, then the transcendental knowledge of the *Prajñāpāramitā-sūtras* (a well-known part of the Buddhist canon), and, in his old age, the quint-essence of Buddhism in the *Lotus Sūtra* (*Saddharma-pundarīka*), the favourite text of the T'ien-t'ai.

The Hokke or Nichiren sect of Japan exhibited some of the popular and militant tendencies of the Shin sect. Its founder, Nichiren (1222–82), a Tendai monk, was interested in the masses and attacked other sects as heretics who sapped the vitality of the people and corrupted the state. The sect upheld Shākyamuni as the eternal, omnipresent Buddha and believed that faith in the teachings of the *Lotus Sūtra* was the only route to salvation. They contended that the world had entered the *mappō* era (the period of the destruc-tion of the law) and that Nichiren was the *bodhisattva* Vishishtacāritra (Jōgyō), whom Shākyamuni had designated to propagate the faith in that era. Because of their sharp, abusive criticism of government, society, and other sects, they were in constant conflict with the state and rival sects but popular with the poor (see Chapter III).

The Chen-yen (Shingon) or True Word sect was the only Tantric per-suasion in Far Eastern Buddhism. It revered Vairocana, the great sun Buddha, as the eternal Buddha, all other Buddhas, the *bodhisattvas*, and the world being regarded as mere emanations. It divided Buddhist thought into ten classes, the highest of which comprised the 'true-word' tantric practices by which the adept became a living Buddha. Its promise of a short cut to salvation through easily performed ceremonies and magic made it popular and to a considerable extent determined procedure at Chinese funerals. Its practices tended to become diffused in China, but in Japan it acquired power and influence. Its principal scripture, *The Great Sun Sūtra* (*Dainishikyō*), was supplemented in Japan by later writings which developed the theory that Shinto deities were but emanations of Vairocana (Dainichi).

Korea's Buddhism was imported from China along with the main Chinese sects. It exhibited no very original developments and was infiltrated by older native beliefs. Its monastic groups became involved in politics, maintained armed forces, and depended heavily on government patronage. By 1300 Korean Buddhism had to compete with a revived Confucian movement but still enjoyed government support.

Buddhism entered Vietnam from China long before 1300, but really distinctive sects did not develop there. Instead Vietnamese Buddhism became an amalgam of several beliefs. To be sure, Buddhist temples (*Chua*) were distinct from Taoist, Confucian, and Dinh temples (the last dedicated to native municipal gods and heroes), but they also contained Taoist, Confucian, and native deities. The *bodhisattva* Kuan-yin (Quan-am), in the form of legendary heroines, was especially popular.

*   *   *

Tantric Buddhism

Tantric Buddhism had been exported from Bihar and Bengal in its least erotic form, the Mantrayāna, to the East Indies and the Far East, and in a later and more modified form to Tibet (*c.* 747) and Nepal. It readily accepted and incorporated local cults and practices. In its most erotic form, Buddhas and *bodhisattvas* were supplied with female counterparts, union with whom constituted *nirvāna*, the highest state of bliss, which might be attained on earth by the adept. Buddhism thus absorbed Shākta as well as Tantric features, Tārā, the female companion of Avalokita, becoming an influential deity. While the Mantrayāna form used the magic formulas and similar rites of Tantrism, the erotic elements in it were not marked. It considered Vairocana the original and chief of the five celestial Buddhas.

The East Indies seem at one time or another to have been influenced by all three main forms of Buddhism. The principal religion of the Majapahit Empire, which, beginning in 1293, dominated Java and some of the neighbouring islands about a century, was a mixture of Hinduism (principally Shivaism), native practices, and late Tantric Buddhism, the last being perhaps the most important. Shiva-Buddha was a popular deity, and several other Hindu deities were identified with Buddhas. The Old Javanese work *Kuñjarakarna* (perhaps eleventh century) included an exposition of the faith attributed to Vairocana, and the *Kamahāyānikan* (thirteenth or fourteenth century) expounded various Mahāyāna and Tantric tenets, including the doctrine of the void, the utility of magic formulas, reverence for the five celestial Buddhas (with female counterparts), and the evolution of everything from Advaya (apparently Ādi-Buddha). The *Kamahāyānikan* also identified the highest principles of Hinduism with Buddhism.

Tibet about 1300 had four main Buddhist sects. All had adopted many features of the native Bon religion, including its demonophobia, necromancy, shamanism, and magic. The oldest, the Nying-ma-pa (Old Ones), dated from the introduction of Mantrayāna Buddhism in the eighth century; Vairocana was its cosmic Buddha, and it also worshipped its founder. The other three—the Kadampa, Sakyapa, and Kargyupa sects—grew out of the Vajrayāna (Thunderbolt Vehicle) or Kalacakra system, which, having spread in the eleventh century from Bihar and Bengal to the East Indies, was taken to Tibet by Atisha about 1040. The Vajrayāna developed the idea that Ādi-Buddha was the primordial Buddha, from whom everything else evolved. It supplied the Buddhas and *bodhisattvas* with wives and adopted the erotic and other elements of the *Tantras*, with their ensuing effect on monastic and religious life. Atisha himself founded the Kadampa sect. The Sakyapa sect was established in 1071 by a royal prince in a great monastery about fifty miles north of Mount Everest, and from 1270 to 1340 its abbots were the real rulers of Tibet. It mixed the *Tantras* of the Old and Kadampa sects. The Kargyupa sect, also founded in the eleventh century, emphasized the solitary, wandering life. None of the four Tibetan sects insisted on celibacy or abstinence from alcohol, all dabbled in politics, and a major occupation of the monks was summoning Buddhas or *bodhisattvas* to combat demons. Tārā was an especially popular goddess; Avalokita and Maitreya were popular *bodhisattvas*; Amitābha, Shākyamuni, and Vairocana were popular Buddhas. A brand of this late Tantric Buddhism mixed with Hinduism also flourished in Nepal.

CONFUCIANISM

Around 1300 Confucianism as a religion was confined to China, Korea, and Vietnam, but certain of its ideas and practices were also widespread in Japan. In many ways it was more an ethical than a religious system, but since it required certain rituals and beliefs that were theistic in nature, it must be regarded also as a creed. Along with Taoism and Buddhism, it was one of China's leading creeds. Confucianism, Taoism, and Buddhism, the *san-chiao* ('the three teachings') of China, were separate, but they were easily alloyed. A few scholars were exclusively Confucianists, a few adepts exclusively Taoists, and some monks and nuns exclusively Buddhists, but the vast majority of Chinese in 1300 were at the same time Confucianists, Taoists, and Buddhists (as well as animists).

This plural loyalty was a parallel to, and perhaps a reflection of, the current attitude of the Chinese towards life in general. Essentially eclectic and tolerant, they tended to adopt whatever usages seemed to meet their needs and customarily permitted any that did not seem to endanger the state or the social order. Their common pattern of behaviour was at bottom ethical, this-worldly, and social, the supernatural being called upon primarily to promote well-being here below. A practical ethical code like Confucianism was found congenial as contributing to harmony among the living.

Ceremonies and rituals were nevertheless extremely meaningful to the Chinese as a rule. Their ethical code was embodied in a system of ceremonial behaviour, and their approach to the supernatural was invariably clothed in elaborate rites. Ceremonies and rituals were generally assumed to have value in themselves but at any rate were useful as educative devices and as a means of social control. Chinese social attitudes tended to be at once superstitious, optimistic, and sceptical. Although the life of the people was difficult and their world was inhabited by harmful spirits and forces, they usually believed that human nature was fundamentally good, that evil spirits could be vanquished, and that conditions would thus be improved, but they tended to be somewhat uncertain about the power of the various gods and demons. This lack of certainty undoubtedly accounted for their eclecticism in religion; if no supernatural forces should prove totally effective, common sense suggested honour to all that might help and propitiation of all that might harm.

Confucianism was in essence a way of life and a system of social and political control. In this regard it resembled the *dharma* of Hinduism—with the difference, however, that Confucianism was interested in the problems of this life and was little preoccupied with the soul and life after death. It more nearly resembled the religious outlook of classical Greece than of India. The Confucianism of 1300 was the product of a long evolution. In the course of time it had incorporated (1) a group of ideas and ceremonials relating to ancestral and natural spirits that predated Confucius (d. 478 BC), (2) a body of moral principles and practices expounded by Confucius and developed by his early followers, and (3) various accretions and adaptations that had taken place since his time. The whole scheme of thought had been systematically organized and sharply defined by the Neo-Confucian writers of the Sung Dynasty (960–1279).

*   *   *

Ancestors, Heaven, and Other Deities

Ancestor worship, which seems to have been as old as the Chinese people, was the core of Confucianism as a religion. Confucius had strengthened the ancestral cult by building a progressive, this-worldly, ethical order around the family. Emphasis upon filial piety and other family loyalties tended to diminish the importance of the supernatural elements in ancestor worship, without eliminating them. About 1300 ancestral worship thus combined ancient Chinese beliefs and practices with Confucian ceremonial and social ideas. Buddhist and Taoist doctrines relating to the after-life had also entered the combination.

The supernatural elements of the ancestral cult centred in the conviction that the spirits of the dead had the power to befriend or injure the living and that, if they were to be friendly, they must be honoured, fed, and cared for. Funeral ceremonies were designed to help a departed spirit safely to an appropriate resting place as well as to demonstrate filial reverence. Funeral days and burial sites were carefully selected, and funeral processions were elaborate. The more important the individual or the more wealthy the family, the more costly the ceremonies, because the competition in ostentation was keen. They included fasting, mourning costumes, and the offering of wine, food, paper money, memorial scrolls, and other gifts. Friends and neighbours attended to pay their respects. Generally Buddhist monks chanted prayers for the soul or Taoist priests exorcized evil spirits.

The spirits of the dead were worshipped in the home, in ancestral tablets, and at the grave. Worship in the home began immediately after the funeral. An ancestral tablet was installed with ceremonious kowtowing and chanting of

F*

passages from the classics, usually followed by the chants and formulas of Buddhist or Taoist priests. The deceased was next provided with things needed in the future life by burning paper effigies of them in an open place. Further ceremonies were conducted at fixed intervals during twenty-seven months of mourning, after which annual memorial services were required. The spirits of departed forefathers were also worshipped daily, under the supervision of the head of the family, with kowtows, the burning of incense, and the offering of food and wine (which were later removed and used by the family). They were appealed to in times of crisis and were informed of significant events. A high point in the marriage ceremony was the kowtow of the bride and groom before the ancestral tablets, and ancestral spirits were worshipped at the grave site during the spring and autumn festivals and upon other special occasions. Families that were members of a clan which maintained an ancestral hall sent representatives there at the winter and summer solstices to join other clan members in making offerings and requesting the help and protection of their forebears' spirits. In all these ceremonies, the oldest male, as head of the family, was the key figure.

The Chinese state officially worshipped a considerable pantheon of natural forces and heroes. Some far-reaching phenomena such as heaven (*t'ien*) and earth had long enjoyed official reverence, but other deities had been elevated to the national pantheon from a distinctly local ranking. After the coming of Buddhism the tendency to deify legendary heroes and famous persons increased, and such deities were gradually included in the national pantheon, among them Confucius himself. The ancestors of the reigning emperor were also included, since they were worshipped by the emperor, and he himself was worshipped by the officials on state occasions. Worship of some of the pantheon was confined exclusively to the emperor or officials acting for him, while others like the city gods, local gods of the soil and grain, and various mountains and rivers were also worshipped directly by the people. At the head of the pantheon was the god called T'ien (Heaven) or Shang-ti (Supreme Ruler). T'ien was respected as a sort of impersonal power or force from which the emperor's right to rule was supposed to come. Sacrifices to Shang-ti were reserved exclusively to the emperor, but all people might and did call upon Heaven, although they did not sacrifice to it. More will be said below about the State Cult.

*   *   *

Confucian Ethics

The Chinese early developed a theory resembling the Western concept of natural law; man and nature, they held, were harmoniously united, and the welfare of man depended upon the maintenance of this unity. Hence man must follow a course of action (*tao*) that preserved and promoted the harmony between nature and the human spirit. Proper behaviour, including sacrifices to the appropriate spirits, was part of the *tao*, and the emperor, as high priest of the state and intermediary between man and nature, was responsible for carrying out the necessary sacrifices.

The Confucians always emphasized the ethical nature of the *tao*, and it would be extremely difficult to say whether or to what extent about 1300 the supernatural prevailed over the ethical elements of the State Cult. The natural forces and the great men that were worshipped were essentially of an impersonal character, and although supplications were often couched in highly personal terms, the whole sacrificial procedure was routine. The will of Heaven was interpreted to mean the will of the people. The very fact that the emperor promoted or demoted deities in the official pantheon indicated the system's rationalistic nature. Whether or not the majority of the lettered elite, the literati, believed that deities could directly influence the course of human affairs, certainly the more rationalistic Confucians looked upon their cult as primarily a way of showing respect for nature and as a traditional procedure useful in promoting social and political control.

The ethical standard of Confucianism was extremely high. Based upon a patriarchal conception of the family as the key social unit, it extended to the clan, the community, and the state, which was the family writ large. The emperor and his officials were expected to rule the state as a patriarch ruled his family—by virtue, benevolence, reasoned guidance, and, when necessary, appropriate chastisement; if those above set the proper example, those below were expected to respond with respect, obedience, and helpfulness. Moral responsibility began with the individual, who was called upon to perfect his heart and conduct, but the individual, of course, first learned the proper ideals and modes of conduct from his family.

The ethical code that the family inculcated may be considered under six headings—filial piety (*hsiao*), the 'five relationships', the five cardinal virtues (*te*), proper conduct (*li*), the norm of life (*tao*), and the ideal of the gentleman (*chün-tzu*). *Hsiao* meant devotion to the family and its ancestors, and special love, respect, and obedience to parents. A child's first duty was to parents, family, and ancestors, but a girl after marriage turned her devotion to her husband's family. The patriarchal family was organized in a hierarchy of privileges and corresponding responsibilities, ranging from the father as head through the mother, elder brothers, younger brothers, elder sisters, and younger sisters to grandchildren and collateral relatives. A mode of behaviour was prescribed for each member of the family in relation to every other. The head of the family was responsible for all, and they owed him reverence and obedience. The 'five relationships', when fully developed, laid down the principles that should govern one's social relations: probity between ruler and minister, affection between father and son, proper division of labour between husband and wife, proper order of precedence between older brother and younger, and fidelity between friend and friend; justice should govern relations even with one's foes. *Te* (somewhat inadequately defined as 'virtue') was a personal quality everyone was called upon to cultivate. It subsumed the five cardinal virtues: benevolence (*jen*), righteousness (*i*), reverence (*chung*), wisdom (*chih*), and sincerity (*hsin*). *Jen* is variously translated also as 'love', 'altruism', and 'human-heartedness'; it conveyed the idea of reciprocal forebearance and was perhaps best expressed in the Chinese equivalent of the Golden Rule: 'What one does not want done to himself, he should not do to others'. *Li*, propriety or proper conduct, is often given as one of the cardinal virtues in place of *chung*. *Li* involved more than good taste and the proprieties like etiquette, ceremonials, and rituals; it stood also for a type of outward behaviour that reflected an inward grace.

One who properly coordinated all the above requirements would approach the Confucian *tao*, or way of life. This Confucian *tao* (to be distinguished from the *tao* of the Taoists, which will be described below) was essentially ethical rather than metaphysical and consisted of the ideal norms of conduct. Individuals who possessed it would live in cooperation and harmony with their fellow men; states that possessed it would be properly governed. He who possessed it was a *chün-tzu* (ideal man), a prince or gentleman in the highest sense.

Concepts like *li* and *chung* made Confucianism ceremonious and ritualistic. Sacrifices and rites were carried out according to carefully prescribed rules. The way to act and speak in different situations and in accordance with the hierarchy of relationships involved was set forth in elaborate codes of etiquette (*li*). Even in cases where *li* did not in fact reflect an inward grace, the Chinese considered it an efficacious means of both education and social control. Sacrificial rituals were thus often practised for their own sake—for their presumed inherent social value—regardless of whether the participants believed in the spirits to which the sacrifices were offered.

*   *   *

State and Popular Confucianism

The Confucian canon was rather concise and clearly defined. It consisted of the sayings of Confucius and some of his disciples, the writings of Mencius, one of his chief successors, and some supposedly older classical works either used by Confucius or in some way associated with him. By 1300 the canon had been reduced to the Five Classics (*Wu-ching*) and the Four Books (*Ssu-shu*). The Five Classics were the *Shih ching* (*Book of Odes*), a collection of about 300 ancient poems and folksongs; the *Shu ching* (*Book of History*), a collection of early historical documents (some of them unquestionably forgeries); the *I ching* (*Book of Changes*), an enigmatic volume consisting of a rural omen calendar, a divination manual, and other materials; the *Ch'un ch'iu* (*Spring and Autumn Annuals*), a history of Lu, the native state of Confucius, which he was supposed to have edited but probably did not; and the *Li chi* (*Record of Rites*), a collection of ancient rituals and practices, much of which was later than Confucius. Two complementary works on ritual, the *I li* (*Book of Etiquette and Ceremonials*) and the *Chou li* (*Rites of the Chou*), although not among the Five Classics, were almost equally esteemed. Parts of the *I li* were among the oldest ceremonial records, and the *Chou li* was a late idealized description of the government of the Chou dynasty. The Four Books included the *Lun yü* (*Analects of Confucius*), the *Meng-tzu* (*Book of Mencius*), the *Ta hsüeh* (*Great Learning*), and the *Chung yung* (*Doctrine of the Means*). The last two were extracted from the *Li chi* and given special attention by the Neo-Confucians; the *Ta hsüeh* expounded a theory of higher learning; and the *Chung yung* set forth a theory of the golden mean. Still another respected work was the *Hsiao ching* (*Book of Filial Piety*), which although no longer considered a classic, was a basic textbook. The civil-service examinations were based on these canonical books, and the commentaries of the great twelfth-century Neo-Confucian Chu Hsi constituted the authoritative interpretation of them.

In one sense Confucianism lacked organization as a religion: no church of Confucianism existed, and no specific body propagated it. But in another sense it was highly organized. A formally organized Cult of the Scholars, whose patron saint was Confucius, was a part of the State Cult, which was headed by the emperor and formally administered by one of the government's main offices, the *Li-pu*, or Board of Rites. The Cult of Scholars involved all scholars, whether official or not, but was in general confined to the literati; purely military officials without literary degrees had their own patron saint. The official philosophy was Confucian, the civil-service examinations were based on the Confucian canonical books, and the whole governmental system of cults, education, and training was organized to promote and teach Confucianism (see Chapter XVI). Moreover, the patriarchal family, out of which so much of Confucianism grew, propagated Confucianism in almost every one of its activities. China was thus thoroughly and completely a Confucian state and society. If the emperor neglected to worship the state deities or failed to rule in an ethical manner, disaster could be expected to overtake the country, and ultimately Heaven would remove his family from the throne (see Chapter VI).

The deities in the official pantheon were grouped in three classes. At the top were Heaven, Earth, and imperial ancestors, and the gods of the soil and grain. In the second class were the sun, the moon, the year star (Jupiter), the gods of the sky, of the clouds, of rain, of wind, of thunder, and of the ten mountains, the four oceans and the four rivers, some legendary rulers, and other distinguished men and women, including Confucius and several of his disciples. The third class included the city gods and the gods of healing, of literature, of war, of fire, of architecture, and of the gate and door. Worship of Heaven, Earth, and imperial ancestors was reserved to the emperor, and he was also required either in person or by proxy to sacrifice to the sun, the moon, the gods of the soil and grain, and several other gods. He often sacrificed also to Confucius. On the longest night of the year, after appropriate fasting and purification, he tendered to Shang-ti burnt offerings of bullocks, silk, jade, wine, and other things of value in an elaborate, impressive ceremony at the Altar of Heaven. At the summer solstice somewhat similar offerings were buried at the Altar of Earth. The farming season opened in the spring with ceremonial ploughing at the Temple of Soil and Grain. Provincial and local officials sacrificed at local temples, where the city gods, the gods of the soil and grain, and Shen-nung, the patron of husbandry, were particularly revered. All the deities were represented by either symbols or images; the symbol of Heaven was circular, that of Earth square.

By 1300 the worship of Confucius was a highly developed cult, promoted by the emperors. An especially revered temple at Ch'ü-fu, Shantung, the home of Confucius, was maintained by the state under the management of a lineal descendant of Confucius. Kublai Khan had built another august temple in Peking. Every territorial subdivision of the country had a Confucian temple, or *Wen Miao* (Temple of Literature or Culture), in which were placed the names or images of Confucius, Mencius, other outstanding Confucian scholars, and illustrious supporters of the doctrine. Side rooms or separate buildings housed tablets or images of Confucius's ancestors and of famous local scholars and officials. These temples were normally open to the public, and twice a year, in spring and in autumn, sacrifices in honour of the sage were offered, with local scholars, officials, and students participating. Everything about the ceremonies suggested deification except the verbal expressions, which honoured Confucius only as a great teacher. All efforts to give him the title *ti* (god), however, were resisted by the scholars, who apparently preferred to venerate him as a sage.

Confucianism as practised by the people, however, was essentially unorganized and varied considerably from family to family. Popular Confucianism involved (1) worship at the local shrines of the Confucian pantheon; (2) training in Confucian ethics and in the various *li*; and (3) participation in the ancestral cult. The city gods and the village gods of the soil were particularly revered by the common people, who prayed, announced births and deaths, and presented offerings to them. Their temples were community centres. Pilgrimages to Confucian holy places were common. Almost everyone reverenced Confucius and T'ien, was acquainted with the *li* associated with his station in life, was able to quote sayings from the classics, and knew and endeavoured to practise the essentials of Confucian ethics. Figures of the Buddhist Kuan-yin, the female transformation of Avalokita, or of the Taoist Tsai-shen, god of wealth, and of the household gods were likely to be associated with the ancestral tablets, and at times of crisis Buddhist and Taoist priests might be called in. Unless the head of the family were an extraordinarily rigid Confucian, womenfolk in particular tended to utilize the services of Buddhist or Taoist priests at weddings and funerals, during serious illness, and at other periods of stress.

Confucianism had spread from China to Vietnam, Korea, and Japan. In both Vietnam and Korea it was a rather watered-down version of that in

China, but in 1300 it probably was somewhat stronger in Vietnam than in Korea. In both countries the ancestral cult was basic and had become thoroughly impregnated with Confucian ideas of *li* and filial piety, and Heaven was officially worshipped. In Vietnam, there was a state cult which resembled that of China, but the worship of Heaven was not exclusively reserved to the ruler as in China, and territorial officials also took part in it; not only did Confucian temples promote the cult of Confucius but also Buddhist temples displayed images of him. In Korea, where Buddhism was the state religion and was much stronger than in Vietnam, no Confucian cult was prominent at this time, but Confucian ideas and practices had fused with native elements. In Japan the Confucian family cult strengthened certain native tendencies. It contributed to the development of a cult of ancestor worship and filial piety, modelled on that of China, and of Confucian ethical and ceremonial ideas. In 1300 the Chinese impact on Japan's state cult was, however, of minor importance; Buddhist religious ideas were far more influential.

TAOISM

Taoism, strictly speaking, was confined to China. A cult bearing the Chinese name existed in Vietnam and Korea but was, in fact, a local occultism modified by a few Chinese practices and, despite the many Taoist temples in Vietnam, not sharply distinguished in the popular mind from Buddhism. Taoism may also have had a modifying influence upon Shinto occultism in Japan, especially in connection with the mountain priests of the Ashikaga period (1336–1568).

Taoism as a religion has to be clearly differentiated from Taoism as a philosophy. In fact, the religion was antithetical to nearly everything in early Taoist philosophy. Although customarily regarded as a degeneration of Taoist philosophy, more probably the Taoist religion emerged from the activities of priests, sorcerers, and magicians of the animistic folk cults, who used oracles, formulas, alchemy, herbs, charms, breath control, and similar means to divine the future, restore youth, gain superhuman powers, or attain immortality. These cults appropriated to their own use the name *tao* and ultimately deified Lao Tzu and other early Taoist philosophers, canonizing their writings. Outside influences also were absorbed, so that religious Taoism in 1300 was an unrationalized mixture of many things. Among them was perhaps something of Persian Mazdaism and Christian Nestorianism, certainly something of Confucian ethics, and a great many Buddhist ideas, such as those relating to monastic organization, sacred literature, a trinity, *karma*, transmigration of souls, ethics, heavens, and hells. Above all, however, still loomed the ideas and practices growing out of the folk cults of China and the activities of their wonder-working priests and adepts.

In contrast to the dominant this-worldly, rationalist Confucianism,

Taoism, whether as a philosophy or as a religion, reflected the mystical, supernatural, and superstitious side of the Chinese. In some respects it shared Hinduism's mysticism and metaphysics. The transcendentalism of Taoist philosophy somewhat resembled Hindu doctrine; the eternal way of nature (*tao*) did not seem far different from the absolute *brahman*; and the Taoists' search for immortality, their numerous gods, heavens, and hells, and their dependence on yoga, magic, and occultism were superficially reminiscent of Hinduism. The two creeds differed fundamentally, however. The central preoccupation of Hindu thought was with the soul, while Taoism concentrated on the body. Taoist philosophy laughed at death and taught that man could best enjoy life by living in harmony with nature; and if the native Taoist religion feared death and endeavoured to find the key to immortality, it was immortality not of the soul but of the body (the totality of the person). Thus Taoism, like Confucianism and unlike Hinduism, was this-worldly.

Taoism's search for immortality generally took the form of a hope for prolonged life, supernatural powers, and special advantages. The immortality sought was that of the mundane body or personality. The aim was to prolong life as long as possible and then to assure the continued existence of the individual as a genie or an immortal (*hsien*), able to move freely between this world, the heavens, and various earthly abodes of the immortals, such as the Isles of the Blest in the eastern seas, or the K'un-lung Mountain in the west, where the Hsi-wang-mu, the Fairy Queen, resided. Taoist literature was full of stories about humans who, having become immortal, could fly through space or pass through solid walls.

Nevertheless, devotion to a single deity through the intercession of a well-knit hierarchy in order to obtain immortality did not emerge, for separate deities were regarded as having separate jurisdiction over wealth, good fortune, and success of various other kinds. In most situations some adept was needed to serve as intermediary between the layman and the supernatural. This need produced a class of adepts, the Taoist priests (*tao-shih*), who knew the lore and tricks of the trade and the value of their services. The Taoist religion thus became a repository of numerous magical and occult practices devised by the *tao-shih* to promote the wishes of his clients.

Some of the *tao-shih* seriously sought the elixir of life or the pill of immortality; most were content to cater to popular superstitions and dispensed, for a fee, whatever combination of ethical teachings, occult practices, and Taoist lore they possessed. In the search for immortality cinnabar (which contains mercury), gold, jade, pearls, and herbs were used. Herbs, seeds, and various drugs were prescribed to treat disease and prolong life. Potions were concocted to inspire love or hate and to restore virility. On the assumption that evil spirits (*kuei*) were the cause of misfortune, exorcism was widely practised to treat disease and insanity, protect or save the dead, release the living from their troubles or shield them from harm, and stop droughts, floods, and other disasters. Chants, formulas, diagrams, extracts from scriptures, charms, amulets, pictures of deities or of virtuous people, and sudden noises as from gongs or firecrackers were used to frighten away evil spirits. Various kinds of fortune-telling flourished—among them astrology, divination, physiognomy, the interpretation of dreams and omens, and communication with the spirit world by means of trances and the ouija board. Shamanism and sorcery were cultivated, particularly by Wu priests, the sorcerers of the folk cults, in the effort to communicate with deities, spirits, and immortals and to command their services or gain information from them. Self-hypnosis, breath control, and perhaps drugs were used to bring on trances. Yoga practices (or 'cultivating the inner embryo'), comprising meditation, posturing, breath control, fasting, and sex rituals, were deemed effective in the search for prolonged life, immortality, supernatural power, and harmony with the *tao*. Geomancy, or *feng-shui*, was considered the best method of calculating the occult forces of nature and discerning a propitious location for graves, temples, houses, and other sites. Systems of dietetics were devised, mainly to prolong life and cure disease. Most *tao-shih* were vegetarians, but they often avoided the use of grains, too, preferring special herbs or seeds and resins.

Despite the prominence of occultism in the Taoist religion, it contained a moral system. According to Taoist ethics: 'One carries his own fate with him in the process of living. The recompense of good or evil follows one, as the shadow follows the object.'[17] The ethical system enjoined the Five Precepts of the Buddhists, the Ten Virtues (filial piety, loyalty, kindness to all living things, patience, remonstrance against evil, helpfulness to the poor, planting trees and setting free living creatures, digging wells and building roads, teaching the unenlightened, and studying the scriptures and making offerings to the gods), and other precepts. The popular *Kan-ying p'ien* (*Books of Rewards and Punishments*) promised that he who observed the virtues would be preserved by providence, respected by all, and assured success and office, and he might hope for immortality. The record of men's deeds was therefore kept eternally, and if one's rewards or punishments were not balanced out during this life, they were credited or debited to one's descendants or to oneself in the heavens or hells of the future life; evil deeds reduced one's life or brought other punishments, while good deeds extended it, brought other earthly rewards, or helped to make one immortal. To become an immortal on earth 300 good deeds were deemed necessary, and to become one in heaven, 1300. Three spirits that dwelt in the body, as well as the city god and the hearth spirit, or kitchen god, were supposed to report man's acts to the recorder of deeds. The kitchen god was often bribed by smearing the face of his image with something sweet. An elaborate system of heaven and hells was pictured in large drawings and detailed written descriptions, making this scheme of *tao* essentially like the law of *karma*.

Taoist mythology included a cosmology and an elaborate pantheon but remained for the most part unrationalized. No consistent explanation of the origin of things was vouchsafed, but change always involved the interaction of

yin or *yang*, the negative (female) and the positive (male) principles respectively. The universe was sometimes depicted as having come from the *t'ai-i*
(great unity), a personalized idea often equated with *tao* or with the dipper
god (Hsüan-wu) and sometimes depicted as having come from the Heavenly
Honoured One of Origin and Beginning (Yüan-shih T'ien chün), often
identified with Yü-huang, the Jade Emperor. Perhaps the most honoured in
the Taoist pantheon was the trinity (*san-ch'ing*) of the purities (essence, vital
force, spirit), personalized respectively in Yüan-shih T'ien-chün, who presided over the Heaven of Jade Purity populated by holy men, Tao-chen (Lord
of Tao), who presided over the Heaven of Superior Purity populated by pure
men, and Lao Tzu, who presided over the Heaven of Great Purity populated
by immortals. In the popular mind, however, the most important deity was the
Jade Emperor, who was often not only identified with the first of the trinity
but also depicted as the ruler, from his residence in the Great Bear constellation, of the universe and judge of rewards and punishments. The universe was
divided into provinces, districts, and so on, in which the other deities occupied
office as his minions. The pantheon also included Tsai-shen (god of wealth),
Wen-ti (god of literature), Wen-shen (god of epidemics), Ho-shen (god of
fire), Lung-wang (the dragon king connected with floods), the mountains
T'ai-shan in Shantung and Hua-shan in Shensi, the kitchen god, other Confucian deities, Buddhas, *bodhisattvas*, local deities, deified heroes, stars, forces
of nature, and the spirits of animals, insects, and human actions such as
robbery, drunkenness, and fornication.

Secret lay societies were a common offshoot of Taoism. Some of them had a
deep religious motivation—such as the Chin-tan Chiao (Golden Elixir of Life
Society), which, organized during the T'ang period, still exists in China.
Others were harmless vegetarian or self-culture groups. Still others—among
them, the White Lotus Society (Pai-lien-hui) of the Mongol period—were of a
criminal or immoral nature or became involved in revolutionary activities.
The White Lotus Society also had Buddhist elements in it.

The Taoists had a sacred literature (*Tao Tsang*), which was in many ways
an imitation of the Buddhist *Tripitaka*. It included the well-known philosophical works of early Taoism, various later ones attributed to early Taoist
worthies, some Buddhist and Confucian writings, and those of the early
utilitarian philosopher Mo Ti. The greater part of the canon was composed
after the beginning of the Christian era though often attributed to legendary
or mythological figures. Some of it was lost in the general destruction of
Taoist works ordered by Kublai Khan in 1281, but it now consists of 5,200
chüan ('chapters'), as reconstituted in an edition of 1446 and supplemented in
1607.

Since the T'ang dynasty, the descendants of the first-century teacher
Chang Tao-ling had been recognized by the emperors as titular heads of
Taoism. They were in charge of a large establishment on the Dragon-Tiger
Mountain in Kiangsi and had the title of *T'ien-shih*, heavenly teacher. The

T'ien-shih was supposed to possess great power over evil spirits, and charms from him were highly prized. The city gods and guardian deities of some of the territorial units of government were technically supposed to receive their appointments from him. Actually he possessed little control over Taoist organizations, and some of the sects did not recognize his authority at all.

Strictly speaking, the only Taoists were those *tao-shih* who had gone through some form of apprenticeship and had been formally admitted to one of the organizations. Most Chinese, however, were influenced to a greater or lesser extent by Taoist ideas and used the services of the *tao-shih*. These priests generally wore blue robes, let their beards and hair grow, and tied their hair up in a 'bun' on the head. They were divided roughly into three kinds: (1) a relatively small group of wandering ascetics or hermits; (2) a considerable group of celibate monks and some nuns who resided in monasteries, although the monks might spend considerable time in pilgrimages; and (3) a larger group of home *tao-shih*, who were married and had families, presided over some temple or shrine, and made a living largely by selling their services to the public. Monastic organization and discipline, while modelled to a certain extent on those of Buddhism, had to take account of the more individualistic nature of Taoism. Some of the wandering ascetics and hermits were almost certainly irregular *tao-shih*, never formally admitted to the ranks; they were those who, drawn by the mysticism of philosophic Taoism, late in life perhaps, had decided to abandon the world and seek contentment in meditation, solitude, and a life as simple and as near to nature as possible.

During the Yüan (Mongol) dynasty (1260–1368) the regular *tao-shih* comprised four main sects. One was the Chen-ta-tao sect, about which little is known. Another was the T'ai-i sect, which used charms and magic in an effort to recover the Great Unity that had existed before the separation of heaven and earth. Both of these sects gradually disappeared. The Cheng-i (True Unity) sect was orthodox, recognizing the headship of the Chang family. Most of its members were home *tao-shih*. It emphasized man's spirit or true self, using charms, magic, and ceremonials to preserve his original nature and prolong life. It was dominant in the south. The Ch'üan-chen (Preserve Purity) sect did not recognize the headship of the Chang family. It was organized along monastic lines. It emphasized the importance of man's vital force (*ch'i*), using potions, medicine, herbs, diet, meditation, breath control, and sex practices to prolong life. The White Cloud Monastery outside Peking was its headquarters, but it also had monasteries in the great monastic centres, T'ai-shan in Shantung and Hua-shan in Shensi. It had its principal strength in the north.

Most Chinese were acquainted with a considerable smattering of Taoist lore and were plenteously supplied with superstitions, which the *tao-shih* on occasion stimulated for their own benefit. Blocks of stone, allegedly from T'ai-shan, were considered a sure defence against demons. Worshippers and onlookers attended services in Taoist temples, and the *tao-shih* with his bag of tricks was always treated with awe and respect. In times of drought, flood, prestilence, or other calamity the services of the *tao-shih* were invariably utilized by public officials as well as private individuals. The numerous vegetarian and self-culture societies of laymen reflected Taoist influence. As we shall see in subsequent chapters, Taoist mythology and lore profoundly affected Chinese literature and art, and Taoist philosophy exerted great weight upon Chinese systematic thought, political theory, and political practice.

SHINTOISM

In the discussion of animism above, Shintoism was mentioned as the native religion of Japan. By 1300 Shintoism had been so nearly amalgamated with Buddhism as to make its future as an independent creed appear doubtful. It proved, however, to be so thoroughly embedded in the folkways of the people, and its deities, shrines, ceremonies, and mythology so tied up with national traditions and with the affairs of the imperial and other important families, that it never quite lost its independence. Although some of its shrines and rites were taken over by Buddhism, the worship of local Shinto deities, and the ancient rituals, legends, and animistic practices of the Japanese folk, continued.

The Shinto state cult also survived. It subscribed to a rationalized mythology according to which the islands and people of Japan were a special creation of the gods (*kami*) whereof the imperial family as direct descendants of the sun goddess (Amaterasu), chief of the gods, were the divinely appointed rulers. Under the sun goddess, with her principal shrine at Ise, came a pantheon of lesser deities. Okuninushi (Onamochi) was the great earth god of Idzumo. Ukemochi was the food goddess, worshipped at the Outer Shrine of Ise and (under the name of Inari, the rice god) at the Inari Shrine near Kyoto. Hachiman, generally revered as a god of war, was apparently a deification of the Emperor Ojin, with shrines at Usa, Kyoto, and Kamakura. Temmangu, god of learning, was a deified human. And a host of minor deities helped to supervise the welfare of the imperial family, the state, and an agricultural people.

A department of the imperial government had charge of the national Shinto shrines and was nominally responsible for the proper observance of festivals and ceremonials, but because of the decay of the imperial government the shrines were actually supported by pious shoguns, warriors, and commoners. Twenty-two of them were singled out for special imperial offerings, since their deities were often officially consulted and gave replies in the form of oracles. The priesthood attached to these shrines or assigned to the observance of Shinto ceremonies was hereditary. It boasted some of the most important families of Japan, such as the Nakatomi ritualists, the Imibe abstainers, the Urabe diviners, and the Sarume musicians and dancers. The established system of festivals and ceremonials included coronations, prayers and thanksgiving for harvests, appeasement of the deities of epidemic, fire, storm, and other disasters, and the two annual rituals in which the impurities of the people were washed away. In certain of these events the emperor played an important part. Offerings of rice, vegetables, meat, weapons, and implements were made to the *kami*, to the accompaniment of music and dances. Shinto's sacred literature included the *Kojiki* and *Nihonji*, which gave the official mythology and early history; various prayers (*norito*), ceremonials, and oracles were preserved in the *Engi shiki* (*Ceremonials of the Engi Era*) and in the records of the great shrines.

Buddhism early invaded the Shinto state cult, Buddha being identified with the sun goddess as early as 742. The Tendai sect of Buddhists gradually adopted the system of Ichi-jitsu (One-Truth) Shinto, in which Shinto deities were regarded as manifestations of the one transcendent Buddha. Shingon Buddhism penetrated Shinto even more effectively with its system of Ryōbu (Double-Aspect) Shinto. It considered all phenomena, including Buddhas, *bodhisattvas*, and other deities, mere manifestations of Vairocana (Dainichi), the one absolute reality, and fitted the Shinto *kami* into various circles of phenomena of decreasing permanence or reality moving outward from Vairocana; the sun goddess herself was identified with Dainichi, the Great Sun Buddha. More and more Shinto-Buddhist sanctuaries were set up, and an amalgamated priesthood (*shasō*) was established in many shrines. The Tendai centre at Mount Hiyei, near Kyoto, at one time alone had twenty-one large and one hundred small Shinto-Buddhist shrines, with others scattered throughout the country. In some places an outer shrine housed traditional Shinto ceremonials while Buddhist ceremonies were conducted in an inner shrine.

The close association with Buddhism, while threatening Shinto from one direction, strengthened it from another. Early Shinto had lacked a well developed philosophy or ethical system. In Buddhism, as well as in the Confucian ideas widely current in intellectual circles, the Shinto priesthood and other intellectuals whose fortunes were in one way or another associated with the national cult found building material for an effective philosophical foundation for Shintoism. The oracles of the Kamakura period (1192–1333) began to show a much greater ethical content. The priesthood of certain of the major Shinto shrines successfully resisted the encroachments of the Buddhist monks, and in the thirteenth century the Urabe family, which provided the priests for the Hirano and Yoshida shrines in Kyoto, and the Waterai family, which provided them for the Outer Shrine of Ise, began to develop a Shinto philosophy and ethics. The threat of the attempted Mongol invasions (1274 and 1281) and the efforts of the Emperor Go-Daigo after 1333 to establish himself as an actual ruler greatly stimulated Japanese nationalism. Interest in the imperial family grew and hence invigorated the native religion associated with it. A Shinto revival movement followed (see Chapter III).

ISLAM

Let us briefly recall the story, detailed in Volume III, of Islam's remarkable spread from its original domain. Under the leadership of Mohammed's successors (the caliphs), Muslim warriors quickly overran the Tigris–Euphrates valley, Iran, the lands to the east, including Sind, and to the west Syria, Egypt, the Maghrib, and Spain, at the same time threatening Constantinople with great armadas. By 750 the advance had been checked at Tours-Poitiers in Gaul, at Constantinople, in India, and in Transoxania. Another era of gradual expansion began in the eleventh century, and it went on unevenly throughout our period. The Punjab, Anatolia, and parts of western Sudan were among the areas opened to Islamic soldiers, saints, and merchants in the eleventh century, and later the expansion continued in these and other directions despite occasional setbacks. In the thirteenth century parts of Syria and Spain were conquered by Western Crusaders, and larger areas by the pagan Mongols. The Mongols were, however, Islamized and helped to spread Islam.

The god of the Muslims was Allah, the same God the Jews and Christians revered. Although Mohammed was considered his final and most perfect prophet, the holy figures of the Old and New Testaments were likewise respected as prophets and founders of true religions. Allah was worshipped through prayer (especially on Friday), alms, pilgrimages, fasting, and, above all, observance of the ritual law, which governed all aspects of life. This worship was based on the *Koran*, God's words spoken to Mohammed, and the *Ḥadith*, sacred reports of Mohammed's own words and deeds. The mosques were centres of ritual worship, education, and much of civil life. There was no Muslim priesthood, but *'ulamā'*, religious learned men, preserved the faith and usually served as *imāms*, or prayer leaders.

At the beginning of the fourteenth century Islam as a religion and as a social order had largely recovered from the worst immediate effects of the Mongol invasions of the preceding century and was vigorously expanding its hold in all directions. With the end even of the dubious claim of the Baghdad caliphate to general sovereignty, Islam was now undisguisably decentralized politically, as indeed it had long been in practice. The spiritual and intellectual issues that had arisen at the time of the caliphate had by now been in large measure replaced by others. In religious life the orders, or brotherhoods (*ṭarīqas*), of Islamic mystics (Ṣūfīs) had come to be more important, whether as actively creative groups or as disputatious rivals, than the earlier sects and schools of law or doctrine. In intellectual life the Hellenistic philosophical and scientific tradition had ceased to play a major independent role, while Persian, as we shall see, replaced Arabic for most purposes as the prevalent vehicle of culture in the large area stretching from Anatolia to Bengal, carrying with it a rich harvest of Iranian aesthetic and historical ideals.

In 1295, when the Mongol rulers of Iran adopted the Muslim faith of the population, Islam was more widespread than any other religion. It was predominant throughout northern Africa, the Middle East from Egypt and Anatolia through the Iranian plateau, and much of central Eurasia, and it was professed by the ruling minority in the Indus and Ganges basins and also by small groups along most of the coasts of the Indian Ocean and in some parts of China. Yet it was held together effectively as an international social and cultural body (despite the lack for some centuries past of any central political or other organizational ties) by a self-perpetuating system of personal and social law, the *sharī'a*.

The *sharī'a* was the sacred law of Islam. It governed personal behaviour ranging from etiquette, ritual, and profession of belief to points of marriage, inheritance, and civil contract. For generations it had been worked out in minute detail and was regarded as binding on all Muslims, but in fact it had never been the only law in Islamic life, and it had come to be applied with varying degrees of completeness among different Muslim peoples. For instance, many of the Berbers, of North Africa, followed an older customary law in such points as inheritance, and Turkish women were granted greater freedom than was the Islamic norm. Nevertheless, the *sharī'a* secured sufficient uniformity to make it possible for a Muslim from any country to be allowed full civil rights throughout the Dār al-Islām, the vast area ruled on Muslim principles. Accordingly, Islam in this period was not only a religion in the narrower sense but also the legal and cultural nucleus of an entire civilization.

The earlier divisions among Muslims as to the interpretation of their religion had to a large extent been overcome before 1300. Almost everywhere the predominant form of Islam was the Sunnī (or Sunnite) form, marked by acceptance of the principle of *ijmā'*—that agreement on points of law among the broad community of believers in the Koran established the validity of the points agreed upon. Among the Sunnīs four schools, each of which interpreted the *sharī'a* differently in secondary matters, had survived all competition and had become mutually recognized as definitive. The Mālikite school prevailed in the relatively rigoristic west, centred in North Africa. Elsewhere the Ḥanafite school—adopted among most of the Turkish peoples—and the Shāfi'ite school, slightly more active theologically, existed side by side, along with a sprinkling of rudiment-minded Ḥanbalites, who persistently criticized the compromises that Muslims in actuality accepted. The principle of *taqlīd*—that further schools were not to be developed and the already recognized schools were no longer subject to basic changes—insured them stability so long as the general social conditions of the world remained as they were. Their several traditions were by now so close together that they could be taught under a common roof.

Scattered widely among the Sunnī, and in emotional opposition to them, were the Shī'ites. The Shī'ites exalted the special claims of 'Alī, a son-in-law of Mohammed, and his descendants. They were divided into a variety of often mutually hostile persuasions, but the Twelver Shī'a (accepting twelve *imāms*, or spiritual leaders, of the house of 'Alī) was the most common during our period. Though the Shī'ites continued to be distrusted by the majority, their principle of *taqiyya* (pretence of conformity) allowed them to take part in the general Islamic life.

In the late Middle Ages, especially after 1300, arose a number of Shī'ite movements in the form of Ṣūfī *ṭarīqas* (brotherhoods). With the downfall (thirteenth century) of Ismā'īlism as a political power and with the failure of orthodox Shī'ism to gain power under the Mongols, Shī'ite tendencies of an unorthodox type gained wide acceptance among Persians, Kurds, Turks, and Arabs. These groups stressed a secret wisdom which the believer could share and which Islamic orthodoxy merely symbolized in its legalistic doctrine. The Ḥurūfīs, for instance, interpreted the Koran in terms of a letter and number symbolism, with which they expressed a gnostic doctrine. Such ideas were especially popular among the Turkish and the Kurdish tribes, which sometimes attached themselves as units to one or another line of Shī'ite teachers. By calling the teachers Ṣūfīs, they shielded themselves from Sunnī persecution. In fourteenth-century Iran amid the political uncertainties that followed upon the collapse of Mongol power there, a large part of Khurāsān was ruled by a Shī'ite group called the Sarbadārs. Their republican disorders were condemned bitterly by the courts of the surrounding amirs, but they were not finally put down until the fanatically Sunnī Timur (Tamerlane) brought devastation among them.

In its Sunnī form, Ṣūfism, Islamic mysticism, had come to be accepted by most Sunnīs as an essential part of the faith, and as a personal religion Islam was largely dominated by it as expressed through the Ṣūfī *ṭarīqas*. These brotherhoods had been developing in the preceding two centuries, and by 1300 they offered varied channels for emotional or speculative piety. Some of the most important were already widely spread, but all the *khānaqāhs* (convents or local meeting-places) remained under the authority of a common head, resident ordinarily at the revered tomb of the founder. The Qādiriyya, with its tendency to extravagant exaltation of its founder's eminence, was found far beyond its centre in Baghdad. The pattern of *ṭarīqa* organization had been established by orders such as the sensitively ethical Rifā'iyya in Iraq, the Iranian Kubrāwiyya, the wonder-working Aḥmadiyya (recently founded) in Egypt, the at first lay-oriented and then orthodox Shādhiliyya in the west, the ecstatic Mawlawiyya (the 'whirling dervishes') in Anatolia, and the Chishtiyya in India, marked by the humane and unworldly spirit of Niẓām al-Dīn Awliyā' (d. 1325). Quite outside the regular orders there wandered throughout the Muslim territories such ascetic or antinomian devotees as the Qalandars, who rejected even the limited institutionalization of Ṣūfism.

In 1300 Islam was in the midst of an active wave of expansion, the result partly of political activity and partly of individual missionary effort in both

Islamic and other areas. The disappearance of the Baghdad caliphate did not handicap this expansion, for the caliphs had rarely contributed to the spread of Islam beyond their own subjects, and for a long time the caliph's powers, except in a narrow area around Baghdad, had been reduced to purely ceremonial functions. After 1300 the title of caliph lost even ceremonial importance. Many independent and God-fearing Muslim rulers assumed the rather empty title and therewith claimed command over the military and administrative forces of Islam. Matters of worship or doctrine as such remained outside any caliph's province except as he taught by example or enforced by the sword the decisions of the '*ulamā*'. Rulers freely called each other 'caliph' out of courtesy, and the title was never the most important in any ruler's etiquette. Its exact use was significant in our period to none save a few rigorist '*ulamā*'.

As Islam expanded, a number of *ghāzī* (frontier warrior) states carried it into the Aegean and southeastern Europe. Ultimately the greatest of these was the Ottoman state, which in the fourteenth century was ready to absorb the larger part of the Balkan Peninsula. This advance into southeastern Europe was offset by the reduction of the Muslim area in southwestern Europe to a small corner of Spain, but there (and more permanently in the Maghrib) the Muslims stabilized their position for a long time.

Islam was meanwhile being more widely accepted in western Sudan. There Islam replaced not one of the great world religions but tribal faiths. The trade and political organization of western Sudan, already well developed (see Chapter I) before the advent of Islam, was furthered by the Muslims, who were able to offer a broader world outlook and contacts with the international society of civilized peoples. Islam was rapidly adopted in the Sudanese cities and among the ruling classes, and was gradually brought to more backward elements of the population.

By 1300 Muslim political domination of India was already far advanced. Islam had long controlled the Indus valley, and Islamic merchants had been known in Gujarat and other Indian coastal areas for centuries. When Delhi, occupied in 1193, became the capital of a series of Islamic dynasties in the north, all India felt the full pressure of Islam. By 1300 north India except parts of Rajputana had fallen under Islamic rule, and by 1327 the Deccan, and for a time even the far south, was under Muslim sultans. The Islamic conquerors brought with them Afghan, Turk, and Persian soldiers, officials, and fortune hunters, many of whom took Hindu wives; and many Hindus embraced Islam out of conviction or as a means of social advancement. Even so, the number of Muslims in India remained relatively small, though significant in the main cities. Their greatest strength was in the Punjab and Sind, where their influence had been exerted longest. While the Delhi sultans were Sunnites, not all of their followers were. Moreover, quite apart from the activities of the sultans, the Ismā'ili Shī'ite sect won many converts in India, sometimes whole castes.

The tide of Islam also swept into central Asia and farther east. From central Asia, Islamic traders and adventurers reached north China at an early date, and Islamic traders were known in Canton from the T'ang dynasty onward. By 1300 much of the Tarim Basin was Muslim, while important Islamic elements were to be found in Kansu, north Burma, and Yunnan. Islam was first introduced into Malaya and the East Indies by Arabic, Gujarati, and Bengali traders, who had been well-known throughout the area for a long time. It acquired its first political foothold in the Pacific islands, however, only in the late thirteenth century, when the seaport kingdoms of Perlak and Pasai in western Sumatra came under the rule of Islamic sultans. Marco Polo in 1292 noted that many of the inhabitants of Perlak were Muslim.

JUDAISM

Judaism in 1300, as during many previous centuries, was international in scope. Beginning in some instances before the rise of Christianity, Jewish communities had grown up all over the Eastern Hemisphere—in China and India, as well as in the Middle and Near East, Ethiopia, and Europe.

Small communities of Jews or sometimes isolated families and individuals had lived in most of the commercial regions of Europe since the early Middle Ages or earlier. In eastern Europe they were to be found in Byzantine centres such as Thebes (as silk manufacturers) and in the Balkan provinces of the Eastern Empire; in central Europe in Hungary, Poland, the Rhineland (especially at Mainz), Italy, and Sicily; and in western Europe in France, England, and both Christian and Mohammedan Spain. Although sometimes segregated in ghettoes, persecuted as infidels, and occasionally massacred in pogroms (especially during the Crusading period), in most regions of the West they prospered. This was particularly true of the Sephardic Jews (those of Spain and Portugal), who in Moorish territory were permitted to rise in social status and frequently acted as 'cultural middlemen' between Moors and Christians. The Ashkenazim (Jews of eastern and central Europe) were less privileged but generally were permitted, though on a precarious basis, to engage in commerce and money-lending.

To the east the Jews generally found more friendly conditions. An isolated community of *Bene Israel* lived for centuries in Cochin, India, and possibly elsewhere along the Malabar coast. In Syria a remnant of undispersed Jews, having endured the hardships of Roman imperial and Byzantine Christian rule, continued to enjoy relative tolerance under various Muslim dynasties. By 1300 Palestine itself was overwhelmingly Muslim, with only a weak minority of Jews. Under the tolerant rule of Persian Muslims, Judaism had flourished in the Euphrates Valley, developing near Baghdad an intellectual centre of international influence in the Gaonate (see Volume III), but intellectual leadership of the Jews had passed before 1300 to Europe, particularly Spain, France, and Germany. The ravages of the Mongols and the expansion of the Ottoman Turks ended the growth and importance of the Persian wing of Judaism, though until the seventeenth century Persian Jews were not actively persecuted. Smaller settlements of Jews existed in the *mellahs* (ghettos) of North Africa, among the Falashas of Ethiopia, in Arabia, and in the Far East. They were frequently isolated from, and exercised little influence on, Jews elsewhere.

The religion of the Jews was a forerunner of the religions of the Christians and the Muslims, but the Jews accepted neither Jesus as the messiah nor Mohammed as a prophet. They had no explicit creed, but a number of basic beliefs were common to them. Judaism was strictly monotheistic. It held high in the minds of its adherents as the 'chosen people' the hope of an ideal end to history—a messianic era, which some of them conceived as a resurrection at some future time of supernatural judgment and others as a possibly near natural event, the return of the Jews to control of Zion. Their sacred literature comprised particularly the unalterable revelation of God's will to Moses in the *Torah*—i.e. the Pentateuch—and parts of the *Talmud*, which comprises the collection of their oral law (*Mishnah*) and of the commentary upon it (*Gemara*).

The scattered Jewish communities had only a loose hierarchy. The descendants of the ancient priests (*Kohanim*) were honoured wherever they could be found, but the diaspora had created conditions under which any Jew, if he were sufficiently versed in the sacred literature, might take upon himself the leadership in performing religious services. Every community that had a synagogue, nevertheless, had a *hazzan* ('prayer leader') and a *rabbi* ('teacher'). The rabbis by 1300 had become the chief figures in their respective communities, some of them enjoying great prestige in other communities as well. Hebrew was the learned and holy language of the synagogue, but Jews commonly spoke also the vernacular of the countries in which they lived, though they might sometimes write it in Hebrew characters. Among the practices that distinguished them from Christians was their strict observance of their Sabbath (from sundown on Friday to sundown on Saturday) and of the Mosaic dietary code (*kashrut*).

In north Africa and in Spain, Judaism was perhaps beginning to decline at the beginning of the fourteenth century. In Europe the Black Death intensified the intolerance of the Jews, fortifying the traditional hatred of them because they were infidels, aliens, property-holders, and money-lenders with the charge that they were deliberate spreaders of the plague. In the cities of Germany, by the second half of the fourteenth century they were more often confined to ghettoes. Several public disputations regarding tolerance took place between Christians and Jews from 1200 to 1500 in France and Spain. That at Tortosa in Spain (1413–14) was perhaps the most important and the longest, lasting a year and a half,[18] but with foregone conclusions. At best the debates confirmed each side in its beliefs. The expulsion of the Jews from various parts of Europe during the early centuries of our period is noted elsewhere (see Chapters I and III).

CHRISTIANITY

The numerous administrative, political, and theological conflicts that beset Christianity also are noted elsewhere (see Chapters I, III, and IV). Here only certain features of Christian organization and geography will be indicated.

*   *   *

Orthodox Christianity

About 1300 Christianity was dominant in nearly all of Europe. In eastern Europe, Orthodox (i.e. Greek Catholic) Christianity, already divided into national units (Russian, Bulgarian, Serbian, etc.), was on the defensive. From Asia Minor the Turkish Muslims of the Ottoman dynasty were threatening invasion, and the Tatars ruled in Russia. In the Balkans the independent Christian rulers of Serbia and Bulgaria had shattered the already weakened authority of the Orthodox patriarchate of Constantinople. The spiritual influence of Greek Catholicism still prevailed, but the machinery of church administration was controlled by the local rulers, and, in addition, a number of heretical sects weakened the hold of the separate local church systems upon the minds of the people. Of these heresies, in the fourteenth century, the Bogomils (see Chapter I) were the most numerous. Originating in Bulgaria, the Bogomils had spread to Serbia and to Bosnia, where they became particularly prominent. Other heretics with similar Manichaean and gnostic beliefs also challenged the Orthodox faith. The heretical creeds were frequently recruited from malcontents whose dissidence was due less to doctrinal convictions than to protest against ritualistic formalism and patrician control of the church.

Under Tatar domination the Russian church continued, as before essentially independent of Byzantine Constantinople's control, while, thanks to the opportunistic Mongolian religious policy, its metropolitans grew wealthy and powerful. The metropolitan see, located in Kiev until 1299, moved permanently in 1325 to the much younger and thitherto less renowned city of Moscow, where its independence and prestige as a symbol of national unity mounted. The Russian metropolitans were appointed by the patriarch of Constantinople and remained nominally subordinate to him and the Constantinople synod until 1439 (see Chapter III). All in all, however, before the Turks conquered the Byzantine capital, though Orthodox Greek Catholicism remained strong in cultural and spiritual influence, it constituted only a loose federation of regional churches.

*   *   *

Roman Catholicism

In the West about 1300, the Roman Catholic Church was rounding out its most successful century. It had been stronger and more firmly unified during the thirteenth century than ever before or since. The new mendicant orders of

Franciscans and Dominicans had given the papacy an effective army of spiritual warriors. But for the clash of Boniface VIII (1294–1303) with the English and French national monarchs, the papacy might have continued its spiritual supremacy and political domination in Western Europe (see Chapter III).

Even so, the Catholic Church preserved its effective control over doctrine. The Inquisition discouraged heresy, and the preaching friars spread devotion. Canon law was respected, and the church courts were powerful. Universities continued to be strongholds of rationalized but conservative orthodoxy, thanks to the learning and keenness of Scholastics such as Thomas Aquinas (see Volume III). Secular education also was a province of the clergy, who in that realm could enjoy a life that was secure and prosperous. The arts were willing handmaidens of the church, and social life still centred largely in cathedral or parish.

In northern Europe, under the guise of 'crusades', Germans and Poles were continuing the *Drang nach Osten*, expanding eastward and northward into the Baltic regions beyond the Vistula River. In the thirteenth century the Teutonic Knights, recently removed from the Holy Land to Hungary, had transferred their crusading activities to the Prussian frontier. They had suffered serious setbacks at the hands of the Mongols (1241) and of Duke Alexander (Nevsky) of Novgorod (1242) and some bloody revolts on the part of their non-Christian subjects in Prussia and Lithuania. Nevertheless, by 1309, when the grand master of the Teutonic Order established headquarters at Marienburg in Prussia, they had extended an iron Germanic Christian control over the Baltic regions and were dominant in Poland.

The Teutonic regime meant forced conversion and enslavement of the native populations to German landlords. Besides, German immigrants, both peasants and burghers, kept thronging to the east, attracted by favourable conditions of settlement on the land and in the towns. The Teutonic Order reached its greatest power and prosperity during the fourteenth century, only to decline thereafter, and a united Poland–Lithuania was to break its military power at the Battle of Tannenberg in 1410. Nevertheless, until 1466 (the Peace of Thorn), when the order's territories became subject to Polish overlordship, it remained practically a sovereign government. The history of the Teutonic Order bears eloquent testimony to the rapid secularization of Europe's crusading ideals. Though never altogether spiritual, Christendom's earlier failure to capture the Holy Land contrasts vividly with the brutal success of the 'crusades' against the Spanish Muslims and the Baltic heathens.

Catholic expansion during the fourteenth and fifteenth centuries was not impelled by national, secular, or materialistic considerations alone. King Louis IX of France and Raimon Lull of Spain tried to persuade the church of the possibility of converting rather than slaying Muslims in northern Africa. Lull learned Arabic, established a missionary college, and died (ca. 1315) a martyr in Tunis. At the beginning of the fourteenth century Pierre

Dubois, in *De Recuperatione Terrae Sanctae*, set forth detailed suggestions for pacific missionary methods. His programme included the conversion of the heathen not only to the Christian faith but also to Christian civilization. He urged that the training of young men and women for missions should comprise the study of oriental languages and medicine as well as Christian theology. This ideal, of course, was not put into operation.

*   *   *

Christianity in Asia

A considerable number of non-Catholic Christians were scattered throughout Asia from Syria and Mesopotamia to Peking and from Samarkand to south India. The Mongol conquerors of the early thirteenth century had, to be sure, killed or dispersed many of them, but during the following century, the religious tolerance of the Mongols, their policy of employing learned or technically trained personnel regardless of race or creed, and their generally favourable attitude towards trade and travel contributed to the growth of Christian communities in their lands. Among the non-Catholic Christians there were several Monophysite groups—the Armenian Christians of Asia Minor and Iran, the Jacobite Christians of Syria, and the Coptic Christians of Egypt and Abyssinia—and the Nestorian Christians, who were the most numerous. The major Nestorian centres were in Mesopotamia, Persia, and Russian Turkestan, but they were also widely scattered throughout India, and the 'Syrian' Christians of south India, if not Nestorians, were closely related to them. Many of the Uighurs and Keraits of Chinese Turkestan and the Naimans and Onguts of southwestern Mongolia were Nestorians. The Mongol conquests scattered these people as far westward as Persia, but the largest groups probably went to China. In the early fourteenth century Nestorians were widely dispersed in China and at one time or another had flourishing churches at Khanbaliq (today's Peking), Chin-chiang, Yang-chou, and Hangchow. The Alans, who originated in the Caucasus and were introduced into China as Mongol military contingents, seem to have been Greek Orthodox at first but were later won over by the Franciscans.

During the late thirteenth and early fourteenth centuries the Dominicans and the Franciscans were active as missionaries. The former were especially occupied in Mesopotamia and Persia, and the latter in south Russia, Turkestan, and China, while both had missions in India. The Dominican Jordanus (Jordan Catalani) disappeared in the course of some daring missionary enterprise in India in the 1320's and 1330's. The Franciscan Giovanni di Monte Corvino (1246–1328), after some success in Persia and India, went by sea to China, where he established a Franciscan mission in Khanbaliq (1294). In 1307 he was made archbishop of Khanbaliq, aided eventually by suffragan bishops in China, central Asia, and south Russia. The China mission flourished, with imperial support for some time, and the Mongol government created a special bureau to regulate Christians. As reinforcements arrived from the West, other Franciscan centres were gradually established—at Hangchow, Ch'üan-chou (Zaitun, a bishopric), Yang-chou, and probably Nanking, Shantung, and other places. The last successful effort to reinforce the Peking (Khanbaliq) mission seems to have been the expedition in which Giovanni di Marignolli participated as papal legate; he was in central Asia (Almaliq in Ili, a bishopric under Peking) in 1340, Peking in 1342, and India (Quilon) in 1348, and back in the papal see at Avignon in 1353. Although Dominican and Franciscan missionaries made a serious effort to proselytize Muslims, they appear to have given more attention to winning non-Catholic Christians to Roman allegiance than to converting Muslims, for which they ran the risk of capital punishment in Islamic countries.[19] Their zeal often brought them into conflict with the Nestorians, particularly in Islamic countries.

After 1350, as the Mongol kingdoms of western and central Asia disintegrated or their rulers were converted to Islam, conditions grew less favourable to Christianity. Travel became more difficult, and missionary reinforcements failed to reach their destinations. The Ming rulers (1368–1644) proved more hostile to foreign faiths than their predecessors had been, and at the same time Muslim opposition increased in the Middle East, central Asia, and India. Under these circumstances all types of Christianity declined in Asia. Both Roman Catholics and Nestorians gradually disappeared in central Asia, and though Nestorians remained on in Mesopotamia and Persia, their number diminished. Christianity in India was eventually confined largely to the Christians of the Malabar coast. Catholic missionary activity throughout the East fell off from about 1350 until after the great discoveries of the 1490's.

*   *   *

Of all the adherents of the religions that in modern times have proved to have major importance, in 1300, with the exception of the Shintoists and the Jews, the Christians were probably the least numerous. Like the devout almost everywhere, they believed that life was but a brief interval between birth and the hereafter, which might bring eternal reward or punishment but in either case was not reached by human volition alone. This other-worldly view was to be more thoroughly questioned by Europeans than by others in the centuries to follow.

NOTES TO CHAPTER II

1. In Professor O. Lacombe's opinion there is a distinction to be made as follows: 'While all religions are characterized by the feeling that the sacred is quasi-immediately present to the profane, the group of great monotheistic religions—Judaism, Christianity, Islam—emphasizes the transcendence of God, not omitting His immanent presence. In the main religions of the Far East, on the contrary, the emphasis is more frequently placed on immanence.'

2. While this is so, Professor O. Lacombe also stresses that the persistence of matriarchal institutions in more than one region of the world here described should not be forgotten.

3. Juan Comas, 'Principales contribuciones indigenas precolombinas a la cultura universal', *Journal of World History*, III (1956), pp. 196–230.

4. *Ibid.*, p. 227.

5. *Ibid.*, quoting A. Caso, 'El Pueblo de Sol' (Mexico, 1953), p. 18.

6. W. Norman Brown, *The United States and India and Pakistan* (Cambridge, Mass., 1953), p. 28.

7. To Professor O. Lacombe while it is permissible to speak of the monotheistic *tendency* of certain forms of Hindu religious life, Hinduism as a whole makes no claim to be monotheist in the Christian or Islamic sense of the term.

8. Professor O. Lacombe indicates that Kashmir Shivaism, now becoming better known, is of great doctrinal importance and occupies a unique place in the history of Indian philosophies.

9. The literal meaning of the word 'avatāra' is 'descent', that is to say the descent of the divine into the earthly condition.

10. Surendranath Dasgupta, *A History of Indian Philosophy* (Cambridge, 1940), III, pp. 399–402.

11. Professor O. Lacombe emphasizes that whatever the differences in theological concept as to the nature of the Christian cult which distinguish Protestant 'congregationalists' from preceding Christianity, the essence of the Christian cult is to be at once communal and personal. Hindu temple rites cannot be viewed in this perspective. The domestic rites referred to on pp. 123–24, on the other hand, concern essentially the family group.

12. The word *skandha* describes literally a major ramified articulation such as a shoulder or a tree trunk. This leads us to the idea of a class-determining group. The five *skandhas* of Buddhism are the five main differentiated groups into which are divided the physical and psychic elements of the universe. (O. Lacombe.)

13. Nirvāna means literally 'extinction': that is the extinction of the miseries and servitudes of transmigration.

14. Bodhisattva: a being destined to Awakening, a future Buddha.

15. Professor O. Lacombe points out that despite the empiric resemblances pointed out here, it is important not to lose sight of certain essential differences between Christian, Islamic, Hindu, and Buddhist concepts concerning the relationship between spiritual and temporal powers.

16. Professor O. Lacombe emphasizes, however, that after attaining Awakening, Buddha deliberated within himself whether it was opportune to show others the difficult way of deliverance he had discovered. Despite the danger of misunderstanding, he opted for the way of compassionate preaching.

17. From the *Kan-ying p'ien*, as quoted in K. L. Reichlet, *Religion in Chinese Garments* (London, 1951), p. 91.

18. Salo W. Baron, 'Some Recent Literature on the History of the Jews in the Pre-Emancipation Era (1300–1800)', *Journal of World History*, VII (1962), pp. 145–6.

19. R. P. Beaver, 'Recent Literature on Overseas Missionary Movements from 1300 to 1800', *ibid.*, I (1953), pp. 142–3.

CHAPTER III

MAJOR RELIGIOUS EVENTS (1300–1500)

BEFORE 1300, religion and politics were, generally speaking, so closely bound together that, despite the frequent clash of temporal with spiritual authority, they constituted a natural and unquestioned association, separable only by a more or less conscious intellectual effort. Europeans, however, had begun to depart to a conspicuous degree from this common pattern even before 1300. In the succeeding ages the Christian church was to be relegated in some areas to a position subordinate to the state, and in others to a sphere altogether separate, at least in theory, from government. Still, in Christian as in other countries religion retained a close identification with society and politics. (Map V.)

HINDUISM

By 1300 all of north India except parts of Rajputana was under Muslim control, and in 1310–11 a great raid overran the extreme south. By 1327, of the southern kingdoms only the Pāndyas in the extreme south and Warangal and Orissa on the east coast were fully independent. In 1336 around the city of Vijayanagar a Hindu empire began to rise, and from 1373 until the city's destruction in 1565 it was the centre of Hindu power and influence in the south. From the middle of the fourteenth century onward, most of the rest of India except for Orissa and the knightly Rajput clans, which were never fully subjected, was under Muslim rule.

The Koran was less friendly to the eastern religions than it was to Judaism and Christianity, and, at least partly for that reason, most of the early Muslim rulers in India were more fanatical than their counterparts to the west. No systematic effort was made to wipe out Hinduism or convert all Hindus to Islam, but sporadic attacks, varying in intensity from place to place and ruler to ruler, were frequent. Muslim rulers destroyed the temples, images, schools, monasteries, and religious books of Hindus, Buddhists, and Jains alike. They persecuted Hindus in general and slaughtered monks and priests in particular. They forbade or discouraged Hindu religious festivals and pilgrimages and subjected non-Muslims to the *jizya* (poll tax) regularly and on occasion to a pilgrim's tax besides. Since, however, the invaders were relatively few, they had to run their government with the aid of submissive Hindu princes and administrators, who contrived to blunt the cutting edge of Muslim persecution. At times influential groups escaped the poll tax altogether or paid it at a reduced rate.

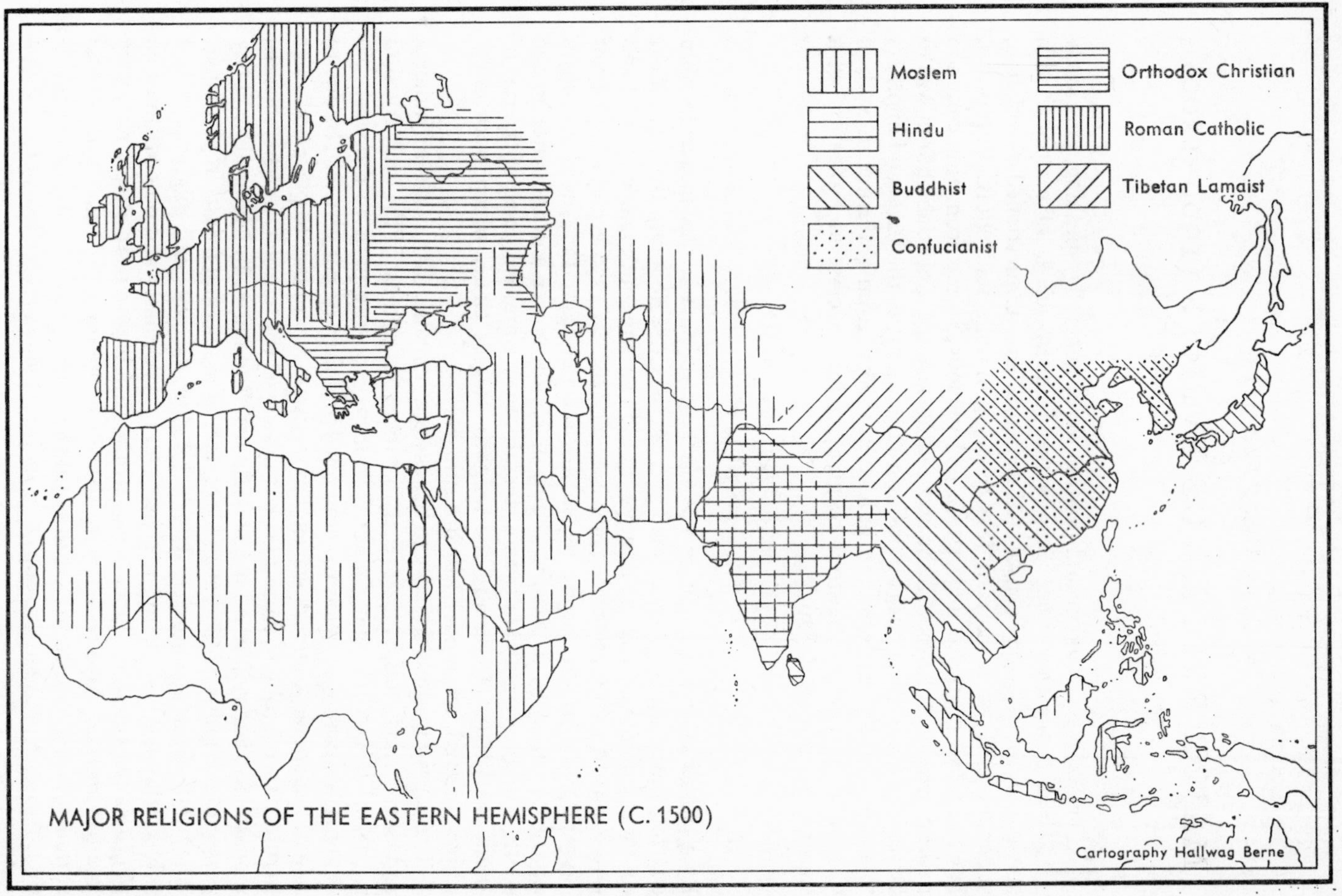

MAJOR RELIGIONS OF THE EASTERN HEMISPHERE (C. 1500)

MAP V

Legend:

- Moslem
- Hindu
- Buddhist
- Confucianist
- Orthodox Christian
- Roman Catholic
- Tibetan Lamaist

Cartography Hallwag Berne

The Muslim conquest affected Hindu religious developments in a number of ways. (1) Hinduism lost ground to Islam, which gradually became established as a major religion in north India. The immigration of Afghans, Persians, Turks, and Arabs, and the offspring of mixed marriages (usually Hindu women to Muslim men) augmented the Islamic ranks. Besides, many Hindus, usually from the lower castes, became Muslims, sometimes out of religious conviction, sometimes to avoid the poll tax or persecution, often to escape the caste system itself. (2) Both Hinduism and Islam gained at the expense of Jainism and especially Buddhism. Buddhism, already declining in India when the Muslim conquest began, had become concentrated in monastic foundations and popular Tantric cults. The destruction of monasteries and monks dealt the *coup de grâce* to the older forms of Buddhism in India. The Tantrics, when they did not turn to Islam, adopted Shāktism or the most emotional forms of Vishnuism. All three religions are still strong in Bengal and Assam. (3) The popular *bhakti* cults grew in numbers and influence. The monotheism of Islam and the miseries of constant war and persecution seem to have encouraged emotional surrender to a god through whose grace salvation could be attained by loving devotion. The Brahmans, perhaps in order to maintain their position against Islamic competition, conceded more and more to the need of the masses for a simple, emotional solution of the problem of salvation. Many of them accepted the *bhakti* ideas, which became less austere and meditative, more emotional, and even sensual. The more personal and lovable *avatāras* of Vishnu—Rāma and Krishna—came to the fore, as did also the terrible but personal goddesses of Shāktism. (4) Cults arose which borrowed from both Muslim and Hindu. Hindus under Muslim rule eventually took over Islamic ideas about dress, ceremonials, the seclusion of women, and other features of Islamic culture, and some Persian Ṣūfīs who settled in India found in turn much of interest and merit in Hindu thought and religion. Leaders then arose who tried to unite Muslim and Hindu in cults that combined elements from the religions of both. (5) Finally, Hinduism gave way to Hīnayāna Buddhism or Chinese influences in the Indo-Chinese peninsula and to Islam in Malaya and the East Indies.

Developments within the several Hindu sects differed considerably. The Smārta traditionalists, for example, underwent few major changes during this period. The Muslim persecutions and the growing emphasis on *bhakti* seem to have caused a reduction in their ranks, since some of them tended to concentrate their affections on Shiva as the most intellectual of the *bhakti* deities, but they continued as a strong group. They unquestionably flourished in the Vijayanagar Empire, which apparently protected all Hindu cults including the Jains. Many of Vijayanagar's emperors were traditionalists or Shivaite, though some were Vishnuite.

Northern Shivaism appears to have suffered considerably at the hands of the invaders. Kashmir Shivaism ceased altogether except among a few scholars. The Pāshupatas vanished from the north and survived only as relatively isolated groups in the south. Despite persecution and massacres, however, northern Shivaism remained a powerful cult, imbued by hardship with greater devotion. It probably also began at this stage the process of absorbing the local Nāth cult of Bengal.

In the south the Shiva Siddhānta school continued under the protection of Vijayanagar. Great Shivaite temples prospered at Madura, Tinnevelly, Tanjore, and elsewhere despite Muslim raids. The theologian Umāpati (fl. 1313) completed the Tamil canon with eight doctrinal treatises, which took the form of poetical commentaries on earlier works, discussions of divine grace, and catechisms and critiques of other faiths (see Chapter X). The devotional element remained strong in this school.

Anti-Brahman influences added vigour to the Lingāyats. This sect flourished, while the affiliated sect of the Ārādhyas probably declined. The Lingāyats spread throughout the Kanarese-speaking areas of south India, and their creed is said to have been the state religion of Mysore (1399–1600).

With Buddhism's decline Shāktism seems to have expanded in Bihar, Bengal, and Assam despite Muslim persecutions. Pillage and carnage seem to have stimulated the worship of destructive goddesses, and local goddess cults like those of Chandī and Manasā, which had already become the last refuge of Tantric Buddhism in India, acquired new importance. Brahmans began to serve these cults and to integrate them with Shāktism. Thus Manasā, partly snake goddess and partly Buddhist figure, ultimately became the daughter of Shiva, and Chandī, partly female *bodhisattva*, became Shiva's wife, identified with Durgā.

This process of amalgamation went on until the eighteenth century or later. An extensive oral tradition relating to these goddesses appeared in Bengali writing (see Chapter X). Shakti *tantras*, such as the *Kālikā-purāna* (which gave prescriptions for human and animal sacrifices), became so numerous that digests for the use of Shāktas were compiled. Shākta saints also emerged. One of them, who may have flourished in the late-fifteenth century, was Sharvānanda, a poor illiterate of Mehar, to whom the Divine Mother was reported to have revealed Herself one night as he was repeating a *mantra* in accordance with a particularly dangerous ritual. Mehar has since become a place of pilgrimage, with an annual festival in January.

*　　　*　　　*

Developments in India

The most spectacular Hinduist developments of the period came within Vishnuism. Equalitarian tendencies arose in opposition to the caste system. Devotional intensity increased with the growth of Rāma and Krishna worship. Efforts to unite Hindu and Muslim emerged.

No striking changes took place among the Mādhvas, who remained aristocratic and puritan. Dancing girls were not allowed in their temples; cleanliness was demanded; and although members of most castes could belong to their sect, only Brahmans could be ecclesiastics. The Mādhvas gradually became separated into two groups, the Vyāsakūtas, who accepted only Sanskrit scriptures, and the more numerous Dāsakūtas, who had somewhat more popular tendencies and accepted Kanarese scriptures.

The origin of the Nimāvat or Shanakādi sect of north India is very obscure. We have already mentioned the debate regarding the date of birth of Nimbārka, its founder (see Chapter II). He lived and taught near Muttra, and the sect developed there and in Bengal. If Nimbārka is placed in the fourteenth century, the rise of the Nimāvats coincides with the upsurge of the popularity of Krishna and Rādhā. Because of their devotion to Krishna the Nimāvats were unquestionably connected with the popular Krishna–Rādhā cults of the period.

The widespread adoration of Krishna and Rādhā was expressed by the Rajput poetess Mīrā Bāī and the great vernacular poets of Bihar and Bengal in the early fifteenth century (see Chapter X). So devoted to Krishna was Mīrā Bāī that he is supposed to have engulfed her in his embrace. A Krishnaite sub-sect, generally considered a branch of the Vallabhas (i.e. of the Rudra sect; see Chapter II), bears her name. These earthy poets seem to have had a deep spiritual affinity with the Rudra sect. In fact, their affinity seems deeper than that of the restrained Maratha religious poets, who are sometimes, though with less reason, also associated with the Rudra sect.

The sect to which these Maratha poets belonged centred upon the temple of Pandharpur. Its deity was named Vitthobā, Vitthala, or Pāndurang. The first two of these names were dialectal variations of Vishnu, and the last was an epithet of Shiva, but the Maratha deity was popularly associated with Krishna and his wife Rukminī. The sect, as portrayed by its mystic poets, accepted the pantheistic monism of Shankara but believed intensely in the saving grace of Krishna. It emphasized the importance of knowledge, meditation, humility, preservation of life, moral purity, and devotion, and largely ignored Rādhā and Krishna in his cowherd character.

Of the mystic Maratha poets, Nāmdev (c. 1400) was the outstanding one. His message was that God was everywhere, accessible to all without ceremonials, austerities, philosophy, or pilgrimages through love and steadfast faith, praise, and devotion. At times Nāmdev denounced images as limitations of God. Except for its adoration of Krishna, this school resembled the Rudra sect less than it did the Rāmāt sect of Rāmānanda (see below), and Nāmdev may have been under the influence of Rāmānanda.

The Shrī-Vishnuite sect of Rāmānuja was in the process of dividing into two groups as the fourteenth century opened. The two were known as the Tengalais, or Southerners, and the Vadagalais, or Northerners, although both were confined to south India. The Southerners were inclined to innovation, tending to disregard the Vedas and Sanskrit tradition, and to consider the

Tamil *Nālāyiram* sufficient as scripture, while the Northerners insisted upon the Sanskrit as well as the Tamil tradition. The Northerners held that true surrender to God can follow only upon good works and individual effort; in order to be saved, one must exert oneself and grasp God as a young monkey grasps its mother. The Southerners, on the other hand, discounted personal effort, aside from faith and self-surrender, and insisted that the grace of a forgiving God grasped the soul as a cat does its kittens. The Southerners held that Lakshmī was created and finite, though divine, and hence merely a mediator without power to bestow grace directly, while the Northerners held her to be equal with Vishnu. Both groups laid great stress on guidance by gurus, though each had a different succession of religious teachers and quarrelled with the other for control of the temples which they used in common. Each developed different sectarian marks and ceremonials, although both branded members with the conch shell and discus. Both were scrupulous about caste observances and the ceremonial purity of their food and meals. Although each admitted lower castes (*shūdras*), a special class of priests, called *satanis*, had to minister to them. The Southerners, being, on the whole, more tolerant towards the lower castes, gradually became the more numerous. Pillai Lokācārya (d. 1327), the effective founder of the Southerners, wrote numerous treatises in Tamil, including simple guides for women and the lower castes. Perhaps the Southerners' chief saint and teacher was Manavāla Mahāmuni (*c.* 1370–1443), who wrote numerous commentaries and poems and a small treatise on daily worship in the home. Vedānta Deshika (*c.* 1269–1369), 'the lion of poets and philosophers', was the most famous of the Northerners. Though a poor householder who travelled a great deal, he was the author of over a hundred works in both Tamil and Sanskrit (see Chapter X).

The Rāmāts differed little from the Vadagalais in doctrine, and although the Rāmāts dispensed with branding, both wore the same sectarian marks. Rāmānanda, founder of the Rāmāt sect, probably flourished about 1400. Whether he was a southerner or a northerner by birth, the scene of his main activities certainly was the north. He was a follower of Rāmānuja but, for infringing its rules regarding eating, was reputedly expelled from the Rāmānuja sect—with, however, permission to found a new sect. Although a few hymns ascribed to him have survived, he was not a writer but a popular teacher who voiced a general desire for a more equalitarian and devotional creed. He formulated no new philosophical system but combined the emotional ritualism of the south with the more restrained meditative philosophy of the north. His love of God seems to have been joined with compassion for mankind. His devotionalism, his use of the vernacular (Hindi in his case), and his disregard for caste were to affect all later Indian sectarian developments. His humanity and moral quality led him to oppose the growing sensuousness associated with Krishna and to favour the worship of the knightly hero Rāma. The heroism of Rāma and the virtue of his wife, Sītā, appealed to a Hindu world threatened by Islam and served as rallying symbols for a highly moral *bhakti* cult.

Rāmānanda inspired the founding of many congregations and monasteries, and numerous disciples carried on his work. The Rāmāts emphasized the role of the guru; their ceremonies included initiations, in which the initiates were given the secret *mantra*, and sacramental meals; they believed in salvation through faith in the saving grace of God; and they tended to disregard caste and seclusion in the preparing and eating of meals. They were divided into celibate ascetics, clerical Brahman householders, and laity. The ascetics in turn were divided into several groups, of which one was reserved for Brahmans and three others were open to all castes.

Rāmānanda was supposed to have had twelve principal disciples, some of whom certainly were not his contemporaries. Among them were men of all castes and of different callings (including a raja, a weaver, a cobbler, a peasant, and a barber) and a woman. They propagated the sect throughout north and central India, and some of them established sub-sects. Rāidās, the cobbler, who established a sub-sect especially popular among the caste of leather workers, wrote hymns in praise of the 'One Infinite God, who is above and beyond all religious sects' and who 'resides within the hearts of his devotees.'[1] Senā, the barber, who also founded a sub-sect, became the guru of a raja. The raja, Pīpā, was born about 1425 (i.e. after Rāmānanda's death); he established a monastery at Pipawat near Dwarka, and his wife took up the religious life with him. The most famous of the disciples was Kabīr, the weaver.

Whether Kabīr was a personal disciple of Rāmānanda or only a later follower is uncertain. He seems to have flourished during the middle and end of the fifteenth century. At first, he probably was a follower of the Rāmāt sect, but eventually he sloughed off much of its mythology, emphasized its monotheism, and added elements from Islam in an effort to unite Hindu and Muslim. He was not a systematic writer but a religious poet and teacher. His sayings and poems have been preserved in the *Bījak* (compiled about 1570), the chief scripture of his sect, and the *Ādi Granth* of the Sikhs.

As these sources were compiled only after Kabīr's death, what he actually taught is uncertain. Clearly, however, he believed in one personal God, who was the same whether called Allah or Rāma, although his God, whom he preferred to call Rām, was more Indian than Semitic. Kabīr rejected reincarnation, maintaining that the world of transmigration and illusion existed in men's hearts and no one could free himself from it except by finding God there instead. Kabīr condemned the formalities of both Hinduism and Islam. Human beings, he held, were of one blood, and caste distinctions were prideful, corrupting fictions. He rejected idolatry, circumcision, austerities, ritualism, haughty self-confidence, and the pursuit of wealth and sensual pleasure, and he extolled respect for all forms of life, hard work, helpfulness to others, love of mankind, the moral way, and service to God. His God says:

'If you want me, give up your desire for every other thing and become mine, and then everything will be yours.'[2] For Kabīr external religious observances possessed no truth:

'The difference among faiths is due only to difference in names; everywhere there is yearning for the same God. Why do the Hindus and Mohammedans quarrel for nothing?'[3]

Kabīr attracted both Hindu and Muslim followers, who were known as Kabīrpanthīs. His teachings were particularly popular among the lower classes of north-central India. After his death his disciples organized the movement and, ironically enough, practically deified him. His sect is generally considered as belonging to Vishnuism despite its wide departure from traditional Hinduism, and he is revered by the Vishnuites. Along with Rāmānanda, Kabīr is by some historians numbered among the world's great spiritual leaders. Certainly the emphasis of these two teachers upon human brotherhood and their supreme devotion to God place them high in the ranks of those who helped to develop mankind's religious and humanitarian ideals.

*   *   *

Developments outside India

Forced to give ground to Islam in India, Hinduism underwent even greater losses in the Indo-Chinese peninsula and Malaysia. During the fourteenth century the dominant people of this area were the Khmers of Cambodia, and some of the Khmer rulers were nominally Shivaite. The famous temples of their capital, Angkor, helped to make it one of the lesser centres of Hinduism. Hīnayānaist Buddhism, however, not only was more generally accepted in Cambodia but also became the religion of the expanding Thai, even though the Thai rulers obtained Brahmans from the Khmer Empire as political advisers and accepted the Hindu concept of the god-king. The Thai sacked Angkor in 1431. Thereupon the Khmer rulers abandoned it, and Cambodia completely forsook Hinduism for Buddhism. In the rival kingdom of the Chams in Champa, Hinduism gradually gave ground before the advancing Vietnamites from the north, and by 1500 the quasi-Chinese religious ideas and practices that they brought with them dominated the Cham area.

In the East Indies Hinduism and Buddhism both fared badly. The expansion of the powerful Majapahit Empire throughout Malaysia assured the strength of its mixed Hindu-Buddhist religion during the 1300's. During the next century, however, Hindu-Buddhism began to meet the competition of Islam spreading eastward from west Sumatra. With the rise of Malacca as a commercial power the spread of Islamic influence was hastened, and with the decline of Majapahit after 1470, Hinduism and Buddhism as independent religions of the Indies rapidly declined, ultimately to disappear except in Bali. Nevertheless, they left a residue of practices and ideas, which, mixed with the pervading animistic beliefs, was amalgamated into Islam to form the dominant religion of Malaya and the East Indies.

BUDDHISM

By 1300 Buddhism's great creative and missionary period was over. Although it lived on as an important religious force in eastern Asia, no significant new doctrines or sects appeared. In India and central Asia its struggling remnants gradually vanished, although in south India survivals of Hīnayānaism seem to have persisted until the sixteenth century. In China, Korea, and Vietnam it lost ground to Neo-Confucianism or other native creeds. Sinhalese, Japanese, and Tibetan Buddhism, however, remained energetic.

In Ceylon much of the north was gradually lost to Hinduism as a result of the Tamil invasions. The great Mahāvihāra Monastery at Anuradhapura had to be abandoned, and the monks with their precious relics, including a tooth of Buddha, were shifted to new and less resplendent locations in the south. The Mahāvihāra brand of Hīnayānaism continued to dominate the south, however, and the prestige of Sinhalese Buddhism remained high in other Hīnayāna lands as well. Pilgrims and students came to Ceylon from Burma and Siam to observe and study. In 1361 Siam asked Ceylon for learned Buddhists, and in 1476 Pegu sent a large group of monks and its highest prelates to be taught and properly ordained by the Mahāvihāras. The process of accepting various Indian *devas* as guardian deities in Sinhalese Buddhism no doubt went on during this period.

In Burma the fourteenth and fifteenth centuries formed an era characterized by sectarian disputes. The collapse of Pagan (*c.* 1298) as the political centre of a united Burma and the invasion of the Shans probably caused some decline of monastic activities, but Pegu remained an important monastic centre, and for a time Pagan, too, revived as such. Besides, various Shan rulers and nobility in the north soon became patrons of the monks, and new centres developed; after 1364 Ava gradually emerged as the political and monastic capital of Upper Burma. In Pegu, King Dhammaceti or Rāmādhipati (*c.* 1472–91), a former monk, succeeded in putting an end to the rivalry between the Talaing and Sinhalese sects and tightening monastic discipline. It was he who sent some monks and prelates to Ceylon for study and ordination. After their return all the monks in Pegu and many from upper Burma, estimated to have numbered together 15,666, were re-ordained. The conflicting sects were thus united, and the Sinhalese school remained the standard for all Burma thenceforth.

In Siam Hīnayāna Buddhism continued to flourish as the national religion under the Thai rulers. In 1361 the ruler of Siam sent to Ceylon for an abbot, or *sangharāja*, who was received with great pomp and ceremony. This abbot no doubt helped to secure the dominance of Pāli (Hīnayāna) Buddhism and reduce the Mahāyāna elements in Thai Buddhism. Also about this time a

G*

bodhi-tree (holy wild-fig tree) was brought from Ceylon, and some sacred relics from Patna. Great monasteries prospered under royal patronage. When after 1350 Ayuthia eclipsed Sukhothai as the political centre of Siam, the rulers continued to be great patrons of Pāli Buddhism, which spread down the Malay Peninsula with the Thai conquests. Ayuthia's rulers remained liberal patrons of Buddhism, as the ruins of Wat Somarokat and Wat Chern with their huge bronze Buddhas testify, until its destruction by the Burmese in 1767.

By 1300, although the Mahāyāna-Brahman cults still flourished at Angkor, Pāli Hīnayānaism, generally accepted by rulers and peoples alike, spread as the national religion. In 1358 the Laotian king was converted to Hīnayāna Buddhism through the influence of his Khmer wife and the ruler at Angkor. A statue of the Buddha known as the Luang Prabang is said to have been sent to the Laotian king from Angkor, and it became the palladium of the Laotian kingdom. After the abandonment of Angkor in 1432, the Mahāyāna-Brahman cults were not revived at the new Cambodian capital of Phnom-Penh, and Cambodia became almost entirely Hīnayānaist.

*   *   *

Developments in China, Vietnam, and Korea

Under the Mongol (Yüan) dynasty (1260–1368) the fortunes of the Buddhists reached an apogee in China. Kublai Khan (1260–94) adopted Lamaism and imposed it on the Mongols. The Tibetan lama, Pagspa (Pa-ssu-pa), was given the title of *Kuo–shih* (National Teacher) and placed at the head of China's Buddhist hierarchy. The ninth collection of the *Tripitaka*, published in 1285–87 under Pagspa's supervision, was in 1312 ordered to be translated into Mongol. Lamas continued to fill Pagspa's post and were favoured in other administrative positions for the duration of the Yüan dynasty. Lamaist temples were established in Peking and elsewhere in north China, and Kublai and his successors generally acted as lavish patrons of other forms of Buddhism as well. Old restrictions on Buddhists were removed, and their buildings and lands were exempted from taxation. The lamas sometimes abused their privileges by allowing the wealthy to register lands in their name in order to escape taxation.

Most rulers of the Ming dynasty (1368–1644) also patronized the Buddhists, giving them lands, endowments, and at times, through the favouritism of eunuchs, special advantages. Still, the Ming emperors did not favour the Buddhists so much as the Mongol emperors had done. The official philosophy of the Ming was Neo-Confucianism, and the administrative hierarchy was controlled by Confucian scholars. Since all religions were officially under the supervision of the government, a Buddhist office (*Seng-lu Ssu*) regulated and supervised the Buddhist monastic establishments, and two Buddhist patriarchs (*Shan-shih*) were officially maintained with a staff of subordinates. Ming religious policy in general was to conciliate the lamas of Tibet because of their influence over the Mongols, to patronize all religions more or less impartially, to restrict the number of monasteries, monks, and nuns, and otherwise to keep a tight control over the clergy. This policy was instituted by the founder of the dynasty, the Hung-wu emperor (T'ai-tsu, 1368–98), who had spent some time in a monastery. He received Buddhist monks, appointed them among others as tutors to his sons, decreed that all monks should study the *Prajñāpāramitā* and certain other revered works, ordered the compilation of commentaries on these works, and patronized the publication of the tenth collection of the *Tripitaka*.

The third Ming ruler, the Yung-lo emperor (Ch'eng-tsu, 1403–24), was still more friendly to Buddhism. He elevated his Buddhist tutor, Yao Kuang-hsiao, to high office. He brought lamas to the capital, restored to them the title of *Kuo-shih*, and made them the highest prelates in Buddhism. He wrote prefaces to the eleventh collection of the *Tripitaka* and to several other Buddhist works and had a *sūtra*, allegedly revealed to his empress, included in the *Tripitaka*. Yet he also restricted the number of persons that might be ordained.

Under the lax administration of the lamas, clerical celibacy had not been enforced, and under the Hung-wu emperor the number of secular clerics (that is, priests who were married and did not live in monasteries) was considerable. They probably had already begun to be numerous during the Mongol period, and they continued to increase under the Ming despite decrees against them (1394 and 1412), for married priests filled a popular need and provided a means of exceeding the limitation placed on the total number of monks. In 1458 a decree restricted the number of ordination ceremonies to one a year. The Ch'eng-hua emperor (1464–87) was under the influence of eunuchs and Buddhist monks (bonzes), but his successor (1487–1505) cleared the monks and eunuchs out and otherwise restricted Buddhist influence.

Despite official patronage, Chinese Buddhism lacked creative qualities in the fourteenth and fifteenth centuries. A few new translations from Sanskrit were made during the Mongol era, but none under the Ming. Nor did native scholarship contribute anything original in theology, confining itself to the preparation of histories, lives of saints, eulogies of the three religions (Confucianism, Taoism, and Buddhism), collections of poetry, and various compendia. During the Ming period, among the intellectuals Buddhism lost ground to Neo-Confucianism. No new sects appeared, and the old ones tended to assimilate, absorb general Chinese practices, and cease to be distinctive. The Sudden Enlightenment or Ch'an (Zen) sect remained the strongest and most original; among the monks the T'ien-t'ai (Tendai) was next in importance; and for the laity the ideas of the Pure Land or Ching-t'u (Jōdō) were by all odds the most significant. Mantrayāna practices spread among all the sects.

Much the same is true of Buddhism in Vietnam and Korea. In both countries, and especially Vietnam, it tended to lose distinctiveness and fuse

with Confucianism, Taoism, and the native cults. In Korea, after the fall of
the Mongols, a revolt deposed the native dynasty, which had submitted to
them, and set up the Yi dynasty (1392). The leaders of the revolt favoured
Neo-Confucianism, and identifying Buddhism with the old regime, subjected
it to persecution. They issued a set of decrees that restricted Buddhist learning, obliged marriages and burials to conform to Confucian rites, required
Buddhist statues to be melted down, and (1472 and 1512) closed monasteries
in the capital and other cities, limiting them to rural areas.

*   *   *

Developments in Japan

In Japan, Buddhism during this period showed some energy and originality, but, largely because of the contemporary political instability, it became
militarized and intolerant. The Kamakura Shogunate suddenly collapsed in
1333 as a result of the Emperor Go-Daigo's efforts to restore imperial
authority. He was unable, however, to establish control, and soon there were
two royal courts, one at Kyoto under the control of the Ashikagas, who set
themselves up as shoguns, and one at Yoshino under Go-Daigo and his
successors. Thus ended a long period of relative peace. The bitter struggle
that ensued came to a close only in 1392, with a compromise that brought
seventy-five years of relative stability. The civil war that then began (1467)
inaugurated a period of relentless feudal strife that lasted until Hideyoshi
united the country in 1590.

During most of this age of strife, compromise, and renewed strife the
Ashikaga shoguns were in power, and it is known as the Ashikaga or Muro-
machi period. It brought several important changes to Japanese Buddhism.
(1) Many sub-sects were established and widely distributed throughout the
country, serving as centres for the spread of Buddhist ideas and a modicum of
learning. (2) Higher learning and culture were kept alive largely by the Zen
monks, who served as advisers to the shoguns but kept largely aloof from the
military conflict, maintained trade and contact with China, and became
eclectics in learning and masters of landscape painting. (3) A code of military
ethics, *Bushido*, emerged that was an amalgam of Zen ideas of discipline,
Confucian ideas of loyalty and family responsibility, and Japanese ideas of
bravery and clan loyalty. *Bushido* somewhat offset a contemporaneous moral
depression characterized by extreme pessimism, intolerance, persecution,
obscene cults, magic, sorcery, exorcism, and divination. (4) Many of the
Buddhist sects became militarized, maintaining considerable armies, turning
their establishments into fortresses, and waging war with one another and
with the feudal lords.

The Zen sect emerged as probably the most important Buddhist group in
Japan, with five great monasteries in Kamakura and five in Kyoto. Its discip-
line appealed to the military, and its monks gained prestige as advisers of the
Ashikaga shoguns. Soseki (Musō Kokushi, 1275–1351), tutor and adviser of

Ashikaga Takauji and abbot of the Tenryuji Monastery, initiated the Zen-Ashikaga commercial voyages to China in 1342 and persuaded the shogun to order the establishment of a Zen monastery and pagoda in every province. Eisan (1268–1325) and Gazan (1275–1365) also laboured to extend Zen in the provinces. Zen monks were record keepers, accountants, tutors, teachers at the Ashikaga college, librarians, chroniclers, essay writers, painters, art collectors, and masters of the tea ceremony. They introduced Neo-Confucian ideas from China and wrote sophisticated works like the *Tsuré-zuré-gusa* of Yoshido Kenkō (1283–1350), which spoke sympathetically of Shinto, Confucianism, and Taoism. In addition, they produced collections of moral maxims, poetry, and devotional tracts suitable for children and common people, and they were instrumental in initiating the transcription of the *Tripitaka*, which was begun in 1354.

Of the other sects the competing Shin and Nichiren were the most militant in the provinces. The Shin sect was especially active in central and north central Japan. Its hereditary clergy dominated it, but it divided into ten sub-sects, each with a different abbot as administrative head, although they all paid general allegiance to the abbot of the Hongwanji Temple in Kyoto, established in 1272. The abbot Ryōgen (1294–1335) was known for promoting Shin influence around Kyoto and the central provinces, but the pre-eminent Shin leader was Rennyo (1415–99). Forced to leave Kyoto in 1465, when the Tendai sect destroyed the Hongwanji, he spent many years wandering and teaching throughout Japan and established a major centre at Yoshizaki in Echizen. In 1480 he rebuilt the Hongwanji at Yamashina, near Kyoto. His *Ofumi*, or Epistles, and *Ryōgemon*, a sort of creed, did much to unify the sect upon a sound moral basis, gradually putting an end to the internal faction called 'Evil Doers', who argued that deeds did not matter if one's belief was correct. The Shin had large groups of poor lay followers and engaged in constant conflict with other sects and with feudal lords. Its congregations, each with its own fortified temple, spread throughout the land. It virtually dominated the province of Kaga and in 1496 established a centre at Osaka. It was driven out of Yamashina in 1532 by the Nichiren sect, whereupon it turned its centre at Osaka into an impregnable stronghold.

The radical Nichiren sect was reported to have established as many as 80,000 centres throughout the country. In 1440 its leader Nisshin (1407–88) won broad renown for withstanding the tortures heaped upon him by the shogun as punishment for criticism. It expanded especially in central and eastern Japan under an effective organizer, Nitchō (1422–1500). The belligerent social philosophy and quarrelsome character of the Nichiren kept them in constant conflict with the feudal lords and other sects. After they drove the Shin sect out of Yamashina, the Bakufu (the government of the shogun) and the Tendai sect joined forces with the Shin (1536). The coalition destroyed twenty-one temples of the Nichiren in Kyoto and drove them from the city. This catastrophe, coupled with internal dissensions and the attacks of feudal lords, caused the Nichiren to decline as the century advanced, while the Shin became probably the most numerous sect in the land.

Only a few other sects continued to thrive. The Tendai monks of Mount Hiei, Kyoto, were not active in the provinces, but in the capital their military forces had to be restrained on numerous occasions by the shogun. The Shingon sect entrenched on Mount Koya, Kyoto, was also turbulent, and a branch developed in Kii province which controlled 2,700 temples, a great fortified centre at Negoro, and a large army of mercenaries. It remained for Ryōto Shōgei (1341–1420), of the relatively inactive Jōdo, or Pure Land, sect, to formulate the most important new religious doctrine of the period. In his *Jugi*, he asserted that the Pure Land was not in another region but represented a change of mind and condition here below. At the other extreme the Mountain Priests, or Yamabushi, a group of wandering teachers, appealed to ignorance and superstition, promoting occult practices and Chinese *yin-yang* ideas.

★   ★   ★

Tantric Buddhism

In north India, although the main centres of Tantric Buddhism in Bengal and Bihar were destroyed by the Muslims, some monasteries seem to have survived. Tibetan sources indicate that a king of Bengal about 1450 restored some others and that *sūtras* were still being copied in Bengal in the fifteenth century. Undisguised Buddhism probably survived longest in Orissa, which was not fully conquered by the Muslims until 1568. Although one of Orissa's rulers persecuted Buddhists in 1529, its last Hindu ruler was reputedly a Buddhist. Elsewhere, fusion with Hinduism or acceptance of Islam had already gone a long way by 1300 and continued during the succeeding centuries. Groups of wandering monks and nuns, generally in pairs, propagated a degenerate sort of Buddhism for a long time. Other unedifying forms of Buddhism, mixed with local practices and Hinduism, survived in Bengal's local cults such as those of Chandī, Manasā, and Dharma (a form of the Buddha). These cults were gradually absorbed by Shāktism, Shivaism, or the Chaitanya movement (see Chapter IV). The Dharma cults were especially strong in western and southern Bengal.

Tantric Buddhism languished in several other regions also. As already indicated, the mixed Buddhist-Hindu religion of Majapahit rapidly declined after 1470. A form of Tantric Buddhism mixed with Hinduism existed in Nepal when in 1324 the Hindu king of Tirhut, fleeing from the Muslims, seized the Nepalese throne. Later in the century his successors, under Brahman influence, organized Hinduism and Buddhism in parallel groups, which tended to become more and more alike and to absorb new Hinduistic elements from India. In the fourteenth century wandering ascetics, or Nāthas, who combined elements of both creeds and were honoured by both, came into prominence.

Tantric Buddhism developed its maximum strength in Lamaism, its Tibetan form. In Tibet the abbots of the Sakya Monastery continued to dominate until around 1340, when the decline of Mongol power enabled other sects and various temporal princes to establish their independence. The Ming dynasty after 1368, apparently content to see authority in Tibet divided, did not interfere actively but recognized the abbots of eight monasteries as well as a secular dynasty.

Coincident with the rise of the Ming dynasty was the career of Tsong-ka-pa (c. 1358–1419). He studied at a number of monasteries and may have known something of Christianity. He was convinced that Lamaism was not in harmony with its own scriptures and undertook to reform it. Originally a member of the Kadampa sect, he reorganized it, making it into the Gelukpa, or Order of the Virtuous Way. He instituted stricter monastic discipline, insisting on celibacy, frequent prayer services, the reduction of tantric and magical elements, and the carrying of the begging bowl. Since his sect wore yellow robes and hats, it was known as the Yellow Bonnets, to distinguish it from the old unreformed sects, or Red Bonnets. He established a close-knit organization and a highly ritualistic service. He founded the Gandan Monastery near Lhasa, his disciples established others, and his sect rapidly developed into the most powerful in Tibet.

About this time the belief emerged that each of the abbots of the Gelukpa was the incarnation of some Buddhist figure and that upon death he was reincarnated in a child who was to be found by oracular means and installed as the new abbot. Tsong-ka-pa came to be considered the incarnation of the *bodhisattva* Mānjushri, while his nephew, Geden-dub, who became the first grand lama of the Gelukpa at Lhasa in 1439, was considered the incarnation of Avalokita. One of Tsong-ka-pa's disciples, as first abbot of Tashilhunpo (founded 1447), was considered the incarnation of Amitabha. The Yung-lo emperor (1403–24), at whose court the *Kanjur* was printed in 1410, greatly advanced the political fortunes of the new Tibetan group in China, and the Ch'eng-hua emperor (1465–88) recognized Lhasa and Tashilhunpo, in that sequence, as superior to the other monastic sees of Tibet. The second grand lama (1479–1541) put the hierarchy in good order, distinguishing clerical posts, to be filled by incarnations, from merely administrative ones.

CONFUCIANISM, TAOISM, AND SHINTOISM

No arresting changes occurred within Confucianism during the period here under consideration, which covers much of the Mongol dynasty (1260–1368) and the first half of the Ming dynasty (1368–1644). Neo-Confucianism had come forward during the Sung dynasty (960–1279) as a genuine effort to revive the ancient thought of China, blurred by centuries of competition with Buddhism and Taoism. The Sung Neo-Confucians, however, did not themselves escape the Buddhist and Taoist influences they sought to throw off. In their efforts to develop a system of thought that would retain the moral, social, and political aspects of the ancient doctrine and yet appeal to a more sophisticated age, they borrowed freely from the very systems they were fighting. Their cosmology, metaphysics, and meditative practices drew heavily upon Taoism and Ch'an Buddhism, introducing much that was alien to early Confucianism. This new Confucianism was accepted under the Mongol rulers as the formal philosophy of the Imperial College but had less effect upon the national bureaucracy than might have been expected, since civil-service examinations were held only intermittently.

The Mongol rulers carried on the official cult much as usual. Although they themselves favoured Buddhism, most of them endeavoured also to please China's scholars by honouring Confucius and supporting the Confucian cult. Kublai built a Confucian temple in Peking, in 1308 Confucius received a new and higher title, and in 1316 the emperor sacrificed to him. In 1313 the names of Chu Hsi and a number of the other Neo-Confucians were added to those honoured in Confucian temples. Sacrifices in these temples became more elaborate, and the tendency to deify Confucius grew.

Under the Ming dynasty, despite the predilections of some emperors, Neo-Confucianism became the unquestioned philosophy of the state (see Chapter VI). The official cult, meticulously carried on, occasionally added a new deity and raised or demoted old ones. Thus, in 1409, new titles were conferred on the T'ien-fei, or Celestial Spouse, a guardian deity of sailors, because of aid supposedly rendered to imperially sponsored voyages into the Indian Ocean. The Yung-lo emperor had the Neo-Confucian writings condensed into the Hsing-li ta-ch'üan, or Great Philosophy, and in 1416 ordered that, together with the Five Classics and Four Books, the condensation should be the basis of instruction in the official schools and in civil-service examinations (see Chapter XVI). The rationalistic tendencies of Neo-Confucianism steadily gained ground, finding expression not only in edicts against yoga, exorcism, Buddhist, and Taoist masses for the dead, and various other allegedly superstitious practices but also in the tendency in the Cult of the Scholars gradually to replace deification of Confucius by respect for him as a mortal sage.

Elsewhere in the Far East Confucianism also flourished. In Korea after the establishment of the Yi dynasty (1392), it became the official philosophy and was liberally patronized by the state. For a time its high ethical and moral principles contributed to good government and a flowering of culture, but as time went on, the bureaucracy forgot its high ideals and became corrupt and grasping. The forms were maintained, but the spirit died. Nevertheless, ancestor worship and Confucian family ceremonials and ethics remained an important part of Korea's popular religion. In Vietnam it also received official patronage. In Japan, its ethics and philosophy contributed to the warrior's code (Bushido) and to Japanese ideas in general.

Taoism likewise underwent no profound change in the Mongol and early Ming periods. Kublai Khan ordered the destruction of Taoist books about 1281, and some Taoist writings were lost as a result. Otherwise the Taoists appear to have suffered little from the Mongols, who indeed were attracted by its shamanistic elements. The Ming dynasty subjected Taoists as well as Buddhists to restrictive legislation, requiring the registration of monks and nuns, limiting the number that could be ordained, prohibiting the building or enlarging of monasteries and temples without official permission, specifying the age at which men and women could enter monastic life, fixing the number of pupils that the married secular clergy could have, and placing all Taoist affairs under a national board, the Tao-lu Ssu, with branches in the local subdivisions. Restrictive legislation was not, however, rigorously enforced, and some emperors were veritable patrons of Taoism. Both Mongol and Ming rulers recognized the position of the Chang family as *T'ien-shih* (see Chapter II), but the Mings seem to have recognized also a rival patriarch. Under imperial patronage publication of the Taoist canon began in 1446, but with the Hung-chih emperor (1487–1505) further destruction of Taoist books took place. During the Ming period, though Taoism seems to have discarded some of the practices that had invited criticism—among them orgies in their monasteries on certain festival occasions, it appears to have generally declined. At least two of its sects, the Chen-ta-tao and the T'ai-i, gradually became extinct.

✶   ✶   ✶

The Revival of Shintoism

During the Ashikaga shogunate, when the fortunes of both the imperial house and the native religion of Japan reached their lowest point, Shintoism began to develop a clearly independent system of thought and to assert its freedom from Buddhism. The roots of this revived Shintoism can be traced back to the thirteenth-century *Shinto Gobusho* (*Shinto Pentateuch*) of the Waterai family priests of the Outer Shrine at Ise. Waterai Yukitada (1236–1305) and other members of the family vigorously asserted the superiority of their deities and ceremonials at Ise over the Buddhist ones, and the new spirit was taken up by officials attached to the imperial court as well as by the priestly families.

The revival of Shinto was soon associated with the restoration of the divine emperors to their position as actual heads of the government. In the formulation of the philosophical basis of Shintoism the work of Kitabatake Chikafusa (1293–1354), a court noble and warrior, stands out. He supported the efforts of the Emperor Go-Daigo to regain control of the government upon the overthrow of the Kamakura Shogunate in 1333. In his various works, especially the *Jinnō shōtōki* (*History of the True Succession of the Divine Emperors*), Kitabatake expounded the uniqueness of Japan as a country of the gods (*kami*) properly ruled only by direct descendants of the Sun Goddess. The three sacred treasures of the imperial regalia—mirror, necklace, and sword—were symbolic of sun, moon, and stars and represented respectively sagacity (or intelligence and veracity), benevolence (or mercy), and courage (or strength and justice). These virtues were the Shinto national inheritance from the Sun Goddess; they were the living facts of national life—the foundations of the state. If the government were to be successful, Shinto ways and the descendants of the Sun Goddess had to be restored and revered. Actually, Kitabatake's ideas were eclectic, for he borrowed heavily from Confucianism and Buddhism, but he presented his borrowed ideas as an essential part of native Shinto.

As Japan's feudal disorders worsened in the fifteenth century, another court noble, Ichijo Kaneyoshi (1402–81), developed the symbolism of the imperial regalia further. In the effort to promote national unity under the divine emperors he fused Buddhist, Confucian, and Shinto ideas and presented them as the Shinto tradition. He identified the cosmic soul of Buddhism and Shinto with the individual soul and argued that ethics consisted of bringing the individual soul and everyday life into harmony with cosmic unity. Although the Shinto *kami* were many, they were in reality but individual manifestations of the universal soul (*kami*) and shared alike the three qualities symbolized in the imperial regalia, which he equated with the three aspects of Buddhahood, wisdom (*prajñā*), emancipation (*moksha*), and truth (*dharma*). The duty of mankind as individuals and of the Japanese as a people was to live in harmony with these Shinto virtues, thus realizing the unity of man with the cosmic *kami* through the divine emperor. This was true Shinto —the Way of the Gods.

Probably the first Shinto school of thought to be formed in distinct opposition to the Ryōbu Shinto of the Buddhists was the Waterai or Outer Shrine Shinto, based on the teachings of Waterai Yukitada and other priests of the Outer Shrine at Ise. It taught an ethical, pantheistic Shinto. Outer Shrine Shinto's high development was not to come until the seventeenth century, but the position of the Ise Shrine was strengthened during the period of imperial poverty before 1500 because its priests formed lay associations for its support and attracted widespread interest and devotion. It thus changed from an imperial-family shrine into a national one, to which the faithful tried to make at least one pilgrimage.

Another early school to oppose Ryōbu Shinto was the Yui-itsu (One and Only, or Unique) Shinto. Since it was developed by the Urabe diviners of the Yoshida and Hirano shrines at Kyoto and most fully by Urabe (Yoshida) Kanetomo (1435–1511), it was also called Urabe or Yoshida Shinto. It was a pantheistic creed that claimed to be a direct revelation from the Japanese gods. It stressed sorcery and divination, laying less emphasis on ethics than previous writers had done.

This Urabe system too was a compound—of Shingon and Tendai Buddhism, Taoism, Confucianism, and native ideas and practices. Contrary to Ryōbu Shinto, however, it asserted that the Japanese *kami* were the original deities, the Buddhist deities being mere manifestations of them. The original *kami* was the self-existent, eternal absolute from which the other *kami*, the universe, and all its manifestations came. *Kami* was soul (*kokoro*), and the soul was *kami*. Japan and her people, by virtue of their more intimate connection with the *kami*, were uniquely divine, and the emperor, as the direct descendant of the Sun Goddess, was a *kami* in human form, who ruled by virtue of his unique descent. Urabe Kanetomo used this doctrine not only to strengthen native Shinto but also to extend the influence of his family in Shinto affairs; ultimately the Urabes virtually monopolized the ordination of Shinto priests and the establishment of sanctuaries.

ISLAM

Between 1300 and 1500 Islam established firm roots in India and spread widely throughout Malaya and the East Indies. In India its spread was largely due to military conquest, which opened up a field favourable to proselytizing, and farther east to the missionary activity of merchants and teachers and to matrimonial alliances. Shī'ite and non-orthodox elements were influential in Muslim conquests and conversions in India, but, whether Shī'ite or Sunnite, the brands of Islam that developed were often heavily intermixed with Hinduistic practices. Many of the traders and teachers who carried Islam to the East Indies were from Gujarat and Bengal, and they generally were willing to accept converts upon a simple affirmation of faith. Hence local practices persisted, and the type of Islam that developed in the East Indies differed markedly from the orthodox Islam of the Near East. Shī'ite elements were also strong in the East Indies during this early period. In central Asia and northwestern China Islam gained some ground, but its cultural advances in China were relatively inconsequential.

During the two centuries under review, Islam grew slowly in north India and the Deccan. Teachers, mystics, merchants, refugees, and adventurers of all sorts accompanied or followed the conquerors. Most of the newcomers were Persians and Afghans, but some were Turks and even Arabs. A majority belonged to one or other of the four main orthodox Sunnite schools, the Ḥanafites predominating, but some were Shī'ites, and many of both groups had only imperfectly assimilated Islam before their entrance. Some brought wives with them, but many took Hindu wives or concubines, and a considerable portion of the Islamic growth was due to natural increase. The children of Muslim fathers were reared as Muslims, even though their beliefs might be thoroughly coloured by Hindu views. Some converts came from the Brahman and other upper castes, but most from the lower classes, who saw in conversion a chance to escape from the Hindu caste system as well as the poll tax (*jizya*) imposed by the conquerors. Converts were especially numerous in Bengal, where many of the leaderless Tantric Buddhists turned to Islam. Islam likewise became significant in the Punjab, which was more thoroughly subjected to Islamic invasion and colonization than other areas. In addition, a considerable Islamic commercial element developed in Gujarat, and Muslims moved also into the Deccan, though the number there was not large. Among those in Gujarat and the Deccan the Shī'ite elements seem to have been strong.

The most important Shī'ite group in India was the Imāmiyya, or Twelvers, whose major strength lay in the Bahmani kingdom of the Deccan. Shī'ite influence was evident from the very founding of this kingdom in 1347, and the ninth ruler, Aḥmad Shāh I (1422–36) openly embraced the Imāmiyya faith. Rulers of some of the states that replaced the Bahmani kingdom were Shī'ites and promoted the faith there.

Of the Ismā'īliyya, another branch of the Shī'a, there were two sects in India. The Tayyibīs (or Bohrahs, as they were called in India) had been established in the Cambay area of Gujarat by missionaries from Yaman before 1300. They were persecuted by the Sunnite rulers of Gujarat after 1396, and a large group became Sunnites in the fifteenth century. The Nizārīs (or Khojahs, as they were called in India) were established in the Multan area of the Punjab and in Sind, Gujarat, and Kashmir by missionaries, principally from Persia, at various times between the twelfth and fifteenth centuries. Both groups recruited heavily from Hindu converts, were active in mercantile affairs, and accepted many Hindu customs, ideas, and legal practices. Each had its separate literature and paid its tithe directly to its respective religious head. The Bohrahs retained their Hindu laws of inheritance, but their literature, mainly in Arabic and Gujarati, generally continued the tradition of Fatimid Egypt. The Khojahs tended to consider 'Ali the tenth incarnation of Vishnu, as set forth in *Das Avatar (The Ten Incarnations)*, written in the fifteenth century by Ṣadr-ud-Dīn, a Khojah missionary. They regarded their head very much as a god. Their literature was in Persian and Gujarati or other Indian vernaculars. Both groups seem to have been active as traders and missionaries in the East Indies and east Africa.

Islamic Ṣūfism became popular in India. Most of the Ṣūfīs were Sunnites, for the Shī'ites generally held that spiritual oneness with God could be attained only through the *Imām* and not through mystic practices. Large numbers of Islamic *faqīrs* (mendicant Ṣūfīs) appeared in India, and their mystic approach led many Ṣūfīs to be receptive of pantheistic Hindu ideas. Two of the regular Islamic *faqīr* orders—the Chishtiyya and the Suhrawardiyya—were introduced into India immediately after the conquest, and the Shaṭṭāriyya order was inaugurated in the late-fourteenth century by Abd Allāh Shaṭṭārī. In 1482 the Qādiriyya order was introduced to Sind, which had already become famous as the home of Indian Ṣūfism. Many Ṣūfīs were important as missionaries. Numerous irregular Ṣūfī orders that did not emphasize learning or observe the Ṣūfīs' customary ritual of fasting, prayer, and other stringent practices also appeared in India during this period. Some of them were founded by outright charlatans, and their begging, singing, magic, fortune telling, amulets, charms, and other unsavoury practices wholly misrepresented the regular orders of *faqīrs*.

In general, Islam took firmer hold in India's towns and cities than in the rural areas. It ranged in form from the most orthodox of Sunnite practice to mere lip-service to Allah and his prophet Mohammed. The Islamic conquerors were not generally accompanied by a well-organized company of teachers and missionaries. Hence, although the essentials of Islam—the confession of faith, daily prayers, giving of alms, the month's fast of Ramadān, and pilgrimages to Mecca—gradually took hold among most of the converts, many elements of Hinduism persisted, particularly among the groups that only nominally embraced Islam. A host of new saints, some of whom were borrowed from Hinduism, appeared; Hindu festivals were incorporated into Islam, as were Hindu godlings and demons and the methods of revering or propitiating them; Hindu rather than Islamic law regarding property was applied in many areas; caste attitudes were often retained, as were Hindu customs relating to family life, eating, marriage, worship of ancestors, and the burning of widows. Pantheism and Hindu ideas regarding the absorption of the individual soul into the divine being affected Indian Ṣūfism in particular. Even Sunnite and Shī'ite differences were sometimes obscured.

*　　*　　*

Developments in Malaya and Malaysia

In the East Indies around 1300 Islam centred in the two petty sultanates of Perlak and Pasai at the western end of Sumatra. Since the Hindu-Buddhist kingdom of Majapahit dominated Java, while that of Malayu (Jambi) dominated south Sumatra, and the Hīnayānaist Thais were expanding in the Malay Peninsula, the spread of Islam at first was slow. But from 1400 onward, and especially after 1440, as the power of Malacca rose while that of Malayu and Majapahit declined, the political domination of petty Islamic rulers spread. The success of Islam was closely associated with the development of trade between the East Indian areas on the one hand and India (especially Gujarat and Bengal), Persia, and the Red Sea region on the other. Islamic merchants from western Asia, and especially from the Cambay area of Gujarat, either settled or spent long periods of time in the trading cities of the East Indies. Encouraged by the local rajas and their overlords for economic reasons, they became influential in many of the cities and, together with the Islamic teachers associated with them, began the process of conversion. In some cases the local rajas were themselves converted or married daughters of Muslim merchants, and so, sooner or later, Muslims sat on their thrones. Once this stage was reached, matrimonial alliances between the petty kingdoms, commercial pressure, or outright conquest extended the sway of Islam. By 1500 most of the commercial towns of Malaya and the East Indies that were the capitals of small kingdoms were Muslim and were ruled by Islamic sultans.

Two major centres of dispersion developed. One was Malacca, the other the trading cities of Grisek and Tuban in the Surabaya area of East Java. Islam spread from Perlak and Pasai to the Malaya peninsula and thence to

Malacca. The kingdom of Malacca was founded about 1403. It soon developed into an important commercial city, in which many Gujarati and Javanese merchants settled, and its first ruler, Parameshvara (Megat Iskandar Shah, 1403–24), embraced Islam at the time of his marriage to a Pasai princess. Despite the threat of an expanding Siam, Malacca maintained its position and from the time of Muzaffar-Shah (c. 1446–59) was a spearhead in the Islamic advance. It extended its dominance to the lower Malay Peninsula, the north-eastern coast of Sumatra as far south as Jambi, and Borneo. Its connections throughout the Indies and especially with East Java made it by 1511 the strongest commercial power in the area. The Gujarati merchants at Malacca were said at times to number a thousand, and it always had a large contingent of East Javanese.

Grisek, the commercial port of Majapahit, to which Gujarati merchants came directly from India, became a distributing centre for the spice trade. With the neighbouring commercial town of Tuban it early developed some important Islamic communities. The oldest Islamic tombstone of Grisek is of 1419. In this area about 1450 appeared Raden Raḥmat (Sunan Ampel), who, together with his sons and foster son, was to be numbered among the most famous *walīs* (Islamic saints) of Java. Raden Raḥmat came from Champa, where an important Islamic community had arisen. He was a nephew of the queen of Majapahit and the son of an Islamic merchant and a princess of Champa. On his way to Majapahit he had converted the Javanese governor of Palembang on the island of Sumatra. After he reached Majapahit, its Hindu-Buddhist ruler gave him a large estate near Grisek, and his estate became a training centre for Islamic teachers. His son rose to be the first Islamic ruler of Tuban, and his foster son, Raden Pahu (d. 1482), founded the ecclesiastical power of the priestly princes of Giri near Grisek, which exerted enormous influence throughout the Indies for centuries. A son of the governor of Palembang married a daughter of Raden Raḥmat and made Demak, to the west of Tuban, another important Islamic centre (c. 1468). About this time the rulers of Majapahit, yielding to a combination of forces, retired to the island of Bali, although Majapahit itself fell into Islamic hands only after 1516.

In the meantime, Islamic rulers had established themselves at Brunei, in northern Borneo, and other points. Moro chronicles place Islamic teachers in ihe Sulu Islands as early as 1380, and the islands were certainly under effective Islamic control shortly after 1450, when Abu Bakr of Palembang, who had married the raja's daughter, established himself as sultan of Jolo (or Sulu). Islam was brought to Mindanao about 1475 by a band of Islamic conquerors from Johore under a leader whose father, Ali Zainul-Abiden, had himself been an immigrant to Malaya from Hadramut in south Arabia. It also spread to points in south Borneo, and before 1500 sultanates had been established at Tidore and Ternate in the Moloccas.

Islam was largely confined, however, in Malaya and the Indies to the coastal commercial towns. In the interior most of the islands, little affected by the Koran, preserved their mixed animistic-Hindu-Buddhist beliefs. Furthermore, many of the coastal inhabitants, though they had crossed over to Islam, retained a large part of their traditional beliefs and practices. Of the few Islamic teachers available, some spread an Indianized Islam of a Persian background, and many of the merchant-missionaries, being Shi'ites, brought to the Indies their Shi'ite practices. Certain so-called mystical elements of Islam, often consisting of faith in charms, spells, and the yoga magic of the irregular *faqīrs*, had a particular appeal for the Indonesians, while the incentive of commercial gain had been important among rajas, officials, and aristocracy. The Islamization of Malaya and the Indies thus was far from complete or whole-souled when the Portuguese arrived.

* * *

Developments from Transoxania to Grenada

Much the same factors that brought about Islam's advance in Malaysia held good also farther west. Sometimes this advance was achieved by the conversion of rulers. Thus, the Mongols of Transoxania soon adopted, as had the rulers of Iran, the religion of their Muslim subjects, and in 1326 the dynasty of hitherto Hindu Kashmir also embraced Islam. Sometimes advance came by the expansion of strong frontier powers. Thus, when most of India south of the Ganges was conquered by the Delhi sultanate and the Balkans by the Ottomans, in each area converts were attracted by the prestige of the new faith. Sometimes expansion was more attributable to individual penetration by merchants and mystics. In one way or another, Islam continued likewise to push on in the Sudan and to extend along the east African coast at the same time that it spread in Malaysia, so that most of the Indian Ocean trade with the Middle East came to be in Muslim hands.

The advance of Islam into Europe under Ottoman banners began about 1350, when one of the warring factions in Constantinople made a marriage alliance with the Turkish ruler Orkhan I (1326–59). Within ten years the Turks were in possession of both Gallipoli and Adrianople. In spite of the Byzantine emperor's appeals to the Avignon popes for western aid, the Turks soon took over most of his European provinces and subjected the independent states of Bulgaria, Bosnia, and Serbia as well. Thus the Islamic faith was introduced into the Balkans, in parts of which it still survives. Sultan Murad (1359–89) began the imposition of the 'blood-tax', training Christian boys to become hardy warriors (Janissaries) and civil servants. At the same time Turkish immigrants spread the faith and civilization of the conquerors throughout the Balkans. The Byzantine Empire was essentially conquered long before the fall in 1453 of its already isolated capital city, Constantinople.

Both before and after this storied event Hungary remained crucial in the Christian defence. Under their general Janos Hunyadi, Hungarian armies drove back the invaders and crossed the Danube into Turkish Bulgaria. The treachery of his allies and the inadequacy of western assistance paved the way to his final defeat. Only one vigorous stand was made—at Varna in 1444, where 'crusading' forces fought along with King Vladislav of Hungary-Poland and Hunyadi. The king did not survive the defeat, and Hunyadi was forced to retreat. His last exploit before dying of the plague was to raise the siege of Belgrade, invested by the Turks in 1456. The Hungarian resistance continued until it collapsed at the Battle of Mohacs in 1526.

In contrast, the Iberian Muslims were being overwhelmed by the Christians of Portugal, Castile, and Aragon. By 1300 Islamic rule survived in Iberia only in the little southeastern kingdom of Granada, which maintained a precarious existence until 1492. In the regions taken over by the Christian conquerors, Muslims who held to their faith were called Mudejars. Like Jews they were forced to wear a distinctive garb, live in segregated sections of the towns, and pay special taxes. Even though they were an economic asset, they were expelled from Seville in 1248 and from Castile late in the fifteenth century.

After the fall of Granada in 1492, followers of Islam were subjected to persecution. The terms of the surrender of Granada provided for toleration, but they were disregarded by Archbishop Ximenes de Cisneros of Toledo (1436–1517) and Queen Isabella. A Muslim revolt ended in a decree (1502) giving the Muslims of Spain a choice between becoming converts (Moriscos) and going into exile. Many ostensible Moriscos remained in Castile, holding secretly to their Muslim beliefs and customs. Mudejars were suffered to remain in Aragon, but only as serfs on the estates of exploiting landlords.

*   *   *

The Great Age of the tarīqas

All over Islam during the fourteenth and fifteenth centuries the Ṣūfī movement grew. The number of ṭarīqas multiplied, especially from the branching-out of established ṭarīqas, and some, old as well as new, were particularly enterprising. The Suhrawardiyya, for example, rivalled the Chishtiyya in India after the time of the lordly Makhdūm-i Jahāniyān in the mid-fourteenth century; the Qādiriyya maintained its lead in Islam as a whole; the Naqshbandiyya, more recently founded, became prevalent especially in Iran and Turkestan; the Shīʿite Bektāshī order rose to prominence in the growing Ottoman domains and in the fifteenth century grew dominant among the Janissaries.

The ṭarīqas disputed with each other for pre-eminence. Each tended to take the position that it alone possessed the full inner truth of Islam and that its heads ruled the mystical saintly hierarchy in which Ṣūfīs had come to believe. In fact, the several ṭarīqas often stood for quite diverse approaches to the problems of the time. The Suhrawardiyya in India tended toward greater orthodoxy in relation to the sharīʿa and to the acceptance of government office than the more ascetic Chishtiyya. Likewise, orders like the Qādiriyya

and the Naqshbandiyya stood by a relatively cautious orthodoxy. Some
bī-sharʿ (without law) orders, on the other hand, asserted, on the model of the
Qalandars, their freedom from the whole *sharīʿa*. Some orders catered more
to wonder-working and popular superstition, like the Saʿdiyya in Egypt. Some
made concessions to the non-Islamic customs of peoples newly won to Islam;
thus, the Bektāshīs in Anatolia and the Balkans, who seem to have played a
significant role in converting part of the Christian population, retained in their
ritual and cult certain pre-Islamic elements. The *ṭarīqas* differed also in their
attitude toward the manner of life of their members. Celibacy was recommended by some but not by others; some required Ṣūfīs to engage chiefly in
wandering, while others gathered them into fixed convents; the Khalwatiyya
of Turkey demanded of each member a solitary retreat once a year. The
ṭarīqas differed also in their hospitality to mystical speculation and in the
degree of freedom with which they treated the philosophical problems then
exercising the Muslims (see Chapter VI).

Significant opposition to the *ṭarīqas* arose from time to time among the
ʿulamāʾ (repositories of the *sharīʿa*). Some *ʿulamāʾ* felt that the popular
reverence for the Ṣūfī saints, around whose memories and tombs the *ṭarīqas*
were organized, went ill with the basic Islamic emphasis on a simple obedience
to the impersonal sacred law. Thus in Syria in the fourteenth century the
Ḥanbalites Ibn-Taymiyya and Ibn-Qayyim-al-Jawziyya held forth tur-
bulently against the prevailing alliance of Ṣūfīs with the more complacent
majority of *ʿulamāʾ*. Their lead was followed much later by the reforming
Wahhābīs of Arabia (see Volume V), but their protest at first was not widely
heeded. Not only did the saints in their tombs receive the often superstitious reverence of the masses, but the popular following of the Ṣūfīs
increased. Large numbers of people who were not themselves under the full
mystical discipline of a *ṭarīqa* formed a lay affiliation with it, reciting its
prayers and accepting guidance from its leaders. Though most of the actual
members of the *ṭarīqas* were men, some convents were at this time founded
for women also.

The Shīʿite *ʿulamāʾ* were generally more hostile to Ṣūfīsm than were the
Sunnite *ʿulamāʾ*, but even the Shīʿite tradition was at this time largely
expressed through *ṭarīqas*. The growing Bektāshī order taught allegiance to
the *imāms* of the Twelver Shīʿites as well as other esoteric Shīʿite doctrines.
The remains of the Ismāʿīlī movement in Syria and Iran took the outward
form of a Ṣūfī *ṭarīqa*. Many Sunnī orders showed Shīʿite influences, but one,
the Ṣafawiyya, turned frankly Shīʿite and was the instrument of the subsequent conversion of Iran to the Shīʿa.

During this great age of the *ṭarīqas*, the Dār al-Islām was fragmented
politically into numerous and, for the most part, unstable powers, but the
resulting political divisions were of less importance than ever before or after.
As a social order, Islam continued to gain territory as well as more complete
adherence within territory already gained. During the two centuries after 1300

Muslim rule receded seriously only in the far south of India and at the western end of the Mediterranean; otherwise, Islamic power and the Muslim religion gained as compared with rival religions till the end of the fifteenth century.

JUDAISM

The years just before and after 1300 marked a new era of Judophobism in western Europe. Exiles from England and France and refugees from the pogroms of Germany and Austria searched for comparative security elsewhere. East European rulers, seeking to repeople their countries after the Mongolian ravages of the mid-thirteenth century, encouraged immigration from the west. For example, the code of King Casimir III of Poland (1333–70) granted religious toleration and local self-government. Thus Poland became an asylum for persecuted Jews. Although again restricted in many ways and subjected to sporadic persecution in the fifteenth century, the Polish Jews enjoyed a degree of prosperity and of religious and intellectual freedom unknown to Jews farther west. The Jewish population of Poland at the close of the eighteenth century is estimated at somewhat more than ten per cent of the total—about 900,000 out of 8,790,000; they nearly all lived in the towns, where they outnumbered the Christian population by about 9 to 5.[4]

The Spanish Jews (the Sephardim) were well treated until the late thirteenth century. A turning came in that century with the conquests in the Muslim south by the Christian kings. As Spanish cities passed from Muslim to Christian control, the generally tolerant attitude of the Muslims of that day toward Jews gradually gave way to Spanish resentment. The new rulers preferred to chasten the Jews as infidels, sometimes as wealthy competitors, and in any case as aliens. In Aragon Jews were excluded from governmental offices (1283), and in Castile segregation decrees were so rigid as to forbid them to employ Christians as servants (1313). The Castilian law code (*Siete Partidas*), initiated in 1256 but not proclaimed until 1348, formalized the new policy, obliging Jews, among other restrictions, to reside in ghettos. These restrictions, however, were not strictly enforced, largely because the rulers found the Jews useful, whether as sources of loans and taxes or as civil servants, in their conflict with the nobles. Hence, in contrast to the rest of western Europe, Spanish Jews remained, despite sporadic outbreaks, relatively safe from mass violence through most of the fourteenth century.

The first epidemic (1347–50) of the Black Death rekindled slumbering anti-Semitism in Germany and elsewhere, but in Spain, although occasionally mercenary troops plundered the ghettos, no mass attacks took place until late in the century. Then, in 1391, at Seville, the preaching of an eloquent court clergyman named Fernando Martinez roused the populace to frenzied action. His attacks started a chain of pogroms, which swept through Castile and Aragon. Jews who accepted conversion were alone spared, and most of them preferred baptism to death. Later pogroms increased the number of converts, popularly referred to as *Marranos* (i.e. *pigs*). Many of the Marranos were converts in name only, continuing their Jewish worship in secret. Thus freed from legal restrictions, Marranos recovered their former places in government and society. Some genuine, or at least zealous, converts became Christian clergymen, fanatically dedicated to the eradication of crypto-Judaism.

With the advent of Ferdinand and Isabella as the 'Catholic sovereigns' of Spain, the pseudo-Christians were considered so serious a problem that the Inquisition was established (1478), primarily to extirpate heresy among the *conversos*. It did its work so well that most of the *conversos* quickly were eliminated, and many Marranos eventually migrated to more tolerant countries. The Inquisition, which had authority over heretics but not infidels, nevertheless advocated the expulsion of the remaining unconverted Jews, whose public practice of Judaism was a bad example to their converted brethren. Accordingly, in 1492 all unconverted Jews were expelled from the Catholic sovereigns' possessions—Castile, Aragon, Sicily, and Sardinia. Navarre followed suit, and Portugal, not permitting emigration, tried forcibly to convert its Jews. Thus, formally Judaism came to an end in the Spains. The exiles settled in North Africa, Palestine, and (in large numbers) in the northern regions of the Turkish empire, where Sultan Bayezid II (1447–1512) gave them a place of refuge comparable to that in Christian Poland, which now harboured the largest Jewish population.

Instances of tolerance sometimes brighten the contemporary record of the vendetta against the Jews. Where the rulers were friendly, as in Poland and, until the fifteenth century, Spain, Jewish scholarship and business enterprise prospered. Among the Avignon popes some advocated the study of Hebrew, although their purpose often was only that Jews might be confuted or converted. Humanist scholars such as Pico della Mirandola saw good in Judaism and tried to reconcile it with Christianity, Islam, and Platonism (see Chapter VI). In northern Europe Johann Reuchlin (1455–1522) not only studied and taught Hebrew (at Orleans and Stuttgart) but also defended Judaic scholarship against clerical extremists who would have confiscated all Jewish books. Other German humanists likewise encouraged the intensive study of the Old Testament in Hebrew and the collecting of Hebrew manuscripts. In some parts of the Islamic world Judaism held on, though its cultural achievements were not so remarkable in this period as in preceding centuries.

GREEK ORTHODOX CHRISTIANITY

During the fourteenth and fifteenth centuries, the Byzantine Empire with its Greek Orthodox populations gradually was subjected to Turkish rule. The outlying provinces succumbed first, Constantinople and its environs last.

Various groups of Balkan Christians had seceded from the harsh control of Orthodox Constantinople long before the Balkan countries were overrun by the Turks. Serbia was the first to do so. Tsar Stephan Dushan (1331–55) made that country the centre of a west Balkan empire, and he set up an independent patriarchate at Ipek (Pec) in 1346. In a striking exhibition of politico-religious ambition, he raised Serbia to equality with Byzantium. The archbishopric of Serbia became a patriarchate, and Stephan himself became tsar and emperor of Serbs and 'Romans' (i.e. east Romans). The ceremony took place at Uskub in northern Macedonia and was attended by the head of the monasteries at Mount Athos. Stephan intended that his Balkan empire and patriarchate should supersede the decadent Byzantine Empire and patriarchate of Constantinople, but all that he accomplished was a secession.

Stephan's ambitions died with him, and by the end of the century Serbia was subject to the Turks. His patriarchate, like his empire, comprising heterogeneous peoples, disintegrated into semi-autonomous communities of Orthodox Serbs, Orthodox Greeks, Roman Catholics, and Bogomil heretics. These irreconcilable ethnic and religious groups failed to co-operate with Janos Hunyadi in his heroic stand against the Turks in the Danube valley immediately after the fall of Constantinople. One by one they succumbed to the victorious Sultan Mehmet II, and the Bosnian Bogomils turned whole-sale from heresy to Islam. The dwindled Serbian patriarchate at Ipek was repressed in 1459, and for nearly a century Serbs as well as Bulgars had to look to the archbishopric of Ochrida (Ohrid) in Macedonia for spiritual guidance. After the Ipek patriarchate was restored (1557), it persisted until 1690, but the Serbian Church passed under the ecumenical patriarchate at Constantinople only in 1766.

The Bulgarians, when dominated by Stephan, were compelled to transfer both their religious and their political allegiance from Constantinople to Belgrade, but upon his death and the disintegration of his Serbian empire, they regained an independent Bulgarian church and state. Within half a century, however, Bulgaria fell to the Turks, and the Bulgarian church like-wise came under Turkish control (1393). It recovered a fleeting independence during the Hunyadi episode (1456), only to fall permanently under Turkish rule later. The Ochrida archiepiscopate was not abolished, however, until 1767. Thereafter, according to a popular saying, just as the Turks governed the bodies of the Bulgarians, the Greeks ministered to their souls. By the end of the eighteenth century the disintegration of the Eastern church, begun in pre-Turkish times, had in a sense been checked; at any rate the Orthodox Christians within the Turkish empire tended to accept the leadership of the sultan-controlled ecumenical patriarchate at Constantinople.

★   ★   ★

The Failure of Union with Rome

The patriarchate at Constantinople had meanwhile suffered serious local crises. Long before 1300 it had inherited a factional conflict over the relationship of the priestly with the monastic clergy. In Constantinople, as elsewhere in Christendom, monks were the nucleus of organized movements for rigid, puritanical reform. Under the leadership of the monks of Mt Athos, the 'Zealot' faction was particularly determined to preserve the faith of the fathers. They had successfully organized a violent opposition to union with the Roman Catholic Church despite the fact that such a union had been arranged in 1274 (see Volume III). In the succeeding century they gained control of the patriarchate so completely that invariably the patriarchs were chosen from the Mt Athos congregation.

The Zealot monastic party was further strengthened by a wave of mysticism. Under the name Hesychasts (i.e. Quietists) ascetics who stressed silent contemplation in complete seclusion from the world came to exercise a powerful influence on Orthodox religious thought and action. Their strength was shown in conflict with Barlaam, a learned pro-Roman Greek monk from southern Italy who criticized the regime at Mt Athos and the Hesychast movement. The specific issue was Barlaam's accusation that Hesychasts who attained the highest degree of contemplative ecstasy claimed to be able to see 'with corporal eyes the divine and uncreated light'[5] which was identical with that which had transfigured Jesus. If so, God was directly visible to men—a doctrine unacceptable to the Roman Catholic Church and to the secular clergy of the Eastern Orthodox Church.

War between rival claimants of the imperial throne, the steady nibbling away of the empire's territory by Stephan Dushan, the Turks, and other neighbours, the decline in Constantinople's trade in competition with Venice, and the complaints of the empire's numerous poor mixed with the dispute over mystical dogma to create an explosive internal atmosphere. The Hesychasts, led by Archbishop Palamas of Thessalonica, won the support of a leading contender for the Byzantine throne, John Cantacuzene, and after an indecisive council in the Church of St Sophia (1341), Baarlam returned, defeated, to Italy. The populace of Constantinople in contempt and anger dragged the dead body of one of the leading anti-Hesychasts about the streets. Revolt broke out also, for mixed religious, social, and political reasons, in Adrianople; and in Thessalonica, the second city of the empire, the Zealots took control for seven years (1342–49), during which they confiscated the property of the nobles and the church and massacred or expelled a number of nobles before the rival emperors combined and restored peace.

Mystical and ascetic influences remained strong in the fifteenth century and inspired violent popular opposition to all proposals of union with the Roman Church. The fruitless efforts of the Roman Catholic pope to bring the Greek Church into the Catholic fold is part of the story of the conflict of the popes with the councils, which will be described below. Any hint of compromising ancient Orthodox dogmas so as to make them acceptable to western Christians whipped the populace of Constantinople into a religious frenzy in which there were mingled bitterness over social and economic grievances and an intense desire for continued cultural independence. So it was with regard to the addition of the words *and the son* (*filioque*) to the portion of the Nicene creed concerning the procession of the Holy Spirit 'from the Father (and the Son).⁶' The additional phrase raised the question of the nature of the Trinity and remains for some a fighting shibboleth to this day. It was accepted as permissible, along with other compromises, by Byzantine diplomats at the Council of Florence in 1439, and thence issued an Act of Union intended to combine the two churches and assure western aid against the Turks. When announced in the East, however, the agreement precipitated outspoken condemnation on the part of ecclesiastical leaders and violent protests from the populace. Many churchmen refused to sign the Act of Union, and those who had signed it were forced to withdraw their signatures. In Alexandria, Jerusalem, and Antioch the action of the ambassadors at Florence was disavowed. In Constantinople and Moscow the conflict of opinions was more violent still.

Emperor John VIII Paleologus (a convert to Roman Catholicism) and the patriarch had negotiated the Act of Union. Emperor John and his successor, Constantine XI, along with the patriarch, now led the Unionists, and thanks to their commanding position they were able to maintain the external formality of union and alliance with the West. Below the official level, however, allegiance to ancient orthodoxy was unbending. In the forefront of the opposition were the monastic Zealots. No matter what price must be paid in political or military defeats, the Athos-led orthodox masses insisted on keeping the faith. In 1450 (according to historical records that some scholars reject) a council in the Church of St Sophia condemned the Act of Union and restored the Orthodox creed and organization.

If (as some insist) such a condemnation did not actually take place, it was because of the imminence of the Turkish attack on Constantinople, which forced the emperor to appeal to the West once more for immediate aid. In 1452 he welcomed a Roman cardinal (the exiled Metropolitan Isidore of Moscow), who proclaimed in St Sophia the union of the Roman and Greek churches under the primacy of Rome. The reaction of the Orthodox bishops and their flocks to the decree of union showed how intense was their dislike of imperial church policy. Even though the city was already in a state of siege, Orthodox mobs cursed the 'Romanists', and one of the imperial princes expressed an unabashed preference for turbans (of the Turks) rather than red hats (of the Roman cardinals) in Constantinople. He got his wish. After the Turkish conquest of the city the new patriarch, George Gennadios, chosen by the sultan, denounced the hated union. Obviously, whatever their political and ecclesiastical leaders might do in the name of expediency, the populace and their monastic-mystic leaders preferred to go down to defeat with their orthodoxy intact.

*   *   *

Autonomy for the Russian Orthodox Church

Only in Russia did Orthodox Greek Christianity emerge from the era of Asiatic conquests independent and powerful. The seat of Russian Orthodox Christianity moved from Kiev to Moscow early in the fourteenth century. Here, in a frontier region, the Holy Church of Russia grew to maturity. As elsewhere in Christendom, a strong, mystically ascetic impulse led missionaries to build wilderness monasteries that developed into dynamic centres of Christian culture. A close alliance of church with state favoured the growth of a strong ecclesiastical hierarchy. Moscow, from which the metropolitan and the prince ruled their respective spheres, became an active capital of religious and political nationalism. By the third quarter of the fourteenth century, Metropolitan Alexis, a man of noble birth in close alliance with other nobles of the royal council, constituted the real power behind the throne. By the middle of the next century, having broken the power of the Golden Horde, Moscow combined a rapidly expanding political regime with an effective ecclesiastical organization.

This vigorous development resulted in final emancipation from the patriarchate of Constantinople. In 1436, the noted Greek humanist Isidore was named metropolitan of Kiev, then dominated by Lithuania, and temporarily was accepted as metropolitan of all the Russias. In 1439 Isidore accepted the Act of Union with Rome. but it proved repugnant to the Russian grand prince, Basil II, and to the Russian clergy, since it required recognition of the primacy of the Roman pope. On his return from the Council of Florence to Moscow, Isidore was put under arrest and subsequently deposed by a synod of Russian bishops. The Unionist patriarch of Constantinople thereupon excommunicated the Russian Church, which in turn refused to accept the patriarch's authority. Thus began the complete autonomy of the Russian Orthodox Church.

ROMAN CATHOLIC PAPACY

A century after Innocent III and his successors had triumphed over the kings of Europe and the Hohenstaufen imperial dynasty (see Volume III), the Catholic papacy suffered defeat and humiliation at the hands of a rising temporal power, the king of France. Boniface VIII, pope from 1294 to 1303, might have maintained a semblance of papal authority over all Christendom had he not alienated those whose help he sought. To begin with, Boniface imprisoned his predecessor, Celestine V, whose abdication smacked of undue influence on Boniface's part and led to charges of illegality. The new pope's Italian policy reflected secular ambitions. In the south he strove, though vainly, to take Sicily by force of arms from its intractable Spanish rulers and restore it to its former Angevin rulers and thus to papal vassalage. Meanwhile he manoeuvred with greater success to keep under his control the Angevin rulers of Naples, a traditional fief of the papacy. Furthermore, in order to round out the properties of his own family in the region of Gaeta, he planned to take over the nearby holdings of the Colonna family.

The Colonnas were formidable foes. They were firmly entrenched both materially, with huge holdings in south Latium, and politically, with two members of their family in the college of cardinals. Cardinal Giacopo Colonna, an energetic opponent of Boniface's Sicilian ambitions, was dangerous also because he questioned the legality of Pope Celestine's abdication. Both Boniface's position as pope and the aggrandizement of his family demanded the elimination of Colonna power. Young Sciarra Colonna by raiding papal property provided a pretext for action. Boniface retaliated by depriving the two Colonna cardinals of their ecclesiastical benefices, and they in turn proclaimed the illegality of his pontificate and appealed to a general church council. Boniface responded by preaching a crusade against them, destroying their Palestrina stronghold, and confiscating all Colonna lands, merging them into a feudal state for one of his nephews. The Colonnas sought refuge in France.

Boniface was less successful in his ambition to gain control of Tuscany. There the bitter strife between the pro-papal party, the 'Blacks' or Guelphs, and the anti-papal party, the 'Whites' or Ghibellines, provided ample opportunity for papal intervention, ostensibly in the interests of peace and amity. A May Day brawl in 1300 between young 'Blacks' and 'Whites' precipitated an uproar in Florence and provided the pope with a pretext for action. First he sent a cardinal to 'mediate' the feud between the in-power 'Whites' and the out-of-power 'Blacks'. When the 'White' rulers (including Dante, who was one of the priors) refused to withdraw their condemnation of the 'Black' conspirators or to agree to the selection of priors from both factions, the papal mediator interdicted the city and departed. Disorder infected other Tuscan towns, and Boniface could, with ostensible justice, send his partisan, Charles of Valois, with an army to pacify Tuscany (1301). Charles entered Florence, 'unarmed', as Dante expressed it (*Purgatorio* 20, 73), 'save with the lance of treachery with which Judas tilted.'

Charles' mediation clearly favoured the 'Blacks'. Exiled members of the papal faction returned in force and, in the name of public reconciliation, virtually took control. Over five hundred 'Whites' were sentenced to death, others to confiscation and fines. Dante went into exile rather than risk trial by prejudiced officials. Early in 1302, having restored the papalists to control, Charles left Florence. But complications elsewhere were to render Boniface unable to reap the fruits of his intrigue in Italy.

Shortly before the accession of Boniface, Edward I of England and Philip IV ('the Fair') of France drifted from diplomatic tension to war. Both kings, in desperate need of funds, applied financial pressure to clergymen as well as to nobles and merchants. In 1296 Boniface precipitated an open conflict with both monarchs by issuing his famous bull 'Clericis Laicos' (see Volume III), which forbade laymen to make or clerics to pay levies except by papal permission. Edward countered by outlawing the recalcitrant clergy and taking over their temporal holdings, and Philip cut off all export of coin from France. The pope admitted defeat by acknowledging the legality of clerical 'gifts' to the crown in times of national emergency.

Boniface might have hesitated to challenge monarchical nationalism a second time but for the accident that 1300 was a centenary year. The jubilee of that centenary was a spectacular success. The promise of spiritual rewards brought throngs of pious pilgrims to Rome, and Christian rulers sent embassies to pay their respects to the spiritual head of Christendom. With coffers and prestige replenished, the pope's self-confidence revived. But Philip IV was equally confident. The year after the jubilee he demanded of Boniface the degradation of a troublesome French bishop on various charges. The pope felt obliged to refuse but ordered that the trial, as one involving clerical jurisdiction, be remanded to the papal curia at Rome.

Had Boniface been content with this plausible legal stand, he would have had a strong case. Instead, he broadened the issue to the moot question of papal *versus* royal authority. He renewed the prohibition of clerical contributions, condemned royal encroachments of various kinds, and summoned the French clergy to Rome for consideration of a programme for reforming the realm of France, and in a papal bull reflected a determination to discipline the king. Philip promptly burned the bull in public and circulated through the realm a garbled version, along with his reply, which opened with the phrase, 'Philip to Boniface, who pretends to be sovereign pontiff, little or no greeting'.

The case of the offending bishop was promptly pushed into the background. The cardinals and the French clergy attending the papal conference at Rome protested against the outrageous language of the French proclamation, and the pope in the bull 'Unam Sanctam' asserted that 'it is necessary for salvation that everyone be subject to the Roman pontiff'. In response, Philip and his lawyers persuaded the three orders (clergy, nobility, and commons) attending the Estates General of 1302 to send open letters denying the pope's political authority over France and questioning the validity of Boniface's election.

For a time the pope seemed to have the better position. In an invasion of Flanders in 1302 Philip's knights suffered an ignominious defeat at the hands of the embattled burghers of Courtrai, and shortly afterward about fifty French clergymen arrived in Rome to attend the council called by the pope. The low state of Philip's cause was revealed by his tactful response to the demands presented by a papal legate. But again Boniface pressed his opponent too far. He demanded unconditional surrender, on pain of excommunication, and Philip, upon the advice of an aggressive counsellor, Guillaume de Nogaret, determined to fight on. The three orders of the Estates General and the populace were flooded with violent charges against Boniface, notably the illegality of his election, and with demands for a general council of the church to judge him for his irregularities and crimes. Scriptural passages were

H *History of Mankind*

broadcast to make it appear a Christian duty for the French king and people to correct the pope and purge the papacy. Thus the pope's council, a weapon forged for the correction of Philip, was to be matched with the king's council, a weapon to be forged for the correction of the pope. While Boniface sought allies, Nogaret found an eager collaborator in Sciarra Colonna. Nogaret set out for Italy with about 1600 men, intent upon bringing the pope either to terms or to trial by a general church council.

The affair came to a climax in 1303 at Anagni, the pope's summer retreat near Rome. Nogaret's little army forced its way into the town and took possession of the pope. Despite Colonna and other bitter enemies, Boniface apparently was not manhandled, although he refused to consider resigning or submitting willingly to arrest and trial. While his captors hesitated for several days to carry him off by force, papal partisans among the townsfolk took up arms, and the invaders beat a hasty retreat. Boniface was escorted by a senatorial delegation to safety in Rome, where, however, he died within a month.

The short pontificate of Boniface's successor, Benedict XI (1303-4), was dominated by his desire for peace. Benedict, instead of condemning the attack on the spiritual head of Christendom, compromised. Nogaret and the Colonna were excommunicated, but King Philip was officially exonerated. Meanwhile Italy split into pro-French and pro-papal factions. When Benedict died, the choice of a successor took place only after a year of manoeuvering between the Italian majority of the cardinals and the French-Colonna faction.

*   *   *

The 'Babylonian Captivity'

Finally Philip's lobbying won the election for Clement V, a Gascon nobleman who had served as archbishop of Bordeaux. On Philip's invitation Clement was crowned pope at Lyons, with the king holding his stirrup in token of royal subservience to spiritual authority. Nevertheless, the pope soon found himself in a royal trap. Philip created complications that induced Clement to postpone departure for Rome. Thus began the so-called 'Babylonian Captivity' of the Avignon popes. It lasted for over seventy years (1305–78).

One of Clement's most notorious complications was the dissolution of the Knights Templars. At the opening of the fourteenth century that order was powerful, wealthy, and corrupt. Unlike the Hospitallers and Teutonic Knights, they could boast no active crusading after the loss of the Holy Land to Islam. Refusing to consider union with the Hospitallers, who were entrenched as far east as Rhodes, they came to be known as luxury-loving aristocrats. Philip decided that it was high time to reform the order, incidentally replenishing the royal treasury by appropriating Templar wealth. Accordingly, he suddenly (1307) ordered an investigation on charges of heresy and immorality. All Templars in France, about two thousand, were arrested and subjected to rigorous examination, first by royal officials, then by inquisitors. Under orders to get confessions, by torture if necessary, the examiners extracted admissions of immoralities, heretical initiation rites, and other secret misdeeds. So impressive was the list of confessed crimes against God and man that Clement sent a papal commission to take over the investigation.

The papal investigation appeared to be objective in purpose and method. In all Christian lands governmental officials were ordered to take the Templars into custody for examination or re-examination, high officers to be given special examination by the pope. The new investigations revealed that many of the original confessions had been obtained by torture or fear of torture. One victim testified that after seeing cartloads of fellow Templars on their way to be burned alive, he would have admitted having killed Christ himself. Many of the prisoners retracted their forced confessions.

Philip and his henchmen now felt obliged to defend their procedure. This they did by inflaming the Estates General and the public to demand punishment of the Templars as secret subverters of religion and morality. Their propaganda prevailed. After four years, the pope gave in and abolished the order, declaring, however, that the evidence was not conclusive. Two years later, Grand Master de Molay and another aged Templar of high rank, both unbroken by their examiners, were executed for protesting against the injustice of the investigations. All Templar property was ordered transferred to the Hospitallers or (in Spain) to other military orders. Eventually, with reluctance, Philip complied with this order, and so his victory over the Templars was less profitable financially than politically. It had warded off penalties for the 'crime of Anagni,' and it placed the papacy still further under royal influence.

Clement V died at Avignon in 1314. Although the town and the surrounding Comtat Venaissin were papal enclaves, the papacy was anything but independent of French control. In his seven-year pontificate Clement created twenty-eight new cardinals, of whom all but three were Frenchmen, and the papacy could presumably be counted on to avoid antagonizing the king of France. The hearings on Nogaret and the other 'criminals of Anagni' dragged on and ended eventually in virtual absolution. The memory of Boniface was blackened by the pope's formal approval of Philip's zeal in endeavouring to purge the church of heresy and corruption.

Although several of Clement's French successors were high-minded, pious, and upright men—for example, Benedict XII (1334–42), Innocent VI (1352–62), and Urban V (1362–70)—they had to keep constant vigil against the mounting bane of wealth and politics in ecclesiastical affairs. John XXII (1316–34) sold church offices and squeezed money from all possible sources so effectively that he left a well-filled treasury to his successor. Clement VI (1342–52), a luxury-loving nobleman from Limoges, expanded the money-raising machinery of the curia and spent freely on artists, poets, women, horses, and other worldly amusements. Urban V completed, in regal magnificence, the papal palace at Avignon. Erected amidst similarly worldly establishments of cardinals, envoys, lawyers, secretaries, lobbyists, sycophants, and prostitutes, and manned by armies of servants, the palace elicited pious condemnation from Petrarch: 'Babylon of the West'; 'hell on earth'; 'sinkhole of vice, glorying not in the Cross of Christ but in feasting, drunkenness, fornication, incest'. Catherine of Siena compared the worst aspects of Avignon to 'the odours of hell'.

The fundamental defect of the papacy even before the 'Captivity' had been the increasing secularization of church administration. It was revealed most spectacularly in two kinds of activity—papal elections and finances. The packing of the electoral College of Cardinals by Clement V was but an accentuation of an older practice rendered still more notorious by the pope's residence in France. Secular influences and interest were perhaps even more crassly revealed in the election of Clement V's successor. Little effort was made to hide that the major issue was not who was the best man but whether he was French or Italian. Twenty-three cardinals met in conclave at Carpentras, near Avignon, in 1314. Lest the minority of Italian cardinals should hold out for an Italian pope or at least for a pope who would return to Italy, the French faction organized pressure groups that mobbed the conclave, threatening death to Italians. Barely escaping with their lives, the cardinals proved stubborn and procrastinated for two years. Finally, convening at Lyons under a guard of French troops, they elected John XXII, a cobbler's son from Cahors.

The financial complications of the papacy had been rendered perhaps even more corrosive than its electoral irregularities by the removal to Avignon. The papal income was diminished by disorder and disaffection in Italy and by the hostility of anti-French nations such as England, while papal expenses increased because of not only the rise in price levels throughout the West but also the vastness of the building programme at Avignon. To meet the demands the popes created a highly successful money-raising machine. The papal chamberlain and his *camera apostolica* became the most important section of the evolving bureaucracy, which comprised departments of revenue (*camera*), correspondence (chancery, or *cancellaria*), and judiciary (*consistorium*, *audentia rota*, *penitentaria*, etc.).

The Avignon department of revenue made tax collections, never popular, particularly odious by its very success. The power of the pope as supreme pontiff to overrule any clerical appointment was turned to profit even where vested electoral rights of long standing were injured, as in the selection of new bishops and in promises of appointment to offices not yet vacant. Candidates were obliged to contribute to the papal treasury a considerable portion of their first year's income, in addition to paying fees and gratuities to all concerned with their actual taking of office. The exploitation of such provisorships, reservations, and expectatives led to violent protests everywhere. In England the reformer John Wycliffe (see below) voiced the resentment which led Parliament to pass the Statute of Provisors (1351), declaring invalid all papal appointments and provisions to English benefices, and the Statute of Praemunire (1353), forbidding the removal of suits to foreign (including papal) courts. By and large, however, the popes were successful in asserting their rights, though often they saw fit to compromise with local authorities by appointing (for a consideration) the candidates of influential patrons.

The financial machine also squeezed out existing dues, fees, taxes, and other levies more vigorously. A papal appointee to a bishopric or abbacy surrendered a *servitium* of about one third of the first year's revenue. Archbishops gave an additional fee for the *pallium*. Appointees to local benefices paid annates (the first year's income) and (for ensuing years) *decimae*, or *tithes*, amounting to about a tenth of the annual income. On the death of an appointee, his personal effects and the income of the office pending occupancy by a new incumbent went to the papal treasury. If an incumbent died leaving debts to the papal treasury, his successor was held responsible for them. Special gratuities and fees to members of the papal bureaucracy, great and small, local and central, contributed to the steady stream of revenue toward Avignon. Resentment of the increase of taxes to an absentee officialdom necessitated strict, often harsh, measures on the part of papal collectors. Severity, in turn, led to the deepening of hostility. Thus, the very success of the revenue machine was a source of misfortune. Worse than public resentment was the deterioration of church officialdom. In every locality absentee beneficeholders, foreign clerics, or pluralists cropped up. At Avignon office seekers and litigants for promised positions swarmed, and petty parasitical officials thrived upon graft, bribes, and fees.

Yet this commercialized system had its good points, too. Papal and temporal patrons often collaborated peacefully in the selection of church officials. Under honest, well-meaning popes, church revenues were put to constructive uses, such as foreign missions, literature, art, and education. For example, Petrarch, though he condemned the luxury and worldliness of the Avignon popes, lived on the benefices they bestowed. Many a university student owed his education to papal grants, and some universities sent to the pope lists of scholars deserving of benefices so that they could complete their education. Clement V and John XXII encouraged medical studies in Greek and Arabic as well as Latin at Montpellier and other universities. They urged the establishment of professorships of Hebrew, Arabic, and other oriental languages, although more for the purpose of combating infidel religions than of increasing human knowledge.

From a political point of view, the Avignon papacy recorded some noteworthy achievements. In addition to deriving political advantage from their cultural patronage, the French popes restored the morale of the papacy as a factor in international affairs. They were not browbeaten or insulted with impunity. To be sure, on occasion papal legates who threatened wayward communities might be roughly handled (at Milan in 1362 they were compelled to eat the papal bull of excommunication, parchment and all). Yet no hostile force invaded the walled town of Avignon, while papal forces reconquered several rebellious towns of Italy.

The Avignon popes carried on a vigorous drive against heretics. Remnants of ancient sects felt their displeasure, notably the Waldenses of the French Alpine regions, who, however, retreating farther into the mountains, managed to survive. In addition, stern decisions were enforced against intramural heretics. Some mystical Franciscans, having in the thirteenth century begun to preach that the era of the Holy Spirit was at hand, practised a strict poverty and the *vita contemplativa*. These 'Spiritual Franciscans' soon fell under suspicion of heresy, and after the accession of Boniface VIII at the turn of the century, those who refused to submit (viz., the Fraticelli) were harshly treated, not merely as heretical but also as rebellious. Nevertheless, numerous sects of 'poor men' sprang up. John XXII excommunicated all who advocated poverty as a fundamental tenet of Christianity, whether the older Beghards and Beguines or the newer Fraticelli. This measure raised a debate over absolute poverty in which the whole Franciscan order became involved, since some within the order favoured strict observance of St Francis' ideal of poverty. In 1323 the pope denounced as heresy the claim that the Apostles had practiced absolute poverty. Still, a number of Franciscans, the so-called 'Strict Observants', chose to follow the rule of St Francis rather than the pope's decree. Here again papal determination, backed by the efficiency of the Inquisition, won a decisive victory. By the end of the century the order had been purged of the heresy of its founder.

The papacy's policy regarding heretics was a logical outcome of its determination to organize effectively all sections of the army of Christ to defend the faith. Strict regimentation aimed at the elimination not only of well-meaning idealists but also of charlatans and vagabond monks. All the monastic orders were forced to regularize their customs in keeping with ideals considered practicable, and several of the popes (e.g. Clement V and John XXII) added valuable disciplinary rules to the existing law of the church. But international disturbances, including the calamity of the Black Death, prevented anything resembling a thorough reformation.

The Avignon popes also organized missions for the penetration of the East. John XXII's and Clement VI's naval expeditions gave allied Christian forces a temporary foothold in Smyrna and made secure the Hospitaller stronghold at Rhodes. By mid-century it was evident, however, that the combined forces of Byzantines, Hospitallers, and Venetians could not battle effectively against the rising strength of the Turks in Asia Minor. John XXII revived a foreign missionary society, first organized in the thirteenth century, and staffed it with Dominicans and Franciscans. In the Holy Land the Franciscans established permanent monastic centres at Jerusalem and Bethlehem. In Armenia monks of the early native Christian orders merged with the Dominicans under the name 'Uniats' (or United Brethren). Still greater success (as we saw in Chapter II) attended the work of missionaries farther east, in regions as distant as China. Until the 1350's the Avignon papacy could boast marked missionary progress in Asia. But in the second half of the century serious setbacks were suffered both in China, because of the fall of the friendly Mongol dynasty in 1368, and in western Asia, because of the ravages of Tamerlane.

★　　　★　　　★

Temporary Returns to Rome

Various considerations continually directed the absentee popes' attention to Italy. Italian sources of income assumed growing importance as English and German recalcitrance increased. The exhortations of mystic or patriotic Italians such as Catherine of Siena, Dante, and Petrarch reinforced this interest in Italy, but more cogent was the practical consideration that papal political control in the peninsula was in jeopardy. In the Papal States local despots and town authorities paid little heed to their French overlord. In Rome, deprived of its attractiveness as Christendom's centre for pilgrims and church politicians, the citizens threatened to set up their own pope. In 1328 they actually crowned the excommunicated emperor, Louis IV of Bavaria (1314–47), and for a time they supported an anti-pope of his designation. Throughout northern Italy the towns profited by this new struggle between church and state, since, to win support, both the absentee emperor and the absentee pope granted them rights which neither was anyway in a position to veto.

Innocent VI paved the way for the prodigal's return by sending (1353) Cardinal de Albornoz, formerly a Spanish warrior, to restore papal authority in Italy. With marked success Albornoz persuaded or forced the independent rulers in the Papal States to submit, eventually promulgating a code of law known as the Aegidian Constitutions (1357). In Rome itself he used the popular leader Cola di Rienzi to win the supporters of the revived Senatus Populusque Romanus to the pope's cause. Urban V actually returned to Rome for a time (1367–70) at the urging of a friendly emperor, Charles IV, amid the applause of the populace and the congratulations of Italian patriots. Three years in devastated Rome amid restive Italians, however, discouraged him, and he returned to Avignon, notwithstanding the protests of Petrarch, the saintly Bridget of Sweden, and the emperor, who had humbly submitted to coronation at his hands. He died shortly after his return.

Italian disappointment at the pope's desertion and resentment at oppression by his French agents were keen. Revolts broke out even in pro-papal Florence. Gregory XI (1370–78), Urban's successor, sent bands of mercenaries to crush the rebels, but the brutalities of the papal soldiery served only to enflame Italian hostility. Catherine of Siena, entrusted by the Florentines to negotiate with the pope, urged him, 'for the love of the crucified Saviour,' to employ weapons of peace rather than war and return to Rome. The threat of the Romans to join the revolt and set up an anti-pope was more convincing. In 1377 Gregory consented to go to Rome, and he spent several months there, but, finding it too dangerous to remain, he went back to Avignon. Resorting to diplomatic tactics, he won Italian city after city by promising self-government under papal supervisors. The Florentines were isolated by these tactics, and the victorious pope finally returned to Rome, where he soon died.

*   *   *

The Great Schism

The regulations governing conclaves required the election of a pope in the town in which the last incumbent had died. At the time of Gregory's death he was preparing to leave once more for Avignon, and the Romans were determined to prevent it. The dying French-born pope had authorized the cardinals to disregard regulations so as to prevent Roman domination of their conclave, but the Romans, officially and spontaneously, blocked all ways of escape from the city, even confiscating the oars of boats in the Tiber. The cardinals were threatened with death if they failed to select a Roman or, at least, an Italian. After ten troubled days they went into conclave at the Vatican. The next morning the crowds were so menacing that quick action was judged necessary, and Bartolomeo Prignano, archbishop of Bari, was elected. Without any apparent question as to the legality of the election, he was crowned pope as Urban VI (1378-89).

Soon, however, Urban's inflexible behaviour alienated most of the cardinals. As soon as they could, some of them left Rome. Within four months after the election, sixteen had escaped, and thirteen of these met at Fondi to declare Urban's pontificate illegal. A month later they elected one of their own number, Robert of Geneva, as Pope Clement VII (1378-94).

Arguments as to whether Urban or Clement was legal pope led to an open schism. It continued for over thirty years as a merely two-part schism, and then for eight years more (until 1417) as a three-part schism. The schism exacerbated the animosities created by 'the Babylonian Captivity'. Rival popes now excommunicated each other and each others' supporters. Duplicate officials were appointed to church positions. Duplicate revenues were claimed. The French generally supported Clement VII, the Italians and the English, Urban VI. The Spanish kingdoms declared for Clement, but Portugal shifted to Urban by reason of English pressure. The German emperor recognized Urban, but not all of the imperial states followed his example. Some Italian states that originally had favoured Urban were driven into Clement's camp because of Urban's fanatical and sometimes brutal treatment of any who differed with him. Neither pope and neither college of cardinals would resign, arbitrate, or even recognize the legal existence of the other. No general council could be called legally without papal consent, and that was unobtainable.

Since no orthodox solution of the muddle was possible, scholars resorted to unorthodox ones. As we shall see (Chapter VIII), the theory of popular sovereignty was widely expounded. Marsilius of Padua and John of Jandun had already set it forth in their *Defensor Pacis* (1324). This work argued that papal authority was dependent ultimately on the faithful or their representatives and, hence, that a general council called even by representatives of the laity might judge the pope, inasmuch as he was the responsible executive rather than the autocrat of Christendom. Rienzi, in defence of his republic in Rome, and William of Ockham, in defence of the Franciscans, likewise questioned whether the pope was supreme in certain temporal and spiritual matters. As the schism moved from bad to worse, theologians, such as the Germans Heinrich von Langenstein and Conrad von Gelnhausen and the Frenchmen Cardinal Pierre d'Ailly and Jean Gerson, rectors in turn of the University of Paris, applied this line of reasoning to the problem of eliminating the double papacy. Thus the idea spread that a general council called by a temporal ruler might remove a pope.

Such unorthodox views received more and more attention as the double papacy was prolongated. After the two original rivals died, the Roman cardinals elected Boniface IX (1389–1404) and the Avignon cardinals Benedict XIII (1394–1423), a Spaniard. In 1395 a council of French clergymen recommended the abdication of both popes, but neither pope would consent. In 1398, on the advice of professors from the University of Paris, among whom were Ailly and Gerson, a second French council adopted stronger measures. Charging Benedict with heresy, both clergy and king withdrew French support, financial as well as spiritual. Affairs in the separate dioceses that had been subject to papal authority were now handled by the bishops. Thus, at one stroke, the papal perquisites in the French church were taken over, ostensibly at first by the French clergy, ultimately by the king and the local nobility. Royal and aristocratic officials exploited local churches unmercifully, benefices and treasures were plundered, and the clergy profited little from their emancipation.

Benedict refused to yield to French pressure. He took refuge at Marseilles, where he received promises of renewed fidelity from outside powers including the king of Castile, and tried to initiate negotiations with his rival. Boniface refused to negotiate, condemning his rival as an obstinate rebel. On his death shortly afterward, the Roman cardinals elected an aged Venetian as Pope Innocent VII (1404–06), but he too refused to negotiate. Benedict thereupon seized the opportunity to press for a conference and, on further refusal, took the drastic step of calling on the temporal princes of Christendom to remove the obstinate Roman pope forcefully. Nothing came of the appeal, however, and on Innocent's death the schism continued, for the Roman cardinals elected Gregory XII (1406–15).

Popular pressure and especially the resentment in the Papal States induced Gregory to be less stubborn than his predecessors. He offered to abdicate if Benedict would do the same, thus permitting both sets of cardinals to unite for the election of a single pope. The two popes haggled until April 1408, when Gregory, temporarily absent from his capital, heard that Rome had been occupied by Benedict's champion, the king of Naples, and broke off negotiations.

H*

By this time the patience of many in the rival camps was exhausted, and each college of cardinals, consenting to desert its pope, agreed to a general council. This startling decision, threatening to take the initiative from both popes, was checked by Benedict, who still hoped to determine the outcome. Retiring to Perpignan, he called his own general council. Pope Gregory shortly followed suit. Both offered to abdicate but on conditions that each was sure would not be fulfilled. Meanwhile a general council had actually met at Pisa and had deposed both popes, and the united college of cardinals elected the cardinal-archbishop of Milan as Pope Alexander V (1409–10).

The choice of a third pope proved to be no way to restore the unity of the church. The failure was partly due to the clever tactics of the other two popes, who refused to give up, but even more to the Pisa papacy's own weaknesses. Before election Alexander had been forced to promise radical reforms in the interests of the local clergy and to the detriment of the papacy. Once he was installed, he ignored his promises. He died within a year, to be succeeded by John XXIII (1410–15). (In 1958 the late pope took the same name, indicating repudiation of the fifteenth-century claimant.) John, the most ruthless of the cardinals, was a fighting man from Naples. He conquered Rome and summoned a council to meet there and sanction his manoeuvres, but it was sparsely attended and quickly adjourned.

*   *   *

The Rise of the Conciliar Movement

Sigismund, the new German ruler (chosen king in 1410 and crowned emperor in 1433), soon voiced the widespread demand of western Christians for a settlement. Ambitious to become a secular leader of the West, he promoted the now familiar idea of conciliar control of popes. He persuaded John XXIII, whose temporal enemies had driven him from Rome, to issue a formal summons to a general council. The Pisa pope consented, not only because he was hard pressed in his wars, with Sigismund presenting his only hope of survival, but also because his cardinals insisted.

Late in 1414 a general council met at Constance, in Imperial territory. Sigismund devoted his attention to the council's relations with secular powers. His efforts to win over the lay adherents of the several recalcitrant popes helped to solve the council's practical difficulties. Its theoretical problem, the justification of the doctrine of conciliar supremacy over the papacy, was the concern of the Scholastics, i.e. the university men. Some of them, notably Dietrich von Niem and Cardinal d'Ailly, thought that general councils ought to be the continuing sovereign power in church government, while Gerson and Francesco Zabarella, of the Bologna law school, thought that they ought to be merely a check on the pope's executive power. All were of one mind, however, as to the necessity not only of eliminating the schismatic popes but also of instituting drastic reform in the papal bureaucracy.[7]

The Council of Constance dragged on for four years. At one time it comprised as many as six hundred representatives, and the total number that attended is estimated at six thousand. Medieval towns were not ordinarily equipped to accommodate so many visitors, and food shortage threatened at the outset, but efficient management, to the point of enforcing schedules of maximum prices, achieved satisfactory local arrangements. International congresses were uncommon in those days, and for a time procedural issues were paramount. The proposal of John's Italian contingent to confirm the Pisa decision (thus recognizing John as pope) and merely to provide for general councils every quarter century was rejected. Two French cardinals, Ailly and Guillaume Fillastre, argued persuasively for the resignation of all three popes and a declaration of the supremacy of the council. They also opposed another Italian proposal to give votes only to bishops and abbots, of whom many were Italian. Instead, decisions ultimately were reached, as was then the custom at the universities, by a vote of the 'nations' present (Italian, German, French, and English), each 'nation' being free to decide who should vote within its own grouping. As a result voting was not restricted to the higher clergy but was extended to clerical university professors, representatives of secular powers, and a few others. The division of a Catholic Church council into 'nations' was an unmistakable sign of the times.

Early in the year 1415 the Pisa pope, John, finding the council indocile, fled from Constance and withdrew his support. This defiance unified the four 'nations'. They decreed that the council held its authority from Christ, was supreme, and must be obeyed by all Christians including a pope. John was summoned, refused to appear, was tried *in absentia*, was found guilty on seventy charges (including simony, varied immoralities, murder, and heresy), and was deposed. Soon thereafter representatives of the Roman pope, Gregory XII, submitted his resignation. But the Avignon pope, Benedict XIII, safe in his native Aragon, remained obstinate. Thereupon Emperor Sigismund left the council in order to try to solve the dispute by diplomatic negotiations. Eventually he was able to win over Benedict's Spanish and Scottish supporters, and they sent representatives to Constance to join the council.

Meanwhile the council also dealt with heresy. The heretics John Huss and Jerome of Prague (whose heresy we shall describe below) were tried, condemned, and burned at the stake. Their archetype, John Wycliffe, already safely dead, was tried *in absentia*, and his remains were ordered removed from an English churchyard. The council's uncompromising handling of the three heretics, even its disregard for Sigismund's safe-conduct for Huss, was generally approved as a necessary if harsh measure for the crushing of treason against God and the Faith. With the council's consent, the new pope, when finally elected, issued a bull condemning specific tenets of Wycliffe and Huss and required a loyalty oath of suspected heretics affirming their acceptance of the council's decrees on church doctrine.

The more subtle problem of church reform met with many differences of opinion at the Council of Constance. Like all other important matters, it was presented to each 'nation' for discussion and vote before consideration in full session. Here the conciliar procedure broke down. While the council was in session a lengthy truce between the English and the French ended, and the Hundred Years' War was renewed. To make matters worse, the French, both at home and at the council, had already split into rival factions, the Armagnacs and the Burgundians, and were at sword's point over the murder some years earlier (1407) of the Armagnac leader, Duke Louis of Orleans, by emissaries of Jean sans Peur, duke of Burgundy. Jean Petit, a French theologian, had defended the murder as justifiable tyrannicide, and Jean sans Peur had himself appealed to the Avignon pope, the still obdurate Benedict XIII, for vindication. Gerson, who had been prominent in the prosecution of Huss, led the opposition to Jean sans Peur and Petit. The issue now came before the council, where it precipitated a feud within the French 'nation' that was at least as bitter as the hostility between the French and English 'nations'.

Other regional issues aggravated the divisions in the council, drawing attention away from church reform. Even when the councillors seriously grappled with that problem, criticism of papal administration proved easier than practical remedy of bureaucratic abuses. A special commission representing the several 'nations' assembled a number of proposals for reform, which it submitted to each of them for discussion. For about two years the commission and the several 'nations' considered proposed reforms, especially of papal financial practices. In general, the German, the English, and for a time the French were more favourable, and the Italians more opposed, than the others to serious change.

The prolonged absence of Emperor Sigismund while negotiating with the schismatic factions added to the delay. On his return Sigismund found the council badly divided. The French cardinals, formerly leaders in the cause of conciliar reform and supremacy, had grown suspicious of him. He and the German 'nation' were pro-English in the Hundred Years' War and were thought to be planning to elect a pope who would be an anti-French puppet. Gradually the council degenerated into two camps, the Teutonic (English and German) 'nations' versus the Latin (French and Italian) 'nations', supported by the newly-arrived Spanish 'nation'.

After more than two years' deliberation, the council deposed the still defiant Benedict XIII and at last took up the question of choosing a new pope. The reformers preferred postponement of a choice until their programme should be adopted, but the French-Italian-Spanish coalition urged an early decision and by the old method—selection by the cardinals. A compromise was reached providing that election should be by a joint conclave of the cardinals and six representatives from each of the five 'nations' and that to be elected a candidate must receive the votes of at least two thirds of the cardinals and of each 'nation's' representatives. An additional compromise stipulated that the election and the reform programme should proceed simultaneously.

The first decision (October 1417) was a decree calling for frequent councils in the future. It was also decreed that, in event of a new schism, a council must be held within one year. Furthermore, certain unpopular papal practices were prohibited, and the new pope was required, with the assistance of the council. to make eighteen specified reforms, chiefly concerning papal revenues and appointments. A new pope was elected without undue delay. On the first vote in the joint conclave, Cardinal Otto Colonna had a two-thirds majority in the English and Italian 'nations' and some support in the others and in the college of cardinals. After three days he was chosen and became Pope Martin V (1417–31).

Martin immediately undertook to consider the specified recommendations for reform. Each 'nation' presented its views on them, and a conciliar reform commission consulted with him. Inevitable differences of opinion, combined with general weariness, played into Martin's hands. He was able to limit the programme to seven of the recommendations, and those of no great import. The council ended with a tacit recognition that universal reform was impossible. The 'nations', on the other hand, were able to make separate treaties with the pope toward the same end. By 'concordats' they tried to limit local abuses in the collection of papal revenues, the making of papal appointments, papal interference in judicial matters, and other papal prerogatives. Like much of the council's later achievements, the concordats were relatively ineffective and short-lived.

★   ★   ★

The Decline of the Conciliar Movement

The adjournment of the council (April 1418) was marked by certain ominous developments. The pope's announcement that the next council would meet at Pavia in Italy displeased the French 'nation'. Several minor problems, such as Petit's defence of tyrannicide, were left unsettled; the doctrine of tyrannicide was denounced as heresy, but the council, which had condemned Huss, left Petit untouched. Gerson, thus partly repudiated, temporarily exiled himself from France, dominated by the Burgundians, Petit's protectors. Many representatives departed with a sense of frustration, and immediate events justified their gloom. After the council formally adjourned, Martin proclaimed to the cardinals, in the presence of Sigismund, that the pope was the supreme judge and that none might appeal from his decisions. This view was not promulgated as a bull only because of the hostile reactions of leading churchmen such as Gerson and the suggestion that the proclamation verged on heresy. For the Italians and the Colonna pope, however, the outcome of the council was most satisfactory. Papal control was restored in Rome and most of the rest of the Papal States. Thus the Colonna family, ruthlessly ousted by Boniface VIII over a century earlier, not only returned to their patrimony but returned to it as leaders in the revival of the papacy, which Boniface had started on the road to Captivity, Schism, and degradation.

Once Pope Martin V was firmly in office, he showed no interest in carrying out the conciliar decrees. His programme was to strengthen the papacy, and that meant to undermine the doctrine of conciliar supremacy. He could not well refuse to call the promised Council of Pavia, but he could minimize its significance. Since Pavia was in the realm of the hostile duke of Milan, he did not attend in person but gave the presidency to four legates and empowered them to move the council to another place if necessary. An epidemic provided them with the pretext for removal to Siena. The poor attendance at the council, an eloquent testimonial of the apathy engendered by the last days at Constance, permitted Martin's legates to control the proceedings. Heresy, especially that of Wycliffe and Huss, was re-condemned, union with the Orthodox Greek Catholic Church was approved but found impracticable, and the reform programme of Constance was revived. When certain drastic reformers of the French 'nation' became uncontrollable, the papal legates left the council and from a safe distance in Florence dissolved it. Determined to spike the guns of the reformers, Martin appointed a commission of cardinals to investigate abuses. The result, a bull condemning some well-known abuses, accomplished nothing except to cover up the pope's aversion to reform.

All parties realized that the fate of real reform and of conciliar influence still hung in the balance. Sincere reformers, notably the scholars of the University of Paris and Sigismund, called on the pope to fulfill the expressed will of the 'nations' at Constance. The rulers of England and France also favoured a council, if for no other reason than to protect their peoples from a revival of papal exploitation. The demand grew louder as the Hussites in Bohemia successfully resisted the crusade that Martin had proclaimed against them. Two German princes went so far as to have placards posted in Rome setting forth the need for a council to combat the victorious Hussites and threatening to depose the pope and the cardinals if they refused to act. Hostile though he was to councils, Martin felt impelled to act. Accordingly in 1431 he appointed Cardinal Giuliano Cesarini, who was en route to Germany to lead the crusade against the Hussites, as his legate to open and preside at a council at Basel. Shortly thereafter Martin died, to be succeeded by Eugenius IV (1431–47), a Venetian cardinal.

Like the abortive council at Pavia, the Council of Basel was poorly attended —at least, at the outset. In fact, it seemed about to expire altogether when the collapse of Cesarini's crusade against the Hussites, impelling him to turn his major attention to Basel, saved it. He sent out a call for the pope and the clergy to attend and invited the Bohemian Hussites to send a delegation to discuss reunion with the church. Then suddenly, in December, word came from the new pope dissolving the council and forbidding negotiations with the heretics. Thereupon the members of the council, thoroughly aroused, taking matters into their own hands, renewed the Constance decrees concerning conciliar supremacy and frequent reform councils.

For two years thereafter council and pope played a desperate game.

Eugenius' plan was similar to that of his predecessor—to use evasive tactics. The council was convinced that the salvation of the church demanded reform, a constructive solution of the Hussite problem, and the establishment of conciliar supremacy. It called upon the pope to revoke his decree of dissolution and to appear in person at Basel. It ordered the cardinals likewise to appear and announced that, should the papacy fall vacant, the election of a successor would take place at the council. Cesarini, now a sincere conciliarist, accepted these decrees. The pope yielded partly, agreeing to allow the council to continue at Basel until the Hussite problem was solved, but after that he proposed to call a new council somewhere in the Papal States to end heresy, reform the church, and restore peace in western Europe. The council responded by reasserting its supremacy.

For a time, the council steadily gained in prestige and attendance. Most of the cardinals appeared. The pope did not appear, but he finally gave sanction to the council and called on all lay and ecclesiastical powers to send representatives. Eventually the attendance reached five hundred. Emboldened, the councillors called on the pope to legalize their actions from the beginning and threatened to depose him if he failed to come or to send official representatives. Eugenius temporized by naming six cardinals to preside in his absence. One of them, Cesarini, refused the appointment. By the middle of 1433 the council began seriously to consider deposing the pope, but Sigismund, whom he had recently crowned emperor at Rome, objected to such drastic action, thus encouraging the pope to take a stronger stand. In several bulls Eugenius condemned any conciliar action save on the three issues which he had named—heresy, reform, and peace. He also annulled all acts against himself and his curia and demanded recognition of his presiding officers. He was perhaps only testing his strength, for he withdrew the demands that evoked violent opposition. By the end of the year both parties seemed content with a stalemate.

Meanwhile conciliar business dragged on. This council was not organized by 'nations', though they functioned informally with considerable vigour and some serious differences of opinion. In general, the Council of Basel was less manageable than that of Constance had been. Voting was by 'head' (i.e. by individuals) rather than by 'nations', and many voting members had low rank. In the long run, the council's efficiency was hampered by this 'democratic' factor as well as by its very success in diplomatic exchanges with the pope, for democracy and success made for extreme measures that undermined public confidence.

Extremism was exemplified in the handling of the delicate problem of church reform. Not only did the council condemn generally recognized abuses and restrict blatant evils of papal finance and bureaucracy but it also made changes that were less easily justified. It set up a system of provincial and diocesan councils with a view to extending conciliar controls to the archbishops, bishops, and other regional bureaucrats of the ecclesiastical hierarchy. Any payment of fees to papal officials for appointments, ordinations, annates, and the like was prohibited. Such officials were thenceforth to depend solely on salaries, although the council not only made no specific provision for salaries but even stipulated that, for the time being, all local revenues due the pope were to be sent to Basel for conciliar supervision. Eugenius took this revolutionary blow at his financial resources with remarkable calm, merely attempting to obtain a compromise. He was encouraged by reports that many conservative members of the council were alarmed at the rising tide of radicalism. His opportunity for decisive action came with the offer of the Eastern emperor and church to negotiate concerning possible unity of the Roman and Greek churches.

The Easterners, concerned over the growing menace of the Turks, seemed willing to buy western aid at the price of reunion with the Roman Catholic Church. For some time the pope and the Council of Basel competed with each other for the right to carry on the negotiations. The Greeks, however, finally refused to go to Basel and insisted that, wherever the meeting took place, the pope must be present. This was Eugenius' first tactical victory over the council. He gained a further advantage when the council split over the place for negotiations. A majority, led by the French faction, voted to meet at Avignon or thereabouts; Cardinal Cesarini and the Italian minority held out for Florence or some other Italian city that would be agreeable to the Greeks and the pope. Differences of opinion degenerated into bitter words and physical violence, with rival spokesmen struggling for the presiding officer's chair and shouting each other down. To make matters worse, the conciliar majority renewed its charges against Eugenius, accusing him of disobeying its decrees, contributing to schism, and resisting reform. This denunciation drove Cesarini and his minority to secession. They adjourned to Ferrara, where the pope opened formal negotiations with the Greeks in January 1438. The Baselites, condemned as a rump council, continued their meetings, futilely denouncing the pope and futilely negotiating with the Hussites.

Dragging on for a decade, the Basel majority demonstrated the weaknesses of a divided parliament if pitted against a centralized authority. When already outmanoeuvred in the Greek negotiations, the council suspended Eugenius, at a time (1439) when his prestige was rising. Temporal bodies were quick to take advantage of the rent in the ecclesiastical system. Albert, who had succeeded Emperor Sigismund in 1437, and the leading German princes, the electors, took a neutral position in the struggle between council and pope, but a German diet exploited the anti-papal decisions, formally adopting the decrees on conciliar supremacy and the restrictions of papal authority in finances and local appointments. Similarly a French ecclesiastical council, convoked by Charles VII at Bourges in 1438, turned the Council of Basel's actions to France's national advantage. Without repudiating papal authority, the Pragmatic Sanction of Bourges (1438), revealing the desire of the French king and clergy for the administrative independence of the French church, declared that the king was free to nominate candidates for French benefices to the cathedral chapters, religious communities, and other ecclesiastical electtoral bodies, and limited French appeals to the papal courts and French payments to the papal treasury. Successive popes refused to honour this unilateral declaration, until a compromise was reached in the Concordat of 1516 (see Chapter IV), but it served as the basis of what later came to be called 'the Gallican Liberties'.

In the face of diminishing ecclesiastical prestige, the rump council at Basel put a finishing touch to its negative programme. It deposed the already suspended Eugenius for the heresy of opposing the council and elected a counter-pope, Felix V (1439–49). Felix at first gained some support in Germany, but Albert's successor as ruler, Frederick III, went over to the papal side in return for the generous Concordat of Vienna (1448), a highly pragmatic arrangement by which the pope purchased the support of a national prince and clergy with concessions on local ecclesiastical revenues and offices. Although the council was still three hundred strong, Frederick expelled it from Basel. It prolonged itself ineffectually at Lausanne, where Felix resided, until he abdicated.

The decade of the decline of the Conciliar Movement was a decade of ascent for Pope Eugenius. The Greeks, having accepted his Ferrara Council as the authentic one, sent to it an impressive embassy, comprising Emperor John Palaeologus, the patriarch of Constantinople, Metropolitan Isidore of All the Russias, and some seven hundred other Greek Orthodox clerics and subordinates. The papal negotiations with the Greeks were outwardly impressive but accomplished nothing permanent. The Greeks were on the defensive at home against Turkish conquest, and their real purpose at Ferrara was to obtain military aid with as little sacrifice as possible of their ecclesiastical independence. All differences except two were settled with relative ease. Both at Ferrara and at Florence (to which the pope transferred the council after a year and where he personally presided) the council heard protracted arguments concerning the supremacy of the pope and the 'procession of the Holy Spirit'. Finally (July 1439) an Act of Union was signed. The Greeks accepted the Roman doctrine that the Holy Spirit had proceeded from God the Son as well as from God the Father,[8] and also acknowledged the 'primacy' of the papacy (with a vague recognition of the autonomy of the Greek Church). In return, the pope sent two war galleys and three hundred soldiers to aid in the defence of Constantinople.

Furious resentment of rank-and-file Greeks, we have seen, kept the ecclesiastical agreements from being carried out, but, even so, Pope Eugenius gained a decisive advantage in the West. Emboldened by his freshly won prestige, he formally condemned all decrees of conciliar supremacy over the papacy, returned to Rome in 1443, and took the council from Florence to his own Lateran, to serve as a 'rubber stamp' for his decisions. Felix's resignation and the demise of the Council of Basel under Eugenius' successor, Nicholas V

(1447–55) marked a new era. The struggle for government of the Catholic Church by reforming ecumenical councils virtually ended, and in its stead came the absolutism of Italian popes. A new schism threatened briefly when a French-inspired council at Pisa in 1511–12 contemplated forcing the abdication of Pope Julius II (see below), but he counteracted it successfully by calling his own (Fifth) Lateran Council in 1512, which lasted until adjourned by his successor in 1517. This council made a few feeble recommendations for reform but did little to correct the major abuses that were to help provoke the different and deeper kind of schism known as the Reformation.

The greatest achievements of the councils must be classified as pragmatic rather than idealistic. In the end the compulsion of nationalism reduced the reform programme to a mere shifting of control of the papal spoils system from an efficient bureaucracy to scattered kings and their secular underlings. The 'nations' of the councils, the concordats, and the pragmatic sanctions were milestones on the road toward the disintegration of the medieval Catholic empire and the rise of nationally controlled churches. As once the provinces of the western Roman Empire had fallen apart among regional tribal groupings, so now the papal empire was falling apart among national dynasties. At their best, the councils had stood for international harmony, limited monarchy, and spiritual reform, but the main currents of Western civilization pushed strongly in the direction of nationalism, absolutism, and political secularism.

*   *   *

The Popes (1417–1521)

In spite of the Conciliar Movement, the autocratic power of the papacy revived. Pope Martin V was the first of a line of secular-minded popes.[9] True to his Colonna ancestry, he laid solid foundations for papal despotism in central Italy. His successor, Eugenius IV, gave ground in the struggle for control of the Papal States during nine years of absence in Cosimo de' Medici's Florence, but his deputy at Rome suppressed republican revolts and governed with such brutal efficiency that Eugenius, upon returning to Rome (1443), was able to exercise absolute power. By mid-century the pope was one of Italy's many Renaissance despots, and the papacy emerged not only as a worldly autocracy but also as a pseudo-nationalist state with the ambition of uniting Italy under its temporal sway.

The popes provided excellent exemplars of another Renaissance characteristic as well—humanistic culture. Nicholas V (1447–55) even before his election as pope had had an enviable reputation as a scholar. The first humanist pope, he aimed to make the rebuilt Vatican City a centre of learning and art and spent lavishly for Latin and Greek manuscripts, whether Christian or Classical, purchased throughout Europe. Scribes and scholars were subsidized to copy and translate. He lived to see the completion of parts of the Vatican Palace, including a library that housed some 5,000 manuscripts. Venerable churches and ancient monuments throughout the city were repaired, and plans were made for a new St Peter's. While Rome was thus rebuilt in a fashion calculated to make it once more the world's cultural capital, the medieval papal idea of spiritual leadership was eclipsed.

Though dominated by grandiose cultural ideas, Nicholas was also remarkably successful in politics. A man of peace, he was by inclination as well as good fortune to bring to an end the papal conflict with the Council of Basel and to terminate the worst of Italy's internecine wars. His jubilee of 1450 was an unprecedented success; so many pilgrims crowded the streets that hundreds were crushed in panics, and it was deemed necessary to limit each visitor's stay. The jubilee filled the papal coffers, permitting the pope to carry on his expensive programme, and brought prosperity to Rome's citizenry as well. Although he benevolently granted a certain degree of local autonomy to the city, his last years were embittered by a republican plot. The major event of his reign, however, was the fall of Constantinople.

Since about 1300 intermittent appeals had been made for Christian crusades against the rising tide of the Ottoman Turks. Christians were no longer urged to help recover the Holy Supulchre but rather to assist in defending Constantinople and Hungary, which constituted Christendom's outer bastion against the infidel. A French-Burgundian army had been annihilated on the lower Danube in 1396 by Sultan Bayezid I's forces. Constantinople's ultimate fate was thus sealed, although postponed half a century by Tamerlane's temporary destruction of Turkish power in Asia Minor. Tamerlane's onslaught might have given Christendom a golden opportunity to counter-attack and destroy the battered and divided sultanate, but no large-scale crusade was launched, and Constantinople fell in 1453.

The exploits of the Hungarian crusaders a few years later were due to a dramatic revival of the old crusading spirit, but only on a national, defensive basis. Inspired by the Franciscan Giovanni di Capistrano and led by Hunyadi, already revered as a national strategist-statesman, a Hungarian army consisting largely of badly armed but heroic peasants not only checked the Turks at Belgrade in 1456 but drove them back and invaded the Bulgarian provinces of Turkey. The lack of effective aid from the Hungarian nobility and, despite papal efforts, from other Christian nations made it impossible to follow up this victory; and it proved to be the only successful Christian crusade of the entire century. Yet in itself it was decisive. It postponed the Turkish invasion of the middle Danube area until the campaigns that led to the Hungarian defeat at Mohacs in 1526 and the siege of Vienna in 1529, and it may have saved central Europe for Christendom.

Nicholas died in 1455 in the midst of a vain attempt to organize a crusade against the Turks, and his immediate successors carried on his policy. Calixtus III, of the Borgia family, formerly a Spanish cardinal, during a short reign (1455–58) continued fruitlessly to promote a crusade. Pius II (1458–64) compared with Nicholas in scholarly interests and crusading zeal. As Bishop Aeneas Sylvius Piccolomini of Siena, Pius had been a worldly gentleman of the High Renaissance. His varied writings on history, education, and other subjects (see Chapters VIII and XVI) had a facile, piquant, classical flavour. His illegitimate children, his disapproval of celibacy for the clergy, and a risqué novel of his younger days, widely translated, embarrassed his pontificate. His shifting career in Basel and in Germany had been more fitting for an Italian humanist and diplomat than for a candidate for the throne of St Peter. Upon becoming pope, however, he not only adopted the crusading programme of Nicholas and Calixtus but in fact died of a fever while preparing personally to lead a Papal-Venetian armada against the Turks. Not until the reign of Sixtus IV (1471–84) did an expedition go off, but, except for taking a few prisoners, it came to naught, and Western Christendom thereupon took a position of passive defence.

Seven popes followed Pius II in the half century or so before the Reformation and for the most part shed little glory on their hallowed post. Even disregarding the unreliable scandal which was noised abroad about most of them, observers could detect the triumph of secularism in the See of Peter. These seven occupants of the pre-Reformation Vatican, on the one hand, showed less interest in Renaissance scholarship than Nicholas V but, on the other, glaringly promoted the triumph of worldliness. They set a spiritually questionable standard of magnificence in their lavishly decorated palaces. Witness the Sistine Chapel—i.e. the chapel of Sixtus IV.

Spiritual indifference was matched by zeal in secular enterprises as papal despotism advanced. Sixtus IV (1471–84) strengthened his control of the Papal States by nepotism and the diplomatic marriages of his kinsfolk. His efforts to extend his sway elsewhere in Italy, though equally unprincipled, were less successful. In fact, in the midst of his manoeuvres, the Turks captured the Italian seaport of Otranto, commanding the straits between the Adriatic and the Ionian Sea. Nevertheless, he showed Italy and the western world that the papacy was an aggressive political force capable of playing a leading part in Italian affairs.

The tales about the Borgian roué, nephew of Calixtus III, who became Pope Alexander VI (1492–1503) may be fantastic exaggerations, but they illustrate how low was the moral tone believed to be characteristic of the nominal leaders of Christendom. Alexander played a despot's role strikingly similar to that of Sixtus IV except that the Borgia curia was packed with Spaniards instead of Genoese. As in Sixtus' pontificate, foreign invaders hampered the pope's Italian ambitions. In Alexander's case, however, the invasion was the first in a disastrous series that came from the north; it was by Charles VIII's French 'barbarians' instead of by Turkish infidels; and it was complete, penetrating the length of the peninsula to Rome and Naples. Unprepared to resist, the pope rode out the storm with diplomatic skill. Eventually he joined with Spain, the Empire, Venice, and Milan, all of which resented Charles' conquests in Italy, in a 'Holy League', which obliged the French to retreat, and he recovered control of the Papal States. The brutal conquests of his son, Cesare, the able general who was the prototype of Machiavelli's *Prince*, were more spectacular than permanent. The pope's untimely death left the Papal States and the rest of Italy in a turmoil.

The reforging of despotism in the Papal States was left to Julius II (1503–13), an iron-willed 'Machiavellian' who had learned much about papal politics as a cardinal. In contrast to the easy-going, urbane Alexander, Julius was a man of a violent temperament who led troops in person and governed the Papal States with tyrannical efficiency. His unscrupulous diplomacy restored the papacy to its position as an international power. Allying with France and others in the League of Cambrai (1508) against Venice, he made good the papal claim to lands that had been seized by Venice. Then with Venice as one of his allies, he set about to drive the French 'barbarians' out of Italy. He fought and negotiated for three years, undismayed by illness, defeat, or threats of deposition by renegade cardinals at the Council of Pisa mentioned above, and he died victorious, absolute master of the revived Papal States, arbiter of the Italies, a leading diplomat in the melée of European power politics. More lasting than his forging of papal despotism (and at the same time a tool in the process) was his patronage of art, especially architecture (see Chapter XII).

Leo X (1513–21), one of Lorenzo de' Medici's sons, played a similar role as builder of papal despotism and patron of Renaissance culture. He strengthened the University of Rome, especially by the addition of professors of Greek and Hebrew, organized the already extensive Vatican Library more effectively, and rewarded classicists, poets, and dramatists generously. Cardinals and Roman aristocrats followed his example in building private libraries and patronizing literature and art (see Chapters X–XII). Leo's need for funds—to rebuild St Peter's Church, among other things—and the inadequacy of the reform measures undertaken by the Fifth Lateran Council (see above) aided directly to precipitate the Reformation. In March 1517 the council ended its five-year career; in October Luther posted his ninety-five theses (see Chapter IV).

MYSTICISM AND HERESY IN EUROPE

Though, and in part because, the papacy was drifting with the current of secularism, the church was fostering certain contrasting tendencies. One of these was mysticism. A dynamic outgrowth of a quieter development of earlier centuries, mysticism now tended to take at the same time the diverging paths of contemplative and of active religion. In pursuing the active aim, the path diverged again—in the directions of church reform, on the one hand, and heresy, on the other.

Mysticism had its roots in Augustine's Neoplatonism and the contemplative life of monasticism. The mystic, inspired by intuitive experience, might seek to revive some aspect of early church worship such as the veneration of the Virgin Mary, the Eucharist, or some earlier puritanical practice such as apostolic or monastic poverty. Monastic mystics were prone to emphasize the other-worldly life of the Apostles and of the early hermit-monks. Women tended to stress a more spectacular type of mysticism, that of prophetic vision or revelation. The puritanical impulse often proved to be a reaction to the worldliness of the clergy and might end in a charge of heresy, as was the case, indicated previously, of the zealots among the Spiritual Franciscans.

Even the Dominicans, although upholders of strict orthodoxy, produced some mystics. Among them were the Rhineland teachers and preachers Johannes Eckhart of Cologne (1260–1327) (generally known as Meister Eckhart), Heinrich Suso (1295–1365), and Johann Tauler (1290–1361). All three were strongly influenced by Neoplatonism (see Chapter VI). Although Eckhart was personally orthodox, certain of his doctrines were condemned as heretical, and undoubtedly they affected those German monastic mystics who followed the heretical path marked out by the Spiritual Franciscans. Suso's influence became noteworthy in Dominican nunneries of the Rhineland and (along with Tauler's) among the fourteenth-century Rhenish and Bavarian mystics known as the 'Friends of God'. Prominent in this loosely organized but effective movement were middle-class laymen and women. Perhaps because of their Dominican connections, the 'Friends of God' held firmly to orthodox doctrines and practices, intent on making themselves an inner church of dedicated souls in direct communion with God. They vigorously opposed the excesses of earlier and more radical German and Flemish groups such as the Beghards, Beguins, and 'Brethren of the Free Spirit'. Out of their midst (c. 1350) came *Eine Deutsche Theologie*, a sort of textbook of mysticism, once mistakenly attributed to Tauler. Widely circulated in manuscript, it was not printed in full until Martin Luther's approval of it led him in 1518 to supervise its publication under the title *Ein geystlich edles Buchlein*. Thus the role of mysticism as a forerunner of Protestantism was made fairly explicit.

A more radical form of mysticism was exemplified in Flanders, where Jan Ruysbroeck (1295–1381) and his disciple Geert Groote (1340–84) taught, preached, and wrote. Even though Ruysbroeck vigorously attacked the Beguins and other such heretical groups in and about Brussels, his own pantheistic tendencies were suspect in his own day and later were condemned by orthodox theologians. He and Groote were concerned to strengthen the people's faith against heresy by enlivening their spiritual lives. For that reason Ruysbroeck wrote in the vernacular, and Groote was, for a time, a popular lay preacher. Both, however, were criticized by the orthodox clergy for their condemnation of clerical faults.

Groote's principal contribution to Flemish mysticism was the establishment of the Brothers of the Common Life at Deventer. The strength of this organization lay in the teaching and practice of the 'New Devotion' (*Devotio*

Moderna), a deep inner spirituality combined with simple honest living. The movement spread widely, as branch houses and schools were established throughout the towns of Flanders. The Brothers' literature of Christian devotion extended still farther—even to Scandinavia, where Gerlac Peterson wrote the *Fiery Soliloquy of God*. With the *Imitation of Christ*, now generally attributed to Thomas à Kempis (1379–1471), the Brothers won an undying influence upon those who sought a secluded, contemplative, and devout Christianity.

England produced a few great mystics, but no English movement arose comparable to those of Flanders and the Rhineland. Richard Rolle (1300–49) came closest to the continental model. An Oxford student turned wandering preacher, he taught both orally and in writing a simple doctrine, strongly Biblical and often highly critical of the clergy. His appeal reached all classes of lay men and women, and he left behind a saintly reputation. His disciples are often unidentifiable or of little renown, but two works of contemplative devotion came from among them—*The Scale of Perfection* by Walter Hilton, which approaches the sublimity of the *Imitation of Christ*, and *Revelation of Divine Love* by Juliana of Norwich.

Juliana was far from being the outstanding woman among the mystics of the fourteenth century. The life span of Bridget of Sweden (1303–73) synchronizes almost exactly with the Avignon papacy. Born into a noble family, she lived a relatively normal life (except for mystic visions, which began at an early age) and became the mother of eight children. The death of her husband on their way home from a pilgrimage to Compostella induced her to embark upon a career that combined spiritual introspection with organized monastic service strikingly similar to that of the Franciscans. Her revelations, written down in the vernacular, included a vision of the Passion, which eventually was known in lands as far distant as Coptic Egypt and Abyssinia (perhaps as a result of her pilgrimages to Jerusalem). Her revelations also involved her in practical reforms: the temporarily successful importuning of Pope Urban V to return to Rome and the founding of the women's Order of St. Saviour (sometimes known as the 'Bridgettines'). This order exemplified the amazing increase of feminine influence in the era after St Francis. His 'Poor Clares', of which Bridget became a member, had been merely a 'tertiary' adjunct of the men's orders of Franciscans. The 'Bridgettines' were an independent order, of which Bridget's daughter Catherine became the first official head.

Bridget's younger contemporary Catherine of Siena (1347–80) is sometimes referred to as a 'politician' as well as a mystic and reformer. Catherine was the youngest of twenty-five children of a Sienese textile worker. When only seven years of age, she became a member of the Dominican tertiaries. Mystic visions led her at nineteen to become a spiritual bride of Christ and impelled her to the task of ending the 'Babylonian Captivity', reforming the church, and uniting the Italies. Like Bridget (and with more lasting effects), by personal intervention she helped to persuade a pope (Gregory XI) to go from Avignon back to Rome. Equally important was her role as peacemaker in war-torn Italy. She negotiated between the rebellious Florentines and the pope. She pleaded for a cessation of the brutalities of war, and doubtless her saintly influence was more immediately effective than the literary appeals of Dante and Petrarch in the vain cause of Italian peace and unity. She died in Rome at the beginning of the Great Schism, leaving in her *Dialogue* a passionate record both of inner spiritual love and of outspoken criticism of clerical vices.

The year of Catherine's death was that of the birth of a townsman, Bernardino of Siena (1380–1444). Bernardino helped found the Observant (i.e. relatively propertyless) Franciscans and by his eloquence persuaded calloused Romans to burn the tokens of their vanity. The Observants were ultimately (1517) recognized as a separate order by Pope Leo X. Mysticism attained great political significance with Bridget and Catherine of Sweden and Catherine and Bernardino of Siena, all of whom were eventually canonized. Yet it did not cope successfully with the church problems of the day. One of the most perceptive of the contemporary churchmen, Jean Gerson, disapproved of the political efforts of Brigdet and Catherine: by persuading the popes to return to Rome they had, in his opinion, precipitated a worse situation, the Schism.

At least in part because of this disillusionment, in the fifteenth century mysticism tended to appear in a different guise—as either the literary spiritualism of individual writers or the social radicalism of heretical or near-heretical groups. The heretical groups, we shall see below, fared badly. Literary spiritualism was exemplified in the works of Thomas à Kempis, the scholarly yet inspirational treatises of Denis the Carthusian (1402–71), and certain writings of Cardinal Nicholas of Cusa (1401–64). The only woman mystic of this century who can compare with the saints of the preceding century (Jeanne d'Arc excepted) was Catherine of Genoa (1447–1510), a cultured Renaissance lady who presided over a spiritual 'salon' and a well-organized hospital.

The belief in witchcraft of the late fifteenth and succeeding centuries may be described as a sort of mysticism in reverse—a belief that men and women could and did commune directly with the Evil Spirit. In earlier Christian times many a learned scientist (e.g. Albertus Magnus and Roger Bacon) had been popularly suspected of occult relations with the Devil. In 1405 a treatise appeared which, among other things, described and condemned seven major classes of magic, all invented by the Devil for the seduction of mankind; they were geomancy, hydromancy, aeromancy, pyromancy, chiromancy (palmistry), aromancy (by animals' shoulder-blades), and necromancy. The climax of this strange aberration came during the High Renaissance. An epidemic of witch hunting commenced during the last quarter of the fifteenth century, and death penalties for witchcraft (thitherto rare) rapidly became more common. This severity seems to have stemmed from a papal bull of 1484. Quoting the

Biblical mandate to the primitive Hebrew tribes, 'Thou shalt not suffer a witch to live' (Exodus 22: 18), the bull urged inquisitors to be more alert in prosecuting witches. Popular suspicion and imagination added oil to the fire. Never before, in Christian lands, had so many innocent women been hounded to death for imaginary crimes. In one Italian town (Como) forty-one women were burned during the next year; and in 1514, three hundred more. The religious dissensions of the Reformation were not to quench—perhaps were even to add to—the blaze.

★   ★   ★

Heresy and Discontent in Western Europe

Mysticism was not the era's only source of heretical persuasion. Censure was also a pitfall for the individualist irked by the regulations of a religious organization, since deviation from organizational norms is likely to be considered heresy.

Long before 1300 the Roman Catholic Church organization and creed had become relatively crystallized. Somewhere between the parish priest with his catechism, confessional, and other direct contact with his flock and the pope's curia at Rome, authoritative judgments could be pronounced on nearly everything of importance in the Christian's daily life. Canon law was a well organized and highly technical code, explained and annotated by authoritative handbooks such as Gratian's *Decretum* (c. 1140), and a long line of eminent theologians had reduced Roman beliefs to a set of fundamental dogmas. To be sure, differences of opinion arose from time to time concerning details, and commentaries of marvellous complexity had been written upon them. Nevertheless, summaries by scholars like Thomas Aquinas and Albertus Magnus had reduced the major points of Christian faith to specific statements on which one could be reasonably certain, and an episcopal inquisition in each diocese permitted bishops to distinguish dangerous divergencies from orthodoxy. As the training of ecclesiastical officials improved in theology and canon law, they became more expert in detecting perilous trends. The strict schooling of Dominican friars made them particularly competent as inquisitors. The centralization of power in the papacy permitted a strong executive in Rome to check lesser officials, enforce ecclesiastical regulations, and otherwise give direction to an effective bureaucracy. This machinery of control, taking shape for a century or more before 1300, thereafter improved its efficiency.

Like every machine, however, the church bureaucracy had its weaknesses, and papal control failed at various times and in various regions. During the fourteenth century, even though the Avignon popes perfected certain parts of the machine, national monarchs sometimes were lax in obedience to papal instructions, and laxity became still more common during the Schism, when two or three rival popes were issuing contradictory orders. At such times heresies flourished with less danger of suppression.

Expanding urban life provided a most favourable atmosphere for heresy.

Commerce, industry, town schools, universities, business, travel, and other mundane relationships that town life fostered helped to promote a desire for secular justice and for reform of the more blatant evils of an increasingly worldly church. In addition, the growing number of persons exposed to a secular education in secular institutions brought an increase in the inclination to question ecclesiastical authority. Merchants schooled in business and graduates of university schools of civil law were little inclined to accept submissively every ecclesiastical judgment based on other-worldly dogmas. Their disinclination developed into heresy at times. The zealous questioner was tempted to become a social reformer, and then a religious heretic. With poverty all around him among the masses, with luxury and immorality rife among the clergy, a reformer felt impelled to speak out boldly. On the other hand, a local ecclesiastic, faithful to his organization and perhaps also confident of its essential rightness, might feel bound to suppress troublemakers.

If the mystic-reformer-heretic was a cleric, he might easily be constrained by withholding the episcopal licence to preach. At a crucial point in a mystic's career he might have to decide whether to obey the will of God (as vouchsafed to him personally) or that of man (as presented by an unsympathetic bishop). In this manner many of the Spiritual Franciscans became heretics, and eventually the Observant Franciscans, too, parted company with the Conventuals (see above). To the more mystic among the Spirituals obedience to God meant the practice of absolute poverty; in the eyes of the official head of the church this practice was heresy. Many pious Christians, judged heretical by 'Christ's vicar', were single-heartedly following what seemed to them to be the precept and example of Christ. Still, the official judge of the law of Christ's church was the pope; therefore his decision must be obeyed or the penalty for disobedience paid. To cite one particularly horrible example, Dolcino of Novara, the messianic leader of the Apostolici, was executed by being slowly torn to bits with red-hot pincers (1307).

The mere enforcement of an orderly legalism, however, did not get at the underlying cause of many heresies, social discontent. 'Poor Men' (Waldenses), whether in Dauphiny or Piedmont or elsewhere, multiplied (until nearly exterminated by a 'crusade' in the 1480's); likewise Apostolici, Beghards, Beguins, and a host of other mendicant groups. Even in earlier times heresies had appeared in industrial regions, especially textile towns. With the expansion of commerce and industry in the thirteenth and fourteenth centuries, industrial workers tended to form a more or less self-conscious proletariat. The Black Death accentuated their discontent, evidenced by a series of revolts in industrial centres throughout the West; and an added incentive to social heresy came from the division, for over a century, of Christian loyalty and papal leadership at the time of the Babylonian Captivity and Great Schism. The grinding poverty of the masses was not so basic to social discontent as the stark contrast between the wealth of some pastors and the hard lot of their flocks. Petrarch expressed in literary indignation what many a heretic felt: the painful difference between the Christ of Galilee with his foot-sore disciples and the luxury of Avignon, 'Babylon of the West'.

At the end of the fourteenth century, Wycliffe spearheaded the widespread resentment. Using the vernacular of the English, he popularized his attacks upon the wealth of the church, his doctrine of 'civil dominion' over church property, and his doubts regarding the sacramental system and the authority of the pope, and he translated the Bible. His followers, the 'poor priests' and the Lollards, were attracted more often by his views upon wealth, whether ecclesiastical or lay, and upon clerical abuses than by his theology, and for much the same reason he lost his support in Parliament. He was condemned by the English clergy as a heretic and banished from Oxford. After his death in 1384, the Lollards remained active, but in 1401 a fearful Parliament passed the statute *De haeretico comburendo*, requiring the temporal authorities to co-operate with the church in seizing, trying, and burning heretics, and forced the movement underground.

Urban and clerical discontent was accompanied by peasant discontent. The English Peasants' Revolt (1381) under the leadership of Wat Tyler and John Ball, who was a follower of Wycliffe, sprang from a combination of both elements. Directed primarily against legal restrictions on wages, servile dues, and poll taxes, it won the sympathy of many in London and other cities. It was, however, a short-lived explosion without significant outcome save for some widespread destruction.

In certain parts of the West national sentiment was also a factor in the rise of heresy. In Bohemia the ground had been prepared during the fourteenth century by several native Czech leaders for a favourable reception of radical religious ideas, but the demand for church reform was in part also a protest against the German influence in the University of Prague and other institutions of Bohemia. The doctrines of Wycliffe were well known at the University of Prague, where Huss was rector in 1402–3, because the political ties of Bohemia and England at that time were close. Jerome of Prague had studied at Oxford. Huss and Jerome preached Wycliffe's views and won wide adherence not only because they echoed Bohemia's discontents but also because the Germans tended to oppose them. After the German ruler Sigismund delivered Huss and Jerome at the Council of Constance (see above), the national solidarity against the Germans was greatly enhanced, to the point where it was embodied in the first great representative assemblies on the European continent—those at Cheslov in 1421 and 1422. Some German Waldenses joined forces with the Hussites. The rebels achieved their major military successes when stirred by patriotic spirit to heroic effort against hated German 'crusaders'. It was also in keeping with the times that their ultimate downfall was in part due to an internal rift between the relatively conservative middle-class Utraquists, primarily concerned with ritual, and the relatively radical, peasant Taborites, primarily concerned with social justice (see Chapter VIII).

In Spain, on the contrary, nationalism worked in favour of orthodoxy. The nationalist monarchs used the legal machinery (the Inquisition) provided by the international ecclesiastical organization to crush infidel minorities (Jewish and Muslim). But, since in this case the unorthodox were social outcasts (even though many of them were wealthy), the royal-papal machinery of suppression was approved with enthusiasm by a national-minded populace. Furthermore, the leaders of the persecution, Ximenes and Thomas Torquemada (1420–98), won support because they were also diligent reformers of the evils of church and clergy.

Two mystics of the fifteenth century provided a sharp contrast to the social-minded heretic, the usual type. A curious Dutch mystic, Wessel Gansfort (1419–89), was a spiritual reformer concerned with individual salvation rather than social reform. Educated by the Brethren of the Common Life, he imbibed more of their Biblical piety than their humanism. His individualism and reliance on the Holy Scriptures as the sole guide for Christians led him to reject the necessity of priestly intercession. The individual Christian, he held, had direct access to God. In a later century he might have joined the Protestants. The same seems plausible in the case of Jeanne d'Arc. Her execution, though essentially politically motivated, had distinct theological overtones. Among the numerous offences held against her by her English captors and their theological henchmen a major one was that she held stubbornly to the conviction that she was responsible for her actions directly to God and not to the church.

*   *   *

Mysticism and Heresy in Eastern Europe

Of the mystics in the Eastern Orthodox Church perhaps the outstanding example is provided by the Hesychast movement of fourteenth-century Byzantium. The way in which it merged with social and political discontents has already been indicated. When the movement was fully systematized by the monks of Mt Athos, the aspirant Hesychast had to pass through several earlier degrees before he became 'perfect' and worthy of the highest degree of ἡσυχία (contemplation). Only the perfect were worthy enough to see the light that was identical with that which had transfigured Jesus on Mt Tabor (Matthew 17: 1–9). The hierarchy, both Roman and Eastern had good reason to suspect this doctrine of direct contact with God as potentially dangerous to the church, whether united or divided.

Of several heretical sects that survived in eastern Europe around 1300, the Bogomils (see above) were the most numerous. Their views resembled those of the Socinians and the Anabaptists of a later period (see Chapter IV). Subsequently, heretical movements occurred in the Russian church. In the second half of the fourteenth century Novgorod and Pskov, and possibly also Moscow and Tver, were the scene of a heresy that took its name from one of its champions, Carp Strigolnik (i.e. Carp the Barber). The 'Barbers' or

'Shearers' (the Strigolniki) not only accepted the heterodox theology of the Bogomils but also denied the need of a special priestly order and ritual, and decried the wealth of the clergy. Their heresy was ruthlessly put down by the church. About a century later a new heresy arose in Novgorod and Moscow. This time its adherents were known as Judaists; they drew their creed from the Old Testament and were familiar with medieval Hebrew literature, and the church contended that their strange doctrines were brought into Russia by the Jews. A church council in 1490 anathematized the Judaists, and some were executed.

The Russian clergy itself split on the question of the material wealth of the monasteries. The overwhelming majority advocated that the monastic lands should be retained and were known as *Nyestyazhateli* ('non-abstainers'); a minority of *Styazhateli* ('abstainers') opposed church ownership of land. Judaists and Styazhateli at first evoked a certain sympathy from the reigning grand prince, Ivan III (1440–1505), at least in part because of the attractive prospect of distributing church lands among the lesser feudal lords whose good will he courted. The church, however, eventually won the support of the state, which ultimately acted in the interests of centralized administration and against the further enrichment of the feudal aristocracy. A church council in 1503–4 condemned the 'abstainers', and several of them were burned at the stake, providing a distinct victory for the alliance of tsar and church against princes, boyars, and heretics. Nowhere in Europe was heresy triumphant before the sixteenth century.

NOTES TO CHAPTER III

1. *The Cultural Heritage of India* (Calcutta, 1936), II, p. 252.
2. R. G. Bhandarkar, *Vaisnavism, Saivism and Minor Religious Systems* (Strasbourg, 1913), p. 73.
3. *The Cultural Heritage of India*, II, p. 255.
4. R. F. Leslie, *Polish Politics and the Revolution of November 1830* (London, 1956), p. 9, n. 1
5. A. A. Vasiliev, *History of the Byzantine Empire* (Madison, Wisc., 1929), II, pp. 376–77. See also Charles Diehl *et al.*, *L'Europe orientale de 1081 à 1453* (Paris, 1945), pp. 254–55.
6. The Act of Union (Council of Florence, 1439) was expressed in the following terms: 'The Holy Ghost proceeds eternally from the One and from the Other [Father and Son] as from one principle and by one aspiration. . . . The procession of the Holy Ghost from the Son is through the Father by whom He is eternally begotten.' In the absence of these details, without the formula 'as from a single principle', the Florence agreement would have been inconceivable. It was no political compromise but a theological explanation upon which the two parties were able to reach agreement. (O. Lacombe.)
7. For a discussion of recent literature on the Conciliar Movement, see Hubert Jedin, 'Nouvelles données sur l'histoire des conciles généraux', *Journal of World History*, I (1953), pp. 164–78.
8. See note 6 above.
9. Professor O. Lacombe points out that these popes, who were temporal rulers, bent upon Italian and universal politics, were none the less obliged to deal daily with a host of strictly religious problems, the religious nature of which was perfectly apparent to them. Neither individual predilections nor historical circumstances, nor yet the upsurge of lay humanism, could blind their innermost consciousness to these facts.

CHAPTER IV

CATHOLICS AND PROTESTANTS IN EUROPE (1500–1775)

DEMANDS WITHIN THE CATHOLIC CHURCH FOR REFORM

THE tribulations of the Catholic Church during the Avignon Papacy and the Great Schism stirred many clergymen and lay Christians to demand reform of the church 'in head and members'. The Council of Constance and its successors drew up lengthy reform programmes, which, however, remained empty promises thanks to the inability or unwillingness of the Renaissance popes to implement them. The Apostolici, Lollards, Waldenses, Hussites, and other heretical aggregates of the fourteenth and fifteenth centuries reflected the widespread discontent but occasioned only further vain efforts at reform.

Economic conditions combined with religious discontent to popularize the demands for reform. In an age of rising prices, the papacy had managed to establish a financial system that enabled it to live in a luxury befitting its position as one of the leading powers of Christendom. To the lower classes those who lived in luxury, whether laymen or clergymen, were suspect, the spiritual leader of Christendom more than any other. This suspicion was especially rife in the northern countries, where the pope and his Italian bureaucrats seemed to be foreigners living off the contributions of the native population, and Rome was pictured as the headquarters of an unreformable ecclesiastical hierarchy of luxury-loving exploiters.

Long before Luther the financial system of the papacy had been subjected to severe criticism. The mercenary aspects of such religious practices as relic cults, pilgrimages, and indulgences had been condemned; the Conciliar reform programmes, for example, had called for correction of the commercial aspects of indulgences.[1] The repeated demands seemed, however, to have fallen on deaf ears, and more and more Christians came to feel that the church hierarchy was callous to the physical suffering and spiritual needs of the faithful. Popular resentments helped lay princes, if indeed they needed such help, to encroach on the property and patronage of the church with impunity.

Early in the sixteenth century the French king provided a pat example of secular encroachment by gaining formal recognition of some of his extensive powers over the French church. Since the Pragmatic Sanction of Bourges (1428) a dispute had raged between France's kings and the popes over the method of selecting French prelates. To many benefices the conflict had brought great confusion, worse confounded by French invasions of Italy and the attempt of King Louis XII to depose Pope Julius II (see Chapter III). When Francis I came to the throne, he undertook to bring order into this chaos by a compromise with Pope Leo X. The result was the Concordat of Bologna (1516), which finally put an end to the French phase of the Conciliar Movement. It provided that the French crown would designate French archbishops, bishops, abbots, and priors to the pope, who would then invest them with canonical authority. Thus ecclesiastical electoral bodies were bypassed. In addition, Francis further expanded his authority over the French church by getting the power to collect an ecclesiastic tithe and to restrict appeals to the Roman curia. In return for this papal surrender the king acquiesced, at least by silence, to the right of the pope to continue to receive annates (the first year's income from new appointees) and certain other dues, and recognized—what was now a fact—the superiority of the pope over the councils. The Concordat of 1516 was bitterly opposed by the Parlement of Paris, the University of Paris, and some of the French clergy on the ground that the king had yielded too much, but in the end he had his way.[2]

In Spain a shift of control of ecclesiastical domination to the state likewise took place. The Inquisition, under monarchical control and with public approval, served as an effective instrument for purging the nation of ethnic and religious minorities. A sincere desire for reform heightened the fanaticism of the Spanish inquisitorial regime. Cardinal Ximenes de Cisneros, the pious and austere Franciscan who became primate of Spain and inquisitor-general, pressed for drastic measures not only against heretics and infidels but also against clerical abuses. After being appointed (1492), despite his reluctance, to the influential position of spiritual guide to the queen, he tried to remodel the Spanish church after his own Franciscan ideals. In an effort to improve the educational as well as the moral standards of the clergy, he made the University of Alcala the centre of the new learning in Spain. Its most remarkable achievement, a tribute to the excellence of humanist scholarship in Spain, was the *Complutensian Polyglot Bible* (so-called because the Latin name of Alcala was Complutum). Published in 1522 in six large volumes, this work was essentially a scholarly edition of the Vulgate with the texts of the component parts in the original languages. It was a formidable scholarly and religious achievement, in some ways surpassing a more famous contemporary work of Biblical scholarship, Erasmus' several editions of the Greek text of the New Testament with his own annotated Latin translation (1516–52).

Whereas the Spanish reformers remained solidly orthodox, the North produced one group composed of moderate reformers and another prepared to run the risk of rebellion. For a time, the moderate reformers, most of them humanists, dominated the northern scene. Unlike the typical Italian humanist, they combined humanistic scholarship with piety. Their very piety made them formidable critics of the bureaucrats in the church administrative system and of the Scholastic theologians in the old-line universities. The persistent religious trend of northern humanism emanated in large part from the *Devotio Moderna* of the Brethren of the Common Life. Erasmus received part of his training at perhaps their leading school, the one at Deventer; Luther at Magdeburg and Calvin at Paris were also among the fairly large number of illustrious men who as boys had gone to the Brethren's classes.

At first some of the northern humanists were allied with the radical reformers in lamenting the shortcomings of the clergy. A case in point is Johann Reuchlin (1455–1522). As an influential and tolerant professor at Heidelberg, he came into conflict with a fanatical converted Jew named Johann Pfefferkorn and his Dominican supporters, who were determined to suppress all Jewish books. In the subsequent war of ink, Reuchlin's *Eyes' Mirror (Augenspiegel)* and his *Letters of Famous Men (Clarorum Virorum Epistolae)* drew many of the German humanists into the camp of the critics of the clergy. The conflict became one of humanists *versus* Scholastics and of tolerant literary men *versus* authoritarian theologians. The humanists employed the weapon of satire with deadly effect. Ulrich von Hutten, Crotus Rubeanus, and others compiled the *Letters of Obscure Men (Epistolae Obscurorum Virorum)*, which pretended (1515 and 1517) to be the work of ignorant clerical bigots. The clergy came in for a goodly share of satire also in *Das Narrenschiff (The Ship of Fools*, 1494) of Sebastian Brant (1457–1521) and the *Encomium Moriae (Praise of Folly*, 1511) of Desiderius Erasmus (1466?–1536).

With his keenly satirical pen, Erasmus was not perhaps so good an example of humanistic piety as some of his contemporaries—his English friends John Colet and Thomas More, for example. Colet (*c.* 1467–1519), having studied the Classics in Italy, returned to his old school at Oxford and developed a humanistic interest in the actual texts of the Holy Scriptures. He was lecturing on the Epistles of Paul as early as 1496, about twenty years before Luther concentrated his attention on them. He preached sermons denouncing the clergy and demanding drastic clerical reforms as early as 1512. At the same time he encouraged in London a humanistic type of secondary education under lay control (see Chapter XVI).

Sir Thomas More (1467–1535), a barrister and a member of the House of Commons, exerted a somewhat similar influence, though in less vigorous fashion and on the broader front of both political and social reform. His *Utopia* (1516) indicates his more secular approach; in depicting an imaginary country that was admirable in many regards though not altogether ideal, it presented a critique of English society of the day. More, Colet, and some of their fellow humanists exemplify the attitude of those humanist reformers who, though critical, refused in the 1520's to join the revolt against the church. Erasmus got to know these 'Oxford Reformers' during several visits to England (1499, 1505, and 1509), and their mutual admiration and influence was unusually strong and lasting. The prince who was to become King

Henry VIII encouraged the activities of this friendly association of learned men.

In general Erasmus was to prove more inclined than his English friends to hold aloof from the struggle of the faiths. To him religion was a guide to right living rather than a set of established beliefs and ritualistic practices. He was intensely interested in the New Testament, especially the Sermon on the Mount, but his interest was ethical rather than devout. The contrast between Jesus' precepts and the practices of the clergy of his own day provided him with a point of origin for a double reform programme—the building of a good life for laymen and the betterment of the clergy. His *Praise of Folly* made a plea for reform of the church; his *Handbook of the Christian Soldier* (*Enchiridion Militis Christiani*, 1503) expounded the way by which a sincere Christian might attain a good life. Education, intelligent Christian effort, and careful self-training in good works, he contended, could produce right living (see Chapter XVI). Holding this philosophy of patience, Erasmus could hardly be expected, when the issues arose, to approve of doctrines like Luther's 'bondage of man's will' and 'justification by faith' or of rebellion against the church, no more than Luther could be expected to approve of Erasmus' belief in salvation by self-training and in the cure of church abuses by slow reform.₃

LUTHER AND LUTHERANISM IN GERMANY (TO 1529)

When, on October 31, 1517, Martin Luther posted his ninety-five theses on the door of the castle church at Wittenberg, he did no more than follow a general practice of announcing an intention to debate with a fellow-theologian certain religious propositions. Yet this act reverberated throughout Germany, indeed throughout western Christendom, and signalled the final break-up of the traditional unity of the medieval church. Why this prompt reaction? Dissatisfaction in Germany with papal ultramontanism and the lax morality of the clergy was widespread. Resentment at the draining of German wealth into the papal treasury at Rome was fanned by a nascent sense of German unity. Social unrest was rife among German peasants and the impoverished German imperial knights; and the rising German middle class, long dissatisfied with clerical abuses and mismanagement, looked to the princes of the Reich rather than to the frequently absent emperor for protection and support.

Luther himself, when he proposed his theses, seems to have had no thought of provoking a general revolt or of breaking with the papacy. He had entered the Augustinian Order in 1505 against the wishes of his ambitious father. Though his zeal, piety, and learning had won him general respect, he remained forever troubled by the problem of divine justice. Neither the strictest observances of monastic discipline nor the most ascetic practices could deliver him from a conviction of utter sinfulness, which made him despair of salvation. In a moment of sudden inspiration, while teaching the Bible at the recently founded (1502) University of Wittenberg, he became convinced that justification must come through faith alone, not through good works. This denial of the efficacy of good works meant the abandonment of a cardinal tenet of Catholic doctrine, which looked upon good works as an indispensable part of its system of penance.

Indulgences were prominent in this system of penance. They were based upon the doctrine of the *thesaurus meritorum*, the inexhaustible treasury of merits accumulated by Jesus and the saints and dispensed by the pope for the benefit of Christians of insufficient merit. Originally indulgences were intended by the church to grant remission only of temporal punishment and only for the truly penitent sinner, but preachers of indulgence claimed for them the power of reducing punishment in purgatory as well and, following a papal bull issued in the fifteenth century, extended this power to include the souls of the departed. Purchase of indulgences thus became an act of pious concern for the dead as well as a matter of personal welfare for the living. The doctrinal errors and the practical abuses in the sale of indulgences had been sharply criticized by theologians long before Luther. In Germany it was viewed with special dissatisfaction as one of the several papal schemes to drain the national wealth into Roman coffers.

A flagrant confusion of financial and spiritual ends was involved in an indulgence issued in 1515 by Pope Leo X, ostensibly for the building of St Peter's in Rome. Albrecht of Hohenzollern, archbishop of Mainz, was made its chief commissary. Contrary to canon law, Albrecht, who was not even of the required age, had brought under his control three German bishropics. He had received papal dispensation in return for a large sum of money, which he, in turn, had borrowed from the Fuggers. In orders to enable him to repay this debt, Albrecht was authorized by a secret provision of the indulgence to pocket half of the proceeds.

To push the sale of this indulgence, grossly exaggerated claims were made about its power. Luther attacked these claims, and his sovereign, Frederick the Wise, elector of Saxony, prohibited the sale of the indulgence throughout Saxon territory. In 1517, when one of Bishop Albrecht's ablest subcommissaries, the Dominican Johann Tetzel, approached the Saxon border, Luther posted his ninety-five theses to challenge him to a public debate. The debate never took place, but the impact of the theses, soon printed and broadcast all over Germany in the vernacular as well as in Latin, was immediate. The theses indeed went far beyond attacking indulgences; they unmistakably suggested limitations of the power of the pope and upheld the Gospel as the only divinely inspired basis of Christianity. Thesis no. 36, for example, read: 'Every truly repentant Christian has a right to full remission of penalty and guilt, even without letters of pardon.'[4] Such bold propositions touched fundamental concepts of Roman Catholicism, for in Catholic doctrine the salvation of Christians depended largely upon the clergy as the ordained administrators of the sacraments.[5]

Luther enjoyed the constant protection of his sovereign, Frederick the

Wise. Neither Emperor Maximilian nor Pope Leo X could well afford to alienate this powerful prince, especially since the emperor hoped to win Frederick's vote for his grandson, Charles of Spain, as successor to the imperial crown. Private efforts in 1518 to make Luther retract his attack failed; he refused to recant unless he could be convinced by arguments from Scripture before an impartial tribunal of theologians. He later converted this demand for a tribunal into a call for a general council of the church, thereby giving Frederick justification for continuing his protection until such a council might take place. Backed by his sovereign, Luther thus became the spokesman of the conciliar party, still strong within the church even among some otherwise opposed to his views.

As public tension deepened, Luther came to deny the importance of the clergy with increasing vehemence. In a crucial debate at Leipzig (1519), a celebrated theologian, Johann Maier Eck, skilfully led him on to deny the infallibility not only of popes but, by admitting agreement with certain principles of the condemned heretic John Huss, also of ecumenical councils. In June 1520, the pope, urged by Eck and the Dominicans, issued a bull (*Exsurge Domine*) threatening Luther with excommunication unless he recanted within sixty days. By that time Maximilian had died, and Charles had been elected and crowned Holy Roman emperor. Charles's diplomatic involvements, however, tied his hands in domestic affairs. Moreover, public sentiment was overwhelmingly in Luther's favour, and drastic measures against him could be expected to provoke large-scale unrest. Luther was therefore in a relatively strong position.

In August–October 1520 Luther, without yet formally replying to the threat of papal excommunication, set down his principles explicitly in three brochures: *An Open Letter to the Christian Nobility of the German Nation, The Babylonian Captivity of the Church,* and *A Treatise on Christian Liberty.* In these works he proclaimed the essential priesthood of all Christians, thus repudiating the distinction between clergy and laity and directly attacking the sacrament of ordination by which the priest becomes endowed with the spiritual power of his office. The true believer, he further contended, needed only one source of truth, the Gospel, and only one means of salvation, faith. The good Christian, though 'the perfectly free lord of all, subject to none', voluntarily acted in accordance with the law to become 'the perfectly dutiful servant of all, subject to all'.[6] The performance of good works was pleasing to God if undertaken freely without the expectation of future rewards. Divine justice was not a simple saving of the righteous and damning of the unrighteous, for all men are sinners. It was rather the working of divine grace, of which man could be assured only by a faith that made him confident of the goodness and mercy of God: 'Good works do not make a good man, but a good man does good works.'[7]

For Luther, therefore, certain external practices were non-essential to true Christianity. He rejected outright four of the seven traditional sacraments as not justified by Gospel, retaining only baptism, communion, and penance, but he later abandoned penance also. Baptism was for him the most fundamental sacrament, for through it the Christian was reborn from his original sinful state, became truly a member of the Christian community, and thus might hope for ultimate forgiveness. Essentially Luther conceived of faith as a mystical bond between man and God and of the priesthood as a mere ministry of God's word.

In December 1520, long after his sixty days' grace was up, Luther burned the papal bull, along with some volumes of the canon law, in a public ceremony. It now devolved upon the young emperor, Charles V, to implement the papal excommunication with an imperial ban. According to imperial law, however, no subject of the Empire could be placed under ban unheard. Charles agreed to grant Luther a hearing before the Diet, which assembled in 1521 at Worms. Protected, at the insistence of Frederick the Wise, by an imperial safe-conduct, Luther arrived at Worms after a triumphal journey. Before the assembled princes and notables of the Empire he refused to retract his writings and asserted the authority of conscience over dogma and canon law:

'I am held fast by the Scriptures adduced by me, and my conscience is taken captive by God's Word, and I neither can nor will revoke anything, seeing that it is not safe or right to act against conscience. God help me. Amen.'[8]

The Edict of Worms, signed by Charles after the close of the Diet, pronounced the ban of the Empire upon the intransigent heretic.

*   *   *

Political and Social Complications

So far Luther's cause had been only a movement for church reform, but the forces that he had unleashed now ran an independent course, at times outrunning his leadership. On his return from Worms to Wittenberg, he was abducted on the order of his prince, and for a year he was kept safely hidden in the Wartburg, Frederick's castle near Eisenach. In a unified country ruled by a strong monarch such defiance of papal excommunication and imperial ban would speedily have been foiled, but the particularism of Germany, leaving to the emperor only a limited and begrudged authority, permitted his opponent, Frederick, to come to an understanding with rival German princes. Moreover, Charles was not free to deal with only German affairs. Though a devout Catholic sincerely eager to crush Luther and eradicate heresy, he was preparing a military campaign against the French king, Francis I, whom the pope was supporting. Frederick, skilfully manoeuvreing between pope and emperor, was able to shield Luther, all the while protesting his desire to comply with the laws of both church and empire.

Behind Frederick stood the formidable strength of incipient German nationalism, and anti-clericalism was a dominant theme in this nationalist sentiment. The establishment of strong dynastic monarchies in France, England, and Spain had left Germany one of the few western European countries still wholly subject to papal authority in church affairs, as well as a most important source of papal revenue. Papal domination had long been resented, and successive German diets had drawn up lists of grievances against the papacy. At the very Diet of Worms which in 1521 had banned Luther, feeling against the church ran so high that the papal nuncio lamented: 'The whole of Germany is in open revolt. Nine-tenths of it shouts for Luther and the other tenth, if it cares nothing for the Reformer, cries 'Death to the Roman Curia.' "9

Luther's *Letter to the Christian Nobility* had contained a calculated appeal to this national fervour. He sought to evoke the pride of his 'fellow Germans' against exploitation by unnecessary papal officials who 'lie in wait' for German benefices 'as wolves lie in wait for the sheep'.10 He called for national legislation to prevent the removal to Rome of the monies collected in Germany. He went still further in appealing to the political interests of the German princes. His concept of the essential priesthood of all believers led him to assert not only the complete separation of temporal from spiritual power but also, since all Christians are equal and temporal power is divinely ordained, the supremacy of the secular government: 'On this account the Christian temporal power should exercise its office without let or hindrance, regardless whether it be pope, bishop, or priest whom it affects.'11 With this assertion of the supremacy of the temporal power, Luther in effect commended the reform of the church to the secular rulers of Germany.

Charles V at Worms made unmistakably clear that he considered himself the champion of the traditional faith, but Luther could count not only upon Frederick of Saxony and certain other powerful princes but, more decidedly, upon the lesser nobility, as well as large sections of the middle class and peasantry. The church was one of the largest landholders in Germany; it commanded vast material wealth and was feudal lord over many nobles and multitudes of peasants and serfs. The Imperial knights, often poor and always proud, were especially prone to look upon the concentration of vast estates in the hands of a few magnates, whether ecclesiastical or lay, as a threat to their well-being. Peasants and knights readily vented their discontents in a deep-seated anti-clericalism and anti-Romanism. Among their grievances were the diminution of the knights' prestige as the cities grew and military techniques changed, and the hardening of servile status for the peasants as Roman law was substituted for traditional German law (see Chapter VIII) and as prices rose for all classes. The demand for reform of the church became also a demand for reform of the society.

Urged on by the knight-humanist Ulrich von Hutten, the knights were the first to take up arms. Hutten published in 1520 a *Complaint and Admonition against the Power of the Pope*, in which he openly espoused the cause of Luther, called upon the emperor and the German estates for a war against Rome, and called for an alliance of the nobles and the cities, if the emperor and the estates failed to take the lead in the national cause. A subsequent publication, the *Exhortation to the Free and Imperial Cities*, revealing the position of the knights more clearly, advocated an alliance of cities and knights alone against their common enemies, the great secular and ecclesiastical princes, who were usurping the rights of burgher and knight. Hutten won over Franz von Sickingen, the most renowned and powerful Imperial knight of his day.[12]

Armed revolt, however, had never been part of Luther's creed. On the contrary, he re-affirmed the ancient doctrines of unquestioned obedience to ordained authority and denied the right of revolt. In his view, where misrule and oppression occurred, they were divinely ordained punishments, to which Christians must patiently submit. His *Ernest Exhortation for All Christians, Warning Them against Insurrection and Rebellion* (1521), issued from the Wartburg when disturbances broke out in Wittenberg and elsewhere, made quite clear that for him reform of religion was the task of the ordained secular power alone and no part of a scheme for general social and political reform.

Despite Luther's exhortations the knights went to war in 1522-23. This Knights' War ended in Sickingen's death, Hutten's exile, and the destruction of the knights' power. Luther saw in their failure a terrible yet just decision of God, but he did not thunder against them so violently as he was soon to thunder against the peasants.

To a degree Luther sympathized with the demands of the peasantry. The Swabian peasants voiced their grievances in the *Twelve Articles*, deliberately phrased in a moderate tone so as to influence him in their favour. One article demanded that peasants be taught the Gospel and have the right to choose their own pastors. Another based the demand for emancipation from serfdom upon a concept that he approved: 'Christ has delivered and redeemed us all, the lowly as well as the great.'[13]

Yet Luther's sympathies with the peasants did not make him waver in his rejection of violent action. To be sure, his treatise *Secular Authority: To What Extent It Should Be Obeyed* (1523) warned the princes of the consequences of misrule; still he clearly denied to suffering subjects the right of revolt and approved of only passive resistance in matters of religion. In part his restraint was due to the growing difficulty of his situation. By this time he had returned from Wartburg to Wittenberg. Shortly after his return a first Diet of Nuremberg (1522) had deferred enforcement of the Edict of Worms against him, demanding the convocation of a general council to deal with the problem; after the knights' defeat, however, a second Diet of Nuremberg (1524) agreed to enforce the Edict 'as far as possible'. This noncommittal compromise reflected the delicate balance between conservative and reformist forces in the Empire, but the same delicacy of balance placed Luther in a dilemma. On the one hand, powerful princes charged him with responsibility for the revolt of the knights and the ferment among the peasants; on the other, a radical wing of the reformers wanted him to side openly with social revolution.

At length (1524) the peasants rose in revolt in Swabia and Franconia. In this perplexing position Luther issued (1525) his *Admonition to Peace: A Reply to the* Twelve Articles *of the Peasants in Swabia*. It denounced the tyranny of secular and especially of ecclesiastical princes, blaming them for the uprisings, yet at the same time turned against the 'false preachings' of radical reformers. It not only did not concede the right of disobedience; it went so far as to assert that the demand for freedom from serfdom was not supported by the Gospel. Despite Luther's appeal to religious principles and moderation, the Peasants' War spread throughout southern and central Germany, marked by all the savagery that characterizes warfare in any age. To Luther the peasants seemed guilty of sinning grievously against the Gospel and of endangering his reform programme. He vented his indignation in a tirade *Against the Robbing and Murdering Hordes of Peasants*, in which he called upon the princes and 'everyone who can [to] smite, slay, and stab, secretly or openly, remembering that nothing can be more poisonous, hurtful, or devilish than a rebel.'[14] The bloody repression of the peasants that followed might very well have come without Luther's appeal, for the princes scarcely needed prompting from him to protect their interests with the sword, but his appeal alienated many who identified religious with social reform.

Luther's proclamation of the religious equality of believers without conceding social and political equality thus helped to promote disunity in the reformist camp. A number of his earlier followers accused him of sacrificing principles to political expediency, and the mass support he had hitherto enjoyed vanished, taking with it all hope of making his movement truly national in scope. His stand, though revealing the essentially non-political intent of his reforms, had political implications. It forced him to rely more and more, in his efforts to organize a new church, upon friendly princes and free cities.

* * *

The Widening of the Rift

During Luther's months of hiding in the Wartburg, the traditional forms of worship had come under attack in reforming communities throughout Germany. In Wittenberg Luther's colleague Andreas Carlstadt (1480–1541), who had independently arrived at a position that approximated the chief reformer's theology, was a leader in a brief radical movement. Unlike Luther, Carlstadt accented the connection between religious and social reform. When Luther returned to Wittenberg, he cut short Carlstadt's ascendancy and, in the end, drove him into closer rapprochement with the more radical reformers or Anabaptists (see below). Yet Carlstadt's activities had forced the Wittenberg town council to adopt the first practical measures of reform—revision of the service, communion in both kinds (wine as well as bread), and abandonment of clerical celibacy.

Luther had at first been willing to grant a certain latitude in religious observances as long as faith and the Gospel were held superior to ritual, but the necessity for uniformity became apparent if reformist strength was not to be dissipated. Gradually the general aspects of a reformed service evolved. Mass was abolished. Regular gospel readings and sermons, both in the vernacular, became the core of religious worship. Communion in both kinds was given to those approaching it in true faith. To make the congregation active participants in the service, Luther advocated community singing of hymns in the vernacular to replace the chants and responses of traditional liturgy. He himself composed a number of hymns for this purpose (see Chapter XII).

Of necessity Luther's reforms carried beyond liturgical conventions. His attacks upon monasticism and the celibacy of the clergy led to large-scale defections from monasteries and convents and to the resumption by monks and nuns of secular life. As early as 1522, the Wittenberg chapter of the Augustinian Order voted its members the privilege of renouncing their vows; Luther himself, after some hesitation, married in 1525. The disorganization within clerical ranks in Saxony caused a disruption of schooling and other social services that the clergy had customarily performed for the poor, the sick, and the orphaned. An early step in some reformed communities was to prohibit begging, which Catholic doctrine had condoned because it offered an opportunity for charity, but as poverty did not shrink before this prohibition, Luther authorized reformed congregations to appropriate ecclesiastical funds and place them in a common chest for the support of the reform (or, as it soon came to be called, 'the evangelical') clergy, the poor, and such social enterprises as hospitals and schools. He thus transferred to the community responsibility for the social no less than the spiritual welfare of its members, as had been true of the early Christians.

By thus assigning the maintenance of the school system to the reformed community, Luther was constrained to give some thought to pedagogical problems (see Chapter XVI). His writings on education plainly reveal his intellectual debt to humanism. That indebtedness was clear also in his translation of the Bible. His searching studies of Scripture would have been impossible without the Hebrew studies of Reuchlin and others and without Erasmus' Greek edition of the New Testament, which became the basis of his translation of the Old and New Testaments into German. The translation was an inescapable consequence of his theology, for if the Gospel was to be the sole source of Christian faith, it had to be read and understood by all. The vernacular Bible became a common bond among reformed Christians. The wording of Luther's translation also had a decided impact upon German literature and the development of the German language (see Chapter XI). Its distribution throughout Germany laid the foundation for a common Schriftsprache that eventually became the vehicle of a truly national German literature. Despite his huge debt to humanism, however, Luther was not wholeheartedly a humanist. His repudiation of rationalism and his religious intolerance clashed with humanist secularism and cosmopolitanism. A rift shortly separated him from the leading humanists and widened as the Reformation progressed.

Many humanists in Germany and abroad—among them Crotus Rubeanus, Hutten, Johannes Oecolampadius, Martin Bucer, and, most important of all, young Philipp Melanchthon—rallied to Luther's support. Melanchthon (1497–1560) was at twenty-one professor of Greek at Wittenberg. He took part in the Leipzig Disputation, was Luther's trusted surrogate in Wittenberg during the period of hiding at the Wartburg, assisted him in translating the Bible and organizing the reformed church, and published the first systematic summary of reformed theology, *Loci Communes Rerum Theologicarum* (1521). In successive diets and at meetings with other reformers he acted as Luther's adviser. Less obstinate and more tolerant than Luther, he was inclined to make greater concessions, but he allowed himself to be overruled. Two years after Luther's death Melanchthon confessed: 'In Luther's time I was often compelled to give in and found it more than humiliating.'[15] He remained, however, a loyal lieutenant throughout Luther's life and then shouldered the leader's mantle.

A similar loyalty and community of purpose was lacking in Luther's relations with some other humanists. What at first drew most of his humanist supporters to him was a common opposition to Scholasticism and Catholic dogma, and a common desire for reform of the church. When Luther went beyond those objectives and proceeded from reform to open revolt, not all humanists could concur. His increasing popular following, some anticipated, would lead to tumult, and his deepening bitterness, intransigence, and intolerance separated them from him more and more.

The rift became unbridgeable as a result of Luther's controversy with Erasmus. Erasmus had at the outset joined Luther's appeal for freedom of individual faith. Luther never thought highly of Erasmus as a theologian but in the beginning was careful to court his support, since Erasmus was the most influential man of letters of the age. Gradually Erasmus was alienated by Luther's religious zeal, while Luther became more and more impatient with Erasmus' cautious conservatism. Erasmus' behaviour was partly motivated by a certain opportunism, for he was worried by attacks from both sides upon himself as a moderate. Yet other, perhaps more compelling, considerations influenced his attitude. His cosmopolitan spirit was offended by Luther's appeal to nationalism. His conviction that gradual education, not quick, spontaneous, popular action, was the surest way of reform constrained him to condemn the passions released by Luther's revolt. Moreover, a fundamental philosophical difference estranged the two men. Luther's pessimism made him picture mortal man as incapable of good without the saving grace of God; a captive will bent by original sin toward evil was a presupposition of the doctrine of salvation by faith alone. For the more optimistic Erasmus, such

I*

religious determinism not only cast doubt upon the possibility of educating man toward good but also implied the responsibility of God for evil. In 1524 Erasmus published *De Libero Arbitrio (On Free Will)*, which attacked the core of Luther's theology, and Luther answered it in 1525 with *De Servo Arbitrio (On the Bondage of the Will)*. Their alienation became final when Erasmus, although still defending Luther against Scholastic attacks, publicly refused to abandon the traditional church.

The current of the time was now against the moderation of Erasmus and his sympathizers. Luther's call for religious reform was closer to the mystical heresies of the Middle Ages than to the reforming humanism of the Renaissance. It led to a renewed preoccupation with religion all over Europe, and thus to a growing theological partisanship—to the neglect of the more secular, rational interests of the humanists. The Reformation indeed is sometimes thought to have brought a marked decline in the influence of humanism in parts of Europe as learned men turned their minds from literary pursuits to theological polemic.[16]

*   *   *

Inauguration of an Evangelical Church System

The preoccupation of Emperor Charles with diplomatic and military complications had given the reformers a relatively free hand to organize their church, and a diet at Spires in 1526 postponed action again. This (the first) Diet of Spires ended with a resolution (generally called the Recess of 1526) foreshadowing the eventual solution of the religious question—that until a general council had been convoked, each state 'should live, govern, and conduct itself as it is willing to answer before God and the Imperial Majesty'.[17] Luther interpreted the Recess to mean that each evangelical prince had the right to organize the reformed church on his own lands. Accordingly, with his chief adviser Melanchthon, he drew up plans for the administration of evangelical churches, giving the prince the functions of a bishop in administrative though not in spiritual affairs. The first 'visitation' (inspection of churches), ordered by the elector of Saxony in 1527, found church affairs in a state of confusion. Melanchthon thereupon worked out a *Kirchenordnung* (Church Ordinance), which, when revised by Luther, provided uniformity of service and supervision of the clergy through regular visitations. The *Kirchenordnung* was a major step toward the subordination of the Lutheran church to the state. The visitations provided the beginnings of a consistorial system through which ecclesiastical government was placed in the hands of a body of state officials, composed of theologians and jurists acting under the temporal authority. (The first consistory was not established, however, until that of Wittenberg was set up in 1539.)

In 1529 Charles V, having defeated his enemies and having made peace with Pope Clement VII and Francis I of France, was at last in a position to press for the strict application of the Edict of Worms throughout the Empire.

The German representatives, meeting that year at the Second Diet of Spires, revoked the latitude tentatively allowed to the local princes by the Recess of 1526 and thus placed Luther and Lutherans again under the Imperial ban. This reversal of policy met with so vigorous a protest from the evangelical princes and cities that their followers were known thenceforth as Protestants. Their protest was in favour of the right of a government (not of the governed) to choose the religion of a state.

ZWINGLI AND CALVIN

German Protestantism was able to achieve no union with a reform movement going on contemporaneously in Switzerland. The leader of the German–Swiss phase of that movement was Ulrich Zwingli (1483–1531). Although reform in Switzerland did not begin until two years after Luther published his ninety-five theses, Zwingli had developed the basic principles of his theology independently. He had become increasingly familiar with the writings of Erasmus, especially the Greek edition of the New Testament, and under the influence of that great humanist, whom he visited in Basel, his religious ideas took on a clearer shape. Although a humanistic bent made Zwingli's approach to reform more intellectual than Luther's, his decision to proceed to an open demand for reform came only after he underwent an emotional crisis during a plague that ravaged Zürich in 1519.

From the beginning Zwingli's reforms combined the political with the religious in a way that distinguished them sharply from Luther's. In fact, the Swiss reformer first became antagonistic to the papacy over a political issue— the plight of Swiss mercenaries in the service of popes and secular princes. As chaplain of Swiss troops on several expeditions into Italy, he had gained first-hand knowledge of their distress and, in verse as well as prose, tried to rouse his countrymen against the trade in human flesh, condemning their greed on theological no less than humane grounds.[18]

Like Luther, Zwingli preached the Gospel in the vernacular, attacking the validity of indulgences, pilgrimages, and similar pious works. After Luther's explicit denial of papal primacy in his disputation with Eck at Leipzig, Zwingli wholeheartedly associated himself with the efforts of his Saxon colleague. In 1519, upon recovering from the plague, he preached a series of sermons that marked the beginning of open reform in Switzerland. These sermons upheld the Gospel and ancient Christianity as the sole basis of Christian worship and church organization and denounced the veneration of saints, fasting, clerical celibacy, and other Catholic practices. Unlike Luther, Zwingli was concerned to give his measures a popular and legal footing through the assent of cantonal and municipal authorities. In a series of public and private disputations in 1523–24, he induced the Zürich town council to vote in favour of preaching the Gospel in all the canton's churches and of separating from the jurisdiction of the bishop of Constance.

By the same kind of civic assent the Zwinglian reformation spread into other cantons. After a nineteen-day disputation in 1528, Zwingli, assisted by Bucer and Oecolampadius, won an especially important ally in the canton of Berne. The backing of the civic authorities in the reformed communities gave his movement a collective sanction that the Catholic Church could not easily deal with, especially since the pope stood to lose his major source of mercenaries in case of open conflict. The fight was, therefore, left to local bishops and lower clergy. Zwingli's insistence upon majority vote proved singularly effective against them, and at the same time it greatly reduced friction within the reformed communities.

With the help of laymen as well as reformed clergymen, the Swiss reformer thoroughly simplified the content and form of the church services. Though not himself a violent iconoclast, he led groups of civic and guild representatives in a usually orderly removal of decorations from the reformed churches. Relics were burned or buried. Priests were allowed to marry, as Zwingli himself did. Permission was given to eat meat during Lent. Mass was abolished, and the service, stripped of all pomp, was built around the reading of the Bible in the ancient tongues with sermons in the vernacular. Zwingli himself collaborated in the translation of the Bible into Swiss German. In 1523 he first began to celebrate communion in both kinds, the entire congregation participating.

The Zürich leader went beyond the Lutherans in the reform of the church. He abolished all practices not sanctioned by the Gospel, including organ-playing and the singing of hymns (which were not reintroduced into the Reformed service until long after his death). He looked upon the church not only as a spiritual but also as a political democracy and placed its external direction in the hands of the constituted civic authority, which he made also the guardian of a strict moral code. He envisaged an identity of church and community that was much closer than had been achieved under the Lutheran princes of Germany. He thus prepared the ground for Calvinist governmental theory and puritanism.

With religious reform Zwingli also sought to combine political and social reform. Under his leadership Zürich for the first time refused to send mercenaries to fight in Italy. He attempted to remove the inequalities that gave the older forest cantons a certain predominance in the Swiss Federation —a proposal that would also have increased the voting strength of the Reformed cantons. He had poor laws passed in Zürich and had begging outlawed. Although he did not condone the violence of the Peasants' Revolt in 1525, in striking contrast to Luther he called for leniency and for measures to improve the peasants' lot, moving toward the abolition of serfdom.

In matters of doctrine, Zwingli's humanism made for greater optimism and rationalism than Luther revealed. Zwingli did not deny the concept of 'original sin' but softened its impact by interpreting it as man's inclination to sin; and while he also preached justification by faith alone, he did not exclude the great teachers of non-Christian societies from salvation. In his *Exposition of the Faith* he wrote: 'We may expect to see [in eternal life] the communion and fellowship of all the saints and sages and believers and the steadfast and the brave and the good who have ever lived since the world began.'[19] Unlike Luther, he did not despair of recognizing the elect, for he identified the chosen with those who had the true faith, thus making all of a reformed congregation potentially members of the true, invisible church. Like Luther, Zwingli accepted only two sacraments, baptism and communion, but, unlike Luther, he saw in them merely symbolic acts rather than true miracles. The conflict over the Eucharist proved to be the most divisive doctrinal difference between Lutheran and Zwinglian theology. For Zwingli the Lord's Supper was but a symbol of Jesus's suffering; Luther, on the other hand, while denying the Catholic doctrine of transubstantiation (i.e. that the bread and wine of the sacrament actually changed into the body and blood of Jesus), believed in consubstantiation (i.e. that Jesus was only—but really and materially—present in the bread and wine during the sacrament).

In Switzerland the balance between the contending forces of Catholics and reformers was no less precarious than in Germany. The old forest cantons in the south resisted all efforts at religious reform; only in the northern cantons (and in some neighbouring areas of southern Germany) did Zwingli and his followers make significant gains. Berne accepted the Reformation in 1528. Next to Berne, the most important canton in the north was Basel. A centre of humanism, especially since the arrival of Erasmus in 1521, it long resisted open reform. Its conversion to Zwinglianism was the work of Oecolampadius. Like Zwingli he had maintained close contact with Erasmus at first but then had actively supported Luther, and when, in 1522, he was called back from Germany to Basel as preacher, he immediately began to press for reform, allying himself closely with Zwingli. After years of preaching and stormy public disputations, his efforts met with success (1529). Erasmus and other humanists left the city for quieter precincts.

The struggle between the reformed and the Catholic cantons had by that time become so embittered that violence broke out. The Catholic cantons formed a league and made an alliance with the Habsburgs, the traditional enemies of the Swiss Federation. War was actually declared between the Reformed and Catholic forces in 1529, but peace was concluded at Kappel without bloodshed, and unity within the federation was temporarily reestablished. Yet each side continued to distrust the other. Suspecting a resumption of the alliance between the Swiss Catholics and the Habsburgs, Zwingli proposed to join forces with the Reformed cities of southern Germany and the Lutheran princes of the Empire.

This plan concurred with that of the newly converted Landgrave Philip of Hesse, who hoped to unite the two Protestant sects. He invited the leaders of both to a colloquy at his residence in Marburg in the fall of 1529—to no avail. Despite a large measure of agreement, the two parties could reach no understanding on the meaning of the Lord's Supper. On the first day of their colloquy, Luther chalked on the desk before him the words from the New Testament: 'This is my Body.' He was unwilling to allow any but the most literal interpretation of the verb *is*, although Zwingli and Oecolampadius insisted that the same verb in other passages of the Bible repeatedly had the meaning *represents*. Zwingli was ready to concede a spiritual, though not a real, presence of Jesus at the Eucharist, but compromise on this basis was blocked by the usually moderate Melanchthon. Melanchthon, possibly swayed by Charles V's recent attempt at the Second Diet of Spires to play the Zwinglian party against the Lutherans, persuaded Luther not to compromise, on the grounds that concessions in a radical direction might forever thwart reconciliation with the Catholic princes of Germany. Realizing the need for at least a show of unity, the Colloquy of Marburg issued a public declaration expressing mutual respect and listing points of agreement. The rift was nonetheless complete, for the declaration also reaffirmed their continued disagreement on the crucial issue of the Eucharist.

The failure of the Colloquy of Marburg weakened the political and military effectiveness of the entire reform movement. Check came soonest in Switzerland, where in 1531 war again broke out. It ended in defeat for the Zwinglian forces in a battle at Kappel, with Zwingli, who had gone forth as field chaplain, among the killed in action. The Second Peace of Kappel followed and put an end to the spread of religious reform in German Switzerland by accepting the emergent principle of territorialism—that the church affiliation of a people was to be determined by its civic authorities.

*   *   *

Calvinism in Geneva

Zwinglianism won adherents in a number of towns in southern Germany, the most important of which were Ulm, Augsburg, Constance, and Strasbourg. The development of Strasbourg as an important centre of Zwinglian reform was largely the work of Martin Bucer (1491–1551). On the crucial doctrine of the Eucharist, though he decidedly shared Zwingli's view, he strove for unity within the reform movement. He therefore developed a middle position between Lutheran and Zwinglian doctrines that was to influence both Anglican and Calvinist theology. For King Henry VIII of England consulted the Strasbourg theologian on his impending divorce from Catherine of Aragon, and Calvin spent three years (1538–41) in Strasbourg in close association with Bucer. In 1549, on the invitation of Archbishop Thomas Cranmer, Bucer went to Cambridge as professor of divinity and subsequently collaborated in the revision of the Book of Common Prayer.

Jean Calvin (1509–64) had originally preferred the contemplative life of the humanist scholar to that of the active reformer and had studied law, Latin, Greek, and Hebrew with notable scholars. His conversion to evangelical Christianity occurred sometime between 1532 and 1533, when he helped to prepare for his friend Nicholas Cop, recently chosen rector of the University of Paris, an address which clearly revealed the influence of both Erasmus' humanism and Luther's belief in the saving grace of faith alone.

Sorbonne orthodoxy reacted to Cop's address with wrath, and Cop fled. After vain attempts to win support, Calvin also fled, eventually reaching Basel. There he completed and published (1536) the Latin version of his *Institutes of the Christian Religion* (*Christianae Religionis Institutio*), which he repeatedly revised until it reached its definitive form in 1559, his own French version appearing in 1541. Dedicated to Francis I, the *Institutes* were originally designed to promote the Reformation in France. In 1536, the very year the *Institutes* appeared, Calvin was persuaded by his compatriot Guillaume Farel, who was in the midst of the struggle for reform in Geneva, that it was his divinely ordained duty to take part in that struggle.

Geneva was particularly fertile ground for reform. Located between two aggressive neighbours, France and Savoy, it sought to maintain its independence by an alliance with the Swiss cantons of Berne and Fribourg. Berne was reformed and Fribourg Catholic. The assistance of Berne had given Farel a strategic advantage when he began his ardent campaign to evangelize Geneva. A public disputation led to no conclusive victory, but soon political dissatisfaction reinforced religious dissent. The citizens of Geneva sought greater self-government, and the Catholic bishop of Geneva, a descendant of the Savoy family, resisted, counting upon armed support from his Savoyard relatives. Continued ferment provoked Fribourg to withdraw from its alliance with Geneva, forcing Geneva into closer ties with Berne. In the midst of this tense situation a second disputation was held (May 1535) and ended in victory for Farel, but it took an iconoclastic riot of the reform party to force accession to the demand for evangelical worship. The House of Savoy now intervened, and Berne was forced to move to Geneva's defence. The Bernese defeated the Savoyards (1536), and the victory of the reformed cause was assured in Geneva. When subsequently nearby Lausanne became Protestant, Fribourg remained the only Catholic canton in French Switzerland.

Thus the circumstances were favourable when Calvin went to Geneva and decided to remain there. His task appeared to be simply to give substance and organization to the newly victorious Protestant creed. His early efforts were only partly successful, however, and in 1538, when he and Farel proposed to re-establish excommunication as a disciplinary measure and sharp disagreement broke out over the ritual of the Lord's Supper, both were banished. Calvin then spent three years in Strasbourg, where Bucer exerted the influence already noted upon his further theological development. Meanwhile Geneva was rent by opposing factions. In 1541 its desperate council recalled Calvin, giving him a free hand to put into practice his stern ideas, which had become even less flexible during exile.

Although Calvin sometimes went far beyond both Luther and Zwingli in his departure from Catholic theology, he was indebted to both. He particularly acknowledged Luther's leadership in formulating the cornerstone of Calvinist, or Reformed, belief—that justification came through faith alone and not through faith and good works. Like Luther and Zwingli, Calvin retained only two sacraments, baptism and communion, but differed from his predecessors in his interpretation of them. In its outward simplicity Calvinist worship was heir to Zwingli; yet, like Luther, Calvin believed in the efficacy of congregational singing, though of psalms in preference to hymns. Under the influence of Bucer he adopted a middle position between Luther and Zwingli in the interpretation of the sacraments. Baptism, in agreement with Zwingli, was for him a simple rite by which one became a member of the Christian church. His interpretation of communion, however, was a compromise between the Lutheran and the Zwinglian positions, similar to that which had been suggested to Luther at Marburg in 1529. Calvin retained Luther's concept of the real presence of Christ but divested that presence of all materialism and, in closer agreement with the Zwinglian concept, declared it to be a spiritual presence which the partaker could, if he had faith, appropriate, although spiritually only.

In Calvin's theology the doctrine of predestination received a more radical formulation than in either Luther's or Zwingli's. Luther had attempted to overcome any starkness implicit in the doctrine by counterbalancing his conviction of man's unworthiness with his faith in God's grace; Zwingli had admitted as potentially included among the elect all those who sincerely embraced his creed; but Calvin pursued the doctrine to its most logical conclusion. His major premise was the absolute omnipotence and omnipresence of God, Whose wisdom and will were beyond human comprehension. Convinced, no less than Luther, of the utter sinfulness of man, he considered salvation an inscrutable mystery. No man could have full assurance of his worthiness to be among the elect and therefore could find hope only in unquestioning faith in the goodness of God: 'For it is unreasonable that man should scrutinize with impunity those things which the Lord has determined to be hidden in Himself.'[20]

Calvin's doctrine of absolute predestination gave to his concept of the church a decided dualism, making it a political and a religious instrument at the same time. For Luther, the sacrament of baptism provided a bond that united all the baptized in one invisible church. Zwingli had accepted the existence of an invisible church of the elect but had regarded membership in the visible church as an outward sign of election. Calvin placed the invisible church of the elect completely outside the ken of man; yet man was saved from despair by his membership in the visible church, which not only united both elect and nonelect in this life but also was a church of equals, for the doctrine of absolute predestination made no special allowances for noble birth or privileged status. Membership in this church provided three possible tests of election; it was the outward sign of the individual's faith, permitting him to hear and preach the word of God; it enabled him to partake of the sacraments; and it bore witness to his righteousness and Christian discipline. Through this emphasis upon the righteous life (which was not the same as, but was reminiscent of, the Catholic doctrine of 'good works') the church became the moral as well as the religious guardian of the Reformed commonwealth and therefore an integral part of its government. Where Luther had subordinated the church to the state and where Zwingli had made his church the expression of the majority will, Calvin placed the civic side by side with the spiritual authority. Even if tyrannical, rulers must be obeyed, Calvin taught, except when they order impiety. The temporal government thus became also a functionary of divine power: 'Civil government is designed . . . to cherish and support the external worship of God, to preserve the pure doctrine of religion, to defend the constitution of the Church, to regulate our lives in a manner requisite for the society of men, to form our manners to civil justice, to promote our concord with each other, and to establish general peace and tranquility.' [21, 22]

The visible church thus was conceived by Calvin as a sort of theocracy, a government according to God's law, but it was a theocracy based upon a representative system. Its powers were laid down in the *Ordonnances ecclésiastiques* of 1541. Church discipline was put in the hands of a Vénérable Compagnie des Pasteurs, a board of ministers, who also were to watch over doctrinal purity. An Order of Teachers was made responsible for teaching the pure doctrine and securing a succession of well trained ministers. A Consistory, composed of six ministers and twelve elders elected by them from the city councils, was to supervise the conduct and opinions of the population. Public welfare was placed in the charge of appointed deacons. Together these orders (ministers, teachers, elders, and deacons) made up the government of the church, which held its authority directly from Christ. At first the authority of the civic bodies of Geneva (councils, assemblies, syndics, etc.) over the ecclesiastics was safeguarded, but the magistrates gradually yielded power and deference to the church orders, particularly the Consistory, and Calvin dominated the Consistory. Eventually civic and ecclesiastic authorities were inextricably intertwined. The republican tradition of Geneva was reinforced by Calvin's at least theoretical preference for an elective theocracy. Moreover, by implication the concept of predestination, no respecter of titles, power, or pelf, was democratic, for the community of the elect (the invisible church) cut across class lines.

The theocracy that Calvin eventually established in Geneva ruled public as well as private life with an iron hand. It discouraged amusements and diversions, outward adornment and manifestation of pride, and often severely punished infractions. Calvin even reintroduced, though against much opposition, excommunication and exile as forms of punishment but, like the Catholic Church, left to the civic authority the execution of the church's sentences. The expression of thought was strictly policed, and a network of informers aided the Consistory in imposing its will. As the number of cases cited before the Consistory indicated, resistance to Calvinist puritanism was widespread, but in 1555, the opposition party (which became known as 'the Libertines') was destroyed by the torture, flight, or execution of its leaders. On the surface at least, Calvin succeeded in his aim of making Geneva the goal and haven of Reformed Christians from all over Europe. John Knox, who visited the city during his exile from England, looked upon Calvinist Geneva as the perfect example of a Christian commonwealth.

In the *Institutes*, Calvin had written: 'I am not an advocate for unnecessary cruelty, nor can I conceive the possibility of an equitable sentence being pronounced without mercy.'[23] The quality of Calvin's mercy nevertheless sometimes was strained, and most conspicuously in his treatment of Michael Servetus (see below). The execution of Servetus (1553) provoked a stinging indictment by the French humanist Sebastian Castellio, whose treatise *On Heretics and Whether They Ought to Be Burned* (1554) presented an uncompromising defence of religious tolerance. Yet it was an era when humanism was being engulfed by the new dogmatism, and the replies of Calvin and Theodore Beza, his adjutant at Lausanne, who ardently sought to justify the punishment of heretics, sounded louder and more persuasive than Castellio's well-reasoned plea.[24, 25]

Despite Calvin's dogmatism, he propounded a thoroughly humanistic system of education. In Chapter XVI we shall describe the curriculum that he provided for the College and Academy of Geneva. Almost from their inception, these schools became the rallying point of students from all over Europe, many of whom were to become leaders of the reform movement in their native countries. Their presence in Geneva testified that Calvin and his commonwealth had become the focal point of the Reformation.

THE TUDORS AND ANGLICANISM

In Germany and Switzerland political action followed from the concern of theologians and humanists with religious reform. In Tudor England the reverse was true: the foundations for reform were laid by an absolute monarch who used theologians with reformist leanings to further his political and personal designs. The one theological issue at first involved, the problem of a king's divorce, entailed little more than a technicality of canon law. In seeking annulment of his marriage to Catherine of Aragon on debatable grounds, Henry VIII was moved by more than infatuation with the dark-eyed Anne Boleyn. Of greater moment were the political considerations that the Tudor succession might be endangered because Catherine was—or, at any rate, was thought to be—too old to bear him a male heir and that the absolutism to which he aspired could hardly be perfected so long as the English clergy recognized in Rome an authority outside his own.

Henry originally had no intention of provoking a rupture with Rome. He had been—and persisted in being—a professed Catholic who allowed no marked deviations from the accepted creed. His *Defence of the Seven Sacraments*, written against Luther in 1521, had, in fact, earned him the title 'Defender of the Faith', conferred by a grateful pope and still borne proudly by Henry's successors. Nevertheless, after Luther's revolt any opponents of the papacy became potential allies of the evangelical camp. Thus Henry's decision to push through his divorce with or without papal sanction gave to a family dispute a profound international significance.

As had been the case with Luther, a delicate diplomatic situation played into Henry's hands. Pope Clement VII not only had genuine religious scruples against annulling King Henry's marriage but also was victimized by the conflict between Emperor Charles V and Francis I. Clement could not well afford to offend the emperor (who was not only Catherine of Aragon's nephew but also a more willing defender of the faith than Henry), especially after imperial troops had occupied and sacked Rome (1527); and yet he also hoped to retain Henry's support in his efforts to counter Habsburg supremacy on the Continent, especially in Italy. He therefore did his best to delay a final decision concerning Henry's divorce. His temporizing tactics did not work to his benefit. Years of waiting only increased Henry's impatience and at the same time gave him the opportunity to devise measures that would give a legal semblance to his divorce if papal assent were not forthcoming.

Meanwhile Henry prepared his subjects for such an eventuality. In 1529 he summarily dismissed his lord chancellor, Cardinal Thomas Wolsey, who had failed to secure the annulment of his marriage. He then attacked some of the clerical abuses most highly resented among the English people. A series of acts forced through Parliament between 1529 and 1532 diminished the economic advantage of the clergy. They regulated charges for clerical services, limited both the number of offices and the amount of property that could be held by members of the clergy, and drastically reduced the annates paid to Rome.

Sure of popular support, Henry concurrently attacked the political position of the clergy also. He accused them in 1529 of having violated the Statute of Praemunire when they had recognized Cardinal Wolsey, archbishop of York and lord chancellor of England, as papal legate—an office that, ironically, Wolsey had accepted with Henry's consent in the hope of furthering the king's divorce. In addition to paying a substantial indemnity for this offence, the Convocation of the English clergy that year had to acknowledge the king as their 'singular protector, only and supreme lord, and, as the law of Christ allows, even Supreme Head'. In 1532, Henry renewed his attack with the 'Supplication against the Ordinaries', which denounced the legislation passed in the Convocations and the clerical administration of ecclesiastic courts. The Convocation answered with a 'Submission of the Clergy', which, in effect, made all future church legislation subject to royal approval and that of the past subject to review. Parliament was then (1533) induced to pass the

Restraint of Appeals Act, which prohibited appeals to foreign (i.e. papal) jurisdiction from decisions of English courts.[26]

Thomas Cranmer, a humanist scholar from Cambridge and a devoted advocate of royal absolutism, had recently won royal approval, for it was he who had suggested an appeal of Henry's case to the European universities, a majority of which had replied in the king's favour. Still acting with papal consent, the king made Cranmer archbishop of Canterbury (1533), and after his installation, Cranmer dissolved Henry's marriage. This action brought the final break with Rome; the pope excommunicated Henry. The authority of the English ruler over church affairs, already implicit in the 'Submission', became explicit when Parliament passed the Act of Supremacy (1534), which unconditionally recognized the king as the supreme head of the Church of England. Prominent dissenters were punished; Sir Thomas More, who in 1529 had reluctantly agreed to be Wolsey's successor as lord chancellor, was executed as a traitor (1535).

Henry was able to accomplish his religious revolution without encountering significant organized resistance. An important factor in weakening the opposition was the strength of national sentiment that had characterized English attitudes since the Hundred Years' War. The War of the Roses had eliminated the English nobility as a serious rival of royal power, and the middle class, anxious to avoid the hardships and devastation of that war, believed a strong monarch to be the best guarantor of domestic peace. Clerical reform and a national church were, besides, welcome in principle to the people of England, while Henry's confiscation and redistribution of monastic lands converted the beneficiaries of royal favour into grateful recipients who replenished the diminished ranks of the English landed nobility with powerful advocates of royal paternalism. The fate of the monasteries between 1536 and 1539, nevertheless, provoked the only serious show of resistance. The struggle was short-lived. It culminated in the so-called Pilgrimage of Grace in 1536–37, an insurrection in several northern shires by thousands of Catholic laymen and clergy, which was put down by a few dozen executions.

Another reason for the weakness of the opposition was that Henry's religious reforms were restrained. They did not impugn Catholic theology but only matters of ecclesiastical organization and administration. They, therefore, did not excite religious passions to the same extent as the Continental reform movements. Henry, in fact, assiduously avoided giving the impression that he favoured doctrinal reform. He persecuted both recalcitrant Catholic clergy and avowed reformers with apparent impartiality. In the Ten Articles, issued by the Convocation of 1536, a deliberate attempt was made to pacify doctrinal disputes and 'to stablish Christian quietness and unity'.[27] The Articles sought to appease not only the more moderate Catholics at home but also the more moderate reformers, for Henry was for the moment courting the German Lutherans. Yet no new doctrine was explicitly proclaimed, and whatever change could be read into the Ten Articles was attributable to omission rather than commission. Thus, while they mentioned only three sacraments, they did not deny validity to the other four. After the open rebellion of the Pilgrimage of Grace, however, Henry opposed even implicit accommodation to reform doctrines. The Six Articles of 1539 reasserted the basic tenets of Catholic theology except papal authority, confirming as dogmas of the Anglican Church hitherto suspect principles and practices such as transubstantiation, celibacy of priests, auricular confession, communion in one kind, vows of chastity, and private masses. Henry's divorce in 1540 from his fourth wife, Anne of Cleves, signalled the complete abandonment of his pro-Lutheran policy. Until the end of his reign, the Six Articles remained the religious law of the land and were firmly enforced.

★ ★ ★

Doctrinal and Liturgical Reform

The phase of the English Reformation which ended with Henry's death constituted little more than the secession of the Church of England from the jurisdiction of Rome and the establishment of the king as the supreme head of the church. Doctrinal and liturgical reforms were accomplished during the short reign of Edward VI, the son born to Henry from his third marriage (to Jane Seymour). The first step in these reforms is identified with the boy-king's uncle, Edward Seymour, duke of Somerset and lord protector, a convinced Protestant of Lutheran persuasion, who exerted a decided influence upon his ward.

Despite Henry's opposition to reformed ideas and his persecution of known Protestants, the writings of Luther, Zwingli, and Calvin had become widely known in England. The Oxford Reformers had helped promote the scholarly study of the Christian tradition, and the still lively persistence of Lollardy had prepared the ground for the popular acceptance of many reformed ideas. A centre of reformed opinion had developed at Cambridge, where the Lutheran leanings of William Tyndale, Cranmer, and other theologians became so well known that their meeting-place was nicknamed 'Little Germany'. Henry had kept these reform advocates in check; Somerset found a willing ally in Cranmer when he set out to add liturgical reform to the political and legal reform of Henry.

So complete now was the submission of the ecclesiastic to the secular power that the authority of the lord protector sufficed to bring about the changes that Henry himself had wanted to forestall. As a first step, the Six Articles were repudiated, and with the Order of Communion, issued in 1548, the year after Henry's death, communion in both kinds was legalized. In 1549, the first Book of Common Prayer was published, substituting English for Latin, and through an Act of Uniformity worship was standardized throughout England. Neither Somerset nor Cranmer, however, was willing to risk civil war, and they revealed their caution in the ambiguity with which they worded important parts of the Prayer Book. Many outward elements of the traditional service were retained, and new ones did not expressly controvert Catholic teaching, although they were so phrased as to enable Protestants to interpret them according to their consciences. Despite the ambivalence in high places respect for the old tradition was still profound in England, and enforcement of the Act of Uniformity led to sporadic outbursts, notably in Cornwall, where English was a foreign language. As on the Continent, the borderline between religious and economic discontent was none too clear, and the hardships caused by the enclosure movement (see Chapter 1) were undoubtedly also important factors in these uprisings.

Somerset's inability to maintain domestic peace coupled with several diplomatic failures led to his downfall and to the ascendency of the Earl of Warwick, afterward Duke of Northumberland. Northumberland cast his lot with the more radical reformers. The ambiguities of the first Prayer Book, while avoiding provocation of traditionalists, were offensive to convinced reformers, who not only pressed for a clearer statement of doctrine but also objected to the persistence of Catholic symbols in the service. They found telling support among several illustrious refugees whom the victory of Emperor Charles V over the Protestant Schmalkaldic League in 1547 (see below) and the consequent threat of persecution had forced out of the Holy Roman Empire. The Pole Jan Laski in London, the Italian Peter Martyr at Oxford, and the German Martin Bucer at Cambridge lent distinguished support to the Protestant cause. Bucer especially, although his willingness to compromise between Lutheran and Zwinglian theology was not acceptable to many, was an influential critic of the first Prayer Book.

Northumberland initiated the final phase of the Anglican revolt, making the break from Rome more definitely a break also from Catholic theology. A new Act of Uniformity, passed in 1552, imposed a second Book of Common Prayer, which went farther than the previous edition in the reform of worship and theology. The service was simplified, marriage of the clergy was permitted, and language and ceremonial more clearly approximated a Protestant interpretation. The rite of communion underwent the most important change. Cranmer, even before Bucer's arrival in England, had been converted to the Zwinglian concept of the Eucharist. Whereas the first Prayer Book had been deliberately phrased so as to allow for a varying interpretation, the second Prayer Book stated expressly that Holy Communion was merely an act of 'remembrance', for 'the natural body and blood of our Saviour Christ . . . are in heaven and not here'.[28] The ceremonial itself was changed to conform with that of the Swiss Reformed Church.

With the second Prayer Book the Church of England took its place decisively on the Protestant side, but the Anglican revolt was—and remained —the least radical of the reform movements. Changes of liturgy and service were less far-reaching than in either Germany or Switzerland, notwithstanding a sudden wave of iconoclasm during Somerset's protectorate. On the Continent, Protestant church administration had been reorganized along either consistorial or presbyterian lines; in England continuity was unbroken in both ritual and organization through the maintenance of the episcopal system. In the relationship of church with state, the English Reformation consequently differed notably from its Continental counterparts; the king was acknowledged as the supreme governor of the Church of England, though without any further spiritual function or office. The crown thus symbolized the identity, almost complete, of the Anglican Church with the English realm. Tudor absolutism had established the most truly national church in western Christendom, but the studied ambiguity of Anglican doctrine contributed in no small degree to a flexibility that permitted men of different convictions to remain loyal subjects and Anglicans. Those who refused to conform altogether, however, were to create future complications.

Emphasis upon national unity at the expense of religious uniformity moulded the strength of Anglicanism. Only a year after the second Act of Uniformity, the death of Edward VI permitted the accession of Mary (1553–59), the Catholic daughter of the repudiated Catherine of Aragon. Anglicanism was to prove that it was capable of surviving Catholic reaction and retaining its predominance in English religious life. Thus to the insularity, dynastic loyalty, historical tradition, and other peculiar institutions bolstering Englishmen's national sentiment was now added the potent force of religious solidarity in an evangelical creed that distinguished them from other nationalities.[29]

THE ANABAPTISTS

The most radical reformers of the century were commonly designated as Anabaptists because advocacy of adult baptism emerged as the chief bond among them. While reform in England, Germany, and Switzerland is clearly identified with outstanding individuals, the diversity of the Anabaptist background beclouds their theological and even their geographical origins. In the Rhineland, Switzerland, Bohemia, Moravia, Poland, the Baltic provinces, and the Low Countries, elements of Anabaptist doctrine were disseminated by preachers who, though they frequently were aware of each other's views and activities, sometimes appear to have had no direct contact with one another. This diversity accounts at least in part for the fact that, while at various moments in Anabaptism's tumultuous history a number of influential preachers came to the fore, no one individual became its acknowledged theologian.[30]

The other religious groups, whatever issues divided them, were unanimous in the violence they directed against this radical wing of the Reformation. Reformers and humanists like Zwingli and Melanchthon joined hands with Catholic inquisitors and untutored feudal lords in demanding the execution of Anabaptist preachers and their followers. In 1529 the Diet of Spires, in the midst of the struggle between Catholic and Protestant factions of the Empire, took time to pass an imperial law commanding the princes on either side to remove Anabaptist 'men and women of rational age from natural life to death by fire or by the sword . . . without prior inquisition before spiritual judges'.[31] Thus Anabaptists were denied even the slender safeguard which the Inquisition, by giving offenders the chance to recant, offered to other heretics.

The passion with which Anabaptists were persecuted cannot be explained solely by the religious doctrines that distinguished them. The very name (meaning 'believers in rebaptism') by which they have become known gives undue emphasis to one of those doctrinal differences and seems to have been deliberately assigned to them by their enemies in order to bring them under the provisions of an ancient Justinian law that made repetition of baptism punishable by death. As a matter of fact, the Anabaptists, to whom this issue was not cardinal, referred to themselves simply as Baptists. The cardinal tenets of their theology were the literal interpretation of Scripture and a firm conviction of the efficacy of divine revelation. These tenets led them to assert the true believer's ability to interpret Scripture for himself and so make religion a personal matter and membership in the church voluntary. As a result, among the Anabaptist arose a host of self-appointed preachers, both men and women, and a marked diversity of teachings. None of them, however, could find in Scripture authority for infant baptism. Hence, but only as a result of their more basic tenets, they advocated adult baptism (not rebaptism).

The faith of the Anabaptists was essentially mystical. It centred upon an intimate relationship of the believer with God that was mediated not by institutions but by Christ alone and could be achieved only through the active desire of the individual. Anabaptists, therefore, revised the doctrine of predestination and insisted upon the existence of free will. Christ, they believed, had died for all men; baptism, therefore, was not a prerequisite of salvation but merely the outward expression of a free-will conversion to Christ. Infant baptism was meaningless, for only adults could knowingly symbolize by baptism their acceptance of the True Church. The True Church thus was composed of voluntary adult believers, the 'saints' who had vowed to live in imitation of Christ. No other reformed creed was ready to go so far in emancipating the immature or unwilling from institutionalized religion or to place so few formal bonds on the mature and willing. To find the true principles of Christian living, no institution or outward rites were needed—only piety and spiritual understanding, which came to the truly pious as an act of revelation. An enthusiastic fringe of the movement preached the imminence of the second coming of the Christ, and their prophesies kept the masses agitated and won adherents who did not necessarily grasp the more obstruse tenets of the creed.

Whether chiliasts or not, in general the Anabaptists demanded the most complete 'restitution' of the primitive church. This demand was revolutionary, for it implied the absolute brotherhood and equality of all believers. To maintain the purity of the True Church, a strict, self-imposed moral discipline was expected, and the state was denied all authority in the affairs of the church. The cardinal principle of complete religious freedom led also to rejection of the authority of the state in matters of individual conscience, to a doctrine of separation of church and state. Indeed, participation by the true Christian in the affairs of the state was disapproved. A true Christian would not pay certain taxes, for example, because they might be used to support un-Christian acts of the state; even church taxes were opposed, on the ground that the church should be supported entirely by voluntary contributions. The true Christian would take no oath. Nor would he hold office, since to do so would conflict with the prescribed equality of all believers and might, moreover, lead him to inflict the death penalty, thus violating Christian scruples against taking human life. The same scruples required Anabaptists to oppose war and to refuse to bear arms even in their own defence. Continued persecution induced only the more radical among them to turn from meek submission to a crusade against their persecutors as enemies of the City of God.

The Anabaptists' ideal of restoring the brotherhood of the primitive church involved a radical concept of social and economic justice. Like the Catholic Church and Luther, Anabaptists not only rejected usury but in their emphasis upon a literal interpretation of the Bible went far in the direction of the primitive communism of early Christianity. In the abstract at least, Anabaptism rejected private property, declaring that all possessions were the property of God, to be held only in stewardship by the proprietors and so ministered as to meet the needs of less fortunate brethren. In practice, Anabaptist attitudes with regard to property ranged from private philanthropy on the part of those who considered community of property impracticable to the voluntary communism practised in the Moravian communities, the compulsory community of goods demanded by Dutch and German Anabaptists such as Jacob Wiedemann, and the violent attacks upon wealth and the hierarchic society in the writings and sermons of Thomas Münzer.

The social and political implications of the Anabaptists' religious teachings help to explain the hostility that they evoked. Their very pacifism, at a time when the Turks were threatening Latin Christendom, laid them open to the charge that they were willing to let Christianity perish. Probably most shocking, however, was their insistence upon the absolute separation of church and state. Luther, Zwingli, and Calvin, while with greater or less vigour asserting the primacy of religion, had submitted to or become allied with the existing civic authority and thus had helped to preserve, to one degree or another, unity of church and state. Carried to a logical conclusion, however, Anabaptist teachings might have destroyed not only the established spiritual order of western Christendom but also the established political and social order.[32]

The Anabaptists were in some regards indebted to the earlier religious revolution in Bohemia. The Hussite movement of the fifteenth century had already demonstrated by its splinterings how schism breeds schism. Nevertheless, on the eve of the Reformation in Bohemia, the more conservative, primarily religiously motivated Calixtenes had outlasted the Taborites and the other more radical, politically and socially motivated splinters, with the exception of the so-called 'Moravian Brethren' (*Unitas Fratrum*). Founded by Peter Chelčisky (d. 1460) and enjoying the protection of John Rokycana (d. 1471), the first and last archbishop of the Utraquist (Hussite) Church, the 'Moravians' during the early sixteenth century won the adherence of influential minorities in Bohemia and Moravia. Unlike future Anabaptists, they accepted infant baptism, and of late the influx of upper-class elements had brought a departure from the radical equalitarianism of the founder, but in other regards they were among the significant forerunners of the Anabaptists. Chelčisky believed in the literal interpretation of Jesus' teachings, the democratic practices of primitive Christianity, and the repudiation of war, oaths, and participation in civic matters.

Prior to the peasants' uprising in Germany in 1524–25, most Protestant reformers had viewed with only relative alarm the various extremist groups that had arisen in the wake of their more moderate revolts. One of the first of these groups was the so-called 'Prophets', Nicholas Storch, Markus Stübner, and Thomas Münzer. In the town of Zwickau, Saxony, near Bohemia, they took the lead in a movement that, going far beyond Luther in its reform efforts, revealed distinctive Moravian tendencies. After expulsion from Zwickau, in 1521, Storch and Stübner went to Wittenberg, where, in Luther's absence, they gained considerable influence over Carlstadt, already showing Taborite proclivities, and even over Melanchthon. Their ardent mysticism, chiliastic prophesies, and iconoclastic outbursts incited demonstrations that greatly disturbed Luther. As already indicated, in 1522 he hurried back from hiding on the Wartburg and regained control of the reform movement. From then on, the Prophets and eventually Carlstadt became bitter opponents of Luther, whom they denounced as a traitor to the Reformation. But Luther did not at that time propose that extreme measures be used against them. The Anabaptist movement had not yet truly begun, and Carlstadt seemed more a misguided mystic than a subversive rebel.

Münzer, Carlstadt, and a number of other mystics who were popularly, if somewhat anachronistically, later to be associated with Anabaptism made common cause with the peasants. Their influence grew as Luther's denunciations revealed him to be an ally of the ruling classes. Münzer became ever more convinced that God was on his side, would exterminate his enemies, and would soon unite the community of the faithful in an egalitarian kingdom of God on earth. A considerable popular following enabled him to create and to maintain until expelled by the local lords communal theocracies in Allstedt and Mühlhausen in turn. In 1525 he was captured after unsuccessfully leading a force of Thuringian insurgents in the Peasants' War and was executed.

Among the Zwickau Prophets adult baptism had been favourably regarded, and Münzer had openly advocated it, but it had apparently not been practised.

It is doubtful, therefore, whether strictly speaking they are to be considered Anabaptists. Anabaptist teachings are commonly believed to have first crystallized into a coherent theology in Zürich, Switzerland, where Zwingli's reform, though even in its initial phases more radical than Luther's, had not yet, in the opinion of an increasing faction, gone far enough. Among the radical leaders stand out Conrad Grebel, well educated scion of a patrician family, and Felix Manz, a humanist and Hebrew scholar. Disputations in 1523 and 1525 revealed the gulf that separated Zwingli from this group, which meanwhile had developed such tenets of Anabaptism as freedom of conscience, adult baptism, free will, and opposition to church taxes. In 1525 at Lake Zürich, Grebel performed the earliest known adult baptism, and the practice spread. With the Peasants' War resounding on the borders of Switzerland, the Zürich town council, fearful of the growing radicalism within its own domain, in 1526 made punishable by drowning not only adherence to Anabaptism but even attendance at Anabaptist meetings. In January 1527, Manz was so executed.

Confirmed now in the belief that Anabaptism was synonymous with rebellion, Luther stiffened his attitude, and Lutherans and Catholics concurred, as we have seen, at the Diet of Spires in 1529 in condemning Anabaptists. In an exegesis of the Eighty-second Psalm written in 1530, Luther distinguished two types of heretics, and with pointed reference to Anabaptist teachings said: 'There are . . . heretics who hold that one should tolerate no authority; . . . that one should own no possessions, but run away from wife and child, leave house and home, or should hold and keep all things common. Such are not only heretics but rebels, and therefore without doubt should be punished.'[33] A year later, the 'gentle' Melanchthon in a memorandum to the elector of Saxony demanded the death penalty for Anabaptists as rebels against the state church, and Luther added: '*Placet mihi Luthero.*'[34] In a letter written to the town council of Münster in 1532, he warned against leniency toward Anabaptists, 'who are always bent on rebellion, mix in political affairs, and arrogantly desire to rule'.[35]

Meanwhile Anabaptist influence had spread into the south German cities, traditionally in close association with the Swiss cantons. The prosperous commercial and industrial city of Nuremberg became a centre of Anabaptism, and several other communities soon contained more Anabaptists than Lutherans and Zwinglians combined. The Anabaptists found a particularly ripe soil in Moravia, where they established one of their earliest communities, but in 1526 Ferdinand of Austria, an ardent Catholic, became king of Bohemia and shortly ended toleration of them. The Moravian Anabaptists, ever victims of persecution, moved through Bohemia and into more tolerant Poland. By 1532, the most capable leaders of the Swiss-German Anabaptists, the men whose restraint had guided their followers and whose high standards of morality had gained for their sect a measure of respect, were dead, often at the hands of executioners.

A faction had long existed that did not accept the absolute pacifism first associated with Anabaptism. These men emphasized the mystical aspects of Anabaptist theology, its chiliastic ideas, and its correlation of religious with social reform. Hans Hut by his militant preaching of pacifism had split the Anabaptist community in Moravia even before Ferdinand's decrees dispersed it. Hut himself soon went to a horrible doom in Augsburg, but under stress of persecution the fanatical element took firmer hold, recruiting its largest following among the common people. Most of its leaders, themselves from the common class, were without formal education. Inspired chiefly by their understanding of the Bible, they derived their authority from the Anabaptist doctrine of divine revelation. Among them arose powerful preachers whose essentially nonrational appeals and prophesies kept their followers in constant agitation. Typical, and perhaps most prominent, was Melchior Hoffmann, a furrier from Swabia. Having first espoused Lutheran, then Zwinglian ideas, he was converted to Anabaptism in 1529 and became one of its most successful itinerant preachers. After wandering and preaching through northern Germany and East Friesland, he arrived in Holland in 1530, where soon a number of Anabaptist communities emerged.

Persecution now spread into Holland. The Anabaptist communities were dissolved, and their leaders were executed. Persecution, however, only raised chiliastic hopes, since according to Scripture persecution of the True Church would precede the second coming of Christ. Hoffman, self-styled prophet, predicted that the millennium would come in 1533 and that Strasbourg was to be the new Jerusalem. In 1533 he confidently entered that city, was promptly arrested, and after ten years of indignities and torture died in prison. His imprisonment having been part of his own prophesies, the expectations of his followers continued to run high. His disciple Jan Matthijszoon, a baker from Haarlem with a somewhat questionable past, became the new prophet of Anabaptism.

The role for which Hoffman had selected Strasbourg eventually went to the city of Münster in Westphalia. Largely Lutheran, Münster was in the midst of a struggle with its spiritual and feudal overlord, the Catholic bishop. That this struggle was not a purely religious one is evident from the citizens' demand during disturbances in 1525 that the clergy should refrain from trade and should surrender the tools they used in industry. Bernhard Rothmann, a teacher and preacher of wide renown, and Bernard Knipperdollinck, a wealthy cloth merchant, led the opposition to the bishop. They found strong Lutheran support, especially among the guilds. A compromise, forced upon the bishop in 1533 by the threat of open warfare, divided the city and its churches among Catholics and Lutherans, granting toleration to both. Rothmann and Knipperdollinck soon embraced Anabaptist doctrines, and Rothmann in increasingly popular sermons emphasizing the social teachings of the creed won a large number of followers. Münster was now split into three factions—the Catholics, composed mostly of the old clergy and the aristocratic element of the town; the Lutherans, strongly entrenched among the guilds; and the Anabaptists, backed mostly by the common people.

Matthijszoon, having proclaimed Münster the New Jerusalem, commanded all members of the True Church to congregate there to witness the coming of Christ. At the same time he preached abandonment of pacifism, declaring that the Anabaptists were destined to prepare the Kingdom of God by the sword. From the neighbouring towns and from Holland, Anabaptists converged upon Münster, among them one of Matthijszoon's chief disciples, Jan Beukelszoon, an adventurous but eloquent and courageous tailor, sometimes known as John of Leiden. In February 1534, after a bloodless demonstration of armed might, the Anabaptists gained control of Münster, forcing their opponents into exile, and established a theocracy under the leadership of Matthijszoon. But his reign was short-lived. The soldiers of the bishop laid siege to the city, cutting it off from the outside world. Sallying forth on Easter Day with only a few men, like another Gideon, to route the enemies of Israel, Matthijszoon was hacked to pieces. John of Leiden became prophet and ruler of the beleaguered City of God.

The new leader attempted to re-establish primitive Christianity. Community of goods was required, by force if necessary; the guilds were abolished; workers were fed and clothed by the community; meals were eaten in common. Absolute obedience to the prophet was demanded, and Knipperdollinck as 'bearer of the sword' enforced discipline by terror. For over a year the city was able to stand off the combined financial and military forces of princes and Empire, even to inflict stinging defeats upon them.

At the height of his military successes, John had himself proclaimed king of Zion and thereafter affected a regal pomp that contrasted sharply with the austerity required of his people. Soon after, he introduced the most widely execrated measure of the Münster regime, polygamy. The tremendous excess of women over men in Münster (about three to one), added to the strain of continuous war, apparently made such a step appear desirable, especially because strict laws against adultery and prostitution remained in force. Moreover, in the Anabaptist view acceptance into the True Church dissolved all previous relationships, including marriage, in order that the Church might preserve its purity by complete isolation from non-members, and so remarriage did not necessarily mean to an Anabaptist that he was taking an additional spouse. Nevertheless, the introduction of polygamy was followed by an uprising intended to overthrow John and to restore private property. The uprising was ruthlessly suppressed.

In an attempt to win relief for his beleaguered forces, John sent twenty-seven 'apostles' through enemy lines to rouse the neighbouring cities. The apostles were all captured and executed, but not before northern Germany and Holland underwent a series of rebellions and demonstrations of sympathy, attesting the widespread social dislocations and the appeal of the Anabaptist movement to the common people. The tight ring that encircled Münster prevented any support from reaching it, and when it was clear that the city was doomed, John permitted all who desired to do so to leave. The end came, hastened by treachery, in June 1535. Retaliation followed. John and Knipperdollinck were among the captured and, after brutal and prolonged torture, were executed in 1536. Their bodies, locked in iron cages, were hoisted to the top of St Lambert's Church, where they remained until 1881. The bishop's soldiers restored Catholicism as the only authorized religion.

Through the efforts of Menno Simons[36] (d. 1561) in the Netherlands and elsewhere and of Jakob Huter (executed in 1536) in Moravia moderate Anabaptism survived, dissociated from revolutionary activity. These men insistently repudiated the Münster type of Anabaptism, remained loyal to the principles of pacifism and community of property, refused to take oaths, and, in order to maintain their version of the Christian life and discipline, banned marriage with dissenters. After decades of persecution under the Spanish régime in the Low Countries, the Mennonites (i.e. the followers of Menno Simons), who were especially numerous in the northern provinces, won tolerance when the Dutch Republic became an independent state and even shared in Holland's prosperity. Holland is still a centre of their faith. From there they spread into England. In the course of time, the constantly dwindling remnants of the Anabaptist sect were hounded out of Switzerland, Moravia, Poland, and elsewhere. At the end of the seventeenth century they began to migrate to North America, where, as Mennonite, Hutterite, and Amish communities, they still flourish.

SOME OTHER PROTESTANT CREEDS

Certain other minor creeds that still survive reflected the splintering tendency of the Reformation without vitally determining the course of the Reformation. The numbers of their adherents were relatively negligible, and the very individualism they preached prevented their maturing into well organized and disciplined churches. Their importance lies rather in the fact that, despite the persistence of dogmatism and intolerance in both new and old churches, they reveal the freedom with which daring individuals began to approach traditional doctrines and the everlasting question of salvation. A marked mysticism is characteristic of some of these fringe movements, spurned alike by Catholic and Protestant because of their opposition to institutionalized religion and their refusal to submit to either new or old dogma. While some mystics, like the Spaniard Juan de Valdes (c. 1500–41) in Naples and Guillaume Postel (1510–81) in France, despite their heretical ideas remained within the Catholic fold, others showed, at least in the beginning, a preference for Protestant affiliations.

Among the most mystical ideas of the time were those of two prominent German thinkers, Sebastian Franck (1499–1543) and Kaspar von Schwenkfeld (1490–1561). Franck, an ordained priest, shortly after Luther's break with the papacy became a Lutheran preacher. His rejection of slavish dependence upon the written word and his insistence upon the greater validity of the inner light soon brought him into conflict with Lutheran authorities. Franck believed in a subjective spiritual interpretation of the Bible, and piety was for him a personal matter whose direction could not be prescribed except by the inner spirit. God was so all-embracing, he thought, that the most diverse conceptions of the Deity were compatible with His existence. This position led him to advocate complete religious tolerance, even for infidels and pagans: 'Wherefore my heart is alien to none. I have my brothers among the Turks, Papists, Jews, and all peoples.'[37] Outlawed by Lutherans as well as Catholics, he had to gain his livelihood successively as soap boiler and printer while engaged in historical and theological writing.

Individualist that he was, Franck did not found a school; Kaspar von Schwenkfeld, a Silesian nobleman, did. Schwenkfeld had at first harboured Lutheran ideas, but his mysticism brought him into opposition to the new creed. During Lutheranism's brief career between revolt and establishment as a new orthodoxy, in Schwenkfeld's eyes it had lost its spirituality and had become too dependent upon Scripture. To him the word of God had two equally valid manifestations: the external Word and the internal Spirit. The internal Spirit was everlasting and removed from the outward symbolism of ritual and sacraments such as baptism or Lord's Supper; its important element was inner experience, not formal practice.

Schwenkfeld recruited a scattered following among Anabaptists to whom his opposition to baptism appealed, and among the pietist Bohemian congregations, to whom his mysticism appealed. Forced to leave Silesia, he wandered to Strasbourg and, driven from there, to Ulm, where he died, outlawed and in hiding. His followers, now known as Schwenkfelders, broke entirely with the Lutheran Church. Persecution by all sects thinned them out and dispersed them into Silesia and elsewhere. They retained their identity, however, despite close association with the mystic Jacob Boehme in the seventeenth century and despite a special effort by the Jesuits to convert them in the eighteenth. The majority of them eventually found refuge with Count von Zinzendorf (see below), whose Moravian Brotherhood some of them joined. A very small group found their way to America, where they still preserve their identity as one of the religious sects among the Pennsylvania Dutch. Schwenkfeld's mysticism, reinforced by the ideas of Boehme, contributed to the development of the Pietist movement (see below).

Perhaps a greater danger to the established Christian churches than that derived from Franck's and Schwenkfeld's views was early reflected in the writings of Servetus. Servetus, an advocate of adult baptism, had still more daring views upon a dogma which is cardinal in Christian theology, Catholic as well as reformed, although subject to debate throughout the ages. It is the dogma that makes the Father, the Son, and the Holy Ghost a trinity and a unity at the same time. It requires faith in the pre-existence of Jesus as the

Son of God before becoming a mortal and, therefore, in his eternal divinity. As Servetus, a physician and humanist of acknowledged reputation, read Scripture, he could find no justification for belief in the Trinity. His studies led him, on the contrary, to a kind of unitarianism that identified Jesus with God. The mysticism of this position was underlined by Servetus' belief that man could conquer mortality by his union in faith with the divine. Few heretics were ever hunted with greater persistence than was Servetus by Calvin. Calvin had a hand in the denunciation of Servetus to the Inquisition at Lyons; and when Servetus, escaping from prison in France, passed through Geneva, Calvin had him arrested and tried (1553). Even after Servetus was burned at the stake (though Calvin had favoured decapitation), the discussion of his principles continued and led to their further elaboration and currency.

An unmystical Anti-Trinitarianism, emphasizing the human character of Jesus and the concomitant dignity of man, was especially strong in the countries east of the Holy Roman Empire. In Poland, Transylvania, and Hungary, the feudal nobility was still powerful, and the defence of the frontier against Turkish advance continued hazardous. Feudalism and military hazards combined to give political influence to the local lords and princes, while king and middle class remained weak and the peasantry powerless. The feudal nobility often were of a faith different from the king's. The resulting political and religious decentralization contrasted sharply with the dynastic centralization that had developed in western Europe and the larger principalities of Germany. As a consequence, radical sects—Anabaptists, for example—were sometimes able to win a local lord's favour and to find at least temporary asylum in these eastern lands.

Among the diverse peoples of the kingdom of Poland religious unity scarcely existed. While the Poles of the west were Roman Catholic, the White Russians and Ukranians of the east were Orthodox. The Reformation at first made striking gains, particularly with the conversion to Lutheranism (1525) of Albrecht of Brandenburg, grand master of the Teutonic Order. On the advice of Luther, Albrecht transformed the order's huge Prussian domain into a hereditary dukedom, which he accepted as a fief from the king of Poland. As we shall soon see, an exceptional degree of toleration of religious differences was to this stage permitted in Poland and the neighbouring principality of Transylvania. It led to an influx of Anabaptists, who added to Poland's religious disunity. And a reform movement in the form of Anti-Trinitarianism also burgeoned in both Poland and Transylvania.

The Anti-Trinitarians quickly split into two factions, one of the leaders of the more moderate splinter being Georgio Biandrata, Italian physician at the courts of Poland and Transylvania. He called upon Fausto Sozzini or (as he is more commonly called) Socinus to help him counteract the extremists. Scion of an Italian patrician family in which the practice of canon law and jurisprudence was a long tradition, Socinus had become interested in the problem of the Trinity through the controversy over Servetus. While denying Jesus' prior existence as the son of God, Socinus retained the practice of invoking—but not worshipping—him. The extreme wing of Anti-Trinitarians denied any divinity at all to Jesus and refused to worship him in any way. Their radicalism was enhanced by the support of many among Poland's and Transylvania's numerous Anabaptists.

Socinus first went to Transylvania (in 1578) and reached Poland in 1579. He was able to win a considerable following even among the extremists in both countries and succeeded in establishing at least the semblance of an ecclesiastic organization, sometimes referred to as the Socinians and sometimes as the Minor Church. Its precepts were laid down after his death in the so-called Racovian Catechism of 1605, drawn up at the communal settlement which the Anti-Trinitarians had created at Racow. Despite a distinct element of mysticism, the Socinian creed stood out for its rationalism. Although the Socinians considered Scripture, especially the New Testament, the authoritative record of divine revelation, they held that the truth of Scripture could be rightly understood only by the application of reason. While they thought God to be omnipotent and the embodiment of the supreme free will, they believed that man, too, possessed a free will, and they accepted neither original sin nor predestination. They held that religion could dispense with both rigid doctrine and sacraments, sharing the Anabaptist view that baptism was simply a rite marking initiation into the Christian community. Possibly Anabaptist influences played a part in the Socinians' appeal for a revival of primitive Christianity and in some of their social tenets; they denounced war and considered it wrongful for a Christian to hold office in a secular government.

Anti-Trinitarianism was especially vigorous in Transylvania, where the Calvinistic bishop Francis David of Transylvania preached the extremist doctrine that conceded neither divinity nor adoration to Jesus. He had made the capital, Kolozvár (Klausenburg, Cluj), the seat of a numerous Anti-Trinitarian sect. Although David, denounced by Biandrata, ended his days in prison (1579), his followers struggled on and even grew in numbers. The name 'Unitarian', apparently first applied to them in debate, came to be used officially and eventually proved acceptable to them.

In Poland and Transylvania the strength and conviction of the Protestant minority, the apprehension of Catholic nobles over the Catholic clergy's power, the weakness of the kings, the tolerant humanist proclivities and the diversity of religions among the nobility, and the need for a united front against the Turks led the diets at first to concede freedom of conscience to Catholics, Lutherans, Calvinists, Hussites, and Socinians alike. In 1572–73 Poland found itself in the midst of an interregnum, and a repetition of the recent French Massacre of St Bartholomew (see below) was to be feared because of the persistent intensity of religious rivalries and the momentary lack of royal authority. Despite some opposition, the nobility drew up a

Confederation of Warsaw (1573) confirming the spirit of religious freedom, and for a long time the succeeding kings upheld it. And so until 1658 the Polish Socinian centres remained, so to speak, the capitals of Europe's Anti-Trinitarians.[38]

Then a series of domestic crises and foreign wars wrought a change in the Polish atmosphere. Perhaps the most critical of these untoward events was the uprising of the Cossacks under their hetman Bogdan Chmielnicki (d. 1657). With the Tatars as allies they fought the Poles in a war (1648–54) that began as a struggle for an independent Orthodox Ukrainia. But soon Tsar Alexis of Russia stepped in as protector of the Orthodox faith, and then King Charles X of Sweden as claimant of Poland's coastal regions. The result was a ruinous Thirteen Years' War (1654–67), which ended with a set of treaties that foreshadowed the eventual partition of Poland among its neighbours.

During this war Orthodox Cossacks massacred Jews, Catholics, and others fairly indiscriminately, and the religious policy of Poland's government changed from toleration to persecution of those who differed from it in creed. Along with other Protestant refugees, the Polish Unitarians fled. They went to western Europe, especially Holland and England, where local Unitarian movements were already under way, and Unitarianism practically vanished from Poland. It persisted, however, though not without difficulty, in Transylvania as one of the four officially tolerated creeds, and today's Unitarians of Rumania are its offspring. An offshoot of the Unitarians known as the Sabbatarians because they celebrated Saturday as the Sabbath and borrowed or were accused of borrowing other Jewish tenets were not formally tolerated at any time, but they managed to survive until the middle of the nineteenth century.

PROTESTANT EXPANSION AND CATHOLIC RESISTANCE 1521–98

The Holy Roman Empire provided an outstanding example of a state where particularism impeded the achievement of national unity and hence of a national church, and the religious reform movement in the Empire was from the beginning partly dependent upon this particularist attitude. The Protestant cause as a whole was able to hold and gain ground mainly because several important cities and powerful princes, especially in northern Germany, were won over. Under the influence of Melanchthon, Philip of Hesse was converted to Lutheranism in 1524, and other Lutheran preachers brought over Margrave Casimir of Brandenburg and Duke Ernest of Lüneburg. The exiled Duke Ulrich of Württemberg, who had much to gain from any embarrassment of the imperial authority, likewise declared his allegiance to the new faith. The spread of Protestantism was, in fact, limited to those territories where powerful converts could resist papal and imperial pressures. In southern Germany and the Rhineland, principal seat of the ecclesiastical electors, the spread of Protestantism met the determined opposition of

Catholic princes. The ardent Catholicism of Charles V, and the equally ardent, although more politic, Catholicism of his brother, Archduke Ferdinand, succeeded in keeping Lutheran ideas from conquering the Habsburg possessions, and persecutions of Lutherans began there early. *Cuius regio eius religio*, the compromise eventually adopted to halt religious strife in the Empire, was applied in practice long before it became an official formula.

The Protestant footing in Germany was further consolidated by a circumstance already mentioned: in the very year of Luther's condemnation at the Diet of Worms (1521) Charles V engaged in his first war (1521–26) with Francis I of France. The Reichsregiment was reconstituted in the hope of carrying on the affairs of Germany efficiently during the emperor's absence, but this effort to bring national unity to the Empire was hampered by the princes' determination to preserve their traditional privileges. Thus two divergent factors, the national consciousness fanned by Luther's appeals and the self-interest of the German princes, joined to build resistance to papal as well as imperial demands for enforcement of the Edict of Worms. Nearly unanimously the German estates demanded reform of the church, though not necessarily Luther's Reformation. At the Diet of Nuremberg in 1522, enforcement of the Edict of Worms was delayed. In fact, a resolution was adopted—and in the emperor's absence issued as an imperial edict—demanding convocation of a council to meet on German soil.

Earnestly concerned about some of the shortcomings of the church, Pope Adrian VI preferred to seek the support of the Catholic princes of the Empire. Some of the most important among them were persuaded to meet at Ratisbon in 1524. There they considered plans for resisting Lutheranism, discussed serious measures of reform, and concluded the first anti-Protestant alliance. Led by Archduke Ferdinand and the Duke of Bavaria, it was supported by a number of south German bishops. The alliance was instrumental in suppressing the Peasant Revolt, which broke out mostly in Catholic principalities, although the Lutherans were blamed for it. During the violent reprisals that followed, known or suspected Protestants frequently were punished along with rebellious peasants. Nevertheless, by 1525 Protestantism commanded a minority strong enough to prevent drastic legislative action by its enemies in the imperial Diet.[39]

The coalition formed at Ratisbon was counterbalanced by one formed at Torgau in 1524 among the principal Protestant princes. As we have seen, at the Diet of Spires the Protestant coalition won the Recess of 1526, but at the Second Diet of Spires in 1529, when Charles felt strong enough not to compromise with the Lutheran faction, the Catholic majority voted to rescind the Recess of 1526 and required strict enforcement of the Edict of Worms. Eight years had elapsed, however, since the Edict first was issued, and Lutheranism had meanwhile grown strong. When the reformers issued the joint protest that gave them the name of 'Protestants', the emperor simply could not disregard it. Much though his power and prestige had increased with his victory over the alliance of his French and Italian enemies in the League of Cognac, he had to move cautiously. He had no assurance of the continued submissiveness of either the pope or the French king, and the threat of the Turks was ever present. A Turkish siege of Vienna in 1529 was broken only by the concerted effort of all German estates, Lutheran as well as Catholic. Charles could ill afford the antagonize to German estates, and Archduke Ferdinand, heavily engaged in his struggle for Hungary, felt constrained to a conciliatory course.

In 1530 the emperor was able to be present at a diet for the first time since 1521. It met, with unparalleled pomp, at Augsburg. The Catholic party, emboldened by the presence of the victorious emperor and a papal legate, at first seemed ready to consider the use of armed force in suppressing the Lutheran heresy. Despite the failure of the Marburg Colloquy in 1529 to achieve the unity of Lutheranism and Zwinglianism, Protestant resistance was also determined. A formal defence of the Lutheran position was introduced at the Diet—the so-called 'Augsburg Confession', which has since become the norm of Lutheran doctrine. It was based upon seventeen points—the so-called Schwabach Articles—which, after Marburg, Luther had drawn up, firmly distinguishing the more radical Zwinglianism from his own creed. Under Melanchthon's influence, the Augsburg Confession became an effort to draw close to Catholicism, thus completely isolating Zwinglianism in the struggle between Catholicism and Lutheranism. The Lutherans at the same time declared their determination to abide by the Recess of 1526 until the religious controversy should be resolved by a general council.[40]

Despite Charles's hardly veiled intention to resort to arms in order to enforce obedience, he was not yet in a position to jeopardize the internal peace of the Empire. He could not feel sure of the support of all the Catholic princes, some of whom indeed supported the Recess of 1526. Moreover, he was concerned with securing support for the election of his brother Ferdinand as king of the Romans and thus successor to the imperial crown. He therefore had to compromise and so issued the Recess of Augsburg, which betrayed his dilemma. Under threat of severe penalties it demanded immediate enforcement of the Edict of Worms but at the same time moved from the use of force in the direction of judicial action. The highest tribunal of the Empire, the Reichskammergericht, was reconstituted and empowered to hear suits for the recovery of church property secularized in the Protestant principalities. Simultaneously Charles pressed Pope Clement VII for convocation of a general council. So strong had the emperor's ascendancy become that Clement, though reluctant, agreed, and Charles promised a council within a year.[41]

In December 1530, the Protestant princes and cities met at Schmalkalden to discuss measures of joint defence on the principle that legal action against one of them in the Reichskammergericht should be considered action against all. The more aggressive Protestant princes at Schmalkalden proposed an armed defensive league and, early in 1531, under the leadership of Philip of Hesse formed the Schmalkaldic League. Meanwhile the threat of court condemnations had led Bucer to promote a rapprochement between Zwinglians and Lutherans, which met with sympathy even from Luther. A number of Zwinglian communities in southern Germany were ready to join the proposed league, but the Swiss cities now refused to make common cause with the Lutherans. Zwingli's death in the second Battle of Kappel (1531) halted the advance of Zwinglianism in Switzerland and gave to the Lutheran forces undisputed leadership of the Reformation in Germany.

Just as the time began to seem favourable for a full settlement in Germany, Clement VII's fear of a general council and the emperor's preparations for another Turkish threat once more brought delay. At Nuremberg in 1532 a religious peace was concluded suppressing all suits against the Protestants before the Reichskammergericht and guaranteeing a truce until a new diet or a church council might make other arrangement. In 1534 came the first armed effort of the Protestant princes, and it was victorious; led by Philip of Hesse, they forcefully restored Duke Ulrich of Württemberg to his ancestral throne. At almost the same time the Lutherans ceased temporarily to be the major threat to the Empire with the outbreaks of Anabaptists revolts in Münster and other German cities, in the suppression of which Protestant and Catholics joined forces. For the next twelve years, the military and political involvements of the emperor vouchsafed a religious truce throughout the Empire.[42]

Meanwhile the Protestant cause in Germany steadily grew stronger. In 1539, Joachim II, elector of Brandenburg, openly adopted Lutheranism. Albertine Saxony likewise was converted under Duke Henry in 1540. In 1542, the reckless Duke Henry of Brunswick lost his territories, the last stronghold of Catholicism in northern Germany, by provoking a war with the Schmalkaldic League. A number of cities and minor princes, encouraged by the early successes of the league, also espoused the Protestant cause. Thus practically all of northern Germany formed a Lutheran bloc, backed by the growing strength of the solidly Lutheran Scandinavian countries (see below). Finally, twenty-six years after the Edict of Worms had called for the repression of Luther and Lutheranism, the religious controversy erupted into open war. The Schmalkaldic War of 1546–47 ended in an easy victory for the emperor, but it was now too late to root out the heresy. In parts of Germany a whole generation had grown up that knew only Lutheranism.

*   ★   ★

The Spread of Lutheranism to Scandinavia

In Scandinavian Europe, as in England, the Reformation was achieved by the political action of the ambitious monarchs. Ever since the Union of Kalmar (1397) the Scandinavian countries had been ruled in personal union by the Danish kings, who also ruled Schleswig and Holstein as principalities in the Holy Roman Empire. This union had always been disturbed by sporadic unrest in Schleswig-Holstein (united in 1386) and Sweden, and unrest grew upon the accession (1513) of Christian II, who tried to make himself an absolute ruler.

Christian's policy required that he break the power of the nobles, allying himself with the merchant class and peasants. An important step in that direction was the *Landelove*, the Danish code of 1521. Among other things the code laid the framework of a national church independent of Rome, and since clerical abuses were all too rife, this objective received popular support. The code placed ecclesiastical affairs under the jurisdiction of secular judges, prohibited the clergy from owning property, required residence of priests in their parishes, and established certain criteria for their education. It also curtailed the prerogatives of the nobility and limited serfdom. Furthermore, Christian regulated trade in such a manner as to favour domestic merchants over both domestic landlords and the Hanseatic League, which hitherto had held a near monopoly of trade in the Baltic regions.

Since he was careful to avoid antagonizing his brother-in-law Emperor Charles V, Christian kept his clerical reform within the framework of correct Catholic doctrine. Nevertheless, his ruthlessness antagonized the Catholic clergy no less than others. In Sweden he encountered open hostility, which he squelched by force in 1520, and after being crowned king of Sweden, he had the most important secular and ecclesiastic princes executed in flagrant violation of an amnesty he had granted. This 'Stockholm Blood Bath' provoked new unrest in Sweden at the very time that the king's reform measures were increasing upper-class antagonism against him in his native Denmark. In 1523, he was deposed by the rebellious clergy and nobility of his entire realm, and his uncle, Frederick of Schleswig-Holstein, was proclaimed in his place. Rapidly spreading revolt and a war with Lübeck, retaliating as leader of the Hanseatic League for his discriminatory trade regulations, forced Christian and his family to flee.

Although the new king of Denmark, Frederick I, had promised loyalty to the traditional church, he was personally inclined toward Lutheranism. Some of the Danish nobility, because they either shared his principles or coveted ecclesiastic properties, also favoured religious reform. Pope Leo X played into their hands by proposing to appoint an Italian to the important archbishropic of Lund. The general outcry against this foreign interference enabled Frederick to proceed with reform. Supported by the nobility at the Diet of Odense (1527), he forced the clergy to accept an ordinance that brought the Danish church completely under the authority of the crown. The ordinance contained a provision unusual for that age: Lutherans as well as Catholics were granted freedom of conscience, and the king was proclaimed protector of both denominations. Toward the end of his reign Frederick was able to restore peace to his uneasy realm.

Civil war broke out again upon Frederick's death (1533). The Danish

Catholic peasants and towns, supported by Lübeck, which was trying to establish a union of Baltic cities, united in an effort to restore the refugee Christian II. The nobility and the Lutherans, in alliance with the now independent king of Sweden (see below), supported Frederick's son, also named Christian. The victory of the Lutheran nobles in this so-called 'Counts' Feud' doomed Catholicism in Denmark. Frederick's son ascended the throne as Christian III (1534–58), a Danish national church was established, and shortly thereafter the Augsburg Confession was adopted as the official creed of the Danish kingdom.

In Norway and Iceland, popular sentiment was distinctly on the side of the Catholic Church, and the crown found significant support only in the towns, where Lutheranism had been introduced through foreign, mostly Hanseatic, traders. During the Counts' Feud Norway, led by Archbishop Olaf Engelbrektssön, rose in revolt against Denmark, recognizing a German Catholic claimant as the legitimate heir to the Norwegian throne. Christian III thereupon issued a proclamation (1536) depriving bishops of their power in the government and forfeiting their possessions. When no help came from Germany, the archbishop fled, and the remaining Norwegian bishops were unable effectively to resist the victorious Danish monarch with his Lutheran Church. Yet remnants of the old faith long persisted in Norway, since the scarcity of Lutheran pastors greatly delayed the spread of the new faith among the common people. In Iceland, too, years of revolt, led by the bishops of the island, followed upon the effort to establish the Reformation by royal decree. Only in 1554 did revolt end and the royal will prevail.[43]

Meanwhile, the turmoil had enabled Sweden to break completely away from the Union of Kalmar. Indignation over the 'Stockholm Blood Bath' brought on an uprising which soon turned into a war for national independence. It was led by Gustavus Vasa, a young nobleman who himself had spent some time in prison as a victim of Christian II's perfidy. Supported by Swedish peasants and Lübeck's naval forces, Gustavus emerged victorious and upon the deposition of Christian II in 1523 was crowned king of Sweden. The advent of the Reformation was closely linked to these political developments. Gustavus Trolle, archbishop of Uppsala, was widely discredited as the instigator of the Stockholm massacre. When he and the other Scandinavian Catholics abetted Christian II's attempt to regain the triple crown, the cathedral chapters voted Trolle's removal from office. Pope Clement VII not only refused to sanction this removal but, repeating Leo X's blunder in Denmark, also attempted to appoint an Italian to the see of Skara.

The consequent resentment gave Gustavus the opportunity to introduce reform in the guise of national resistance to the pressure from Rome. Secretly an adherent of Lutheranism, Gustavus took into his service Olaus Petri, a minister who had studied at Wittenberg, and Lars Andersson (Laurentius Andreas), archdeacon of Uppsala Cathedral and an ardent reformer, who became the royal secretary. Through Petri's translation of the New Testament and other theological writings, Lutheranism began to spread among the Swedish people.

Matters came to a head when it became clear that the king's financial needs could well be met by the confiscation of church properties. In the struggle for independence, most of the old nobility had perished, and the free peasantry stubbornly refused to pay the taxes needed to bring order to the exchequer. At the Diet of Västerås in 1527, by a threat to abdicate Gustavus was able to push through his demand for sequestration of church property. The resulting Recess of Vasterås gave to the crown all ecclesiastical property that in the king's judgment the church did not need, and restored to their original owners all taxable and some tax-exempt properties previously granted to the church. Subsequently the Västerås Ordinances completed the subordination of the clergy to the king by giving him, among other controls, the power to appoint and dismiss bishops. Gustavus made no attempt to decide matters of dogma by official action, but under the influence of the king and devoted preachers Lutheranism spread throughout the land. The Augsburg Confession, however, was accepted as the official creed of the Swedish Church only in 1593. Finland, as a possession of the Swedish crown, was also subject to the royal religious policies.

★   ★   ★

From the Augsburg Confession to the Heidelberg Catechism

The spread of Lutheranism in northern Europe was not matched by a similar expansion of the Reformed Church in the south. After Melanchthon in the Augsburg Confession had emphasized the differences between the Lutheran and Zwinglian creeds, Zwingli addressed to the emperor (July 1530) a personal profession of faith in which he, too, sharply drew the line between them. Thereupon, four German cities, Strasbourg, Constance, Memmingen, and Lindau, also dissociated themselves from the Augsburg Confession by presenting to the emperor their own joint confession, the so-called *Confessio Tetrapolitana*. Though essentially Zwinglian in character, its wording betrayed the hope of its chief author, Bucer, to bring about some measure of agreement between the two leading reform parties. Political exigencies made such a rapprochement seem desirable, and for a while it looked feasible. Luther agreed to receive Bucer at Coburg in September 1530, and Bucer's Strasbourg joined the Schmalkaldic League in December. But the Zwinglian position stiffened even as the Lutherans became less adamant. In the end the Swiss cities refused to join the Schmalkaldic League, and Berne rejected the Tetrapolitana. Reconciliation of Lutherans and Zwinglians thereafter became still more difficult.

About the same time the victory of the Forest Cantons in the Battle of Kappel brought about a considerable degree of religious tolerance in Switzerland. Despite his goal of a democratic reformed commonwealth, Zwingli had been willing to use force to secure the victory of the Reformation throughout

Switzerland. In Zürich and other Reformed cantons Catholicism was suppressed and Catholic dissenters were persecuted. Zwingli had provoked the second war with the Forest Cantons largely by his attempt to force them into submission by an economic blockade. His defeat and death marked the end of such forcible methods, and the Second Peace of Kappel secured freedom of worship for Catholics in the Reformed cantons. Eventually Catholicism was restored in the canton of Glarus, and through the efforts of Cardinal Carlo Borromeo (1538–84), who founded a Swiss College at Milan, Jesuits and (later) Capuchins gained influence in Catholic Switzerland, especially Lucerne. In 1586, Lucerne joined the six other Catholic cantons in a defensive alliance, the so-called Borromean (or Golden) League. The check of militant Protestantism was thus assured in Switzerland, but without destroying the traditional freedom of the Swiss cantons. Decisions concerning religious as well as political affairs remained subject to a majority in each canton, making Switzerland one of the first countries where a degree of religious diversity was sanctioned. The practice became the law of the land as the result of a series of *Landfrieden* (national peace treaties) from 1529 to 1712.

Under the leadership of Zwingli's successor, Heinrich Bullinger (1504–75), the Reformed Church, though not permitted to expand, was able at least to consolidate its position. Steps to mediate the difference between Zwinglianism and Lutheranism meanwhile continued. Bucer, generally recognized as a mediator, took an active part in these efforts. In 1536 some Swiss theologians formulated at Basel the First Helvetic Confession, which attempted to bridge the gulf between the two creeds. Later that year in the Wittenberg Concord a gathering of evangelical divines made an attempt to compromise on the doctrine of the Eucharist. Although the German cities of Strasbourg, Ulm, Constance, and Augsburg were ready to accept the compromise, Luther still hesitated. A second conference at Basel rejected the Wittenberg Concord, and Zürich took a similar step in 1538.

In an effort to strengthen Swiss Protestantism, Bullinger now turned to Calvinist Geneva. The Zwinglian view of the Eucharist, which saw in the sacrament merely a symbolic act, was abandoned in favour of the Calvinist doctrine, which held to the spiritual presence of Christ. In 1549, Bullinger and Calvin concluded an agreement at Zürich, the so-called *Consensus Tigurinus*, in which the Calvinist view was formally adopted. It became the basis of the Second Helvetic Confession (1566). The unity of Swiss Protestantism became complete eighty years later, when Basel finally adhered to it. The boundary between the Lutheran and the Reformed Church in the Alps region thus came to coincide with the political boundary between the Empire and the Swiss Confederation, while at the same time Protestantism and Catholicism within Switzerland were stabilized between urban and rural sections respectively.

The void left among the Protestant masses by Luther's alliance with the

K*

ruling powers was generally filled by the more democratic Calvin, who became the outstanding theologian of European Protestantism and gave to the Reformation its world-wide significance. After Luther's death, Calvin's Geneva became the undisputed centre of the Reformation to a degree never true of Luther's Wittenberg. The academy Calvin founded became the centre of Reformed learning, a magnet drawing from all over Europe reformers who desired to study with Calvin or its other famed teachers. Geneva became also the base of Protestant missionary activities, which, directed by Calvin, spread throughout Europe and beyond.

Even during Luther's lifetime a personal friendship had developed between Melanchthon and the Geneva reformer, confirming the Wittenberg humanist in his growing sympathy with Calvinist views. After Luther's death Melanchthon permitted his followers for a time to become 'adiaphorists'—i.e. uncommitted on those things which, though condemned by Luther, the Bible seemed neither to condemn nor to approve. One of Melanchthon's disciples, Zacharias Ursinus, was instrumental in making a most significant concession to Calvinist influence. Under the auspices of Frederick III, Calvinist elector of the Palatinate, he participated, after Melanchthon's death, in the formulation of the so-called 'Heidelberg Catechism' (1563). This catechism found wide acceptance as the definitive statement of the reformed creed. Though opposed by dyed-in-the-wool Lutherans, it was adopted by either the governments or a fair share of the population (or both) not only in other parts of Protestant Germany (Hesse, Anhalt, Nassau, Bremen, Branden-burg, and elsewhere) but also in the Netherlands, Poland, Hungary, and Transylvania.

*   *   *

The French Wars of Religion

In France the first phase of the reform movement was represented chiefly by a group of humanist reformers that gathered around the learned bishop of Meaux, Guillaume Briçonnet. Their intellectual leader was a famed humanist and translator of the New Testament, Lefèvre d'Étaples. For a while this group enjoyed protection in high quarters—the king's sister, the future Marguerite of Navarre, and even Francis I himself. But Francis, though a humanist, was not a reformer. The Concordat of Bologna in 1516 had more or less satisfactorily resolved the ancient dispute between kings and popes regarding the primacy of authority over the French church, giving the French kings significant control over episcopal appointments. The king, therefore, not only had no fundamental conflict with the established church but had, in fact, a vested interest in its preservation, while the upper clergy, dependent upon the crown for appointment and benefices, was a staunch ally of the monarchy. The established order was at first supported also by the nobility and the wealthy bourgeoisie. The Meaux group was forced to disperse in 1525.

Francis I's policy toward the reformers vacillated between suppression and leniency, according to the exigencies of his conflict with Charles V. Neither by conviction nor by policy was he ever interested in reform beyond the correction of certain clerical abuses. In his later years, in fact, he took increasingly violent measures against religious dissenters in reprisal for sporadic outbursts of Reformed fanaticism in Paris and other French towns. Under his son, Henry II (1547–59), persecution increased in violence, and *chambres ardentes* awaited the avowed heretic with the death penalty.

Reform persisted, however, among the small artisans and merchants in the towns and among the lower clergy, who, mostly of poor origin themselves, were familiar with the physical and religious needs of their flock. For them the French translation (1541) of Calvin's *Institutio* was a milestone. Calvin had never abandoned his attempts to carry the Reformation into his native country. His *Institutio* had been dedicated to Francis I; in subsequent pamphlets and letters he tried to guide the course of French reform. Geneva received money from France to finance Protestant missions, and several French preachers returned from Geneva devoted apostles of Calvinism, ready to accept martyrdom. The first Reformed church in Paris was founded in 1556, and in 1559 the first national synod was organized and drew up a strictly Calvinist confession of faith. Despite persecution, censorship, and book burnings, Protestant churches multiplied.

The movement remained essentially middle-class and became increasingly urban. Its strongholds were in the coastal towns of Normandy, which were in constant contact with England, in the region along the Loire River, in southwestern France, and along the Mediterranean coast, but the eastern regions, despite their closeness to Germany, proved relatively immune. Rouen, Dieppe, La Rochelle, Tours, Lyons, Montauban, and Nîmes were among the most important Calvinist centres. A significant segment of the wealthy bourgeoisie joined the smaller merchants and tradesmen, and so did a few among the military and administrative officers of the kingdom. This link with the grand nobility gave to the Huguenots (as the French Protestants came to be called) a strategic position out of all proportion to their numbers. It transformed a minority middle-class movement for religious reform into a powerful party, whose religious and political aspirations became inextricably interwoven. Bourgeois, fighting against the royal bureaucracy for administrative and economic reforms, and noblemen, fighting against royal encroachments upon their feudal privileges, united under the banner of religious reform in common enmity to the devoutly Catholic Guise family, which used its mounting power behind the ever weakening Valois throne to further its own dynastic ambitions.

On a provincial scale at first, then on a national scale, and eventually on an international scale, the Huguenots met armed resistance. A Catholic League was organized inside France, sanctioned by the pope and assisted by the king of Spain but dominated by the Guises. The League's power soon overshadowed that of the French king. The short-lived reigns of Henry II's three young and weak sons made the French throne the object of an intense struggle for mastery between France's two most powerful noble families— the Guises, who dreamed of restoring Catholicism to undisputed power in the kingdom, and the Bourbons, who had assumed leadership of the Protestant party. Since the Bourbons, as 'princes of the blood', might become the legitimate heirs to the throne if the Valois line were to die out, rivalry for succession became a salient motive in this religio-political duel. Eight religious wars, in reality forming one long and violent civil war interrupted by a series of armistices, ravaged France between 1562 and 1589.

Hoping to prevent the religious struggle from destroying France, the moderates formed a party known as the *Politiques*. Loyal Catholics, the *Politiques* yet preferred non-conformity in religion to civil anarchy. They therefore advocated religious toleration as a means of safeguarding the continued existence of the state. Their tolerant attitude was frustrated by the plotting of Catherine de Médicis, queen-mother and regent, and the Guises. Perhaps out of fear, perhaps out of cool calculation, they gave the signal for, may even have prepared, the Massacre of St Bartholomew's Day (1572), in which many Protestant leaders and thousands, by some estimates tens of thousands, of lesser Protestants were slaughtered all over France. While surviving Protestant leaders fled abroad, some Catholic rulers ordered *Te Deums*, and the pope had a medal struck to commemorate the destruction of the heretics.[44]

In the end, massacre only intensified fanaticism and increased the violence of the civil war. In its final phase, it became an open war of succession—'the War of the Three Henrys' (the Valois king, Henry III; the Catholic pretender, Henry of Guise; and the Bourbon heir-presumptive, Henry of Navarre). The Huguenots owed their military and political strength to effective organization. They formed a confederation held together by a written instrument of government that provided for the orderly and efficient conduct of governmental functions and for unity in the conduct of the war. Even before their ultimate victory, their organized power won them important religious and political concessions.

Upon the assassination of the other two Henrys, Henry of Navarre, having consented to become a Catholic, was crowned King Henry IV of France. He then made a daring bid for religious peace. His Edict of Nantes (1598) placed France among the first countries (along with Poland, Transylvania, and Switzerland) to establish some sort of religious toleration by law. It confirmed all the privileges previously granted Protestants, conferred upon them complete freedom of conscience and of private (though not public) worship, and accorded them full civil rights. The king provided money for Protestant schools and colleges, and, of gravest import for the future, the Huguenots were ceded control over numerous towns and castles, which they were permitted to fortify and garrison at royal expense. The most important among the fortified towns were Montauban and La Rochelle. The Huguenots thus became a quasi-independent power, a political and military stumbling-block on the calculated road to royal centralization.[45]

*   *   *

Calvinism in Scotland and England

In Scotland in the sixteenth century a unique combination of social, political, and religious factors led to one of the most significant triumphs that Calvinism achieved outside Geneva. Barely emerging from its clan society and still dominated by a feudal nobility, Scotland was torn by internal feuds and ravaged by repeated wars with England, whose kings coveted the Scottish crown. Fear of English aggression threw Scotland into alliance with France, involving the Scots in the intermittent duel between the French and the English rulers and making resistance to English purposes a main tenet of Scottish patriots. At the beginning of the Reformation, the Franco-Scot alliance was a leading factor in preserving Catholicism, despite some Protestant sentiment, as the essentially undisputed faith of the Scots. Still, the Scottish clergy, largely recruited from the powerful noble families, had become notoriously lax in behaviour and uneducated to the point of illiteracy. Desire for reform—at least within the Catholic Church—spread, especially among the common people and the slowly emerging merchant class.

Scotland became more closely tied to France (and therefore to the Catholic cause) when in 1538 its King James V married Mary of Guise, whose family was rapidly assuming leadership of political Catholicism in France. Upon the king's death, Mary, surrounded by French advisers, whose patronizing demeanour in Scotland was widely resented, became one of the regents for her six-day old daughter, Mary Stewart. The queen-regent's government, refusing her daughter's hand to the future King Edward VI of England, arranged instead a prospective marriage to the French dauphin. Before she was six Mary, queen of Scots, went to France (1548). She was to marry the dauphin ten years later, and in 1559, when he became King Francis II, the queen of Scotland was to become the queen of France as well but to remain such only a little over a year, for her husband died in 1560.

Meanwhile in many Scottish patriots' minds France had begun to supplant England as the major threat to Scottish independence. The queen-dowager, they thought, ruled the country, protected by unpopular French soldiers, as if it were a province of France at war with England. The Protestants grew in number, and in 1557 the Protestant nobles formed the self-styled 'Lords of the Congregation', a 'covenant' for mutual protection and advantage. In their minds Catholicism rather than Anglicanism became identified with the national enemy.

The leader of the Protestants in Scotland was John Knox (1505 ?–72). A Scottish Catholic cleric in his youth, he had become a Protestant and had been a chaplain at the court of Edward VI of England. When a Catholic reaction (1553–58) took place in England under Queen Mary Tudor ('Bloody Mary'), daughter of Henry VIII and his divorced wife, Catherine of Aragon, Knox went into exile. Eventually he reached Geneva, and there he developed into a zealous and fearless apostle of Calvinism. He became the chief adviser of the Lords of the Congregation both from exile and during a brief sojourn at home. Upon the accession (1558) of Elizabeth I, daughter of Henry VIII and Anne Boleyn, to the English throne, the Catholic reaction ceased in England, but some Catholics there and elsewhere, insisting that Elizabeth was illegitimate, recognized Henry VIII's grand-niece, Mary, queen of Scots and bride of the dauphin of France, as the true ruler of England.

Knox returned to Scotland in 1559. That year the Lords of the Congregation declared Mary of Guise deposed as queen-regent and asked Elizabeth to act as protector of their country against France. A year later, a series of laws established the Reformed Church in Scotland. The Scottish Parliament decreed that papal authority in Scotland had come to an end, that the statutes against heretics were illegal, and that celebration of the mass was punishable by death. A confession of faith drawn up by Knox was adopted as the law of the land. In 1561, the *First Book of Discipline*, prepared mostly by Knox and based upon Calvin's *Ordonnances*, prescribed the organization of the Scottish Church. Local churches—or kirks—were to be governed by presbyteries (or councils of ministers and elders), which were vested with the right to arbitrate matters of doctrine, to control education, and to ordain and induct ministers; final authority rested with the General Assembly of the Universal Kirk, in which all local presbyteries were represented. When first her mother and then her husband died (1560), Mary, still in her teens, returned to Scotland (1561). A widowed queen of France, a cultured French-woman of Catholic faith, a rallying symbol of the Catholic cause in England, she found herself the reigning monarch of a predominantly Protestant country.

Although Elizabeth greatly disliked Knox because of his *Against the Monstrous Regiment* [*i.e. rule*] *of Women*, she had little choice but to help the Scottish Protestants. Mary was widely suspected of aiming to restore Catholicism in Scotland and, eventually, in England, and though she was not herself actively engaged in such a purpose, she was supported by Catholic nobles at home and in England who were. The French, preoccupied with their own religious wars, failed to give Mary effective aid. Kidnappings, marriages, divorces, and murders now further poisoned the Scottish political atmosphere, with Mary as victim rather than perpetrator of most of the intrigues. A general uprising in 1567 forced her to abdicate and eventually to seek a forlorn refuge with her rival and cousin, Elizabeth. Twenty years more of plots and counterplots and finally Mary, accused of complicity in a plan to murder Elizabeth, was executed. With her died the hope of Catholic restoration in Scotland and England.

Calvinism also gained an important foothold in England. Calvin himself attempted to influence the English reform movement by correspondence with influential men. Upon her accession, to be sure, Elizabeth, largely for political reasons, confirmedre the Anglican compromise through the Act of Uniformity (1559). Nevertheless, many of the English reformers who returned from exile after her accession were active Calvinists, seeking a more radical break with Roman dogma and ritual, and Calvinism acquired a certain vogue. Agitation for a more thorough 'purification' of the Anglican Church gave rise to even more audacious 'Puritan' movements such as the Separatists and the Presbyterians (see below). Elizabeth decided, however, that political exigencies demanded caution in religious matters, and the Thirty-Nine Articles, adopted in 1563, confirmed the reestablishment of the Anglican compromise.

★   ★   ★

The Dutch War of Independence

In the Low Countries, the eventual triumph of Calvinism was linked with the drive of the Dutch Netherlands toward freedom from Spanish domination. Here the reform sentiment had beginnings independent of Lutheranism and Zwinglianism. Inspired by the humanist demand for a more spiritual religion, the doctrine of sacramentarianism, anticipating the Zwinglian interpretation of the Eucharist as entirely symbolic, spread among the Dutch, especially the wealthy bourgeoisie in the flourishing trade centres. For a time Anabaptism, too, gained a considerable following among the lower bourgeoisie and peasantry. The two trends reinforced the resistance to Lutheranism with its doctrines of the real presence in the Eucharist and of infant baptism.

Moreover, the Lutheran subordination of religion to the princely authority held little appeal for the Low Countries, fiercely jealous of their traditional privileges. They had small use for a church organization that might counterbalance their weight in the conduct of their own affairs through their old provincial states (or legislatures) and their more recently granted States General (representative of the provincial estates). Moreover, Emperor Charles V, who had inherited the Low Countries from his paternal side, considered them an entity separate from Spain, Austria, or the Holy Roman Empire. Having been born and brought up in the Netherlands, he had encouraged their national unity. Though he attempted to suppress religious dissent in the Low Countries through the establishment of the Inquisition there in 1522 and the publication of the so-called *Placards* against heresy, he did so in a manner consistent with the provinces' traditional privileges. His effort to suppress the Netherland Anabaptists was violent but did not provoke unrest on a large scale, since, as elsewhere, this sect was generally hated as extremist.

The relatively calm Dutch atmosphere changed after the abdication of Charles in 1555. His son, Philip II, received both the Spanish crown and the Low Countries as hereditary possessions. Philip's attempts to establish in the Low Countries the religious unity to which he was accustomed in Spain eventually alienated large sections of the Netherland nobility. His efforts to increase the number of bishropics and to turn the Inquisition into an instrument of state policy patterned after the dreaded Spanish model met with widespread opposition. The commercial classes were provoked by the new taxes and commercial restrictions imposed upon them in order to promote Spanish military and political ventures. Even among Catholics Philip's peremptory order to enforce the decrees of the Council of Trent (see below) was resented as an invasion of provincial privileges. Though Catholic, the local nobility, educated in the humanist tradition, were opposed to forcing conscience. Philip thus became identified not only with Spanish domination but also with intolerance.

Meanwhile Calvinism, introduced from England, France, Germany, and Geneva, had spread through the provinces, especially in the north. Unlike Lutheranism, Calvinism preached the absolute supremacy of 'the Word of God', even over the authority of the ruler. This doctrine appealed to the growing patriotic sentiment in the Netherlands, since it seemed to justify resistance to the ordained overlord on religious grounds. Opposition crystallized in the Compromise of Breda, concluded in 1566 and signed by over two thousand individuals, in which suspension of the Inquisition and of the *Placards* against heresy was demanded. From the epithet *Gueux* (beggars), supposedly applied to those who presented a petition to Philip's regent in the Netherlands, Margaret of Parma, the movement derived its name and emblems of solidarity (the beggar's wallet or bowl).

Among the signers of the Compromise were a number of Catholics. Violent outbursts of iconoclasm quickly alienated many of them, but the ruthless policy of repression applied by the Duke of Alba, Philip's lieutenant in the Netherlands, and the excesses of his Spanish troops rallied the Catholics once more to the support of the rebellious Protestants. In 1574, the Netherland Confession and the Heidelberg Catechism, both unmistakably Calvinist, were officially adopted in the largely urban province of Holland, though the other provinces left the religious question unsettled. Through an agreement known as the Pacification of Ghent (1576) mutual toleration, warmly advocated by William of Orange, leader of the *Gueux*, himself until recently a Catholic, was agreed upon in a common struggle against the Spanish invader. And the next year on William's instigation toleration was extended to the Dutch Anabaptists.

Toleration, however, proved hard to achieve in fact. Dissensions between the predominantly Protestant and Dutch north and the predominantly Catholic and Flemish or Walloon south were frequent and were skilfully exploited by the new regent of the Netherlands, the Duke of Parma. They led at last to the abandonment of the Pacification of Ghent. The Union of Arras, concluded in 1579, created a Catholic nucleus for the eventual reconquest of the southern Low Countries (modern Belgium) and was counterbalanced a few days later by the Union of Utrecht, creating a confederation of the seven largely Protestant provinces of the north. After a solemn abjuration of allegiance to King Philip in 1581, the Union of Utrecht became the United Provinces, whose independence, however, was formally confirmed only after decades of war by the Treaty of Westphalia in 1648 (see below). The creation of this independent, kingless confederation was a victory not only for Calvinism but also for republicanism. More prominently than in the winning of Swedish independence, the quest for religious freedom had rallied the builders of the new Dutch nation. The partial victory of Calvinism in the Dutch Republic had a special political significance besides; it prompted Johannes Althusius (1557–1638) and other Calvinists to seek to justify rebellion on more than religious grounds (see Chapter IX).

* * *

The Reformation in Eastern Europe

In eastern Europe, the Protestant reform movements were unable to develop the strength requisite for lasting victory. In both Poland and Hungary the ever-present tension *vis-à-vis* the Empire worked against the adoption of Lutheranism, which, suspect because of its German origin, appealed mainly to the urban population. Calvinism thus became more attractive to those who entertained a reformed opinion. In Poland, it spread among the nobility and for a while was supported in the Diets even by Catholic members of the *szlachta*, the Polish gentry, because they considered the hierarchy a threat to their political interests.

Among the important Polish reformers were the humanists Andrzej Frycz Modrzewski (see Chapter VIII) and Jan Laski. Laski during his travels in western Europe had come to know Erasmus, had embraced the ideas of Calvin, and had been a leader among the foreign refugees in England. Laski's attempts to unify Lutherans, Calvinists, and Bohemian Brethren in Poland into a national Reformed Church were frustrated by the intense rivalry among the reforming sects, especially the Anti-Trinitarians, and by the loyalty of the Polish kings and common people to the traditional faith.

In spite of occasional edicts directed against non-Catholics, Sigismund I and particularly Sigismund II generally granted them tolerance. The Catholic recovery of Poland was assured, however, when the childless Sigismund II accepted the decrees of the Council of Trent (1564) and gave up the idea of divorcing his third wife and when Cardinal Stanislaus Hosius, the leader of the Catholic reform movement, brought the first Jesuits to Poland (1565). In the brief interregnum that followed the death of Sigismund II, toleration, as narrated above, was formally guaranteed to most dissenters by the Religious Peace or Confederation of Warsaw in 1573. The Jesuits' subsequent success in restoring Poland to Catholicism was a striking example of their skill in combining political pressure with missionary zeal.

The Ruthenians (White Russians and Ukrainians) of the Polish-Lithuanian Commonwealth had been Orthodox Christians on the eve of the Reformation. But the frustrated Union of Florence (see Chapter III) was still remembered among them, and when many prominent Ruthenian families turned to Catholicism of the Latin rite or to Calvinism, the Orthodox hierarchy decided in favour of a regional reunion with Rome—one that would recognize papal primacy but would retain the Slavonic liturgy, the Eastern ritual, and the right of the clergy to marry. That union was proclaimed at the Vatican toward the end of 1595 and ratified the next year at the Synod of Brest-Litovsk by the metropolitan of Kiev and most of the Ruthenian bishops. It had the support of the Polish government but was regarded as an apostasy by Moscow and Constantinople. In Poland this 'Uniate' church was generally accepted by the formerly Orthodox at the beginning of the eighteenth century, but many peasants and a few noble families remained Orthodox, giving Russia a pretext for future intervention in Polish affairs.

After the Battle of Mohacs (1526) Hungary was divided into three parts. The Habsburgs retained a narrow strip known as Royal Hungary; the Turks took the rest, but they governed only the western part of their area directly, granting to Transylvania a large degree of autonomy. In Royal Hungary Catholicism always remained dominant, but the Reformation made speedy progress in the districts under Turkish control, for the sultans cared little what creed their Christian subjects professed. The peasants of Transylvania, being largely Rumanian, were to that extent Greek Orthodox and little affected by the schism in the Roman Church. The Turkish government and the Hungarian nobles alike, however, were opposed to the Catholic Church as the Habsburgs' ally. At the same time, the Hungarian nobles rejected Lutheranism, which vested religious supremacy in the ruling prince. Thus Lutheranism made pronounced progress only among the 'Saxon' (German) element in Hungary. The Szeklers, descendants of the ancient Magyar frontier guard in eastern Transylvania, accepted the Socinianism of the Polish reformers; and among the Magyar nobility of Transylvania, Calvinism found greatest favour, broadcast through the efforts of reformers like Peter Melius and Kasper Karolyi, translator of the Bible into Magyar. In Transylvania Calvinists at first were outlawed, but in 1546 they gained tolerance under the semi-independent prince John Sigismund. Catholics, Lutherans, Calvinists, and Socinians all gradually acquired legal status by a series of decrees of the Transylvanian diet, eventually formally included in a corpus compiled in 1669.

In the Austrian holdings of the Habsburgs, the dual problem of religious conflict and princely particularism continued to embarrass Charles V's successors. More politic than his brother Charles, Ferdinand I was a constant advocate of conciliation and compromise. Despite his own Catholic orthodoxy, he placed the unity of the Empire in the face of the Turkish aggression above religious conformity. He adopted a policy of compromise with the Protestants, and his policy at first was carried on by his son, Maximilian II. Ultimately Maximilian resumed an aggressive Catholicism in order to insure his succession to the imperial crown, and a chance of election to the throne of Poland made him still more zealous in the Catholic cause. His son and successor, Rudolf II (1576–1612), whose Spanish mother was a devout Catholic, had been reared in Spain by Jesuits. Under Rudolf Habsburg Catholicism became increasingly militant, especially in the family domain, sharpening the religious conflict.

The Jesuits had already begun their labour of education and conversion in Austria, and although Protestantism had spread widely, they were remarkably successful. In 1552 Ferdinand had summoned Father Peter Canisius from his pedagogical triumphs at the universities of Cologne and Ingolstadt, and Canisius repeated his success in Vienna. In 1556 a Jesuit college was established also in Prague. Under Rudolf II and his successors, Jesuit educational efforts were reinforced by the secular authority with a programme of persuasion, persecution, and forcible conversion of Protestants. By 1597, Catholicism was re-established in Austria and was well on the way to recovery in the other Habsburg territories.

*   *   *

Efforts to Restore Religious Unity by Force

The Reformation had early produced civil wars, as in Switzerland and Denmark, and foreign governments had not hesitated to intervene in them, as Lübeck intervened in Denmark. Full-scale international conflict, however, did not become a decisive factor in the course of the Reformation until Charles V undertook to suppress German Protestantism by force. He thus initiated a century of armed clashes that sooner or later involved all of western Christendom. They began with the Schmalkaldic War in 1546 and closed only with the Thirty Years' War in 1648. In these struggles political rivalries cut across religious lines and hindered concert of action by those who might have been expected to support the same religious cause. Where expediency suggested, Protestants fought on the side of Catholics against Protestants, and Catholics on the side of Protestants against Catholics, for territorial or political advantages.

The mixture of political aspirations with religious convictions was clearly apparent when (as previously noted) the Protestant duke Maurice of Saxony first allied himself with Charles V against the Schmalkaldic League and then, fearful of imperial supremacy, turned against his erstwhile ally. By the Treaty of Friedwald (1552), Maurice secured the assistance of France in the renewed struggle against the emperor, their mutual enemy. Maurice thereby established a precedent for a long series of alliances by which German princes made a willing France the guardian of their particularism against Habsburg domination. Despite the emperor's initial victory over the Schmalkaldic League, the conflict ended with a formal recognition of the compromise that had long existed *de facto* in Germany. The Religious Peace of Augsburg (1555) proclaimed liberty of conscience in the Empire for Lutheran and Catholic rulers but not for Calvinists, Anabaptists, Socinians, or others of the new creeds. Lutheran princes and free cities were granted freedom of worship and the *ius reformandi*, the right to introduce the Reformation into their territories. This legal confirmation of the principle of territorialism—*cuius regio eius religio*—was a belated recognition of a truly revolutionary break with medieval religious tradition, which had regarded the Universal Church as the supreme guardian of Christians. Luther's concept of the authority of the prince over his church thus emerged victorious in the Empire, foreshadowing the heyday of divine-right absolutism.

The effort to restore religious unity to Europe was transformed from the several domestic scenes to the international theatre by Philip II of Spain, groomed for this task by his father, Charles V. In Spain, where particularist interests and constitutional restrictions were not so strong as in the Empire, Charles had been able to impose his sovereign will, and his son inherited a centralized realm in which religious uniformity was enforced by the Inquisition. The Moriscos were to rise up ultimately against forcible Christianization (1609), but that was not to be until the reign of Philip II's successor, and then it was to result only in their expulsion.

Philip II saw in his secure national position the means of achieving an ambitious programme—Spanish predominance, his own political leadership of Catholicism, and the restoration of religious unity throughout Europe. We have already encountered some of the national antagonisms and political rivalries that frustrated him. In England his marriage (before he became the Spanish king) to Mary Tudor was highly unpopular, and his and the queen's policy of Catholic restoration was doomed to failure there. His desire to support Mary, queen of Scots, and to keep Elizabeth I from intervening effectively on the side of the rebellious Netherlands induced him openly to attack England; the ill-fated Great Armada of 1588 was the outcome. His efforts to wipe out the Protestants of the Low Countries led to rebellion and the eventual independence of the United Provinces. The fear of Protestant success in France forced him, now married to a French princess, to take an active part in the French Wars of Religion, but the inveterate competition of Spain and France for supremacy on the Continent made him reluctant to give adequate support to the Catholic side lest its clear-cut triumph make France too united and strong. Upon the victory of Henry IV in France, Philip by the Treaty of Vervins (1598) had to yield all his French conquests and more. Philip nevertheless won great prestige from the major part his navy played in temporarily checking the Turkish advance in the Mediterranean (by the victory of Lepanto in 1571), and he annexed Portugal in 1580. His policy of militant Catholicism was to be continued, but with even less success, by his son, Philip III.[46]

THE CATHOLIC REFORM MOVEMENT

Catholic humanists, clergy, popes, and princes all realized that the spread of Protestantism could not be halted by political or military measures or by persecution alone but had to be met also with a moral and spiritual regeneration of church and papacy. They therefore pressed for reform—as Luther himself originally had done—within the established church.[47]

The Catholic reform movement received a strong impetus from late-fifteenth-century Spain. As devout Catholics, the Spanish monarchs, Ferdinand and especially Isabella, had zealously supported the reform measures of Cardinal Ximenes (see above). Their Most Catholic Majesties' desire to cement the absolutism with which they ruled the national church as well as their people was an effective political spur to their interest in religious reform. Ximenes, combining religious zeal with a thorough education in the new learning, favoured church reform as much as he opposed revolt. Through his efforts, the Spanish church became perhaps the strongest and best disciplined of the national churches in the age of the Reformation. It was able to resist, spiritually as well as politically, the threat of Protestantism and to play a leading role in the Catholic reaction to it. Spanish national sentiment, which was largely identical with Spanish Catholicism, was contemporaneously intensified by the continuing struggle to eradicate the Moors and the Jews. The Spanish Inquisition (a national rather than papal institution) had been founded originally (1480) to investigate converts from Islam and Judaism, but its operation culminating (long after Ximenes' death) in the multiple executions called *autos-da-fé*, initiated in 1559, also made the dissemination of Protestant ideas exceedingly hazardous.

Nevertheless, Erasmian thought found a fairly wide acceptance among Spanish scholars and theologians. As revealed in the case of Servetus, its attacks upon the abuses of the church prepared the ground for the infiltration, even the further elaboration, of Protestant principles. Many Spanish humanists and reformers were forced to seek refuge in neighbouring Italy or Switzerland. Most prominent among them was Juan de Valdes. Influenced by the Dutch humanist and apparently also by the German mystic Tauler, Valdes became a leader of the reform movement in Italy.

Several centres of Protestant thought prospered for a time in Italy. In Ferrara, the Duchess Renée, daughter of King Louis XII of France, aided a group of Calvinists despite her husband's opposition. In Venice, Lutheran sympathies reached into the ranks of the clergy and the populace. In Milan, Lucca, Modena, and several other cities the number of Protestants was also significant. Often the most illustrious reformers were not heretics but were linked with heresy in official or popular thought because they favoured some of the things for which the Protestants stood. Profiting from this atmosphere of reform, Valdes gathered near Naples a group of devoted followers.

Valdes's theology is best formulated in his *Hundred and Ten Divine Considerations*. He accepted the Lutheran doctrine of justification by faith but deepened its mysticism with the precept that divine inspiration could be found through introspective contemplation. He taught a simple Christianity reflected in noble and righteous living. Some of his disciples eventually took the final step into the Reformed camp, but in general, they worked quietly and devotedly within the Catholic Church for a spiritual regeneration. They took no vows and followed no formally accepted rules but found inspiration and fulfilment as individuals in contemplation and lofty discourse. Recruited mostly from among the Italian nobility, they were held together chiefly by admiration of their mentor. After his death (1541) they dispersed throughout Italy.[48]

More formal in its organization and more direct in its approach to reform was the Oratory of Divine Love, which claimed among its members some of the most distinguished priests and laymen of Italy. It was founded in Genoa about 1500, before Lutheranism became a threat, and similar communities were shortly established in Rome (1517), Naples, and other Italian cities. Its aim was the reform of religion through both personal devotion and acts of charity. Most of the Italian leaders of church reform were in one way or another associated with the Oratory. Among its prominent members was Giovanni Pietro Caraffa (later cardinal and still later Pope Paul IV), who as bishop of Chieti had brought strict reform to his diocese even before Luther's revolt. In 1524 a new order appeared—the Order of St Cajetan. An off-shoot of the Oratory of Divine Love, it was a strict order, composed mainly of Italian nobility and devoted predominantly to the education and moral improvement of the clergy. Caraffa became its first superior, and in his honour it became known as the order of the Theatines (Thiete being the Latin name of his see, Chieti).[49]

The Theatine order scattered after the sack of Rome in 1527 but was reconstituted in Venice. Under the guidance of Senator (later Cardinal) Gasparo Contarini, Venice already contained the nucleus of a reform order. At various times the order blossomed, counting among its members such partisans of reform as the humanist Cardinal Jacopo Sadoleto, once secretary of Pope Leo X, and Cardinal Reginald Pole, who had fled England during the controversy over Henry VIII's divorce. These men, entertaining a certain respect for some Lutheran ideas, at first showed a cautious willingness to compromise, but their conciliatory attitude gradually faded. Caraffa himself became a zealous defender of papal authority, and when he became pope, was to persecute both the Oratory and the remnants of the Valdes circle. Meanwhile, however, it was largely from members of the Oratory and the Theatines that the papacy recruited the men through whom it sought to effect reconciliation with the Protestants.

The death of Leo X (1521) and the election (January 1522) of Adrian VI brought to the Holy See a pope of sincere devotion and uncompromising austerity. Born in Holland, Adrian was to be the last pope of other than Italian birth. He had been educated in the simple piety of the Brethren of the Common Life. As tutor of the future Emperor Charles V and bishop of Tortosa, he had been associated with Cardinal Ximenes, whom he succeeded in 1518 as inquisitor general of Castile and Leon. His unanimous election to the papacy seemed to augur a change in the conduct of papal and church affairs, but the reforms he attempted were resisted by papal courtiers and church officials who resented his measures of economy, his caution in bestowing gifts and offices, and his endeavour to halt the corruption that pervaded the Curia. His Dutch manners increased his unpopularity among the Romans.

Aiming to restore unity among the Christian princes, Adrian made a sincere effort to assess the clerical abuses that contributed so greatly to Luther's success. He instructed his nuncio at the Diet at Nuremberg in 1523 to accept the Curia's responsibility for ecclesiastical conditions and to announce the pope's intention to bring about reform. The need for such a step was recognized by an important segment of Catholic opinion; in 1523 Dr Eck, Luther's opponent at the Leipzig debates, paid a visit to the Vatican in order to persuade Adrian that immediate reforms alone could prevent the further spread of Lutheranism. Adrian's death later that year, however, halted the work of reform before it could get under way.

Adrian's successor, Clement VII (Giulio de' Medici), though able as an administrator and well-intentioned as a reformer, was preoccupied with preserving the temporal power of the papacy (and of his family). He therefore became heavily involved in the conflict between the Habsburg emperor Charles V and the Valois king Francis I over the control of Italy. His ill-fated alliance with the League of Cognac against Charles led to the capture and sack of Rome by imperial troops in 1527. This catastrophe shook the Renaissance papacy to its foundations and may have had some influence on Clement's refusal to grant Henry VIII's divorce. Even the most reluctant members of the Curia were now sufficiently shocked to submit to reform.

Reforms finally were initiated under Clement's successor, Paul III (Cardinal Alessandro Farnese). Although the new pope continued the sharply criticized practice of nepotism and openly strove to increase his family's power and wealth, he was genuinely concerned with reform of the Curia. He signalled his intentions by elevating to the cardinalate some of the most conspicuous advocates of mediation and reform, most of whom were or had been associated with the Oratory of Divine Love—among them Caraffa, Sadoleto, Contarini, and Pole. In 1536 a commission, composed exclusively of known reformers, was established to report on needed reforms. Again members of the Oratory were prominent.

In 1537 the commission presented a secret proposal for reforming the church (*Consilium de Emendanda Ecclesia*). The *Consilium* began with a frank admission of the ills that plagued the Curia, giving a long list of them, specifying unbridled greed and papal absolutism with consequent favouritism and nepotism as the chief causes of the corruption. The commission insisted that papal dispensations be dissociated from money payments and that the rule of law and justice be reinstated in the government of the church. Contarini minced no words in urging this unvarnished view upon Paul III:

'The law of Christ . . . is a law of freedom and forbids a servitude so abject that the Lutherans would be entirely correct to compare it with the Babylonian Captivity. . . . A pope . . . must command, forbid, or grant dispensation not according to his own pleasure but in accordance with the rule of reason, of divine commands, and of love. . . . For positive laws are not imposed by arbitrary will . . . but by bringing natural law and divine commands into harmony with existing conditions.'[50]

The *Consilium* resulted in the naming of several later commissions with the express purpose of reforming the Curia. In 1540, Paul III ordered that their proposals be initiated without delay throughout the entire church.

★   ★   ★

The Failure of Attempts at Reconciliation

While these efforts to reform the church from within were going on, liberal Catholic reformers tried to seek a reconciliation with the Protestants. The zeal of members of the Oratory for reform and their willingness to compromise on doctrine so long as the unity of the church was acknowledged made them the logical mediators between the papacy and the dissenters. In 1539, Sadoleto, at the suggestion of Pope Paul III, tried to win strife-torn Geneva back into the Catholic fold by means of a letter addressed to the city authorities and inhabitants. In a conciliatory tone, he stressed their common tradition and faith, but to no avail. His letter inspired Calvin, then in exile in Strasbourg, to answer with a cogent defence of the Reformed position.[51]

A more concerted attempt at reconciliation, on the initiative of Charles V, led finally to a colloquy at Regensburg (Ratisbon) in 1541. Preliminary conferences had induced the leaders of both parties to hope that they might find a common ground and restore unity. Political considerations also rendered a colloquy imperative. Charles V, though momentarily not engaged in open war, wanted unity within the Empire in his two-front struggle against French and Turks. The papacy, too, desired to present a united Christian front to the Turkish advance. Paul III therefore instructed his successive nuncios in Germany to take a conciliatory position and to demonstrate the new spirit of reform in the Roman Curia. Charles V likewise chose for the imperial delegation theologians known for their moderation. On the Protestant side Melanchthon and Bucer were the most active participants; Calvin attended as an observer from Strasbourg. In an early atmosphere of amity and optimism a surprising degree of agreement prevailed on four doctrinal points—the nature of man, original sin, salvation, and justification. Contarini as the papal legate made important concessions on the last point, admitting justification by faith alone, if by faith was meant a living, operative faith (which thus implied good works).[52]

In the end, however, Protestant dogma proved too widely divergent from Catholic dogma to make a reunion possible, and other than religious considerations further complicated the negotiations. The Reformation by that time had become so integral a part of the political constellation of western Christendom that, even if a theological compromise had been possible, it probably would not have resolved the controversy. For all his desire to reassert papal authority over a unified Christendom, the pope feared the power of a Germany united under Habsburg rule. A united Habsburg empire would be a grave threat also to the emperor's opponents both within Germany, such as the duke of Bavaria, and abroad, such as the king of France. Advice, protests, and warnings therefore went to Rome that could not fail to have an effect. When the discussion turned to the question of papal authority, the pope refused to consider anything but unconditional acknowledgement. Ultimately he rejected the conciliatory formulation of doctrinal points that at first had given so much hope. Nor was the Protestant camp—especially Luther—convinced of the sincerity of Catholic concessions or reform. After four months, the Regensburg Colloquy ended in failure.

*　　*　　*

Increased Demand for Reform within Catholicism

In Rome the failure at Regensburg brought a reaction in favour of reform in accordance with the tradition of the Catholic Church. This movement centred around heretic-hunters like Cardinal Caraffa, who now definitely opposed appeasement of those who seemed to him to be rebels. The pope repudiated Contarini's concessions and inaugurated the Roman Inquisition (1542), making it one of the most powerful weapons against Protestantism in the Italian principalities. After 1550 Protestantism survived nowhere in Italy as a serious menace.[53]

The Inquisition alone, however, did not account for that outcome. Among the other factors was the Catholic reformers' concern with revitalizing Catholic theology and its didactic method, Scholasticism, which had long been under attack by the humanists as obscuring rather than clarifying the meaning of Christianity. We shall soon encounter leading Scholasts of the sixteenth century—such as Melchior Cano and Francisco Suárez. A leading role in this revitalization was played by the Dominicans, one of whose principal domains was the teaching of theology (see Chapter XVI).

Improvement of the traditional orders and the inauguration of new ones was another part of the internal reform programme of the church, especially in Spain and Italy. The Theatines, though few in number, had already provided an imposing precedent. Gregorio Cortese reorganized the Benedictine community, and Paolo Giustiniani, a Venetian nobleman, reformed an ancient offshoot of the Benedictine order, the Camaldulians.

Matteo di Bassi, an Observant Franciscan, was not content with mere reform of an existing order. Repelled by the secularism that by the sixteenth century characterized even this stricter branch of the Franciscan friars, he led a secession from his old order. The subtleties of theological disputes were less meaningful to him than the everyday workings of the Christian spirit. If the church were to be effectively rehabilitated in the minds of the common people, he maintained, then the orders, whether old or new, must combine preaching and teaching with social service among the poor and the sick, giving a visible demonstration of the traditional concept of Christian charity. Bassi therefore aimed to restore the original Franciscan practices of poverty and austerity. Despite the opposition of his old order, he was able to win recognition of a new one, which was formally confirmed by Pope Clement VII in 1528. Members of the new order were called Capuchins because of the hood—*cappuccio*—which they wore. They not only preached to the poor but also ministered to the needy, performing especially valiant work in the trying times after the sack of Rome. Despite the withdrawal of some of their leaders to the Observant Franciscans or to Calvinism, they steadily increased in numbers and influence. Their missionary work eventually reached to Africa, Asia, and the Americas, and they played a leading role in reviving the common people's affection and respect for the Roman Catholic Church.[54]

New charitable orders followed one another in quick succession. Girolamo Miani founded the Order of the Somaschi (so-called from their centre, Somasca) to help repair the devastation wreaked by the wars of Charles V upon northern Italy; it established orphanages for the care and education of destitute children. The Barnabites (officially, the Clerics Regular of St Paul), organized (1530) in Milan by three noblemen, combined care of children with preaching and missionary work among the poor. Filippo Neri founded the Oratorians in Rome for secular priests; originally dedicated to relieving the plight of the pilgrims to that city, they sought to revive an informed piety through simple, exegetic services (they gave their name to the oratorio as a musical form), preaching, and the confessional. The Fathers of a Good Death, of Camillus de Lellis, and the Brothers of Mercy, of John of God in Spain, ministered to the sick, buried the dead, and founded hospitals, orphanages, and schools.[55]

Women, too, took an active part in these efforts at religious reform and social relief. Influential missionary and educational work was carried on by the Ursulines, founded by Angela Merici at Brescia, (1535) officially approved by Paul III (1544, and later on patronized by Cardinal Carlo Borromeo). The Ursulines were mainly devoted to the care and education of children, especially girls, as well as to the care of the sick. In Spain St Theresa was instrumental in the reform of the Carmelites, working with John of the Cross in creating an especially ascetic branch called the Discalced (barefoot) Carmelites. Notwithstanding their emphasis upon practical social work, nearly all the new orders stressed education as an important instrument of social rehabilitation and religious reform (see Chapter XVI).

A number of these Catholic reformers lived exemplary lives that were to lead eventually to sainthood—for example, Neri, John of God, Theresa, and

John of the Cross. At the Curia this saintly spirit was represented by Cardinal Borromeo (1538–84), nephew of Pius IV and archbishop of Milan. Despite the high offices he held at Rome, he scorned the opportunities for a brilliant career and, instead, devoted his life to the reform of his diocese, to the care of the sick—especially during the plague that ravaged Milan in 1576—and to the establishment of colleges and seminaries. Canonized in 1610, he belonged to a new group of saints who were sanctified by neither martyrdom nor miracles but by self-sacrificing labour among the sick and destitute and by unceasing efforts to bring to men once again the message of hope.[56]

*   *   *

The Organization of the Society of Jesus

Perhaps the most effective instrument in rebuilding the power of Catholicism was the order of the Jesuits, founded by Inigo Lopez de Loyola (now generally known as St Ignatius). Born in 1491 of Spanish nobility, Loyola led the life then typical of courtier and soldier until in 1521, during the siege of Pamplona by French troops, a cannon ball shattered one of his legs. In the long confinement that followed, he submitted unflinchingly to the rudimentary orthopedics of the day. To distract his mind from the agony, he turned to reading and thus came under the spell of religious books. Their spiritual message merged with the tales of chivalry that once had inspired him, and he began to dream of himself as a knight-errant consecrated to the defence of Jesus and Mary. He vowed to go to Jerusalem and fight for conversion of the Turks.

Upon his recovery and after some time spent in the most severe ascetic practices, Ignatius travelled to Italy to obtain permission for a pilgrimage from Pope Adrian VI. Finally, having survived a difficult and hazardous voyage, he arrived in Jerusalem in 1523. The Franciscans, fearful lest Loyola's proselytizing zeal incite violence from fanatical Turks, forced him by a threat of excommunication to leave. Returning to Venice in 1524, he determined to acquire the education prerequisite for priesthood and successful missionary work. After two years at Barcelona, where he studied Latin in the company of small boys, Ignatius went to the universities of Alcala and Salamanca. Already conspicuous by his ascetic life, utter poverty, and strange, ragged garb, he roused suspicion among the clergy by his public discussions of Scripture, and he and his followers were repeatedly cited before the Inquisition. Acquittal followed his courageous defence of his orthodoxy, but he decided nevertheless to move to the less inquisitorial Paris, where he enrolled in 1528 at the College of Montaigu and later at that of Sainte Barbe.

In Paris, Ignatius formed the nucleus of the future order of the Jesuits. One night in 1534, in a little church on Montmartre, he and six devoted companions took holy communion and vowed to go forth together to convert Turks or, if that mission should prove impossible, to place themselves unquestionably at the disposal of the pope. His six companions were Pierre Lefèvre (Peter Faber), once a Savoyard shepherd, who had been his tutor and room-mate at Sainte Barbe; Francis Xavier, of an aristocratic family in Navarre, who had long resisted Loyola's efforts but was to become the most ardent and effective Jesuit missionary; Diego Laynez, of Spanish-Jewish ancestry, who was to become prominent at the Council of Trent and to succeed Loyola as general of the order; Alfonso Salmeron of Toledo, who was destined to be equally prominent at Trent and to become a foremost theologian; Simon Rodriguez, a Portuguese, who was eventually to return to his native land as head of the Jesuit mission there; and Nicholas Alfonso, named Bobadillo after his home in Castile, who was to carry on important missionary activities in the Holy Roman Empire.

Shortly after their inaugural meeting the seven men dispersed. When, two years later, they reunited in Venice, their membership had increased to ten. In Venice Loyola, again suspected of heresy, drew upon himself the wrath of Cardinal Caraffa by his criticism of the Theatines, of whom Caraffa was the superior, and by his refusal to merge with them. The renewal of the Turkish wars kept Loloya and his disciples from departing for the Holy Land. In Rome, where they went in 1538, they were openly accused of heresy, but Loyola in a long audience with Pope Paul III defended his stand so skilfully that he gained the pope's approval. A trial, begun at Loyola's own request, ended in complete vindication, bringing wide recognition to the 'Inigists' (as the band was called, after its founder's Spanish name). The learning and the effectiveness of their preaching attracted the attention of Catholic princes everywhere, and they were soon in demand throughout Europe to aid in reforming Catholic institutions and strengthening the Catholic party. Laynez and Lefèvre were appointed to the University of Rome, where their success as teachers and theologians was so great that a papal decree in 1530 commanded all teachers in the holy city to adopt the new order's methods of instruction (see Chapter XVI).

If conversion of the Turks no longer seemed practical, Europe, rent by the Reformation, seemed to cry aloud for missionary devotion. When, therefore, Loyola and his followers met again (1539), they decided to reorganize their brotherhood. This meeting marked the formal founding of a new *compania* of militants for Christ, thenceforth known as the Society of Jesus. To the vows of chastity and poverty was now added that of absolute obedience to the pope and to the general of the order. The strange rules of the new order encountered stubborn disapproval in the Curia, and it took the most subtle manoeuvres on Loyola's part to overcome opposition. The new order received papal sanction only in 1540, and the next year Loyola, against his will, was unanimously elected its general. Membership was at first limited to sixty, but in 1543 a papal bull removed this restriction and unconditionally recognized the order as operating under its own rules. Loyola spent the rest of his life revising these rules, and only in 1558, two years after his death, were the society's 'Constitutions' adopted by its first General Congregation. The 'Constitutions', together with other crucial documents of the order, form 'The Institute of the Society of Jesus', which regulates it to this day.

In the Institute the church was conceived as the Church Militant, served by the order with absolute obedience and soldierly discipline. The stringent training by which the aspirant Jesuit became a full-fledged 'professed of the four vows' will be analyzed in Chapter XVI. Obedience was maintained not only through binding vows but also through the acceptance of the obligation to report infractions of rules or expressions of rebellion. Highest constitutional authority rested with the General Congregation of the Order, a body of officers recruited exclusively from the 'professed'. They elected the general, and, if paramount considerations required, might depose him. Otherwise, actual authority rested with the general—checked, however, by a body of 'assistants' representing the geographical subdivisions ('assistancies') of the order, by a special confessor, and by a monitor who brought to the general's attention the assistants' criticisms of his actions. All of these officers were appointed by the General Congregation without interference from the general. The assistancies of the order were organized into 'provinces', each headed by a 'provincial', who was appointed by the general and assisted by a body of advisers similarly appointed. The provinces had jurisdiction over the order's colleges, seminaries, novitiates, houses, and missions within their boundaries. All branches of the Society were under the centralized administration at Rome, where the general was required to reside.

While all the Jesuits took vows of obedience to the pope, they also vowed obedience to their general. In cases of conflicting interests the general might thus successfully thwart papal policies for which the efforts of the Society were required. Even so, Popes Paul III and Julius III further strengthened the general's power, but after Loyola's death Paul IV actively interfered in the affairs of the order. In addition to insisting upon greater conformity in Jesuit religious services, he issued a decree (1558) that limited the general's term of office to three years.

The Society found supporters among the most influential Catholics of Europe. The Jesuits' austerity and strict conduct, their devout obedience, their willingness to sacrifice themselves, and the obvious success of their labours made them indispensable allies in the struggle for the preservation of Catholicism. After Paul IV's death (1559), Pius IV restored the provision by which the general held office for life. Under Pius V all privileges formerly bestowed upon the Jesuits were confirmed and even extended to include all benefits enjoyed by the traditional orders. For the next two hundred years, until their temporary suppression in 1773, the Jesuits remained the most active allies of the papacy. In 1773 they numbered around 24,000, divided into 49 provinces, in which there were 669 colleges.[57]

From the outset the Jesuits purposefully concentrated upon effective control of men's minds. Jesuit aspirants were carefully trained and over a period of years were weeded out step by step until only the best adapted candidates remained (see Chapter XVI). When they were fully trained, education, both formal and informal, became one of their major activities (with dramatic results that will likewise engage our attention later). Their missionary work was perhaps still more dramatic. Even before the official recognition of the Jesuits in 1540, their assistance was requested by King John III of Portugal in converting the inhabitants of his newly acquired colonies. Francis Xavier spread the Gospel under the most difficult circumstances in India, the Indies, and Japan. In subsequent decades Jesuit missions were established in many parts of the world, including Africa and America. A key to their success was the flexibility with which they accommodated Christian teachings to the beliefs they encountered. Xavier himself did not employ this expedient of 'accommodation' though he frequently used other kinds of worldly pressure, such as promises of financial reward, commercial advantage, and threats of punishment by the civil authorities. His successors in Asia, as also those in the New World, went much farther in this direction, appearing in the religious garb familiar to the locality or permitting elements of the old religion to become part of the new as long as they seemed not to offend essential Christian doctrine. While these methods were frequently criticized both within the church—by Pascal, for instance—and by Protestant opponents, they were successful in prompting conversions *en masse* though perhaps not in depth.

A similar flexibility was in no small degree responsible for the Jesuits' success in their inner missions. As militant defenders of Catholicism, expert pamphleteers against Protestantism, and skillful organizers of the Catholic party throughout Europe, they fitted their methods to the situations confronting them. Loyola himself, though aware of the need for missionary work among the masses, had early realized the importance of gaining support among persons of authority and influence. Accordingly, Jesuits became tutors of princes and, particularly under Loyola's successors, court confessors in Catholic countries, capable by their knowledge of a ruler's mind and soul to give to their spiritual guidance a decisive political turn. Jesuits addressed themselves to all classes of society, sometimes wearing no distinctive garb and accommodating themselves even in appearance to the milieu in which they laboured. They preached sermons tailored to suit the merchant as well as the farmer, the soldier as well as the criminal. Flexibility, though a source of strength, was ultimately also a source of weakness, for it made them vulnerable to never-ending accusations of opportunism or even hypocrisy, which eventually, in the age of the Enlightenment, were among the factors that led to their temporary dissolution after 1773. The Jesuits' devotion to the cause of Catholicism, and especially of the papacy, was to be amply tested in the long and tortuous conferences known as the Council of Trent.

THE CATHOLIC COUNCILS AT TRENT (1545–63)

The Fifth Lateran Council, we have seen, lasted until 1517, the year of the Ninety-Five Theses. It accomplished little in the way of reform, for neither Julius II nor Leo X permitted any interference with papal authority or with the secular interests of the Holy See. The council, in fact, reaffirmed the doctrine of the superiority of popes over councils in the affairs of the church, thus confirming the failure of the Conciliar Movement. The idea of conciliar supremacy retained many adherents, however, especially among those who were persuaded that papal absolutism was a stumbling block in the way of religious reform.

Luther's appeal for a general council found a strong echo in Germany, where Protestant and Catholic princes alike felt the need of defending their opposing causes before a forum of all Christendom. Emperor Charles V himself at times supported the idea of a council. A devout though not fanatical Catholic, he was fully aware of the need for reform. Nevertheless, his reform efforts, like his policy toward the Protestant Reformation, were geared to the exigencies of his political problems. Habsburg rivalry with Valois France and campaigns against the Turks obliged him to be cautious in dealing with the German princes, whether Protestant or Catholic. A general council, in which conceivably Catholic strength would prevail, thus seemed to afford a possible solution of his dilemma. Furthermore, he was heir to the traditional rivalry between the emperors and the popes and therefore intent upon limiting the papel power. His sympathy with the demand for a general council thus not only betrayed his desire for moderate religious reform but also implied that in the affairs of Christendom he recognized an authority higher than the pope. This very implication, however, was the major reason why the contemporary popes for a long time refused to convoke a general council.

The papal strategy, perhaps wise for Italy, led in Germany to a louder demand for a national council to resolve the religious affairs of the Empire. Although the most powerful ruler in Europe, Charles was unable to assert full power anywhere because of the numerous involvements his very power entailed, and he was only gradually induced to take a definitive stand. When Pope Clement VII joined the alliance against him (1526), he demanded a council to arbitrate Catholic and Protestant differences; he even appealed to the cardinals to convoke it in their own name if the supreme pontiff refused. Then when the fortunes of war placed the pope for a time in his power (1527) he dropped this policy.

The accession of Paul III (1534) at first brought a change in papal attitude. Paul actually convoked two councils between 1536 and 1538, at Mantua and Vicenza respectively, but both were prorogued without material achievement because of hostilities between the emperor and the kings of France and England as well as the refusal of the Protestant princes, organized since 1531 in the Schmalkaldic League, to participate. In the heat engendered by the increasingly complex political situation Paul's willingness to convene a council withered. His desire to reform the church, though real, was not so deep as to permit him to jeopardize the papacy's prestige and power as one of the great temporal states of Europe. And so, until 1545 convocation was frustrated, chiefly by the antagonistic aims of the principal Catholic rulers. Charles V, however, continued his attempts to compromise with the Protestants, with or without papal sanction, and his tactics made it imperative— as several papal legates repeatedly pointed out from Germany—that the pope should not veto a council.

Some of the most jealous manoeuvring that preceded the actual convocation of a council revolved around the issue who was to control it. The emperor and the pope were the leading contenders, with the king of France skillfully playing one against the other to further his own purposes. The pope's main concern was to confirm the position of the Fifth Lateran Council that popes were superior to councils and thus to frustrate the emperor's attempts to make the council rather than the papacy the authoritative instrument of reform. The preliminary jockeying in this race for control pivoted upon the location of the forthcoming council. The pope naturally preferred Italy, where the majority of attendants would probably be Italian bishops, who, looking to the Curia for benefices and privileges, might be counted upon to support the papal cause. German public opinion, for parallel reasons, clamoured for a location somewhere in Germany, forcing Charles to oppose the papal preference. In the end a compromise solution was agreed upon; the council was to be convoked in Trent, a city in southern Tyrol, close to the Italian border but at least nominally within the Holy Roman Empire.[58]

The rival Catholic parties also wrangled over what policy to follow regarding the Protestants. A reconciliation was for a time considered conceivable, but after the failure of the Regensburg Colloquy, as noted above, the pope considered the heretics beyond compromise and in 1542 inaugurated with the Roman Inquisition a policy of repression. Political considerations, however, forced Charles, engaged in war with Francis I, to maintain a conciliatory attitude and to acquiesce in Protestant demands for tolerance—at least until a general council might settle disputed points. Thus the emperor was concerned to delay a council until Paul might show greater signs of moderation, while the pope, wary of German reconciliation, shifted his stand, declaring his readiness to convoke a council at an early date. Charles agreed, assuring the German estates that he would convene a national council in Germany if the prospective general council should fail.

Long negotiations followed between papal legates and imperial ambassadors. The pope vainly tried to change the announced location for the council, but a summons to meet at Trent in November 1542 was finally issued. Then war between France and the emperor once more intervened; only three papal legates and the imperial chancellor appeared; and a papal bull in July 1543 suspended the council. Whether it would reconvene was left to the pope's discretion.

Charles' defeat of France and the consequent Peace of Crépy in September 1544 considerably reduced the international tension. The pope, once more in at least outward rapport with the emperor, summoned the council to assemble again at Trent in March 1545. Its formal opening was delayed until December, but even then attendance was small. The Italian and Spanish delegations outnumbered the Germans, because the German bishops were preoccupied at home by the threat of war with the Schmalkaldic League of Protestant princes. Attending the council by express order of the emperor (who, as king of Spain, was their sovereign), the Spanish delegation represented the imperial power as well as the Spanish national church. They not only pressed for reform of the Curia but also persistently defended episcopal—and by implication, conciliar—privileges against papal encroachment. Their opposition was formidable, because since the reforms of Ximenes the Spanish church had not only become the strongest and most unified in western Europe but also could boast some of the most learned theologians of the age. Their unquestioned orthodoxy and their loyal support of the papacy in matters of doctrine made their challenge of the papal legates and their emphasis upon reform doubly effective.

No Protestants participated in the council, and for a number of reasons. Although Luther and his followers had constantly appealed from the pope to a general council, their emphasis had always been upon a 'free' council not dominated by the Curia, and they declared that this one was neither general nor free and not even Christian. Political calculations likewise hindered their attendance. Various temporary agreements allowed them the exercise of their religion in the Empire until a general council should reach a definitive doctrinal settlement, but the decisions that were to be anticipated from the Council of Trent might put an end to tolerance. They, therefore, wished the emperor to guarantee in advance that the truce would continue. This, of course, the emperor would not do, and so, despite his assurances of peaceful intentions, the Protestants stayed away.

The struggle for control of the council began at the outset. Three forces openly contended with one another—the Curial party, jealous for papal prerogatives and eager to reassert papal authority over all of western Christendom; the Imperial party, still hesitant to break completely with the Protestants and intent upon reform and restriction of papal power; and the episcopal party, mostly non-Italian bishops, eager to defend their prerogatives against the pope, the most radical among them ready even to question the primacy of the bishop of Rome. The episcopal movement, identified most readily with the Spanish bishops, could have succeeded only in conjunction with a strong conciliar movement, and its advocates were indeed conspicuously conciliar in sentiment, but the conciliar theory was essentially incompatible with the concept of hierarchic priesthood, which even the most radical bishops were loath to abandon. Despite the widespread opposition to papal absolutism, the papal legates had the upper hand because the assembled bishops were unwilling to attack in any fundamental way the hierarchical structure of the church.

The first meetings of the council decided three issues in a way that portended the eventual victory of the papacy. When the full name of the council was considered, a number of delegates proposed that the words *universalem ecclesiam representans* be added. These words seemed to imply that the council, as fully representative of the church, was superior to the pope, and the papal legates induced the council to reject them. A second issue concerned the system of voting. At previous councils, votes had been counted by nations, with lesser clergy and theologians voting along with princes of the church. This method permitted a significant number of voters to avoid direct papal influence. At Trent voting by nations was rejected in favour of voice voting, only bishops and generals of orders being allowed to vote, no proxies permitted. Thus the Italian bishops, being the largest delegation, could almost alone assure the eventual success of the papal cause.

On the third issue the papal preferences met with a setback but only a partial one. Upon the express orders of the pope, who considered reform a papal prerogative, his legates insisted that dogma be made the first business of the council. This move encountered determined opposition from the Imperial camp, which was under orders to place reform first. The Spanish bishops proved their strength when against the most determined papal opposition they forced a compromise. In January 1546, it was decided that dogma and reform should be considered simultaneously by special commissions and their findings brought before the council in alternate sessions. The partial defeat of the papal party on this issue was softened when the pope's counter proposal that no reform of the Curia be discussed without his prior consent was accepted. It was further agreed that only after being prepared, discussed, and approved by preliminary bodies should a measure be brought before the general assembly, and it was to be promulgated as a definitive act only if adopted in a solemn public *sessio* (meeting) of the entire council.

The debates on dogma were the most heated. The Jesuit fathers Laynez and Salmeron played a vital part in them as the pope's theologians. Although they were not delegates, they alone among the assemblage had been granted the privilege of preaching, and their general learning and familiarity with Scripture and canon law won deep and wide respect. Although originally instructed by Loyola to mediate between pope and bishops, they were also instructed to make no concessions on dogma. Thus they became in effect the vanguard of the papal forces. Their learned discourses—especially those of Laynez—were instrumental in solidifying the front against innovation. The fact that the Jesuit theologians were Spanish offset the Spanish opposition.

The very wording employed by the papal legates in formulating doctrinal disagreements usually seemed designed to make reconciliation with the Protestants impossible. Almost every point of Protestant theology was branded from the outset as heretical and appeared to be cited only to be anathematized. The attack began with the discussion of the sources of faith and revelation. Against the Protestant conviction that Scripture was the sole source, the council decreed that tradition (i.e. the writing of the church fathers) was of equal validity and that the church alone had authority in the interpretation of both. At the same time, obviously in repudiation of Luther's translation of the Bible, the Vulgate was decreed the only authentic version, even though the more learned among the delegates, as indeed Paul III himself, realized that the work of the humanists had raised doubts concerning its adequacy.

The discussion of the sources of faith led logically to the discussion of justification. Justification by faith alone, the principal creed of Protestantism, was defended even by some of the delegates. One of the papal legates, Cardinal Pole, noted for his moderation, pleaded with the council not to reject a tenet merely because it was held by the Lutherans. Cardinal Seripando, general of the Augustinians, made an impassioned plea for a rapprochement, expounding an opinion that approximated the Protestant doctrine of justification by faith alone. In reply, Laynez made one of his longest and most effective speeches, and in the end prevailed. Justification by faith alone was anathematized.

The ancient dogma thus clinched implied many corollaries, and the public *sessio* on justification resulted in no fewer than thirty-three canons of key importance. Good works were now logically reconfirmed as a necessary part of justification. With equal logic, free will, which enabled man to choose the path of good works, was retained as part of the Catholic creed. All seven traditional sacraments were reaffirmed, and the council declared that, with the exception of baptism, they could have their true efficacy only if performed by ordained priests. Thus the dependence of the laity upon the priesthood, in opposition to Luther's assertion of the essential priesthood of all believers, was reasserted. Still later, when the sacrament of ordination was discussed, the council anathematized any who maintained that 'sacred ordination is not truly and properly a sacrament instituted by Christ' and repudiated the doctrine that priests might be elected from and by the laity; 'those who, being only called and instituted by the people, or by the civil power and magistrate, ... are not ministers of the church, but ... thieves and robbers, who have not entered by the door'.[59]

The pope was eager to publish the canonical findings of the council, since they bade fair to become a telling weapon against Protestant heresy. On the other hand, the emperor betrayed growing dissatisfaction. The Schmalkaldic War had broken out soon after the council opened, and he had won such important victories that he had reason to hope for concessions from the

Protestants. He, therefore, tried to delay publication of the conservative decisions on dogma while pressing for supplementary measures of vital reform. Thus the issue was joined whether the council was to become an instrument of reform or of counter-reform.

Though Paul III, through his legates, was determined to maintain full control over the Catholic reform movement, he had to face a significant number of non-Italian bishops. The Spanish delegation proved its strength a second time and forced another compromise. The debate on the rules for preaching and religious instruction brought a decision that members of the regular clergy would be free to preach in the churches of their respective orders but must not preach in diocesan churches without the bishop's permission. During this debate an issue arose that repeatedly dominated discussion of episcopal jurisdiction: Were episcopal privileges and obligations founded upon divine law (*iure divino*) or ecclesiastical law (*lege ecclesiastica*)? The Spanish bishops maintained that all episcopal duties existed *iure divino* —thus implying that bishops derived their obligations and authority directly from God, as did the pope himself (as bishop of Rome). This view was naturally opposed by the papal legates—to whom, besides, the corollary that bishops should reside in their sees was personally embarrassing since it called in question the papal practice of bestowing benefices in distant parts upon cardinals living in Rome. The origin of episcopal rights was so passionately argued that otherwise dignified prelates exchanged insults and came to blows. A decision was not to be reached even in the final stages of the council (1563), when the question was evaded by intentional ambiguity.

Meanwhile political considerations added to the tensions created by the disputes over theology and church administration. Shortly after the Council of Trent began, the Protestants showed some signs of becoming tractable. Luther died in February 1546, thus depriving them of their most unbending spokesman, and their military power was broken by the emperor's victories over the Schmalkaldic League. Charles still had to take into account, however, the legal rights of the Protestant princes, and he was anxious not to provoke the outbreak of new hostilities. Moreover, he saw in the Protestant opposition to the pope a means of strengthening his own bargaining position at the council.

Paul III had good reason to fear the emperor's improved position, and he urged the council to move to Italy, where he could better balance imperial influence by his personal presence. A few cases of the plague aided the papal legates to win a majority, and despite the vehement protest of the minority, composed mostly of Spanish bishops, the council adjourned, and most of the delegates reassembled at Bologna (March 1547). This move came close upon a sudden burst of public approval for the council's decisions on dogma, putting further obstacles in the way of the emperor's peace efforts. Wrathfully Charles forbade the Spanish bishops to leave Trent, and so a rump body held out there. Although it was careful, on the emperor's orders, to avoid action that might lead to schism, the council was none the less split, and no effective action could be taken at either Trent or Bologna. Charles summoned the Diet to meet in Augsburg in September and in due course (May 1548) proclaimed his own tentative compromise with the Protestants, the Augsburg Interim. But no more definitive agreement could be reached and finally in September 1549, Paul III prorogued the council at Bologna. Two months later he died.

The new pope, Julius III, while continuing to assert the power of the Holy See, proved willing to appease the emperor, even on the delicate issue of Protestant attendance at a council. The German princes demanded that the council resume at Trent, for they wanted the Protestant problem in Germany solved on German soil, and after displaying considerable reluctance, Julius consented. Two further obstacles to Protestant attendance at the council remained to be overcome—an unconditional safe conduct that would be better honoured than the one promised to Huss over a century earlier and a decision whether the new assembly was a continuation of the prorogued Council of Trent. If the new assembly was to be regarded as merely a continuation of the old, it would feel bound by its earlier decisions on dogma, rendering attendance by Protestants futile. Julius III at first left this question open, but toward the end of the new set of meetings it came to be regarded *de facto* as a continuation of the earlier council. By that time, other events had once more made apparent that debate, however free, would not alone suffice to heal the schism in Christendom.

Some lay representatives of a few German Protestant states were finally admitted to the fifteenth public *sessio* of the council (January 1552). In expounding the conditions on which Protestant theologians might agree to attend, they made stipulations that could hardly be compromised. They wanted to resume the debate on dogma, insisting at the same time that Scripture be the sole authority for further deliberations. Bishops should be freed from their oaths of papal allegiance, they argued, for otherwise the pope in effect would sit in judgement of his own case, and they insisted that the papal legates, who normally held the presidency of the council, should surrender that prerogative. The principal speech setting forth these demands, probably written by Melanchthon, made a profound impression, especially upon several Spanish delegates. 'In full session', the Bishop of Orense exclaimed, 'they have stated what we [Spaniards] dare not say'.[60] It appeared for a moment as if the entire papal opposition at the council—Spanish bishops, emperor, and Protestants—might form a united front.

Once more political forces interfered, abruptly stifling any slim chance there might have arisen of forcing papal concessions and restoring Christian unity. Certain German Protestant princes were worried by the emperor's conciliatory policies, which seemed designed to repeal territorialism, unite the Empire, and break their power. The devious Maurice of Saxony was one of them. Coveting the title and prerogatives of his kinsman the Saxon elector, he had recently changed sides and had fought under Charles V in the Schmalkaldic War. At this juncture he changed sides once more, resuming leadership in the militant Lutheran cause and taking up arms against Charles. His victorious advance forced the emperor to seek refuge in Innsbruck, only to flee again when Protestant troops converged upon that city. Fear spread that Maurice might march on Trent, about eighty-five miles away, and the council precipitately suspended its meetings again (April 1552). It had done little more since reconvening than discuss the sacraments, anathematize Protestant doctrine concerning the Eucharist, and postpone a decision on the question of communion in both kinds.

Almost ten years were to pass after the second prorogation of the council before it reconvened. In that interval several popes had succeeded to the papal throne. Julius III (d. 1555) was followed by Marcellus II, who survived his election only three weeks, and after his death, Caraffa received the tiara. During his austere reign as Paul IV he initiated no move toward reopening the council. Though as cardinal he had been a most ardent advocate of reform, he proved as pontiff to be conspicuously political-minded. His deep-seated mistrust of Spain involved him in war with that country, staunchest supporter of orthodox Catholicism in Europe, and led him to make overtures even to Protestants and Turks in a vain effort to avert military disaster. The nepotism that he practiced to the dismay of the reform party in Rome was closely related to his anti-Spanish policy, for members of his family insinuated themselves into his favour as staunch supporters of his diplomacy. Dis-illusioned by defeat and the realization of a favoured nephew's unworthiness, he at last concentrated on reform but did so with such fanaticism that rejoicing was general in Rome when he died (1559).

By that time, the political situation had changed materially. Charles V had abdicated, and his son had become King Philip II of Spain, and his brother Holy Roman Emperor Ferdinand I. The successes of Maurice of Saxony and the intervention of France had evened the balance between German Catholic and Lutheran princes, and (as we saw above) they had agreed to the compromise Peace of Augsburg (1555). Armed conflict ended in Germany for over half a century.

Within a year of Pius IV's accession (1559) to the papal throne, he summoned the council to reopen at Trent. But his initial willingness soon evaporated because of apprehension that a new assembly might undo some of the earlier work. Once again the threat of a separate national council—this time from France—was needed to prod the hesitant pontiff into confirming the convocation. An anticipated conflict quickly arose: Was this a continuation of the old council and therefore committed to previous decisions (as desired by the uncompromising Philip II of Spain), or was it a new one and free to revise previous decisions (as demanded by the Emperor Ferdinand and by Francis II of France, who had powerful Protestant groups among their subjects)? Pius resorted to the now familiar device of leaving the question undecided. When in January 1562 the council finally opened, the hope of reconciliation seemed dim indeed, and it soon vanished entirely. The Protestants, although safe conduct had been granted them, again stayed away, and after deliberations were well under way, Pius decreed that this assembly was a continuation of the old Council of Trent.

During this third period of the Council of Trent the constellation of powers differed from the earlier ones. France and the Holy Roman Empire were united in favouring not only a thorough reform of the Curia but also changes in ritual and religious practices, such as communion in both kinds, mass in the vulgar tongue, permission for priests to marry, and stricter observance of residence by bishops and priests. The Spanish bishops, no longer under a king identified with the Empire, while still demanding stringent reform of the church, were unwilling to make any concessions in dogmatic matters. As a result papal diplomacy was again successful in dividing the opposition, and the papal legates, having the sole right of initiative, achieved considerable control over deliberations. After a year or so of this third period, the council seemed to be headed toward a conclusion. Philip of Spain was convinced that the council was seriously contemplating reform; in fact, Cardinal Morone, who became first legate in 1563, introduced a project in July intended to satisfy some of the various national demands. Emperor Ferdinand, faced with frustration of his desire that the chalice be granted to the German laity, heeded his adviser, the Jesuit Canisius, and decided to negotiate directly with Pius IV rather than to prolong the council's discussions on the subject. Canisius's advice proved justified, for the pope eventually (1564) granted the chalice in Germany, though under specified conditions. The Cardinal of Lorraine, leader of the French delegation, also was won over to adjournment. On December 4, 1563, at the close of its twenty-fifth *sessio*, the council, having accepted Morone's project, formally terminated amid the unconcealed rejoicing of the delegates.

In the bull *Benedictus Deus* (January 1564) Pius IV confirmed the decrees of the council but asserted the pope's exclusive prerogative of interpreting them and giving them their true validity. He appointed a special commission of eight cardinals to serve as a Congregation of the Council of Trent to help him carry on its work, and later that year he published the 'Tridentine Profession of Faith' (now generally known as 'The Creed of Pius IV'), to which all holders of ecclesiastical offices still must subscribe. This creed no longer left much room for discussion. It not only restored the traditional faith but in fact reinvigorated it by the clarity and definitiveness with which it repronounced Catholic doctrine. In the centuries that followed, deviations from the Tridentine Creed were synonymous with heresy and exposed their proponents to the displeasure of the Inquisition. Thus the Council of Trent, after its many years of fierce debate and intermittent search for compromise, provided in effect an arsenal of weapons for a counter-reformation.

The papal victory probably could not have been won without internal reforms that strengthened the church as a militant organization and blunted the fittingness of its opponents' criticism. The reform decrees of the Council of Trent were intended to correct the patent abuses that had contributed to the outbreak of the Reformation. Although those decrees did not always have the desired effect, they considerably improved discipline throughout the church. They made preaching a solemn obligation of ordained priests, gave to the training of priests a firm and lasting foundation by instituting a seminary in each diocese, enjoined bishops to reside in their dioceses and priests in their parishes, denounced plurality of offices, strengthened the authority of bishops over regular and secular clergy, abolished the sale of indulgences for money and specifically restricted the conditions under which indulgences might be granted, reaffirmed the celibacy of priests, excluded the illegitimate sons of prelates from certain benefices and pensions, and prohibited clandestine marriages even for laity. The council itself did not establish a new *Index of Prohibited Books* although it appointed a commission to revise the *Index* of 1559, but it referred this matter along with other important decrees to the pope for implementation.

PAPAL POLICIES AFTER TRENT

If the Council of Trent left western Christianity irrevocably split into several sects, the Roman Catholic Church emerged stronger than it had been before. The Church, to be sure, had narrowed its geographical boundaries, but at the same time it had drawn its faithful together in a tighter, more authoritative bond. The Council of Trent not only provided added momentum in the counter-attack upon the Protestant heresy but also marked the end of the Conciliar Movement. No ecumenical council was called again until 1869, and then it was completely under papal domination (see Volume V). The authority of the pope as the spiritual overlord of the Roman Catholic fold was more fully established by the Council of Trent than ever before, and if in Europe that fold was diminishing, overseas it gained many new adherents.

Active reform was intensified under the austere Pius V (1566-72), a former Dominican monk. He issued the Roman Catechism called for by the Council of Trent. He also gave Catholic liturgy a marked degree of uniformity. Both breviary and missal had thitherto varied greatly in the different parts of Catholic Christendom, since bishops had the right to determine details of liturgy for their dioceses. A commission established by the Council of Trent had undertaken the task of revising and unifying them. Under Pius V these revisions were formally promulgated as the officially sanctioned liturgy, except for churches which could claim an unbroken local usage for two centuries. This exemption was intended in the main for the French and German Catholic churches, but so great became the influence of the papacy upon an increasingly unified Catholicism that Pius's 'reformed' missal and breviary gradually supplanted most local versions. He became a staunch ally of Philip II of Spain in his determination to wipe out the Protestant heresy and stem the advance of the infidel Turk, and, except for Rome and Ancona, he expelled the Jews from the Papal States. He made the Inquisition a powerful weapon in the struggle against Protestantism, enforced the strictest morality and discipline throughout the hierarchy, put an end to some of the more glaring types of nepotism, and thoroughly revised the system of justice in the Papal States. He prohibited future investitures in perpetuity with fiefs from the papal possessions, and to give this reform measure lasting stability, he compelled his cardinals by solemn oath to support it.

Like liturgy, canon law took final and official form as a consequence of the programme laid down at Trent. Shortly before the council ended, Pius IV had established a commission (the Correctores Romani) to compile a definitive edition of canon law, but it completed its work only in the days of Gregory XIII (1572–85). In 1582 appeared the first edition of this new compilation, which later became known as the *Corpus iuris canonici* and, together with the decrees of the Council of Trent, forms the basis of the *ius novissimum*, the latest law. Augmented by the rulings and decrees pronounced since the Council of Trent, this *ius novissimum* has remained the basic code of Roman Catholicism to this day.

Gregory's main attention was focused upon improving religious instruction, particularly for the clergy. He was an especially generous patron of the Jesuit colleges, helping to found the Roman, German, and English colleges at Rome, as well as those at Vienna and Graz and on the Greek islands. His best known contribution was the reform, in keeping with a recommendation of the Council of Trent, of the calendar (see Chapter XIV); the Gregorian calendar gave greater regularity to religious holidays by establishing a more accurate correlation between them and the four seasons of the year than had been possible under the Julian calendar. Gregory also spent vast sums of money for public works and for subsidies to Catholic princes who were fighting Protestantism, especially in the Netherlands, France, and England. To compensate for the drain on the papal treasury he resorted to such measures as the confiscation of fiefs of doubtful title. Widespread unrest resulted among the nobility in the Papal States, and the curse of private warfare with resultant large-scale banditry returned to Italy.

On Gregory's death his successor, Sixtus V (1585–90), faced with the problem of restoring peace and financial solvency, crushed brigandage and private warfare with brutal severity and replenished the papal treasury by means that could not easily be reconciled with his reforming zeal. While he cut down the expenses of the Curia, he also increased old taxes, devised new ones, and raised both the number and the price of offices put up for sale. He debased the currency and, when his tampering led to speculation in currency exchange, sold permits to the speculators. These measures provided the vast sums needed for his numerous public works in Rome and for the defence and propagation of the faith. In 1586, Sixtus gave the College of Cardinals its

L*

definitive form, and in 1588 he reorganized the Curia by establishing fifteen congregations of cardinals, each having a special advisory capacity in a specified field of ecclesiastical administration.

The Council of Trent had left to the popes the responsibility not only of interpreting but also of enforcing its decisions. To place spiritual conformity under the desired discipline, it had proposed control of the minds of the faithful. Censorship had long been known in the Catholic Church, but not until 1559, under Paul IV, was an official *Index Librorum Prohibitorum* issued with full papal authority. This *Index* was regarded as inadequate by the Council of Trent, and a commission was appointed to propose revisions. The new *Tridentine Index* was published under Pius IV in 1564, along with the famous 'Ten Rules' setting forth the criteria of censorship adopted by the Council of Trent. Under Pius V a Congregation of the Index was established, and the formal publication of lists of prohibited books ended only in 1966.

The Inquisition became an even stronger weapon in the arsenal of Roman Catholicism. The papal Inquisition had lost considerable power and prestige during the Great Schism, but the Spanish Inquisition, established by Ferdinand and Isabella, had become formidable. Yet outside Spain Catholic princes, even Charles V in his role of emperor, were reluctant to follow the example of Spain, where the Inquisition had become a power rivalling that of the crown. Moreover, popular opposition was so violent in the most important Spanish possessions in Italy that attempts to establish the Spanish Inquisition at Milan and Naples had to be abandoned. The spread of Protestantism, however, led Pope Paul III to establish the Inquisition at Rome (1542), and Paul IV and Pius V, himself once an inquisitor, used it ruthlessly and successfully not only to ferret out known or suspected Protestants but also to enforce discipline among the faithful.

The church did not rely on reform and compulsion alone to fortify Catholicism. As will be indicated in Chapter XII, church architecture and church music became part of a studied effort to make a dramatic appeal to the eye and the ear. The paganism that had characterized some of the great accomplishments of Renaissance art gave way increasingly to a new piety in which the artist again sought inspiration from Christianity. This development was at least in part consciously in opposition to the austerity of Protestant church service and church architecture. The schools, too, became an effective instrument in the battle for men's minds, especially in the hands of the Jesuits (see Chapter XVI).

Thus, a little over half a century after the first impetus of the Reformation, Catholicism rose again in a new militancy under a revitalized central authority. For all that, the attempts to make the decisions of Trent binding throughout Catholic Christendom met with considerable defiance. Catholic princes, though willing to submit in matters of dogma, were reluctant to accept the decrees on discipline, which frequently infringed cherished interests of national governments and churches. The decrees on discipline were withheld in the Empire (although Ferdinand adopted them for his hereditary dominions) and in France; Spain and Venice adopted them only with stringent reservations; in effect, only Portugal and Poland among the Catholic powers approved them outright. Yet even in those Catholic countries where, out of national or dynastic considerations the Tridentine decrees were not regarded as binding, in a very real sense the effect of the Protestant revolt had been to cement the bonds among those who had remained loyal.

RELIGIOUS CONFLICT AND NON-CONFORMITY (1598–1775)

War weariness and an emergent rational spirit led to various attempts to restore Christian unity by irenic means. We have already referred to the humanists' efforts (e.g. those of Modrzewski and Laski in Poland) to harmonize conflicting doctrines on the basis of a common Christianity. Harking back to such humanists, various conciliators of the seventeenth century sought to merge Lutheran and Calvinist, Protestant and Catholic, Roman and Greek Orthodox theologies. Hugo Grotius explored the common ground of Catholics and Protestants in his *De Veritate Religionis Christianae* (1627) and its sequel, *Via et Votum ad Pacem Ecclesiasticam* (1642). The 'pansophy' of John Amos Comenius (Komenský) (1592–1670) was designed to end the conflicts of at least the evangelical creeds through a common core of learning (see Chapter XVI). The Lutheran theologian Georg Calixtus of Helmstedt took an active part in a religious conference at Thorn (1645) that vainly tried again to reconcile the Protestant creeds. Though attacked by all parties, especially by orthodox Lutherans, he inspired the Great Elector to attempt a union between Lutherans and Calvinists in Prussia, though without avail. A disciple of Calixtus, Gerhard Molanus, participated in the most far-reaching efforts at conciliation. One of these was the negotiations between the French bishop Bossuet and the German philosopher Leibniz, whose *Systema theologicum* (1687) advocated the accommodation of all Christian creeds and whose *Théodicée* (1710) was partly intended to cut across the differences among Christian sects and present a fundamental Christian theism. Another was the overlapping efforts of Bishop Spinola, who, in the service of Emperor Leopold I, negotiated with the Archbishop of Mainz, Protestant theologians in Berlin and Hanover, and Leibniz. Watched by the papacy and supported by the emperor, who sought Protestant aid against a new Turkish advance in the 1680's, these efforts ended in an abortive religious colloquy at Hanover in 1683. In the end, all these syncretic schemes, and parallel ones in England and Sweden, failed.

In the Germanies the Religious Peace of Augsburg (1555) lasted for over sixty years. Nevertheless, the truce was a precarious one. Some Protestant princes—mostly Calvinists, from whom official recognition was withheld in the Peace of Augsburg—formed a Protestant Union, abetted by Henry IV of France; the Catholic princes, resenting the frequent secularization of their church's properties, which they considered a violation of the treaty, formed a Catholic League. Each alliance looked for support abroad among co-religionists or others who might benefit from cooperation. Germany was thus split into hostile and alert factions. Several crises nearly led to armed conflict, and a full-fledged civil war broke out in 1618.

The Thirty Years' War began that year with the rebellion of the Bohemian Protestant estates against Habsburg attempts to abrogate their religious and political liberties. It quickly broadened into an unequal struggle (1618–20) between the Protestant Union and the Catholic League and then (1620–25) merged with the age-old conflict between German particularism and imperial authority. First (1625–29) Christian IV of Denmark and then (1629–35) Gustavus Adolphus of Sweden intervened directly on the side of the German Protestants. Spain's Habsburgs supported the Catholic League and the Austrian Habsburgs, and the Habsburg compact brought in on the other side their long-standing enemy France. Meanwhile the confederation of the United Provinces continued its struggle for independence from Spain. The German war thus spread into a general conflagration in which the battle between Protestantism and Catholicism became inextricably mixed with political rivalries that at times eclipsed the religious issues. Germany remained the principal battleground, ravished by the mercenaries on both sides. Among their commanding generals the adventurer Wallenstein was one of the few moved by a far-sighted political goal—German unity based upon religious freedom and a strong, centralized monarchy.

Disunited and faced with vastly superior Catholic power, German Protestantism was almost overwhelmed but was saved by Cardinal de Richelieu. For the very reason that he sought successfully to weaken the Huguenots of France (see below), Richelieu wished to keep the German Protestants strong —i.e. as a menace in each case to the respective central authority. It was for that reason that he had induced Gustavus Adolphus of Sweden to intervene in Germany, and when the intervening Swedish forces stalled after their king's death in the Battle of Lützen (1634), he brought France into open military alliance with the Swedish forces. The final phase of the Thirty Years' War thus in a sense became a Bourbon continuation of the long duel between Habsburg and Valois.

The peace, signed in the Westphalian towns of Münster and Osnabrück in 1648 after years of negotiation, was a series of treaties adjusting a vast complex of religious and political disputes. The religious settlement extended the provisions of the Religious Peace of Augsburg to German Calvinists and removed all distinction in the affairs of the Empire between Protestant and Catholic states. Ecclesiastical properties secularized before 1624 were allowed to remain in the hands of those who had secularized them. Previously granted religious liberties were reaffirmed, but Protestants under Habsburg family rule were specifically excluded from this provision. The Treaty of Westphalia did not grant full religious toleration but accorded the right of emigration to those denied the exercise of their religion, and Lutheran as well as Calvinist princes agreed upon mutual freedom of worship in their domains. Habsburg dominance was counterbalanced by increasing French power in Alsace-Lorraine, by increasing Swedish power in the Baltic area, and by formally recognizing the independence from the Habsburg crowns of Switzerland and the United Provinces. The gravest setback to Imperial union, however, was the complete restoration of territorial sovereignty (*Landeshoheit*) to the German states, including the right to enter into alliances among themselves and with foreign powers. The holocaust of the Thirty Years' War, though perhaps sometimes exaggerated, nevertheless left the Empire materially and spiritually weakened for over a century. Moreover, with France and Sweden as its guarantors, the Treaty of Westphalia became the thin end of a wedge for constant foreign intrusion in imperial affairs.

★   ★   ★

Fragmentation and Individualism in Protestantism

Protestantism manifested a strong tendency toward fragmentation. English Protestant opinion, for example, inclined increasingly toward Calvinism, and many of the subjects of Elizabeth I's successors resented the retention of certain Catholic elements in Anglican worship. While some of these 'Puritans' never broke with the Anglican Church, others became Presbyterians or Separatists. They all strove for a greater simplicity in church service and sought to cleanse the national church of doctrinal and vestiary externals incompatible with Reformed beliefs. They tended to believe that one who was among God's elect would lead a life of practical Christianity, outwardly demonstrated by a kind of temporal asceticism, and they opposed the subordination of religion to political exigencies. The Presbyterians of England and Scotland differed from other Puritans chiefly on the issue of church administration. Presbyterians opposed government of the church by the state (Erastianism) or by bishops (episcopalianism) and advocated government by its members through a hierarchy of assemblies, representing at each step a widening circle of churches. Presbyterianism was a logical outgrowth of the Protestant belief in the essential priesthood of all Christians. It occupied a middle ground between the monarchic episcopalianism of the Anglicans and the democratic congregationalism of the Separatists, or Independents, who believed in separate organization and independent government for each congregation.

Calvinist doctrines also contributed to the development of Baptist groups. Under Mennonite guidance, the Anabaptists had abandoned their earlier radicalism, and some English Brownists (Separatists), exiled in Holland, easily fell under Mennonite influence. They soon divided into 'General Baptists', who rejected Calvinist views of predestination, and 'Particular Baptists', who accepted them. Congregationalist in matters of church government, Baptists went further than the Presbyterians in their demand for freedom of religion from civil authority. In their 'Declaration of Faith', published in 1611 in Holland, English Baptists were the first to include in a formal creed the demand both for the absolute independence of congregations and for absolute freedom of the individual conscience.

The ultimate manifestation of Protestant individualism came with the rise of the Society of Friends (or Quakers). In Quaker theology doctrinal pre-occupations and formal ritual were abandoned. Worship was freed of all external and material ritual in order to make the religious experience as inward and personal as possible. Quakers built no churches and, though the first to recognize the ministry of women, ordained no ministers, believing that communication with God cannot be limited to particular places, times, ceremonies, or intermediaries. Their tolerance of doctrinal heterogeneity did not prevent their accepting a certain code of religious and social ethics expressed in such outward manifestations as pacifism, refusal to take oaths, philanthropy, and full support of civil liberty. Under the leadership of George Fox and William Penn, Quaker colonies were established in Pennsylvania, New Jersey, and Delaware, and Quakers, despite persecutions, went to live in nearly every other Anglo-American colony. They were the first religious body publicly to advocate the friendly treatment of Amerindians and the abolition of slavery. They did so before the close of the seventeenth century, and by the end of the eighteenth century, slavery virtually had ceased to exist among them. The Quaker John Woolman's *Some Considerations on the Keeping of Negroes* (1754) was the first important American abolitionist tract.

Strict personal conduct as an expression of practical Christianity became characteristic especially of the Bohemian Unity of Brethren (Unitas Fratrum). All but wiped out during the Thirty Years' War, the Bohemian Brethren survived in Saxony, where a remnant found refuge on the estates of Count von Zinzendorf at Herrnhut. Under his influence the Brethren became closely associated with Lutheran Pietism (see below) and subsequently took an active part in the religious revival of eighteenth-century German Protestantism and in the foundation of the 'Pennsylvania Dutch' communities in America. Through John Wesley's contacts with them, the 'Moravians', as they were called in America, were also to influence the development of Methodism in England and the Anglo-American colonies.

The emphasis upon active endeavour became part of an ascetic Protestant ethos that sought to realize Christian principles in all spheres of life. The good Protestant was conceived as abiding by strict standards of family discipline, morality, honesty, thrift, austerity, and philanthropy. Idleness and waste were rejected as dangerous to the Christian's state of grace, but the honest accumulation of wealth and power through toil and enterprise was regarded as a possible outward sign of an inner grace. It has long been argued pro and con whether this list of virtues made Calvinism especially attractive to the rising capitalist class,[61] for Protestant ethics seemed to give a religious incentive to 'business virtues' and 'substance', and thus sanctioned the profit motive that Catholic scruples about 'just price' and 'usury' had tended (rather unsuccessfully) to discourage. Civic philanthropy in Protestant countries tended to take the place of ecclesiastical 'good works'. The elect would engage in good works, the Westminster Confession (see below) said, as 'the fruits and evidence of a true and lively faith'.

* * *

Protestantism and Political Dissent

Greater perhaps than the social significance of Protestant sectarianism was its impact upon political developments. The emphasis on active endeavour also has its political phase. As Calvinist synods became larger or representative of greater numbers, they grew in power and assertiveness, uniting their adherents, taking sides on all kinds of issues, influencing public opinion, and yet speaking, though in the name of the sovereign God, as delegates of the faithful. Representative and responsible government thus became associated with Calvinism in an age which ordinarily took for granted a close union between church and ruler and in which religious nonconformity, tantamount to political subversion, was often punished as disloyalty to the ruler in his capacity of leader in the national religious organization. In fact, in Lutheran monarchies, as also in England, the ruler formally became the supreme head of the church, thus burnishing the image of monarchy. Even in Calvinist countries presbyteries, consistories, and synods sometimes tried to dictate in civil affairs as well as theology and church matters. And yet in most states, whether Lutheran, Calvinist, or Roman, a monolithic church structure was a thing of the past. Though (with a few previously designated exceptions) intolerant of one another and of dissent within their own ranks, the various sects by seeking religious toleration for themselves became actively engaged in the struggle for freedom of conscience, political liberty, and civil rights. Even persecution indirectly served the cause of toleration, for the enforced emigration of nonconformists spread fragments of sects through much of Europe, notably the enlightened province of Holland, and to a few of the English settlements in the New World, where they gradually acquired the right to worship as they pleased.

Toleration came to the United Provinces only after a tragic political struggle. Once victorious there, Calvinism developed a schism in which political issues merged with doctrinal disputes, centring upon the divergent views of predestination held by two theologians of the University of Leyden, Franciscus Gomarus and Jacobus Arminius. The Gomarists, representing most of the preachers and Reformed congregations, stood for a strict interpretation of predestination; the Arminians (later called Remonstrants, after the 'Remonstrance' in which, in 1610, they defended their position) advocated a liberal interpretation. The Remonstrants demanded a national synod to be convoked under the authority of the States General, but the Gomarists insisted upon submitting the dispute for decision to a church synod only. The Remonstrants thus became Erastians (i.e. followers of the view, somewhat erroneously attributed to a late Swiss scientist and theologian, Thomas Erastus, to the effect that the state was dominant in ecclesiastical matters), and the Contra-Remonstrants (or Gomarists) strict Calvinists in both theology and church polity.

The dispute became a matter of personal conflict between the leading statesman of the young Dutch union, John Oldenbarneveldt, advocate of Holland, who sided with the Remonstrants, and Prince Maurice of Nassau, son of William the Silent, stadholder and a foremost general of his time. In 1614, on the initiative of Hugo Grotius, the States General attempted to grant toleration to both sides and to win mutual forbearance. The conflict in the end, however, was resolved by Maurice's military might, and the Gomarist party made captives of its opponents. It assembled a synod of churchmen at Dort (or Dordrecht), which conferred from 1618 to 1619 in a sort of Council of Trent of the Reformed Church. While most of the synod's more than one hundred members were from the Netherlands and it was intended to deal with the Dutch domestic controversy alone, a number of observers came from Switzerland, Germany, Scotland, England, and other areas where Calvinism had taken hold. It adopted the Netherland Confession and the Heidelberg Catechism. Thus orthodox Calvinism became the official faith throughout the United Provinces, and the Dutch Reformed Church set a pattern for other Calvinists. Oldenbarneveldt was executed on a trumped up charge of treason in 1619; his young colleague Hugo Grotius was imprisoned but managed to escape. The Remonstrants won official toleration in 1632, however, and the United Provinces embarked upon an extraordinary record of religious liberty that was to be one of the crowning glories of its 'Golden Age'.

The political import of religious dissent was especially evident in England, where the struggle against the Anglican episcopacy and for presbyterian or congregational government in church affairs contributed to the origin of a rebellion. A principal aim of the rebels was to limit Stuart absolutism by the establishment (or, from the point of view of some of their apologists, the retention) of constitutional government. The 'Solemn League and Covenant' concluded between Scottish Presbyterians and English dissenters in 1643 sealed the doom of Charles I. The resulting Parliamentary government and Cromwellian rule did not last. Nevertheless, the Westminster Assembly (1643–49) drew up the Westminster Confession, which has remained the creed or at the basis of the creed of Presbyterian churches ever since.

With the restoration of the Stuarts, the Anglican episcopacy was restored, and the struggle against the renewed danger of royal absolutism was resumed. After the Glorious Revolution of 1688, no English king dared openly to attempt to rule without Parliament. The Declaration of Rights and the Act of (limited) Toleration, which lifted the penalties that Protestant dissenters had had to incur for non-attendance at Anglican services, both issued within a few months of the Glorious Revolution, indicated that political liberty and religious freedom might be a logical outcome of the Reformation. Still, after the Act of Settlement (1701), none but a Protestant could hope to sit on the British throne; complete abolition of religious disabilities for subjects of the United Kingdom was not to come until the nineteenth century.

Henry IV, made king of France by civil war, assassination, and conversion, was himself assassinated in 1610. In the troubled reign of Louis XIII, Richelieu undertook the destruction of Huguenot independence, which he considered detrimental to the absolute monarchy that he wanted to establish. He succeeded largely because he was willing to use superior force while the Huguenots failed to muster the unity and organization that had made their past successes possible. Among them, as throughout the rest of France, the influence of the nobility had considerably decreased as the bourgeoisie grew in wealth and power. The Huguenot Duc de Rohan tried in vain to win the concerted support of the Huguenot cities in his fight against the threat of royal absolutism. The bourgeoisie, whether Catholic or Protestant, tended to support the king, from whom they expected protection and the promotion of their economic enterprises. The fall of La Rochelle in 1628 enabled Richelieu to take from the Huguenots their armed strength as an *imperium in imperio*, but he left them still a tolerated sect. Louis XIV, on the mistaken assumption that their number had dwindled to negligibility, first tried to force them into conformity and then revoked the Edict of Nantes (1685). The Protestants remained an outlawed sect until Louis XVI granted them toleration once more (1787).

A similar ebbing of numbers and standing came to the Protestants of Transylvania. Despite the legal equality of Catholics, Calvinists, Lutherans, and Unitarians in Transylvania, after the Thirty Years' War Protestantism gradually diminished there and in Royal Hungary. The ambitious ruling families of Transylvania joined with the Habsburgs against the Protestants. They not only got the help of the triumphant Jesuits but also relied upon the sword to root out the threat that Magyar Calvinism presented to their rule. In 1679, an uprising in Royal Hungary led by Imre Thököly revealed not only the union between the Magyar aristocracy and Protestantism but also the readiness of Magyar Protestants to ally with the Catholic king of France and the infidel sultan of Turkey against the Habsburgs. This Magyar rebellion was a phase of the war against Turkey (see Chapter I) that brought King Jan Sobieski of Poland to the relief of Vienna and resulted in a Holy League against the Turks. When the war ended (1699), Royal Hungary was no longer an elective possession of the Habsburgs but had become hereditary; Transylvania and large parts of Turkish Hungary had been annexed to Austrian Hungary; and the Hungarian Protestants were practically defence-less. Religious and political liberty was restored in 1711 only as a result of a Magyar rebellion during Austria's preoccupation with the War of the Spanish

Succession, but the Protestant population was by that time considerably reduced in size.

Other Protestant sects fared equally badly in eastern Europe. The Bohemian Brethren, having spread from Bohemia and Moravia into Poland, barely survived the Thirty Years' War under their bishop Comenius (see Chapter XVI). Unlike the Brethren, the Socinians had little following among the common people, drawing their support mostly from the Szeklar (i.e. Magyar) landowners of Transylvania, where they still survive. In the great Catholic counter-offensive that in the wake of the Thirty Years' War swept Poland, Bohemia, and Hungary under Jesuit leadership, Socinians and Brethren were practically extirpated from eastern Europe. The Socinians who found their way to England helped to found present-day Unitarianism. From England the movement spread to the Anglo-American colonies, and despite efforts to repress it, Unitarianism flourished in the English-speaking lands. In 1774 its adherents opened a chapel in London. The Bohemian Brethren, as we have seen, became the 'Moravians' of America.

*   *   *

Jansenism

Within Catholicism the quest for personal religious identification had political connotations somewhat similar to those implicit in the Protestant emphasis upon individual freedom of conscience. At the bottom of this quest lay a concern with the problem of predestination newly stimulated by Protestant, especially Calvinist, preoccupations with the teachings of the Church Fathers. At the Council of Trent the question of predestination had been touched upon by implication but never fully settled. At the same time that the issue separated Arminians and Gomarists in the United Provinces it became a focal point in a long controversy that raged between the Jesuits, who propagated an orthodox Scholasticism, and a group of theologians at the Belgian University of Louvain who demanded a more mystical approach to religion that they found in the writings of the Church Fathers. Cornelius Jansen, bishop of Ypres, took a prominent part in the controversy and presented his views in a voluminous treatise on St Augustine, in whose theology predestination had played an important part. Jansen's work, entitled *Augustinus*, was published posthumously in 1640. It attacked Jesuit rationalism and formalism, emphasizing inner experience and an active love of God rather than reason and formal devotion as the way to salvation. Love of God could come to man, Jansen held, only through an act of divine grace completely beyond human volition. Jansen's teachings thus gave a new prominence to the doctrine of predestination, softening it, however—as compared to the eternally fixed election of Calvinism—by a belief in conversion, holding forth the hope of attaining election, if God so willed, during one's earthly existence. The Jesuits subscribed to a theology which put greater stress upon freedom of the will. The Jesuit theologian Luis de Molina (1535–

1600) had in 1588 published a work entitled *Concordia Liberi Arbitrii cum Gratiae Donis, Divina Praesentia, Providentia, Praedestinatione et Reprobatione*, which, as the title indicates, undertook to show that the freedom of the human will was compatible with belief in divine grace and predestination. The Jesuits' emphasis upon the Molinist doctrine of free will led them to see in Jansenism a rank heresy, even though the Jansenists did not deny that good works were also a mark of God's grace and were in the keeping of the Catholic Church.

Jansenism spread into France through Jean du Vergier de Hauranne, abbot of St Cyran, and his disciple, Antoine Arnauld, the ablest spokesman of the rapidly growing movement. Together they established a Jansenist centre at Port Royal, site of a Cistercian convent which had been revivified by Arnauld's sister, Abbess Angélique. Dedicated to a life of practical labour and ascetic devotion, the Jansenist colony at Port Royal through its vigorous intellectual activities and its model schools (see Chapter XVI) became a great influence in French literature. Racine was educated there, and writers like Pascal and scholars like Tillemont were among its illustrious members.

Arnauld's book *De la fréquente communion* (1643), which attacked Jesuit confessional practices, was the signal for a long conflict between Jansenism and orthodox Catholicism. It was condemned as heretical by the Sorbonne and eventually by Pope Innocent X. Though never wholly adopting the ascetic life of the Port Royal solitaries, Pascal espoused the cause of Jansenism. In defence of Arnauld, he began his *Lettres écrites . . . à un provincial*, generally known as the *Lettres provinciales* (1656–57), which added to his already secure fame as a scientist (see Chapter XIV) a glorious reputation as a philosopher, moralist, and writer of prose. Before the last of these *Lettres* was published, Arnauld was expelled from the Sorbonne, but the *Lettres provinciales* have remained a quiver of ironic shafts to aim at the Jesuits, especially for their alleged casuistry and 'probabilism' (readiness to accept debatable tenets and practices).

The Jansensists' views on predestination and their advocacy of a personal religion proved welcome to the large number tired of mere dogma and ritual. At the same time, they appealed to Gallican sentiment—that is, the desire for a French national church, independent of Rome—by their refusal to accept the decisions of Rome. Pasquier Quesnel's *Réflexions morales sur le Nouveau Testament* (1671), which was both a commentary on and a translation of New Testament texts, further popularized Jansenism. The clarity with which he explained the Jansenist position made it both an effective appeal to the laity and a prime target of Jesuit theologians and the papacy.

The Jansenists' non-conformism was bound to bring them into disfavour with Louis XIV, who regarded as disloyal those who did not accept his church. Yet for years no official condemnation was forthcoming. Several factors combined to delay drastic repression: the protection of the king's cousin Madame de Longueville, the moderate attitude of Pope Clement IX, the ability of Jansenists (Arnauld above all) to temporize on all decisions by adroit legalistic arguments and manoeuvres, and widespread doubts as to whether the Jansenists were in fact as heretical as the Jesuits claimed. The death of Madame de Longueville in 1679 ended the protection Jansensists had enjoyed at court, and the French king joined hands with the pope to exterminate this new dissent. Arnauld had to go into exile in the Netherlands, followed six years later by Quesnel. The Jansenists nevertheless refused to break with the papacy, contending that 'respectful silence' without interior assent was sufficient to meet papal condemnation. The pope, they argued, might be infallible regarding questions of heresy but was not infallible regarding the 'facts', such as what was in an author's mind when writing a book. Clement issued the bull *Vineam Domini* (1705), denying the sufficiency of 'respectful silence'.

Meanwhile Louis XIV, urged on by the austere Madame de Maintenon, who was now his wife, and his Jesuit advisers, determined to uproot Jansenism as he believed he already had uprooted Calvinism from the soil of France. Port Royal was destroyed in 1709, after the recusant nuns had been forcibly removed. Importuned by the king, Clement issued a second bull, *Unigenitus* (1713), intended to deprive Jansenism of all theological justification. It anathemized one hundred and one propositions contained in Quesnel's *Réflexions* and condemned popular Bible reading, which had become a practice even among devout Catholics. The bull *Unigenitus* was considered by convinced Gallicans a distinct victory of Ultramontanism (i.e. of papal supremacy), and an important segment of French Catholics refused to accept it. Some of them migrated to Utrecht, where a Jansenist church has maintained itself since the early eighteenth century.

*　　*　　*

Gallicanism and Febronianism

Foremost among the French clergy who refused to accept *Unigenitus* was Cardinal de Noailles, archbishop of Paris and a leading Gallican, to whom a recent edition of Quesnel's book had been dedicated. Gallicanism thus became an ally of Jansenism. The doctrine of 'Gallican Liberties' had been in the air since the Pragmatic Sanction of Bourges (see Chapter III). An aftermath of the Conciliar Movement, it held that the king's temporal authority was not subject to papal approval and that the pope had only limited jurisdiction over French ecclesiastical affairs. With the intensification of absolutism, the Gallican Liberties had become of mounting concern to the French kings.

At the beginning of the seventeenth century, Edmond Richer, a famous Sorbonne theologian, had gone so far as to claim a voice in Gallican Church affairs for the lower clergy as successors to Jesus' disciples. This doctrine, known as 'Richerism', was dangerous, since it combined a political and social philosophy with dogmatic Gallicanism. It had been condemned by

Cardinal Richelieu and was recanted by its author. The classic formulation of Gallicanism was rather a pronunciamento of upper clergymen; it came from Bishop Bossuet in 1682 at a special assembly of the French clergy. A conflict had arisen between Louis XIV and Pope Innocent XI over the king's right to collect the *régale*, the income from vacant ecclesiastical benefices. The pope's unwillingness to permit this unilateral action led Bossuet to draw up a Declaration of Gallican Liberties, which the assembly unanimously accepted. The declaration reasserted, more explicitly than ever before, the independence of temporal sovereigns from the pope, the superiority of a general council to the pope, the powerlessness of the pope to make decisions contrary to the rules of the Gallican Church, and the fallibility of papal decisions not acceptable to an ecumenical council. In the end, Louis' numerous foreign complications obliged him to withdraw the declaration without pressing for a victory. Gallicanism, nevertheless, had served temporarily to revive conciliarism in France against ultramontane pretensions and in support of divine-right absolutism.

Contrary to Louis XIV's intention, the appeal to a general council became a weapon in the Jansenists' fight against the *Unigenitus*. A brief respite in Jansenist persecution ensued after the death of the Grand Monarch, when the indifferent Duc d'Orleans was regent, but was followed by renewed persecution when Louis XV began to reign in his own right. Gallican sentiment was strong, however, and many members of the Parlement of Paris called themselves Jansenist, though more out of political anti-clericalism than religious conviction. In 1730, when Louis XV ordered the *Unigenitus* to be registered as law, the Parlement of Paris refused to comply.

The essence of Gallicanism—that is, the politico-religious struggle against ultramontane supremacy and papal infallibility—spread beyond the borders of France. In the Holy Roman Empire the movement for national independence from Rome appeared as 'Febronianism'. The name is derived from a book entitled *De Statu Ecclesiae et Legitima Potestate Romani Pontificis*, published in 1763 (under the pseudonym Justinus Febronius) by Nikolaus von Hontheim, auxiliary bishop of Trier. Febronianism denied that the church as instituted by Jesus was a monarchy ruled by the pope. The constitution of the Catholic Church, Hontheim contended, rested upon the common episcopacy of all bishops, with the pope merely *primus inter pares*, having the role of coordinator and collaborator. Attacking the False Decretals, upon which he maintained that the pretensions of the papacy were based, Hontheim reasserted the supremacy of a general council over the pope.

Despite almost immediate papal condemnation, Febronianism was very influential in Catholic Germany and in all the Habsburg dominions. It was generally favoured by German bishops, who since the sixteenth century had enjoyed special privileges, and by the so-called 'enlightened despots' of the eighteenth century, whose reform programmes encompassed domination of the church. Devout Catholic though she was, Empress Maria Theresa refused to prohibit Hontheim's work, and Febronian principles guided Emperor Joseph II, her son, in his attempts to reform state and church. From his vigorous support of Febronianism came the name *Josephism*. Josephism relegated papal authority strictly to the domain of dogma and spiritual guidance, reserving to the state all other measures pertaining to the welfare of its subjects and the government of the church. Joseph thus promoted religious tolerance in the interest of internal peace and emphasized the practical work of the secular clergy among the people above the *vita contemplativa* of the regular orders. Hundreds of new parishes—in the emperor's view, centres of social and religious life—were established, hundreds of religious houses and oratories were closed, and theological seminaries were attached to the secular universities as part of his effort to achieve educational and other reforms. Thus the principle of Erastianism became a weapon also for Catholic monarchs seeking to make the national churches a branch of the dynastic service.

*   *   *

Quietism

Despite Jansenism's emphasis upon the intimate relation of man with God, and despite the occasional devotional outbursts and miracle working that it developed under the pressure of persecution, it was not essentially mystical in nature. In the seventeenth century Catholic mysticism took the form of Quietism. The roots of Quietism go back to the devotionalism that, under the influence of Theresa of Avila and John of the Cross, flourished in Spanish Catholicism during the sixteenth century. Both of these mystics, while stressing an essentially passive love of God, had also insisted upon an active life of practical good works and considered the mediation of the church as necessary. In France a profound religious revival followed the wars of religion. Cardinal Pierre de Bérulle (1575–1629) founded the French Oratorians, Vincent de Paul (1576–1660) the Congregation of the Mission (Lazarists) and the Sisters of Charity, and François de Sales (1562–1622) the Order of the Visitation. These men eloquently preached, in sermons and in books, a personal piety through prayer, love of God, charity, and personal service.

A later manifestation of this widespread Catholic piety was the creed known as Quietism, which, in contrast to the earlier movements, rejected the active life and need for a mediator between man and God. It taught, instead, a love of God so complete and unquestioning that self was utterly submerged and, in the highest stage of communion with God, became, without deliberate intention, the recipient of divine inspiration. This experience, attainable only in moments of most passive contemplation, was considered so personal and so far beyond the power of human reason that neither the church nor man's active desires could guide him toward it. Quietism thus carried to its logical conclusion the mystic's repudiation of the mediatorship of the church. It further asserted that supreme oneness with the divine could come only through a selfless love of God and a submission to the divine will so perfect that intentional preoccupation with the merits of good works, even consciousness of sin, must give way to a sublime indifference to all self-interested concerns. These tenets seemed to Quietism's opponents inveterate heresies alarmingly close to Protestantism.

The essence of Quietism is contained in the *Guida Spirituale* (1675) of the Spanish priest Miguel de Molinos. He resided in Italy, where elaborate ecclesiastical ceremonials provoked him to deny the importance of ritual, dogma, and church, and to emphasize 'contemplation' and 'inner peace' instead. His teachings, widely influential in Italy, remained unopposed for years, until they aroused the opposition of Jesuits, ever alert to threats to the ecclesiastical structure. After other attempts at censure had failed, Father François de La Chaise, Jesuit confessor to Louis XIV, persuaded the French king to instruct his ambassador at Rome to insist upon action. A papal bull in 1688 condemned Molinos' teachings, and he himself languished as a prisoner of the Roman Inquisition until he died in 1697.

Meanwhile Molinos' ideas had spread across the borders of Italy. The most ardent advocates of Quietism in France were the wealthy widow Guyon and her confessor, Father Lacombe. Continuing waves of devotionalism had swept France since Bérulle, François de Sales, Vincent de Paul, and others had founded their new religious societies and charitable orders, making it easy for Madame Guyon and Father Lacombe to recruit a considerable following. Both of these Quietist advocates were imprisoned about the time that Molinos was condemned, but Madame Guyon was subsequently freed and introduced by an influential friend into the circle around Madame de Maintenon. During a brief period of prominence in court society the devout widow won over the famed archbishop of Cambrai, Fénelon (1651–1715). Her writings and proselytizing in Madame de Maintenon's school at St Cyr aroused the disapproval of Bossuet, who on three separate occasions condemned Madame Guyon's teachings and attempted to silence her. Finally, after imprisonment in the Bastille, she went into exile at Blois, devoting her remaining years to piety and philanthropy.

Meanwhile Fénelon had risen in her defence and in his *Maximes des saints* (1697) undertook to explain the Quietist position of disinterested love of God. He insisted that the Quietist doctrine of the love of God required a serene passivity that might become the sole basis of a truly personal religious experience. To his opponents Quietism implied an abandonment of self so complete that the individual might become absolutely indifferent even to his own salvation. Bossuet meanwhile was producing his *Instruction sur les états d'oraison* in defence of an active, personal desire for salvation, and a prolonged and bitter controversy began between the two bishops. Eventually Fénelon's teachings were officially condemned by Pope Innocent XII, and Fénelon submitted, without, however, formally retracting his writings. His submission and exile from the court, Madame Guyon's arrest and exile, and

Louis XIV's support of Bossuet heralded the end of Quietism as a significant movement.

*   *   *

Pietism

The quest for the 'inner light' of a personal religion found more lasting form as a Protestant movement. Whereas the Catholic hierarchy was able to reassert its doctrinal supremacy over Jansensists, Quietists, and other dissidents, Protestant theology as it became formalized in its several established churches was more defenceless. One reaction against established Protestant orthodoxy took the form of Pietism, which exerted an impact upon both Calvinist and Lutheran Protestantism.

Calvinist Pietism spread from the Netherlands into the Reformed territories of Germany. Under the leadership of Jodocus van Lodenstein the first organized sect of Pietist leanings was formed within the established Calvinist church as a protest against the materialism that prosperity had brought to Holland. More radical, Jean de Labadie, a former Jesuit aspirant converted to French Calvinism, founded a religious community that was intended to constitute a 'pure church'. German Pietism merged the less shocking tenets of the Labadists with Quietist and Jansenist ideas, the mysticism of Jacob Boehme, and the poetic spirit of Friedrich von Spee, the Jesuit opponent of witch-hunting.

Phillip Jakob Spener, the founder of Lutheran Pietism as a distinct movement, became convinced through Labadie's sermons and the writings of Boehme of the necessity of reforming the Lutheran Church. In 1675 he published his *Pia Desideria*, which presented the basic tenets of Pietist devotion. His major premise was Luther's concept of the universal priesthood of all Christians, which assigned an important function to the laity. The personal religious experience that alone could give meaning to this priesthood, he taught, was a living, active Christianity, which could be achieved only through the application of Christian principles to everyday life; the essential Christian principles could be grasped only through a loving familiarity with Scripture. To combat the doctrinal inflexibility that held sway over Lutheran theology, he directed the Lutherans back to the foundation of their creed, the Bible.

Perhaps the most lasting achievement of Pietism was that it liberated the study of the Bible from the theologians and placed it in the homes of the laity. Spener advocated the formation of private devotional and study groups such as the *collegia pietatis* (which he initiated in his own house), and the *collegia philobiblica*, seminars for students of the Bible. Such groups and seminars, he held, should lead ministers as well as laity from deadening doctrinal preoccupations toward a practical devotional life, which was the outward manifestation of spiritual regeneration. Congregational singing also became an important phase of lay participation in Pietist religious activity, and Paul Gerhardt, one of the most prolific of Protestant hymn writers, provided Lutheran Pietism with some enduring hymnal expressions of religious devotion.

The University of Halle, founded in 1694 under the patronage of Frederick III, elector of Brandenburg, became a centre of Pietist learning through Spener's influence and the efforts of August Hermann Francke and Christian Thomasius (see Chapter XVI). Lectures on Scripture were made the basis for the training of ministers, who were to be practising Christians rather than orthodox doctrinaires and whose sermons were to inspire rather than to expound. Francke was called upon to help train the missionaries whom Frederick IV of Denmark proposed to send to the Danish possessions in India. Pietism thus became a factor in the Protestant missionary movement, and under Pietist influence (for Zinzendorf was a godson of Spener and an ardent Pietist), missionary work formed an important aspect of the activities of the Bohemian Brethren (see Chapter V).

Pietism was not intended by its founders to be a separatist movement and did not long outlast Spener and Francke (d. 1727) as such. Nevertheless, spiritual pietism—i.e. the call for personal devotion and a living Christianity, the emphasis upon direct communion between the individual and God, and the reliance upon feeling rather than intellect as the way to achieve this communion—continued in pious circles. Distrust of organized religion prevented effective coordination among the Pietist congregations, leaving room for the accusation that their *ecclesiolae in ecclesia* disrupted the unity of the Lutheran Church. On the whole, however, Pietism reasserted the importance of the laity, thitherto rendered almost negligible through the hardening of Lutheran orthodoxy at the hands of the clergy.

Despite its stress upon the intuitive and the sentimental in religious devotion, the very individualism of Pietism was a foretaste of the Enlightenment. The opposition to dogma and to rigid church organization as well as the emphasis upon freedom of conscience and upon personal independence provided a common ground for both Pietism and enlightened philosophy. Though closely identified with Pietism, Thomasius was also an influential exponent of enlightened ideas. In his studies of natural law, he tried to define the role of state and religion in the society of men, and echoing Spee, he attacked the persecution of heretics and the trial of witches. Where, however, the philosophers of the Enlightenment relied upon Reason, Thomasius was more likely to rely upon Revelation (see Chapter IX).

*　　*　　*

Freethinkers and Devotees

A great Puritan awakening inspired by Richard Baxter in seventeenth-century England in some ways paralleled the Pietism of Germany. Though relatively free of the mass emotionalism which revivalism acquired in later years, these movements were essentially revivalist. To the concern with Christianity as a personal experience and an active way of life, revivalists added a deep-seated loyalty to what they conceived to be the fundamental teachings of Christianity and a desire to impart that loyalty to the populace.

Their appeal to the masses was in large part a reaction against the several rationalist trends and the rising indifferentism of the seventeenth and eighteenth centuries (see Chapter VII). One of the rationalist trends was Latitudinarianism, an effort of English clergymen, like the Cambridge Platonists, to find a common ground upon which Protestant Christians could unite despite their doctrinal differences. Another was Deism, which developed in England and France in the seventeenth century. Deism was a 'natural' religion, free of dogma and church, in which the Deity became First Cause and little more. Some went in that direction only so far as to seek a rational Christianity; others, like Lord Herbert of Cherbury, laid the basis for the rationalist, natural, free-thinking religion of the eighteenth century.

A still more sceptical trend was that of the coterie of French poets of the seventeenth century known to their enemies as 'Libertines'. They were free-thinking, unconventional, even atheistic writers, of whom one of the most prominent was Théophile de Viau (d. 1626). They rejected, along with traditional religion, much of the faith in man, his morality, and secular authority, thus appearing to the devout in the midst of the contemporary revival in France of a prayerful, active Christianity, to be in conspiracy against God, man, and government. The state, egged on by the Jesuits, took vengeance on Viau; after a lengthy trial (1623–25), he was sentenced to exile. 'Libertinage' did not disappear, however; it merely resorted to subtleties. New writers came to be charged with it, Cyrano de Bergerac (d. 1655) among them—composers of light verse, risqué or even obscene poems, irreligious burlesques, and broad satires. Claude Le Petit was executed in 1662 for 'divine and human lèse-majesté'. Still the movement persisted until, in the eighteenth century, literary 'libertinage' merged with the Enlightenment (see Chapters IX and XV).

Revivalism was not the only reaction to the extensive corrosion worked by these rationalist trends upon orthodox theology and the minds of the un-schooled. In Catholic France, with the connivance of influential nobles, officials, and prelates, the Duc de Ventadour in 1629 founded the Compagnie du Saint-Sacrament de l'Autel, a pious, secret society. It was intended not only to combat libertines, Protestants, the less devout workers' organizations (compagnonages), the more arbitrary employers, the poverty and paganism of the rural districts, and other threats to orthodoxy but also to bring pressure to bear upon lax or hesitant authorities. The Compagnie operated, with great secrecy but with conspicuous success, through branches in Paris, Lyons, Marseille, and other cities, even abducting and imprisoning arbitrarily women who had incurred its displeasure. In 1660, angered by its usurpations, the government arranged to have the Parlement of Paris suppress unauthor-ized societies, but the well organized 'conspiracy of the devout' continued, sometimes under other names, reaching even into Louis XIV's cabinet.

At the beginning of the eighteenth century, in Protestant England a mass attack on irreligion began. Charles Wesley, John Wesley, and George Whitefield were among a number of Oxford students who were induced by reaction against Latitudinarianism, Deism, and other contemporary religious innovations to study Anglicanism systematically. Their derisive fellow students called them 'Methodists'. John Wesley's concern led him to visit Herrnhut and the Bohemian Brethren, and eventually to become convinced of full salvation by faith in Jesus. Although the two Wesley brothers died (Charles in 1788 and John in 1791) as Anglican ministers, and Whitefield, breaking from the Anglican Church, died a Presbyterian (1770), they were in part responsible for the founding of a new evangelical sect. Wesley lived to see the Wesleyan Methodist Church arise in England, and the Methodist Episcopal Church in the United States. Whitefield's followers had meanwhile organized the Calvinist Methodists, especially strong in Wales. During their lifetime they travelled as evangelists in Europe and America hundreds of thousands of miles, wrote thousands of hymns, and preached scores of thousands of sermons to huge spontaneous congregations in open fields, barns, and specially constructed tabernacles, calling upon their hearers to repent their sins and to revive their faith in salvation. Anglo-America proved to be the land *par excellence* of religious revivals (see Chapter V).[62]

NOTES TO CHAPTER IV

1. Professor A. Dupront points out that the proliferation of indulgences, and in particular, towards the end of the medieval period, the development of indulgences applicable to the dead, is attributable not merely to the inventive cupidity of the Roman Curia but also to a firmly-anchored religious desire to guarantee, by all means available during this life, the life of the future, that is to say, eternity.

2. Professor A. Dupront believes that for modern France a vital consequence of the Concordat was the integration of the church into the growing apparatus of absolutism, the arrogation to royal power of larger material wealth, and also, as a consequence of the system of benefices, that other form of the power of the nobility represented in the seventeenth and eighteenth centuries by the aristocratization of the church. As for the formal aspect, the concordat settlement of 1516 provided a definition of co-operation between the two powers which, while restating but abating the authority of the 'Christian body', in fact served to disintegrate it.

3. Professor A. Dupront feels that here a fundamental aspect has been left aside, the central consciousness of a *philosophia Christi*—a grandiose attempt at a Christology immanent to the century, which, while adamantly refusing all pagan ambiguity, rediscovered the dual discipline of a rhetoric and a σοφια. And again, without trying to multiply Erasmism as the French school in particular has done, there existed in the Nordic and German world, centred around the person of the young emperor, an almost eschatological hope of an imperial, secular, and Christian rule, animating for a few years certain circles among the high authorities at court, in the chancelleries of princes and nobles as well as in the cities. Erasmism was also an attempted synthesis of the two powers in the order and administration of the Empire, just as the *philosophia Christi* was the profoundly religious union of the two halves of history—Classical and Christian.

4. *Works of Martin Luther*, ed. Henry Eyster Jacobs (Philadelphia, 1915), I, p. 33.

5. To Professor A. Dupront this point might be amplified as follows: A 'linear' account of facts does not seem sufficient to convey the extraordinary correspondence existing between Luther's religious crisis and the sudden repercussions of the Ninety-Five Theses and their rapid translation into the vernacular—theses which, moreover, go far beyond a denunciation of the exploitation of indulgences. The traditional historiographer sees no more than a relatively banal causality, whereas there is, in fact, a conjunction between a 'case' of religious exigency, powerful and entirely unbridled, and the reactive spirit of the German nation, temporarily roused against the *gravamina*. That these two should have coalesced, mutually fortifying one another, is no reason to confuse them, or yet to fail to distinguish them sufficiently. For the case of Luther, see Lucien Fèbvre: *Un destin: Martin Luther* (Paris, 1945), and more particularly a work remarkable for its spiritual penetration: Joseph Lortz: *Die Reformation in Deutschland* (2nd ed., Freiburg, 1941).

On the state of mind of Germany during the second decade of the sixteenth century, see Maurice Gravier: *Luther et l'opinion publique. Essai sur la littérature satirique et polémique en langue allemande pendant les années décisives de la Réforme (1520-30)* (Paris, 1942).

Moreover, is it possible to describe Catholic doctrine to the point of saying that 'the salvation of Christians depended largely upon the clergy as the ordained administrators of the sacraments?'

Such extra-temporal schematism seems to forget that the sacramentary doctrine of the church had, in fact, been perfectly proclaimed only in the canons of the Council of Florence, just over a half a century before Luther. On the other hand there exists a theology of the church, linked with the actual history of the church, and there has never been any question but that Christ gave to Peter and the Apostles power to bind and unbind. See Matthew XIX, 18: 'Whatsoever thou shalt bind on earth shall be bound in heaven; and whatsoever thou shalt loose on earth shall be loosed in heaven.'

6. 'A Treatise on Christian Liberty', Luther, *Works*, II, p. 312.

7. *Ibid.*, p. 331.

8. Quoted in James MacKinnon, *Luther and the Reformation*, 4 vols. (London, 1925-29), II, pp. 237-38.

9. *Ibid.*, p. 277.

10. Luther, *Works*, II, p. 84.

11. *Ibid.*, pp. 70-1.

12. Professor A. Dupront stresses that Hutten's interest in the Augustine monks dates only from after his excommunication. All that went before was for him mere clerical squabbling, and the occasion one for championing Germanic liberties in the face of the essentially Roman antichrist, whereas Luther's struggle was for the essential freedom of the Christian.

13. Quoted in J. S. Schapiro, *Social Reform and the Reformation* (New York, 1909), p. 139.

14. Luther, *Works*, IV, p. 249.

15. Quoted in E. W. Zeeden, *The Legacy of Luther* (Newman Press, Md., 1954), p. 15.

16. Professor A. Dupront agrees that, from the point of view of formal classification, the heresy represented by certain major aspects of Lutheranism is still medieval. The new phenomenon is that the heresy became the church. The *Loci Communes* is already a church book. On modern heresy, reference may be made to A. Dupront, 'Reflexions sur l'hérésie moderne', *Archives de Sociologie des Religions*, No. 14 (1962), pp. 17-25.

Moreover, is it justifiable to reproach Luther for a certain decline in humanism and the proliferation of theological controversies? The truth would seem to be that

(1) the fate of humanism was of very little interest to Luther and his followers, who were profoundly religious men;

(2) Lutheran attitude and dogma faced modern religious experience with the problem of direct relations between man and God, outside all church institutions, that is to say, forced into the open the whole drama of Divine Grace.

17. Quoted in Leopold von Ranke, *Deutsche Geschichte in Zeitalter der Reformation* (Munich, 1925), II, pp. 289–90.

18. Oskar Farner, *Zwingli the Reformer*, translated by D. G. Sear (New York, 1952), p. 24.

19. G. W. Bromley, ed., *Zwingli and Bullinger*, Vol. XXIV of the 'Library of Christian Classics' (London, 1953), p. 275.

20. *Institutes of the Christian Religion*, translated by John Allen (6th American ed., Philadelphia, n.d.), II, p. 142 (bk. III, ch. XXI, par. 1).

21. *Ibid.*, p. 634 (bk. IV, ch. XX, par. 2).

22. Two aspects of the demands of Calvinism, quite properly treated in this context, could with advantage be further clarified. One is the ethical demand: to the Calvinist ethics are a style, that is to say a matter for the individual. In practice they became stereotyped: good actions and good works becoming susceptible of reconciliation. This, however, was not a fundamental religious attitude but a social mechanization. It is certain, on the other hand, that a spiritual discipline distinguishing works from faith can spread its teaching only by means of ethical rules more or less stamped with values conforming to the society concerned.

The other aspect is the sharp distinction between the two powers, rapidly obliterated by the Geneva experience. This distinction, lucidly formulated by the reformer, perhaps as a lesson of the Lutheran development, is essential to modern religion. But in this Calvin is more a deliberate clarifier than an innovator: dualism was implicit in the rule so often invoked by canonists from the fourteenth century onwards: 'Render therefore unto Caesar the things which are Caesar's; and unto God the things that are God's.' Matthew XXII, 21. (Alphonse Dupront).

23. *Institutes*, p. 645 (IV, ch. XX, par. 10).

24. For the recent literature on this controversy see George Sarton, 'Deux Centenaires: Servet et Chateillon', *Journal of World History*, II (1954), pp. 140–41.

25. Professor A. Dupront points out that the Genevan theocrat was much more political than is suggested by the traditional image, lit by the flames which consumed Servetus; the man himself was more sensitive than is generally supposed, particularly in his often tender reverence for God, and he was a closer follower of Christ than a blind servitor of a severe and powerful deity.

His genius for organization deserves special emphasis. As regards the teaching of the doctrine contained in the *Institution*, the training of pastors, the foundation of churches, this theologian was a man of action and a first-class educator. Far more than Lutheranism, Calvinism was, down to the last detail, the work of its founder. See André Bieler, *La pensée économique et sociale de Calvin* (Geneva, 1959), which is an indispensable guide on this subject.

26. To Professor A. Dupront behind all these events and actions which mark the progress of Henry VIII's appropriation of the English church, lies the policy of Thomas Cromwell. In 1536, Henry appointed him his vice-gerent in 'spirituals', thus providing complete confirmation of the spiritual omnipotence of the sovereign.

27. Quoted in *Cambridge Modern History* (Cambridge, 1934), II, p. 446.

28. *The Second Prayer-book of King Edward VI (1552), reprinted from a copy in the British Museum* (London, n.d.), pp. 169 and 172. (The spelling of the quoted words has been modernized above.)

29. Professor A. Dupront stresses in this context the originality of the Anglican tradition as it appeared in the middle of the sixteenth century. As a national church and as an essential tool of Tudor absolutism, the Church of England was 'administrative' by definition, that is by secular authority and by Acts of Uniformity. Whether the source of its dogma was traditional or derived from continental heresy, it constitutes the first experiment in the history of the modern Western world of a state church, administering spiritual affairs. If we compare the small number of men who created it, highly situated as these were in the state hierarchy, with its historical success—despite, as the present authors aptly remark, the test of the reign of Mary Tudor—it must be recognized that this

collective form corresponded to the needs of insular society, 'dissent' finding expression later in the proliferation of religious sects.

30. To Professor A. Dupront the fact that there were no theologians was one of the anomalies of Anabaptism, which we must accustom ourselves to treating as a religion of panic, and thus wholly different from modern religions or at least established modern religions. All the more panic-stricken for its pretension to lucidity particularly in regard to adult baptism and the idea of a church of 'Saints' in which childhood had no part.

31. Quoted in Paul Wappler, *Inquisition und Ketzerprozesse in Zwickau zur Reformationzeit* (Leipzig, 1908), p. 56.

32. To Professor A. Dupront the verdict of history, even more brutal than the collection of reasons here judiciously advanced, was the intense violence of the repression, a clear avowal of panic fear. Did panic breed panic? The root of the matter seems to be—we shall find it again in very different forms in Jansenism—the absolute refusal of the other eschatological, divine, utopian, democratic society, the true City of God, which the Anabaptist preachers proclaimed and worked for, with every sort of revolutionary threat. The fact that the Tyrol became the refuge of the Anabaptists as persecution grew, right up to the end of the century, reveals, besides the obvious protection afforded by the mountains, the demand for a primitive religion, which, if not peasant, was at least non-urban. Naturally the sign of the kingdom was to be the conquest of the cities. Hence the New Jerusalem announced by the Anabaptists in their eschatological sermons.

33. P. Wappler, *Inquisition und Ketzerprozesse in Zwickau zur Reformationzeit*, p. 58.

34. *Ibid.*, p. 62.

35. Quoted in Georg Tumbült, *Die Wiedertaüfer* (Bielefeld & Leipzig, 1899), p. 63. For Calvin's attitude see George Huntston Williams, *The Radical Reformation* (Philadelphia, 1962), pp. 580–614.

36. At the age of forty, Menno Simons, until then a Frisian priest, began a wandering life in the course of which he was to show himself a remarkable and wise organizer of Anabaptists in northern Europe. (Alphonse Dupront.)

37. Quoted in Roland H. Bainton, *The Reformation of the Sixteenth Century* (The Beacon Press, Boston, 1952), p. 129.

38. Professor A. Dupront points out that it has rightly been remarked that Anti-Trinitarianism developed essentially on the fringes of Europe under the influence of men exiled from their native lands, where such beliefs had little hold. In the wake of Servetus, itinerant Italians or Spaniards, doctors or humanists, benefitting from the complicity of Calvinist communities, were to establish in Poland and Transylvania this 'pre-rationalist' doctrine, non-violent in character, deeply imbued with human sensitivity, but, on account of certain analogies with Anabaptism, often anarchic at least in regard to established authority.

On the subject of this complex group in which men, milieux, and ideas are inextricably tangled, two authoritative studies are by Delio Cantimori, *Per la storia degli eretici italiani del secolo XVI in Europa* (Rome, 1937) and *Eretici italiani del cinquecento, ricerche storiche* (Florence, 1939).

39. To Professor A. Dupront Adrian VI was a northerner and servitor of Charles V, and like other members of the imperial circle, particularly the Erasmians, he believed in the utility of a confession of Roman sins before the Diet. Once Rome admitted the *gravamina* anything was possible. This is the explanation of the quite extraordinary mission of the nuncio Chiergati to the Diet of Nüremberg in 1523, as was underlined by Fra Paolo Sarpi, earliest historian of the Council of Trent, a man of penetrating mind, well informed, and unlikely to be guilty of complaisance towards the papacy.

40. Professor A. Dupront adds two observations which may throw some light on the evolution and meaning of this story. One is the leitmotiv of the convocation of a council. As long as it was demanded with some instance of sincerity, it is clear that there was as yet no split in the 'seamless robe', a fact of the utmost importance for the subsequent general evolution of the process of separation. The other is the 'phenomenological' aspect of the Augsburg Confession: an improvised document, skilfully negotiated and to some

extent determined by the threat of more radical confessions, it came to be the very definition of Lutheranism. With the *Loci Communes* and the *Confessio Augustana*, Melanchthon assumed the role of a wise father of the church.

41. Professor Dupront notes that the scene of negotiations between emperor and pope was Bologna, where the coronation of Charles V also took place: equally sincere, neither protagonist was duped.

42. To Professor A. Dupront the facts presented here (each perfectly correct in itself) suggest, when considered collectively, a 'wait and see' policy on the part of Charles V, completely resolved to resort to force. The emperor was too religious a man, in the most traditional sense of the term, not to do his duty as an extirpator of heresy, but it cannot be established that he accepted and encouraged for at least ten years the effort of religious *colloquia*, which were to culminate in the immense hope inspired at Ratisbon in 1541, followed by failure. It is easier to appreciate at its just value the historical role of Charles V if he is judged not by events, but in relation to his genius, his complexity, his faith, his concept of his duty and of Empire. For recent studies, putting forward different hypotheses, see 'Charles-Quint et son temps,' *Colloque du Centre National de la Recherche Scientifique* (Paris, 1959) and José Antonio Maravall, *Carlos V y el pensamiento politico del Renacimiento* (Madrid, 1960).

43. Language was another important element in Norwegian resistance: the Bible was in Danish, the only official language. (Alphonse Dupront.)

44. Professor A. Dupront notes that we are today revolted by what was normal in a world still permeated by the *habitus* of holy war. The reigning pope, Gregory XIII, a Jesuit from Bologna, was far from resembling his predecessor Pius V. And the rites of thanksgiving and commemorative medal were not innovations, any more than was the special jubilee, prescribed by the bull of September 1572. It is, moreover, clear that the Massacre of St Bartholomew seemed to serve the policy of the Holy League in the crusade against the Turks, which the former pope had been endeavouring with some difficulty to continue after the glories of Lepanto, less than a year before.

45. Professor A. Dupront stresses that in his opinion the Edict of Nantes was, of course, an edict of religious tolerance guaranteed by law. But also and above all it was a basic act of absolutism. As guarantor of religious peace, the state became the supreme power and religion a part of the order of the state. This was well understood at the time, by contemporaries invoking the peace and unity of the 'kingdom'. During the wars of religion the concept of kingdom remained the foremost collective value.

46. To this picture of the religious proselytism of Philip II should be added the specific attempt at 'caesaro-popism' which he never ceased to pursue, often fiercely against Rome. He felt that he was upholding the church within the framework of traditional orthodoxy. (Alphonse Dupront.)

47. The text here sometimes seems to adopt an outdated position: that of a *reformatio* defined as the result of the evolution of the Protestant Reformation, i.e. as a Counter-Reform. In point of fact the demand for reform was much older, the normal act of a healthy, living organism. This is proved by the interior dialogue of the *reformatio* which, during the first half of the sixteenth century was to oscillate between *reformatio in capite* and *reformatio in membris* without coming to any final choice, or, what was more serious, any actual fulfilment. In line with the genius of the Roman Catholic Church, Catholic reform was more an adjustment brought about by a series of successive gestures and without major incitations than a 'Reform' with all the apparent radicalism that this word implies. (Alponse Dupront.)

The authors wish to call the reader's attention to the initial section of this chapter entitled 'Demands within the Catholic Church for Reform' (pp. 222–25) and to like passages passim.

48. Professor A. Dupront notes that besides Erasmism—a recent historiographical concept, perhaps in need of revision—another fact, clearly brought out by Delio Cantimori, is worth underlining: namely that the new ideas penetrating into Italy from across the Alps circulated in Italy in almost all milieux, perhaps not with enthusiasm but at least received with great readiness and persistent sympathy.

Among the towns which were centres of Protestantism, Vicenza, in the Venetian 'terra firma', should be mentioned. As Cantimori has observed, while the new ideas circulated freely all over the peninsula without any compartmentation by state or diocese, the capital of Anabaptism and Anti-Trinitarianism was Venice. Naples, on the other hand, was the city of the Valdesians, that is to say the disciples of Juan de Valdès.

Among the Valdesians should be remembered Ochino, the Capuchin general, who became Anabaptist. The whole movement, difficult to circumscribe, was characterized by its aristocratic clientèle, almost exclusively Italian, and from the spiritual point of view, by its platonizing tendencies. The only man in contact with the masses was Ochino, and, as far as the nostalgia for Platonism was concerned, one has only to follow the career of Vittoria Colonna, her exaltations with the aging Michaelangelo, her relations with Reginald Pole and his group at Viterbo, to understand what 'chiaroscuro' powers they encountered in these circles marked by a spiritual quest which neither Aristotelianism nor Thomism could satisfy.

49. Professor A. Dupront indicates that the Oratorio del Divino Amore was organized under the influence of Saint Catherine of Genoa. Destined to serve as a model, it nevertheless takes its place as part of a movement for the foundation of charitable brotherhoods in many Italian cities at the end of the fifteenth and beginning of the sixteenth centuries. The aim of these brotherhoods founded for charitable purposes, was a communal spiritual life among its members. Their main inspiration was secular, and at the Oratorio itself, in the beginning, the number of priests was limited: a clear indication of a strong current of religious spirituality in peninsular life before the Reform. Contemporary Italian historiography is in process of discovering this at the same time as it emphasizes the wide influence of certain important figures such as Paolo Giustiniani, and the role of certain prelates also pre-reformers in their respective dioceses even before Gianmatteo Giberti in Verona, a model of Catholic reform prior to the Council of Trent.

50. Quoted in Leopold von Ranke, *Die romischen Päpste in den letzten vier Jahrhunderten* (2 vols.; Hamburg, n.d.), I, pp. 89–90.

51. To Professor A. Dupront von Ranke's interpretation needs supplementation: the Consilium was essentially a repertory of abuses, the important factor being its drafting by a commission of cardinals, thus representing an act of *reformatio in capite*. Its fundamental rule, however, was in no way new: true reform—the return to 'the old sublimity' meant the application of canon law; i.e. the reinstatement of church order. Sadeleto's letter to the Genevans marks the end of a whole series of epistolary attempts on the part of the Bishop of Carpentras, among them the famous letters to Melanchthon (June 1537) and to Sturm (July 1518), perhaps a doomed but sincere aspect of a 'pre-irenic' tendency.

52. Professor A. Dupront feels that the effective participation in the Diet of Ratisbon is here somewhat obscured. The Protestant protagonists were Melanchthon and Sturm: Luther was in safe custody in the hands of the Elector of Saxony, who was opposed to the conciliation.

53. The bull *Licet ab initio*, foundation of the future Holy Office, should not be considered as establishing a Spanish-type inquisition. In point of fact it arose, in conjunction with certain panic reflexes against the contagion of heresy, from a need for centralization, establishing Roman authority throughout the peninsula to counteract the weaknesses of diocesan officialdom. It is true that Gian-Pietro Caraffa succeeded in appropriating the institution from the very beginning. (Alphonse Dupront.)

54. Professor A. Dupront thinks that it is not desirable to place on the same plane all the religious families born of the so-called Catholic Reform. For example, the foundation and early development of the Capuchin order was typically medieval as was also their habit of seeking to establish themselves in the countryside, in hermitages, in fulfilment of their original vocation of being, in the actual terms of their Constitution of 1629, '*Fratres Minores Vitae Eventuticae*'. The other congregations of the Catholic reform were, by their very nature, urban.

55. Professor A. Dupront finds that more characteristic of most of their founders are the imprint of advanced spirituality, a kind of spiritual aristocracy, and, in almost every case, the influence of a female mystic, vowed to sainthood. Their precipitate appearance during

the first half of the cinquecento confirms the latent desire for spirituality fermenting in Italian society since the end of the fifteenth century, and even more deeply felt at the time of the foreign occupation of the peninsula.

Filippo Neri, though Florentine in origin, the Roman saint *par excellence*, constitutes a case apart. In founding the Oratorio he sought to create a centre of total religious life, intimately bound up with the life of the city—on the borderline of the regular and the secular—inspired by the desire to incarnate a 'Christian humanism'. An experiment lasting for two generations at the most, but serving to attract a number of noble and attractive non-Oratorian personalities, such as Agostino Valiero, bishop of Verona.

56. To Professor A. Dupront the historical figure of St Carlo Borroméo is here presented somewhat hagiographically. Did he really exercise so great an influence in the Roman Curia, even during the pontificate of his uncle Pius IV, who was in no way a religious character ? As for his retirement in Milan, it is certain that there was no further place for him in Rome during the pontificate of Pius V, while at Milan he found his family and also a diocese in which to carry out his apostolic and defensive action against the Spanish power and the authority and liberties of the church. An ascetic, but, aside from certain Spanish influences, little inclined to mystic meditation. Regrettably the great Lombard prelate, destined after the Council of Trent to become the 'good bishop', has not yet found the biographer demanded by what is still the enigma of his personality and his historical importance.

Must we accept the authors' suggestion as to a new type of saint of the Catholic reform ? The social tendency is evident, and there are no more martyrs. What is most striking about the cohort of saints borne upon the altars during the first decade of the seventeenth century is the great diversity of 'mortals'—bishops, founders of orders—represented, indicating a demand on the part of different milieux for a renewal of exemplary images. The canonization of founders of orders in particular was for each of the new orders a final consecration of their power and of their virtue of collective sanctification.

57. These figures are taken from a study prepared for this volume by the Spanish National Commission for UNESCO through the mediation of Professor Joaquin Perez Villanueva.

58. Hubert Jedin, 'Conciles généraux', *loc. cit.*, discusses the literature dealing with the Conciliar Movement and the Council of Trent.

59. The decrees of the twenty-third *sessio, The Canons and Decrees of the . . . Council of Trent,* translated by J. Waterworth (London, 1848), pp. 172–74.

60. Ranke, *Deutsche Geschichte im Zeitalter der Reformation,* V, p. 108.

61. For a recent discussion of this controversy and its bibliography, see Sidney A. Burrell, "Calvinism, Capitalism, and the Middle Classes: Some Afterthoughts on an Old Problem', *Journal of Modern History,* XXXII (1960), pp. 129–41.

62. *In the course of printing this volume, the distances between the publishers (London), the editors (Paris), and the author-editor (Chicago) prevented the inclusion of the author's rejoinders to Professor Dupront's comments (except the one in n. 47 above). A general remark, therefore, seems called for. While the authors are indebted to Professor Depront for the details he has provided, they do not think that their interpretation of the reform spirit within the Catholic Church before, during, and after the rise of Protestantism differs markedly from his. Nor, despite their emphasis at times upon political considerations and his on religious convictions, do they find themselves differing widely from him, or he from them, even in those regards—as other chapters of this volume will make still clearer.*

CHAPTER V

OTHER RELIGIOUS EVENTS (1500–1775)

CHRISTIANITY OUTSIDE EUROPE

WITH varying degrees of success, Christianity accompanied Europe's explorers and settlers to Africa, Asia, and the Americas (Map I). The Spanish and Portuguese kings, looking upon their new lands east and west as papal grants, felt under special obligation to spread the Christian gospel among them.[1] Cardinal Ximenes in 1516 required every expedition to the Indies to carry missionaries, and famous missionaries sometimes accompanied famous conquistadores. The first effective group of missionaries were twelve Franciscans, who were solemnly welcomed to New Spain by Hernan Cortes in 1524; others reinforced them soon. By 1531 the Franciscans claimed to have baptized about 1,000,000 natives. The Dominicans followed shortly after the Franciscans, and among the Dominicans was Bartolomé de Las Casas, champion of the Indian slave, who for a time was bishop of Chiapa in Guatemala. The Augustinians went out in smaller numbers. And after the Jesuit order was founded, it became the most active of all. Within a century the Spanish-American patriarchate included six archbishropics, thirty-two bishoprics, and two abbeys. In 1676, the archbishopric of Brazil was created, with its seat at Bahia; Portuguese America comprised nine bishoprics at the close of the eighteenth century.

In 1568 Philip II called a Junta Magna to consider the problems of the clergy in the new Spanish lands. This congress proposed the establishment of a patriarchate in New Spain. To the question whether the colonial clergy was responsible to pope or to king it answered largely in favour of the king: a bishop was to be named by the Holy See only on presentation by the king, and a colonial bishop was to name his subordinates only after presentation to the royal provincial representative. In the Antilles dioceses tended to coincide with the royal boundaries; in Mexico they tended to correspond with the missions.

The Junta Magna also limited the missions in America to four orders—Franciscans, Dominicans, Augustinians, and Jesuits, although others already engaged in missionary work nevertheless stayed on. The Franciscans after 1682 established a special missionary branch of their order, of whom Junipero Serra (1713–84) was perhaps the most celebrated; some of the important cities of modern California owe their beginnings at least partly to him. The Dominicans carried on their work mostly in already founded missions and cities. The Jesuits began with the coast settlements of Brazil but spread from there to Mexico, Peru, and elsewhere. Among their Brazilian missionaries José de Anchieta (1530?–97), founder of São Paulo, was probably the most successful. At first they worked within settlements but eventually undertook to establish new missions on the frontiers, especially among the Guarani and Araucanian Indians. Missionaries also worked among the *encomendados*, for the *encomendero* was required to provide instruction in the Christian religion. As the *encomienda* disappeared (see Chapter I), the state, regarding the Indians as its wards, assumed responsibility for continuing their religious education.

Some of the clergy made a special effort to protect the Indian from exploitation. Hence the Indian sometimes received privileges that the Negro rarely enjoyed—in education and office-holding, for example. In Pedro Claver, Jesuit missionary to the Negro slaves, the Negro, too, found a champion, as had the Indian in Las Casas. Over a period of forty years, Claver baptized and befriended around 300,000 of the slaves who arrived on the monthly slave ship at Cartagena. The Inquisition was introduced into Spanish America in 1569 but was not permitted to try Indians, since they were regarded as incapable of valid judgments. Hence many local customs were allowed to enter into the Indians' Christian ritual.

The work of the missionaries necessarily led them toward educational efforts. They studied and wrote books upon local ethnology. They learned the native language and customs, and prepared dictionaries and grammars. They founded schools and universities, such as the technical college of Santa Cruz in Mexico and the College of San Andrés in Quito. They encouraged local artistic talents in the building and maintenance of their churches and cathedrals. To a considerable extent, the eighteenth-century idea of 'the noble savage' was an outcome of their reports, particularly of Las Casas's, upon their experiences with the Indians. Without their investigations and writings, knowledge of the history and culture of antecedent Amerindian societies would have been largely lost.

Perhaps the most celebrated missionary effort in Spanish America involved the Jesuit *reducciones* (settlements of converted Indians) in Paraguay, begun early in the seventeenth century. At their highest point, the 1730's, there were thirty of them, estimated to have about 140,000 inhabitants. Fantastic stories arose about the rich Jesuit kingdoms in Paraguay, and Brazilian slave raiders made attacks upon them, forcing them to move to areas farther south, with consequent interruption of their prosperity. They also suffered from the frequent defensive wars that they had to fight with the warlike, unconverted tribes, who martyred a number of Jesuit fathers. In 1750 seven of the Paraguay *reducciones* were required by treaty to transfer bodily to a part of Uruguay under Portuguese control, but the Jesuits and their wards resisted in the War of the Seven Reductions, yielding only in 1756. When the Society of Jesus was suppressed in Spanish America (1767), the remaining *reducciones* in Paraguay were placed under the Franciscans, but they soon deteriorated and eventually disappeared. The Portuguese annexed much of the territory previously controlled by the Jesuits.

*   *   *

Catholics and Protestants in North America

In North America, the first Christian settlement that lasted was founded by the Spanish at St Augustine, Florida, in 1565. Whether it could survive as a Spanish Catholic community was at first doubtful, for a French Huguenot settlement was about the same time established at Fort Caroline, Florida. The Spanish admiral Pedro Menéndez de Avilés wiped out the male population of the French colony, however, and shortly afterward slaughtered the Huguenot admiral Jean Ribault and his crews, shipwrecked in an effort to attack Menéndez by sea. Even though a French force two years later retaliated by massacring the Spanish garrison left at Fort Caroline, Florida remained relatively safe for Catholicism until the eighteenth century.

The English soldier James Edward Oglethorpe founded Georgia in 1733 largely in order to keep the area north of Florida out of Spanish hands. Then he took the offensive against the Spanish in Florida, but his siege of St Augustine in 1740 was futile. Florida later fell to the English by the Treaty of Paris (1763), which ended the Seven Years' War, but in 1783 it was returned, still Spanish and Catholic. Hundreds of the French Catholic loyalists of Acadia, which was surrendered to the British in 1713 and renamed Nova Scotia, were in 1755 deported to Georgia, but they soon voluntarily went elsewhere. Georgia, along with North and South Carolina, excluded 'papists' from office until well past our period. On the other hand, these colonies gave full rights to French Huguenots, Moravian Brethren, and other Protestant refugees from Europe.

The other Anglo-American colonies in North America, with the exception for a time of Maryland, were even more exclusively dominated by Protestants. The Protestants came after the Reformation was clearly irreversible in England and at a time when in England feudal obligations were essentially a thing of the past and the individual was relatively free to move about. They brought with them notions of freedom of movement and of conscience (at least for themselves) that probably were less familiar in other parts of Europe and that were bound to become more firmly entrenched among frontiersmen as they tamed a wilderness. Some things the wilderness did for them that Europe could not well do; it cracked the cake of custom, it thinned the influence of overseas authorities and institutions, and it offered them room to go elsewhere if they disagreed with their neighbours.

And disagree they did. The colonists who settled Virginia accepted the Church of England. So did the settlers of the other English colonies eventually established south of Virginia. The Pilgrims who settled in Massachusetts in 1620 were Separatists—i.e. Congregationalists—and other Puritan critics of the established church of England. The Mayflower Compact which they drew up on board ship to serve as their fundamental law was perhaps the first example of 'a social contract' that was expressly written down as such and actually adopted by all those it was intended to govern. Plymouth was the first of several Separatist settlements in Massachusetts. Massachusetts was a strict Puritan state, but the rest of Anglo-America tended toward greater religious flexibility. Strict Calvinism forced Roger Williams and others of a more Arminian view out of Massachusetts and led to the establishment of new colonies in Rhode Island, Connecticut, and New Hampshire—colonies of individualists who not only insisted upon free popular consent as the basis of government but also were ready to extend to other Protestants a greater degree of toleration than they themselves had enjoyed in Massachusetts. New York was built upon the basis of the Dutch colony of New Amsterdam, captured (1664) at a time when Dutch toleration had permitted peoples of many tongues and of various religions (including Jews) to live there. Under King James II it even had a Catholic governor for a time, but Catholicism was all but stamped out after the 'Glorious Revolution.' Pennsylvania and Delaware were the proprietary colonies of William Penn and his descendants, who were Quakers, pacifists, friends of the Indians, advocates of tolerance, and opponents of slavery. Not only Mennonites and Moravians but also Jews and Catholics received asylum there.

Except for Maryland during its early history, Catholics nowhere dominated any of the Anglo-American colonies, and even in Maryland they were not the majority. Maryland was founded by George Calvert (afterward Lord Baltimore), a recent convert to Catholicism. It was politically controlled by Catholics until the English Civil War, when the Puritans ousted the proprietor and seized control of the government (1652). Religious liberty had, however, been permitted from the start and was formally proclaimed in 1649. Terminated by the Puritans, it was restored in 1658. The Baltimores retained their proprietary rights until after the 'Glorious Revolution' and the reign of William and Mary. In 1692 Maryland became a royal colony with the Church of England as its established church, and in 1713 the Baltimores became Protestant. In 1718 Catholics were disenfranchised, and in 1754 the property of the Catholic clergy was confiscated. Catholics continued, however, to live in Maryland unmolested, and Irish immigrants were numerous. The accepted estimate of the number of Catholics in the Anglo-American colonies on the eve of the American Revolution is 25,000, mostly in Pennsylvania and Maryland. Philadelphia had the first and largest organized parish. North Carolina tolerated Catholics but excluded them from office.

As already noted (Chapter IV), the Protestants of Anglo-America were particularly susceptible to religious revivalism. Among the sparse populations of frontier settlements a man was likely to be measured by what he could do rather than by his religious preferences. The indifferentism thus imposed was fundamentally incompatible with orthodoxy, which was strictly enforced only in New England under Calvinist influences, and New England's Calvinists themselves were vulnerable to the appeal of Arminianism, with its liberal view of predestination and forgiveness of sin. To counteract Arminianism and sin, Jonathan Edwards (1703–58), Congregationalist minister of Northampton, Massachusetts, began a series of fiery sermons that started a wave of religious revivals. It spread from 1734 to 1740 throughout New England, culminating in the 'Great Awakening', a chain of devotional meetings and movements that after 1740 moved from New England over the entire Atlantic seaboard, greatly aided by the powerful sermons of the strictly Calvinist George Whitefield.

The Great Awakening was characterized by mass conversions on an unprecedented scale. In the process it was constrained to adapt itself to large numbers of men of different persuasions, especially in the frontier towns, whose inhabitants flocked to hear the revivalists. The message and eloquence of an Edwards or a Whitefield could fill the churches, but sermons such as Edwards' famous *Sinners in the Hands of an Angry God* (1741) and books such as his *Freedom of the Will* (1754) painted too lurid a picture of man's depravity, placed election too far beyond human endeavour, and painted too deterministic a philosophy to satisfy the religious needs of frontiersmen conscious of their own worth and will power. Many a man who had been indifferent or had belonged to the older Puritan creeds joined the Baptist Church, equally evangelical and more Arminian, or the Methodist Church. Edwards himself paid dearly for his inflexibility, since his insistence upon admitting to holy communion only the truly converted led to his dismissal from the congregation which his labours had revitalized and increased. He went out as a missionary to the Indians.

The Great Awakening had implications beyond the realm of theology. For one thing, it made the nonconformist sects of Anglo-America conscious of their strength, and it gave them reason to question the supremacy in America of the established Church of England. For another, it led to the increase in the number of colleges and academies in America (see Chapter XVI). In addition, it had a significant impact upon the literary development of a colonial people. Edwards was the first notable American writer to deal philosophically with the problems of mind, will, and virtue. An upsurge of sermons and other edifying prose and of pious poetry and hymns revealed the spread and intensity of religious emotion, the overpowering joy of a personal faith. Edwards had himself given the cue in a sermon in 1734: 'There is such a thing as a Spiritual and Divine Light, immediately imparted to the Soul by God, of a different nature from any that is obtained by natural means'.[2] The Great Awakening thus helped to articulate the hopefulness and self-reliance that were important ingredients of an American political creed that was contemporaneously taking hold. The spirit of self-determination in the religious sphere was to be translated into the political language of anti-colonialism when the occasion arose (see Chapter IX).

★ ★ ★

Missions to the Eskimos and Indians

Danish missionaries, especially Hans Egede (1686-1758) and his son Paul (1708-89), carried the Gospel to the Greenland Eskimos, and the various Protestant sects that peopled the colonies of England in America carried on missionary work among the Indians. Presbyterians, Anglicans, and Moravians were particularly conspicuous among them. Nevertheless, although 'the propagation of the Gospel' had been declared to be 'first' of the 'Principal and Maine Endes' of the Virginia Company (founded 1606), few North American Indians were converted out of their 'almost invincible ignorance'[3] by the English-speaking colonists. One of the outstanding English missionaries was John Eliot, who preached to the Massachusetts Indians in their own tongue and translated the Bible (1661-63) and other sacred literature for them. On his initiative Parliament incorporated the Society for the Propagation of the Gospel in New England (1649), and before his death he and his helpers converted several thousand Indians.

Large-scale conversion of North American Indians, however, was rather the work of the Catholic missionaries of New France. A few Recollects (Franciscans) arrived in 1615, and in 1623 Champlain sought the assistance of the Jesuits. Until Richelieu founded the company known as the Hundred Associates (1627), little progress was made even by the French; the Associates were pledged to bring the natives instruction in the 'Catholic, Apostolic, Roman religion'. The British capture of Quebec (1629) temporarily delayed their efforts, but after it was returned to the French (1632), the Jesuits began missionary work in earnest (1635). Subsequently (1664) the Recollects returned, but the conversion of large numbers of Hurons and some Iroquois was mostly the work of Jesuit martyrs like Father Bréboeuf and Father Jogues, massacred by the Iroquois in the Iroquois-Huron wars (1646 and 1649 respectively) because the Iroquois considered them allies of the Hurons. In part as a missionary to the Indians Father Marquette canoed down the Mississippi in 1682 and made the vast valley of that river a French Catholic area (except for a brief Spanish occupancy) until the nineteenth century.

When the British won Canada (1763), they allowed its French population to retain the Catholic religion and hierarchy under the bishop of Quebec. Indeed, in 1774, by the Quebec Act, they even widened Quebec's boundaries to the south in order to keep the Ohio valley from settlement by rebellious Protestant English-speaking colonists. Quebec thus remained French-speaking and Catholic even though Jesuits and Franciscans were suppressed.

In Spanish America the missionary frequently preceded the conqueror into the wilderness. While missionaries often were the agents of the conquerors, they also did much to counteract the cruelty of *conquistadores*, slavers, and exploiters. Las Casas held that 'the way to bring into the bosom of the Christian faith and religion men who are outside the church must be a method which persuades their understanding and which moves, exhorts and gently attracts the will'.[4]

The adaptability of the Amerindian combined with his lack of doctrine and systematic theology to make his conversion relatively easy. Thus, by missionary work as well as by white settlement, the Western Hemisphere became Christian. The Jesuit missions alone are sometimes credited with having brought to Catholicism in the course of time probably more souls in America than were lost to Protestantism in Europe.

★   ★   ★

Catholic Missions in Asia

Christian missionary activity in Asia in modern times began with the arrival of the Portuguese in India in the 1490's and was extended by the Spanish occupation of the Philippines in the 1560's and 1570's. This work was in the hands of the monastic orders, which functioned under the patronage of the Portuguese and Spanish kings, although a secular clerical hierarchy was also set up to minister to Europeans. Archbishoprics were ultimately established at Goa and Manila. Of the missionary orders the Jesuits soon became the most important in the Portuguese area; in the Philippines they shared the field with Augustinians, Franciscans, and Dominicans. Among the missionaries patronized by Spain, Spaniards probably predominated, but among those who acted under Portuguese patronage after Francis Xavier, Italians were for a long time the most influential if not the most numerous.

Franciscans undertook the first serious Catholic missionary work in India, but from the time of the arrival of Xavier in 1542 the Jesuits rapidly assumed the lead. From India and Ceylon Xavier went to Malacca and Amboina in 1545–46; in 1549 he inaugurated missionary work in Japan; and in 1552 he died on an island off the coast of China in a vain effort to plant a mission there. Most influential in developing the Jesuit mission and shaping its policies was Alessandro Valignani (1539–1606), whose activities as visitor (i.e. superior) of the Society (1574–1606) ranged from Mozambique and India through the Indies to Japan and China. During the 1580's Matteo Ricci was the chief figure of the Jesuit mission in China (see Chapter XIV). He mastered the Chinese language. His scientific instruments and knowledge roused the Chinese interest in Europe, and his reports home excited Europeans toward greater missionary effort in China. The Jesuit College at the University of Coimbra became the principal training centre for Jesuits going to the East. During the course of two centuries it sent out about 1,650 missionaries.

After 1622, with the formation of the Sacra Congregatio de Propaganda Fide, commonly referred to as the Propaganda, the papacy took a more direct hand in promoting missions. The Propaganda maintained a college for educating missionaries to and nationals from foreign lands, it kept a formidable printing establishment busy, and it showed a keen interest in training native clergy. The papacy began to assert its authority over the missions through vicars apostolic and bishops and thereby came into conflict with the Portuguese, for the king of Portugal claimed the *padroado*, or right to promote Christianity and control appointments in the East, conferred by earlier papal bulls. The papacy respected the rights of the Portuguese in areas under their immediate administrative control but asserted its own rights elsewhere, while the Portuguese claimed jurisdiction over all the East.

The missionary spirit spread eastward rapidly. In the seventeenth century Germans and other central Europeans began to appear in increasing numbers among the missionaries of the various orders. The Société des Missions Étrangères was formed in Paris in 1663, and then the French moved into the field in increasing numbers. The Paris missionary society sought lay support and put its emphasis upon the secular clergy as missionaries. It called particularly for the training and establishment of an indigenous secular clergy in foreign lands. François Pallu, a leader in founding this society, was himself an active missionary in Siam and Indo-China. By 1700 the societe had sent out 119 priests, and 198 by 1800. The Capuchin order also increasdy its missionary work.

In the East the missionaries encountered difficulties that did not arise in the New World. In Asia the Europeans did not have political control, Islam was a successful competitor, and, above all, highly developed civilizations were well entrenched, each with its own refined systems of religion, thought, and values, expounded and defended by an established learned class. Hinduism, Buddhism, and Confucianism could meet Christianity on its own intellectual level. Only in Malaya, the East Indies, the Philippines, and, to a certain extent, Japan did the lack of sufficient commitment to an existing system offer good conditions for proselytizing. Islam, already politically dominant in India and actively engaged in spreading its political control in the Indies, was more amenable to the extensive cultural adaptations needed to win the uncommitted than was Christianity. Furthermore, partly because of the very lack of theological and moral sophistication on the part of the East Indians, the Jesuits considered them poor prospects and chose to make their major efforts elsewhere. In the long run Catholicism made effective progress only among the relatively uncommitted peoples who came also under European political control.

The high level of the Eastern civilizations posed a problem of missionary policy. The Jesuits quickly realized that their success might depend upon a sympathetic hearing from the political and intellectual guardians of the established systems and that to get such a hearing Christianity must not appear antithetical to the established order. Under the tolerant leadership of some Italian humanists they therefore adopted a programme of cultural

M*

accommodation, based on the postulate that any culture might develop its own Christian forms. They allowed Christian converts to continue in those beliefs and practices which they deemed not positively contradictory to the essential doctrines of Catholicism, while the missionaries themselves studied the local languages, literature, and ideas and attempted to become as much a part of the local culture as possible. They also attempted to make themselves more acceptable by expounding the new science of the West, which seemed to appeal to many Eastern intellectuals. Most of the other missionary groups, however, taking their cue from the unbending Iberian conquistadores, insisted on Europeanizing their converts. In this difference of approach lay the seeds of ultimate controversy.

The two methods reinforced each other at first. Readiness to adapt, aided by favourable political conditions, enabled the Jesuits to make surprising progress during the late-sixteenth and early-seventeenth centuries in Hindu and Mogul India, Japan, and China—all areas outside Iberian political control. The other missionary orders met with their major successes where Spanish and Portuguese political power was strong. By 1600 the number of Christians in the East probably exceeded 1,250,000. The largest single group, if the Syrian Christians, many of whom had come under Catholic leadership, be counted, were in the Portuguese-dominated areas along the Malabar coast and in Ceylon, but Japan and the Spanish Philippines each counted about 300,000 converts. The Christians of the East Indies (found especially in the Spice Islands) probably numbered fewer than 100,000. The successes of the Christian missionaries in China were just beginning.

Modest though these figures were in proportion to the total population, they appeared to indicate great possibilities until some setbacks occurred. In Japan, unification under the Tokugawa shogunate led in 1613–14 to the prohibition of Christianity as potentially inimical to national traditions and the ruling authority. This reversal proved especially disastrous when the prohibitory decrees were followed by savage persecutions, which ultimately wiped out all but a few thousand secret practitioners of Christianity. After the middle of the century the Catholics lost further ground to the Dutch Protestants in Ceylon and the Indies, and about the same time in India the policies of Aurangzīb and internal strife (see below) created conditions unfavourable to Christian missionary activity.

Several propitious developments counterbalanced these losses. Shortly after 1600 the Jesuit Robert de Nobili began a relatively successful mission among the Hindus of south India by adapting Christianity to the caste system.5 A growing stream of devoted men from France reinforced the missionaries in India and elsewhere and initiated new activities in Siam (1662–64). Missionaries banished from Japan met with some success in Cochin-China and Annam. Rapid progress was recorded also in the Philippines. In China, the scientific activity of Ricci was duplicated first by Adam Schall and then by Ferdinand Verbiest (see Chapter XIV), winning for the

Jesuits the toleration of many officials, the patronage of the newly established Manchu emperors, and acceptance of their missionary activity, which culminated in a general edict of toleration for Christianity in 1692. The high water mark of this early period of Christian missionary activity in the East was probably reached about 1700, when the total number of converts was in the neighbourhood of 3,000,000—mostly Catholics. Over 1,000,000 lived in India and perhaps 600,000 (partly Protestant) in Ceylon, 800,000 in the Philippines, 300,000 in China, and 100,000 each (partly Protestant) in Indo-China and the Indies.

Thereafter the vitality of Christian missions in the East, Catholic and Protestant alike, declined, probably reaching its nadir about 1775. The total number of Christians at that time was perhaps as great as in 1700, but the China mission was practically dead, and little expansion had taken place elsewhere, while the morale of the missionaries was generally low. The reasons for this demoralization were numerous. To a certain extent the scepticism that accompanied the Enlightenment in Europe discouraged enthusiasm for missionary activity. More important, however, was the decline of Catholic Portugal and Spain and the concomitant rise of Protestant Holland and Britain as commercial and colonial powers in the East. In a some-times unedifying competition Dutch Protestant missionaries vied with Catholics in Ceylon and replaced them in the Indies, where in addition Islam was busy establishing its hold. In India's constant internal strife, Hindu Maratha nationalists and ardent Muslim princes (like Tipu Sultan) also victimized Christians and destroyed their churches. Jurisdictional rivalries among Portugal, Spain, and the papacy and among the various religious orders and societies further weakened the Catholic effort. These rivalries led to a notorious controversy over ritual that perhaps did more damage to Catholic missionary activity in the eighteenth century than any other single circumstance.

This 'Rites Controversy' resulted from the Jesuits' efforts to make Christianity acceptable to the inhabitants of China, Japan, and India. In India their readiness to accommodate local customs and practices led to the continuation by some of the converts of caste rules and procedures. In China it amounted to the toleration of certain aspects of ancestor worship and permitted Confucian scholars and officials who had become Christians to perform the prescribed rites honouring Confucius. The Christian opponents of the Jesuits were especially shocked that the latter also accepted *T'ien* (*Heaven*) or *Shang-ti* as translations for *God* along with the unobjectionable *T'ien-chu* (*Lord of Heaven*). As early as 1623 the papacy had given a guarded approval of the Jesuit practices in India (the so-called Malabar rites), which were later attacked by the French Capuchins, but the complicated nature of the problem delayed a definitive decision. When Franciscans and Dominicans under Spanish patronage entered China from the Philippines in the 1630's, they immediately found fault with Jesuit latitudinarianism and insisted that their rivals were compromising the basic doctrines of Christianity. The Dominican missionary and world-traveller Domingo de Navarrete (1618–86), among his careful notes on the memorabilia he encountered, told of these controversies, and through him and other correspondents in China, Europe kept well informed not only of Chinese cultural achievements but also of the Jesuits' evangelical 'accommodation' to Confucion rites. A prolonged and bitter conflict ensued, spreading from the Far East to Europe and involving the whole Catholic world, lay as well as clerical.[6]

The Jesuits solicited the K'ang-hsi emperor's opinion, which was naturally in favour of the Chinese rites. On the other hand, in 1704, the papacy finally ruled against the Jesuits, forbidding ancestor worship, participation in the rites honouring Confucius, and the use of *T'ien* as the name of the Divine. A papal legate, Maillard de Tournon, was sent out to enforce the papal decree and to pacify the Chinese emperor. In India he ruled against the Jesuits' Malabar rites. In China the imperial wrath descended upon him when, in 1706, the papal position became known, and the emperor in effect ordered the banishment of those missionaries who did not accept the Jesuit position. Though Maillard de Tournon ordered the missionaries, on pain of excommunication, to conform with the papal decision, the Portuguese-appointed hierarchy in the East refused to recognize the legate's jurisdiction. As a consequence, many Jesuits' chose to remain in China, while members of other orders were forced to leave. Later efforts to work out a settlement came to nothing, since neither the emperor nor the pope would change his position.

This turn of events encouraged hostile Confucian officials to denounce Christians vehemently. Consequently the Yung-cheng emperor in 1724 banished all missionaries except those retained in his service, ordered converts to give up Christianity, and directed that churches be turned into public places. Although this and later anti-Christian decrees were not rigorously enforced, the mission in China rapidly declined. Since the papacy, with minor modifications, upheld the legate's decision regarding the Malabar rites, the Jesuit mission in south India was also handicapped at this crucial juncture. In part, the ill-will engendered toward the Jesuits by the Rites Controversy reflected the increasing opposition for other reasons to the Society of Jesus in Europe. It was banished from the Portuguese domains in 1759, suppressed in France in 1764 and in the Spanish possessions in 1767, and formally dissolved by the pope in 1773. Thus the major Catholic missionary organization in the East ended (at least until the Jesuit order was again officially restored in 1814), and the Lazarists, who tended to take over in its stead, were not prepared to carry on its far-flung activities.

*   *   *

Protestant and Orthodox Missions

Protestant missionaries received feebler support from governments than did the Catholic missionaries and made less headway, but it was a notable headway still, not only in Dutch, Danish, and British America but also in the East Indies. In 1705 the first Protestant mission in India was established by German Pietists at Tranquebar with the aid of the Danish king Frederick IV and of August Hermann Francke. The Moravian Brethren, with little but their faith to sustain them, went out as missionaries to Greenland and Surinam, to Algeria and the Cape of Good Hope, to Ceylon and other distant points, and even sent a mission to the Hottentots (1737). Except, however, for the ancient Coptic Christians of Ethiopia and Egypt and the newer Calvinist Boers of South Africa, Africa felt little Christian influence, Catholic or Protestant, until the nineteenth century, and although Christian Friedrich Schwarz (1726–98), a Pietist missionary, encountered considerable success at Tranquebar in India, Protestant missionary activity by the end of our period had made little progress in Asia.

In the early-seventeenth century Dutch Calvinists were active in Batavia, Amboina, the Spice Islands, the Timor area, Talaur, the Sangi Islands, and Formosa (where the Dutch had an establishment between 1624 and 1661). The Dutch East India Company supported the missionaries and subjected them to regulation, but the Dutch church examined those to be sent out and maintained correspondence with them. In the areas actually under the company's administration, Dutch missionary policy was at first little better than forceful conversion. The Dutch gave considerable attention to translating the Bible. They made the New Testament available in Portuguese in the Indies in 1682; they put out the complete Bible in Malay in Latin script in 1734 and in Arabic script in 1759; and in Ceylon they published the whole of the New Testament in Tamil and parts of it in Singhalese. Their work was handicapped by language difficulties, shortage of religious personnel, their rigidly assimilative and puritanical policies, and the competition of Islam.

The Dutch missions made greatest progress among those natives who had already been converted to Catholicism. Even among these, however, resistance was encountered—for example, in Ceylon, where missionary work was begun in 1642. After 1658, when the Dutch had completed the conquest of a considerable portion of the island from the Portuguese, they used inducements of every sort to convert non-Christians and to force Catholic natives to become Protestant. Effective resistance among the Catholics was organized by Joseph Vaz (1651–1711), a converted Brahman from the Bombay area. Meanwhile a revived Buddhism under the kings of Kandy competed with both Protestants and Catholics. Dutch missionary activity declined in the eighteenth century along with the financial well-being of the Dutch East India Company. About 1775 the number of Protestants in the Indies was probably under 200,000, and the estimated number in Ceylon, which was 425,000 in 1722, was only 342,000 in 1801.

Other Protestant missions were still less impressive. As indicated in Chapter IV, Pietists from Germany, especially Halle, undertook some missionary work. Under the patronage of King Frederick IV of Denmark and with financial support also from Germany and England, they began (1706) at the Danish settlement of Tranquebar in south India and gradually reached out to other colonial enclaves in India. Toward the end of the eighteenth century they claimed some 20,000 converts, principally in Tranquebar, Madras, and nearby towns. Missionaries of this group translated the whole Bible into Telugu and Tamil, and most of it into Hindustani. Schwarz was one of the Tamil translators. He won the friendship of the raja of Tanjore, who, without turning Christian himself, aided him in his missionary endeavours. In 1760 the Moravians, too, came to Tranquebar, but they were regarded as interlopers, and their efforts to plant missions, chiefly in connection with Danish trading establishments, all ended in failure by 1803. The British East India Company showed no interest in missionary activity, although it provided chaplains at its own settlements.

The Orthodox clergy benefitted from the Russian overland advance eastward. They penetrated Siberia and established a permanent residence in Peking. They went to China, however, as students of the language and as priests to the Russian colony at its capital rather than as missionaries.

★   ★   ★

Two-way Results of European Missionary Efforts

The net religious effect of Christian missionary activity in the East until 1775 was not very profound. At that date the total number of Christians in southern and eastern Asia, which, we have noted, could not have much exceeded 3,000,000 (and was probably less), constituted only a small fraction of the area's teeming population. The northern Philippines and Goa and other Portuguese possessions in India were and have continued Catholic, and size-able groups in other parts of India, the Spice Islands, Vietnam, and Ceylon were Christian. Yet many of the converts retained animistic beliefs, the vast majority of eastern Asians remained untouched, and the promising beginnings in Japan and China had ended in ruins. Very few Asian intellectuals had been lastingly impressed by either Christianity or the culture it represented. In India most converts to Catholicism and Protestantism were from among either the Syrian Christians[7] or the lowly and the outcast, and in China and Japan most converts had been from poverty-stricken classes not fully committed to Confucianism or Buddhism. In Vietnam, the Indies, and the Philippines the big Christian successes had been among people uncommitted to any other highly developed religious or philosophical system.

Experience thus demonstrated that cultural assimilation, or Europeanization, when not backed by Western state power was ineffective in southern and eastern Asia, and the failure of Jesuit probabilism left little hope that a policy of accommodation to local culture would be much more successful. The two countries that for a time had shown the greatest interest in the science, technology, and geographical knowledge which the missionaries had to offer decided to reject these suspect advantages (see Chapter XIV). Fear of political and cultural ties with Christianity caused Japan to close her doors to almost all of the outside world, and China to intensify her xenophobia.

In the reverse direction, however, the Christian missionaries promoted a trend that possibly exceeded anything they had intended. They provided the Western world with a large body of literature dealing with the geography, languages, literature, arts, manners, customs, and ideas of the East that enriched Europe and unquestionably affected European thought and institutions of the eighteenth century. To this intellectual trend must be added the effect on the economic and political life of Europe produced by its trade and colonial enterprises in the East. These trends, already mentioned in Chapter I, will receive fuller attention in some of the chapters that follow.

THE ORTHODOX CHRISTIANS

The story of the Orthodox Christians in the Polish orbit has been told in Chapter IV, and the beginnings of Orthodox missionary effects in China have been touched upon above. Here we shall deal with Orthodox Christians in Turkey and Russia.

The Turkish sultans who followed Bayezid I (d. 1403, after defeat and capture by Timur) were even more lenient than he toward the Christians of their empire. Following the ancient Islamic code, they allowed their non-Muslim subjects one of three choices—the sword (for obstinate rebels), the Koran (for sincere converts), and tribute (for peaceful unbelievers). In Turkish Europe most Christians, known under the designation *rā'iya*, availed themselves of the third choice, paying a head tax which was not oppressive. The levies on trade and industry, most of which were in Christian hands, were also not oppressive. The submissive among the Christian population, and also among the Jews (as had been true in Muslim Spain), were economically no worse off under Turkish rule than they had been under the Byzantine emperors.

With the fall of Constantinople and the firm establishment of Sultan Mehmet II's rule (1453–81), Eastern Christians had still more reason to feel that the Turkish yoke was comparatively light. The sultan had the leader of the anti-Romanists elected to the patriarchate of Constantinople. To be sure, this patriarch and his successors were kept under close control, and by their nomination of bishops maintained an indirect Turkish restraint upon the several dioceses. Everywhere, however, the bishops were recognized as the heads of the Christian communities, in civil as well as in religious affairs, and the subject populations enjoyed a kind of local self-government. Thus the astute sultan was able to fashion the Orthodox Church into a valuable instrument for stable government. Internal dissensions were left to the patriarch, and the sultan's government not only was relieved of much administrative detail but besides derived considerable income from the sale of the patriarchate to ambitious clergymen.

The sultans also exploited the military and administrative potentialities of their Christian subjects. We have already indicated (Chapter I) that the 'blood tax' created an elite. Christian boys, selected when young, were brought up in the Muslim faith and trained for governmental or military service in schools of Spartan discipline. Some became civil officials or members of the palace guard. The hardiest were enrolled at twenty-five in the famous Janissary corps of shock troops. In Mehmet II's time this corps numbered about twelve thousand. Inured to a régime of absolute obedience and expected to abstain from marriage and luxury, these Christian-born lads, without families or other loyalties, were for centuries considered the most effective warriors of European Islam.

As the Constantinople patriarchate became a tool of the sultans and the Ipek patriarchate of Bulgaria dwindled away, Russia profited by the Turkish conquests. The fall of Constantinople to the Turks made Moscow the virtual capital of the independent Orthodox world—'the third Rome', as a Russian ecclesiastic expressed it. Eventually (1589) the metropolitan see of Moscow was raised to a patriarchate. The Orthodox religion was one of the main bonds of union among the Russians during 'the Time of Troubles' (*Smuta*) that followed. The Jesuits and the Poles on the one hand and the Swedes on the other supported rival pretenders to the Russian throne, but against them the Orthodox religion stood as both a symbol and a reason for resistance to foreign domination. Finally the national Sobor of 1613 chose Michael Romanov to be the new tsar. He was a compromise candidate, one who was related to the old dynasty of the Ivans and upon whom the clergy as well as cossacks, boyars, and merchants could agree, partly at least because these influential groups anticipated from his youth and weak character that they would have little to fear. They reckoned without Michael's father, who was formally enthroned as the Patriarch Philaret in 1619. Before his death (1633), the patriarch inaugurated a policy that eventually enabled the Romanovs to establish a state in which loyalty to the tsar was a compound of patriotic sentiment for 'Mother Russia' and pious devotion to 'Holy Russia'.

Under Michael's son Alexis the Russian national church underwent an internal crisis. The patriarch of that day was Nikon (1605–81), who tried unsuccessfully to make the church strong and independent of the state. Without intending to effect serious reform of ritual or dogma, Nikon introduced changes in the service that were meant to be in keeping with recent scholarship and with the practice of other Orthodox churches. Such apparently trivial things, however, as the Russian spelling of the name Jesus or the number of fingers used in crossing oneself became major issues, and the Russian clergy soon split between those who favoured Nikon's changes of ikons and liturgy and those who opposed them. The opponents of Nikon created a schism (*Raskol*) and were called *Raskolniki* (*Schismatics*). At first their programme was one of liturgical conservatism as against Nikon's minor reforms. Unsupported by the tsar, who resented the patriarch's efforts to divorce the church from the state, Nikon was tried by a synod in 1667 and confined to a monastery.

The Raskolniki were not appeased, however, and the Raskol spread. Peasant discontents that had added fuel to the social seethings in the 'time of troubles' had not yet been assuaged, and, in fact, they grew more bitter with the legal hardening of Russian serfdom under the new Romanovs. Many of the peasants readily identified themselves with the defence of the 'Old Belief' (i.e. with the *Raskolniki*) in their struggle against the landlords. Thus, ironically, religious conservatism, starting out as non-conformity with ritualistic change, became joined with demands for social reform; an extreme sect of the dissenting Old Believers denied the need of a clergy altogether and became a priestless cult (*Byezpopovtsi*). Religious fanaticism, doubtless confirmed by economic despair, seized large numbers of the *Raskolniki*, and thousands of them committed suicide, often by fire, while others, reinforced by local peasants, fugitives from Stenka (Stefan Timofeevich) Razin's outlaws, and malcontent townsfolk, fled to distant forests, set up communities of their own, stubbornly resisted the tsars' alternating policies of force and conciliation and, despite internal fragmentation, managed to survive. Estimates of the number of Old Believers in the nineteenth century run as high as 20,000,000.

Peter the Great had meanwhile solved the problem in his own high-handed, rationalist manner. He granted the Raskolniki (along with all but Jews and Jesuits) religious toleration, for he saw no reason why they should be outlawed and thus allowed to avoid taxes and work for the state. In order to make certain that no Nikon would arise to question or share his authority, Peter appointed no successor when the Patriarch Adrian died in 1700 but named an 'exarch' (that is, an officer of lower rank and power) instead. Peter practically nationalized the monasteries in 1701, making the monks salaried officials. By ukase in 1718 he required attendance at church every Sunday and holiday on pain of being ineligible for office, but his motive was political rather than religious—that an illiterate people might learn his will as the priests read his ukases. Finally, in 1721, he created a 'Spiritual Department' to explain dogma, regulate the press, and help him to select bishops. This body was presided over by a procurator, who was a layman, but was completely dominated by the tsar. Eventually it became the Holy Synod, and such it remained, dictating the religious life of Russia, until the Revolution of 1917.

Catherine the Great undertook further measures that demonstrated the subordination of religion to the state's purposes. In a series of steps between 1764 and 1786 church lands were secularized, and about 2,000,000 ecclesiastical serfs became directly dependent on the crown (but under conditions that in some respects worsened rather than bettered their lot). Catherine also took a step that made the Russian ruler more obviously the temporal leader of Eastern orthodoxy; by the Treaty of Kutchuk Kainardja with Turkey (1774) she received certain privileges that in the judgment of the Russian foreign office made the tsars protectors of the Christians in the Ottoman Empire. This claim ran counter, however, to French claims of a similar nature and in the next century further complicated the already complex Near Eastern Question.

ISLAM

In the early sixteenth century a series of important changes occurred in the political circumstances of Islam that deeply affected its religious evolution. Previously Islam as a religion had been the chief binding force of the many Muslim peoples, and the local military states that came and went might well have been looked upon as necessary evils. The pious were commonly urged to have as little to do with them as possible, and the governments in turn interfered only sporadically and on a personal basis in the development of religion. The centrifugal force of politics thus failed to disrupt the common loyalty to Islam. By the middle of the sixteenth century, however, a contrary tendency was visible. The central lands of the Muslim faith were traversing separate paths charted by a series of relatively stable Muslim empires, while Islam in the remoter areas was becoming culturally isolated.

At the start of the sixteenth century, Ismā'īl was the head of the Shī'ite Ṣafawiyya order. He set out to conquer as much of the Dār al-Islām as possible and to force the Sunnī populations to adopt Shī'ism. He succeeded in carving out a lasting empire in Iran—the Ṣafavid Empire. There he insisted that everyone should publicly curse such heroes of early Islam as 'Umar and Abū-bakr and follow the Shī'ite form of the *sharī'a*. The Sunnī *ṭarīqas* were suppressed, and many Sunnī were killed; Shī'ite books and teachers were brought in hastily from wherever they could be found; and the autonomous body of Shī'ite *mujtahids*—authorized leading interpreters of the *sharī'a*— gained an undisputed ascendancy. The original Shī'ism of the movement had been for the most part the esoteric faith of a *ṭarīqa*, but gradually the *mujtahids* imposed a Twelver Shī'ite orthodoxy. In the seventeenth century, Muḥammad-Bāqir al-Majlisī, with the aid of the political authorities, was especially effective in putting the doctrine into definitive form (see Chapter IX). The areas incorporated in the Ṣafavid Empire, whether Persian, Turkish, or Arabic speaking, have been insistently Shī'ite ever since; and the Iranians (and with them most Iraqis) were till modern times divided from their Sunnī neighbours in the west, north, and east by an implacable wall of distrust, each side regarding the other as infidel.

The Shī'a paid for its triumph in Iran by suffering great, and equally definitive, massacres in the expanding Ottoman territories, which became for the most part overwhelmingly Sunnī. From a dynamic frontier state in the Balkans and Anatolia, the Ottomans extended their rule to include most of the Arab countries as well. In the new empire the *sharī'a*, always rather a personal and social than a constitutional law, was made in principle the guide of state affairs, which in fact became unusually coloured by it. In contrast to earlier periods, the large non-Muslim population now took little part in public life or cultural matters, even though their sons, if converted, had a part in ruling the empire. The old system of juridically and even socially segregating lesser faiths in their own autonomous communities was strictly carried out. The Muslim '*ulamā*' became methodically organized in an unprecedentedly hierarchical manner (which incidentally entailed the supremacy throughout the Ottoman Empire of the Ḥanafites over the Shāfiʿites, already suppressed in Shīʿite Iran). The head of the '*ulamā*', the *shaykh al-Islām*, rose during the sixteenth century to a constitutional position almost on a level with the sultan, by whom, however, he was appointed. The sultan himself eventually came to emphasize his own caliphal character as head of the body of Muslims—a character assumed by many other rulers as well after the fall of the old titular caliphate at Baghdad—and as their representative against the infidels. And so the expansion of the Ottoman Empire, and at the end of our period its reverses, were regarded as those of Islam itself.

The Ottoman power reached as far as Algeria. Beyond lay Morocco, where the Sharīfian dynasty (i.e. a dynasty of *sharīfs*, 'nobles', descendants of Mohammed) now replaced the degenerate Berber dynasties. Morocco maintained not only political but also religious independence. The sharīf was honoured as a holy personage, and adherence to him became the touchstone of the faith. By the end of the sixteenth century much of Muslim western Africa had accepted this allegiance, and parts of it have tended to look to Morocco for religious leadership ever since. The earlier inclination of Morocco to regard the rest of Islam as apostate was confirmed, as the Islamic far west became almost self-sufficient.

In northern India arose a great state, the Mogul Empire, which rivalled in splendour the Ottoman and Ṣafavid Empires. Within this empire, as we shall soon see, Indian Islam went through its own, and an equally distinctive, evolution. Elsewhere, though continuing to advance in a number of areas, Islam confronted obstacles. At the beginning of the sixteenth century, Christians from the West put the Muslims on the defensive in many parts of the Indian Ocean coasts and in Africa, Malaysia, and even Arabia. The Muslims of the north at the same time became relatively isolated. Those of the Volga came under Russian rule, while Turkestan was divided between the long-pagan Kazaks and the culturally not much more stimulating Uzbeg rulers, who were bitterly at war with Shīʿite Iran. Thus the Muslims of China had little opportunity for contact with vital Muslim centres.

The *ṭarīqas* continued almost everywhere, although chiefly on a relatively local basis now. In the Ṣafavid domain they survived only in impoverished circumstances. In Ottoman territories the *ṭarīqas* favoured by the Turks, such as the various branches of the Khalwatiyya, increased in strength and enjoyed greater pomp than others; the heads of the North African orders were the objects of a devotion near to anthropolatry. One or another order was introduced in every corner of Islam. Thus, with the saint 'Abd al-Ra'ūf in the seventeenth century, the Shaṭṭāriyya gave self-confidence to a strong mystic movement in newly converted Malaysia. The orders came to show less originality, however; many of the ṭarīqas were wealthy and shot through with popular superstition. Yet among the new branches of ṭarīqas now set up there were some devoted to reform. Orthodox 'ulamā' working within a Ṣūfī framework also sometimes carried out reform, as did Aḥmad Sirhindī at the beginning of the seventeenth century in India (see Chapter VII), and so sometimes did simple and pious mystics. In the eighteenth century there arose in Arabia a reform movement which was radically anti-Ṣūfī—that of the Wahhābīs—and it was to have far-reaching effects in the next century.

★   ★   ★

The Moguls in India

In 1500 India was divided between Muslims and Hindus. Most of north and central India was under Muslim rule. The Afghan sultans ruled at Delhi; independent Muslim rulers controlled Bengal, Malwa, Gujarat, Kashmir, and Khandesh in the north; and the Bahmani kingdom and its successor states (Berar, Ahmadnager, Bihapur, Golkonda, and Bidar) controlled the Deccan. The Hindu Vijayanagar Empire, which reached its height under Krishnadeva Rāya (1509–29), dominated the south; Hindu rulers controlled Orissa and Rajputana; and Assam and Nepal were independent of Muslim control. Elsewhere, despite continued persecutions and desecrations, interpenetration of the two cultures was in progress, though slowly and generally unintentionally. In some areas, notably Kashmir, the repeal of the poll tax, the use of Hindu advisers, the patronage of vernacular literature, some relaxation of the restrictions on Hindus, and years of contact had somewhat reduced the conflict between Hindu and Muslim.

In the second quarter of the century the Afghans were displaced in north India by the Moguls, or Mughals, under Bābur (1526–30) and Humāyūn (1530–38 and 1555–56). In the reign of Akbar (1556–1605) Mogul rule spread over Bengal, Orissa, Malwa, Gujarat, Rajputana, Berar, and Khandesh. He improved administration, conciliated the Rajputs, repealed the poll tax and pilgrim tax, used Hindu advisers, patronized Hindu learning, and generally tolerated Hinduism, thus creating an era of rare well-being and good will. Meanwhile, in the south, after the sack of Vijayanagar (1565), Hindu rule declined before the advance of the Muslim kingdoms of the Deccan, and Akbar's successors, Jahāngīr (1605–27) and Shāh Jahān (1627–58), extended Mogul sway into the upper Deccan. Under Aurangzīb (1658–1707) it stretched over all of India except the small southern tip.

The rise of the Mogul Empire brought the widest reach of Muslim political power in India and, with it, the maximum degree of Islamic organization and hence of potential proselytizing power. The head of the Sunnī community in India was the sultan (who, from Akbar on, commonly carried also the title of caliph), an emperor who dealt with the Ṣafavī shāh and the Ottoman sultan on a basis of equality. In 1579, renewing the efforts of certain earlier Delhi emperors to extend control to matters of doctrine, Akbar induced the highest '*ulamā*' to accept his interpretation on points of religion when the theologians disagreed and to consider his decrees final when they were not in opposition to the Koran and were of benefit to the people. His immediate successors maintained this position. Below the sultan the organization of the Islamic community included various law officials, such as the chief justice, canon law judges (*qaḍis*), common law judges ('*ādils*), and subordinate law officers (*muftis*); various financial officials (*dīwān*); various religious officials, such as the *sadr* (in charge of religious endowments and ecclesiastical affairs), the *shaykhs* (heads of the mendicant orders), the *muḥtasibs* (censors of public morals), and the *īmāms* (prayer leaders in charge of the mosques and mosque schools). The highest of these posts were occupied by the '*ulamā*'.

The Mogul conquest brought an influx of soldiers, scholars, and fortune hunters into India, and Akbar's fame and tolerant attitude attracted Sunnī scholars and Shī'ite refugees alike. Akbar tolerated Hindus, Christians, Jains, and other religious groups, as well as differing Islamic sects. He not only supported and debated with their scholars at his court but he even permitted Hindus to proselytize. Badāyūni, an orthodox Muslim chronicler, shocked by Akbar's freethinking and conciliation of Hindus, alleged that Islam died during his reign. To be sure, few famous Islamic missionaries appeared after the fifteenth century; yet it may well be that Akbar's toleration attracted more humble Hindus to Islam than did the militant policies of his great-grandson Aurangzīb. Certainly some of his enlightened policies restricted Muslim zealots, but the charge that Akbar abjured Islam and persecuted Muslims seems extreme.[8] His 'Divine Monotheism' appears to have been not a new dispensation but only an order of devoted courtiers.

Jahāngīr, while continuing some of his father's tolerant measures, promoted Islam more actively. Converts appear to have received daily allowances, and Hindus were discouraged from converting or marrying Muslim women. Jahāngīr also persecuted the Jains and drove many of them from Gujarat into Rajputana. Both he and his son, Shāh Jahān, were zealous builders of mosques and patrons of Islamic religious establishments.

Shāh Jahān was an orthodox Sunnī. During his early years he made some changes in the policy of toleration, but most of them were not enforced after 1638. He did, however, establish a superintendent of converts and permitted compulsory conversion. Moreover, he vigorously promoted Islam, observing festivals, encouraging pilgrimages to Mecca, restoring prerogatives to the '*ulamā*', imposing the Islamic moral code upon Muslims, and improving court relations with the orthodox.

Aurangzīb, a strict Sunnī and militant puritan, completely reversed the policy of toleration. In 1669 he ordered provincial governors to destroy

Hindu schools and temples and to put an end to idol worship. Temples were demolished all over the country—two hundred and fifty in Rajputana alone in a single year. Hindu religious festivals and pilgrimages were stopped. The hated poll tax was reintroduced, even for Rajput warriors, who were essential to Mogul military power. Aurangzīb encouraged proselytizing and compulsory conversion, with the result that, while many prominent Hindus were converted to Islam, even more died resisting. He also tried to impose the Sunnī law on all Muslims, and his censors strictly enforced his prohibition of wine, spirits, public music, singing, long beards, and objectionable clothing. Unorthodox Muslims were particularly hounded, and the Shī'ite Muharram (new year's festival) was banned. Aurangzīb had the system of Hanafite law prevalent in India compiled into the *Fatāwa-i'Ālamgīrī*, which became the first standard legal code for the Muslim community.

While Aurangzīb's policies undoubtedly pleased the orthodox, they also aroused bitter opposition, which did not end until the Mogul Empire crumbled. Even before his drastic orders of 1669 rebellion began, under the leadership of Sivājī, among the Marathas, and a struggle with the Sikhs was also in progress. In 1669 the Jāt peasants in the Mathura area also revolted, and in 1678 the Rajputs joined in. The emperor's last years were given to the conquest of the Shī'ite sultanates of the Deccan and to a fruitless struggle against the Marathas. After his death the empire rapidly disintegrated. Provincial governors revolted; the Persians raided Delhi; and the Marathas built a loose confederacy that dominated much of India. These chaotic conditions created an occasion and an opportunity for British and French intervention.

During the period of toleration India became a major intellectual centre of the Islamic world, attracting Muslim scholars from everywhere. At the beginning of the seventeenth century the Ṣūfī order of the Naqshbandiyya was introduced into India, but it never became so popular as the older orders. Several irregular orders also arose. Numerous Ṣūfī, Shī'ite, and freethinking scholars shared honours with the orthodox Sunnī ones. Outstanding among them were the freethinkers Mubārak and his two sons, Faizī and Abu'l Faḍl. Another of the liberal scholar was Dārā Shikūh, a son of Shāh Jahān, whose *Majma'-ul-Baḥrayn* emphasized the similarities between Ṣūfism and Hinduism. He was executed by his uncompromising brother Aurangzīb in the struggle for the throne.

The Shī'ites generally prospered under the more tolerant emperors, and the Imāmiyya, the major Shī'ite subdivision, gained ground throughout India, particularly under Akbar. His guardian, Bairām Khan, belonged to this group, and so did the Persian scholar, Sayyid Nūr-Allāh bin Sharīf al-Ḥusaynī al-Mar'ashi of Shushtar, whom he appointed chief law officer in Lahore. As such, Nūr-Allāh completed in 1604 the *Majālis-ul-Mu'minīn*, a defence of the Shī'ites, only to be executed for heresy in 1610 by Jahāngīr. Until the time of Aurangzīb, the chief Imāmiyya centres were located in the independent sultanates of the Deccan. In his later years Aurangzīb extinguished these sultanates and persecuted the Shī'ites as heretics, but after his death the ruler of Oudh became a Shī'ite, and in 1732 Lucknow, its capital, became the principal centre of the Imāmiyya.

The most important of the other Shī'ite subdivisions in India was the Ismā'īlīyya. Already split into Khojahs and Bohrahs (see Chapter III), it now added several new sub-sects. In the sixteenth century the head of the Tayyibī Ismā'īlī (Bohrahs) came from Yemen to make Gujarat his headquarters. Sometime after his death a split occurred in his sect (1588); one group, known as the Sulaymāni, followed a new head (Sulaymān) in Yemen, but most of the Indians in the sect, accepting a Gujarati leader named Dā'ud, became known as the Dā'udī. The Dā'udī ultimately established headquarters in Surat, while at Boroda a deputy of the Yemen succession led the Sulaymāni group. Still another offshoot of the Ismā'īlīyya, the Rōshaniyya, was established in the Northwest Frontier in the sixteenth century. Strongly influenced by Hinduism, its adherents believed in transmigration and the pantheistic nature of God and accepted their leaders as divine manifestations. They submitted to Akbar in 1587 and gradually died out. Aurangzīb appointed Sunnī officials for the Bohrah mosques but failed to extinguish them.

Islam began to move out of the cities and into the rural areas during the Mogul period, probably reaching its maximum strength in the reign of Aurangzīb. Improved organization and instruction, the influence of scholars from various parts of the Islamic world, and continual pilgrimages to Mecca all served to deepen the understanding of Islam among its Indian followers and to eliminate some of the unorthodox or local accretions. During the disorders that followed Aurangzīb's death, when the Hindu Marathas were ascendant, Islam apparently made little further progress.

Even while expanding and deepening, Islam generally underwent some Hindu influences, and sects arose that combined Hindu and Islamic ideas (see below). Although Islam frowned upon castes, many caste rules and practices survived among Hindu converts and subtly exerted their spell upon the whole Islamic community. In the popular mind upper-class Indian Muslims were divided into four main groups; the Sayyids, claiming descent from Mohammed through Fatima; the Shaykhs, claiming pure Arab descent; the Moguls, claiming descent from those who came at the time of the Mogul conquest; and the Paṭhāns, found particularly in the Northwest Frontier, claiming descent from Afghans. The unreliability of these designations as a key to origins was represented in the popular saying, 'Last year I was a Julāhā [or weaver], this year I am a Shaykh, next year, if prices rise, I shall be a Sayyid'.[9] Since most Hindu converts adopted the Shaykh designation to gain social approbation, the vast majority of Indian Muslims came to belong to this group.

★   ★   ★

The Spread of Islam in Southeast Asia

Despite the contemporaneous development of Christian influence, Islam spread in Malaya and the East Indies. When the Portuguese captured Malacca (1511), they thereby eliminated one of the most important Islamic centres in the East, but the Grisek-Tuban centre in Java remained, and others quickly developed. Acheh (Achin), in western Sumatra, emerged as a Muslim rival to the Portuguese at Malacca and gradually extended its sway over western Sumatra. The displaced sultans of Malacca established themselves at Johore in south Malaya, threatening Malacca and influencing the nearby areas and western Borneo. From Perak, Kedah, and Patani, Islam penetrated lower Malaya and moved into lands controlled by Buddhist Ayuthia (Siam). From Jambi and Johore it spread to central Sumatra, and from Palembang to southeastern Sumatra and southwestern Borneo. Under Sultan Tranggana (1521–46) Demak emerged as the strongest Islamic power on the north coast of Java, and by 1526 its political and missionary efforts won Bantam and West Java as well. In 1568 Hassan Udin, son of Sunan Guning Jati, the chief missionary in the conversion of Bantam, established there an independent sultanate, which then became in its turn a base for the dissemination of Islam.

Except for Malacca, Islam dominated Malaya and the Malay Archipelago in the sixteenth century. Only in the northern Philippines, after the establishment of the Spanish at Manila (1571), did Christian influence conspicuously turn Islam back. Elsewhere in the area Islamic political control pushed onward from the coastal regions into the interior. Although the actual conversion of the hinterland was a rather slow process, when the Dutch and the English arrived (c. 1600) most of that part of the world was at least nominally Muslim.

The gradual extension of European political control over the Malaysian coasts in the seventeenth and eighteenth centuries did little to shake the hold of Islam. Demak declined, but Mataram rose and by 1601 dominated south and central Java. Under Sunan Agung (1613–45), a fervent Muslim, it conquered the Hindu kingdom of Balambang on the eastern tip of Java and gained control over all of that island but Bantam. Agung crusaded against the Hindu-Buddhist remnants, established close relations with Mecca, brought new Islamic contacts to Java, exerted his influence in southern Borneo, and crossed swords with the Dutch at Batavia. About 1604 a Muslim trader converted the raja of Macassar and thus began the conversion of the Bugis of Celebes. They in turn extended Islam into Borneo and the islands east of Java. From Brunei and the Suli area, Islam spread into Mandanao and the Manila Bay region, where it was stopped by the Spanish conquest. Ternate and Tidore remained Islamic centres for the area of the Moluccas and Banda Islands despite repeated counter-measures of the Portuguese, Spanish, and Dutch.

In this area Islam suffered few defeats. The Europeans succeeded in getting permanent Christian footholds only on Amboina and at some points in the Moluccas and northern Celebes. The Dyaks of central Borneo, the Bataks of west-central Sumatra, and some other isolated tribes were never converted to Islam, the Bataks ultimately becoming nominal Christians. On Bali and Lombak Hindu-Buddhism survived despite all efforts to convert them.

Islam also encountered successes north of Malaya. Sometime after their final conquest by the Annamites (about 1470) the Chams of Cochin-China became Muslim. Intermarriage with Indians introduced some Muslims into the Arakan area of western Burma, while others from Yünnan in China established themselves in northern Burma. But an effort to plant Islam in Cambodia about 1650 failed.

During this expansion Islam underwent a complex process of acculturation, analogous to that of Catholicism in the Latin-American countries. This process resulted in the permanent engraftment upon Islam of numerous native folkways that converts would not give up. In consequence, Indonesian Islam emerged as something different from either Middle Eastern or Indian Islam, although most Indonesians came to consider themselves orthodox Sunnī. Many converts had little understanding of Islam's basic doctrines and looked upon it as a superior form of magic. Others were converted *en masse* upon superficially accepting the faith of a recent conqueror. Still others came in as a result of the work of zealous merchants and mystic *faqīrs*, whose knowledge of Islam was much less impressive than their enthusiasm. The number of missionaries who knew Arabic or Persian and were learned in the Koran and Islamic law was not large.

The seventeenth and eighteenth centuries were a period of purification for East Indian Islam. Some of the more unacceptable native practices were eliminated, and some of the more basic tenets of Islam gained wider currency and deeper understanding or were associated with elements of the native tradition that were too precious to surrender. In this process new teachers and missionaries from India and the Middle East or East Indians who had gone to these areas to study were important agents. Pilgrimages to Mecca also played a part. Many local rulers sent their sons to Mecca, and merchants, nobles, and others who could afford it themselves made the pilgrimage. The mosque schools were also effective media of education, as were the private schools, or *pesantren*, taught by gurus. In rural communities, villagers received elementary instruction in prayer halls from leaders who had received a modicum of training in *pesantrens* (see Chapter XVI).

Gradually a Malaysian Islam emerged which, with local variations, had its own distinctive character. The very form of the mosque was distinct, in some ways resembling a pagoda. The Malaysian's attitude toward the five pillars of faith was far from orthodox. His confession of faith did not convey to his mind the strict denial of other beliefs that it conveyed in original Islam. Daily prayers and purification ceremonies were not rigidly observed, while the giving of alms was transformed largely into the offering of rice on festive occasions, an act generally believed to be efficacious in cleansing away sin. The fast of Ramadān was popular because of the belief that it made up for shortcomings during the rest of the year. The pilgrimage to Mecca (*hajj*) was so generally undertaken when financially possible (although substitutes were often sent) that Malaysian Muslims were reputed for their pilgrim zeal. When Islamic law regarding such things as marriage, succession, and inheritance was in conflict with native customary (*adat*) law, the native custom usually prevailed. Other practices showed marked deviations from orthodox Islam: the high social and legal status of women and the absence of *purdah*; the prevalence of ritual feasts (*slametans*) at times of birth, marriage, conception, death, birthdays, and holy days, at which offerings were made to spirits and ancestors; the use of drums in the call to prayer and of native orchestras (*gamelang*) and dramatic dances (*wayang*); the common substitution of incision for circumcision; the attachment to mosques of a *penghulu*, or religious judge and director of mosque affairs, in addition to the prayer leader and other accepted mosque officials; and the mildness of the restrictions on wine.

★   ★   ★

The Muslims of China

In China, too, the number of Muslims increased, but only slowly. They were to be found particularly in the northern provinces and in Yünnan, most often engaged in cattle, horse, and sheep raising, caravan trading, inn keeping, and mercantile operations, although some were farmers and some served as Chinese officials. They avoided pork, alcohol, and opium and the worship of idols and ancestors. Few made the pilgrimage to Mecca; the Koran was not translated into Chinese; and only a few mosque officials knew Arabic. Except for those in Sinkiang and adjacent regions in northwest China, the Muslims of China tended to become Sinicized. Most of them retained or adopted Chinese names and dress, acquired some Confucian learning, participated in the civil service examination, and approved of the worship of Heaven as identical with Allah. Subject to the same government regulations and restrictions as Buddhists and Taoists, in general they lived in harmony with the other Chinese, but some political disturbances in Yünnan and the northwest were not entirely dissociated from religious questions. Migration into the northwest areas seems to have been considerable in the eighteenth century, and the total number of Muslims in China and Sinkiang possibly exceeded ten million in that century.

HINDUISM

During this period Hinduism experienced several reform movements, unconnected with but, despite marked differences, not wholly unlike the contemporary reform movements of the West. Among them were two important Vishnuite cults, the Vallabhas and the Chaitanyas.

As previously indicated, Vallabha seems to have been the one who effectively developed the Rudra tradition and the system of thought and practice associated with it. He lived somewhere between 1470 and 1533. His activities appear to have centred in Benares and Muttra, although he spent many years travelling and teaching in Vijayanagar and other parts of India. During his travels Krishna is supposed to have come to him and directed him to promulgate the worship of the divine cowherd child.

Vallabha's numerous treatises and theological views will be examined in Chapter VII. Here is will suffice to indicate that he expounded a doctrine in some respects suggestive of, though also widely different from, the idea of divine grace set forth in some European theologies. The Lord, he taught, engendered in some souls the capacity to worship Him for no other reason than that they loved Him passionately and without ulterior motive such as a desire for salvation. The Lord gave such favoured souls a divine body like His and allowed them to dwell eternally in Heaven (*Goloka*). The *Gopīs'* (*milkmaids'*) devotion to the youth Krishna best illustrated this kind of divine love. Those who had received divine favour automatically saw everything in the Lord (while others saw Him as everything); they devoted themselves and their belongings to Him and lost themselves in Him, thus eliminating the mortal obstructions of egoism and possessions. This *pushti-mārga*, or salvation by divine grace, was open to all—women, Sudras (the lowest of the four great castes), criminals, peoples of all creeds—whereas lower levels of bliss, available by *karma* (good works) and *jñāna* (knowledge) were open only to males of the three upper castes. Those who hoped for *pushti-mārga* would normally eschew asceticism and aspire to love the Lord as did the Gopīs; for all souls were essentially feminine and had the Lord as their natural husband. Nevertheless, Vallabha warned, sensualism played no part in the love (*rasa-līlā*) of Krishna and the Gopīs, and worldly matters must be forgotten in the Lord's service.

The Vallabhas were augmented and organized by the missionary efforts of Vallabha's eighty-four principal disciples and two sons. His son Vitthalnātha established the chief Vallabha shrine at Gokul, near Muttra, the scene of Krishna's association with the milkmaids. The sect spread in Rajputana, Malwa, Bijapur, and Gujarat. Vitthalnātha's seven sons, in whom Krishna was said to have been incarnated for five years, exercised authority over separate districts. Vallabha's male descendants controlled the sect as teachers, or *gosāins*, and each took the title of maharaja. During the persecutions by Aurangzīb the most sacred image was transferred from Gokul to Nāthadwār in Rajputana, and the maharaja of that shrine became the head of the sect.

The daily prayer and initiation formula of the sect reflected the founder's spirit of devoted service: 'Krishna is my refuge. I, who suffer the infinite pain and torment of enduring for a thousand years separation from Krishna, consecrate to Krishna my body, senses, life, heart and faculties, my wife, house, family, property, and my own self. I am thy slave, O Krishna.'[10] But in time the noble sentiments of this prayer were perverted by less noble practices. A self-indulgence unfolded that appealed especially to the mercantile classes, but the chief beneficiaries of the idea of submission of body, purse, and spirit to Krishna were his earthly representatives. Like the Renaissance popes, the maharajas became more and more wealthy and powerful, and less and less ascetic. The temples were considered their personal property. Lay members came for instruction and guidance to them, who were looked upon as divine. The sect forgot or largely disregarded the prohibition of caste distinctions and Vallabha's warning against sensuality. Since Krishna was adored particularly as a child, images of the infant Krishna were bathed, fed, and fondled in the maharajah's temples. Many of the sect's hymns and dances were licentious. Women seem to have striven to serve the maharajas as Gopīs and paid established fees for looking at them, touching them, swinging, dancing, sitting, or being closeted with them, washing their feet, drinking the water they had bathed in, or eating food from their mouths. Opposition to the Vallabhas' immorality developed, and in the nineteenth century a new sect arose specifically to oppose them.

★ ★ ★

Chaitanya and the Krishna Sects

The Brahman Chaitanya (1485–1533), a contemporary of Vallabha, founded his Vishnuite *bhakti* cult in Bengal. His sect is said by some to belong to the Rudra tradition, by others to the Nimāvats, and by still others to the Mādhvas. Its Krishna-Rādhā worship is attributed to a Mādhavendra Purī, whose disciple, Īshvara Purī, is in one of the relevant traditions supposed to have transmitted it to Chaitanya, and Īshvara Purī does in fact seem to have been associated with the great change that came over Chaitanya just before he began his ministry. These men and others closely connected with Chaitanya were followers of the Mādhva tradition. The Mādhvas certainly leaned heavily on the *Bhāgavata-purāna*. To be sure, that *purāna*, though it extolled Krishna, did not mention Rādhā, but a Bengali variation by Mālādhar Vasu, called *Shri-Krishna-vijay* (written between 1473 and 1480), had introduced the Rādhā romance. Chaitanya clearly drew upon this Bengal tradition about the love of Krishna and Rādhā and upon other sources that were not related directly to the classical books or the older theology. He was also influenced by the Krishna-Rādhā poetry of Jayadeva (*Gīta Govinda*) and (among more recent poets) of Vidyāpati and Baru Chandīdās (see Chapter X).

Chaitanya was a revivalist, a mystic who swooned at the mention of Krishna, and not a theologian. At the age of seventeen, while on a pilgrimage, he began to show signs of religious ecstasy. At twenty-five he abandoned his family, became a *sannyāsī* ('ascetic') and ultimately settled in Puri near the Jagannath Temple. He toured southern and eastern India, meditating, preaching, and demonstrating his ecstatic worship; apparently thousands flocked to hear him. Swaying, dancing, and gesticulating, he sang hymns or gave theatrical performances. The essence of his teachings was that God (that is, Krishna) was love and must be approached through devotion and self-surrender.

The simple, easy, equalitarian, and emotional nature of Chaitanya's teachings made a profound appeal to the oppressed, and even Brahmans and Muslims were converted. The movement spread rapidly in Bengal, eastern India, and Assam, especially at the expense of Shāktism and through the conversion of disorganized remnants of Buddhism. Chaitanya disregarded such outward religious tokens as caste, rites, ceremonies, and asceticism and extolled such inner graces as honesty, simplicity, and sincerity. Members of his sect were not to covet gain, rank, or esteem and were to refrain from self-aggrandizement, self-indulgences, and jealousy. He favoured marriage, vegetarianism, and teetotalism, and in his theology, the sensual and voracious could not attain salvation. Yet he preached a sensuous devotion to God, which, however, like the love of Rādhā for Krishna, contemplated only the Lord's pleasure and not one's own. He conceived of himself as Rādhā in his devotion.

The philosophy of Chaitanya's sect was essentially that of Nimbārka (see Chapter III). The material world was a manifestation of the Deity, eternally distinct but not separate from Him. The soul was a detached portion of the Deity, yet eternally connected with and dependent on Him. It was deluded by *māyā* and found salvation only through *bhakti*—faith, love, and absolute surrender to the saving grace of Krishna; reason was useless. There were five degrees of devotion: calm meditation, servitude, friendship, love like that of a child for its parents, and the highest love, like that of a woman for her lover, like that of Rādhā for Krishna.

The organization of the sect was largely the work of Chaitanya's disciples. Two of them, Nityānanda and Advaita, and Chaitanya himself were called the three masters (*prabhūs*) and were regarded together as a joint incarnation of Krishna. None of the three wrote anything, but two other disciples, Rūpa Gosvāmī and Sanātana Gosvāmī, who lived at Brindaban (near Muttra) and had at one time accepted Islam, wrote a great deal (see Chapter VII). The sect flourished at Puri and Brindaban and in Bengal. The descendants of the disciples, especially those of Nityānanda, became its teachers, or *gosāins*, and were adored almost as deities. The *gosāins* were nearly all Brahmans.

The sect also had its ascetic orders. They seem to have developed under Nityānanda and his son, who apparently admitted by simple initiation ceremonies groups of wandering ascetics, men and women, remnants of Tantric Buddhism. Out of these unpromising beginnings arose nominally ascetic orders—the Vrikats, who were celibates; the Spashta Dāyakas, whose monks and nuns lived together in the same establishments; the Nerā-Neris, wandering pairs of men and women; and other unregulated groups. The tantric Sahajiya[11] (Way of Nature) cult also became associated with the Chaitanyas; it taught the attainment of salvation through the worship and physical love of a beautiful women regarded as representative of Rādhā.

Despite these associates, the principal sect remained, under the leadership of its *gosāins*, a highly moral, though emotional, group. Adoration of the gurus, singing, repetition of the name of the deity, communal meals, and necklaces and rosaries of *tulasī* beads were prominent in its ritual. Its doctrines were developed by Jīva Gosvāmī and Krishnadās Kavirāja, residents of Brindaban. The latter's biography of Chaitanya in Bengali, the *Chaitanya-charitāmrita* (completed about 1616), became probably its most important work. In the seventeenth century the leader Shrīnivāsa transported the writings of the Brindaban group to Bengal, where they became the sect's chief scripture, replacing the *Chaitanya-bhāgavata*, a biography written in Bengali verse by Vrindāvan Dās shortly before 1550. The new doctrinal treatises stimulated the Bengal-Orissa group to another period of expansion, with leaders from the lower castes, women leaders, and women writers. Later in the seventeenth century Vishvanāth was perhaps the Chaitanyas' foremost figure, and in the early-eighteenth century it was perhaps Baladeva, who wrote an important commentary on the *Vedānta-sūtra* and defended the *gosāins'* sect at a crucial meeting of Vishnuites in Jaipur.

The sensuous elements in the sect's doctrine inevitably conflicted with the moral restraints imposed by the *gosāins*. A controversy arose over Rādhā's relationship to Krishna, the *gosāins* maintaining that she was his wife but others preferring to consider her his mistress and advocating the practice of spontaneous love (*rāga-mārga*). In the early-eighteenth century, the *gosāins'* control weakened, while the Sahajiyās and similar groups that concentrated on the erotic side of Rādhā worship asserted themselves. Women other than wives became companions in the course of *sādhana* (training and discipline), in which the pastimes of Krishna and Rādhā were resumed. The advocates of spontaneous love also abandoned vegetarianism and other restrictive practices, and caste distinctions tended to creep back. The Bauls, a sect of musicians and singers who considered the sex act the most appropriate form of worship, became associated with the Chaitanyas, and the Vrikat celibates appear to have yielded to the sensuous persuasion. In the seventeenth century alleged followers of the mystic Chaitanya started a stream of erotic poetry that rose to a flood in the eighteenth. Nevertheless, the main body of the laity continued under the leadership of the gosāins as a morally restrained sect.

Chaitanya's creed had a certain appeal for Muslims; one of his disciples, Haridās, was a poor Muslim. Although direct ministration to Muslims by gurus gradually ended, a cult called the Kartābhajas, to which both Hindus and Muslims belonged, seems to have developed out of the Chaitanyas in Bengal. The cult's founder, Rām Smaran Pāl (born about 1700), taught that there was only one God, Who was incarnated in the *kartā*, or head of the sect. The *kartā* claimed to be the owner of his followers' bodies and extracted rent for the soul's use of the body. Later *kartās* came from the descendants of the founder. The Kartābhajas recognized no distinction of caste or creed, forbade meat and wine, sang or chanted *mantras* five times daily, and regarded Friday as a holy day.

Other Krishna sects were closely related to the Chaitanyas. The Mahāpurushīyas of Assam were founded by Shankar Deb (died *c.* 1569), whose relationship to the Chaitanya movement is uncertain. He preached the worship of Krishna but not of Rādhā and denounced caste, idolatry, sacrifices, and the eating of meat. His successor, Mādhab Deb, rejected these practices even more completely, and his writings became the scriptures of the sect. The Mahāpurushīyas movement was at first opposed by the Shākta Brahmans and was persecuted by the king of Ahom. It continued to grow, however, and even to put out offshoots, such as the monastic Bamunia and the tribal, politically revolutionary Moamarias.

The Haridāsīs were founded at Brindaban by Haridās (fl. *c.* 1600). His teachings were very close to those of the Chaitanyas. A Hindi poet of merit, he also wrote in Sanskrit. Many of his successors as head of the sect were also gifted poets, some of whom expressed devotional views in erotic verse.

Two other Krishna sects of the period, the Rādhā-Vallabhīs and the Sakhi-bhāvas, are often associated with the tradition of Nimbārka. Both concentrated their adoration on Rādhā rather than Krishna, and their practices were tied up with the idea that mankind should cultivate a female love for Krishna, who was the only male. The Rādhā-Vallabhīs were founded by Harivamsha at Brindaban about 1585. He wrote, in both Sanskrit and Hindi, poems that were notoriously erotic, as did later members of the sect as well. In secret ceremonies adherents of the sect were said to dress as women. The Sakhi-bhāvas definitely imitated feminine dress, habits, and functions, and considered themselves female attendants of Rādhā.

*   *   *

The Vishnuite Sects

A tendency to counteract the flood of Krishnaite sensualism developed within Vishnuism. For one thing, the worship of Rāma was greatly strengthened by the didactic poetry of Tulsī Dās (1532–1623) of Benares. His masterpiece, the *Rāmacaritamānasa* (*Lake of the Deeds of Rāma*), popularly known as the *Rāmāyana*, was but one of his several poems exalting Rāma (see Chapter XI). It became the Bible of the people of north India. Hindu in theology and imagery, it expressed a noble theism and a rare standard of ethics. It depicted Rāma as an omnipotent but kind and tender saviour of all, regardless of caste or position; faith, love of God, and devotion to Him constituted the road to happiness; but the love between the soul and God was no form of sexual passion, nor was salvation mere absorption into the Divine.

The Rāmats continued strong in north India, and several new Rāma sects were formed. Of these the Malūkdāsīs, founded by Malūk Dās (of Allahabad) during the reign of Arangzīb, was perhaps the most important. Malūk Dās was a trader, and in his sect, although monasteries were established, the teachers were laymen and not ascetics. Rāma worshippers generally held aloof from the sensuality of the Krishnaites, but in one of their orders, the Bairāgī, monks and nuns adopted the practice of living as couples.

In the Maratha country, Krishna worship continued, centring around the Pandharpur shrine of Vitthobā (Vishnu), but it was a restrained and elevated creed. Ekanātha (sixteenth century) and Tukārām (1607–49) carried on the devotional, anti-ceremonial, anti-theological tradition of Nāmdev. Tukārām's hymns in Marathi were extraordinarily popular and played a part in the later national revolt under Sivājī. He taught that the way to God was through neither asceticism nor sensual passion but through purity and dedication.

About 1650 Rāmdās (1608–81), the spiritual preceptor of Sivājī, established the Rāmdāsīs sect. His devotion to God and to the equality of all men before Him, expressed in his *Dashabodha* and demonstrated in his monastic foundations, helped to promote Maratha nationalism. The sect flourished especially during the rise and expansion of the Maratha empire. It was devoted to Rāma, accepted the absolute monistic philosophy of Shankara, and taught that faith (*bhakti*), knowledge, and works were necessary to salvation.

Another Vishnuite sect, the Shrī-Vishnuites, while continuing to prosper throughout south India, became further fragmented. After the death of Vedānta Deshika's son, the Vadagalais (or Northerners) tended to separate into autonomous congregations. In the attempt to combat this tendency Ādi Vana-Shathakopa (Shrīnivāsa, died *c.* 1559) established various temples and *maths*, including the famous Ahobhila Monastery, gave privileges to the lower castes in the temples, and endeavoured to unite the northern and southern groups. His attempt failed; though the largest group of the Vadagalais accepted his successors as leaders, other groups, known as the Munitraya-sampradāya, remained independent under local gurus. The Tengalais (or Southerners) continued to expand, especially among non-Brahmans, and became the strongest of the Shrī-Vishnuites. No changes of importance seem to have occurred among other Vishnuite sects.

*   *   *

Shivaism and Shāktism

Nor in general did Shivaism undergo major modifications. The Pāshupatas shrank to a negligible number, but Southern Shivaism remained strong, and its philosophy (see Chapter VII) and literature were developed by a significant group of writers, including the poet Rāmalinga. The devotional aspect of Shivaism reached its zenith in the Tamil songs of the Sittars (Siddhas), or Perfect Ones. Despite their anti-Brahmanism and anti-sacerdotalism, their hymns are held in reverence still by the southern Shivaites. They reflected severe monotheism, contempt for the *Vedas*, *shastras*, images, and priests, disbelief in transmigration, and interest in alchemy. Perhaps influenced by Islamic Ṣūfism, they breathed a mystical devotion to a personal deity. The Lingāyat creed continued and apparently was the religion of the viceroys of

Bednūr (Keladi, Ikkeri), who carved an independent kingdom (1550–1763) out of the Vijayanagar Empire. Although the Lingāyats gradually established centres at Kadur, Ujjeri, Benares, Shrisailam, and Kedarnāth in the Himalayas, they seem to have had little strength in north India. In general, Shivaism, patronized by the upper castes and non-sectarian ascetics, despite its pronounced *bhakti* features did not develop the sensuous tendencies of Krishnaism.

Shāktism, having gathered great strength in Bihar, Bengal, and Assam, was expanding its influence there when our period ended. As an organized group it was not strong in other parts of India. The Shāktas appear to have suffered from the competition of Chaitanyaism and to have lost ground during the sixteenth and seventeenth centuries. Conflict and recrimination were frequent between the two creeds. In the eighteenth century, however, as the Chaitanya movement declined or became infected with elements of Shāktism, the Shāktas experienced an upsurge, which correlated also with the economic and political chaos that accompanied the disintegration of the Mogul Empire and the rise of British power in India.

A good deal of Tantric literature devoted to the Shaktis was produced in the centuries under consideration in this chapter. Compilers of the *tantra* digest were especially active in Bengal, their work perhaps reaching its culmination in the *Āgama-tattva-vilāsa* (c. 1687) of Raghunātha Tarkavāgīsha. New *tantras* were composed, among them the sixteenth-century *Yogini*, clearly connected with the well-known Shakti shrine at Kāmarūpa, which, having been destroyed by the Muslims, was rebuilt (somewhere between 1550 and 1565) with dedicatory ceremonies at which one hundred and forty men were said to have been sacrificed. In the seventeenth century the flow of Tantric literature was reduced, but in the eighteenth perhaps the greatest of the *tantras*, the *Mahānirvāna*, or *Tantra of the Great Liberation*, appeared. In many ways it resembled the *purānas*. Shiva declared in it that Shakti was the mother of the universe and made the worship of her as the creator, preserver, and destroyer necessary for salvation. It also contained hymns to Kali, instructions for the householder, ceremonials, *mantras*, high ethical precepts, and instructions for the erotic circle worship. Many Shākta poets, too, wrote in praise of the goddesses (see Chapter XI).

*   *   *

Nānak and the Sikhs

During this period Sikhism emerged and ultimately failed as an effort to unite Hindu and Muslim. Its founder, Nānak, was born (1469) a Hindu but at some point in his career came under Muslim influence. Attracted by Kabīr's mixture of Hinduism and Islam, he did not at first aim to establish a new sect but travelled around India appealing to both Hindus and Muslims. He described his followers as Sikhs, or disciples. His teachings and rituals were more Islamic in tone than were Kabīr's, but they included some elements of

Vedāntism also. He believed that there was only one God, the Creator, called Hari, who ruled the world; that God had made the illusions (*māyā*), such as desire, passion, and self-assertion, which condemned souls to be born again and again; but that He was also gracious, and salvation (blissful union with God) could be attained through His grace by those who loved, feared, served, and believed in Him and practised righteousness. Moderation, temperance, honesty, hard work, humility, gentleness, patience, and faith were the elements of righteousness. Forms and rituals were useless, and idolatry and inequalities of caste and sex were wrong; all mankind were brothers and equal before God, whose power and mercy were infinite. Nānak's hymns and sayings, collected only after his death (1538), promoted this monotheistic, pacific, and equalitarian creed.

Nānak and the subsequent leaders of the sect were called gurus. Nānak appointed his own successor, and so did the next two gurus. They spread the faith, adopted a common kitchen to eliminate caste, and abolished the seclusion of women. The fourth guru, Rām Dās (1575–81), acquired a tank at Amritsar and began the construction of the Golden Temple in it. From Amritsar he organized associations of disciples in different parts of the country. He appointed his son Arjun (1581–1606) guru, and thereafter the office became hereditary.

Arjun collected tolls from the faithful and completed the organization of the Sikhs into a community governed from Amritsar. He complied the *Ādi Granth*, the original scriptures of the Sikhs, which consisted of hymns, prayers, and sayings by thirty-five authors including Kabīr, Rāmānanda, Nānak, and Arjun. It was written in a special alphabet and contained pieces in different languages, of which Western Hindi, Punjabi, and Marathi were the most important. Arjun's union of temporal with spiritual power aroused the ire of Emperor Jahāngīr, who charged him with harbouring the emperor's rebellious son and had him cast into prison, where he died.

The union of church and state within the Sikh sect, and the persecutions by bigoted emperors from without, gradually transformed the tolerant religion of Nānak into a creed antagonistic to both Muslims and Hindus. Later gurus undertook to make the Sikh's a military community, bringing on internal dissensions and attacks by imperial troops. The ninth guru, Tej Bahādur (1666–75), was martyred by Aurangzīb. In retaliation, Govind Singh (1675–1708), the tenth and last guru, transforming the Sikhs into a military caste called the Khālsā, engaged in almost continuous warfare with the Moguls.

The ideals of the Khālsā were high. A member was expected to be a 'pure one, who did not believe in caste, colour, sex or credal differences; who believed in the oneness of God and the brotherhood of man; who endeavoured to live a life of usefulness, charity and purity; . . . and who dedicated his life to God and the Gurus, to the service of humanity and to the protection of the weak and the oppressed'.[12] Anyone could, in theory, join the Khālsā, and within it all were equal. Their initiation ceremony, resembling baptism, was performed with sugar and water stirred with a double-edged dagger. The initiate vowed not to worship idols, to bow to none except Sikh gurus, and never to turn his back on the enemy. Sikhs were to salute no Hindus and to destroy all Muslims. All men were to carry swords and wear their hair long and their trousers short. To strengthen the order, Govind Singh compiled a supplement to the *Ādi Granth* incorporating his regulations and ideas, and the combined work was known as the *Granth*. He refused to appoint a successor and told the Sikhs thenceforth to consider the *Granth* their guru.

Internal dissensions and the conflict with Aurangzīb and his immediate successors nearly led to the extermination of the Sikhs. But fanatical leadership kept the movement alive, and as the Mogul power declined, that of the Sikhs rose. By the middle of the eighteenth century they were masters of the Punjab.

*   *   *

Other Followers of Kabīr

Other followers of Kabīr remained more loyal to his apcifist and equalitatian philosophy. The Kabīrpanthīs, concentrated in central and west India, drew support mainly from the lower classes. Their centres at Benares and Maghar, where Kabīr had died, were under a *mahant*, or superior, who traced his descent back to Surat Gopāl, an early follower of Kabīr; the *mahant* at Chattisgarh traced his to Dharm Dās, another early follower. At Maghar Hindus and Muslims had different monasteries but followed very similar practices. The *Bījak*, the Kabīrpanthīs' main scripture, was compiled about 1570, and to it were added the *Sukh Nidhan* (attributed to Surat Gopāl but probably written sometime between 1729 and 1750) and the *Amar Mūl* (written perhaps as late as 1800). As these works revealed, the Kabīrpanthīs tended to revert to traditional Hinduism. Although they abjured caste and idols, they identified Kabīr with the Creator, and he became an object of worship whose help was necessary to salvation. They emphasized the doctrine of the Divine Word, or understanding of the essence of God hidden behind the word *Rām*, but pantheistic Vedāntism, somewhat reminiscent of Ṣūfism, also asserted itself.

A number of Kabīr's followers founded sects of their own, and ultimately no fewer than ten traced at least some of their teachings back to him. In the beginning most of the new sects likewise rejected caste and idolatry and were rather rigidly monotheistic, but in time they too tended to revive Vedāntism and caste, though they were generally open to Muslims as well as Hindus. Some used the word *Rām* or *Rāma* to refer to the Supreme Being, while others used different names; some admitted only ascetics; most of them emphasized the importance of gurus and developed a considerable literature in the vernaculars.

*   *   *

Hinduism about 1775

Nānak and Chaitanya take a prominent place alongside the great spiritual leaders of an earlier period such as Rāmānanda and Kabīr as exponents of the higher religious and humanitarian ideals of mankind. For all that, the story of Hinduism from 1300 to 1775 is of a religion on the defensive, giving ground to Islam both in India and farther east. In the East Indies (except Bali) and the Indo-Chinese peninsula it had ceased to exist as an independent force and had been replaced by Islam and Buddhism respectively. In India Islam had superseded it as the dominant religion in the northwest and parts of Bengal, Muslims were to be found everywhere, and Islamic rulers controlled many states. Nevertheless, Hinduism remained the prevalent creed of the Indian peninsula as a whole and even expanded its influence into Assam.

Confronted by Muslim persecution and competition, Hinduism closed its ranks, reorganized, and assumed the offensive. Some of the new Hindu sects, like the followers of Kabīr, borrowed considerably from Islam, particularly from Ṣūfism. To meet persecution and to compete for popular support the *bhakti* element was stressed, and particularly in Vishnuism a large number of new sects arose, splintering Hinduism in a manner that recalls the contemporaneous splintering of Christianity. *Bhakti* Hinduism reached out to encompass many castes and local cults and practices that the older, more aristocratic faith, with its emphasis on knowledge and works, had ignored. It absorbed most of the remnants of Buddhism in India and reduced the ranks of the Jains. The Smārtas (traditionalists) undoubtedly declined somewhat in relative importance, but they remained strong. Despite the fact that the Brahmans' services became much less essential in many of the *bhakti* cults, as a group the Brahmans managed to maintain their status. By amalgamating many local cults with Hinduism and by assuming the leadership of most of the new *bhakti* and Shakti cults, they made their influence much broader than it had been in 1300.

Whether Shivaism or Vishnuism was the stronger about 1775 is impossible to say. Shivaism was less fragmented than Vishnuism but certainly was also less well organized in north India. Shivaism, being more ascetic, less emotional and erotic, and perhaps more intellectual than Vishnuism, was probably more favoured by the learned and tradition-minded. Among the Vishnuites the sects with the highest moral tone worshipped Rāma or older forms of Vishnu, but Krishna-Rādhā and Shakti worship, tending more and more toward emotional escapism, produced perhaps the most significant trend in Hinudism from 1550 to the end of our period. That escapist trend was evident not only in the rise of new sects and adaptations in the practices of old ones but also in the current vernacular literature.

Until beyond our period, however, no new sects or philosophical ideas of major importance appeared after 1550. Despite this apparent decline in creative power, Hinduism of the eighteenth century was nevertheless better organized, more broadly based, and probably more equalitarian than it had been in 1300. At any rate, it was sufficiently cohesive and dynamic to resist the appeal of Islam and Christianity alike.

BUDDHISM

During this period Buddhism lived on as a religious force, moribund in some countries but in general active enough to have a direct effect upon the lives of at least one third of the people of the world.

Hīnayāna Buddhism suffered in the end only slightly from the inroads of Christianity and Islam. Sinhalese Buddhism, which had previously lost considerable ground through the Tamil invasion, was nearly extinguished by the Portuguese but recovered under the Dutch. The Portuguese arrived in 1505, and between them and the various kingdoms of the island a long and bitter struggle for mastery ensued. The Portuguese, gaining control of the coastal areas, undertook to convert the population to Christianity and by financial considerations and torture induced some Sinhalese to accede. In 1560 the invaders got possession of a relic they believed to be the Buddha's tooth. King Bayin Naung of Pegu (Burma) offered to ransom it, but the Portuguese ecclesiastical authorities of Goa rejected his offer, pounded the tooth to bits, burned them, and scattered the ashes over the sea. This blasphemy resulted in a miracle; two teeth appeared, each alleged to be the original. One was purchased by the king of Pegu from the king of Cotta, while the other, two inches long, remained in Ceylon in the hands of the king of Kandy. Though Kandy remained independent, in 1597 large parts of the rest of the island submitted to the Portuguese, but the chiefs successfully insisted that they should be allowed to retain their religion and customs.

Ceylon's Buddhism had sunk to its lowest level when the Dutch appeared (1602). Joining with the king of Kandy, they succeeded by 1658 in expelling the Portuguese. Once masters of a considerable part of the island, they, too, attempted to force Christianity upon it, but their opposition to Catholicism and their desire to court the favour of the Sinhalese rulers led them ultimately to assist local governments to restore Buddhism. Independent Kandy's later kings were patrons of Buddhism. In the seventeenth century, the monastic succession having failed, Kandy sent to Arakan (Burma) for properly ordained monks (*theras*), but this importation proved inadequate, for King Kittisiri Rājasiha (1748–81) again found no properly ordained monks; many proclaimed themselves as such, to be sure, but had they had families. With the aid of the Dutch he obtained ordained monks from Siam in 1752 and 1755 and reconstituted the order. The new Siamese order, however, was aristocratic and would admit only members of the highest caste.

In Burma Buddhism had a varied career. About 1525 the Shan king of Ava attempted to exterminate the Buddhist monks of his realm, burning their temples, monasteries, and libraries. This policy of persecution did not last long, however, and when King Bayin Naung (1551–81) of Toungoo captured

Ava (1555) and united all Burma, the tide turned. A Buddhist zealot, he constructed and endowed numerous Buddhist establishments, especially in Pegu, and forced the Shans and Muslims in northern Burma to make a formal profession of Buddhism. Until 1752 his successors at Ava acted as patrons of religion and literature, encouraging Pali commentaries upon the *Abhidhamma*, as well as Burmese translations and paraphrases of it. Toward the end of the seventeenth century, as civil conflict rent the country, a dispute divided the monks over whether the monastic robe should be worn upon both shoulders, as was traditional, or whether the right shoulder should be left bare. The Ekamsika, or One-Shouldered, faction found support only in late authorities and Ceylonese practice, but the controversy was so bitter that royal interention, though twice called upon, failed to settle it.

The unification of Burma by King Alaungpaya (1752-1760), founder of Rangoon, led to something of a religious and national revival. He was popularly considered to be a *bodhisattva*, and his court piously observed the holy *Uposatha* days, but he also failed to settle the controversy between the Ekamsika and the Pārupana (Fully Clad) faction. Since his chaplain, Atula, was a One-Shouldered supporter, he tenatively ordered the monks to leave one shoulder bare but took no measures against the Fully Clad faction. His successor continued this policy; he also persecuted a heretical sect called the Paramats, who objected to the use of shrines and images. Eventually the Fully Clad group won out, and a royal decree in their favour (1784) was generally accepted.

In Siam Buddhism continued as the national religion under the patronage of the kings of Ayuthia. In 1602 marks were discovered on the rocks at Phrabat, north of Ayuthia, which were identified as footprints of Shākyamuni. Siam thus claimed the honour of having been visited by him, and a legend developed that he had died at Praten (north of Phra Pathom). In the late seventeenth century, a Greek adventurer named Constantine Phaulcon gained power at the court of King Narai. Having turned Roman Catholic, Phaulcon allowed French missionaries to carry on their activities and exchanged embassies with Louis XIV's France. He was eventually executed for treason, however, and after King Narai's death a reaction set in against the French. Considerable Buddhist literature was produced in Siamese, particularly the *Pa: thŏmma sŏmphŏthiyan* (*Wheel of the Law*), a popular life of the Buddha. In the 1750's, as already noted, it was to Siam that Ceylon sent for properly ordained monks. In 1767, when the Burmese destroyed Ayuthia, the Buddhists of Siam suffered a grievous blow, but the Siamese, rallied by the able general P'ya Taksin, drove the Burmans out and established a new capital at Bankgok. During the accompanying disorders the church became disorganized and somewhat corrupt, and in the process of reforming it P'ya Taksin asserted such strenuous authority that the monks participated in his overthrow. A new dynasty, established in 1782, was more co-operative with the Buddhist orders.

In Cambodia and Laos, despite hectic political events, Buddhism suffered little change as the national religion during this period. In the late sixteenth century Spanish and Portuguese missionaries entered Cambodia, but in 1603 a king, subservient to Siam, put an end to Christian missionary activity. Rama Thuppdey Chan (1642–59) became a Muslim, but with the help of the Vietnamese he was deposed. Vietnamese aggressions provoked severe retaliation in 1730 when a Laotian, claiming to be inspired by the Buddha, collected bands of fanatics and attempted to massacre all the Vietnamese in Cambodia.

* * *

Buddhism in the Mahāyāna Lands

In the Mahāyāna lands Buddhism revealed less vitality, on the whole, than in the Hīnayāna lands, but, nevertheless, during the late Ming period Chinese Buddhism began to show some signs of a renewed vigour. The Cheng-te emperor (1506–21) was friendly and seems to have somewhat relaxed the restrictions on the number of monks. His successor, more inclined toward Taoism, had the Buddhist images in the Forbidden City destroyed but on several occasions participated all the same in Buddhist ceremonies. The Wan-li emperor (1573–1620) distributed copies of the *Tripitaka* to monasteries, repaired the famous P'u-t'o sanctuary in Chekiang, and in one of his edicts compared Confucianism and Buddhism with the two wings of a bird, each requiring the co-operation of the other. When Christian missionaries issued a number of tracts refuting Buddhism, which they considered their chief competitor, the Buddhist monk Shen Chu-hung put forth replies in its defence. The Ch'an sect, in particular, and various lay societies and brotherhoods connected with the Pure Land sect exhibited new vigour. The lay brotherhood that showed the greatest religious energy was the Wu-wei-chiao, founded about 1620 by Lo-tsu, who claimed to have received a special revelation. It was strictly vegetarian and objected to images, incense, candles, and other ritualistic usages.

The policy of the Manchu, or Ch'ing, dynasty (1644–1911) was much like that of the Ming, although the emperors were not equally friendly to Buddhism. They regulated Buddhism by an administrative board and limited the number of its monasteries and monks. The Shun-chih emperor (1644–61) showed some interest in Buddhism, and though the Sacred Edict of K'ang-hsi (see below) denounced heterodox doctrines including Buddhism, he took no action against it and at times even patronized it, praising some of its doctrines and publishing the Tibetan *Kanjur*, for which he himself wrote a preface. The Yung-cheng emperor (1723–35), although likewise a staunch Confucian, began the publication of the last imperial collection of the *Tripitaka* (1735–37), and the Ch'ien-lung emperor (1736–95) reputedly had it printed in Mongol, Manchu, and Tibetan. He at first proposed to eliminate the unordained secular clergy by requiring them either to enter monasteries or to become laymen, but he later modified this requirement, allowing them to continue under certain conditions. The Manchus tried at first to get along with the lamas of Tibet, but in the end the Ch'ien-lung emperor occupied it, placed a Chinese resident at Lhasa, and regulated the process by which the reincarnations of the grand lama were picked.

The Buddhism of Korea and Annam was certainly more corrupt and moribund than that of China. Yet even in China it lacked originality and power, and tended to decline in discipline and moral tone. Ignorance and laziness too often characterized its monks, while superstition and the search for special advantages infected its lay followers. Ch'an monks, probably the most active during the Ch'ing period as before, are supposed to have published some 230 works.

In Japan also Buddhism tended to deteriorate, despite official support. Its deterioration is part of the story of sixteenth-century feudal strife, which ended in the rise of the great military leaders who united Japan (see Chapter I). These national leaders destroyed the military power of the Buddhist sects with the aid of the provincial lords. In 1571 Oda Nobunaga (1534–82) stormed and demolished the three thousand Tendai monasteries on Mont Hiei at Kyoto, killed thousands of the inmates, and banished the rest. A few years later he routed the Shin forces from Kaga, but he was able to obtain their surrender at Osaka only in 1580. In 1581 he forced the submission of the Shingon monks of Mount Kōya. In 1584–85 his successor, Hideyoshi (ruled 1582–98), routed them from Kii province and destroyed their stronghold at Negoro. Other military establishments were likewise demolished in the culminating feudal struggle. Meanwhile, in Kyushu and the central provinces the Buddhists lost ground to the Jesuits. Nobunaga and many of the lords of Kyushu were friendly to the Jesuits, and although Hideyoshi, after taking Kyushu (1587), formally banned them, he made no real effort to enforce his decree. In 1591, in the same lenient spirit, he permitted Kennyo Shonin of the Shin Buddhists, who had resisted him at Osaka, to rebuild the Hongwanji Monastery at Kyoto.

Subsequent rulers more vigorously favoured Buddhism, now that it was disarmed, as a state religion. Tokugawa Ieyasu (1598–1616), founder of the Tokugawa shogunate, had family connections with the Jōdō (Pure Land) sect, and Tenkai, a Jōdō monk, and Denchōrō, a Zen monk, were among his close advisers. He clearly used Buddhism to advance his political purposes. He formally recognized the Jōdō sect as independent and built for it the Zōjōji Temple in Edo (Tokyo) when he established a new administration there. He weakened the rival Shin sect, dividing it into two main branches by building a second Hongwanji Monastery at Kyoto for one of Kennyo Shonin's sons, and in 1614 he proscribed the most militant branch of the extremist Nichiren sect. In decrees of 1613–14 he also banned Christianity as a menace to the stability of the state and made Buddhism in effect the state religion (without proscribing Shinto, which he identified with Buddhism). These and later decrees provided that every Japanese was to register at the Buddhist temple of his native district, whatever the sect to which that temple might belong, and to receive a certificate of registration as an identification card; thereafter he or she was to attend the parish temple on certain days, particularly the day of an ancestor's death, on pain of forfeiture of the certificate; and every Buddhist was to be buried according to the rites of his parish temple. Those who had no certificates or who wished to change their burial rites were automatically suspect of being Christians. Buddhist priests were held responsible for visiting their parishioners and reporting on suspected Christians. A separate branch of the Tokugawa administration was set up to supervise Buddhist and Shinto temples, shrines, and monasteries; and funds were provided for their support.

The anti-Christian policy continued under the Tokugawa shoguns. Iyemitsu (1623–51), who was especially vindictive against the Christian remnants and inaugurated the isolation policy, was a generous patron of the Buddhists. During his regime the *Tripitaka* was reprinted (1633–51), and he built many Buddhist temples. Tsunayoshi (1681–1709), who believed that the loss of his son and his inability to have another heir were due to his having been guilty of bloodshed in a previous incarnation, issued many decrees protecting animals, especially dogs. Other shoguns, however, were less fanatical in their Buddhist proclivities.

Along with the establishment of Buddhism as the official religion the shoguns promoted the study of Neo-Confucianism among the samurai. Neo-Confucianism led to criticism of Buddhism and to a school of historical studies that promoted the rise of the Shinto nationalists, who, in turn, criticized Buddhism and Confucianism alike as alien influences that had corrupted the pristine purity of native Japan (see below). Ensconced in their official position, however, the Buddhists seem to have accepted this criticism without vigorous response. A new Zen sect, the Ōbaku, was established in 1655, but it was the work of a Chinese monk, Yin-yüan (Ingen), and remained distinctly Chinese in character. The Zen priest Hakuin (1685–1768) was noted for the style and vigour of his sermons, and the Zen monk Bashō (1644–94) was a popular poet, but otherwise the Buddhists produced few outstanding personalities during the seventeenth and eighteenth centuries. The scholarship they exhibited in history, biography, religious tracts, and new editions of the Buddhist literature was respectable but uninspired, and they seem to have produced practically nothing in reaction to the mounting attacks of Confucian philosophers and Shinto propagandists.

*　　*　　*

Tantric Buddhism in India, Nepal, and Tibet

In the Tantric Buddhism of India and Nepal some events of only minor importance took place during the centuries here being considered. Traces of Tantric Buddhism crept into Shāktism and Chaitanyaism, while broader elements survived among the Saraks of Orissa and the Dharma cults of

N*

Orissa and Bengal. In Nepal the chief native Buddhist work, the *Svayambhū-purāna*, was probably produced in the sixteenth century, and the Hinduiza-tion of Buddhism seems to have been speeded up when the Gurkhas, a Hinduized tribe of Tibetan stock, conquered Nepal in 1769.

For Tibetan Lamaism, however, the period was notable. To begin with, the Mongols were reconverted. The previous conversion had affected mainly the Mongols in China, who, however, when driven back into Mongolia by the Ming, rapidly relapsed. In the 1570's, upon the invitation of the Mongol ruler, Altan Khan, Grand Lama Sodnams (Sö-nam Gya-tso, 1543–86), of the Gelukpa (Yellow) Church, visited Mongolia, and Altan Khan and his tribesman accepted Lamaism in 1577. A lama who was considered a rein-carnation of the *bodhisattva* Mañjushri (the personification of thought, wisdom, and meditation) was put in charge of a temple and monastery at Kuku-khoto. When Altan Khan died (1583), the grand lama returned to Mongolia to consolidate his position; and the Ming dynasty, to assure them-selves of his support, conferred the same titles on him that Pagspa had received. When Sodnams died, his reincarnation appeared in a new-born child of the Mongol royal house, and when this new grand lama moved to Lhasa (at the age of fourteen), another lama was established at Urga as his vicar and primate of Mongolia. The grand lamas of Mongolia came to be considered the reincarnation of the Tibetan Buddhist historian Tāranātha and through him of the *bodhisattva* Maitreya. The Chinese, however, required that future Mongolian grand lamas should be reborn in Tibet, and this requirement seems to have been followed.

Tibetan Lamaism made some strides in other lands along the Tibeto-Chinese and Tibeto-Indian frontiers. The *Kanjur* was translated into Mongol between 1604 and 1634 and was published in China by the K'ang-hsi emperor. Lamaism spread to the Kirghis and Kālmuks of Russian Turkestan, the Buriats of the Lake Baikal area, and the Mongols and related peoples in Manchuria and Inner Mongolia. It moved southward into Sikkim (*c.* 1650), and into Bhutan apparently after its conquest by Tibet (*c.* 1670). The Red Church dominated in these two areas.

Grand Lama Lozang (1617–80) was able, with the aid of the Mongols, to make himself and his successors temporal as well as spiritual rulers of Tibet. A temporal prince of Tibet who was a follower of one of the unreformed sects seized Lhasa about 1630 and threatened to destroy the Yellow Church. Lozang appealed to the Mongols under Gushi Khan, who thereupon seized all of Tibet (*c.* 1640) and turned it over to Lozang as temporal ruler. The grand lama proceeded to consolidate his position, building an imposing fortress-residence, the Potala Palace, at Lhasa. In 1652–53 he went to Peking, where the newly established Manchu dynasty heaped honours upon him. He retained control of Tibet during a long lifetime, and his successors remained its rulers. They were, however, gradually brought more and more under Chinese control.

The rise of the reformed Yellow Church to both political and ecclesiastical dominance in Tibet did not mean the end of the older sects or of the native Bön religion. The older sects of the Red Church divided into numerous subsects or offshoots, the Nying-ma-pa (Old Ones) being particularly strong in eastern Tibet. Most of the Tibetan monasteries were large and well supported, almost every family anxious to have a son in the monkhood. Celibacy was not enforced in most of the monasteries of the Red Church, and the position of abbot was generally filled by hereditary succession. Tantrism, magic, and superstition were more prominent in the Red Church than in the Yellow, while learning, discipline, and moral standards were higher in the Yellow Church.

CONFUCIANISM AND TAOISM

During this period Confucianism continued along the lines laid down under the early Ming dynasts. Neo-Confucianism remained the official philosophy of the state, and all China's emperors, regardless of their personal inclinations, publicly acted as its patrons; and so the official cult was meticulously preserved without material change. Popular Confucianism spread into the far recesses of the empire as a code of behaviour and an ethical system; and while continuing as a system of ancestor worship, it tended to slough off its supernatural elements and emphasize its social and ethical precepts. Although some scholars opposed such changes, the Cult of the Scholars became more rationalist, eliminating images from the Confucian temples and abandoning forms and titles which inclined toward the deification of Confucius in favour of those which extolled him as a mortal sage.

In 1530 the scholar Chang Tsung (1475–1539) induced the Chia-ching emperor to sanction a series of reforms. Images were withdrawn from the official Confucian temples and replaced by wooden tablets; the term 'king' was removed from Confucius' title, and instead he was called 'Master K'ung, the Perfectly Holy Teacher of Antiquity'; titles of nobility were eliminated for other Confucians in the temples and replaced by titles meaning 'illustrious' and 'scholar'; several names were removed from the temples and replaced by those of Sung Neo-Confucians; and the ritual was somewhat simplified. Most of these reforms remained permanent, indicating that the rationalist trend was generally sanctioned by the literati. The absence of images from the temples led the Jesuit missionaries of the next century to look upon most Confucian practices as mere civil and family ceremonies honouring great teachers and ancestors rather than as religious rituals.

During the late Ming period a tendency toward syncretism and eclecticism led some Confucians and Buddhists to emphasize the essential similarity of the 'Three Teachings'. Perhaps the most famous of the free-thinking Confucians was Li Chih (1527–1602), who ultimately adopted Buddhist garb, rejected Confucius and the classics as standards, and proclaimed the individual as the judge of right and wrong. Many regarded this attitude as personal moral laxness, which they believed had also infected government. In reaction to it emerged the Tung-lin movement, often referred to as the 'Righteous Circles', founded by Ku Hsien-ch'eng in 1604. This movement reasserted the basic ethical values and behaviour patterns of Neo-Confucianism, calling for a scholars' moral crusade to maintain them.[13]

Under the Manchu dynasty, Neo-Confucianism remained the official philosophy. The laws suppressing heresy and limiting Buddhists and Taoists were re-enacted and reinforced, and Confucian ethics received new emphasis as the underpinning of state and society. In fact, the Manchu emperors were more sedulous in promoting the official creed than their native predecessors had been. They fostered the Cult of the Scholars, built many new and beautiful Confucian temples, and honoured Confucius as a great teacher and sage. No ruler did more to support and expand the ethical principles of Confucianism than the enlightened K'ang-hsi emperor. He generally permitted freedom of thought and tolerated not only Christianity (for a time) but also the School of Han Learning, which, although critical of Neo-Confucianism, emphasized the rational and humanistic aspects of the Confucian system. His Sacred Edict (1671), re-issued and elaborated by his successor in 1724, breathed the moral principles of Confucianism, disparaged unorthodox doctrines, and encouraged the reverence of Heaven. It was publicly read twice monthly in cities and towns, and colloquial versions were prepared for circulation among the masses. K'ang-hsi's successors repressed both Christianity and unorthodox Confucian schools.

★   ★   ★

Taoism under Later Ming and Early Manchu

Although the great days of Taoism were past, the creed nevertheless showed some signs of vitality. Under the later Ming rulers, who were more friendly to Taoism than their predecessors had been, this vitality was demonstrated especially in the field of literary publication. During the Cheng-te reign (1506–21) Taoism's enormous canon, after many years of preparation, was published. The Chia-ching emperor (1522–66) appointed some Taoists to high office and instituted a search for their books on immortality. Taoist adepts had ready access to the Wan-li emperor (1573–1619). A supplement to the Taoist canon was published in 1607, and numerous Taoist pamphlets and tracts were piously disseminated during the later Ming (see Chapter XI). The early Christian missionaries testified to the popularity of Taoist lore and practices and to the search for immortality among the court circle and scholars of the late Ming period, but they obviously did not consider Taoism so serious a competitor as Buddhism.

None of the early Manchu rulers seems to have shown any predilection for Taoism, and the creed underwent a decline. As under the Ming, the

Taoists were regulated through an office at the capital with branches in the provinces. Restrictions upon Taoism and Buddhism, many of which had been relaxed during the late Ming, were re-imposed and more rigorously enforced. One of the first acts of the Ch'ien-lung emperor (1735) was to order secular Taoist and Buddhist priests either to return to lay life or to give up their families and enter monasteries; they were not to have pupils, and most of the property controlled by them was to be confiscated. This decree stirred up so much trouble that by 1738 it had been modified in several regards: many of the secular clergy were given certificates without having to enter the cloisters; property administered by them for temples and monasteries was not to be touched; and each priest, after the age of forty, was permitted to have one pupil to train as his successor. The official attitude toward Taoism as an organized religion nevertheless remained unfriendly, and the Taoists diminished in number. A government enumeration of Buddhist and Taoist monasteries and temples in 1667 indicated a total of 79,622 (of which only 12,482 had been established with imperial permission); the Buddhists numbered 110,292 monks and 8,615 nuns, and the Taoist 21,286 monks and no nuns. These figures did not include the secular clergy; between 1736 and 1739 some 340,000 of these received certificates of registration, the far greater part probably being Buddhist. In other words, the total of registered Taoists seems to have been not much over 100,000—an estimate that does not compare favourably with those for earlier centuries.

Although organized Taoism seemed to be on the decline, Taoist lore and practices apparently remained influential among the masses. Secret and semi-secret vegetarian and self-culture societies of laymen, at least partly inspired by Taoism, were numerous. The Tsai-li Chiao, or Rationalistic Religion, organized in the seventeenth century, advocated, among other things, abstention from tobacco, snuff, and alcohol. More sinister groups also masqueraded under the cover of Taoist or Buddhist practices.

Taoism's two main divisions each divided into two sub-sects. The Cheng-i, or orthodox division, which recognized the headship of the Chang family and was dominated by the home *tao-shih*, split into the Fu-lu (Charms) sub-sect, which emphasized exorcism and necromancy and used amulets, spells, cryptic monograms, ouija boards, and other charms for producing spiritual and psychic phenomena, and the K'o-chiao (Ceremonials) sub-sect, which depended more on religious forms and rituals. The Ch'üan-chen division, strongest in the north, stressed monastic organization. It split into the Lien-yang (Hygiene) sub-sect, which counted on physical and mental hygiene, including meditation, yoga, and sexual practice, to strengthen the body and spirit and to prolong life, and the Fu-shih (Diet) sub-sect, which put faith in the power of herbs, medicine, and potions to maintain and restore vigour.

Taoism maintained itself also in Vietnam and Korea, where its forms and ideas were mixed with local practices.

SHINTOISM

During the Tokugawa period several schools or sects, built around certain shrines or growing out of the teachings of certain families, helped to revive and popularize Shintoism. The Yui-itso Shinto of the Urabe priests held its ground, and with Watarai Nobuyoshi (1615–90), of the priestly family in charge of the Outer Shrine at Ise, the Watari (or Outer Shrine) Shinto blossomed as a competitor of Buddhism. Although he attempted to repudiate Buddhism and Confucianism, he borrowed many pantheistic ideas from Buddhism and drew upon Confucianism in formulating his ethical system. Asserting the superiority of the deities, ceremonials, and teachings of the Outer Shrine over all others, he insisted that the Shinto deities were the source of government and of the principles of human conduct. His emphasis on divination, while showing Taoist influence, also brought native Shinto practices to the fore.

New Shinto schools arose in the seventeenth century. The Suiga school was founded by Yamazaki (1618–82) of Kyoto, a student of Buddhism, Chinese science, and Japanese classics and head of an educational institution for young samurai at Edo. His school so openly espoused Confucian ethics and philosophy that a later (Pure Shinto) writer insisted that it was only a scheme to use Japanese classics to promote Confucianism. The word *Suiga* is composed of the last syllables of the words *shinsui* (divine grace) and *myoga* (divine protection). Suiga emphasized the doctrine that divine grace depended upon prayer and divine protection began with uprightness. Yamazaki taught, too, that *kami* (the basic stuff) was the soul of the universe and that Japanese mankind, as descendants of the *kami* (gods), were the god-stuff of the world; ultimate reality was the identity of God and man. According to Yamazaki, the Sun Goddess, Amaterasu, had taught the system he expounded, which must, therefore, be standard for the nation; reverence for its teachings, the goddess, and her imperial descendants was the highest virtue. Out of the Suiga School grew Tsuchimikado Shinto, founded by Tsuchimikado Yasutomi and his family. It gave special emphasis to the interaction of positive and negative principles (as Suiga Shinto had also done) and to the role of divinition in procuring the well-being of the state and people. Hakke (Head Family) Shinto was allegedly derived from the teachings of the Shirakawa family, which for centuries was in charge of the Department of Shinto Affairs, but its principal expounder was the eighteenth-century figure Mori Masatane. It stressed ritual, propriety in human relations, ceremonials for the dead, and the careful expounding of ancient Shinto texts.

Fukko or Pure Shinto (sometimes called Ancient Learning or Renaissance Shinto) was the most important of the new Shinto schools, though it reached its prime only in the eighteenth century. In keeping with the isolation policy of Japan, it sought to throw off alien influences and to return to the unadulterated Shinto of primitive Japan. An emperor-centred, nationalistic movement, it revived the study of ancient chronicles and other early Shinto documents. It sprang from the ideas of Kada Azumamaro (1669–1736), a member of the priestly family in charge of the Inari Temple near Kyoto, who insisted that the safety of Japan lay in a revival of the ancient 'Way of the Gods'. He, therefore, favoured the study of the ancient language and literature, and denounced interest in Chinese learning.

Kamo-no-Mabuchi (1697–1769), who came from a long line of Shinto priests and was a pupil of Kada for a short time, was the true founder of Pure Shinto. Continuing Kada's linguistic studies, especially of early poetry and the *norito*, or Shinto liturgies, he came to the conclusion that Chinese ways and ideas had corrupted the Japanese. The ancient rulers, he argued, had reverenced their divine ancestress, Amaterasu, and had intuitively ruled with love and benevolence in accordance with her will, while the people, needing no moral code to guide them, had, with matching intuition, avoided corruption. This was the true Way of the Gods. The importation of Chinese political institutions and practices had destroyed these simple mores, separating the divine rulers from the people and destroying their mutual loyalty and self-sacrifice. Nevertheless, Japan, alone having an unbroken line of rulers descendant from the Sun Goddess, possessed a unique national character and polity, and would return to them once corrupting foreign influences were discarded and ancient ways restored.

Mabuchi's work was carried on by Motoori Norinaga (1730–1801). A physician but also trained in letters and one of the most celebrated scholars of his day, Motoori produced about fifty-five separate works and actively propagated his ideas in lectures and tracts. His major opus was an edition (posthumously printed) of the *Kojiki*, Japan's oldest surviving book, which in his opinion set forth the true story of creation. The Japanese, according to him, were a divine race ruled over by the descendants of the Sun Goddess, who had instituted the state and the true Shinto; the chief duty of man was to follow unquestioningly the teachings of the Sun Goddess and her descendants. Moral ideas were implanted by the Gods and resembled instincts; hence the original Japanese had unerringly followed the moral way without special instruction. Motoori was resentful of foreign influences, although he considered them part of the divine plan, for he held that they had corrupted the Japanese: 'That Japan ranks far above all other countries is a natural consequence [of its origin]. No other nation is entitled to equality with her, and all are bound to do homage to the Japanese sovereign and pay tribute to him'[14]. Motoori's philosophy of life—a hopeful one, contrasting sharply with his gloomy picture of life after death—will engage us in Chapter VII.

With the Pure Shinto revival Shinto passed from a religious to a political stage. Japanese independence from and superiority to other peoples now was asserted with religious conviction, and the restoration of the divine emperors to real power was demanded, along with explicit obedience and loyalty to them. The unity of church and state was thus affirmed. Although the movement did not succeed in disestablishing Buddhism during the Tokugawa period, it helped not only to reduce the prestige of Buddhism and Confucianism but also to undermine the foundations of the Tokugawa shogunate.

JUDAISM

The story of the Jews from 1500 to 1775 is one of persistent persecution in western and central Europe and of relatively favourable treatment in Poland (except, as we shall soon note, from Cossack rebels and their allies) and in the Turkish empire. The tolerant stand of Johann Reuchlin and a few other humanists toward them did not pass on to Protestantism. Luther, who had at first attacked the Catholic practice of compulsory conversion and was regarded by the Jews as a champion, later turned against them, holding that 'if the Jews refuse to be converted, we ought not to suffer them or bear with them any longer'.[15] The one great exception to the general rule of intolerance in western European countries was the Low Countries, where many Spanish, Portuguese, and German Jews settled and prospered. The Jewish communities of the southern provinces began to decline at the time of the conflicts with Spain in the sixteenth century, but Dutch Amsterdam continued to be a refuge for Jews comparable in some ways to Turkish Constantinople and Salonika, and yet different too, since Dutch tolerance did not reflect mere indifference to or contempt for infidels. During the seventeenth century the United Provinces set a new standard of toleration for the West. Rembrandt perpetuated the contemporary Jews' features on canvas, and Grotius inaugurated the fight for their rights. Dutch colonies in the New World, like Curaçao, Dutch Guiana, and New Amsterdam, received not only Dutch Jews but Marrano refugees from Spanish and Portuguese America. When, about 1620, the Dutch temporarily conquered some Portuguese settlements in Brazil, about a thousand Marranos openly declared themselves Jews, but their number quickly diminished when the area was reconquered by the Portuguese.

Even the Dutch Jews did not have full toleration. During the controversy between the Gomarists and the Arminians at the beginning of the seventeenth century, the presence of the Jews aroused unfriendly comment, and from 1616 onward they were made subject to certain disabilities. In 1632 all trades not necessary for providing for themselves were closed to them, with certain exceptions such as printing, the sale of drugs, and money-lending.

The insecurity of the Jewish community in Amsterdam explains in part their severity toward two famous heretics in their midst—Acosta and Spinoza. Uriel Acosta (1590–1647), a descendant of a Christianized Portuguese family, became Jewish of his own volition and left Portugal for the Jewish community of Amsterdam. There, his rationalism, his belief in the mortality of the soul, and his criticism of the community led to his being arrested and fined by the civil authorities and excommunicated by the Jewish community.

He recanted but again incurred disfavour and, being again excommunicated and exposed to severe corporal punishment, finally committed suicide. Spinoza's rationalism (of which we shall say more in Chapter VII) was among the factors that led to his excommunication likewise by Amsterdam's Jews. In both instances, not only the excommunicates' unorthodoxy but also the desire to avoid Christian disapproval appear to have been motives behind persecution of Jews by Jews.

Not until the seventeenth century was the Dutch policy of limited toleration of Jews imitated by any other western country. England was the first to follow the Dutch example. Despite the exclusion initiated by Edward I in 1290, some Jewish families seem to have continued to live clandestinely in London, and under Elizabeth I an influx of 'neo-Christians' had taken place. Shortly after coming to power, Cromwell took some cautious steps toward reversing the exclusion policy. He invited the Amsterdam rabbi Menasseh ben Israel to England and allowed other Jews, mostly merchants, to enter openly. The city of London conformed to, without regularizing, the new attitudes, not so much out of Christian charity as out of mundane considerations. The Jewish community of London soon could boast some influential merchants, especially active in the East and West Indies trade, and some outstanding financiers. Their prominence as well as the malaise it caused was indicated in 1697, when the number of Jewish members of the Royal Exchange was limited to twelve. Various legal restrictions also kept professing Jews from holding office under the crown. A Jew Bill passed by Parliament in 1753 proposed to naturalize them as citizens, but popular clamour soon caused its repeal.

Elsewhere in western and central Europe the plight of the Jews was worse than in the United Provinces or England. They were not allowed to live in Spain and were not allowed to leave Portugal—which meant in both instances that they became crypto-Jews, or Marranos, if not completely converted, though in greater numbers in Portugal than in Spain. Guilds did not readily admit them to membership, and so they were rarely found in the crafts. More often they sold things to each other or followed the old clothes trade or (if they had the means) engaged in money-lending and banking or (if they could get licences) practised the learned professions. They frequently had to wear distinctive clothing or badges and to pay special taxes. In the German cities and principalities, *Schutzjuden* (protected Jews) were special wards of government, for which status they paid *Schutzgeld* (protection money). Even Frederick the Great, for all his enlightenment, found *Schutzgeld* too good a source of revenue to abandon. In a *Schutzbrief* issued in 1750, he divided the already strictly limited number of Prussia's *Schutzjuden* into two classes, allowing some (the 'extraordinary *Schutzjuden*') to will their privileged position, each to one and no more than one son, while others (the 'ordinary *Schutzjuden*') could enjoy it only for life. Other Jews, of course, had no special protection at all, but Frederick at least allowed a number to settle in his domains and usually did not permit maltreatment of them. Prussia's extraordinary *Schutzjuden* collectively paid 70,000 thalers in 1763 for the privilege of passing their protection on to second sons. Prussia's Jewish population increased when Prussia annexed her shares of the Polish partitions. Russia, where no Jews had been allowed before 1772, also acquired a large number of Polish Jews after that date.

In Austria Jews were considerably more restricted. Driven out in 1420, many had gone to Poland. Others, however, had stayed behind, sometimes as crypto-Jews, sometimes in hiding. From time to time the climate grew less unfriendly, but they nearly always had to wear distinctive badges, pay special taxes, and stay out of certain economic activities. In 1670 Emperor Leopold I drove them out of Vienna and some other parts of Austria again. About fifty families found refuge in the Great Elector's Prussia. Others went eastward to Poland and Turkey. Some once more risked staying behind, and others returned, especially those who could claim to be 'Turkish' Jews entitled to favoured treatment by the mutual concessions which, by the Treaty of Passarowitz, Austria and the Porte entered into for the reciprocal protection of each other's subjects.

Even before the 1780's, when Emperor Joseph II cancelled some of their special disabilities, the Austrian Jew had gradually regained some standing. The skill that a number of Austrian and German Jews acquired in finance and commerce led to their becoming royal financial advisers and purveyors to the military. Such Jews became known as 'court Jews' and enjoyed great favour and influence, which sometimes remained in the family. Samuel Oppenheimer and Samson Wertheimer were especially well known court Jews in Vienna in the eighteenth century, but others were equally influential both in Vienna and other German capitals. By the end of the eighteenth century the Jews of the German-speaking lands were well started toward that prominence which had been one of the factors of their ruin in fifteenth-century Spain and was to be again in twentieth-century Germany.

Another kind of influence in Jewish and German affairs was achieved by Moses Mendelssohn. As a philosopher, scholar, and man of letters Mendelssohn had come to know and to be admired by many prominent men in the German-speaking world. He therefore was able to intervene, sometimes with good results, on behalf of his co-religionists who were being persecuted. The German dramatist and critic Gotthold Ephraim Lessing (1729–81) was his lifelong friend. In his play *Die Juden* (1749) Lessing held up to scorn the ignorant man who for no reason condemned the Jews, and thirty years later in another play entitled *Nathan der Weise* he had a Jewish sage (whom critics generally recognize as Mendelssohn) plead convincingly for toleration. Mendelssohn's philosophical writings emphasized the common essentials of Judaism and Christianity—one God, immortality, and the law. He translated the Pentateuch (Torah) into German and had the translation printed in Hebrew characters, thus providing, as a sort of Jewish Luther, an avenue leading from the original Hebrew text through Yiddish (which is essentially medieval German written in Hebrew characters) to modern German. Before he died (1786), he had gone far toward identifying the German Jews with Western culture and toward interesting Enlightenment thought in the plight of the Jews.

*　　*　　*

Jews in the Ottoman Empire and Poland

The favourable treatment that earlier Jewish refugees from the West had received in the Byzantine Empire continued, and even more noticeably, under the Turkish successors of the Byzantine emperors. The careers of several prominent Jews vividly reflected the general situation; they fled from persecution in western Europe to toleration and even honours in the Ottoman Empire. Joseph Nasi (d. 1519) was an especially striking case. Born in Portugal of a wealthy and influential family of Marranos, he migrated with his family to Antwerp, where he continued the family business as a prosperous banker. Resentful of the pseudo-Catholicism he was compelled to practice in Habsburg-ruled Antwerp, he again migrated, first to Venice, which proved little better than Antwerp, and finally to Turkish Constantinople. Here, openly proclaiming his Judaism, he rose to high rank in the sultan's service. As duke and governor of the island of Naxos from 1566 onward, he exercised such profound influence that Christian rulers of the West sought his advice and aid in diplomatic and commercial relations with Constantinople. Among his several plans was a proposal to establish at Tiberias on the Sea of Galilee a settlement of Jews exiled from Italy, but his scheme, perhaps never seriously intended, failed when he fell from power.

Another case in point was Juan Rodrigo de Castel-Branco (1511–68), better known as Amatus Lusitanus. A Portuguese Marrano, he had acquired a distinguished reputation as a physician, scientist, and teacher of medicine. Finding it obnoxious to conceal his religious convictions, he moved first to Holland, then to France, and then to Italy, where in several cities he followed his profession of doctor and scholar. Settling for a time in Rome, he listed among his patients Pope Julius III and his sister. The anti-Jewish measures of Pope Paul IV forced him to migrate once more, and he went to Turkish Salonika, where there was a relatively large and thriving Jewish community. Here, openly avowing his Judaism, he carried on his humanitarian work until he fell victim of the plague.

The strange story of Sabbatai Sebi (1626–76) would hardly have been possible in Christian Europe but was intelligible in the atmosphere of Turkish indifferentism toward religious disputes among non-Muslims. Whether Sabbatai was a charlatan, as some maintain, or a mystic, he believed or pretended to believe that he was the Messiah and—possibly because his father, who had lived in England, knew about the English Millennarians (see Chapter IX)—that the year 1666 was to be the year of salvation. From his birthplace in Smyrna he moved freely about among the Jewish communities in the Ottoman Empire, sometimes urged or forced on by his opponents but always finding willing disciples and a hopeful following. The Jews of Constantinople, Cairo, Jerusalem, Salonika, Smyrna, Buda, and other cities in the Ottoman Empire were electrified but torn between believers in Sabbatai and sceptics. The fame of 'the Messiah' spread to Jewish and Marrano communities everywhere, and many gave away their worldly goods, did penance for their sins, and awaited the Messiah or sought to go to the Holy Land. Early in 1666 Sabbatai started for Constantinople with a band of his followers, only to be arrested by Vizier Aḥmed Köprülü. Imprisoned at Abydos through a large part of the year 1666, he was treated as a martyr by his followers and as a privileged inmate by the government until a Polish rival, Nehemiah-ha-Kohen—whether to test Sabbatai's sincerity or to strike a bargain with him is unknown—came to see him and decided to denounce him as a traitor to the sultan. Sabbatai was thereupon given a choice between Islam and death and chose Islam. So did a number of his followers, and to this day these *Dönmeh* (Turkish: *apostates*) survive, outwardly professing Islam but also practising many Jewish rites and customs.

Sabbateanism did not wholly end with Sabbatai's conversion. His followers had been especially numerous in Poland. In part, he seemed to be the answer to their prayers for a deliverer from the Cossacks, who were massacring Polish Jews (and Catholics) in a prolonged struggle (1648–67) that foreshadowed the ultimate decline of Poland (see Chapter IV). Sabbateanism also appealed to the poor, unlettered, pietistic Jews who found the dry formalism of the rabbis hard to comprehend and discouraging. Nehemiah-ha-Kohen, upon his return to Poland, seems to have been accepted as Messiah by some of the still undaunted Sabbateans until (the sources disagree) he either died or was disgraced and driven out.

Jacob Frank (1726–91), another self-proclaimed prophet, found a following even in the eighteenth century among the Polish Sabbateans, though only a few went along when he preached conversion to Catholicism. Many more turned to the contemporary mystic who was known as Baal-Shem-Tov (Master of the Good Name). This simple man preached a pietistic religion of direct communication with a pantheistic God through fervent prayer, ecstasy, dance, song, and joy, rather than through learning, jejune ritual, and asceticism. His followers, borrowing an ancient name, called themselves Chassidim, and Chassidism remained a live movement among the eastern European Jews thereafter.

Ritual, however, did not lose its force or its effectiveness as a uniting trait among a dispersed people. Safed, near Jerusalem, was a thriving Jewish community, and a group of Hebrew scholars had established themselves there in the sixteenth century around the learned Isaac Luria (1534–72). In 1535 Joseph ben Ephraim Qaro (1488–1575), an exile from Portugal, joined this community. For fifty years he had frequent visions of a heavenly visitor who spoke to him about Talmudic questions. Qaro kept careful notes of these conversations, and from them came two significant studies of Jewish law. *Beth Josef* was a lengthy commentary on the Talmud and on earlier Talmudic authorities; *Shulhan 'Arukh* was a code of rabbinical practice and ritual. For many years the *Shulhan 'Arukh* was disputed among the rabbis of widely scattered communities, but gradually the very disputes made it better known. By the middle of the seventeenth century most rabbis regarded it as authoritative, and in the eighteenth century they considered it the final word on matters of which it spoke. Thus, even as Mendelssohn's emancipation movement in Germany and Baal-Shem-Tov's Chassidic movement in Poland were taking form, rabbinical ritual and Talmudic learning as codified by Qaro in Palestine acquired authoritative standing. The future of Judaism as a religion lay along those three lines.[16]

NOTES TO CHAPTER V

1. The passages on missionary efforts in South and Central America are largely borrowed from a study especially prepared for this volume by the Spanish National Commission for UNESCO.

2. *The Works of President Edwards*, 8 vols. (Worcester, Mass., 1808–09), Sermon XXVII, Vol. VIII, p. 293.

3. Quoted in Alexander Brown (ed.), *The Genesis of the United States* (Boston, 1890), I, p. 339.

4. Quoted in R. P. Beaver 'Recent Literature on overseas missionary movements from 1300 to 1800', *Journal of World History*, I, (1953), p. 148.

5. Professor O. Lacombe points out that the missionary activity of a Nobili or his kindred Jesuits did not rely only on an adaptation of the caste system. They 'divined' the way by which they might penetrate the 'inner' India (J. Monchanin and H. Le Saux, *Ermites du Saccidânanda* [Paris, 1956], p. 40). The Tamil texts of Father Beschi are considered literary monuments of high value in this particularly difficult language.

6. To Professor O. Lacombe the difficulties involved in the question of Chinese, Japanese, Indian, and other 'rites' were due not to the principle itself (according to which the Church might allow the faithful to observe rites of purely human and social significance, uncontaminated by superstition and not contradictory to faith and morality) but to the frequent absence of any clear distinction between 'civil' and 'religious' rites among the peoples to be evangelized. The missionaries therefore found themselves here treading on slippery and shifting ground and the differences of appreciation in individual situations were considerable. See p. 363.

7. The early Indian Christians, the 'Christians of St Thomas' (here called Syrian Christians), enjoyed a high social status; for the new Christians this was far less frequently the case. (Oliver Lacombe.)

8. Sri Ram Sharma, *The Religious Policy of the Mughal Emperors* (London, 1940), pp. 41–60.

9. Quoted from Ja'far Sharif, *Islam in India*, as translated by G. A. Herklots and revised by William Cooke (Oxford, 1921), p. 10.

10. C. N. E. Eliot, *Hinduism and Buddhism, an Historical Sketch*, 3 vols. (London, 1921), II, p. 250.

11. The literal meaning of the Sanskrit word *sahaja* is 'congenital, innate, connatural, natural'. The translation of the neo-Indian word *Sahajiyā* by 'Way of Nature' should not be interpreted in a naturalistic or empirical sense. The expression in question refers principally, if not exclusively, to that deep, metaphysical blessed spontaneity which is innate and immanent in the heart of man. (Oliver Lacombe.)

12. *Cultural Heritage of India*, II, p. 227.

13. Heinrich Busch, 'The Tung-lin Shu-yüan and Its Political Philosophical Significance', *Monumenta Serica*, XIV (1949–55), pp. 1–163; Charles O. Hucker, 'The Tung-lin Movement of the Late Ming Period', *Chinese Thought and Institutions*, ed. John K. Fairbank (University of Chicago Press, Chicago, 1958), pp. 132–62.

14. Ernest Satow, 'The Revival of Pure Shintau', *Transactions of Asiatic Society in Japan*, Appendix to Vol. III (rev. ed., 1883), p. 32.

15. Quoted in H. Graetz, *History of the Jews*, 6 vols. (Philadelphia, 1891–98), Vol. IV, p. 551.

16. For bibliographical detail, see Baron, as cited for Chapter II, n. 18.

CHAPTER VI

THEOLOGY AND METAPHYSICS
(1300–1500)

GENERAL REMARKS

IN this period, as before, Chinese, Hindu, Buddhist, Jewish, Christian, and Muslim thinkers generally based their theological-metaphysical speculations on certain absolute religious values and confirmed them by orthodox systems of dialectic. Aristotelianism in a 'Christianized' form, for example, dominated western European thought with a rigidity that Aristotle himself would perhaps have disapproved. His syllogistic system of logic, dominant first among east Christian, Muslim, and Jewish scholars and later also among west Christians, had brought to all of them the problem of how to use it in order to rationalize their religious dogma. Aristotelianism was followed by an anti-Aristotelian reaction. During the fourteenth and fifteenth centuries, the highly sharpened tools of Scholastic logic were brought to bear on the products of the older Aristotelian logic.

As Aristotelianism waned, Neoplatonism waxed. The Neoplatonism of this age laid special emphasis upon the intuitive, mystical elements in Plato's philosophy, adding the sympathy of an elite to the ancient urge of the unlettered toward a more irrational mysticism. Mysticism serves, among other things, as an escape for sensitive or troubled souls from the pressure of spiritual or physical hardship, and this was a period of unusual hardship for great numbers of people. Mysticism is also a counterpoise to rationalism. The marked increase of mysticism during the fourteenth and fifteenth centuries coincided with the heated Scholastic rationalistic controversies of the time and in part was a reaction to them. If the mystic was less of a philosopher than the Christian Thomist or the Hindu Advaitist or the Chinese Rationalist, it was not because life presented him with different questions but rather because his method of arriving at answers relied more upon inspiration than upon his own frail intellect.[1] The mystic, whether European or Asian, trusted in intuition, personal revelation, and other highly individualistic inner processes that often ran counter to organized codes of belief and conduct and to conventional ethics. In western Europe the Roman Catholic hierarchy was likely to be suspicious at first of such individualistic mystics, though it eventually sainted some of them.

Rationalistic theological conflict during the fourteenth and fifteenth centuries tended toward ever greater subtleties of logic. Within Islam theological thought ran to systematic compendia of doctrine regarded as settled—except in Ṣūfism, in connection with which a richly imaginative literature elaborated the themes developed in the two preceding centuries. Judaism especially in the West carried on the old disputations with the Gentiles and inwardly was divided over the problems of Aristotle, Maimonides, and Qaballism. China and Japan, perhaps more than any other region, were melting pots of rival theologies and philosophies—Buddhism, Neo-Confucianism, Taoism, and various shades of rationalism and mysticism. Christianity was torn by schisms, heresies, and schools of logic.

And yet in all major civilizations, the period between 1300 and 1500 seems to have been less outstanding than earlier or later ones in producing new and lasting systems of theology. Instead, as a general rule though with notable exceptions, it was marked, in Europe and to a lesser degree elsewhere, by the application of secular logic to bolster the approved answer to the eternal question of man's place in God's scheme. What was the source of knowledge; whether space, time, and matter were finite or infinite; what was the cause of evil; whether body and soul were the same or different; whether man's will was free or predetermined; whether faith alone or faith only if coupled with some variety of good works would save him—such were the theological and metaphysical problems to which mankind all over the world sought solution. Men's problems were similar even though their vocabularies were diverse.

HINDU DEVELOPMENTS

The six traditional systems of Indian philosophy were already highly developed by 1300, and the thinkers of the period seemed to confine themselves to elaborating, developing, refining, or defending them. The apparently derivative nature of their commentaries, expositions, and polemics might lead to the conclusion that little original was produced after 1300, but, in reality, works whose avowed purpose was either to expound or to criticize an old system sometimes set forth what amounted to a new one. Philosophical speculation continued at a high level into the seventeenth century, and only after that did originality disappear and speculation drop to low levels.

By 1300 the six systems of philosophy had become grouped into three pairs. Within two of these pairs the paired systems were for practical purposes syncretized inseparably. These two were the Nyāya-Vaishesika and the Sānkhya-Yoga. The third was the Pūrva-Mīmāmsā, better known simply as the Mīmāmsā system, and the Uttara-Mīmāmsā, better known as the Vedānta system. Some of these systems were themselves divided into several schools.

Although the six systems differed considerably and much of their literature consisted of mutual polemic, they held certain ideas in common. All six respected the authority of the Vedas, although the third pair, the Vedānta and Mīmāmsā systems, were more dependent upon them than the others. All accepted the doctrine of karma and the idea of *mukti* (*moksha*), or final liberation from the chain of rebirths. How to attain this liberation was in fact the central problem of all Indian theological speculation of the period. The theistic schools, of course, found the answer in devotion to a personal, accessible God, while other schools found it in some form of identity of the individual soul with the absolute, impersonal *brahman*. All the systems believed also in the existence of the soul or self, a permanent and pure element which in some way had become entangled in impurities and passions without their forming a real part of it. Each system had different ideas as to the nature of the soul, but all agreed that final release from the earthly form was attained through removal of the impurities, permitting the soul to realize its own essential, unsullied nature. Each system was rather pessimistic in its attitude toward mundane life, yet optimistic in the belief that ultimate enlightenment and release could be attained. Life on earth was but a succession of sorrows and sufferings brought on by ignorance, the search for pleasure, and 'selfness', or self-centredness. All systems agreed upon the general principles of conduct that should be followed, which included control of the passions, non-injury to life, and restraint of the desire for pleasure. The theistic schools found the next and highest step in *bhakti*, or devotion to a personal deity, while the non-theistic schools found it in meditative yoga practices, which also formed a part of *bhakti* devotionalism. While Hindu philosophy was vitally concerned with moral issues, it devoted little speculation (as distinct from religious instruction) to ethics as conceived in the West or China, perhaps because ethical conduct was taken for granted as part of the search for enlightenment. Enlightenment could be fully attained only through a late stage of knowledge (whether acquired by reason or yoga) or of devotion to God.

The Nyāya-Vaishesika system was realistic and pluralistic. It held that the external world was real and that ultimate reality consisted of many eternal entities. Among them were atoms (which combined to form matter), time, space, mind, souls (self), and the supreme soul, or God (Īshvara). God originally had not played a prominent part in the two systems that had paired to form this one, but before 1300 He had come to be regarded as the efficient, if not the material, cause of the universe, as its architect and controller. Release from the consequences of karma came through recognition that the soul was not dependent on body, mind, or external factors. At first, this knowledge was considered attainable through correct thinking and living, moral detachment, and ultimately higher meditation (yoga), but as theistic ideas penetrated the system, the higher states of enlightenment were deemed possible only through the grace of God, who was generally identified with Shiva.

The Vaishesika system was fundamentally a metaphysical atomic philosophy, and the Nyāya was fundamentally a system of logic and dialectics emphasizing the importance of perception, inference, verbal testimony, and comparison in validating knowledge. Gangesha of Mithilā (*c.* 1200) had presented the logical aspects of the Nyāya-Vaishesika system in so masterful fashion that thereafter its logic was emphasized while its metaphysical features were neglected.[2] The Mithilā school of logic and its method of expression spread in Bihar and Bengal and for a time had great influence, especially with the Vedānta philosophers. Among the proponents of the system were Shankara Mishra (variously dated between 1425 and 1650) and Vāsudeva Sarbabhauma (c. 1450–1525). The former was famed for his commentaries on the *Vaishesika-sūtra* (*Upaskāra*) and on Gangesha's work; the latter also wrote a commentary on Gangesha and was the first exponent of the rival Nadia school of Nyāya logicians, which gained strength in Bengal as the Mithilā school declined.

The Sānkhya-Yoga doctrine may be described as a sort of mechanistic dualism.[3] The Sānkhya system as interpreted in the ninth century was essentially atheistic. It was in accord with a few isolated statements of the *Upanishads* but was fundamentally at odds with their dominant concepts in that it posited the eternal existence and separateness both of matter (*pakrti*) and of an infinity of souls or spirits (*purusa*). In this dualistic scheme, matter had the power to evolve, bringing into existence the material world; the mechanical contact of souls with matter produced consciousness, egoism, and striving, and hence the belief (false in this chain of reasoning) that the soul was enmeshed in matter; release from the consequences of karma could come only when knowledge revealed the unreality of the connection between soul and matter.

The Sānkhya posited but did not develop methods for the attainment of this knowledge. They were developed in the Yoga system of Patañjali (fl. c. 150 BC), which outlined meditative practices that would lead to release from karma. It also posited a theistic principle—the existence of a perfect soul or God (Īshvara), Which prompted the process of evolution and salvation and Which was not, like ordinary souls, deluded into believing that It was in bondage to matter. The release of ordinary souls could be attained either by knowledge achieved through yoga practices or through devotion to Īshvara.[4]

By 1300 this theistic view was most generally accepted by the followers of the Sānkhya-Yoga system. Nevertheless, several books of this period still advocated the atheism of the ancient Sānkhya system. One of the most important was the *Sānkhya-sūtra*, unknown before the fourteenth century and probably compiled only during that century from previous Sānkhya works though attributed to a writer named Kapila. It was first commented on by Aniruddha in the late-fifteenth century. Its philosophy did not differ essentially from that of the early atheistic Sānkhya system, and it attempted refutation of other doctrines. It seems not to have increased the popularity of atheistic Sānkhya at the expense of the theistic Sānkhya-Yoga system.

The Mīmāmsā system (Pūrva Mīmāmsā) was a type of pluralistic realism having much in common with the Nyāya-Vaishesika. It early split into two schools with certain differences of detail. Of these two during our period the Bhatta school, following the teachings of Kumārila Bhatta (c. AD 700), was the more important. Mīmāmsā was a product of the ritualistic features of the Vedas, its object being to provide a proper method for interpreting the Vedas and, in doing so, to posit a philosophical justification for their rituals. It produced no outstanding contribution to metaphysics but propounded a theory of knowledge and a methodology of interpretation that were widely used by other schools, especially the Vedānta. According to Mīmāmsā, knowledge was derived from perception (through the senses, mind, and other internal organs), inference, comparison, presumption or postulation, non-perception, and verbal testimony. All knowledge was considered as self-validating and hence acceptable as soon as cognized, although illusion and error had to be explained away by technical distinctions. This theory of self-evident knowledge was necessary to confirm the testimony of the Vedas, which along with souls, the material world, heavens, hells, and Vedic deities were considered real and eternal: they had never been created and would never be destroyed. Such a system had no place for a supreme God or absolute, since nothing could be superior to the eternal Vedas. Mīmāmsā held that the law of karma governed the world and rebirth arose from the bondage of the soul or self to the body, the senses, and the material world. *Moksha,* or release from rebirth, came when the soul, having destroyed its bad karma by abstaining from deeds left optional or forbidden in the Vedas and by performing those prescribed, recognized that it was in reality separate from material things. Mādhava (*c.* 1350) and Laugāski Bhāskara (after 1400) produced the most significant of the works on the Mīmāmsā philosophy that appeared between 1300 and 1500.

*   *   *

The Advaita School

The Vedānta system (Uttara-Mimāmsā) showed more originality during those centuries than any other of the six systems. Several schools had arisen within it. All of them claimed to follow the *Upanishads,* and specifically the *Brahma-* or *Vedānta-sūtra* traditionally attributed to Bādarāyana, and each, whether absolutistic or theistic, claimed to present the only true interpretation of this ancient *sūtra.*

Though Vedānta also contained several theistic schools that were growing in importance and popularity, particularly during the period covered by this volume, the school of absolute monism—or, perhaps more accurately, non-duality (*Advaita*)—was the most widely known and influential of all Vedānta schools, and many think of it as synonymous with the whole Vedānta system. Based upon the *Upanishads* and the *Vedānta-sūtra,* the Advaita school had been given its classical monistic statement by Shankara in the ninth century and had been expanded by a host of commentators before 1300. It insisted that the absolute, unitary, impersonal *brahman* was the sole reality and was identical also with the *ātman* (*self* or *soul*), which was pure consciousness and bliss. *Brahman* appeared in the form of the manifest universe (*māyā*) and as individual souls (*jīva*). As the manifest universe, the world we know, it was an illusory phenomenon, similar to the illusion that occurs when a rope is mistaken for a snake; as the individual ego or soul it was the real *ātman* but was perceptible only with the modifications that came inevitably from an illusory universe, much like the yellowness of a white conch when viewed through yellow glass or like the reflection of the sun in a pool.

Māyā thus connoted illusion itself, the power to obscure or to create illusion, and the capacity to create a sense of multiplicity where unity was the only reality. It was inherent in *brahman*. When operating in the causal capacity of *māyā*, *brahman* might be personalized as Ishvara (or God), the efficient and material creator of the illusory multiple universe, and as such was known as the lower or qualified *brahman*. God the Creator was thus a super-illusion produced by the reflection of *brahman* through *māyā*. The *jīva* was a further reflection of Ishvara, and the sense of individuality was but a mirage created by ignorance or nescience (*avidyā*), a component of *māyā*. Salvation or escape from rebirth (*moksha*) was to be obtained through true knowledge (*jñāna*), recognition that individuality and multiplicity were unreal and that the individual soul was actually the changeless, eternal *ātman* or *brahman*. To attain *moksha* required the performance of one's ordinary duties in a detached manner without desire for worldly gains and the taking of the steps necessary to acquire *jñāna*. These steps included formal study of the Advaita under a teacher, reflection, and meditation (*yoga*). The enlightened soul would become completely free and be *ātman* when it cast off the physical body, the last trammels of *māyā*, at death.

By 1300 several branches of the Advaitins had arisen. Most writers belonged to either the Vivarana or the Bhāmati branch, but the differences between them were minor. The Advaitins' major controversies were with the theistically inclined Vedāntists or with the adherents of the other systems. Their dialectical skill steadily improved during the period; as already stated, the monists generally accepted the Nyāya method of logical analysis and a theory of knowledge and a methodology of interpretation similar to those of the pluralist Mīmāmsā school.

Among a host of Advaitin exponents prior to 1500 two are especially noteworthy. Rāmādvaya (probably before 1350) was the author of the *Vedānta-kaumudī*, dealing with Shankara's commentary on the *Vedānta-sūtra*. He elaborated the monists' theory of perception and consciousness, defined right knowledge as experience which did not misrepresent its object, and accepted the Mīmāmsā theory of the self-validity of knowledge. Probably the greatest Advaitin figure of the period was Vidyāranya (fl. 1350), generally known as Mādhava (not to be confused with Madhva, founder of the dualist school of the Vedānta). Mādhava was particularly celebrated for his clear, forceful style and excellent diction. He wrote a compendium of the existing systems of thought (*darshana*) entitled the *Sarva-darshana-samgraha*. Although later writings summarized individual systems or commented on various aspects of one or more of them, Mādhava's work has remained probably the outstanding epitome of Indian thought produced by traditional Indian scholarship. In his writings on the Advaita he followed the Vivarana interpretations. His *Pañcadashi* was a popular presentation of the monistic system; his *Vivarana-prameya-samgraha* was a scholarly commentary and exposition of the work of an earlier Vivarana writer; his *Jīvan-mukti-viveka* was a clear exposition of the monists' view of emancipation and of the training and meditation leading to it. As became increasingly characteristic of monist writers, he gave *māyā* almost an independent existence, even though he considered it still a part of *brahman*.

* * *

The Vīrashaiva Philosophy

The theistic Vedānta schools grew out of the religious sects as a reaction to the impersonal monism of Shankara's followers. The monists' transcendent *brahman*, their complete identification of the soul with *brahman*, their doctrine that individual souls and the manifest universe were but illusory phenomena, and their denial of incarnation were essentially incompatible with a personal religion in which God could save the souls of those devoted to him. In the latter view God, individual souls, and matter had to be real and in some way distinct, and God had to be perfect, all-powerful, and immanent.[5] In the twelfth century both Vishnuite and Shivaite philosopher-theologians had worked out systems of thought that, while meeting the needs of the theists, could compete on intellectual grounds with Shankara's monism; Rāmānuja had provided Vishistādvaita, or qualified monism, the Vishnuite system (which we shall examine a little later), and the Shivaite philosopher Shrī-kantha (Nīlakantha) provided another type of qualified monism. In the next century Meykandar (Shvetabana) and Arunandi perfected the philosophy of Southern Shivaism. It reached definitive form shortly after 1300 in the writings of Umāpati (see Chapter X), the most significant philosophical works among them being the *Shivappirakāsham* and the *Pauskar-āgama*.[6] Several important commentaries were written on the works of Arunandi and Umāpati after 1300.

The Shivaite qualified monists accepted the *Upanishads* and the *Vedānta-sūtra* as the fountain of authority but gave them a theistic interpretation compatible with the Shivaite *Purānas* and *Āgamas*. While they maintained that God, souls, and matter were discrete and real, they endeavoured to maintain a monistic position by asserting that souls and matter, though separate, were in fact identical with God. *Pati*, the Lord (that is, Shiva), was identical with *brahman*, although personal. He was pure, eternal, all-powerful, always present, and free. *Pāsha* (matter) was also eternal. *Pashu*, the eternal individual soul, bound by the fetters of matter, had become separated from the Master. The fetters of matter were *ānava* ('inborn impurity' or 'ignorance'), *karma* (which inevitably resulted from *ānava*), and *māyā* ('illusion').

Although all three were binding, they helped the soul through experience to liberate itself by realizing its true identity with Shiva. To make this possible, Shiva carried out His five-fold function of creation, preservation, destruction, concealment, and bestowal of grace. Concealment was necessary in order to make souls active in seeking experience. When, through the long experiences of transmigration, the devoted soul gradually wore away its fetters and began to comprehend its true identity, the stage was set for release through divine grace. The Lord revealed Himself to the soul, instructed and purified it, and led it to full realization of its identity with Him. While the idealistic school of Kashmir held that the released soul merged with Shiva, the majority of Shivaites believed that the released soul both became a Shiva, although dependent on Him, and retained its distinct identity. Shivaite qualified monism is in some regards analogous to Christianity: *ānava* suggests 'original sin', *bhakti* 'faith', *moksha* 'salvation'.[7]

In the latter half of the fourteenth century Shrīpati Pandita put the philosophy known as Vīrashaivaism into definitive form. His *Shrīkara-bhāsya*, a commentary on the *Vedānta-sūtra*, was perhaps the most original theistic treatise produced by the Shivaite schools. The Vīrashaiva philosophy insisted that God, souls, and the universe were real. God (that is, Shiva) was the physical and spiritual material of the universe; He was pure consciousness and will; He was energy and action; and He had created the universe out of himself as a spider spins a web. *Brahman* was the essence (*sthala*) of Shiva. By its innate power (*shakti*) *sthala* created the *linga*, individual souls, and material objects. The *linga* was Shiva, and because of its divine nature was to be worshipped. The individual soul was *bhakti* (or devotional) and was the worshipper. The devotional soul, with the aid of Shiva as instructor and guide (redeemer), passed through six stages leading from indifference concerning this world to blissful union (without complete loss of individuality) with Shiva. Love of God and moral and spiritual discipline were essential to redemption.

*   *   *

The Vishistādvaita School

The Vishnuite Vishistādvaita, the qualified monism of Rāmānuja, also found a number of able propagators and defenders. Few of them, however, adopted the logical methodology of the Mithilā school, and hence they seldom reached the critical heights of the Shankara and Mādhva schools. Their polemical works were directed mainly against those who were not qualified monists. In the Vishistādvaita system, Nārāyana (that is, Vishnu), the personal God, and *brahman* were identified, and both matter and souls were considered the body of *brahman*, which comprised and pervaded everything. Matter and souls were thus not *māyā* but the substance of God, and were distinct and eternal. Salvation was obtainable by good works, knowledge, devotional meditation (*bhakti*), and self-surrender, assisted by the grace of God, and meant a personal blissful existence near Vishnu, partaking of his qualities without being merged with him. God revealed himself not only as the supreme spirit and as the ruler within the soul but also in various manifestations and incarnations (Rāma and Krishna), and in duly consecrated images.

In the fourteenth century some noteworthy followers of Rāmānuja's qualified monism appeared. The earliest of them was Pillai Lokācārya, who was associated with the development of the doctrine of the Tengalai sub-sect (see Chapter III). This doctrine held that salvation was attainable not so much through good works and effort on the part of the individual as through devotion and self-surrender, after which the Lord parentally grasped the soul. It tended to emphasize not only the omniscience of God but also His kindly, merciful, and blissful nature.

The greatest of the qualified monists after Rāmānuja was Venkatanātha (mentioned in Chapter III as Vedānta Deshika). Venkatanātha (or Vedānta Deshika) was a fine poet and a prolific writer. His numerous treatises on religion and philosophy did so much to clarify and expand the ideas of Rāmānuja that the two rank almost equally high as architects of the Vishistādvaita system. In his *Nyāsa-vimshati* Venkatanātha developed the idea, associated with the Vadagalai sub-sect, that successful self-surrender to God must be preceded by good works and individual effort to grasp God for help and protection. His *Nyāya-parishuddhi* expounded the logical principles of the qualified monist school. He accepted the idea of the self-validity of knowledge and explained illusion as the appearance of one thing in the form of another. He recognized only three sources of knowledge—perception, inference, and scriptural testimony; and he described intuitive yoga knowledge, which had been accepted by Rāmānuja, as a form of higher perception, thus dividing perception into three classes, namely God's, the yogi's, and the ordinary man's. He insisted that some propositions must by nature be valid, because if nothing were considered valid, there would be no basis for any reasoning process. The existence of God, nevertheless, could not be established by reason but must be accepted on the basis of scripture. He also (compare the contemporary European nominalists) denied the reality of universals or categorical concepts, maintaining that they arose only out of human perception of similarities in different and specific things. His *Shāta-dūsanī* was devoted principally to refutation of the views of the Shankarites (among others) about the nature of *brahman*, the soul, reality, and emancipation. He denied their doctrine of *māyā* and insisted upon the reality of the world, but he did not accept the atomic theory of the Vaishesikas.

Perhaps Venkatanātha's greatest work was the *Tattva-muktā-kalāpa*, in which he set forth his own version of qualified monism. To him God was everything—the instrumental and material cause of the world, its controller and director. Individual souls and material things were created by God out of Himself to form His body. They were, therefore, a part of God, yet real, distinct, and eternal. Despite the dependence of the individual on God,

Venkatanātha insisted, God gave man freedom to make his own choices. Although *bhakti*, the joyous adoration of God, was essential to salvation, it must be accompanied by deliberate effort on the part of the individual. The emancipated soul participated in the omniscience and bliss of God but did not partake of His power to create and control the world or to emancipate souls. In the late fourteenth century Varadārya and Shrīnivāsadāsa, Venkatanātha's son and pupil respectively, carried on the master's message, and in the fifteenth century Rāmānujadāsa (also called Mahācārya) not only wrote commentaries on Rāmānuja and Venkatanātha but also as an advocate of Vishistādvaita attempted a refutation of the Mādhva dualists, on the one hand, and of the Shankarite monists, on the other.

⋆   ⋆   ⋆

The Dvaita School

The dualistic (Dvaita) Vedānta school, founded by Madhva in the thirteenth century and elaborated by Jaya-tīrtha in the first half of the fourteenth,[8] was also a reaction to the Shankara system. Jaya-tīrtha wrote many books expounding, defending, and elaborating the rather cryptic writings of Madhva. His two most important works, the *Nyāya-sudhā* and the *Tattva-prakāshikā*, were commentaries on and elaborations of Madhva's principal philosophical works. The former book has sometimes been described as the most masterful commentary in all Sanskrit literature.

The Dvaita school was theist and realist as well as dualist. It developed a distinctive logic and theory of knowledge. Perception, inference, and scriptural testimony were regarded as the sources of valid knowledge, but each, especially perception, was defined in a way peculiar to the Mādhvas. They held certain things to be real and eternal but distinct—God and soul, different souls, God and matter, soul and matter, and variant forms of matter. In sum, however, they conceived of only two kinds of things in the world—independent and dependent. God alone was independent, everything else was dependent on Him. The existence of God could be established only by revelation. He was identified with *brahman* and called Vishnu or Nārāyana, but he might appear in diverse forms. He was the perfect, all-powerful, omniscient, omnipresent, all-merciful controller of the world; He was its efficient but not its material cause. God and souls were considered related as father to son or master to servant, and each soul was real, eternal, unique, and marked by its own ignorance and imperfections. The substance of the manifest universe (including the human body) was matter (*prakrti*), which was controlled and directed by God. The destiny of souls was predetermined—whether to eternal bliss in the presence of Vishnu, to an eternal round of transmigrations, or to an ever downward course of suffering (as in the case of demons and sinners like the monists). The rebirth and the suffering of souls destined for salvation were caused by the ignorance and imperfections adhering to them, which obscured their true nature and prevented them from acquiring the knowledge essential to salvation. Proper living, study of the scriptures, and detached contemplation and meditation were essential to knowledge of self and God, but the final, indispensable step in salvation was a loving devotion (*bhakti*) that grew out of a realization of God's majesty and goodness. Such devotion led to the bestowal of God's grace, without which salvation was impossible. Salvation was a blissful existence, but even saved souls enjoyed bliss in different degrees, depending on the intrinsic worth of each.

A number of subsequent defenders of the dualist position showed great ingenuity and subtlety in elaborating details, but they added little that was fundamental to Jaya-tīrtha's thought. Probably the greatest controversialist of this period was Vyāsa-tīrtha, who seems to have lived in the fifteenth century. His *Nyāyāmrta* took up the arguments of various monists from Shankara on and refuted them, only to be refuted in turn by Madhusūdana in the sixteenth century. Vyāsa-tīrtha attacked the doctrine of the illusory nature of the world (*māyā*) and questioned the monists' conception of *brahman*, knowledge, ignorance, perception, inference, and liberation. He upheld the reality and distinctness of God, souls, and the material world, supported the idea of a personal God as opposed to the absolute *brahman* devoid of all qualities, and insisted that God or *brahman* could not be the material cause of the world but only its instrumental or efficient cause.[9]

* * *

The Dvaitādvaitamata School

If Nimbārka lived in the fourteenth rather than the twelfth century,[10] then, as the founder of the Dvaitādvaitamata, the school of dualistic monism, he was perhaps the most original, although not necessarily the best, of the Indian thinkers who flourished between 1300 and 1500. His ideas were set forth in a commentary, entitled the *Vedānta-pārijāta-saurabha*, on the *Vedānta-sūtra* and in a brief compendium of doctrine, entitled the *Dasha-shlokī*. Like other theists he was dissatisfied with the system of absolute monism, but he could not entirely cast off its spell. He was also committed to an intensely emotional dedication to God. The result was a qualified, pluralistic realism grafted upon a theistic monism. This philosophy borrowed much from Rāmānuja but developed its own distinctive features. Nimbārka's school accepted the self-validity of knowledge and admitted perception, inference, and scriptural testimony as the sources of knowledge but defined them in its own way.

According to Nimbārka the impersonal *brahman* and the personal Krishna (Vishnu) were the same. God was pure being, bliss, and consciousness; He was all-powerful, all-pervading, and all-merciful. He was both the instrumental and the material cause of the world, for, like the familiar spider spinning its web, he had created souls and the material world out of himself without altering. The world and individual souls were thus a part of him, created out of his energy, or *shakti*. They were dependent on him and could not exist without him, but they were also separate, distinct, eternal, and real. Their relationship to him was like that of waves to water; they existed potentially within God and became manifest in a gross form in the phenomenal world. The monistic texts in the scriptures were thus harmonized with the dualistic ones, in that *brahman* was conceived of as at once different from and yet identical with the world of spirit and matter.

Nimbārka preached a doctrine of salvation by enlightenment and faith. Every soul was encumbered with its own ignorance, impurity, and material body, which caused it to act independently, thus suffering pain and misery. Salvation came when the soul realized its true relationship to God, ceased its striving, and found its place as a participant in God's nature and in blissful, devout contemplation of and servitude to Him. This state of enlightenment, however, could come only as a result of the mercy of Krishna, and grace would be bestowed only on those who felt their helplessness and in faith surrendered to Him. Self-surrender, when accompanied by God's grace, engendered an intense love of and devotion (*bhakti*) to God, which made possible carrying on the routine duties of life, studying the scriptures under an enlightened teacher, and meditating on the nature of God in the manner necessary to the attainment of complete enlightenment.

Shrīnivāsa, Nimbārka's pupil, was his immediate successor as head of the sect. He wrote a commentary, known as the *Vedānta-kaustubha*, on the first of Nimbārka's works, and elsewhere expounded and upheld the master's teachings. After Shrīnivāsa dualistic monism found few able expounders, although some of the heads of the sect were reported to have been great scholars and controversialists.

CHINESE AND JAPANESE DEVELOPMENTS

In contrast to the Indian interest in metaphysics, theism, and salvation, Chinese thought was basically practical, moralistic, and secular. Although Chinese concern with metaphysics was conspicuous during this period, it was regularly subordinated to moral and practical considerations. Since neither Taoism nor Buddhism (with the possible exception of certain Ch'anist writers) produced any thinkers of renown, the only significant system of thought was Neo-Confucianism.

Two major schools of thought had developed within Neo-Confucianism during the Sung period. One was noted for its monistic idealism and is generally known as the Hsin-hsüeh, the School of the Mind, or, simply, the Idealistic school. It looked upon the mind (*hsin*) as everything—as principle (*li*), as the source of knowledge, as the ultimate reality; and it placed great stress upon intuition and the 'investigation of mind' (rather than external things) through meditation. In its emphasis upon the mind as the source of concepts of reality, it bore some resemblance to the subjective idealism of Bishop Berkeley in Europe in the eighteenth century (see Chapter VII). It did not obtain many able followers during the Mongol and early Ming periods and was not to be of much importance until later.

The other major school believed in a sort of dualistic idealism, emphasizing the interaction of principle (*li*)—that is, moral law or reason—and substance (*ch'i*)—that is, matter or material force. Since this school considered *li* the determinant factor in this interaction, it was known as the Li-hsüeh, or Rationalistic school. In emphasizing the 'investigation of things' rather than ideas of the mind as the source of truth (but not in much else) it resembled the empiricists of seventeenth- and eighteenth-century Europe.

Despite their differences, both schools subscribed equally to the unity of the universe and the interdependence of all things within it. Both considered the old Confucian ethical term *jen* (denoting goodness, benevolence, love or human reciprocation) fundamental to their thought, but they also gave it a metaphysical quality, making it the source or unifying principle of the universe. The *jen* of heaven was a principle shared by all things, tending to unite them and, in fact, making them one. They conceived of it not only as 'forming one body with the universe' but also as the 'life force' or 'generative principle'. It was likewise 'the character of mind and the principle of love,' comprehending all the virtues and generating in them the spirit that made them 'real, social, and dynamic'.[11]

*　　*　　*

The Li-hsüeh

Chu Hsi (1130–1200) was regarded as the greatest exponent of Li-hsüeh, and the Confucian books accepted as classical by him, together with his commentaries on them, were made standard for civil-service examinations in 1313 and remained so until the twentieth century. During the Yung-lo period of the Ming the writings of Chu Hsi and the Rationalists were condensed into the *Hsing-li ta-ch'üan*, or Great Philosophy, and this work, along with the classics and Chu's commentaries, became the basis of instruction in the official schools as well as of the examinations. Official support induced every scholar with ambition for office to turn to the study of Rationalistic philosophy. That philosophy taught that governments, too, had their *li* and that bad government arose because the ruler and his officials, not comprehending that *li*, did not follow it as truly enlightened rulers and officials should. The Rationalistic school completely dominated Chinese thought during the Mongol and early Ming periods until the sixteenth century and continued to exert a profound influence into the twentieth.

The Rationalistic dualists maintained that everything was made up of *li* and *ch'i*. The concept of *li* was much like Plato's doctrine of 'ideas' or 'forms'. *Li* was the governing principle or essence of things—abstract, eternal, and without form itself, but determining the nature of all things. It was, in short, abstract truth. *Ch'i* provided the substance of things. Thus, all being had two levels—the one abstract, absolute, eternal, and 'beyond shapes', and the other concrete, destructable, and 'within shapes'. Everything—the world, human nature, bamboo, motion, bricks, government—had its *li* but became embodied in a particular form only when combined with *ch'i*. *Li* was perfect, but *ch'i* varied in quality; and thus when they were combined in forms, the forms were subject to imperfection and evil. *Li* was superior and prior in the sense that the principle of all things had to exist before the things themselves could be embodied in particular forms. *Li* by itself was potential but inactive; *ch'i* possessed the power of movement and action, and in combination with *li* produced particular forms, the nature of which was determined by their *li*. Differences within the same categories were explained as due to varying amounts or qualities of *ch'i*.

For a thing the standard was *li*, and for the universe the standard was the great *li*, or supreme ultimate (*t'ai-chi*), of which all particular *li* were a part. The supreme ultimate thus contained within itself the potential of everything. It was often equated with *tao*, the way, or cosmic moral law. Furthermore, the supreme ultimate, without losing its unity, was present in every separate thing. Creation and destruction, growth and decay were explained in terms of the interaction of *li* and *ch'i*. The *li* of movement or the *li* of quiescence combined with *ch'i* to produce *yang* or *yin* respectively (action or repose, male or female, light or dark, good or evil), and *yang* and *yin* through their interaction produced the five elements (earth, water, fire, wood, and metal) from which the physical universe arose.

The *li* of each individual within the same category was exactly the same. Hence all humans were endowed with the same *li*, or nature, which consisted of the four fundamental virtues: righteousness (*i*), courtesy and propriety (*li*), wisdom (*chih*), and reciprocal goodness or love (*jen*), which, we have seen, was also the bond of cosmic union. The *li* of mind by itself was incapable of thinking, feeling, or having emotions, but combined with *ch'i* it formed mind (*hsin*), which possessed these capacities. Evil in the world and among men arose because of defective *ch'i*, which tarnished the perfect *li* of man's nature. To triumph over evil, man's purpose should be to strive to attain his true nature, which was good, by understanding the perfect *li*, which united him with all things, and thus to recover his 'lost mind'.

Toward this end the Rationalistic school advocated certain spiritual exercises. They included both 'the extension of knowledge through the investigation of things' and 'attentiveness of the mind', or study and meditative thought. The true nature of the great *li* or of oneself was to be discovered first through the investigation of particular things. After long study and careful investigation with the proper 'attentiveness of the mind', complete enlightenment was likely to come rather suddenly. The enlightened person understood his true nature and his oneness with other men and the universe, and was able to follow the *tao* with equanimity and impartiality. The ideal human way was that of the householder who, practising the four fundamental virtues, lived in harmony with man and nature. The Rationalist philosophy was thus essentially optimistic in its outlook; it believed in the moral perfectibility of man (in this regard resembling the *philosophes* of eighteenth-century Europe) and the possibility of approximating the ideal human society ('the heavenly city') that was supposed to have existed under the sage kings of the dim past.

The Mongol and Ming periods produced a number of able commentators on the Rationalistic system, and most scholars and officials parroted its basic principles, but few undertook to expand it. Chu Hsi, like Thomas Aquinas, appeared to have done his work so well that within its own premises the system could not be improved. Probably, too, the fact that it not only was the official philosophy but also tended to look backward to the classics and to a presumed golden age for inspiration had a stultifying effect. For whatever reason, many fell in with the view that since the time of Chu Hsi the truth had been manifest, further exposition was unnecessary, and nothing was left but to practise it. In consequence, later scholars did not fully apply the injunction to 'investigate things', which might have led them toward experimentation in natural science. On the contrary, they tended, far more than Chu Hsi, to disregard the world about them and, like the contemporary Scholastics of Europe, to investigate and expound the 'things' of their classics.

*   *   *

The Hsin-hsüeh

Although the Idealistic school accepted the same classics as the Rationalists and shared many of their ideas, it differed from them on certain fundamental points. To the Idealists mind was pure *li*, and they insisted that nature (*li*), mind, and feelings were different aspects of the same thing. For them there was but one realm of being or reality, namely that of the world of time and space, and what was 'above shapes' and what was 'within shapes' constituted a common realm. They accepted the view that the supreme ultimate was present in everything and argued that since it was present in the mind, the mind was everything: 'The universe is my mind, and my mind is the universe.'[12] The mind was at the same time the source of knowledge and of moral perfection, and one should concentrate on the study of one's own mind through introspection and reflection in order to find the principle of things, the *li* or the *tao*, rather than waste time investigating things. Evil arose because the mind was led astray by external things and became attached to desire. These externals must be shut out, and through concentrated, meditative, introspective study the 'lost mind', which held complete knowledge and understanding within itself, must be sought, and it might be recovered in a burst of sudden enlightenment. This conclusion brought the Idealists close to the Buddhists and Taoists, and indeed they were accused by their opponents of being Buddhists in disguise.

The Rationalistic school remained dominant until the sixteenth century. To be sure, compromise with Idealism was sometimes suggested. For example, during the first half of the fourteenth century Wu Ts'ao-lu and Cheng Shih-shan inclined toward a synthesis of the Rationalistic and Idealistic schools. But later Sun Lien (1310–81) and Fang Hsiao-ju (1357–1402) upheld the Rationalistic school against dilution. The Rationalists thereupon enjoyed a sort of renaissance, despite the martyrdom that Fang and all his relatives suffered for protesting, in proper Confucian fashion, against the seizure of the throne by the Yung-lo emperor.

★   ★   ★

Possible Synthesis of the Two Schools

Ts'ao Tuan (1376–1434) was the leading Rationalist of the early-fifteenth century. He was followed by two younger contemporaries, Hsüeh Hsüan (1392–1464) of Shansi and Wu Yü-pi (1391–1469) of Kiangsi. Actually, neither Hsüeh nor Wu appear to have fully distinguished between Rationalists and Idealists. Both emphasized investigation of things less than attentiveness of mind and hence, while considering themselves followers of Chu Hsi, promoted views which, strictly interpreted, belonged rather to the Idealists. Nevertheless, while the influence of the Idealist school was increasing, Hsüeh's followers, the so-called Hotung school, made strenuous efforts to uphold the Rationalistic position.

On the other hand, Wu's followers tended more and more toward an Idealist position. Wu, a sort of farmer recluse who shunned official position, himself had emphasized self-denial and self-perfection through meditation. One of his pupils, Hu Chü-jen (1434–84), came very close to the Idealistic school on many points but still loyally upheld the idea of investigating things. Another, Lou Liang (1422–91), was virtually Idealistic. Still another, Ch'en Hsien-chang (1428–1500) of Kwangtung, moved completely over to the Idealistic school. He himself described what happened when he failed to get satisfactory results from the method of study taught by Wu:

'Thereupon I cast aside the complexities of his [method], and sought for a simple one of my own, entirely through "quiet sitting". After a long time I finally came to perceive the very structure of my mind, which mysteriously became visible to me, even as if it were a concrete object. . . . Thereupon I came clearly to have trust in myself. . . . Comprehending this [the all-embracing activities of *li*], I find that Heaven and Earth are established by me, their myriad transmutations issue forth from me, and the whole universe lies within myself.'[13]

In this way some of the more original thinkers emancipated themselves from the orthodox Rationalists and paved the way for a great Idealist revival (see Chapter VII).

★   ★   ★

Theological Developments in Japan

In Japan Zen Buddhist priests introduced Neo-Confucian ideas from China before 1500, but these ideas were to bear fruit there only after that date.

Before 1500 the most original and interesting theological developments took place in connection with the efforts of court officials and Shinto priests to restore the position of the emperor and revive the native Shinto religion. Their thought was eclectic, borrowed from Buddhism, Confucianism, and Taoism. It was also monistic and pantheistic, the Sun Goddess being identified with the absolute from which all else emanated. It helped to provide eventually the metaphysical and ethical foundations for a theocratic and absolute system, although actual political power during the period remained in the hands of independent feudal lords. The ideas of the chief writers, Kitabatake, Ichijo, and Urabe Kanetomo, have been discussed in connection with Shintoism in Chapter III. In addition, Ryōyo Shōgei, of the Pure Land sect of Buddhism, developed the doctrine that salvation did not mean transportation to the Western Paradise (Pure Land) but represented a change of mind and condition here and now.

ISLAMIC DEVELOPMENTS

In Islam, no less than elsewhere, intellectual life was subservient to religion; and philosophy, along with law and the sciences, was held by the pious to be a handmaid of theology. Muslims distinguished sharply between *kalām* and *falsafa*. *Kalām* corresponds somewhat to theology, but it touched all philosophical questions as well, always from a religious-dogmatic point of view; and *falsafa* was in principle totally natural in method, but it sometimes touched upon questions regarding the nature of God. During our period mysticism was more intensively developed than systematic theology, which, however, was now being put into definitive form by commentators. Like other religions, Islam produced radical, moderate, and conservative factions, and probably in greater diversity and with more distinctive sects than Christianity did before 1500.

In contrast to the contemporary trend in Western Christendom and Judaism, the Muslim states of the West brought forth almost no great theologians, but in the rest of Islam theology flourished. The contrast can be explained, at least in part, by the fewness of the Muslim provinces in the West. The career and posthumous reputation of Ibn-al-'Arabī illustrate the fact that the centre of Muslim intellectual life was in the main areas of Muslim population, for this thirteenth-century Spanish-Muslim visionary migrated to Hijāz and Syria. He gave theological expression to the Neoplatonic and pantheistic aspects of Muslim mysticism and laid the philosophical foundations of one sort of monistic Ṣūfism. His influence, momentous in Islam, even made itself felt in Christendom. Some of his work, notably a chapter in the *Futūhāt Makkiyya* that describes a twofold ascent into Paradise, is considered by some scholars a significant source of Dante's *Divine Comedy*, although perhaps Dante merely reflects the mystical tendencies common in the literature of all the religions of those times. Some scholars assert also that

Ibn-al-'Arabī's mystical treatment of womankind inspired Dante's *Banquet*. It is more widely agreed that the Muslim mystic exerted a strong influence on the writings of Ramon Lull, one of the best Arabists of Christian Europe in his day.

Ibn-al-'Arabī's teachings became one of the subjects of controversy in Islam. Muslim theologians had come to terms with Aristotelian rationalism long before Christianity made its great Thomistic compromise with it, and before 1300 Aristotle had been reconciled with the Koran and other Islamic religious writings. Commentaries were compiled under the influence of the rationalism exemplified by Avicenna and Averroes (see Volume III). But Ibn-al-'Arabī's mystic monism became popular, and his writings raised more keenly than the less explicitly philosophical writings of earlier Ṣūfīs a problem that could scarcely be solved through Aristotelian logic—the significance of cosmic unity for personal experience. The controversies that now arose centred on the concept of *waḥdat al-wujūd* (*unity by existence*), which, while some decried it as in effect negating the identity of God, the majority of Ṣūfī philosophers defended.

Many scholars of the fourteenth and fifteenth centuries in Middle Eastern Islam reacted strongly against the scholasticism of the Aristotelians and in favour of the mysticism of the Ṣūfī. Such was the attitude of 'Abd-al-Karīm al-Jīlī (d. 1428), representative of a famous Iraqian family of conservative theologians; he reduced Ibn-al-'Arabī's visions to a consistent doctrine that presented the ideal man as a microcosm realized in mystical experience. An outstanding champion of the Ṣūfīs among the theologians was 'Abd al-Razzāq (d. 1329), a Persian mystic; he engaged in a controversy with Rukn-al-Din 'Alā' al-Dawla, a contemporary writer who attacked the orthodoxy of Ibn-al-'Arabī. A revived Arabian kingdom in the Yemen produced some theologians of note, prominent among whom was al-Yāfi'ī (*c*. 1300–67), a staunch defender of the mystical tendencies of the Ṣūfīs against the reformism of the Syrian Ḥanbalite Ibn-Taymiyya (1263–1328). Ibn-Taymiyya and his disciple Ibn-Qayyim-al-Jawziyya developed an incisive critique of both philosophy and Ṣūfism in favour of a social and historical puritanism which emphasized the responsibilities of man-in-community. They also attacked the orthodox *'ūlamā'*, for like other Ḥanbalīs they rejected the traditionalist limitations of *taqlīd* (binding by legal precedent) and called for what they regarded as a return to primitive Muslim orthodoxy. Their attacks, whether philosophical or social, were largely ignored.

Mysticism's dominance in Islam was manifested likewise by the Mawlawiyya *ṭarīqa*, the 'whirling dervishes' of the Turkish lands. Organized by the thirteenth-century Persian-born poet, Jalāl-ud-dīn Rūmī, who was a professor at the *madrasa* of Konya, they were merely one of the more spectacular of the numerous Muslim fraternities of practising mystics. Their members helped to give social prestige to monistic philosophical doctrines.

Probably the most vital line of intellectual endeavour, as might be expected, was the development and the critique of Ṣūfī theosophy. At the beginning of this period, the Syrian school of Ibn-Taymiyya was noted for its all-out opposition to Ṣūfism. Most of the Ṣūfīs' positive work, however, was done not in Syria but in Iran, developing both the Ishrāqī metaphysics of light and the cosmic monism associated with Ibn-al-ʿArabī. The most prominent presentation of mystical monism was in the writings of poets such as Jāmī in the fifteenth century, who produced prose commentaries on mystical texts and embodied such ideas in his verse (see Chapter X).

JUDAIC DEVELOPMENTS

Judaism inherited from the centuries before 1300 numerous theological controversies that resulted in factions of conservatives, moderates, and radicals in much the same fashion as in other religions. One of the oldest of the controversies concerned the fundamental basis of faith: Should sacrosanctity be restricted to the Pentateuch (Torah) or should it also extend to other holy scriptures such as the Talmud and to oral tradition?

The relationship of Aristotle to orthodox theology, which had become crucial among Judaism's problems in the eleventh and twelfth centuries, was still highly debated in the fourteenth century. Aristotle's logical treatises circulated widely through the Hebrew world, and his ideas were adapted to current philosophical disputes, often with violence to their original meaning. The conservatives of Judaism under the leadership of some of the rabbis opposed Aristotelianism and the rationalization of faith implicit in it. A moderate faction of intellectuals, on the other hand, adopted the Aristotelian ideology associated with the name of the twelfth-century philosopher Maimonides. A third category, comprising Jewish theologians of a still more moderate, even neutral attitude, was probably the majority group. A fourth group, extreme radicals, even sceptics, opposed Maimonidism as vigorously as did the conservatives.

The strict-constructionist role had for centuries been filled by the Karaites, 'children or followers of the Scripture'. They wrote commentaries on the holy books but vigorously rejected the lore and authority of rabbinical works, holding that each man was free to interpret Torah for himself. In this respect they resembled the later Protestants of Christianity, who rejected the doctrines of the Roman Catholic clergy and church fathers, relying solely on the Bible as their religious authority. This resemblance led certain Roman Catholics in the sixteenth century to refer to the Protestants as 'Karae' (i.e. Karaites).

Aaron ben Elijah of Constantinople (1300–69) is often called the 'Maimonides of Karaitism'. Aaron differed with Maimonides, however, in at least one essential; he questioned Maimonides' attempt to reconcile Aristotle with religious orthodoxy. Aaron's *Tree of Life* rejected Aristotelianism in favour

o*

of the earlier orthodoxy of Judaism. Along with his other works it stressed the freedom of the human will and the importance of the ancient prophets. He was influential among the Jews in the West as well as the East, but he was the last outstanding Karaite. Karaitism declined during the late Middle Ages, and conservative ideologies, even in the once-great French, Spanish, and North African centres of Jewish theology, were eclipsed by the ever-increasing forces of skepticism and secularism.

During the fourteenth and fifteenth centuries Maimonides' rationalistic approach to religion continued to be attacked from other quarters. Among the most assiduous of the attackers were the mystics—especially in Spain. A sect of mystical extremists, the Qabbalists, had arisen there in the thirteenth century. The first outstanding Qabbalist, a Catalan Jew named Azriel ben Menahem (1160–1238), had adopted an old theory of emanation, adding to it certain Aristotelian ideas concerning the eternity of the world, and the Biblical account of creation. About a century later, a work (attributed to Moses ben Shem-Tob of Leon by modern scholars) entitled *Sépher ha-Zohar* (*Book of Splendour*) synthesized the prevailing mysticism and became the mainstay of Qabbalism. Qabbalism was an amalgam of magic, pseudo-science, and religion. Strange beliefs and practices from Zoroastrianism, Neoplatonism, and ancient Babylonian mythology were mingled with genuine spiritual idealism. At its worst, with its demonology, lore of numbers, and astrological superstitions, it marked a decline in the ancient faith. On the other hand, its high spiritual aspirations encouraged idealists to rise above the legalism and ritualism of rabbinical Judaism. Qabbalism became immensely popular with those moderate Jews who could accept neither the conservative nor the radical extremes of theology and also with those who sought in an extravagant, visionary lore escape from the tribulations of life.

Qabbalism contributed to the waning of Jewish thought after 1300. Even in Spain, where it had once flourished brilliantly under Muslim rule, Judaic theology declined. The decline was due also in part to the restrictions placed upon the Jews by Christian rulers. As the Christians extended their sway over the lands of the south, Jewish scholars often found it safer to restrict themselves to commentaries on the Old Testament and the Talmud. Such commentaries appeared in great numbers, not only in Spain but also in southern France and north Africa, where large colonies of refugees sought safety from Christian persecution. Another indication of the cumulative flight of Jewish scholars from original thought on Judaic subjects was the rise in the number of translations of Latin works into Hebrew.

In southern France and Spain rival groups of radicals and conservatives built up a vast controversial literature, especially concerning the merits and shortcomings of Maimonides. Some of this literature transcended mere pedantry. Joseph Kaspi (1280–1340), a south-French Jew, wrote brilliant treatises quoting extensively from Aristotle (and sometimes from Plato) and defending the moderate rationalism of Maimonides. Kaspi's contemporary,

Levi ben Gerson, sometimes known as Gersonides (1288–1344), one of Judaism's outstanding scholars, wrote a treatise entitled *The Wars of the Lord*, in which he reconciled Judaism with Aristotelianism. In this and his commentaries on Aristotle and other philosophers, he is sometimes considered more logical and certainly was more truly Aristotelian than Maimonides. Naturally he stirred up violent opposition. During his own lifetime he was charged with heresy, and later Jewish scholars attacked both him and Maimonides. Strange to say, although Gerson was an Aristotelian rationalist, he upheld the 'realist' position of medieval thinkers with regard to universals (see below). The leader in the attacks on Maimonides and Gerson was Hasdai ben Abraham Crescas of Barcelona (1340–1410). Crescas' works mark the climax of the anti-Aristotelian movement in Judaism, and his *Light of the Lord* was appealed to also by anti-Aristotelian Christian scholars in their attacks on Thomist rationalism. Attempts (by Simon ben Zemach Duran Joseph ben Shem-Tob, and others) were made to reconcile the Crescas school with the moderate rationalism of the Maimonidans but proved vain.

Italian humanists and neo-Hebraic writers sometimes mutually influenced one another. A fourteenth-century Italian Jew, Immanuel ben Soloman, wrote, though in a lighter vein, a Hebrew poem modelled in part upon the *Divine Comedy* of his friend Dante. In the fifteenth century, many humanists saw a kinship of Jewish and Christian thought in Qabbalism, with its anti-Aristotelian, Neoplatonic bias, and its reliance on individual instinct rather than logic. Pico della Mirandola, the Neoplatonic humanist (see below), was a friend and student of Jewish scholars in Italy, particularly of Elia del Medigo. He earnestly studied the Qabbalist writings with the help of a less scholarly Jew from Constantinople, Jochanon Aleman. In these works he thought he found proofs of the divinity of Jesus and other Christian doctrines, and with these arguments in hand he hoped to convert Jews to Christianity. Furthermore, he endeavoured to achieve a great syncretistic triumph, reconciling Judaism not only with Christianity but also with Islam, Platonism, and even Aristotelianism.

Pico della Mirandola exerted an unmistakable influence on Judah Leon Abravanel, also known as Leo Hebraeus. Judah was the son of Isaac Abravanel, Jewish philosopher and onetime financial adviser to the Spanish throne, who had preferred exile to remaining as a specially privileged Jew in Spain. Judah was a physician. Both men, after the expulsion of 1492, had found refuge in Italy. Judah Abravanel's *Dialogues of Love*, written in Italian and widely read in Italy, combined the stylistic beauty of literary humanism with fanciful erotic imagery. The lover's desire to be absorbed physically and spiritually into his beloved symbolized for him the mystical union of the human intellect with divine intelligence. Ficino and other Hellenophile mystics of the Platonic Academy in Florence (see below) were somewhat less enthusiastic over Qabbalism than Pico, but they too found in it an ally for their Neoplatonism. It gave them ground for their efforts to synthesize various theological and philosophical schools of thought under one all-embracing mystic essence of Divine Truth.

DEVELOPMENTS IN CHRISTIANITY

Volume III has indicated that when, early in the thirteenth century, Aristotle's *Physics* and *Metaphysics*, with Averroes' rationalistic commentaries, reached Paris, Scholasticism (i.e. the logical method of the Schoolmen) entered a new phase. At first, the church tried to prohibit the teaching of any of 'the philosopher's' writings except those on ethics and logic, but when the prohibition proved unenforceable, the Dominican theologian Thomas Aquinas undertook to harmonize Aristotle with orthodox Christianity.[14] His *Summa Theologica*, the principal work in his aim to organize Christian doctrine into a theological system, provided a formidable defence against free thought on the one hand and thoughtless reaction on the other. His brand of Scholasticism came to be generally known as Thomism. It was widely accep-ed in the schools around 1300, when it was still possible to expect that a tstable society, a common weal based upon the proper admixture of scripture, church tradition, and Aristotelianism could be indefinitely preserved.

Though in a sense the culmination of medieval Scholasticism, Thomism was challenged from several directions. In Thomas's own day, the deductive method in science was winning persuasive adherents; then Schism and Councils lessened the unity of the church; meanwhile, urbanization and commerce gave power and prominence to a bourgeois class that stressed individual initiative, achievement, and worth rather than birth and stability of social status. Thomas's contemporary Roger Bacon, Franciscan friar and scientific empiricist, rebelled violently against Aristotelian authority as 'a fountain of error' and against its Dominican exponents. The Catalan scholar and missionary Raimon Lull (*c*. 1235–1315) attempted to combine mysticism with reason by a Platonic or Pythagorean rather than an Aristotelian scheme for proving the truths of Christianity; he sought to do so by mathematical logic, equations, and diagrams. The conservative branch of the Augustinian order upheld the supremacy of faith in all matters theological.

Conservative Franciscan theology proved more formidable immediately as a foe of Dominican Scholasticism than empiricism or mystic mathematics or Augustinian faith. Thomas's works were charged with containing over two hundred heretical statements, and a French Franciscan corrected more than half of these so-called heresies. Subsequently the Franciscan archbishop of Canterbury formally condemned 'Thomism'. A more philosophical attack came from Duns Scotus (1266–1308), an English Franciscan who had been schooled at Oxford by empiricists like Bacon. Endowed with one of the keenest minds of his day, trained in logic and mathematics, Duns Scotus, a Schoolman himself, attacked Thomist Scholasticism with a paradox: the very acceptance by Thomas of the major premise that God was the omnipotent

Creator indicated the inadequacy of reason and the primacy of faith, since such a premise was not rationally demonstrable and must be accepted on faith. Furthermore, if God is omnipotent, he must be the cause of evil, and freedom of the human will is an illusion; reason unassisted by faith thus would lead logically to what seemed to Scotus a *reductio ad absurdum*—that God is responsible for the choice of evil by some mortals. Similarly Duns Scotus claimed to have reduced to rational absurdity Thomas' argument that man's immortality is proved by his desire for it and by his resistance to death: animals show similar tendencies. Though unprovable by reason, Duns Scotus argued, the justice of God and other Christian dogmas are necessary for man's morality and must be accepted on faith as a practical necessity. Against Thomas' preference for a rationalizing of religion, Duns Scotus maintained the desirability of keeping religion separate from rationalized thought.

Thomist Scholasticism survived the attack. Shortly after Thomas's death (1274) his old master, Albertus Magnus, persuaded the Dominicans to defend Thomism against the charge of heresy. Early in the fourteenth century, Dante also came to Thomas's defence, making him in the *Divine Comedy* one of his guides in the ascent of the highest steps of Paradise. In 1323 Thomas was canonized.

Yet personal vindication did not carry immunity from further criticism. A younger contemporary of Duns Scotus, William of Ockham (*c.* 1300–49), likewise a Franciscan trained at Oxford, continued the attack. Under papal suspicion for a critical commentary on one of the classics of Scholasticism, Peter Lombard's *Sententiae*, and for a defence of the Spiritual Franciscans, Ockham took refuge with a leading political opponent of the Avignon popes, Emperor Louis of Bavaria. The last twenty years of his life were spent in exile under the emperor's protection, and the philosophical dispute of Thomists and Ockhamists thus became merged with the political disputes between pope and emperor. Ockham's extensive writings and rigorously independent thinking brought to a climax the Franciscan attack on Thomism. With Ockham, as with Duns Scotus, it took the form of a markedly sceptical approach to the validity of Thomas' rationalized universals.[15]

Scepticism regarding the validity of universals is known as *nominalism*, since it holds that universals are merely convenient names without reality; belief in the reality of universals is known as logical *realism*. Coming on the heels of Duns Scotus' questioning of the use of reason in theology, Ockham's nominalism resulted in temporary eclipse of the Thomist brand of 'realism'. We shall discuss Ockham's contribution to logic below. Despite his intention to promote faith as a source of theological truth, his nominalism tended to promote descriptive science by pointing an accusing finger at the weaknesses of the deductive method of reasoning and by carefully indicating the limitations of the inductive method.

Ockham's doubt of Thomas's 'realism' infected the University of Paris, birthplace of Thomism. The fame of Jean Buridan (*c.* 1297–*c.* 1358), professor and later rector at Paris, spread Ockhamist nominalism among students not only of France but also of the new universities of Germany. Buridan's contemporary, Nicole Oresme (1323–82), shared his attitude. A major interest of both men was science (see Chapter XIII), and as philosophers and scientists they were both interested also in the works of Aristotle. Buridan wrote commentaries on Aristotelianism and (at the request of his king, Charles V the Wise) produced the first vernacular (French) translation of Aristotle. Scientific studies brought empirical questioning, which in turn induced philosophical nominalism and led Oresme particularly to support the Scotist-Ockhamist attack on Thomism and on those who would impugn faith by argument. Later French intellectuals, notably Chancellor d'Ailly (1350–1420) and Jean Gerson (1363–1429), his student, colleague, and successor as chancellor, adhered to the nominalist tradition of the University of Paris, impelled in part at least by their openly proclaimed concern for papal reform (see Chapter III) in the course of the Conciliar Movement.

Despite the steady drift from medieval religiousness to what we are accustomed to call 'modern' secularism, Thomism persisted through the fourteenth and fifteenth centuries and regained some of its lost prestige during the sixteenth (see Chapter VII). Scholasticism, especially in its Thomist form, continued as a rallying point for believers who were moderate rationalists. Serving as a buffer between Averroist extremists, unyielding advocates of reason, on the one hand, and conservative Augustinians, equally unyielding advocates of faith, on the other, it strove for the reconciliation of faith with reason.

★   ★   ★

Mysticism

At the time (mid-fourteenth century) when the German emperor Ludwig the Bavarian was providing a refuge from which the Franciscan William of Ockham delivered his assaults on Thomism, Meister Johannes Eckhart, a Dominican of independent spirit, was preaching doctrines that savoured of pantheism (see Chapter III). Although Eckhart seems to have known no Hindu theological works, a modern Hindu has commented that Eckhart's sermons constituted 'an Upanishad of Europe'.[16][17] The analogy brings vividly to mind the similarity of mysticism in all parts of the world, but Eckhart's mysticism was rooted in the Augustinian-Neoplatonic philosophy of the West, in a soil that knew more of Jewish and Muslim than of Hindu mysticism. Some of his doctrines were formally condemned upon his death.

Eckhart's disciples John Tauler and Henry Suso were also Dominicans. Less philosophical than he, they did more to spread mysticism through the Germanies. Preaching, teaching, and writing in the vernacular, Suso in particular gave Eckhart's ideas a poetic, yet practical turn that made them immensely popular, especially in the Rhineland. Doubtless the poetical trend of Suso's mysticism saved him from charges of heresy such as had plagued Meister Eckhart; in the nineteenth century Suso was beatified. The work of these German Dominicans was continued late in the fourteenth century by the 'fathers' of Flemish mysticism, Jan van Ruysbroeck and Gerhard Groot. Both men, and Groot especially, were closely connected with the Brothers of the Common Life at Deventer and gave that order its mystic flavour. Their direct influence on systematic theology was slight, however, except as illustrating the reaction against the rigid Scholasticism of the day.

Mysticism would seem to be rare among scientists, yet one outstanding mystic of the fifteenth century was found among them. Trained at Deventer, Nicholas of Cusa (1401–64) became an ecclesiastical administrator, a reformer during the Conciliar Movement, a Scholastic logician, and a cardinal. Although he attained an enviable reputation in mathematics and other sciences (see Chapter XIII), he was also a Platonic mystic. His loyalty to Scholasticism and mysticism at the same time illustrates the prevailing dilemma of scholarly churchmen of the late Middle Ages. He escaped from the dilemma through his doctrine of intuitive faith. Denying the validity of human reason as a solvent of theological problems, he went so far as to maintain in his *Learned Ignorance* (*De Docta Ignorantia*, 1439–40) that all human knowledge is mere conjecture and that man is wisest who most readily acknowledges his ignorance. This line of reasoning may well lead directly to scepticism or agnosticism, but it led Cusa to a mystical concept of the Divine, which he set forth particularly in *De Visione Dei* (1453). Only by speculative contemplation and intuitive cognition, he held, can one attain God, Who is infinite, in Whom opposites like maxima and minima coincide, and Who is the sum-total of everything. Although these ideas in turn laid Cusa open to the charge of pantheism, he managed to avoid the accusation of heresy. Until his death he served the papacy faithfully.

*   *   *

The Platonic Revival

During Cusa's lifetime the Platonic abstractionists grew in numbers and influence, reinforced by the humanist revival of Plato. In the Middle Ages Plato's writings, save portions of the *Timaeus* in Latin, were unread in the West. Platonism in its modified, Neoplatonic form, however, had exercised a powerful influence on early medieval theology, especially through Augustine's works. During the centuries of triumphant Aristotelian Scholasticism after Thomas, Neoplatonism persisted vigorously only among mystics such as Eckhart and his disciples, and weakly in a few learned circles where the works of medieval Neoplatonists were studied. Petrarch possessed some of Plato's works but could not read them in the original Greek. Contenting himself with lauding Plato highly, he devoted serious study almost exclusively to the Latin classics. Boccaccio likewise lauded Plato, along with other Greek writers, but made no significant study of Platonism. To both of these fathers of Italian humanism, Plato was little more than a fellow-fighter in the feud with the deadening logic of Scholasticism. Nicholas of Cusa's Neoplatonic strain was tempered by Scholastic logic and given a humanist's touch by his schooling at Deventer.

Neoplatonism might perhaps have disappeared entirely into vague mystic abstractions had it not been for the revival of Plato in the 'Greek Renaissance'. At the end of the fourteenth century the Greek scholar Chrysoloras lectured upon Greek literature and translated some of it into Latin at Florence and other north Italian towns, and Plato's works were prominent in his repertoire. Early in the fifteenth century, one of Chrysoloras' Florentine disciples, Leonardo Bruni, translated several Greek writings including several of Plato's *Dialogues*. A Greek émigré, John Argyropoulos, added to the number of available translations late in the century. Thus Plato's philosophic ideas became known to Westerners at first hand.

Moreover, numerous second-hand interpretations of Plato were made available by fifteenth-century Byzantine émigrés. Notable among them were Gemistos Plethon and his disciple Bessarion, both members of the Byzantine embassy to the Council of Florence of 1439 (see Chapter III). These two scholars made a favourable impression on Cosimo de' Medici; Bessarion remained in Italy, eventually becoming a cardinal in the Roman church. To Italians the two men's knowledge of Greek philosophy was very impressive indeed. Plethon, who had written learned works on both of the great Greek philosophers, leaned strongly toward Platonism, even Neoplatonism. Bessarion was more moderate. Having translated Aristotle's *Metaphysics* into Latin, he endeavoured to mediate between the sometimes unphilosophically violent protagonists of Aristotle and of Plato. When, however, one of the radical Aristotelians, George of Trebizond, vilified both Plato and Plethon, Bessarion wrote a treatise condeming George in turn (*In Calumniatorem Platonis*). The preference for Plato over Aristotle on the part of Plethon and Bessarion seems, in a century when the adherents of Platonism, Aristotelianism, and nominalism were vying for domination, to have turned the intellectual tide in favour of Platonism in Florence and other Italian centres.

Although Bessarion deserted Greek Orthodox Catholicism, Plethon devoted himself for a time to the creation of a system of Neoplatonic theology that he hoped would reinvigorate the Byzantine church and society. In this role he became the rallying point for Greek as well as Italian Platonists in their attacks on Aristotelianism. Aristotle found vigorous defenders not only in George of Trebizond but also in Theodore of Gaza and Gennadios, the first Turkish-appointed patriarch of the Greek Orthodox Church. The feud raged throughout the latter half of the fifteenth century, interrelated with the ill-fated programme of union of the two churches (see Chapter III). Plato, Plethon, and union became confused with one another, for Platonists generally supported union. Platonist Plethon, on the one hand, was excommunicated by Aristotelian Patriarch Gennadios, while, on the other, Aristotelian

George of Trebizond was dismissed from his papal secretaryship because of his violent anti-Platonic propaganda.

Some humanists made a genuine effort to reconcile Platonism and Christianity. Bessarion, after his conversion to Roman Catholicism and his promotion to the cardinalate, emphasized the Christian implications of Platonism. In contrast, Marsilio Ficino (1433–99) carried doubt of revelation so far as to become orthodox in his Platonism. He was interested, among other things, in finding a solution of the problem of the Christian scholar who loved the pagan classics. All religions, he thought, could be reconciled. Encouraged spiritually and subsidized financially by Cosimo de' Medici to translate Plato, he became secretary of the *de luxe* Platonic Academy of Florence.

Under the leadership of Ficino the Academy gave Platonism its greatest vogue in Italy. Immersed in the labours of translating and commenting on Plato and the third-century Neoplatonist Plotinus, Ficino tended to become a worshipful admirer of the great pagan philosopher. Plato became for him a saint whose pronouncements were no less important than the scriptures. His bust of Plato was treated like a holy image, with candles and other ceremonials. He developed the themes of Platonic love and of the contemplative life by which the spirit can eventually attain oneness with God. The immortality of the soul became the central idea of his philosophic synthesis.

Eventually Ficino summarized his blend of Platonism and Christianity in a treatise with the revealing title *Theologia Platonica*. It was a medley of mystical abstractions in which the Renaissance emphasis on the dignity of man served as an underlying theme. This philosophy satisfied the cosmopolitans of the Platonic Academy; it was intelligent and at the same time orthodox, for Ficino was careful not to push his views too far. An individualist such as Pico della Mirandola, another leading figure in the Neoplatonic movement, might stray into the realm of pantheistic, Judaistic, or Islamic speculation (see below), but Ficino and most of the Academists kept clear of heresy. They covered their deviations from strict orthodoxy, such as the pantheistic concept of God and His relation to the soul, with abstract pronouncements, rhetorical embellishments, and tactful compromises. Reconverted in middle life, Ficino took priestly orders and, when he died, he believed that he had reconciled Platonism and Christianity both spiritually and practically, and many poets and humanists of his time agreed with him.

*   *   *

Stoicism and Epicureanism in Renaissance Italy

The intellectual climate of the Renaissance, which, especially in Italy, was so favourable to the revival of Platonism, was unfavourable to Stoicism. The stern ideals of self-control and uncompromising virtue for which the Stoics stood were suited only to the sturdiest ascetic souls. Had it not been for the Petrarchian cult of Cicero, Stoicism might have had no vogue at all in Renaissance Italy. Petrarch was familiar also with Seneca's letters, which presented a form of Stoicism more in keeping with Petrarch's Christian philosophy than did Cicero's works. Furthermore, Petrarch's humanism rested on a substratum of medieval asceticism, which in his *Secretum* appeared as a Stoic code of virtue, tempered by Ciceronian rationalism. In his literary masterpieces he solved the dilemma of the semi-fictitious Laura as body and soul by resort to a Ciceronian compromise, rejecting Augustine's extreme asceticism in favour of Stoic self-restraint.

In the fifteenth century, Lorenzo Valla's *De Voluptate et Vero Bono* focused attention on both Epicureanism and Stoicism in a spectacular fashion. Epicurean ideals had been anathema throughout the Middle Ages. A philosophy which taught that the external world was only a fortuitous interplay of void and atoms and that pleasure, no matter how simple and restrained, was the highest good was bound to appear heretical to those who held the Neoplatonic ideal of the plenitude of God and shared the Christian eschatology. Conservative clergymen condemned as atheists those who denied the resurrection of the body or quoted Epicurus and Lucretius to justify living solely for enjoyment. Valla was careful to provide his book with an outward orthodoxy but presented Epicurean ethics in a favourable light. Using the literary device of the dialogue, he presented a defence of Epicureanism by Antonio Beccadelli (author of a series of pornographic Latin epigrams), a defence of Stoicism by Leonardo Bruni, and a reconciliation of Christianity and Greek philosophy by Niccolo de' Niccoli. Since God had created human nature, the book argued, natural desires must be good; therefore the instinctive quest for pleasure should be satisfied; chastity was no virtue; courtesans were better for mankind than nuns.

Along with Beccadelli, Valla and his book were condemned. Nevertheless, during the pontificate of Nicholas V he was made papal secretary, worked as a translator in the Vatican Library, and died (1457) as a respectable canon of the Lateran Church. Similarly amazing was the career of the Florentine humanist Carlo Marsuppini (1399–1453), whose admiration for Classical antiquity led him to reject Christianity and to refuse the last sacrament but who, nevertheless, had served as a papal secretary and was buried magnificently in the Church of Santa Croce. Like Valla, many humanists of the Italian upper classes seem to have sought a pleasure-loving life. Yet few traces of systematic hedonism appear in humanistic writings before the sixteenth century, and the scientific implications of Epicurean atomism received no significant attention until the seventeenth century (see Chapter XIV).

★   ★   ★

The Attack on Aristotelianism

Hard and fast classification of the humanists into philosophical schools is difficult because of both their intense individualism and the wide range of Renaissance thought. The dilettantism of the humanist mentality is perhaps best exemplified in Pico della Mirandola. A wealthy nobleman, widely travelled, he could afford to be eclectic in his interests and ideologies. He studied sympathetically and unsystematically several different philosophies— Christian, Classical, Muslim, and Jewish—appropriating from each whatever he considered worth-while. He found some good even in Scholasticism, to which most humanists from Petrarch onward were hostile, thus providing a striking example of the searcher for compromise between rational scepticism and orthodox tradition. Tolerant of many ideas he had learned about from both Scholastic works and the writings of Jews and Muslims, he attempted to reconcile them with one another as well as with both Platonism and Aristotelianism. He published a list of nine hundred theses, among which some were dangerous, such as that the dogma of eternal punishment was false because inconsistent with the dignity of man and the goodness of God, and he offered to defend them against all comers at his own expense. In the end he retracted those theses which smacked of heresy, and Pope Alexander VI forgave him. A firm believer in the limitless potentialities of mankind and in the inherent power of human mentality, Pico was nevertheless modest about his own accomplishments and generous to others. Having dedicated his fortune to the indigent, he ended his career at thirty-one as a devout Roman Catholic ascetic, a follower of the fervent reformer Savonarola. Such a man cannot easily be classified as Platonist, nominalist, Stoic, Epicurean, Scholastic, or orthodox.

Despite the diversity in their ranks, humanists exhibited a certain unity in their general disapproval of the formal syllogistic logic of the Schoolmen. In fifteenth-century Italy Valla made an effort to simplify and humanize it, and in the sixteenth century the Spanish-born Juan Luis Vives and the Frenchman Petrus Ramus in his *Aristotelicae Animadversiones* were to insist upon the perniciousness of its errors, particularly its indifference whether major premises were consistent with reality so long as the resulting conclusions were logically derived from it. Humanists also objected to the otherworldliness of Scholastic thought, but the common assumption that humanists were necessarily, like Petrarch, sworn enemies of Scholasticism is suspect, since there were notable exceptions to the general rule, and some of its firm critics saw real hope in its logical method even when they disapproved of its premises. In the universities Scholasticism was well entrenched although in several the division between *moderni* (Ochhamist nominalists) and *antiqui* (Thomist 'realists') was intense. The universities of Bologna and Padua were hotbeds of Scholastic conflict between Thomism and a materialistic Averroism taught by a succession of professors who prepared the way for Pomponazzi (see below). Of these Nicoletto Vernia, professor at Padua from 1468 to 1499, maintained that the truth of science was independent of the truth of theology.

The nominalist neo-Scholastics of Oxford and Paris and the mystic Neoplatonists of Florence and elsewhere may have helped dethrone

Aristotelianism, but Aristotle uncrowned continued to be revered and imitated. Some Platonists, conceding that Aristotelianism could not be destroyed, worked, like Bessarion and Pico della Mirandola, to reconcile the two Greek philosophies but with Aristotle in a minor role. Meanwhile Aristotelians, like George of Trebizond and Theodore of Gaza, vigorously defended Aristotle against Plato and wrote commentaries intended to put Aristotle back in the ascendant. Aristotle's works were, in fact, translated into Latin in both camps—by Platonist Bessarion and by Aristotelian Theodore. In 1495 the Aldine Press at Venice began the printing of a Greek edition of Aristotle. Italian scholars joined in the contest, in which, although the Aristotelians were in a minority, they had strong supporters. Among the open admirers of Aristotle were Federigo de Montefeltro, duke of Urbino, the historian Francesco Guicciardini, the physician Girolamo Cardan, and the scholar Ermolao Barbaro. The commentaries of Jacopo Zabarella (1532–89) and the attacks of humanists such as Ortensio Landi and Ramus testify to the persistent influence of Aristotelianism in the sixteenth century.

The career of Pietro Pomponazzi (1462–1525) vividly illustrates the strength of Scholasticism at the climax of the Italian Renaissance. As professor first at Padua and later at Bologna, Pomponazzi lectured on Aristotle, commenting freely on philosophical problems. Citing 'the philosopher', he used Scholastic logic to prove that the soul was not immortal. Since this position had already been condemned by a Lateran council, charges of heresy ensued. Pomponazzi defended his orthodoxy by resorting to the Averroist argument of double truth: as a Christian he accepted the doctrine of the soul's immortality even though he could not accept it philosophically. In similar fashion he denied supernatural healing (he was a trained physician) but accepted Biblical miracles. He also justified the use of edifying myths, false though they might be, as pragmatic methods of controlling man's natural waywardness. Charges and counter-charges resulted, but the professor continued to teach at Bologna for the remainder of his life, with increases in salary obtained because of flattering offers from other universities. In contradistinction, Giordano Bruno (1548–1600), with his strongly Neoplatonic ideas, was to be driven from one university to another before ending his career at the stake (see Chapter VII).

*   *   *

Ockham, Lull, Oresme, and Cusa

Despite the disputes between Aristotelians and Neoplatonists, orthodox and sceptics, ancients and moderns, realists and nominalists, Averroists and Thomists, Scholastics and humanists, and other conflicting schools of thought—and, indeed, in part because of them—notable contributions were made to the tools of philosophy during the Renaissance. The newness of William of Ockham's logical method lay not in its originality but in its stringent application of old principles to specific theological problems. Aristotelian logic, enthroned by the thirteenth-century Scholastics as a limited monarch, became a self-destroying tyrant in the ensuing period, thanks to the Ockhamists and Scotists. This trend was more pronounced in the north than in Italy, where Petrarchian humanism exerted a restraining influence on the so-called 'logic-choppers.' Duns Scotus' keenly logical synthesis of philosophical problems dealt a heavy blow, possibly not intended, to Thomism. Ockham's rigid application of logic to certain of these problems was so effective that it undermined, although it failed to destroy, the Thomist structure and led in some quarters to something akin to agnosticism. This outcome was certainly not Ockham's intention. He did not consider himself one of the *moderni*; he questioned not the doctrine so much as the method of proof of the doctrine.

The 'new logic' of Ockham's *Summa Totius Logicae* was merely the sharpening of the weapons that had been shaped by northern thinkers in the thirteenth century. Even the famous logical principle which in the eighteenth century came to be known as 'Ockham's razor' had been earlier used in one form or another by other Oxford Franciscans. In the seventeenth-century form now most commonly but not altogether accurately quoted it reads: *Entia non sunt multiplicanda praeter necessitatem* (loosely translated: *work with the fewest entities necessary*), and is now generally known as 'the law of parsimony'; avoid introducing into any explanation unnecessary hypotheses, principles, or laws. The idea of a law of parsimony, in one wording or another, was emphasized again and again in the works of Ockham.[18]

'Ockham's razor' was meant to shave off the expendable details in the Thomist compromises (which to Ockham appeared more elaborate than substantial) between essence and existence, universal and particular, real and nominal. By purging Thomism of generalizations and abstractions that to him seemed not only unproved but needless he meant to expose what he believed to be its logical barrenness. When we consider epistemology below, we shall see that for Ockham 'singular' things might have reality but the words that substitute for them in speech (i.e. generic nouns) were mere symbols; generalizations from such symbols were mere abstractions, but they led in Thomist thought, he claimed, to still more abstract abstractions. His careful analyses and definitions of grammatical terms and his clarification of the variability of the *suppositiones* (the several substitutive meanings) that the same term may have gave a new emphasis to an old semantic problem. He also clarified the understanding of *consequentiae* (antecedent-consequent relationships).[19] Faith, he argued, was an intuitive act of will, not of logic, and belief in God's attributes and moral laws must rest in the end on faith whether or not they are logically demonstrable. For Ockham this was not, as it was to be for Pomponazzi in humanistic Italy, escape by the stratagem of 'double truth'; it was rather an insistence that in theological matters, logic was insufficient and faith was a superior source of truth. He thus also contributed, and probably unintentionally, to the separation of theology from philosophy and thus to the growing secularism of his day.

The emphasis upon precision in the new logic won the support of some of those who were interested in mathematics and the natural sciences. Lull's effort to improve theological reasoning by the rigorous application of mathematical processes, including complicated diagrams, has already been mentioned; with exaggerated optimism he hoped thus to synthesize all knowledge into a verifiable unity. A century and a half later, Oresme provided another example of the inquiring mind, stressing both the importance of precise logical methods and the unity of knowledge—to the point of an Ockhamist disbelief that faith needed to be harnessed to reason. Although he translated certain of Aristotle's works into French, his logic was not Aristotelian; his concern was rather with mathematics and natural science (see Chapter XIII). His *Quodlibeta* was devoted largely to arguing that a resort to a supernatural explanation was often logically less satisfactory than a natural one.

In Nicholas of Cusa, in contrast, a mathematical mind reacted piously against Ockhamist nominalism, reverting to the fundamental aims of thirteenth-century Scholasticism, the reconciliation of reason and faith. Under the mystical influence of his training at Deventer, he made a virtue of the shortcomings of logic. Criticized by the Aristotelians, he replied by glorifying 'learned ignorance'—that is, the learned man's recognition of the inadequacy of his learning and reasoning. In his *De Docta Ignorantia* intellectual intuition, though buttressed by mathematical symbolism, took the place of formal logic.

*   *   *

Epistemology in the Fourteenth and Fifteenth Centuries

Logic may be considered a major methodological tool of the philosopher; an understanding of epistemology and ontology is among his major objectives. Epistemology includes the search for the bases of knowing, and ontology for the bases of being. Until modern times these two objectives were rarely considered separately. In Aristotle's metaphysics they were combined in a joint quest for true *knowledge* of man's *being*. This problem, which he called 'the first philosophy', was an important element of Aristotelian Scholasticism, as revealed in the conflicts of the Schoolmen over essences and universals, nominalism and realism. Aquinas relied upon both human reason or intellect and human will for the solution of the problem of the course of knowledge, thus partly tending toward a nominalist rather than a realist epistemology. His ambivalent position brought him into opposition with the strict Averroist Siger of Brabant (1235–81) and other Paris Averroists. Siger favoured the sacrifice of faith to logic as the source of knowledge, if necessary, where Aquinas subordinated logic to faith. The attitude of the church was unmistakable; it condemned Averroism (1270) and Siger (1277) and canonized Thomas (1323).

Once Averroism was driven underground, the major attack upon the Thomists' epistemology, as upon other aspects of their philosophy, came from a more orthodox quarter, the Franciscans. Duns Scotus's attack upon Thomist epistemology was for reasons exactly opposite to Siger's. Posited upon his denial of the effectiveness of reason to reinforce belief in the Christian creed, Scotus's epistemology was voluntarist rather than intellectualist. God, 'the First Being', Scotus said, is the source of all essences, but He is primarily will, beyond the understanding of man, and so man must rely for true knowledge on faith, not on reason. Scotus' followers became known as 'Duns men'; like him they attempted to place various articles of faith, as realities in the mind of God, beyond the realm of human reason. Their zeal in combating reason gave to the Duns men the reputation, and epithet, of 'Dunces'. Nevertheless, until the humanists brought a new worldliness into philosophy, the Duns men's brand of epistemology prevailed in the schools—to the disparagement of reason as a source of knowledge and to the neglect of philosophy in favour of Christian theology.

The 'modern' epistemology of William of Ockham, also a Franciscan, was a natural reaction to the extreme realism of the Scotists. Ockham revived nominalism. His brand of nominalism is called 'terminism' because of his theory that all human knowledge of universals is based on 'terms' (*termini*), which represent but are not the actual objects: Man's knowledge of universals cannot arise directly from essences or even from the individual objects; it can arise only with the semantic 'terms' that represent them. This theory of universals, grown from Classical roots, differed from the earlier extreme nominalist theory of universals as mere *flatus vocis* ('hollow sounds of the voice'). Ockham's *termini* were meaningful class-names that the mind could use systematically to formulate general propositions.

Despite his insistence on simplifying logic by shaving off expendable concepts, Ockham in fact built a complicated structure of epistemology. He did not reject the Thomist concept of the existence of universals in God's mind (the Platonic *universalia ante res*); he merely insisted upon the difference between God's universals and man's. Man could grasp the essences of things only from the things themselves (the Aristotelian *universalia in rebus*) or, more explicitly, from his names for them. Man's universals were therefore *universalia post res*; they could come only after examination of the 'singulars'. Ockham did not deny that universals existed in the plenitude of God's mind as essences before the individual things took form as existences; he contended, however, that man was able to recognize universals only in a greatly limited fashion; without Revelation he would be ignorant of those related to God, the soul, and the most important problems of ontology.

Although no sceptic himself, Ockham led directly to what has sometimes been called 'fourteenth-century scepticism'. He cast doubt upon man's ability to know any reality—least of all, abstractions like 'substance' and 'cause'. His sceptic tendencies made suspect all Scholastic thinking whether based on faith or derived from reason. As previously indicated, they penetrated the universities, notably Oxford and Paris, and successive generations of students at Paris under Buridan, Ailly, and Gerson were infected by them. Ailly doubted that man could be certain of anything beyond self. Gerson, although himself a nominalist, became troubled over the doubts and logical subtleties that were multiplying among the students of the university as a result of the application of Ockhamist methods to theology. The sceptical movement, nevertheless, developed without formal condemnation until Nicholas d'Autrecourt carried the attack on Scholasticism so far as to propound an anti-Aristotelian atomism and the belief that little was certain (though some things were probable) even in inferences derived from immediate experience and principles derived *ex terminis*. Accused of the heresy of extreme fideism, he was condemned in 1346 and recanted.[20] Ockham's brand of nominalism, however, and the *via moderna* in logic and epistemology held its own in fifteenth-century scholarly centres despite setbacks and the constant opposition of Thomists and Scotists.

The natural scientists of this period developed no particular school of epistemology. They were usually zealous exponents of the use of the human intellect in science, but where they were not Scholastics themselves, they left epistemological problems to their theological colleagues. They clung to the traditional ideas of man's ability to know himself. No significant treatise on scientific method was achieved in the fourteenth and fifteenth centuries. Scientists generally were Aristotelians and considered speculation upon Atistotelian principles superior to experiment as a way to attain knowledge. Experiment, using the hands as well as the head, was still carried on mainly by astrologers and alchemists. Most of the physicians and physicists tended to a conservative realism, believing that empirical observation had definite limits as a means of attaining knowledge and that Revelation and intuition must often be relied upon in arriving at truth. The early humanists, too, in their adoration of the Classical masters, were sometimes indifferent or even hostile to original thought and experiment.

*   *   *

Medieval Christian Ethics

Medieval ethics was in large part a heritage from Hebrew morality and Classical philosophy. The Mosaic commandments gave Christianity a ready-made code presumed to be in conformity with God's law, and Aristotelian ethics reflected the Classical emphasis on wisdom as the source of man's virtue. Aquinas organized Christian morality into an ethical system based on Aristotelian rationalism but not excluding entirely Stoic, Neoplatonic, and Augustinian teachings. In treating the regulation of vice by law, he differentiated between divine law, natural law, and human law. His emphasis on natural law was an inheritance from the Roman philosophers. Through natural law, he said, man participates in God's eternal law as a free intellectual being. God has implanted in man the knowledge of divine law and a disposition to obey it, but since man's choice is subject to the free exercise of his will, mistakes occur that must be corrected by human law.[21]

Aquinas' doctrine of the close relationship of intellect with will, and of the close co-operation of God's determining will with man's free will, was, along with other parts of Thomist doctrine, attacked by the Scotists and the Ockhamists. Duns Scotus, like Aquinas, stressed the importance of man's intellect in moral actions but, rejecting Aquinas' imputed compromises of faith with reason and remaining consistent with his voluntarism, held that moral behaviour depended more on will than on intelligence. Furthermore, since divine will is above and beyond reason, divine law is absolute in matters of morals. William of Ockham likewise argued against reason as a source of principles of morality. The questioning of the rational basis for morality pointed to unreasoning faith as the obvious alternative for orthodox Christians.

The trend of Italian humanist thought from the fourteenth century on was more inclined toward scepticism than faith. The humanistic emphasis on the dignity of man, on the importance of this world, and on the worth of the individual tended to bring speculation upon ethics down from eternal law to earthly practice. Some of the works already considered, such as Petrarch's *Secretum* and Valla's *De Voluptate*, indicated that the more puritanical pagan philosophies like Stoicism were also acceptable to some Italian humanists of the fourteenth and fifteenth centuries.

Though its prevalent climate tended to be less religious than that of the northern regions of Europe, Italy, too, had its exemplars of a mystical ethics. Under the most cynical of the Avignon popes, Italy produced and lauded Catherine of Siena, Bernardino of Siena, and Savonarola of Florence. Careers like theirs reveal deep currents of Italian spirituality that stirred the souls both of the populace and of intellectuals such as Pico della Mirandola. Unlike Catherine and Bernardino, Savonarola failed to achieve sainthood. His passionate temperament and uncompromising attitudes drove him to such extreme demands for purity in private life and sacrifice for public welfare that he alienated the conservative Florentines and induced the easy-going Borgia pope, Alexander VI, to excommunicate him. He was tortured and hanged as a heretic with two of his disciples, and their bodies were burned and thrown into the Arno. He attained sanctity only in the opinion of some of his followers in Florence and some Protestants such as Luther. Yet his violent career marks, better perhaps than those of his Sienese predecessors, how deep the currents of spirituality ran in Renaissance Italy's great worldly centres such as Florence, Siena, and Rome. Alexander VI and Savonarola exemplified the extremes—the cynical, secularist pope and the uncompromising mystic who died resisting the prevailingly secular trend.

Thus, even while scorned by some Italian humanists, the Christian bases of ethics found fervent champions. Humanists might well be the protégés of some 'tyrant', noble, or merchant prince, benefiting from the drift toward absolutism or from the emergence of capitalism. Nonetheless, the sermons of

Bernardino of Siena and Savonarola, the letters of Catherine of Siena, and several treatises of Abrogio Traversari and Giannozzo Manetti bear witness to the presence of genuine Christian ideals in high intellectual circles. Furthermore, the ethical teachings of the church prevailed among the masses of devout believers, who sometimes were at least the short-run victims of the very political and economic changes from which the middle class and nobility benefited. Savonarola's temporary sway over the people of Florence provides dramatic evidence of the strong undercurrent of Christian morality in Renaissance Italy, of the popular reaction to the humanists' outward contempt of the traditional ethical code.

In the north, mysticism exerted a curious, and sometimes contradictory, influence on ethical beliefs and practices. The mystics' personal communion and direct spiritual contact with God tended to undermine mere traditional forms and systems of ethics; it also tended to prevent the formulation of new ethical conventions. Christian mysticism, closely related to Neoplatonism,[22] emphasized contemplation rather than action, ecstatic union with God rather than rational comprehension, intuitive inspiration rather than intelligence. The leaders of German mysticism, predominantly Dominicans, were more often preachers and teachers than philosophers; their writings usually were inspired sermons or treatises unrelated to systematic thought. Meister Eckhart's works, however, reveal a collected effort to form a metaphysical synthesis. His exposition of the close union of the human soul and mind with the soul and mind of God was so metaphoric and ambiguous as to subject him to charges of pantheism. In his opinion, knowledge, though an end in itself, was inferior to love, but both were activities of the soul, to which God revealed Himself once the soul had renounced everything, including self, whereupon the soul returned to the bosom of God; the soul that had become reunited with God was above mere human moral values. It is easy to understand why this brand of mysticism might remind a modern scholar of Indian mysticism.[23]

In keeping with this persuasion, a follower of the mystical revelation could hold that the actions of a sincere Christian were subject to no controls save those of his divinely guided individual judgment. This conviction made possible the moral excesses of certain radical peripheral groups. It also laid all mystics open to charges of immoral, or at least uncontrolled, conduct. Nevertheless, oblivious to external authority, sincere Christian reformers, north and south, chose to obey God rather than men (even where the man was clothed with ecclesiastical authority). Those mystics who acted as dedicated individuals fared better than those who organized for group action or who publicly advanced their aims in formal writings. Catherine of Siena and Bernardino of Siena preached a stern morality and a drastic type of reform even to popes without incurring penalties. If Savonarola was less fortunate, it was largely because he made the mistake of acquiring political power in opposition to a pope and of writing on philosophical subjects. Mysticism was relatively safe so long as the mystic held to the fundamental spirit of individualism and maintained an unassailable standard of personal ethics.

On the materialistic front, Christianity confronted an ethical problem that ultimately proved more urgent than mysticism. In the fourteenth century the economic principles of the church remained essentially the same as in earlier centuries. The increasing secularism of Western civilization had led Aquinas to devote some of his logical ingenuity to the conflict between the Christian ideal of brotherhood and the prevailing practice of private gain. He endeavoured to solve the dilemma by a rational compromise. On the one hand, he reiterated the Aristotelian and Biblical condemnations of usury (the taking of interest), insisting that the private ownership of property was a violation of divine and natural law and that property-holding was a public trust. On the other hand, he, and later Scholastics as well, occasionally tempered their disapproval of profit and interest. For example, the ideal of 'just price' (based originally on labour costs) was allowed an alternative interpretation that was more practical and flexible; it might normally be determined by supply and demand in the market place, and only when the free market brought too high a departure from accustomed prices would it be necessary for public authority to intervene and fix prices by fiat. A specific example of this flexible standard of economic ethics can be found in Bernardino of Siena's writings (c. 1400).[24]

Nevertheless, the church's general economic attitude was one of disapproval of big commercial profit. This attitude encouraged conservative Christian businessmen to invest in land and agricultural activities, in which the ecclesiastical authorities saw less capitalistic evil. The church's own wealth set a good example, for it was largely in landed property. Contemporary economic theorists like Oresme and Gerson made no serious objections to the conservative economic principles still prevalent in Christendom (see Chapter VIII). Even in the face of increasing usury, monopolies, and other kinds of commercial profit-making, until the sixteenth century the clergy fairly consistently condemned acquisitive capitalistic enterprise as unchristian (see Chapter IX). To be sure, merchants meanwhile engaged in various kinds of subterfuge to make an 'unjust' profit or to take interest, but social pressure for a 'just' price and against interest, even if not always respected, remained quite respectable, whereas 'usury' and even mercantile wealth, even if respected, were regarded as not quite the proper thing.

NOTES TO CHAPTER VI

1. For Professor Olivier Lacombe Thomist tradition always advocated the union and harmony of the three wisdoms: philosophical, theological and mystic. Thomas and more than one of his followers actually practised in their lives their teaching on this subject. Nor did Thomas ever sacrifice metaphysical or spiritual intuition to dialectics and logic. Similar remarks should be made concerning the Indian Advaita, due allowance being, of course,

made for the essential differences between Thomism and the Advaita. Any shifts in balance occurring during the fourteenth and succeeding centuries (or earlier) should not cause us to lose sight of these valuable achievements.
The authors feel, however, that 'the text does not imply that the Thomist might not also be a mystic; it does imply that the mystic was not likely to be a philosopher'.

2. M. Hiriyanna, *Essentials of Indian Philosophy* (London, 1949), p. 85.

3. It is, however, distinguished primarily by an alternating dynamism, sometimes evolutive, sometimes involutive in direction. (O. Lacombe.)

4. From the very first the 'non-theist' Vedānta had its own methods of spiritual concentration; only later are these confused with Yoga proper. The alliance between Buddhism and the methods of Yoga—of a re-thought-out Yoga—appears, on the contrary, to be fundamental. (O. Lacombe.)

5. Professor O. Lacombe stresses the extreme delicacy which is necessary in employing the terms 'immanent' and 'transcendant' in connection with the great doctrines of the Far East. See also p. (159), n. 1.

6. Dasgupta, *op. cit.*, V, 19, says that Umāpati was the author of the *Pauskar-āgama*.

7. Professor O. Lacombe points out that the resemblances emphasized in this text between Christianity and Shivaism will be found elsewhere in the religious world of India. These, however, rarely exceed the limits of the most generalized categories distinguished by the science of religions.

8. This dating is based on the assumption that Madhva died about 1276. Jaya-tīrtha is generally given as the fifth pontiff of the sect after Madhva.

9. Dasgupta, IV, 215 and 312–13.

10. See *ibid.*, III, 399–402, and p. 119 above.

11. Chan Wing-tsit, 'The Evolution of the Confucian Concept *Jen*', *Philosophy East and West*, IV (1955), 308–16, especially 314–16.

12. Lu Hsiang-shan, quoted in Fung Yu-lan, *A History of Chinese Philosophy* (Princeton, 1953), II, 573.

13. Ch'en's *Pai-sha-tzŭ-ch'uan-chi* (Complete Work of [Ch'en] Pai-sha), quoted *ibid.* pp. 594–95.

14. The work of Thomas is not an 'ambivalent compromise' between faith and reason, Christianity and Aristotelism. Quite the contrary, to quote a now famous expression, it 'distinguishes in order to unite'. (O. Lacombe.)

15. As regards universals, Thomism occupies an original position somewhere between realism and nominalism not accurately covered by the label 'realist'. (O. Lacombe.)

16. Ananda Coomaraswamy, *The Transformation of Nature in Art* (Cambridge, Mass., 1935), p. 61.

17. Professor O. Lacombe writes on this point: 'More than one expert has been struck by the affinities between Eckhartian mysticism and certain forms of Indian mysticism. Since any form of direct historical influence is excluded, we are here faced with the deeper problem of the diversity of mystical attitudes. The univocality of the concept of mysticism is too often taken for granted. It is our opinion that while the mysticism of immanence and that of grace are closely analogous, they are also distinguished by certain essential differences. Meister Eckhart presents a difficult case in so far as his Christian faith puts him in the order of grace while certain moments and aspects of his mystical experience seem to belong rather to the order of immanence.'

18. W. N. Thorburn, 'The Myth of Ockham's Razor', *Mind, a Quarterly Review of Psychology and Philosophy*, XVII (1918), 345–53; Mayrick H. Carre, *Realists and Nominalists* (Oxford University Press, London, 1946), p. 107; A. C. Crombie, *Augustine to Galileo, the History of Science*, AD 400–1650 (London, 1952), p. 231. Ockham's own wording of the so-called razor was: '*Pluralitas non est ponenda praeter necessitatem*'.

19. Philotheus Bochner, *Medieval Logic, an Outline of Its Development from 1200 to c. 1400* (Chicago, 1952), pp. 36–44 and 54–8.

20. See Julius Rudolph Weinberg, *Nicolaus of Autrecourt, a Study in 14th Century Thought* (Princeton, 1948), pp. 4–8; G. M. Sauvage, 'Fideism', *The Catholic Encyclopedia*, VI (1909), 68–9.

21. Natural law, as understood by Thomas, is the immanent expression of the transcending divine law, incapable either of entering into conflict with the economy of salvation which culminates in the person of Christ or of leading it to its ruin. (O. Lacombe.)

22. Professor Lacombe emphasizes that the historical relationship between Christian and Neoplatonic mysticism is well known. But for the reasons indicated in previous notes (pp. 159–60, 221, and 412) such historical links do not, in the majority of cases, imply the essential identity of any two mysticisms.

23. See n. 17 and n. 22 above.

24. See Raymond de Roover, 'The Concept of the Just Price; Theory and Economic Policy', *Journal of Economic History*, XVIII (1958), 418–34.

CHAPTER VII

THEOLOGY AND METAPHYSICS
(1500–1775)

METAPHYSICAL SPECULATION WITHIN HINDUISM AND JAINISM

INDIAN thought after 1500, despite some exceptional individual contributions, did not give rise to any radical cosmological or epistemological departures. The metaphysical questions discussed were still the ones that had long bothered mankind everywhere—monism *vs.* dualism, the nature of cause, the nature of reality, the relation of man to God, and like ancient and mooted problems. The old theistic trends continued to dominate the attempts to answer them, and traditional Indian theistic speculation remained at a relatively high level until well into the seventeenth century. Then it suffered a rather sudden collapse. Among the reasons for the collapse were (1) the decline of Sanskrit as the vernacular literatures displaced it (see Chapter XI) and (2) the disruption of the traditional foundations of society as the Mogul Empire declined, rival European interests in India grew stronger, and warfare accompanied the shifts in the balance of power. During the period 1500–1775 Western influences helped to impede without otherwise modifying Indian philosophical tendencies, and on the whole Hindu philosophers seem to have been immune to Islamic ideas as well.

After 1500 the Nyāya-Vaishesika system showed little originality. Nevertheless, at least two excellent popular manuals of the system were produced —the *Tarkasamgraha* (before 1585) by Annambhatta and the *Kārikāvalī* by Vishvanātha (before 1634), each provided by the author with commentaries. Raghunātha Shiromani (c. 1477–1547), of the Nadia school of logicians, wrote probably the best commentary on Gangesha logic, and it did much to spread the Nyāya system of logic throughout India, but another commentary on Gangesha—this one by Gadādhara Bhattācārya (c. 1650), likewise of the Nadia school, who is often described as the prince of Indian schoolmen— became the standard textbook. Thus, about the time that Francis Bacon was attacking the deductive method of the European Scholastics, in India over-refinement, technical subtleties, formal perfection, and logical quibbling triumphed. The Nadia school was subsidized by Bacon's compatriots, the early British rulers of Bengal.

Of the Sānkhya system of philosophy the chief expounder after 1500 was Vijñāna Bhiksu, an independent thinker of the sixteenth century. He prepared a commentary on the *Sānkhya-sūtra* entitled the *Sānkhya-pravacana-bhāsya*, an excellent gloss on Vyāsa's commentary on the *Yoga-sūtra*, and a commentary on the *Vedānta-sūtra*, which interpreted it along theistic Sānkhya lines. In these works he attempted to harmonize the orthodox schools of Indian philosophy, maintaining that since there were precedents for each school in the Vedas and *Upanishads*, each represented only a different aspect of the same truth. He sought to harmonize the theistic with the absolutistic systems by identifying the personal God with the absolute *brahman*, and to harmonize pluralistic realism with monistic idealism by arguing that the plural elements were both non-existent and yet potential within the absolute, becoming real whem embodied in material form during the process of world development.

Vijñāna Bhiksu's views were not only in general conformity with the theistic Vedānta of Rāmānuja and Nimbārka but delineated the 'dominant view of the Purānas' and of Hindu life and religion in general. He believed in a number of apparent paradoxes:

'the reality of the universe as well as . . . its spirituality, the distinctness of the individual souls as well as . . . their being centres of the manifestation of God, moral freedom and responsibility as well as a spiritual determinism, a personal God as well as . . . impersonal reality, the ultimate spirit in which matter and pre-matter are dissolved into spirituality, . . . the superior value of knowledge as well as of love, . . . [and] the compulsoriness of moral and social duties as well as . . . their abnegation'.[1]

He insisted that although Sānkhya had originally been theistic, its later atheistic system was so rational that it sufficed to explain the universe even without Īshvara. Besides the theistic and *bhakti* elements that he injected into the Sānkhya-Yoga, he contributed several original interpretations— for example, on the reality of the connection between souls and consciousness, and on the independence of the senses in the perceptive process.

During the sixteenth and seventeenth centuries the Bhātta school of the Mīmāmsā system of philosophy popularized its method of logic. The Bhātta logical method was common to Indian reasoning generally. It consisted essentially of five steps—posing a subject for consideration, raising doubts about it, setting forth a prima-facie view, developing a correct decision, and then relating it to other relevant doctrines.[2] Among the more important works dealing with the Bhātta teachings were the sixteenth-century *Mānameyodaya* (sometimes attributed to Nārāyana Bhatta but more recently regarded as the work of two authors),[3] the seventeenth-century *Bhātta-dīpikā* by Khandadeva, and an independent manual and exposition of the system, the *Mīmāmsā-nyāya-prakāsha*, by Āpadeva, also of the seventeenth century.

During the sixteenth century, many writers popularized, expounded, refined,and defended the Advaita (monistic) system. Nrsimhāshrama Muni, though renowned among contemporaries, added little to earlier ideas. He emphasized the identity of *brahman* with the self and the illusory nature of the apparent world. One of his pupils, Dharmarāja Adhvarīndra (c. 1550), perhaps had greater influence, for his *Vedānta-paribhāsā*, a technical and systematic exposition of the Advaita system, especially of its logical and methodological aspects, became a sort of manual for later monists. He continued the growing tendency to treat *māyā* almost as if it were a real and independent substance and in so doing helped to obscure the distinction between monists and dualists.

Of a more original turn of mind was Prakāshānanda, who, in *Siddhānta-muktāvalī* and other works, re-asserted the absolute monistic position by denying that *māyā* was in any sense the real stuff of the world. He was among the first to try to explain Vedānta 'from a purely sensationalistic viewpoint of idealism', denying the objective existence of any matter. The seeming existence of material objects was nothing more, in his scheme, than perception. He preached the extreme view of the Vedānta system, conceding no objectivity whatsoever and maintaining that *māyā* (the illusory world) did not exist, that ideas had no material basis, that self was the only reality, and that there was no causation or creation.[4] Prakāshānanda gained many followers and evoked at least one outstanding commentary on his work.

One of the most prolific writers of the sixteenth century was Appaya Dīkshita (1520–92), an indefatigable and able scholar though not an original thinker. He wrote commentaries on the *Vedānta-sūtra* from varying points of view—the Shivaite, the monistic, and the qualified monistic—but he generally supported the monistic system, trying in particular to refute the dualistic position of Madhva. His *Siddhānta-lesha samgraha* was a collection of the contrasting views of various monistic authors without any attempt to harmonize them or to show his own preference. He wrote a commentary, too, on one of the main texts of the Bhāmati branch of the monists, and this work in part inspired the *Ābhoga* of Laksmīnrsimha (late-seventeenth century), one of the last significant books concerned with the Bhāmatic interpretation.

Probably the best known of the Advaita writers was the polemicist Madhusūdana Sarasvatī, who flourished somewhere between 1500 and 1650. His most important work, the *Advaita-siddhi*, attempted to refute the objections to the monistic position raised by Vyāsā-tīrtha in defence of Madhva's theistic dualism. His *Vedānta-kalpa-latikā* gave brief and often distorted summaries of other systems and contrasted them unfavourably with the monistic. He defended particularly the monistic view of emancipation (*moksha*). Despite his philosophical adherence to monism he was a confirmed promoter of *bhakti* and wrote numerous works supporting the idea of personal devotion to God.

Various writings relative to Southern Shivaism were produced after 1500. Of those in Tamil or other south Indian languages Shivajñāna Munivar's commentary (late-seventeenth century) on the works of Meykandār was perhaps the most important. Of the Shivaite works in Sanskrit the most important was the *Shivārka-mani-dīpikā* of the aforementioned Advaita scholar Appaya Dīkshita, a commentary on the early philosopher Shrīkantha. Although of value in interpreting early Shivaite thought, it was tinged by the author's greater devotion to monism.

About 1500 several prominent writers expounded the qualified monistic (Vishistādvaita) system of Rāmānuja. Shrīnivāsacārya, a pupil of Rāmānuja-dāsa, wrote a clear, simple exposition of that system, in which he upheld the Vadagalai interpretation of the nature of self-surrender to God and repudiated the doctrine of *māyā* and some other propositions of other schools. Shrīshaila Shrīnivāsa wrote many works, of which the *Virodha-nirodha* was perhaps his best philosophical treatise, refuting the arguments of the Shankarites and others; he was particularly interested in upholding *brahman* as the efficient and material cause of the world, the ultimate creator of all, and in refuting the Shankara theory of causality. Kastūri Rangācārya in his *Kāryā-dhikarana-vāda* supported the Tangalai interpretation of salvation and of self-surrender to God; against Venkatanātha's doctrine that emancipation was only temporary if attained through mere self-realization without recognition that self was a part of God, he held that such emancipation was final, although less rich in experience. Later Vishistādvaita defenders were numerous, but none was outstanding as a philosopher.

The Mādhva dualists continued for some time after 1500 as a strong and energetic group. They prepared many commentaries on their earlier literature and many ingenuous and subtle arguments in defence of their system. Perhaps their most illustrious exponent during the period was Rāmācarya, probably a late-sixteenth-century figure, who, in his *Nyāyāmrta-tarangini*, answered the refutations of the well-known monist Madhusūdana. In his attacks upon the monists Rāmācarya covered much the same ground as Vyāsa-tīrtha (see Chapter VI).

As the popularity of Krishna worship spread, the dualistic monism of Nimbārka likewise produced several able supporters. Purusottama Prasāda, who must have lived in the late-sixteenth century, wrote commentaries on most of the works of Nimbārka and Shrīnivāsa. In the *Shruty-anta-sura-druma*, a commentary on Nimbārka's *Shrī-krishna-stava*, he attacked the Shankarites, criticized Rāmānuja for believing that impure material elements were really a part of *brahman*, upbraided Madhva for insisting that the material elements of the world did not exist as potentials within *brahman*, and sustained Nimbārka's view. Since, he maintained, both the monistic and dualistic scriptures were literally true, everything must exist as potentials within *brahman*, although, in the process of creating souls and the material world out of its energy, *brahman's* true nature remained unchanged and what it produced was not identical with it.

Mādhava Mukunda in his polemical *Para-paksa-giri-vajra* covered much the same ground as Purusottama. He attacked *in toto* the monistic scheme of the Shankarites, upholding the reality of the world and the diversity within unity of God, souls, and matter. He expounded the theory of knowledge long held by the Nimivats. Perception, it ran, was of two kinds, internal and external; external perception was of five kinds, each dependent upon one of the senses, while internal perception was of two kinds, ordinary and transcendental; the perception of pleasure and pain was of the ordinary internal variety, while perception of the nature of God was of the transcendental variety; three kinds of inference were valid—from positive instances, from negative instances, and from both positive and negative instances, when both were available.

*　　*　　*

Vallabha, Chaitanya, and Their Followers

Probably the most original religious thinker of this period was Vallabha (see Chapter V), who developed the Shuddhāvaita school of thought, or pure monism. His *Tattvadīpa* with his own commentary on it (the *Prakāsha*), his *Subodhinī*, a commentary on the *Bhāgavata-purāna*, and his *Anubhāsya*, a commentary on the *Vedānta-sūtra*, were his most significant metaphysical works. Although his system was known as pure monism, he was critical of the Shankarites and their idea of *māyā*, and he found a place for a personal god who saved souls. The Supreme Being—that is, Krishna (Vishnu)—was *brahman*; He was possessed of existence (*sat*), knowledge, (*cit*), bliss (*ānanda*) and sentiment (*rasa*); He was complete, perfect, omnipresent, eternal, and personal; He was both doer and enjoyer. In play (sport) He had created the universe with its individual souls out of Himself without undergoing change, and He was thus both the efficient and the material cause of the world, its sustainer and its absorber, and it was part of Him. Hence the material world and souls were real and eternal and not *māyā* in the Shankarite sense, but they differed. The material world had only existence while the soul could feel. It could lack bliss and, because of ignorance of its true nature, suffer from egotism and the idea of possession (mine and thine). The round of rebirths, therefore, would continue until the soul realized its true nature—that the Lord was everything—after which it would be re-absorbed and would attain bliss. But re-absorption might vary in degree or manner depending upon the mode of realization. Those who attained realization through works (*karma*) and knowledge (*jñāna*) were re-absorbed at a lower level of bliss than those who attained it through devotion (*bhakti*), and the highest form of salvation was through *pushti-bhakti*, or divine grace (see Chapter V).

Vallabha, while, like most of the theistic writers, placing great stress upon *bhakti*, denied that it was intellectual in nature. He emphasized it rather as an emotion that expressed itself in a loving devotion and service which produced a sense of oneness with God. (Compare his European contemporary Luther.) Good works and individual effort were not essential to such a state of mind. In manifesting His qualities as the universe without changing Himself, the Lord, according to Vallabha, appeared as Akshara, or the Immutable Brahman, and as time, karma, and nature. Nature was defined as that which produced change. From it arose the twenty-eight long familiar principles or categories (*tattvas*), which were a further unfolding of God. They were purity, activity, inertia, soul (*purusa*), matter, cosmic intelligence, egoism, five subtle elements, five gross elements, five organs of action, five organs of knowledge, and mind (*manas*); and from these a further unfolding of the world took place. Individual souls (*jīvas*) were parts of *purusa*.

Vallabha's son Vitthalanātha (see Chapter V) expounded his father's system in his *Vidyā-mandana*. He affirmed that *avidyā*, or ignorance, which caused the bondage of the individual soul (*jīva*), was an attribute to God. In discussing the nature of the *jīvas*, he made clear how Vallabha's conception differed from that of some other theistic thinkers. Madhva had regarded *jīvas* as parts of God,[5] yet distinct from and not identical with him; Nimbārka had regarded them as different from, yet similar to, God; and Rāmānuja had believed that God held the souls within himself and by his will dominated them; but the pure monist Vallabha held that the *jīvas*, being parts of God, were one with him although certain powers and qualities which belonged to God were obscured from them by ignorance. In his *Bhakti-hetu*, in connection with his discussion of the routes to salvation Vitthalanātha set forth a doctrine of salvation by two methods that are respectively reminiscent of Catholicism and Calvinism. Some, following the *maryādā-mārga*, the route of good deeds, purity of mind, and intellectual endeavour, would ultimately obtain *bhakti* and thus salvation but only because God had so willed it, for God granted His grace with complete freedom and could not be bound or induced to grant it. Others would receive His special grace and automatically follow the *pushti-bhakti* route to salvation (*pushti-mārga*) with or without personal effort.

Another among Vallabha's numerous followers was Purusottama (born *c.* 1670 and not to be confused with Purusottama Prasāda), who was the author of many treatises. His *Prasthāna-ratnākara* discussed Vallabha's concept of *māyā* as contrasted with that of the Shankarites. According to him, *māyā* was a power of *brahman* and thus identical with *brahman*; it was also identical with *avidyā* (ignorance) and with the three categories *sattva* (purity), *rajas* (activity), and *tamas* (interia), and at the same time was their cause. In individual souls *sattva* produced attachment to pleasure and knowledge, *rajas* produced clinging and desire for action, while *tamas* produced a tendency to error, laziness, and sleep. Thus through *māyā* God manifested Himself as manifold and produced ignorance, desire, and confusion, but this manifestation was real and not an illusion, as the Shankarites held. Purusottama discussed at some length also the nature and theory of knowledge. To perception, scriptural testimony, and inference as sources of knowledge he added implication (which he distinguished from inference)— for instance, that an individual is outside the house when he is not found in the house.

Chaitanya, the other great Hindu religious leader of this period (see

Chapter V), did not himself provide a new theistic system, but several of his followers produced works of theological interest. Rūpa Gosvāmī's *Bhakti-rasāmrta-sindhu* (early-sixteenth century), a particularly famous study of the subject, distinguished three stages, each with many sub-stages, of *bhakti*—the performance of the duties of a Vishnuite, the realization of natural attachment to God, and the combination of the sense of possession of God with absolute detachment from other things. *Bhakti* itself was defined as behaviour wholly and exclusively intended to please God; it was the eternal bliss of God and hence could not be created but existed eternally in the heart and could be aroused as an emotion only through the grace of God.

Jīva Gosvāmī, a nephew of Rūpa, was perhaps the most important of the Chaitanya philosophers. His *Sat-sandarbha* (late-sixteenth century) set forth an eclectic philosophy borrowed from all the previous schools. For him *brahman* was a partial manifestation of the total personality of Bhagavān, or Krishna—that is, God. Pure bliss and consciousness were the substance of God, and His other powers were its attributes. Pure consciousness was the true nature of the soul, realizable through *bhakti*, and in realizing it, the soul realized its identity with *brahman*. God manifested Himself as the presiding lord of the totality of souls, as matter, and as the controller within the soul. Through his power of *māyā* God caused different things to have an apparently independent existence, although they were actually one with Him. The material world and the individual soul were neither wholly real nor wholly unreal; they were real in an unmanifested form, just as a jug exists in a lump of clay, but in a manifested form they were a product of God's power of *māyā*. In emancipation all illusory notions about the world vanished, but the world itself remained, for it was not false; emancipation was a subjective reformation, not an objective disappearance of a false world. Jīva's thought, like that of many Vishnuites, was a form of monistic-dualism in which many contradictions were possible because God was conceived as a super-logical, transcendent Being Who could manifest Himself in all kinds of finite forms and yet remain one and identical with His own supreme and unchangeable nature. Jīva assigned to the highest form of *bhakti* six characteristics: it destroyed sin and ignorance; it created happiness through love and friendship; it brought such joy that it left no desire for emancipation; it could be attained only by the grace of God; its joys were superior to those of emancipation through *brahma*-knowledge; and it overwhelmed God so that He was drawn into the service of His devotees.

Another Chaitanya philosopher, Baladeva Vidyābhūsana (still alive in 1764), wrote the *Govinda-bhāsya*, probably the only significant Chaitanya commentary on the *Vedānta-sūtra*. Its train of thought was somewhat different from that of Jīva Gosvāmī: God was everything and controlled everything; yet souls and matter were distinct from Him, although part of Him and completely dependent on Him; the ultimate end of man was to obtain eternal bliss by attaining true knowledge of God, which could be attained only through true knowledge of self, which could be achieved only by the grace of God through *bhakti*; *bhakti* was a species of knowledge by which one turned to God without any ulterior motive, and its practice bound God to the devotee. The soul's ignorance and bondage were more real to Baladeva than to Jīva; in emancipation their destruction was real and the emancipated soul retained its separate individuality. In another work Baladeva attacked the Shankarites' doctrine of absolute monism.

★   ★   ★

Jain Religious Thought

Between 1300 and 1800 the Jains, although a small group, produced a number of active writers. While they added little to earlier Jain doctrine, several of them contributed to the Jain system of logic. Gunaratna (c. 1363–c. 1439) produced a critique of the Nyāya system of logic. Dharma-bhūsana's *Nyāya-dipika* (c. 1600), after taking up the general characteristics of valid knowledge, discussed perception and indirect knowledge, including in the latter category knowledge derived by recollection, recognition, argumentation, inference, and tradition. Yashovijaya Ganī (1608–1688) elaborated Jain logic and dealt with such theological and philosophical questions as the soul, emancipation, substance, time and space, and the nature of knowledge. Having studied at the Brahman schools of logic in Benares, he wrote a detailed criticism of the Mithilā and Nadia logic taught there. Jainism thus continued to assert its own independent tradition.

METAPHYSICAL SPECULATION IN CHINA[6]

In China the dynamic thought of the sixteenth century was dominated by the Idealist interpretation of Neo-Confucianism, although the official schools, the examination system, and the greater part of the scholars and officials still adhered to the Rationalistic interpretation.

Chan Jo-shui (1466–1560), a student and fellow-provincial of Ch'en Hsien-chang (see Chapter VI), founded a new branch of the Idealistic school known as the Chiang-men branch. In his *Explanation of the Diagram of the Mind and of Nature (Hsin-hsing t'u-shuo)*, he maintained that the mind embraced, permeated, and went beyond heaven, earth, and all other things; that nothing was internal or external for the mind; and that those who considered heaven, earth, and other things outside the mind reduced it to something extremely petty. He seems, however, not to have meant to contend that the external world was only a mirage created by the mind; he criticized his contemporary Wang Yang-ming (see below) for teaching that the investigation of things should take place in the mind and insisted that things themselves should be investigated.

For all that, Wang Yang-ming (1472–1529), also known as Wang Shou-

jen), was the towering thinker of the Ming period. With him the Idealistic
school reached its apogee. He was not only a scholar, teacher, and philosopher
but also a successful military leader and statesman. He received the customary
training of the Rationalistic school, at one time making himself ill by an
almost uninterrupted seven-day investigation of the bamboo in an effort to
comprehend its *li*. He also studied both Buddhism and Taoism. In 1508,
while in temporary disgrace at a frontier post for having opposed a powerful
court eunuch, he experienced enlightenment and realized that 'the task of
"investigating things" has to do only with investigating one's own body and
mind'.7

Wang's ideas were fundamentally similar to those of the earlier Idealists,
but he presented them more fully and clearly and added various new concepts.
He began with the basic Idealist premise that principle (*li*) and mind (*hsin*)
were the same. Along with all Neo-Confucians, he believed that the great
principle, or supreme ultimate, was to be found in all things, was their unifying bond, and in fact made them one. He further insisted, with other Idealists,
that principle and nature were the same as mind and feelings, that all things
were therefore to be found within the human mind, and that moral perfection
and complete knowledge thus were potentials within the mind. In addition
Wang emphasized *jen*, a sense of unity with and love of all things, which
made sages able to live in harmony with the world, 'rectify affairs', and follow
the *tao*. All men had this virtue buried deep within their minds or original
natures. The recognition and expression of it Wang called 'the extension of
intuitive knowledge'. Intuitive knowledge—conscience, the inner light of
the mind, the sense of right and wrong—would inevitably produce the right
impulse or answer, if not inhibited, since it was the response of the perfect,
all-knowing, or 'original mind.'

The unique feature of Wang's doctrine was that the 'extension of intuitive
knowledge' was inseparable from practice. He considered the study of one's
own mind through introspective meditation and the elimination of selfishness
and desire as necessary to the 'extension of intuitive knowledge' but not
enough; intuitive knowledge must be put into actual practice, removing any
obstacles which prevented its constant application. Knowledge which was
not put into practice was in fact not knowledge at all, but practice would
make clearer and extend intuitive knowledge, while meditation and flight
from the ordinary affairs of life, as taught by the Buddhists and Taoists,
would not. 'Investigation of things' (*ko-wu*) Wang interpreted to mean
'rectification of affairs' (righting wrongs, correcting errors, etc.). Morality
was no mere metaphysical concept to him; it extended to everyday action.
Filial piety, brotherly love, and other virtues could be understood only
through practice.

While Wang believed intuitive knowledge to be the best guide of all
conduct, he held that it could not be forced. Extremes in either direction
(either too much selfishness or too much effort to eliminate selfishness) were

equally sources of evil and would obscure or inhibit intuitive knowledge; for such knowledge was the initial heaven-inspired response of the perfect principle of the mind and would be blurred or obscured by ratiocination. The instantaneous alarm and desire to save a child about to fall into a well was an example of intuitive knowledge at work, illustrative of the *jen* of all men. The perfecting of mankind consisted of extending *jen* to the utmost. In a discussion of the classic *Great Learning*, Wang elaborated his ideas:

'The great man is an all-pervading unity with Heaven, Earth, and all things. He regards all beneath Heaven as one family, and the Middle Kingdom as one man. Those who emphasize the distinction of bodily shapes, and thus make cleavage between the self and others, are the small men. The reason that the great man is able to be one with Heaven, Earth, and all things, is not that he is thus for some purpose, but because the *jen* of his mind is naturally so and thus makes possible this union. . . . The mind of the small man is exactly the same, only he himself makes it small.'[8]

Wang perceived in the *Great Learning* 'three major cords' and 'eight minor wires'. The major cords were: to 'manifest the illustrious virtue', to 'love people', and to 'rest in the highest good'. The minor wires were: to extend knowledge, to investigate things (or to rectify affairs), to be sincere in thought, to rectify the mind, to cultivate the self, to regulate the family, to order the state, and to foster peace—all of which were but aspects of the extension of intuitive knowledge. Like other Confucians Wang emphasized that gradations of *jen* were necessary in order to distinguish the more important from the less important. Beginning with parents it should extend outward in decreasing intensity to other relatives, other men, animals, plants, and inanimate things.[9] The obvious equalitarian implications of this ethical doctrine will be considered when we take up the history of political thought (Chapter IX).

In 1514 Wang began to teach his doctrine of 'the extension of intuitive knowledge' exclusively. Among his more important writings were the *Ch'uan-hsi lu* (*Record of Instruction*), *Ta hsüeh wen* (*Questions on the Great Learning*), a preface to the *Complete Works* of Lu Hsiang-shan, and the *Chu-tzu wan-nien ting-lun* (*Doctrine Reached by Master Chu [Hsi] in Later Life*), in which he tried to prove that Chu Hsi ultimately adopted the Idealistic position. He attracted a throng of followers, and after his death his disciples spread his doctrine far and wide. They were especially strong in south China.

The upsurge of the Idealistic school, and especially Wang's argument that Chi Hsi had really become an Idealist, provoked the Rationalistic school to reply. Two writers, Lo Ch'in-shun (1465–1547) in *K'un chih chi* (*Remarks Reached after Hard Study*) and Ch'en Chien (1497–1567) in *Hsüeh-p'ou t'ung-pien* (*Analysis of the Prejudices of Philosophy*), attempted to refute Wang's contentions about Chu Hsi, insisted that mind and principle were not the same thing, and charged the Idealists with preaching Ch'an Buddhist doctrines. Despite these arguments and a certain amount of official opposition, the Idealistic school continued to expand.

Wang's followers were known as the Yao-chiang school, after Wang's native place in Chekiang province. Ch'ien Te-hung (1496–1574) was probably the most prominent of them and certainly the most faithful to Wang's teachings. He was the compiler of Wang's dialogues, or *Record of Instruction*. He emphasized the inseparability of knowledge and practice, thus promoting the most dynamic aspects of the Idealist's teaching. Another prominent disciple was Wang Ken (1483–1540). Some of his ideas and practices on meditation were so close to Ch'anism that he was charged with having gone over to Buddhism, but he seems to have remained essentially true to Wang Yang-ming's emphasis on practice and in some respects foreshadowed the practical Confucians of the next century. He gave special attention to the perfecting of one's own conduct, which, once correct, would inevitably, he thought, promote correction of the world about. His political philosophy will be mentioned in Chapter IX.

Some of Wang Yang-ming's followers went to great lengths in advocating the spontaneous following of intuitive knowledge and the dictates of the perfect mind, insisting that the learning and teachings of former scholars would only obstruct the true way (*tao*). Others displayed extreme forms of subjectivism and distinct Ch'anist tendencies. Lo Nien-an (1504–64) advocated 'having no desire'. Nieh Hsuang-chiang (1487–1563) taught 'retiring into silence'. Wang Chi (1498–1583), an especially popular teacher, preached 'absence of thought' and was to have great influence in the late-sixteenth century. In the search for spontaneity he opposed any effort to discipline or organize the thinking process, insisting that the mind was devoid of both good and evil and hence that thinking, knowledge, and things were equally devoid of good and evil; evil arose only from interference with the spontaneous flow of thought and action by creating consciousness and attachment to existence. Having adopted the Buddhist ideas of Nirvana and transmigration, he held that the spontaneous way would bring freedom from the endless wheel of life and death. For him no essential difference separated Confucianism, Buddhism, and Taoism.

None of Wang Yang-ming's immediate followers was sufficiently intoxicated by the strong wine of intuitive knowledge to carry it to irresponsible extremes. Wang Chi and some others, however, disregarding the master's warning that almost no great men had spontaneously acquired intuitive knowledge, tended to overlook his restraining doctrine that it must be acquired, tested, and expanded through practice. A second generation of Idealists, which flourished around 1600, and especially the followers of Wang Chi and Wang Ken, carried the doctrine of spontaneity to a drastic conclusion. They denounced traditional practices, beliefs, and authority; and right or wrong, good or bad, became relative matters for them. They simultaneously advocated both non-active meditation and activism in following one's impulses, becoming incapable of decisive action or consistent policy in affairs of state. They promoted the merging of Confucianism, Buddhism, and Taoism, and mingled freely with Buddhist and Taoist monks. For these free-thinkers friendship and conviviality as well as eccentricities became supreme virtues, and many lived the lives of knight-errants.

Li Chih (1527–1602) was representative of these free-thinking, individualistic relativists. Despite his respect for Wang Yang-ming, he rejected the authority of the Confucian classics and adopted the garb and habits of a wandering Buddhist monk. As a lecturer he attracted a huge following by teaching that everybody was a potential sage and that even the common man had inborn moral faculties which he could use to become a perfect personality or a Buddha. Long before Adam Smith he upheld self-interest and profit as worthy incentives. He favoured equality of the sexes and marriage by free choice; and he praised politicians regardless of what they stood for, if they succeeded. Advocating spontaneous 'living in the present', he denounced the ancient virtues of loyalty, chastity, filial piety, and righteousness as artificial and foreign to the nature of the 'inner essence'. Accused of heresy, he committed suicide rather than face trial at Peking.[10]

Under Buddhist slogans of 'quiet sitting' and 'seeing one's own mind', many of the later Idealists degenerated. They became 'loafers, irresponsible talkers, and shameless seekers after fame and profit' who had no higher aspirations than 'women, money and wine'.[11] They undoubtedly contributed indirectly to, or at any rate reflected, the decline of the Ming dynasty and its inability to act decisively when faced with the rising threat of the Manchus.

* * *

The Tung-lin Movement

The moral irresponsibility of the later Idealists was combated by the Rationalists and by the Tung-lin movement (see Chapter V), a political and philosophical reaction to the laxity in government and society growing out of the increasing relativism of the Idealists. The Tung-lin disciples—the 'Righteous Circles'—insisted upon return to rigorous traditional training in morality and self-discipline and to social and political responsibility; most of them were politically active; some of them had been connected with the official censorate but had found it too subservient and had left it. Emphasizing virtue rather than enlightenment, they rejected the notion that human nature was neither good nor bad; in their ethics it was basically good but could not rely on its 'inner essence' alone and must be constantly buttressed by conscious moral exertion. They accepted the Idealist phrase 'living in the present' but interpreted it to imply moral effort, the practice of traditional virtues, and insistence on principle. They rejected all compromise with Buddhism and Taoism.

Beyond generally subscribing to these practical precepts, the Tung-lin thinkers lacked philosophical unity. Most of them attempted some sort of

P*

fusion of the views of Chi Hsi and Wang Yang-ming. Of these who leaned more in Wang's direction the outstanding ones where Ch'ien I-pen (1547–1617) and Sun Chen-hsing (1565–1636). They rejected Chi Hsi's distinction between ideal human nature (*li*) and material human nature (*li* plus *ch'i*) and accepted Wang's view that there was but one concrete human nature, which was synonymous with mind. They contended, however, that it required conscious cultivation through strict moral discipline.

Ku Hsien-ch'eng (1550–1612), the leader of the group, leaned more to the side of Chu Hsi. While he emphasized the goodness of human nature and favoured Wang's idea of realizing inborn knowledge, he also placed emphasis upon the necessity of investigating things, which he interpreted to include the moral ideas of the classics. He insisted that both Wang's 'extension of knowledge' and Chu's 'investigation of things' required a rigorous morality and practical activity, and amounted to much the same thing.

Kao P'an-lung (1562–1626) was the most original thinker in the Tung-lin movement. For him 'enlightenment' was essential to moral perfection but was of little value without self-discipline. Kao considered himself a follower of Chu Hsi, but he insisted that *li* and *ch'i* were really one and that *ch'i*, as cosmic matter, provided the common unity of all things. Ch'i was 'ultimate reality', 'the complete substance, to whose nature *li* belonged as immanent laws and forms'.[12] While advocating 'quiescence' and 'sitting quietly', Kao, like Ku, held them up as parts of a programme of practical rigorously moral activity.

Liu Tsung-chou (1578–1645) was a friend of Kao but not a regular member of the Tung-lin group, coming rather from the Rationalist school. He was critical of the contemporary trend of the Idealistic school, but many of his doctrines reflected the best of the Idealistic tradition, He developed a theory of the oneness of *ch'i* and *li* similar to that of Kao, giving primacy to *ch'i*.

★　　　★　　　★

Confucian Opponents of the Manchus

The reaction against the relativism of the later Idealists and the demands for moral uprightness and reforms in political practice did not save the Ming dynasty. China's collapse before the onslaught of the barbarian Manchus produced, after 1644, among a group of critical and pragmatic scholars an earnest endeavour to discover the reasons for the catastrophe that had befallen their country. These men came from no one group or school, and most of them mixed elements of Idealism and Rationalism to form their own eclectic philosophies. They organized no unified philosophic movement, and none of them made significant contributions to philosophy. They were generally united, however, in denouncing the moral laxity and ethical relativism of the later Idealists, the majority attacking also the speculative, metaphysical, and deductive nature of Sung and Ming philosophy. They insisted that Neo-Confucianism, by taking over Buddhist and Taoist ideas, had corrupted the true Confucian doctrine and, by failing to concentrate on practical, down-to-earth moral and political problems, had brought on the disaster. Some of them may have been influenced by the scientific technique of the Jesuits and by the Jesuits' contention that Sung and Ming metaphysics were derived from Buddhism.

Most of these critical, pragmatic scholars refused to serve the Manchus. Among them was Huang Tsung-hsi (1610–95), a disciple of Liu Tsung-chou (who starved himself to death rather than work for the conquerors). Huang, too, steadfastly spurned employment under the Manchus. Although a disciple of Liu, he was an avowed Idealist; yet he advocated the active cultivation of 'native knowledge' and had little regard for meditative speculation. He critically re-evaluated Sung and Ming thought in his *Sung-Yüan hsüeh-an* and *Ming-ju hsüeh-an*, condemning its Buddhist and Taoist elements. In his study of the legitimate grounds for imperial rule he attacked autocracy in government. Supporting the monist position of the Idealists, he advocated a theory very similar to that of his teacher: *li* and *ch'i* were really one, but *ch'i* was prime. Chu Chih-yü (1600–82) was likewise interested in practical reform and denounced the Ming scholars for their empty abstractions. He ultimately settled in Japan and, as we shall soon see, had considerable influence on the development of historical studies there.

Wang Fu-chih (1619–92) was another of the critical, pragmatic group who opposed the Manchus. Attacking particularly the Idealism of Wang Yang-ming, he undertook to perpetuate the better aspects of the Rationalistic school. He elaborated the doctrine of the investigation of things in a practical way but, not wholly avoiding Buddhist idealist monism, favoured knowledge obtained through one's moral nature over that obtained through one's senses. In his *Remarks on Reading the Four Books* (*Tu Ssu-shu ta-ch'üan-shuo*), however, he developed a monistic theory of the unity of principle and matter similar to that of Kao, Lui, and Huang and very near pure materialism:

'Within the universe there are only *li* and *ch'i*. The *ch'i* is the vehicle of *li*, through which it derives its orderliness. . . . When speaking of mind, nature, Heaven, or *li*, it must in every case be on the basis of *ch'i*. If there were no *ch'i*, none of them would exist.[13]

Without *ch'i* as instrument *tao* would be impossible.

Yen Yüan (1635–1704) and his pupil Li Kung were also among the critical, pragmatic Confucians. They, too, attacked the ideas of the Sung and Ming schools as abstract, impractical, and inspired by Buddhist and Taoist doctrine, and called for a return to ancient principles. Yen's ideas were set forth in his *Preservation of Learning* (*Ts'un-hsüeh*) and *Preservation of the Nature* (*Ts'un-hsing*). These works described the ancient principles as contained in 'the three tasks', 'the six treasures', 'the six patterns of conduct', 'the six virtues', and 'the six liberal arts' of Confucius and those whom he had considered model rulers. 'The three tasks' were the rectification by the ruler of the people's virtue, his utilization of the country's resources for their benefit, and his abundant provision for their livelihood. 'The six treasures' were water, fire, metal, wood, earth, and grain. 'The six patterns of conduct' were filial piety, fraternal devotion, friendship, marital constancy, forbearance, and compassion. 'The six virtues' were wisdom, *jen*, sageness, righteousness, loyalty, and harmoniousness. And 'the six liberal arts' were rituals, music, archery, charioteering, writing, and mathematics. Yen insisted that the 'investigation of things' really meant the actual practice of the three tasks and the other ancient principles. He wanted scholars to take up some useful calling and to put their learning into everyday practice. Unhappy over poverty and the inequalities of wealth, he advocated the redistribution of land. He attacked the Rationalists' dual system of principle and matter, denied the distinction between ideal or moral nature and physical nature, and expounded a monistic system in which *li* and *ch'i* were 'amalgamated into a single continuum'. Man's nature, good and bad, was thus one. Evil resulted from 'enticement, delusion, habit and contagion',[14] but good could be cultivated by education and the practice of *jen*. In a *Commentary on the Four Books* (*Chuan-chu wen*) Li Kung (1659–1733) expanded Yen Yüan's ideas. Neither writer had a large following, however.

The critical scholar Ku Yen-wu (1613–82) practised what he preached, befriending the people and refusing to serve the Manchus. In a general way, he belonged to the Rationalists, but his opposition to metaphysical abstractions, his accentuation of the original meaning of the classics, and his insistence on verifiable statements in scholarship helped to undermine their position. He attacked the Idealists also—for engaging in abstract Buddhist talk about mind and human nature, while failing to take action against the evils that corrupted government and oppressed the people. Modern scholarship, he complained, preferred words to deeds:

'Confucius seldom spoke about "human nature", "fate", or "Heaven", but present-day scholars constantly discuss them. Confucius and Mencius constantly discussed practical questions of conduct, but present-day scholars seldom mention them. . . . In my humble opinion the Way of a sage is [in the words of Confucius] to be "widely versed in learning" and "in one's personal conduct to have a sense of moral obligation." . . . One should feel deeply ashamed if he does nothing to alleviate the poverty of the common people'.[15]

The critical scholars—in particular, Ku and a younger contemporary, Yen Jo-ch'ü (1636–1704)—were the fathers of a new school of empirical research, which, becoming clearly differentiated in the eighteenth century, was known as the School of Han Learning. An omnivorous student, Ku observed the most critical canons of scholarship. His writings on phonetics and geography expanded their use as tools for historical and philological research. Yen Jo-ch'ü in an *Inquiry into the Authenticity of the* CLASSIC OF HISTORY *in Ancient Character*s (*Shang-shu ku-wen shu-cheng*) demonstrated that many sections of the *Classic of History* used by all Neo-Confucians were spurious. He stimulated a return to the texts of the classics as known in Han times and their critical study and revaluation (see below).

The more traditional-minded scholars remained either Rationalists or Idealists and have been generally referred to as the Sung school. Most of this school were Rationalist, used the text of the classics as fixed by Chu Hsi, and followed his commentaries and interpretations. They remained the orthodox official school, promoted by the government and the examination system. Many of the more able Rationalists, such as Chu Shih (1665–1736), not surprisingly became high officials. Li Fu (1675–1750) was one of the few Idealists in the Sung school worthy of note. The school produced a number of fair scholars and able officials, but it was uninspired and uncreative.

* * *

Han Learning and Moral Law

The School of Han Learning received its name because it considered the classical texts and commentaries of the Han period (206 BC–AD 9) to be the most authentic. It held that the texts, commentaries, and philosophical points of view of the Sung and Ming periods had been corrupted by Chu Hsi and his followers, and it was suspicious also of texts that claimed to be earlier than the Han dynasty.

Han Learning was basically practical and empirical in its point of view. It insisted on studying the texts of the Han period afresh and on using them as a practical guide to moral and political action, and not in a metaphysical fashion. Its scholars, therefore, worked hard to re-establish the original meaning of the classics and in the process developed a scientific methodology for the study and analysis of texts. Hence the movement produced a large number of distinguished scholars in the fields of textual criticism, philology, classical commentary, history and historical criticism, historical geography, and Confucian ethical and political theory. They denounced what they considered the bias and subjectivism of Sung and Ming scholars and attempted to reappraise the course of Chinese civilization from more authentic documentation.

Only a small number of the scholars of the Han Learning were interested in metaphysics. Among this number was Tai Chen (1724–77, also known as Tai Tung-yüan), the outstanding philosopher of the school. His particular brand of philosophy is often called the Tao-hsüeh, or Moral Law School, because of the importance of the term *tao* in it. Tai, as a critical and empirical scholar, was interested in all aspects of learning including mathematics, astronomy, geography, and technology, and he asked much the same kind of questions as those that disturbed his contemporaries of the European Enlightenment. He wrote or edited about fifty works, the most important for philosophy being *The Nature of Goodness* (*Yüan shan*) and the *General Survey of the Meaning of Mencius* (*Meng-tzu tzu-i shu-cheng*).

Tai was critical of both Chu Hsi and Wang Yang-ming. He advanced an essentially materialistic theory, which, although similar to that of Wang Fu-chih and other monists, went far beyond them in scope and organization. In his system *ch'i*, or substance, was the sole constituent of all things. He meant, not that things did not have *li*, but that *li* was 'simply the *manner* in which their substance is arranged and organized'.[16] Denying the separate existence of body and soul, he attacked the whole concept of *li* as presented by the Sung and Ming thinkers:

'Since the Sung dynasty there has grown up the habit of regarding *li* as if it were a veritable object, received from Heaven and present in the mind. The result is that those who are able to do so regard their mere opinions as being *li*. . . . Where in the six classics or in the books of Confucius or Mencius is it stated that *li* is such an external object, existing apart from man's feelings and desires, and designed sternly to repress them ?'[17]

For Tai *li* was not a part of a cosmic absolute implanted by heaven in the minds of men but a principle inherent in the *ch'i*, or the substance of things. It was not something apart from the concrete material world; it did not transcend things but was immanent in them. *Li* was the internal structure or system of a thing—in other words, its governing principle. It could be discovered and understood, not by introspective meditation or sudden enlightenment, but only by 'wide learning, careful investigation, exact thinking, clear reasoning and sincere conduct'.[18] Tai's views were essentially nominalistic as opposed to the realistic position of the earlier Neo-Confucians. Interestingly enough, although he was recognized as a great scholar and employed and favoured by the emperor, he was never able to pass the highest civil-service examination controlled by the orthodox Realistic school.

For Tai's Moral Law school, *tao* was the activity of nature; it was 'movement' and 'the evolutionary operations of the *ch'i*'. '*Yin* and *yang* and the five elements' constituted its true substance. *Tao* was thus immanent in the *ch'i*; in the natural realm it resulted in unending production and reproduction, and in the realm of human affairs, it manifested itself in the relations among men. *Tao* (the proper way of a thing, of the universe, or of human society) was something inherent in things or institutions. It could be discovered and followed by the mind of man, but it was not a substantive entity:

'The unceasing evaluation of the universe constitutes the *tao*. Does not the alternation of the *yin* and *yang* result in production and reproduction ? . . . The process of production and reproduction is that of love (*jen*), and never occurs except according to an orderly pattern. In the orderly unfolding of this pattern we find the highest manifestations of propriety (*li*). And in the distinctions that are laid down in the course of this orderly pattern we find the highest manifestations of righteousness (*i*)'.[19]

Really significant differences between *tao* and *li* are hard to detect in Tai's system, but he seems to have wished to give prominence to *tao* because of the abuses he saw in the applications of *li*. In human affairs, he thought, one found *tao* and *li* by studying mankind, by putting oneself in the place of others and considering how one would then like to act toward oneself. Conclusions reached by this process were to be tested, for one thing, by others' opinions (for that which did not win the approval of others was but personal preference) and, for another, by history (for that which had received confirmation over many generations throughout the world was probably a true principle). Tai clearly believed that most of the principles of the human way had been known to the authors of the classics, but he seemed also to leave the road open for change.

Man's nature, Tzi thought, consisted of blood, breath, and mental faculty and was divided into three particular aspects—feelings, desires, and knowledge. Evil arose because defects in the feelings, desires, and knowledge of men created selfishness, one-sidedness, and delusion. But these defects could be overcome by improved knowledge and by socializing and sublimating the desires rather than repressing them. The desires, if properly understood and guided, could be the foundation of the virtues, which were derived from innate human tendencies and could be developed and strengthened by proper training. Selfishness might be eliminated by strengthening altruism, and delusion by study: 'The benevolent [*jen*] man, wishing to live his own life fully, helps others to live their lives to the full'. Government and society should function in a way to make possible the orderly fulfilment and expression of the desires, and thus the development of the great virtues. The *tao* for Tai, as for Confucius and Mencius, was thus 'a way of human cooperation for the good of all'.[20] In like mood, some contemporary Western thinkers were speaking of the natural order as leading, if correctly understood, to the greatest good of the greatest number.

METAPHYSICAL AND ETHICAL SPECULATION IN JAPAN

In Japan metaphysical speculation was more prevalent after 1500 than before. The earlier trend in favour of Shinto accelerated so rapidly that by the end of the eighteenth century Shinto nationalistic thought became the most dynamic intellectual movement of the country. Motoori Norinaga (see Chap. V) was perhaps the outstanding theologian of the Pure Shinto school at its prime. His views were a mixture of a stark predestinarianism with an optimistic faith. Life on earth, he taught, was a constant struggle between virtue and evil, steadily moving in the direction of the higher good and a sort of best-of-all-possible worlds. All men, however, whether good or bad, must upon death go to *yomi* (the land of the dead), which was a dark, foul, and unpleasant place. No amount of rationalizing or retribution could change this destiny, but absolute resignation to the will of the gods would bring peace of mind.

*   *   *

The Teishu School of Neo-Confucianism

Until well into the eighteenth century, however, the thought that was dominant in Japan was not Shintoism but Neo-Confucianism. Neo-Confucianism was a borrowed system, and its advocates showed no great originality, being generally content merely to restate ideas developed in China. Nonetheless it occupied the minds of most Japanese samurai intellectuals and produced a considerable body of literature, some of which unintentionally promoted Shinto nationalism. Though metaphysics appealed to the Japanese mind perhaps even less than to the Chinese, Japanese thinkers repeated the metaphysics of early Neo-Confucianism but tended to emphasize its practical, ethical, social, and authoritarian aspects. They were particularly interested in its accent on duty, loyalty, and obedience to higher authority, utilizing it to rationalize the *Bushido* code. Neo-Confucianism in Japan was also markedly dogmatic and intolerant; the official school (that is, the branch promoted by the shogunate) in particular encouraged the authorities to repress its rivals. Four main branches of Neo-Confucian thought emerged in the seventeenth century.

The Teishu school, the oldest of these four, became the official school, advocating the dualistic Rationalism of Chu Hsi. Its first great figure was Fujiwara Seikwa (1561–1619). Ieyasu, the founder of the Tokugawa shogunate, patronized him and promoted the study of Confucianism as an intellectual prop to the shogunate and as a device for taming the restless samurai. Fijuwara Seikwa began his career as a Zen priest but ultimately abandoned Buddhism for Confucianism. He was more tolerant than most later members of the Teishu school. While he denounced Christianity, he was less critical of Buddhism and was acquainted with the monistic Idealism of Wang Yang-ming. He emphasized the ideas of *jen* and *te* (virtue), maintaining that people should have compassion for one another (*jen*) and that rulers should be possessed of special virtue (*te*). He insisted that Confucianism and Shintoism were similar and identified the Confucian *jen* with the Way of the Gods (Shinto).

Hayashi Razan (1583–1657), a pupil of Fujiwara Seikwa, was not equally tolerant. As Confucian adviser to the shoguns, he became head of the official academy established at Edo in 1633, and that post thereafter was held by his descendants. He vigorously denounced other systems of thought, including the Idealistic school of Wang Yang-ming. His own thinking led him, to be sure, to insist that *li* (*ri*) and *ch'i* (*ki*) could not be separated—a position that was not very far from the Idealists' monism, but he opposed the doctrine of intuitive knowledge. Emphasizing filial piety and loyalty, he tended to identify Confucianism and Shintoism, with the argument that Shinto was loyalty to the sovereign and loyalty to the sovereign was Confucianism.

Perhaps the most interesting of the Teishu school was Kaibara Ekken (1630–1714). Though he considered himself a supporter of Chu Hsi, he seems clearly to have been influenced by seventeenth-century Chinese writers. He did not accept Chu Hsi's distinction between ideal and material human nature, believing rather that *li* and *ch'i* were one and inseparable. Although he expounded the Confucian virtues and maintained that knowledge and practice should go together, he was also loyal to Japanese institutions and opposed efforts to impose the Chinese system on Japan. His last important work, *My Great Doubt*, reveals that he was no slavish follower of any system. He showed a great concern for the happiness of the ordinary man, popularizing Confucian ideas, travelling a good deal to lecture and teach, and writing his many works in simple Japanese rather than Chinese. A work entitled *The Great Learning for Women*, written by his wife, Token, had considerable influence on the education of women, emphasizing the necessity of their obedience to men.

Kinoshita Junan (1621–98) maintained a private school in Kyoto and was the teacher of three famous Teishu figures—Amamori Hōshū (1611–1708), Arai Hakuseki (1656–1726), and Muro Kyūsō (1658–1774). Not entirely orthodox, Amamori argued for the basic unity of Confucianism, Taoism, and Buddhism, and identified the jewel, the sword, and the mirror of Shinto with the *tao* of Confucius. Arai was a rigid follower of Chu Hsi. As an important adviser of the shogun in the early-eighteenth century, he emphasized the Confucian virtues, expanded court ceremonials and etiquette, and made an effort to apply ethical principles to economic problems. Muro, who succeeded as adviser to the shogun, was less rigid in the application of the Confucian virtues and achieved better results. A staunch upholder of Chu Hsi and of the shogunate, he repeatedly laid stress upon the blessings received from parents, lords, and sages. He identified Chu Hsi's Confucianism and Shinto, insisting that the Way of the Gods was that taught by Chu Hsi.

*　　　*　　　*

The Ōyōmei School

A though the Teishu writers tended to identify Confucianism with Shinto, most of them were supporters of the shogunate, and their emphasis on loyalty helped to buttress the shogunate and foster submission to it. In contrast to the Teishu school was another of the four main branches of Japanese Neo-Confucianism, the Ōyōmei followers of Wang Yang-ming; most Ōyōmei Idealists were critical of the shogunate for not doing more than they did for the welfare of the people. Partly for that reason and partly because their doctrine was unorthodox, their teachings were often under ban, and many of them spent some time in not too onerous house-arrest at the headquarters of some feudal lord. Their criticism helped to weaken the shogunate, while a number of their ideas helped to strengthen Shinto nationalism and promote the demand for the restoration of the emperor. They wanted a government that should strengthen the state and better the lot of the people. Some of them showed an interest in Western thought. Their emphasis on intuition and self-control was similar to that of Zen Buddhism, which had earlier appealed to the warrior class, and samurai with an independent turn of mind were attracted to them.

Nakae Tōju (1608–48) was the founder of the Ōyōmei school. He accepted the characteristic Idealistic Confucian doctrine that everything existed within the heaven-bestowed mind and that man's duty was to develop, articulate, and put into practice the intuitive knowledge that existed as principle in that mind. Nakae's thought was monistic and essentially pantheistic, but at times Heaven took on for him something of the aspect of a personal god. He emphasized the idea of *jen* in human relations and argued for the basic equality of all men: 'Emperor, duke, knight and commoner are not the same socially, but in their dignity as men there is no difference at all.'[21] He became an Idealist only during the last years of his short life, but his views were carried on and given new turns by his most distinguished disciple, Kumazawa Banzan (1619–92).

Kumazawa was especially famous as a critic of the shogun's administration and, as a result, spent considerable time in exile or house-arrest. Although a practical man interested in administrative reform, he strongly supported the idea of intuitive knowledge. He argued that Confucianism and Shintoism were in origin one and the same, that in its original form Shinto was best for Japan, but that Idealistic Confucianism also had certain contributions to make. He also argued, however, that many Idealists were lacking in historical knowledge of Confucianism, that Chu Hsi's ideas did not suit the Japanese, and that Wang Yang-ming placed too much emphasis on *jen*. He likewise criticized both Buddhism and Christianity.

Among the numerous eighteenth-century Ōyōmei scholars were Miwa Shitsusai (1669–1744) and Hayashi Shihei (d. 1793). The former prepared an important edition of some of the writings of Wang Yang-ming. He also laid down a tenfold path toward the attainment of perfection: the first step was to fix one's will on perfection; the other nine comprised a sense of shame, filial piety, nourishment of the body, generosity, control of temper, self-examination, development of intuitive knowledge, carefulness in thought, word, and deed, and the golden mean. Hayashi was interested in Western learning and in order to strengthen Japan advocated opening the country to outside contacts. For him intuitive knowledge of good and evil was conscience, and to obey one's conscience was courage. Most of his books were banned, and he died in prison for his criticism of the shogun's policy.

*   *   *

The Kogakuha and the Mito School

A third school of Neo-Confucianism, the Kogakuha (the Ancient or Classical school), arose in seventeenth-century Japan. It was critical of both the Teishu and the Ōyōmei school for their departure from original Confucianism and, like China's slightly earlier critical scholars, insisted on searching the original texts of the Confucian classics for their true message. Also like some of the Chinese scholars, it preached a monistic materialism in which *ch'i* (*ki*) was the absolute substance to which *li* (*ri*) adhered as guiding principle.

Some doubt arises as to who was the founder of the Kogakuha or Classical school. Yamaga Sokō (1622–85) was the earliest of this group. A student and teacher of military tactics, he laid the philosophic foundations for the knightly code of *Bushido*. An ardent nationalist, he also insisted that Japan was the central kingdom of civilization. In presenting his version of what original Confucianism meant, he attacked the other Confucian schools so violently that he was soon in trouble with the authorities. Itō Jinsai (1627–1705) is perhaps more justly considered a founder of the Classical school. Although, exceptionally enough, he was of mercantile origin, as teacher and writer he developed its characteristic philosophical doctrines.

Like philosophers elsewhere, the Kogakuha school debated the true nature of man. Itō Jinsai believed, with the revered Mencius, that human nature was fundamentally good. Tending to emphasize the practical side of early Confucianism, he exalted the four virtues—benevolence (*jen*), righteousness, propriety, and wisdom—of which he considered *jen* the most important. On the other hand, Ogyū Sorai (1666–1728), following the ancient Confucian Hsün Tzu, insisted that human nature was essentially evil but that the ancient sage-kings had given humanity the proper ethical codes for controlling human nature and that by training in and adherence to the proper ceremonials (*li*) mankind's behaviour could be improved. Although he did not have many disciples, this reasoning, providing as it did a philosophical justification of authoritarian government, found considerable support. His views were opposed by Itō Togai (1670–1736), who, carrying on the teachings of his father, Itō Jinsai, had numerous disciples.

The fourth main branch of Japanese Neo-Confucian thought was the Mito school of historical studies, which will be examined in greater detail in Chapter IX. It too contributed to the rising opposition to the shogunate.

THEOLOGICAL TRENDS IN ISLAM

After 1500, Islam continued to a certain extent to form a single society, of which any member might find himself largely in familiar surroundings no matter how far he might wander within it. Even as Islam expanded in size, travelling Ṣūfīs, merchants, and officials might everywhere encounter the *ṭarīqas* that they knew and find themselves protected and regulated by the same *sharī'a*. Nevertheless, forces were at work that were transforming the essentially apolitical Islamic society of the previous centuries into one dominated by three great political powers—the Ottoman, Ṣafavī, and Mogul empires.

By the middle of the sixteenth century each of these empires was making somewhat divergent changes in the common religious heritage while the remoter areas that did not come under their jurisdiction tended to go their separate ways. In the lands that passed under the control of the Ṣafavī dynasty Shīʿite *mujtahids* (independent learned inquirers) promoted an intensely emotional religion centring upon a ritual of mourning for the martyred *imāms* of Twelver Shīʿites and followed the Shīʿite version of the *sharīʿa*. Al-Majlisī was the outstanding Shīʿite legist of the seventeenth century (see Chapter IX). In India the Shīʿite kingdoms of the south fell under the influence of Persian culture and religious inspiration. On the other hand, the Ottoman Empire bitterly repressed Shīʿism and imposed a militant Sunnism upon its official life: the Sunnī version of the *sharīʿa* was incorporated into the constitution; the *'ulamā'*, guardians of the *sharīʿa*, acquired political and hierarchal status; and some of the *ṭarīqas* were officially favoured.

Within the Ottoman Empire the traditions of the Iranian and Arabic cultural zones met. A standard representative of the Arabic-Maghribī tradition of north Africa was al-Sanūsi (d. 1490), a follower of the theologian al-Ashʿari (873–935). Muḥammad Birgewī, a subtle sixteenth-century theologian, whose catechism became very popular, was a good representative of the Persian-Anatolian tradition; he carried on disputations with Abū-l-Suʿūd Khoja Chelebī (d. 1574), the greatest legal mind of the Ottoman Empire, who advocated the adjustment of tradition to new social and religious realities (see Chapter IX). The mysticism of the Syrian poet and commentator Abd-al-Ghanī al-Nābulusū (d. 1731) well illustrates the confluence within the Ottoman Empire of the Maghribī and Persian-Anatolian traditions.

Despite such confluences the tension between Shīʿite Persia and Sunnī Turkey grew and produced a significant effect upon the variant interpretations of the *sharīʿa*. In earlier centuries the Shāfiʿī school had been the most popular in some central Islamic lands. In the Ottoman Empire, however, the Ḥanafī school was given official recognition, while in Persia the Shāfiʿī school was formally forbidden. Shāfiʿīs still flourished, however, at Cairo and in Arabia, and they acquired new centres as Islam expanded in Malaysia and East Africa.

The *ṭarīqas* retained a good deal of their prestige during this period, and their heads were sometimes the recipients of great devotion, having, as in Persia and Morocco, founded or helped to found illustrious dynasties. The great orders spread their influence as Islam spread, and Ṣūfī mysticism and pantheism went with them. Abd al-Raʿuf, a saint of the Shaṭṭāriyya, took his order to Malaysia in the seventeenth century. New orders arose, too, sometimes in protest against the wealth, superstitious practices, and conventional orthodoxy of the older ones, and tried to bring about reform. In the seventeenth century Aḥmad Sirhindī attempted to reintroduce freedom of speculation and discussion into the *ṭarīqas* of India but won a following chiefly because of the great intensity of his mysticism. He launched the doctrine of *waḥdat al-shuhūd* (*unity by witness*) as against that of *waḥdat al-wujūd* (*unity by existence*), thus attempting to reconcile on the metaphysical level the very personal experience of the mystic with an intensely social activism. As the power of Islam declined in India, his followers were among the most zealous in urging Muslims to restore by words and arms the paramountcy of the *sharī'a*.

For all this activity many *ṭarīqas* of this period produced little new or original thought, and the several movements of reform remained isolated within one or another of the great empires. Not until the anti-Ṣūfī Wahhābī at the end of the eighteenth century (see Volume V) did a reform movement attain wide significance in many Islamic areas at once.

Mogul India produced a series of Muslim thinkers who, like Sirhindī, were concerned with the problems of coexistence with Hinduism. Sometimes they were favourably impressed by Hinduism, as in the case of Prince Dārā Shikūh, who argued the identity of Vedānta and Ṣūfism (see Chapter V). More often they engaged in an attempt to reassert, in historical or psychological terms, the superior social value of a dominant Islam, as in the tradition leading from Sirhindī to Shāh Wali-Allāh (eighteenth century) and his many active disciples. This series of thinkers helped to forge the cultural and intellectual tradition which bound Muslims together as an Islamic community in the Indic subcontinent, a tradition without which the geographical anomaly of Pakistan today would be incomprehensible and the passionate advocacy by many Pakistani leaders of Urdu as a pre-eminently Muslim language would seem absurd.

Philosophy in Islam was not only bound up with theology during this period; it was often, besides, in the hands of poets. The essentially monistic, pantheistic mysticism that has persisted in Arabic letters since the time of Ibn al 'Arabi continued. It has been discussed in Chapter V as theology and will be discussed again in Chapter IX as literature. Arabic prose tended increasingly toward commentary upon and monographic elaboration of older works rather than toward creative or broadly scholarly achievement.

During the years 1500–1800 Iran was an influential centre of philosophical thought, the originality of which, however, was restricted to a limited range of investigation. It developed the implications of themes broached before, particularly in Ṣūfī circles, and treated chiefly by the *mutakallimūn*, men who were theologians first of all and philosophers only secondarily. The trend was toward reaffirming the conventional, though the ban on Sunnism after the fifteenth century led to much effort to formulate and popularize Shī'ite doctrines. Nevertheless, as in the Arabic zone, both in Iran and elsewhere in the Persian-speaking zone scholarship tended increasingly to take the form of commentaries and super-commentaries.

Whether under Sunnite or Shī'ite auspices, the most significant religious thought in the Persian zone concerned the problems raised by the mystical doctrines of the divine unity. Two traditions of thought were chiefly influential—the Ishrāqī metaphysics of light and the mystical monism associated with Ibn al-'Arabī. Even after the advent of the Shī'a, Iran continued to be an influential centre of Ṣūfī-oriented philosophical thought. In the seventeenth century arose a more purely philosophical school of mystical speculators, the teachers and students of Mullā Ṣadrā (d. 1640), in whose system monism was pushed to a subtle extreme. He was a disciple of the relatively freethinking Mīr Dāmād (d. 1631) and of Shaykhi-Bahā'ī (d. 1622), both of whom were speculative thinkers with scientific interests as well as theologians and were protected by Shāh 'Abbās, patron of art and learning. Mullā Ṣadrā was more outspoken than his teachers and wrote with comparatively little regard to theological prejudices. He consequently had much trouble at the hands of the other 'ulamā', who accused him of abandoning the faith. It has been suggested that in the school of Mullā Ṣadrā Neoplatonism with its doctrine of emanations was cast off in favour of a much purer Platonism, but it was a Platonism interpreted nonetheless in terms of the Ishrāqī philosophy of light.

Persian philosophical thought of this period was often tied to special Shī'ite problems, as was suitable in newly Shī'ite Iran. The effort to adapt Shī'ism, hitherto the creed of a minority, to the needs of the whole of a large and prosperous society led to a profusion of both theological and philosophical developments. Twelver Shī'ism as an orthodox legal system came to be divided into two major schools—the Uṣūlīs, who predominated, and the Akhbārīs. The Uṣūlīs insisted on constant reference to the first principles (uṣūl) of faith in the settlement of cases in the sharī'a and therefore stressed the role of the independent inquirer, the mujtahid. The Akhbārīs—not altogether unlike the earlier Sunnīs—stressed dependence on akhbār or ḥadith, certified reports of sayings of the imāms. In the late-eighteenth century the shaykhīs formed a third school with particularly strong philosophical interests. Founded by Shaykh Aḥmad al-Ahsā'ī (d. 1827), they stressed among other things the metaphysical position of the (Shī'ite) imāmate as a means of human access to divine truth, elaborating to this end novel doctrines about time and substance.

THEOLOGICAL AND EPISTEMOLOGICAL SPECULATION IN THE WEST

In Europe, the sixteenth century was a period of intense theological polemic. The Catholic Counter Reformation brought renewed interest in religious disputations and, with them, a reinvigoration of Scholastic logic. Among the works that Cardinal Cajetan wrote as a Dominican scholar when not occupied with affairs of state were commentaries on the Summa Theologica of Aquinas; they are now adjoined to the papal edition of that work. Neo-scholasticism flourished particularly in Spain, where the work of the Dominican Francisco de Vitoria (1480–1546) and the Jesuit Francisco Suàrez (1548–1617), a disciple of Molina (see Chapter IV), bolstered and rivalled the reputation of Aquinas as defenders of Christianized Aristotelianism.

Vitoria, professor of theology at the University of Salamanca, in *Relectiones Theologicae* (1557) expounded a concept of a *ius gentium*, of natural rights and obligations, as based on eternal, divine law and reason and as binding upon all nations. If rationally observed, it would, he taught, rule out war except in self-defence (and therefore he deprecated even religious conversion by force). While it would justify the power of the state, it would lead also to cooperation among the nations and to freedom of movement for individuals from one country to and in another. Vitoria's views seemed to be an apology for Spanish colonization in American and other lands at the same time that it urged moderation—and not merely in religious affairs—upon the colonizers.

Suàrez's *Disputationes Metaphysicae* (1597) became a widely used text of the Jesuits, since it simplified many of the logical problems created by the realism imputed to the Thomists. Abandoning the Scholastic tradition of writing commentaries upon texts from Aristotle, he undertook an original critique of independent issues that he raised, revealing an encyclopaedic knowledge of the relevant sources. Like the Aristotelian professors of Padua (see Chapter VI), though for more orthodox reasons, he separated theology with its supernatural justifications from philosophy, which, avoiding the more abstruse disputes of the Schoolmen, he limited to speculation on the nature of finite things. 'Suàrezianism' was adopted widely in the north also as a Protestant weapon in the conflict with resurgent Catholicism. Suàrez was the last of the great Scholastics. His political theory will engage our attention later (Chapter IX). In his philosophy theology was still queen of the sciences, but her realm had become less ethereal and considerably narrower than before.

The victories of Thomism were defeats for Ockham's brand of Scholasticism, which had to bow not only to Catholic but also to Protestant religiousness and to humanist ridicule as well. In the Rhineland, ever a stronghold of Thomism, in the Italy of the Council of Trent, and in the Spain of the Most Catholic Monarchs, realism defeated nominalism. In France, the philosopher Petrus Ramus, before he embraced Protestantism and fell a victim of the Massacre of St Bartholomew's Day, had in several works vigorously opposed the old Scholasticism in all its branches, working out a humanist 'new logic', based, he claimed, on a truer interpretation of Aristotle and on more rational methods derived from it for the solution of philosophical problems. Ramus's works had a certain vogue in Protestant countries.

The Neoplatonism of Renaissance scholars evoked among western European scholars relative indifference to other schools of Greek philosophy. Both Protestantism and the Counter Reformation especially in northern Europe, proved more favourable to Stoicism than Renaissance Italy had been. At the University of Louvain from 1592 until his death in 1606, Justus Lipsius, a Belgian scholar famous for his edition of Tacitus, lectured to crowded classes on Seneca's moral treatises. In France Michel de Montaigne (1533–92) for a time was an admirer of Seneca and Plutarch, and Guillaume du Vair

(1556–1621) glorified Stoic virtues. And in the early decades of the seventeenth century several Spanish writers, among whom Francesco de Quevedo was perhaps the most eminent, introduced a vogue of neo-Stoicism sometimes designated as Senecism. Stoicism made little progress in Western thought, however, before the end of the seventeenth century, but then and in the next century the Stoic concepts of Virtue, Reason, and Nature moved into and deeply coloured Enlightenment thought (see Chapter IX).

Similarly, few traces of Epicureanism appeared in humanistic writings before the seventeenth century. The fearless and uncompromising Giordano Bruno, who was burned for heresy in 1600, was Lucretian in a way, but he fell far short of the Epicurean theory of an atomistic world. Bruno, one of the boldest of the sixteenth-century thinkers, followed Nicholas of Cusa (whom he called 'the Divine Cusanus') and Neoplatonism rather than Epicurus and Lucretius. He envisaged God as the infinite combination of finite but constantly evolving matter ('monads') and world soul. He was, however, Lucretian in that he held a heretical theory of an infinite universe of innumerable worlds. It was not his philosophy that brought him to the stake; it was, rather, his iconoclastic temperament. Montaigne and Francisco Sanchez (1550–1623) put forward no less sceptical queries about orthodox knowledge than Bruno;[22] and Pierre Gassendi (1592–1655) was more notable as an advocate of the atomistic universe and of Epicurean thought in general. These men, however, were more tactful than Bruno and did not outspokenly attack religion; consequently they escaped condemnation.

Bruno marks an important point in modern thought. With him the scientific method, on which he lectured widely, invaded humanistic philosophy, eventually to put a demand for systematic verification into the loose, individualistic speculation that had prevailed during the Renaissance. We shall speak of him as a scientist later (Chapter XIII).

★　　　★　　　★

The Co-existence of Science and Religion

The European sages of the sixteenth and seventeenth centuries, whether Catholic or Protestant, were almost without exception professing, and generally devout, Christians. When Galileo was accused of having upheld the Copernican theory (which, however, the pope had not *ex cathedra* declared heretical), he was also accused of having been a bad Catholic and of having acted deceitfully; he proved willing to 'abjure, curse and detest' his 'errors and heresies and generally every other error, heresy and sect whatsoever contrary to the Holy Church', but he begged not to be made to say either that he was not a good Catholic or that he had ever deceived anyone, and he was not required to say either.[23] In other words, he was unwilling to risk punishment for teaching what he believed to be true, but he was, it seems, prepared to risk punishment, if he had to, rather than admit to being a bad Catholic. Among other Catholic scientists of foremost rank were Vesalius,

Torricelli, and Pascal, all devout men in their separate ways. Sceptics like Vanini and Hobbes were *rarae aves* in the seventeenth century. Later, during the eighteenth century, scepticism was fairly common among the *philosophes*, but with infrequent exceptions they too openly adhered to some form of Christianity, generally paying it at least public deference. They almost never were outright atheists, even though frequently charged with atheism by their opponents.

Protestants were no less zealous than Catholics in the promotion of science (see Chapter XIV). Some historians have maintained that the Calvinist ascetic spirit furthered the development of science: 'The number of sixteenth century botanists in central and northern Europe who were of the reformed faith is indeed remarkable.'[24] Kepler was a Lutheran. Boyle, Newton, Harvey, and Locke were professing Anglicans. Bayle, though he moved from Protestantism to Catholicism and back to Protestantism, was always a devout Christian. Huygens and Leeuwenhoek were members of the Reformed Church. Examples could easily be multiplied of sixteenth- and seventeenth-century scientists and philosophers, both Catholic and Protestant, whose new knowledge and methods did not seriously disturb their faith in their respective Christian creeds.[25] In general, these men were willing to seek knowledge wherever it could be found. 'If we hold the Spirit of God to be the only source of truth', Calvin wrote, 'we will neither reject nor despise this truth wherever it may reveal itself, provided we do not wish to offend the Spirit of God.'[26]

Part of the quarrel between Jansenists (and also the Oratorians) on the one hand and Jesuits on the other was over the nature of science. Far from thinking of science and theology as at war, these devoutly religious groups differed only regarding the exact nature and value of science in God's plan for man's salvation. To the predestinatarian Jansenists scientific achievement could come only as a result of God's grace and could not affect salvation; it was only a *divertissement* (Pascal's word for it), and the method it employed was not prescribed. To the Jesuits, with their Molinist acceptance of free will, science was a means of drawing upon the treasury of good works, though it could be properly studied only within the Aristotelian framework. For both Jansenist and Jesuit, science was an avenue to the better understanding of the manifestations of God, to greater knowledge of God's Truth, and to a stricter avoidance of Error. The divine mind had, according to many of the sixteenth- and seventeenth-century scientists, Protestant and Catholic alike, best manifested itself through the natural world and could best be studied by studying 'the Book of Nature'.

*   *   *

The Rise of Empiricism

The attacks upon Scholasticism were in large part due to what its critics believed to be the Scholastic practice of feeding on itself. According to them the Schoolmen turned mentally inward, reasoning circularly within a more or less closed syllogistic system, where major premises might have no reference to reality, rather than going out and studying mentally and manually the Book of Nature. In the sixteenth century a group of Italian anti-Aristotelians had begun to preach that knowledge derived from sensory data was superior to abstract reasoning. Bernardino Telesio (1509–88), though his senses led him to a rather specious theory of wet-cold and dry-warm forces as the basic principles of existence, nevertheless in his *De Natura Rerum Iuxta Propria Principia* (1568) laid a foundation for an empirical philosophy of science. His work had a direct influence upon Francisco Patrizzi (1529–97) and Tommaso Campanella (1568–1639). As a Neoplatonist and a believer in the primacy of space and light, Patrizzi in *Nova de Universis Philosophia* (1591) expressed some doubt about the validity of Telesio's teachings on force, while Campanella in *Philosophia Sensibus Demonstrata* (also 1591) defended Telesio, but both men, in these and other works, lifted the anti-Scholastic banner, championing some method of interaction of the senses with the mind (though they did not agree on what method) as a better source of truth than syllogistic argument.

Francis Bacon also knew of Telesio and, without endorsing his findings, admired him as the *primus novorum virorum*. Bacon's emphasis upon the inductive method was a direct reaction to the speculative methods of the Scholastics and their Aristotelianism. Find new information, he recommended, by investigating nature with a new method (*novum organum*), using your own hands or working in cooperation with those who used theirs; consider no time-honoured ideas sacred, and avoid predispositions to error ('idols'), whether they are the anthropocentric predispositions of mankind in general (idols of the tribe), personal prejudices (idols of the cave), rhetorical inaccuracies (idols of the market place) or conventional philosophies (idols of the theatre); begin rethinking ('the Great Instauration') from first principles, from irreducible and observed 'instances' (or elements of fact); do not despise the knowledge of craftsmen, who know from actual experience much that is worth knowing. In this way, he thought, as old knowledge was discarded, new knowledge would not only be accumulated but its accumulation would redound to the benefit of mankind.

Bacon's point of view was favourable not only to inductive reasoning but also to empirical methods, tools, and terms, and to utilitarian objectives—in all three regards, a departure from the prevalent view of the Scholastics. He was, if anything, somewhat unappreciative of speculative judgment and deductive reasoning, and seemed particularly unaware of the importance of the mathematical process in scientific investigation. This indifference to mathematics was all the more striking because he was a contemporary of Kepler and Galileo, who were concurrently applying speculation and mathematical principles to empirical data.

Bacon had no quarrel with theology in its own sphere—the nature of God, the soul, and morals. But the *novum organum* was for him the only method of deriving truth in the material sphere—abstract truth that could be tested by its usefulness in revealing 'new works and active directions not known before'.[27] At the same time, he struck at both the contemporary theologians, who claimed that the church was the ultimate source of truth, and the Scholastic and the humanist worshippers of Antiquity, who claimed that either Aristotle's 'induction by simple enumeration' or Platonic 'ideas' were all that was needed to derive truth. Instead, he favoured a process of induction that also required a logical process—a process that (1) would consider the 'negative', 'positive', and 'comparative instances' of forms (or physical properties); (2) would then derive from this observation of forms an 'axiom' (i.e. a generalization about their regularities regarded as objective in God's nature); and (3) would move step by step from axiom to axiom toward a new provisional principle. He thought the 'true way' of 'searching into and discovering truth' was the one that 'derives axioms from the senses and particulars, rising by a gradual and unbroken ascent, so that it arrives at the most general axioms last of all'.[28] Eventually truth would be able 'to endow the life of man with infinite commodities',[29] for institutions devoted to scientific research, much like the House of Solomon pictured in his *New Atlantis* (1627), would help to establish man's control of natural forces and promote his betterment.

Bacon died of a bronchitis brought on by experimenting with refrigeration as a means of preventing animal decay. In several ways he was an anomaly, but not least in affording the picture of a lofty personage, a lord chancellor, who believed that men of science working with their hands as well as their heads and in company with craftsmen should strive to increase knowledge and improve the physical lot of man on this earth rather than, without transgressing traditional methods, speculate upon the learning already in the books, the hereafter, and the greater glory of God. For all the residue of Aristotelian terminology in his discourse and for all the self-seeking in his aristocratic career, this was a secular philosopher of a modern cast, even in his overconfidence in the empirical method.[30]

Although once an amanuensis of Bacon, Thomas Hobbes was nevertheless ready to philosophize and to speculate mathematically. Hobbes tried to explain human behaviour in deductive terms—not only in his famous political treatise, *The Leviathan*, but also in *Human Nature* (1650) and other works. He concluded, apparently on little empirical basis, that the ultimate realities in the cosmos were matter and its qualities of extension and motion. This concept he perhaps derived from Galileo, whom he knew personally and greatly admired. While Galileo had applied it only to the physical universe, Hobbes reduced all science to a quest for laws of motion. Politics and ethics as well as physics and mathematics were for him but the application of those laws to their respective subject matter. The inevitable conclusion from this deductive philosophy was favourable to empiricism: the mind as a product of the elemental realities of matter and motion was neither free nor innate. If changes in the mind are only the effects of motion on matter, knowledge and other mental processes must originate from impulses or sensations that come from outside the mind and effect modifications (i.e. motion) within it. Hobbes' philosophy seemed so thoroughly materialistic that he was sometimes accused of being an atheist. Certainly, as his political views showed (see Chapter IX), he was cynical of man's capacity to solve his social problems, and yet he ranks with other English empiricists and the French *philosophes* as the founder of a school of thought which held that human affairs no less than the physical universe might be subject to rational, natural law.

The materialistic implications of Hobbes' epistemology, along with other sources of scepticism (see Chapter IV), met with reaction among other English thinkers. Ralph Cudworth and Henry More became the central figures of a latitudinarian and idealist group known as the Cambridge Platonists, who argued that an incorporeal and eternal spiritual quality—an *anima mundi*, or 'world spirit'—filled space and time and pervaded the matter of the cosmos, predisposing the human mind to reason and morality. Beliefs like this were reinforced by William Gilbert's contention that magnetism was animate and by Isaac Barrow's that space and time were but mathematical manifestations of God. Barrow was a teacher of Isaac Newton.

The capstone was placed in the structure of English empirical reasoning by John Locke's *Essay Concerning Human Understanding* (1690). Addressing himself directly to the by-then hotly disputed question of the origin of human knowledge, he boldly took the side of those who contended, contrary to Descartes (whom we shall presently encounter), that the mind had no innate ideas. It did have, however, certain innate capabilities, he claimed: it could receive sensations from without, whether the stimuli were inherent in the external object—as, for example, shape, motion, and plurality (primary, quantitative, or tactile features)—or could be appreciated only with the aid of the animal physiology—as, for example, taste, colour, and smell (secondary features); it could store these sensations in the memory; and it could observe its own internal operations and reflect upon them. Out of the combination of sensation, memory, and reflection came the ability to compare the results of cognition ('ideas'), approve or disapprove of them, imaginatively reconstruct them, name them, and generalize about them. Thus the mind developed from a *tabula rasa* at birth ('white paper, void of all characters, without any ideas', but ready to receive 'simple ideas')[31] into a mature thinking apparatus capable of 'complex ideas' and of various kinds of abstract reasoning. Locke considered some of these complex ideas as at least partly *negative*—i.e. thought *not* derived from sense-experience but resulting from the mind's *inability* to comprehend them—as, for example, the idea of the finiteness of time and space, whence, he reasoned, came the positive idea of 'infinity'. He also believed that human beings have intuitive knowledge of their own minds and wills, and from such knowledge comes 'demonstrative knowledge' of God.

Obviously Locke was a theist. As other writings more fully show, he accepted Revelation and Resurrection on faith and as 'above reason'. He was not even a full believer in the *tabula rasa*, since a mind equipped with the ability to receive sensations, remember them, and reflect upon them is not 'white paper'. His argument for the existence of God, based as it was on the awareness of our own being and beginning was not far removed from Descartes'. But he departed from Descartes in emphasizing the need to begin with elementary sensations received from the outside and with simple ideas independent of introspection in order to arrive at complex ideas and to proceed thence to other kinds of knowledge. He thus fortified the arguments of those who favoured the inductive method of learning and reasoning from accumulated details through categories to generalizations rather than by the deductive syllogistic method of the Schoolmen or the intuitive rationalist method of the Cartesians.

*   *   *

Doubts on Empiricism

When we come to consider the history of social thought (Chapter IX) and science (Chapter XIV), we shall see that the great British scientists among Locke's contemporaries were not full-fledged empiricists. Newton, for all his contempt in the *Principia* for hypotheses and his admiration of 'reasoning from mechanical principles', nevertheless believed that since God had existed 'always and everywhere', He 'constitutes duration and space'. Thus Newton found a satisfying explanation and foundation for his premiss of absolute time and absolute space, which prevailed until Einstein expounded the theory of relativity. Newton was able to accept, though certainly he had no sensory experience of them, both the theory of an all-pervading ether and the corpuscular theory (see Chapter XIV). Boyle was more definitely mechanistic than Newton in his philosophy and more empirical in his method, and yet he was one of the first to explain the cosmic order as analogous to that of a clock somewhat like the astonishing time-machine in the Cathedral of Strasbourg with God as the clockmaker, Who might occasionally intervene by miracles to modify the regular operations of His machine. Locke and contemporary empiricists seem never to have dreamed of postulating a world without God. Their thinking was, rather, in the opposite direction: In a sensate world what is the place of God?

As we shall see when we reach the discussion of the history of psychology during this period (Chapter XIV), a number of writers who examined the problem of knowledge doubted the validity of Locke's epistemology. George Berkeley (1685–1753) accepted Locke's assumption that ideas formed by finite minds were based upon blendings of sensations, but Berkeley turned it into a weapon against materialism. He argued that the finite mind could not distinguish between primary and secondary qualities, that even primary qualities are ideas and so cannot exist outside a perceiving substance or mind. Hence, he concluded—somewhat like the Hindu qualified monists and the Chinese Idealists (of whom he probably did not know) and like Jonathan Edwards (who probably neither knew of nor was known to him)—that, whether or not matter existed objectively, it could be perceived only by a conscious mind, and such perception and, more especially, perception of a regular order in nature was possible to finite minds only because the mind of God could and did posit it. David Hume (1711–76), as sceptical a philosopher as was to appear in England before the nineteenth century, raised the question whether self, cause, and other generalizations needed for human understanding could be derived from observation, whether the mind ever perceived a real connection among discrete things, and whether causal generalizations did not in fact depend upon customary and regular associations, mere conjunctions, which the mind came to accept as cause-and-effect. Building on Locke's *tabula rasa* and a theory of nervous vibrations borrowed from Newton, David Hartley (1705–57) developed a system of physiological psychology generally designated as 'associationist', which, while a product of the empirical school, was also a departure from it in the direction of analysis of the role of nerves and brain in the thought process (see Chapter XIV).

⋆   ⋆   ⋆

Cartesianism and Occasionalism

On the Continent strict materialism—i.e. the certitude that matter was the primary stuff of the cosmos and that mind was a derivative of it—did not flourish until the eighteenth century. Before that, Cartesianism, the school of theist naturalism based upon the rational dualism of René Descartes (1596–1650), was dominant.[32] In the Cartesian scheme matter was inert and continuous but had motion, imparted to it by God. The mind was distinct from matter and contained an irreducible, self-evident awareness of its own existence (*Cogito, ergo sum*) and hence of causality and God. The world of matter was mechanical, since all was a single plenum and continuum, and motions in one part produced circular eddies or 'vortices' that caused respondent motions in all the rest. The essential qualities of matter were for Descartes, as for Hobbes, extension and motion. We shall deal with the scientific implications of this mechanical theory elsewhere (Chapter XIV). The theological significance of it centred upon the contention that God's will alone allowed dead matter (*res extensa*), including animal bodies, to bridge the gap to the animate mind (*res cogitans*) by sensations. Thus Descartes lent his formidable authority to a clear-cut philosophy of dualism—matter and mind, body and soul.

Descartes' dualism was quickly attacked on various religious fronts. The rector of the University of Utrecht, Gisbert Voetius, assailed him in the name of the old orthodox philosophy. Gassendi, as befitted one of the small school of seventeenth-century philosophers who preferred the philosophy of the Epicureans, attacked the idea of the continuum moving by vortices, preferring an atomistic universe. Anticipating Locke (who, also with Descartes in mind, repudiated innate ideas), Gassendi contended that *nihil est in intellectu quod non prius fuerit in sensu* and thus, though himself inconsistently admitting the knowledge of God in the intellect, questioned the logic of Descartes' ontological argument.

The Cartesians themselves felt called upon to modify or expand Descartes' epistemology. The dissociation of matter and mind in Descartes' world raised the question how a change in one could bring a change in the other, how a sensation from the material world could cause an effect in the mind, even when both mind and matter are united, as in man. This problem led to the philosophy of Occasionalism, early broached by Sylvain Régis: when a change occurred in the material world God *occasioned* a corresponding change in the mind. Some of the Cartesians were Complete Occasionalists, who believed that no occurrence whatsoever was independent of God's volition. Others were Restricted Occasionalists, who left to the human mind some limited capacity to act of itself. The Oratorian Nicolas Malebranche (1638–1715) was a Complete Occasionalist, and his most noteworthy opponents among the Restricted Occasionalists were Arnold Geulincx (1624–69) and the Jansenist leader Arnault. The Occasionalists thought of God as, so to speak, a sort of clockmaker who had made *two* clocks that he constantly kept synchronized.

*　　*　　*

Critics of Cartesianism

This explanation of causality went too far for some and not far enough for others. The English philosopher Joseph Glanvill and the French scientist Blaise Pascal (1623–62) doubted that rational speculation on cause could fortify the Christian sense of the belief in God, Who, rather, must be taken on faith, for human understanding was insufficient for the understanding of the Divine. Glanvill became a Cambridge Platonist, Pascal a Jansenist. No theologian but speaking as a student of law and history (see Chapter IX), Giovanni Battista Vico in the *Principii d'una scienza nuova* (1725) questioned the Cartesian assumption that human knowledge came from thinking, or cogitation, and held that it came rather from doing, or action: *verum et factum convertuntur*. Although he had to wait until the nineteenth century for his views to make a wide impression, Vico thus early formulated the school later known as historicism (explanation by historical development) to counteract both rationalism (knowledge from reason) and empiricism (knowledge from experiment).

Dissatisfaction with the Cartesian explanation of knowledge, causality, and God came not only from empiricists and historicists but also from other kinds of rationalists. Although excommunicated by the Jewish community (see Chapter V), Baruch Spinoza (1632–77) had been trained as a youth in the rational tradition of the rabbis, for whom God was 'the space of the world'.33 In exile in Rijnsburg, Spinoza associated with the Mennonites known as *Collegianten*, many of whom were Cartesians, and Spinoza prepared textbooks on some of Descartes' work without wholly sharing his views. He had in fact already begun to develop an epistemology which, after his death, was published in his *Tractatus de Intellectus Emendatione*. His theory of knowledge differed significantly from both the empiricist Bacon and the rationalist Descartes at the same time, for it insisted that the human mind was capable of not only 'opinion', based upon elementary perceptions (or images) derived from the external world, but also of 'reason', based upon conceptions of, or logical connections among, related things, and of 'intuition' (rational cognition) based upon methodically trained insight into nature's universal laws and rules *sub specie aeternitatis*.

Spinoza's epistemology, set forth chiefly in his *Ethica* (first published in 1677), was of a piece with his cosmology, where, too, he repudiated both the materialists and the dualists while building upon the foundations which they had laid. Essentially he was a Western monist, a religious materialist, a Judeo-Christian pantheist. The *continuum-and-plenum* of Descartes, the all-pervading and infinite *extension* of matter of Hobbes, and the ever-present, ever-active Divine Will of the Occasionalists, Spinoza combined in a mystical concept of Substance. Substance was not for him mere matter, as it was for Descartes and Hobbes, nor yet mere idea as, in a sense, it was for Berkeley, but rather that which always had been and always would be, independent of everything else, eternal, infinite, active, from which all other things were in one way or another derived. Hence it was God, or Nature. It was the object of man's 'intuitive' knowledge (for Spinoza, the most highly trained kind of knowledge). This Substance had Attributes, of which the two known to man were matter or extension and spirit or thought, which, while infinite and complete, were not *absolutely* independent and non-derivative as was Substance. Since the two were equally the Attributes of Substance (or God, or Nature), they are at the same time identical with, though independent of, each other, and their connection or correspondence (occasions or causes) can be conceived by human 'reason'. The Attributes, in turn, have Modes (or modifications) that, when finite and temporary, were particular things like individual minds or bodies or events. Of these Modes man could by perception or imagination have 'opinions'.

Spinoza's ethical views were, in turn, also of a piece with his epistemology. Man's higher feelings, for Spinoza, were the 'active' ones, based on conscious desire, and the lower ones were 'passive', based on influences outside himself. The 'passions' are due to 'human bondage' to 'opinion', the lowest, 'inadequate' form of knowledge, and generally cause pain. The 'active' feelings are due to an exercise of 'reason', and because they are the outcome of some form of self-expression, they sometimes are 'adequate' and generally cause pleasure.

If finally the mind by acquiring adequate ideas is attuned to the cosmos and accepts all things as coming from God, it has reached the highest level of insight, the level of 'intuitive' knowledge. Since this *scientia intuitiva* is rare and difficult, in Spinoza's system a political organization was necessary to enable man to avoid the evils that his 'passions' entail and to live a life of reason (see Chapter IX). Despite the enormous reputation of Spinoza in his own day, some of his most important works were published only post-humously and were not widely known until the end of the eighteenth century.

★   ★   ★

Leibniz, Wolff, and Optimism

Gottfried Wilhelm Leibniz (1646–1716), expert in mathematics and mechanics and practiced in history and diplomacy, was too busy ever to set forth his philosophy in a systematic exposition. Yet he wrote several essays and many letters of a philosophical nature, for he knew almost every great thinker of his day. He had met Christian Huygens and several other out-standing Cartesians in Paris, when on a diplomatic mission to divert French aggression from Germany to Egypt, and had gone to Holland to talk to Spinoza, with whom he afterwards kept up a steady correspondence. He also had been to London and knew Newton and Boyle. Besides, Leibniz was more concerned with Chinese philosophy than perhaps any other European scholar of his day. As a mathematician, one of the discoverers of the calculus, he approved of the reasoning method of Descartes and Spinoza—in geometric fashion from simple postulates to complex theorems—and tried to carry it a step further by a universal calculus, somewhat like that advocated today by the symbolic logicians—the reduction of the simple, self-evident truths to symbols which could then by equations of identity or non-identity be used to arrive at more complex truths. Universal truth seemed to him capable of comprehension because the universe was the product of a Pre-established Harmony—'a prevenient divine contrivance, which from the beginning has formed each of these substances [the soul and the body] in a way so perfect and regulated with so much accuracy that merely by following laws of its own, received with its being, it nevertheless agrees with the other, just as if there were mutual influence, or as if God in addition to his general cooperation constantly put his hand thereto'.[34]

Leibniz thus seems to have come as close as a theist could to the concept of a regular order of nature in which all things animate and inanimate work according to eternal, universal, and self-operating laws. He bridged the gap not only chronologically but logically between those of the seventeenth century who spiritualized matter and those of the eighteenth century who materialized spirit. His endowment of matter with spirit was explicitly set forth in a letter to Prince Eugene of Savoy (published as *Monadologie* in 1714), but the problem had already been broached in the *Nouveaux essais sur*

l'entendement humain (1704), a step by step refutation of Locke's sensationalism. To Leibnez, student of mechanics, the primitive stuff of the universe
was not substance but force. He conceived of force as present in the elementary units of the universe, which he called *monads* (a term he probably
borrowed from Bruno). The monads were the atoms of nature, each of which
combines the spiritual and the material, and was perpetual and independent
of all others. Each monad was a microcosm sharing in varying degrees all the
characteristics of the highest monad, God, Who differs from them not only
in being the highest of them but also in being able to create and destroy them.
Autonomous and self-perpetuating, the monads nevertheless 'vary in perfection like different representations or drawings in perspective of the same
town seen from different points'. Hence, though they exercise 'physical action
and passion' (i.e. outward force) on one another, none exercises 'metaphysical
action or influence' (i.e. cause and effect) on another, 'and what we call
causes are . . . only required as concomitants'. Hence no 'vulgar hypothesis
of influence' or of 'occasional cause' is needed to explain the union of soul and
body. Instead he propounded the hypothesis of concomitance: 'For God
has from the beginning so fashioned soul as well as body . . . that from the first
constitution or concept itself of either one, everything that happens in one
corresponds perfectly to everything that happens in the other.'[35]

In an effort to explain how evil could exist in the Pre-established Harmony,
Leibniz wrote an *Essai de théodicée* (1710) and *Principes de la nature et de la
grace* (1714). He argued: 'All spirits . . . .entering by virtue of reason and of
the eternal truths into a sort of society with God are members of the City of
God, . . . where there is . . . as much virtue and happiness as is possible . . .
because by virtue of the perfect order established in the universe, everything
is done in the best possible way'; yet 'since God is infinite, he cannot be
wholly known,' and 'therefore our happiness will never, and ought not,
consist in full joy, where there would be nothing further to desire, rendering
our mind stupid; but in a perpetual progress to new pleasures and to new
perfections.'[36]

This theodicy was the Optimism which Christian Wolff (1679–1754) made
into a more thoroughly anthropocentric philosophy and which Voltaire
would make sport of in his *Candide* (1759). Wolff modified Leibniz's logic
also in a geocentric direction. Leibniz had held that certain propositions are
true because they can logically be reduced to identity with their definitions;
these were for him universally 'necessary truths'. Other propositions rested
in his philosophy upon 'sufficient reason'; they were 'contingent truths'—
true enough, that is, though in an incomplete way, for the present world:
anyone with sufficient knowledge could account for their being so and not
otherwise. Wolff, however, obliterated the difference between necessary and
contingent truth and tried to rationalize all truth into necessary truth.
Several of his works were entitled *Vernünftige Gedanken von . . .* (*Rational
Thoughts upon . . .*). Kant had Wolff (among others) in mind when he wrote

his *Kritik der reinen Vernunft* (see Volume V). Incidentally, like Leibniz, Wolff was greatly interested in Chinese thought.

*   *   *

Indifferentism and Deism

All of this speculation on the nature of cause and reason was going on concomitantly with 'the scientific revolution', which we shall describe in Chapters XIII–XV. As we shall then see, the scientists from Copernicus to Lavoisier, even though they rarely intended to question the foundations of religious faith, raised considerable doubt about the literal interpretation of certain passages in scripture, the reliability of Aristotle's physics, the probability of miracles, and the plausibility of other parts of the Christian credo. At the same time, students of philology and history, like Erasmus and the authors of the *Magdeburg Centuries* (see Chapter IX), were querying the credibility, sometimes the very authenticity, of at least parts of significant pieces of Catholic literature. And Protestant scholars were making the Bible so accessible in the numerous vernaculars that any reader might interpret it for himself, with the consequence that Protestant sects split into so many different fragments that the differences among them appeared sometimes picayune and often confusing to outsiders. Meanwhile explorers and missionaries had made the Christian world aware of highly advanced peoples who lived by venerable ethical codes and righteous concepts of Heaven but who knew nothing of Revelation. More's *Utopia*, Campanella's *Civitas Solis* (1613), and several later works of the same genre revealed the readiness of pious minds at least to idealize for rhetorical effect and perhaps to respect, even to envy, such exotic cultures.

The result of the concurrence of these intellectual developments was rarely complete disbelief by the Europeans in the Judeo-Christian story. Rather it was a widening of the spirit of adiaphorism—a feeling that differences in dogma or ritual were unimportant and that therefore no church should have the power to force its creed upon others or induce governments to do so. The contemporary rise of rationalism led, instead, to the belief that a 'natural religion' could count on man's innate sense of right and wrong for moral conduct and genuine piety.

To the champions of established churches and of the several orthodoxies such indifferentism was shocking, and they seldom hesitated to call it 'atheism'. Though the Pyrrhonic *De Immortalitate Animae* (1516) of Pomponazzi was burned, he himself was spared. His pupil Lucilio Vanini (1585–1619) was less fortunate. He was actually tried and found guilty of atheism (though his books reveal, rather, a pantheistic view) and was sentenced to have his tongue cut out and to be strangled at the stake. Often, too, the offended believer called the unorthodox 'libertines'; and we have seen (Chapter IV) how wretchedly Théophile de Viau and Le Petit fared under such a charge.

Indifferentism nevertheless spread, and in the late seventeenth and the eighteenth centuries a brand known as Deism (or, at first, also Theism) won particular prominence. While Deism found early exponents on the Continent, too, it reached maturity in England after the Civil War—the very war that had produced Fifth Monarchy Men and other millenarians, who based their chiliasm upon a literal interpretation of the Bible (see Chapter IX). Deism, because of its very premises, never became an organized movement or created a unified church; some of its adherents never formally left their respective established churches. Some of them believed in the immortality of the soul, which would be punished or rewarded in a hereafter; others carried free thought so far as to come fairly close to atheism. Despite these divergences they all held in common a belief in a First Cause that had set the universe agoing in accordance with universal laws though It subsequently remained relatively indifferent to the ways of man and was inexorable to prayers or ritual, faith or good works.

This common belief made them all antagonists of organized churches. The English philosopher Herbert of Cherbury (1583–1648), the so-called 'father of Deism', believed, with Descartes, that knowledge of God was innate. Upon that knowledge, he concluded, a 'natural religion', more acceptable than the traditional ones, could be based. The Earl of Shaftesbury (1671–1713) argued that morality, like the sense of beauty, was inborn, and that the highest forms of religion needed no theology or church. Other leading Deists were more direct in their attack upon the Christian church. Matthew Tindal (1656–1733) in *Christianity As Old as Creation* (1730) maintained that the validity of the Christian religion lay in its being, and only in so far as it was, an explicit statement of natural religion. John Toland (1670–1722) in *Christianity Not Mysterious* (1696) and other works undertook to divest it of its mysteries and contradictions, leaving a comprehensible and rational residue. Other Deists, with varying degrees of scholarship in comparative theology and history and of persuasiveness in rhetoric and logic, attacked various parts of what they considered the Christian myth. Viscount Bolingbroke (1678–1751) went so far as to suggest (but posthumously) that church organizations were contrived by the clever only for the purpose of keeping the ignorant in subjection.

French Deism had its native seventeenth-century roots, and it was fortified in the eighteenth-century Enlightenment from England. Voltaire and Rousseau were the most prominent among its proponents. Voltaire found it, and particularly the more cynical brand of Bolingbroke, well suited to his own resentment of ecclesiastical power and intolerance and, after his sojourn in England (1726–29), went on to attack the church, particularly the French Catholic Church, as the chief enemy of enlightenment—witness his *Essais sur les Moeurs* (1756)—and to preach the necessity of 'crushing the infamous thing' ('*Ecrasez l'infame!*') along with all other brands of obscurantism. Rousseau's Savoyard Vicar (see Chapter XVI), though much more of a

Christian than Voltaire, nevertheless propounded in *Émile* (1762) a natural religion without church or clergy. Denis Diderot (1713–84) was so little theist that, without complete justification, he was considered an atheist even by some of his more objective contemporaries. Elsewhere in Europe than England and France the influence of Deism was less marked but none the less familiar in high places. Lessing's pleas for tolerance and the educational theories of Basedow (see Chapter XVI) were perhaps due to both men's acceptance of a similar persuasion. In America outstanding leaders of public opinion—notably Franklin, Jefferson, and the international insurgent Thomas Paine—avowedly believed in a God who needed no church or clergy to rule the universe by ascertainable, even self-evident, laws of nature and natural rights of man.

*   *   *

The Rise of Materialism and Mechanism

Until the 1730's Cartesian rationalism, with its dualistic emphasis upon innate ideas, and Cartesian science were in almost unquestioned dominance of the Continent. The empirical naturalism of Locke and Newton, however, was popularized from the 1730's on by Voltaire and others. In 1734 the annual prize of the French Academy of Sciences was divided between Johann Bernoulli and his son Daniel, the older man defending the Cartesian system and the younger the Newtonian one. After 1740 no Cartesian won the prize again. In the 1740's Condillac actually went farther than Locke in the direction of monistic sensationalism by imaginatively creating a hypothetical mind within a statue, endowing it with each of the senses in turn. Diderot reinforced the sensationalist argument by his *Letter on the Blind* (1745) and *Letter on Deaf Mutes* (1751); reversing the procedure of Condillac, he both empirically and imaginatively inquired what the effects on the mind might be if human beings were deprived of any of their senses. Maupertuis in his *Accord des differentes lois de la nature* (1744), noting the efficiency with which the universe seemed to operate, propounded the Principle of Least Action: within a dynamic system unaffected by outside forces change takes place only with the least possible value of a mathematical expression of the energy involved, which is known as the 'action'. Expressed in theistic terms (as Maupertuis did express it), this meant that God chose the simplest means to achieve his ends. That principle, while well in keeping with the Neoplatonic concept of the plenitude of God and with the Leibnizian concept of a Pre-established Harmony, was not incompatible with the Deistic concept of God as the efficient clockmaker.

At the end of the seventeenth and the beginning of the eighteenth century, the work of Leeuwenhoek, Bonnet, Trembley, and other microbiologists (see Chapter XIV) seemed to provide proof of a close relationship among the various forms of life. Their readiness to accept such a conclusion had a disturbing effect upon Europe's philosophers. Maupertius' Principle of

Least Action, broadly interpreted, was sufficient perhaps to explain a life history which seemed to have begun with forms so simple as to be almost indistinguishable from inanimate matter and in which some plant forms could easily be confused with animal forms. But what if this process should still be going on? What if, along with the kind of 'perfection' that Leibniz envisaged (which contemplated reaching toward the harmony of God) or that Bacon envisaged (which contemplated a steady accumulation of knowledge) or that the Abbé de St Pierre envisaged (which contemplated a studied improvement of men's institutions), a continuous and undesigned perfectibility of man's physiological and even psychological nature were also possible? And what if the perfectibility of man were, whether by the original plan of God or no, now due merely to the contingencies of nature?

Before 1775 no one had yet fully formulated a notion of biological evolution, but in the middle of the eighteenth century several had begun to query whether in fact God had created man and the other living things whole and by a single act. Julien Offray de Lamettrie argued almost atheistically in *L'homme machine* (1747), *L'homme plante* (1748), and *Systeme d'Epicure* (1750) that the Cartesian distinction between man and lower forms of life (because man alone has a soul while lower forms are but machines) was false, for, Lamettrie claimed, man's mind, a mere function of his brain, dies when his body dies, his soul is not immortal, and God is an unnecessary hypothesis. In 1748 Benoit de Maillet's *Telliamed* (the title is the author's name spelled backward) cast doubt upon the Biblical account of Creation with his suggestion that every land animal has a marine prototype. In 1749, Comte de Buffon (1707–88) published the first three volumes of his *Histoire Naturelle*, reinforcing the belief that a sort of vitalism ruled the world of life and enabled it to dispense with God as First Cause. In remote Massachusetts Cadwallader Colden argued (in *The Principles of Action in Matter*, 1751) that ether was the universal substance and that matter was only sublimated force, and mind only spiritualized matter. In 1754 the French version of Maupertuis' *Système de la nature* (first published as *Dissertatio Inauguralis Metaphysica* in 1751) queried whether 'the multiplication of the most dissimilar species might have resulted from two single individuals'.[37] And in the next decade Jean Battiste Robinet's *De la nature* (1763) and *Considérations philosophiques sur la gradation naturelle des formes de l'être* (1767) presented a theory of an eternally continuous process of Creation.

In 1751 the first volume of Diderot's *Encyclopédie* had appeared. Its formal title was *Dictionnaire raisonné, etc.*, and the reasoning, D'Alembert indicated in the *Discours préliminaire*, would be along the empirical lines laid down by Bacon and not along the rationalist lines of Descartes. Several of its articles spoke of the possibility that lower forms of life had given rise to the higher ones. Diderot in a number of other works, some not published during his lifetime, moved steadily toward a theory of a dynamic life force that enabled organisms to evolve in response to their organic needs.

By that time materialism had left behind almost all pretence of theism. The *Testament* of the Abbé Jean Meslier (1664–1729) was one of the most widely read of the numerous manuscripts that circulated clandestinely in France in order to avoid the censorship authorities; it attacked all religion as false and all churches as impostures and denied even the Deists' premise of a First Cause. Although Baron d'Holbach was careful to observe the Catholic forms in private life, he psuedonymously (in 1770), wrote a *Système de la nature* that is sometimes called 'the Bible of Atheism'. The fundamental stuff of the cosmos, Holbach contended, is materialistic and mechanistic— matter and motion. Soul was to Holbach synonymous with brain, and thought with imperceptible motions in the brain; God was synonymous with the natural order operating in accordance with natural law; man was not free in will, and morality should be but the prescriptions of the state or society to protect itself and its members from injury and to achieve their maximum happiness. Helvétius in *De l'esprit* (1758) and *De l'homme* (1773–74) set forth a strictly sensationalist psychology from which he derived the same kind of utilitarian explanation of morality. The moral sense must be based, he held, upon the desire to avoid pain and to incur pleasure; since esteem is pleasant and contempt is painful, the business of government, which has no purpose other than to advance the happiness of the greatest number, is to provide a system of education and of rewards and punishments that will make bad conduct painful or ill-esteemed and duty pleasant.

Goethe declared that his revulsion upon reading Holbach's *Système de la nature* drove him into the Sturm-und-Drang movement. Several *philosophes* (Diderot, in the posthumously published *Neveu de Rameau*, for example) had been profoundly disturbed by the question why men should be moral if the soul was mortal, and Rousseau had earlier broken with the *philosophes* because of his insistence upon the religious basis for morality. From agreement with Rousseau and Hume on the inadequacy of the empirical method no less than from disagreement with Wolff on the sufficiency of the rationalist method, Kant was moved to examine the limitations of human reason (see Volume V) and to propound his conclusions on the necessity for faith.

NOTES TO CHAPTER VII

1. Dasgupta, *op. cit.*, III, pp. 471–2.

2. A. B. Keith, *A History of Sanskrit Literature* (Oxford, 1928), p. 473.

3. M. Hiriyanna, *Outlines of Indian Philosophy* (London, 1932), p. 302.

4. Dasgupta, II, pp. 221 and 224.

5. Madhva is often considered a radical 'pluralist'. His thought, however, remains difficult to penetrate. It is to be hoped that more light may be forthcoming in an important work now in preparation. (Oliver Lacombe.)

6. In Professor O. Lacombe's opinion, this section has the advantage of stimulating the reader to reflection. Particularly interesting is the contrast between the 'middle way' of Wang Yang-ming in which the best of the multiple Chinese traditions is once more found, and the unbalance which ensued. Many of the great themes of the history of human thought are evoked in the course of these pages: quietism, the goodness or wickedness of human nature, the role of spontaneity, of virtuous discipline, etc.

7. Wang's Complete Works, quoted in H. G. Creel, *Chinese Thought from Confucius to Mao Tsê-tung* (Chicago, 1953), p. 214.

8. This quotation is adapted from the translation given in Fung Yu-lan, *op. cit.*, II, p. 599 and in Fung Yu-lan and Derk Bodde, *A Short History of Chinese Philosophy* (New York, 1948), pp. 310–13.

9. Fung Yu-lan, II, pp. 613–14.

10. Heinrich Busch, *loc. cit.*, pp. 81–3, 86 and 89.

11. Chan Wing-tsit, *Historical Charts of Chinese Philosophy* (New Haven, 1955), chart 5.

12. Busch, *loc. cit.*, pp. 130–31.

13. Adapted from the translation given in Fung Yu-lan, II, pp. 641–42.

14. *Ibid.*, p. 645.

15. Quoted in Creel, p. 222.

16. *Ibid.*, p. 228.

17. Quoted *ibid.*, pp. 230–31.

18. Feng Chao-yang's article on Tai Chen in Arthur W. Hummel, *Eminent Chinese of the Ch'ing Period* (Washington, 1944), II, p. 699.

19. Quoted in Fung Yu-lan, II, p. 654.

20. Quoted in Creel, p. 231.

21. R. C. Armstrong, *Light from the East. Studies in Japanese Confucianism* (Toronto, 1914), p. 138.

22. Professor O. Lacombe, however, wonders to what extent did Montaigne's philosophic scepticism affect the orthodoxy of the Catholic faith which he professed? He suggests that the question seems far from having been resolved in the direction the text appears to indicate.

23. Georgio de Santillana, *The Crime of Galileo* (Chicago, 1955), pp. 311–12 and 322–23.

24. R. Hooykaas, 'Science and Reformation', *Journal of World History*, III, no. 1 (1956).

25. For a lengthy list arranged according to fields of study, see François Russo, 'Role respectif du Catholicisme et du Protestantisme dans le développement des sciences aux XVIe et XVIIe siècles', *ibid.*, no. 4 (1957), pp. 854–80.

26. *Institutes*, III, 2, no. 15, quoted in Hooykaas, *loc. cit.*, p. 128.

27. Quoted in F. H. Anderson, *The Philosophy of Francis Bacon* (Chicago, 1948), pp. 81–2.

28. *Novum Organum*, Book I, Aphorisms 3, 4, and 19.

29. 'Mr. Bacon in Praise of Knowledge,' quoted in James Spedding, *The Letters and the Life of Francis Bacon* (London, 1861), I, p. 123.

30. On this point see Alexander Koyré, 'Influence of Philosophic Trends on the Formulation of Scientific Theories', *Scientific Monthly*, LXXX (1955), pp. 107–11.

31. Book II, Ch. I, p. 2.

32. Professor O. Lacombe raises the question why, in the above pages less than a single one is devoted to the founder of a tradition which still numbers many devotees, whereas his principle disciples, Spinoza and Leibniz, receive more extensive treatment. Without displaying undue partiality for Descartes—one could wish the following points had been treated here: (1) the unity of soul and body, by means of which Descartes seeks to counterbalance his dualism, and (2) the voluntarist aspect of the doctrine and his theory of divine liberty, of which far from negligeable traces are to be found in certain forms of contem-

porary existentialism, their atheistic humanism notwithstanding; and (3) it should also be recalled that, despite his ambition to reconstruct philosophy without reference to its past history, Descartes remains to some extent indebted to scholastic tradition.

The authors wish to indicate that they deal with Descartes, as well as with Spinoza and Leibniz, at some length in several other contexts.

33. Quoted in A. Wolf, *The History of Science, Technology and Philosophy in the 16th and 17th Centuries* (New York, 1935), p. 666.

34. 'A Letter of Leibnitz on His Philosophical Hypothesis . . .' (1696) in T. V. Smith and Marjorie Greene, *From Descartes to Kant, Readings in the Philosophy of the Renaissance and Enlightenment* (Chicago, 1940), p. 344 n.

35. *Opuscules et fragments inédits de Leibniz*, ed. by Louis Couturat (Paris, 1903), quoted *ibid.*, p. 343. See Leibniz *Monadology*, para. 51.

36. *The Philosophical Works of Leibnitz*, tr. by George Martin Duncan (New Haven, Conn., 1890), quoted in Smith and Greene, pp. 368–69.

37. Quoted in Lester G. Crocker, 'Diderot and Eighteenth Century French Transformism' *Forerunners of Darwin: 1745–1859*, ed. Bentley Glass, Owsei Temkin and William L. Straus, Jr. (Baltimore, 1959), p. 127. See also Arthur O. Lovejoy, *The Great Chain of Being* (Cambridge, Mass., 1936), pp. 227–87; R. R. Palmer, *Catholics and Unbelievers in Eighteenth Century France* (Princeton, 1939), pp. 157–77; and Preserved Smith, *A History of Modern Culture*, Vol. II, *The Enlightenment, 1687–1776* (New York, 1934), pp. 187–88.

CHAPTER VIII

POLITICAL AND SOCIAL THOUGHT AND PRACTICE
(*c*. 1300–*c*. 1500)

POLITICAL THEORY AND PRACTICE

The Rise of Political Philosophy in Europe

ONE of the most striking characteristics of modern political structure is the sovereign national state. Such a concept was barely recognized in the Middle Ages of western Europe, where pope and emperor claimed dominion in the respective fields of spiritual and temporal matters. In fact, the intellectual spirit of the early Middle Ages had been favourable to no autocracy but theocracy. Until the struggle between church and state came out in the open, the accepted theocratic ruler on earth was the pope, 'servant of the servants of God'. The line of command, according to ecclesiastical theory, was from God by way of the pope (His vicar on earth) to the clergy for spiritual affairs and to emperor, kings, and nobles for temporal affairs.

When the emperors sought to free themselves from papal authority, they resorted to the doctrine of their God-given right to serve as His vicar in temporal affairs. That is, they sought to change the line of command by moving themselves up to a position of equality with the pope, so that God's will in temporal affairs might be assumed to pass from Him to an emperor directly and not by way of the pope. Medieval artists sometimes depicted either Christ simultaneously handing the keys of Heaven to Peter and the standard of the cross to Emperor Constantine or Peter handing the stole to Pope Leo and the standard to Emperor Charlemagne. For all that, at no time in the Middle Ages had temporal autocracy been effectively based on the premise of the divine right of kings.

Nevertheless, the concept of the divine right of kings persisted. Jesus's words, 'Render under Caesar the things that are Caesar's' and the exhortations to obedience by Peter (I Peter 2:13-17) and Paul (Romans 13:1-7 and Titus 3:1), especially the reminder that 'the powers that be are ordained of God' (Romans 13:1), often were quoted, though usually with a disclaimer to the effect that such injunctions did not apply to tyrants. In the fourteenth century, this general line of reasoning won the support of Wycliffe, who in some passages went so far as to assert that man because of his sinful nature must as a Christian duty submit even to tyranny, since the ruler, right or wrong, is God's vicar. A century later, Pope Pius II reiterated the divine-right theory. But not until the sixteenth century was the doctrine widely accepted full-fledged that Christians were bound to obey their rulers absolutely because they were the representatives of God on earth.[1]

If the theory of divine right of kings had to wait longer for full expression, late-medieval scholars found other arguments in favour of autocracy. They found them in Roman law and history. After the revival of Roman civil law (see Volume III), monarchs began to employ as advisers lawyers trained at Bologna and other Italian centres of Roman law. When Philip IV of France clashed with Boniface VIII at the end of the thirteenth century, he had to find some legal justification for his defiance of God's vicar on earth. He used civil lawyers such as Pierre Flotte and Nogaret to formulate and implement his anti-papal propaganda. In a treatise entitled *De Utraque Potestate*, one of Philip's lawyers drew also on ancient history to provide an independent, pre-papal origin for the French monarchy and its royal authority. Another French legalist, Jean de Jandun, argued that whereas God had only one vicar for spiritual affairs (the pope), for temporal affairs He had to have several, including the king of France as well as the emperor. Still another French publicist, Pierre Dubois, in *Supplication. . . . contre le pape Boniface* (1304) asserted the king's right to use force against corrupt popes for the public welfare. Thus Philip's political exigencies, hastening the literary articulation of certain secular views of law, history, and logic, added to their effectiveness in undermining theocratic ideology.

In Italy at this time the interminable conflict of popes and emperors, of Guelfs and Ghibellines, of despots and cities led to a similar secularization of political philosophy. Looking forward to a day of universal peace and justice, Dante in *De Monarchia* cited Roman imperial history, the Bible, Aristotle, Cicero, Aquinas, and other authorities in support of the emperor's right to head a universal empire. Dante claimed that, like the ancient Roman Empire, an ideal universal empire would be in accordance with God's will and should be independent of the papacy. A little later, another Italian, the Pavian lawyer Bartolus de Sassoferrato (1314–57), analysed monarchical government in a more objective fashion. Also citing Christian scripture, classical and Thomist authority, and Roman history and law, he concluded that whereas small states (especially city states) can best be governed by the entire citizenry or by selected representatives, large states need monarchs. For example, he argued, when Rome became an empire it replaced its multiple executive with a single emperor. Since a good monarch's authority was God-given, he had the power to collect taxes, make laws, and engage in other operations necessary for the administration of the state. But even a monarch was subject to limitations: he had no right to deprive individuals of their property unjustly or to serve his own selfish ends, for rulers who exercise power for their own advantage are tyrants, and tyranny is a corruption of government.

Bartolus and other legalists of the period frankly debated the justice of tyrannicide. Some boldly favoured it; others urged caution. In a treatise entitled *De Tyranno*, Bartolus openly asserted that tyrants might be not only resisted and deposed but even killed. The Florentine statesman Coluccio Salutati (1331–1406), although he concurred in the opinion that to kill a tyrant was honourable, urged caution, citing the precedent of Brutus and Cassius; they had killed Julius Caesar unlawfully, he thought, and had justly been relegated to Hell as traitors in Dante's *Divine Comedy*. In a still more cautious vein one of Bartolus' contemporaries argued that a tyrant might not even be deposed legally. The assassination of Louis of Orleans (1407) as a tyrant (see Chapter III) was approved by a French court though tyrannicide was condemned in principle by the Council of Constance.

In time the tendency to defend temporal autocracy increased. Unconditional defence of it was prevalent especially among civil lawyers, naturally intent upon the independence of civil courts and civil law from church courts and canon law. A number of lawyers argued that the people of ancient Rome had irrevocably granted absolute power to their emperors and that when the Roman Empire disintegrated, this power had passed to their successors, the German emperors. Some even asserted that the monarch's will was law and above all other sources of law within his realm. Although it was generally recognized that rulers must not contravene religious and natural law, civil lawyers stressed the practical importance of the state and of strong rulers. Thus the medieval ideal of the king as an agent of God, pope, and people for the fulfilment of the divine purpose slowly gave way to a concept of temporal autocracy. In the process the Thomist ideology of theocracy was steadily undermined. Legalistic politicians might pay lip service to natural law but were inclined to give it a secular, statist interpretation that favoured autocracy. The ideas of these civil legalists paved the way eventually for Luther's support of autocracy as a Christian dogma.

In Italy the growth of an autocratic ideology came less from religious considerations than from political necessity. As despots increased in numbers in the late-fifteenth and the early-sixteenth century, the defence of autocracy became proportionately intense. After the triumph of the revived papacy over the councils, this autocratic trend became unmistakeable. *The Discourses* and *The Prince* of Niccolo Machiavelli (1469–1527), although they reflected his hard-headed reaction to the realistic and frankly cynical quality of the war-torn, conspiratorial politics of his day rather than ambition, ruthlessness, or any other personal characteristic of his own, gave to political philosophy the term 'Machiavellian'. He stands out not only for the originality of his ideas but perhaps even more for the boldness of his exposition, a candid statement that contrasted vividly with the cant and hypocrisy of his day. He proposed, he said in dedicating *The Prince* to Lorenzo the Magnificent, to do for politics what the painter of his day was doing for landscape art—to examine the scene from a good vantage so as to depict the nature of his subject appropriately. As the son of a lawyer, he had learned the practical side of government in the hard school of experience. He had also acquired the humanists' deference to Classical example; the political philosophy of his *Discourses* is based largely on Livy's *History of Rome*. *The Prince*, more famous though merely a by-product, vividly expounded his belief in statism and autocracy as a practicable system of government. With a toughness that shocks modern readers, he stripped the rationale based upon Aristotelian, Christian, and Roman principles from the accepted princely stereotype, leaving the prince little more than a personification of the empirical precept, derived from contemporary Italian wars and turmoil, that might and cunning make right.

Yet Machiavelli was no mere cold-hearted realist. He upheld the ideal of the strong and wise prince who assumes responsibility as he takes power, who protects his subjects against themselves and considers it a duty to use all possible measures for the preservation of law and order. In several pious passages, Machiavelli presented religious faith as a constructive force in government. Man's susceptibility to religion, he proposed, should be encouraged as a means of preventing the disintegration of the state, whether in a republic or in an autocracy. He even lauded republicanism, though he thought it an impractical ideal for contemporary Italy. Beneath the hard surface of his authoritarian programme burned the patriotism of one who was prepared to make great sacrifices of principle for Italian unity and peace, which, for practical purposes and under existing circumstances, seemed to him to require absolute control of the state by the prince.[2]

For sheer realism unrelieved by deference to ethical principles, Machiavelli's contemporary and friend Francesco Guicciardini (1483–1540) surpassed him in both action and theory. As statesman and diplomat Guicciardini practised the cynical 'virtues' with far more consistency than Machiavelli. Although his preferred form of government was aristocracy and he despised the clergy, he served Medici and papal despots throughout most of his public career. In his two histories (of Florence and of Italy) and his political writings (which included a commentary on Machiavelli's *Discourses*) he presented more coldly objective analyses of government and power politics than any of his contemporaries. His estimate of human character was low, and his own private career helped to justify his estimate. Self-interest was for him the chief motive of human beings, and the quest for power the chief impulse of nations. Among the first to write the history of Italy as one people, he was also among the first to speak of a 'balance of power' as a means of preserving a semblance of peace. Better than Machiavelli's, Guicciardini's political theory reflected the disunity, civic unrest, and private demoralization of the Italy of their day.

*   *   *

The Debate on the Limitations of Authority

Unlike Italy, several other states of Europe (see Chapter I) emerged during this period as unified, dynastic realms, England, Spain, France, and Russia being the outstanding examples. The rise of Russia as a huge unified auto-cracy in some ways, despite its peculiar circumstances, illustrates the contemporary process of centralization of governmental power. Practical conditions rather than Machiavellian theories accounted for the central-ization of Russia (as well as of the other above-designated states), and, in addition, its princes—particularly those of Moscow—showed that they were capable of heroic leadership. As Russia recovered from the Tatar ravages and began to struggle in the common cause against the hated alien yoke, its separate rulers tightened their economic and political bonds. Its urban population too, growing in number, power, and prestige, took part in the drama of centralization, playing a particularly prominent role, celebrated in several chronicles and folktales, in an uprising against the Tatar regent (1327). By the end of the fourteenth century Dimitri Donskoi, having behind him the combined strength of several dependent, semi-dependent, and allied states of north-eastern Russia, was able to defeat the once invincible Golden Horde on Kulikovo Plain (see Chapter I). The Russians now had not only a common cause but also a common tradition, almost indispensable factors in unifying a people. In the next century, despite the enmity of the Tatars, Poland, and Lithuania, Dimitri's successors conquered vast stretches to the west, north, and east. As in other centralizing monarchies, all other com-petitors for leadership were overwhelmed—among them the wealthy com-mercial empire of the city-state Novgorod and the powerful principality of Tver—and the prestige of Moscow's major rivals as capital cities was now systematically undermined. After 1480 tribute was refused to the Golden Horde. By 1500 Russia, unlike Italy, was far from a mere geographical expression; among the titles that the Grand Duke Ivan III (the Great) claimed were *samoderzshets* (autocrat) and *gosudar* (sovereign) of all Russia. The cost of Russia's unification was paid not only by the feudal princes, now weakened, and the boyar officialdom, now dependent on the ruler's good will, but also by the peasants, now more thoroughly subjected to their lords. Yet unification had the support of many merchants, artisans, and other town dwellers, and Russia's writers began to talk of Moscow as 'the third Rome'.

Although in Europe absolutism was becoming more firmly entrenched on nearly all sides, it met with a stern opposition. The nobility, following the feudal tradition so well exemplified in the English Magna Carta, as a general rule did not willingly surrender their ancient rights. Even where kings such as Edward I of England and Philip IV of France initiated no new policy but engaged only in furthering the institutions of dynastic control that were already strong when they had inherited them, the aristocratic families defied them and carried on intermittent feudal wars. The clergy likewise, despite periods of ineffective papal leadership such as that of the Avignon papacy and the Schism, resisted royal encroachments on their rights and properties. The burgher element of the third estate, though usually inclined to ally with the king against the nobility, were by no means disinclined on occasion to form alliances with it in order to resist royal encroachments. In the Holy Roman Empire, Bohemia, Hungary, and Poland, where the rulers were elected and, in several notable instances, also were foreigners more interested in promoting their dynastic ambitions than in perfecting internal administration, the nobles were able to obtain Golden Bulls or other charters and concessions from the crown in return for their support. English Parliaments, French Estates, German Electors, Spanish Cortes, and Polish Sejm and Sejmiki during the fourteenth and fifteenth centuries at times displayed a readiness to oppose autocracy actively. Wherever parliamentary or quasi-parliamentary institutions arose, representatives of at least the higher estates claimed and exerted special rights in taxation, tariffs, elections, appointments of ministers, or other governmental affairs.

The theory behind this sort of check upon absolutism was the medieval principle of popular sovereignty, which the theologian Aquinas and the jurist Bracton had set forth in the thirteenth century. Sovereignty, they had said, comes from God and is vested in the people, who delegate it to their rulers; the rulers are not masters but are the subjects of God and law; and if rulers become tyrannical, the people have the right to overthrow them in an orderly and legal manner. Around 1300 this idea, with minor modifications, was well known to Europe's political theorists. In England the works known as *Fleta*, *The Mirror of Justice*, and *The Method of Holding Parliament* asserted the king's subservience to law and stressed the authority of the people, through the members of the *curia*, to enforce the law if the king transgressed it. For further guaranty of the public welfare, the king was bound by a coronation oath. Some even asserted that parliaments should be held twice a year, not only for granting aids but also for presenting petitions to which the king must give consideration.

Two English kings (Edward II in 1327 and Richard II in 1399) were in fact deposed by Parliament during this period. While fundamentally the conflicts that led to their downfall were the consequence of the rivalry among contemporary noble families and personages for power and the royal ermine, they reflected also a marked degree of popular unrest. Despite Wycliffe's assertion of the duty of Christians to obey their rulers, some of the Lollards, his followers, though primarily concerned with reform of ritual and clerical extravagance, had no trouble finding in his writings justification for condemnation of and rebellion against a sinful king who violated law. Richard II successfully mastered the Peasants' Revolt under Wat Tyler (see Chapter III), but his treachery and ruthlessness in so doing and his other transgressions on the rights of the *populus* account, in part at least, for his ultimate doom. The Lollards approved the open resistance of their new leader, Sir John Oldcastle, to the authority of both church and state. They were persecuted as heretics and condemned by parliamentary statute; Oldcastle was hanged and burned (1417); but the movement survived despite persecution.

A popular uprising in France during this period was rooted almost entirely in political and economic considerations divorced from religion. This was the revolt of Paris under the leadership of its political head (*prévot des marchands*), Etienne Marcel. The defeats of France in the Hundred Years' War not only depleted the ranks of the nobility but required the dauphin (the future King Charles V, acting as regent during the captivity of his father) to raise large sums of money. Both contingencies played into the hands of the middle class. Under Marcel's guidance they exploited their advantages, demanding concessions in return for continued financial support of the war, and the concessions were made in a statute known as the *Great Ordinance* (*Grande Ordonnance*). Unlike earlier royal charters, the Great Ordinance was no mere set of restrictions on the king's power but rather a statement of requirements for good government, and it vested temporary political power in a commission representing all three estates of the realm, commoners as well as clergy and nobles. Power, however, gradually passed to the middle class of Paris and to Marcel, who claimed to represent 'the will of the people'. He also supported and in turn received support from the peasantry, who rose in numerous *jacqueries*.

Marcel exercised his power for only a brief period (1356–58) before he was killed by an opposing faction acting on mere suspicion that he was engaged in treasonable dealings with the English and out of a deep resentment of his espousal of the peasant cause. His death marked the end of this effort to rule France through an Estates General dominated by the Third Estate. The Great Ordinance was repudiated by the captive king in London, and nothing came of Marcel's brief dictatorship save a precedent and the legend of Etienne Marcel as a leader of the people. Contemporary literature reverberated with popular complaints. A French treatise (*Songe du Verger*), though addressed to King Charles V, suggested the principle of popular sovereignty as a corrective of unjust royal levies: the king had the right to extraordinary taxes only for a just cause such as the defence of the realm; if he misapplied revenues he might be deposed. Similar opinions were expressed by contemporary philosophers like Jean Gerson and Pierre d'Ailly.

In Germany likewise the limitation of the royal prerogative was debated. In a treatise (*De Jure Regni et Imperii Romani*), written about 1338, Luipold Bebenburg discussed at length the electoral right of the people. He maintained that, as in the ancient Roman Empire so also in the Holy Roman Empire, the electors represented the *universitas* of the princes and the people. At the close of the fourteenth century, Emperor Wenceslaus was actually deposed by some of the German electors (a small and select body, to be sure, but yet with some claim to represent the whole empire) for his failure to govern in the public interest. Later, Nicholas of Cusa entered the argument; deriving the origin of governments from natural law, he contended that all political authority was based on popular consent.[3]

Perhaps the strongest statement of the theory of popular sovereignty during this period came from the pen of Marsilius of Padua (possibly with the collaboration of Jean de Jandun). His *Defensor Pacis* (*c.* 1324), like the political works of Dante, Petrarch, and other Italians, was coloured by resentment of papalism, and his major theme was the need to keep the peace despite the warmongers, notably popes and emperors. He applied the Thomist formula to the definition of sovereignty, contending that sovereignty extended from God to the people and from them to their government, which, he felt, should remain responsible to them. His *people*, however, were not the *demos* but rather those typified by the bourgeoisie of Italian cities like his native Padua. Using the term *principans* (*one serving as prince*) to denote a ruler, he stressed the view that the collective citizenry (*civium universitas*) had the right to elect and control a ruler. In case the executive transgressed his delegated powers, the people either as a whole or through its upper-class representatives, its better (*valentior*) part, might depose him. He clearly described the representative-legislator as superior to the *principans*, or executive.

Since the *Defensor Pacis* was dedicated to the emperor-designate Ludwig of Bavaria, sworn enemy of the Avignon papacy, Marsilius' programme was perhaps meant to apply more to the popes than to the temporal autocrats. It portrayed the papacy and clergy rather than emperors and princes as the chief offenders against peace, on the ground that the churchmen were the aggressors, encroaching on the jurisdiction of the secular rulers. His proposal for the solution of this clerical transgression was to subject the church to the state (anticipating Wycliffe, Huss, and Luther in this view). His plea in favour of limiting papal powers was forceful. A forerunner of a philosophy that was to become prominent during the period of the Schism and the Councils, he argued that councils rather than popes were the supreme ecclesiastical authority, for councils were representative of the people, both lay and clerical, and should be convoked by the emperor rather than by the pope.[4]

The impact of Marsilius's ideas was due not so much to their originality as to their direct application to the stormy problem of papal government. His practical approach to the threatening political crisis helped to provide a philosophical justification for its removal from the realm of abstraction to the realm of action. Public response to Marsilius' work was prompt and vigorous. The *Defender of the Peace* was translated into the vernacular; it was attacked by some but also, especially at Ludwig's court, championed. This and his other works, along with those of Jean de Jandun, were exploited for arguments in later polemics, especially against the popes of the Renaissance and the Reformation.

Some fourteenth-century writers, of course, questioned the concept of popular sovereignty. William of Ockham was certainly less liberal and perhaps more objective as a reporter of current views than Marsilius. Though also a protégé of Ludwig of Bavaria, William of Ockham presented the argument,

Scholastic in form, nominalistic in philosophy, that any type of universal empire, whether temporal or spiritual, was apparently a violation of reality (nature),[5] to which all concepts of sovereignty, popular or other, must bow. This idea was more explicit in Wycliffe, who, as we know, doubted that the people should exercise authority over God's vicar in the person of their monarch. Nevertheless, the Marsilian view persisted in the political theory of western Christendom—the view that the sovereign authority of the people was not only the original source of political power but also a continuing force in government. Those who favoured this view held that during an interregnum or a breakdown of established government authority reverted to the people as a whole. Some writers upheld a theory of contractual relationship between people and ruler and stressed the importance of election as a means of controlling monarchs (see Chapter IX).

Despite prominent exceptions, however, from Aquinas' to comparatively recent times little doubt existed that, except in certain limited areas, the best form of government was some form of effective monarchy. In the sixteenth century, the practical tone that prevailed in Italian political theory tended to justify the autocracy of the Italian 'despot' rather than the republicanism of the city-state. Although Machiavelli admitted the hypothetical appeal of democracy and the superiority of the people as a whole to the nobility, he argued that, inasmuch as man by nature was deceitful, cruel, and corrupt, authoritarianism was a necessary evil. He held God and morality in abeyance, making the ruler responsible only to himself and the necessities of the state.[6] Guicciardini, as behoved perhaps the keenest and most cynical mind of his day, recognized the power of the people but put no faith in them either in his own personal activities or in his political theorizing. For him 'the people is a monster, full of confusion and error'.

*   *   *

How Was Arbitrary Power to Be Resisted?

Yet all thinkers on the subject were inclined to favour some fundamental limitations to the power of the monarch.[7] The question was: How and by whom was arbitrary royal power to be restricted? The papal claims to the right to do so, as formulated earlier by Pope Gregory VII and put into effect by Innocent III, carried little weight during the era of the Avignonese, Schismatic, and Renaissance popes, for society could hardly expect protection against royal autocracy from popes who themselves manifested marked autocratic tendencies. Furthermore, the papal claims had to compete with several other answers to the same problem. For the aristocracy, the prince was but *primus inter pares*, one who by some historic chance or method of selection had become foremost in fact among them but was no better by right than they and might be held in check by them, not only for their own but also for the people's defence against arbitrary behaviour. For the towns and cities the prince was often the source of privileges and rights, contained in charters of his granting, but he was also a potential threat that the burghers and guild members within their walled towns must resist if he repudiated royal concessions or made harsh demands. Burghers and nobles sometimes united in parliaments, estates, or cortes against the common danger of autocracy, and frequently the clergy was on their side, moved not only by humane considerations but also by their self-interest as a corporate body. Yet clergy, nobility, towns, and other corporate or quasi-corporate bodies or estates were on some matters as likely to be opposed to as to be united with each other against the prince's authority. When they were united they could claim to act in the name of the *universitas* or the *natio*. Future events were to render their united action increasingly feasible and so to make more acceptable the idea that the community (*universitas*) of the people was the arbiter of tyranny and the active agent for restraining it (see Chapter IX).

*   *   *

Medieval Republicanism

Before the nineteenth century the premise of popular sovereignty rarely was reduced to its logical extreme of republicanism and democracy. Popular sovereignty was in fact absent from government practice except in some Italian and German city-states, some Swiss cantons, and some Netherland provinces, and even in those instances it took the form of aristocratic republicanism rather than popular representative government. The humanists' favourable attitude toward the republican form of government was derived from the Renaissance conception of the ancient Roman Republic (*Senatus Populusque Romanus*) and from the actual republics in the Italy of their day, such as Florence and Venice. None of the contemporary republics, however, was a true democracy. Their governments were dominated by groups of aristocrats and plutocrats, who often brought the leaders of the middle-class guilds into their organization. *A fortiori* in other political structures, it was taken for granted that, although according to natural and divine law the *populus* was the arbiter of the form of government, the sinfulness of at least some of the people required that the actual exercise of power be in the hands of either the *valentior pars* of the citizenry or a prince. Even when theorists differed as to whether the people's delegation of authority to a prince was permanent and whether or how a remedy was to be applied in case the delegated power was misused, popular sovereignty was more or less attenuated in theory, and in practice almost undetectable. Limitations on royal power, if at all applied, were applicable only by, and usually only for, the upper classes.

The theoretical *Respublica Christiana* of the medieval theologian was no genuine republic but a theocratic monarchy. The example of the Roman Republic, however, kept recurring to political theorists, especially during the centuries when Classical studies were revived and cultivated with an unprecedented and since unequalled enthusiasm. Although some writers like

Dante in *De Monarchia* concentrated attention on the Roman (and German) empires, others like Petrarch waxed enthusiastic over Ciceronian literature with its high-flown passages on the greatness of the Roman Republic. When the medieval citizens of Rome became dissatisfied with papal government, they were likely to turn to ancient Roman republicanism as a historical justification for rebellion. Rienzi as 'dictator' and 'tribune', clad in a senatorial toga, made a vain effort to revive the *Senatus Populusque Romanus*, using its emblems, and proclaimed himself 'illustrious redeemer of the Holy Roman Republic'. Petrarch's pen worked overtime to rouse 'the invincible Roman People' to the defence of Rienzi and the Classical-Christian 'Liberty' he had restored to them. Elsewhere in Italy the persistence of municipal titles such as *consul* and *senator* and of the terms *populus* and *plebs* bore witness to latent Classical republicanism. In fifteenth-century city-states such as Milan, where despotism was well rooted, tyrannicide after the example of Roman Republican heroes became a devout purpose for some extremists. In 1412 Duke Giovanni Maria Visconti was stabbed to death at the doors of the Cathedral of Milan by three patriotic nobles moved by the story of Brutus. Classically inspired legalists, confronted with the conflict between popular sovereignty and imperial autocracy, tried to solve it by a theory of history to the effect that the sovereign *Populus Romanus* of the Republic had delegated its power irrevocably to the Roman emperors. Some of them asserted that the German emperors had inherited this absolute authority; others, with less success, made the papacy its beneficiary. Such historical assumptions did little to fortify republicanism, which fought a losing fight in the fourteenth and fifteenth centuries.

A century after Rienzi and Petrarch, republicanism of a different inspiration manifested itself in northern Italy. An evanescent, three-year 'Ambrosian' Republic was established by the nobles of Milan on the death of a childless Visconti ruler in 1447. Unlike Rienzi's SPQR it was dedicated to a Christian hero, Bishop Ambrose, who in the fourth century had forced the Roman Emperor Theodosius to submit to ecclesiastical authority. In Florence also republicanism drew on Christian sources. When the Medici dynasty was overthrown during the French invasion of 1494, Savonarola already had acquired a weirdly pious influence over the Florentine *populus*. Summoned to join the council of the newly established republic, he soon dominated its policies, primarily with a view to establishing a puritanical theocracy. He was more successful in purging the city of its 'vanities' than of French invaders, and shortly a violent faction, called 'the Mad Dogs' by his supporters, arose in opposition. Savonarola's miniature *Respublica Christiana*, having become obnoxious to the Borgia pope, Alexander VI, and from the outset unsuited to Florentine Renaissance tastes, soon purged itself of its mentor.

Meanwhile, in resplendent contrast to this short-lived, pre-Calvin puritanism and republicanism, Venice (Guicciardini's ideal) continued the long-lived, prosperous regime of its plutocratic aristocracy. The Adriatic city-state

rivalled Constantinople and Genoa for control of the Balkan and Mediterranean trade. It steadily augmented its huge territorial empire on both sides
of the Adriatic until checked by the Turkish upsurge in the Levant in the
fifteenth century, and its commercial and cultural prestige continued even
after its imperial expansion had ceased. Its ambassadors ably took care of
Venetian interests abroad; their fairly regular written reports, inaugurating
what is still a major function of diplomatic corps, remain a mine of information about the events of their day.

★   ★   ★

Hussite Political Philosophy

In northern Europe, an illustrious example of republicanism had religious
rather than commercial or Classic roots. The Hussite revolt was in part a
protest of Bohemian cities, artisans, and craftsmen against imperial, royal,
and clerical autocrats. The Utraquist doctrine, the belief that the communicant should partake of the wine as well as the bread of the sacrament, came
to be a major shibboleth in the fight, for it meant to its adherents not only a
return to scripture and the primitive church but also the elimination of a class
barrier between clergy and laity. In the course of this struggle the Bohemian
nobles on their own initiative in 1415 convened a general assembly to protest
the sacrifice of Huss by Emperor Sigismund and the Council of Constance
(see Chapter III). Four years later, direct action was taken against the anti-
Hussite town council of Prague by a crowd of Hussite demonstrators under
the leadership of Jan Žižka, one of the great military leaders and patriots of
his day. After defenestrating the councillors and killing the unfortunates who
survived this forceful sign of their displeasure, they set up their own municipal
government. King Wenceslas, unable to quell the uprising, died shortly
after, leaving all Bohemia in the hands of the Hussites. Their kingless government consisted of a diet and local councils, and Prague became not only a city
republic but to some extent a democracy.[8]

For a time the Bohemian nation united behind the Four Articles of Prague
(1420)—freedom of preaching, partaking of the wine as well as the bread of
the sacrament, confiscation of church property, and the proper punishment
of sin. In 1421 a National Assembly at Chaslav, specifying fourteen tyrannical
offences of Emperor Sigismund, declared that 'we have never accepted . . .
nor will we accept him' as king, and so set an early example of a declaration
of national independence.[9] The Hussite republic successfully maintained
itself against the German 'crusaders' led by Emperor Sigismund but then
succumbed to its own factional differences. On the one side were the Utraquists or Calixtines—so called because they believed that the communicant
should be passed the *calix* ('chalice') of the Eucharist; they were the new
conservatives led by the nobles, inclined to call a halt to further reform. On
the other side were the Taborites, made up largely of peasants, who were
more radical not only in religious thought, wanting a more thorough return

to the principles of scripture, but also in social philosophy, wanting the abolition of private property, taxes, and feudal obligations. The Taborites were defeated (1434) by a combination of Utraquists and Catholics. Before the Hussite Revolution came to an end, however, it had provided religious, political, and intellectual precedents that made it 'the first in the great chain of European revolutions which helped to shape the character of modern, Western society'.[10]

The fate of both Lollard and Hussite followers of Wycliffe illustrates the general trend of sociopolitical events and thought in the fourteenth and fifteenth centuries. The doctrines of republicanism and popular sovereignty were dangerous if taken seriously by the rank and file of the people, but they were destined not to be put into long-term practice. They were meant rather as pious or Classical themes for academic philosophizing and for justification of the strong (popes, emperors, or princes) in their resistance to each other. Still, so long as that resistance persisted and called for justification, such doctrines were bound to survive and to have a mass impact.

*　　*　　*

Political Thought and Practice in Islam

During the period 1300–1500 Islamic political control spread gradually, taking along with it political philosophies based upon traditional institutions and theology. In the process of expansion political unity became more remote than ever; after 1258, when the Abbasid caliphate collapsed, it could not be envisaged even in ceremonial terms. Within the Dār al-Islām, however, political boundaries were regarded as of little consequence. In fact, the various rulers rarely interfered with the autonomous working of either the local or the international institutions through which Islamic life was chiefly carried on.

The political problems that presented themselves after the Mongol regime had ceased were confronted in two ways. One was the critique of reformers such as Ibn-Taymiyya (see Chapter VII), who insisted on the rights of the sharī'a and its interpreters, the 'ulamā', against the worldly corruptions of the military rulers. The other was the attempt by both 'ulamā' and philosophers to come to terms with the actualities of fragmented and militarized political life. On the part of the 'ulamā' this attempt took the form of an assertion—in effect—that the subjects were not politically responsible for any established ruler, provided he tolerated the private practices of Islam, on the ground that even the most unjust rule was preferable to rebellion and civil war. More commonly, however, an effort was made to distinguish legitimate government (given the name caliphate in this period, no matter how local its power) from government that failed to uphold the sharī'a and was therefore condemned. For philosophers legitimate 'caliphal' government in this sense was grounded in Classical ethics; the Aristotelian ethical tradition (as interpreted by Avicenna) received its definitive Islamic form in Iran by the end of the fifteenth century at the hands of Muḥammad b. Saʻd-al-dīn Dawwāni (1425–1502/3).

Perhaps at no time, however, have Ṣūfīs as a whole come closer to a complete rejection of political involvement. Refusing to compromise with a political situation which went against all Muslim instincts, yet not happy with the rigidity of the more puritan of the 'ulamā', they often forbade all contact with the amīrs. At this time the doctrine of the Quṭb received full popularity: the Quṭb was the mystical head of all the Ṣūfī hierarchies; he invisibly superintended the life of the whole world, and before him any monarch was a mere child.

Ibn-Khaldūn (1332–1406) was Islam's outstanding political thinker during these centuries. He worked out a monumental analysis of the dynamics of the formation of states and of the relation to state power of the development of civilized culture. He made use of Greek concepts of political forms but transformed them in terms of an analysis of effective historical interrelations. After intimate involvement in the political life of the Maghrib, he seems to have developed his unprecedented theories for the guidance not only of the student of history but also of anyone who might suppose himself capable of undertaking political activity in an idealistic effort to improve society. An answer to the problems of political philosophy raised in this period of Islamic history came only with the changed political situation after 1500 (see Chapter IX).

★   ★   ★

Hindu Political Theory

Neither political conditions nor the intellectual climate encouraged political speculation among Hindu thinkers, and they rested content with the traditional political theories set forth in the *Dharma-shāstras* (treatises on *dharma*) and *Artha-shāstras* (treatises on the art of government). These included the *Nānava-dharma-shāstra* (Code of Manu), the *Shāntiparvan* section of the *Mahābhārata*, the *Artha-shāstra* of Kautilya, and the last great treatise on government, the *Shrukranīti*, which was probably a thirteenth-century production although small additions may have crept in later. The fourteenth-century philosopher Mādhava, in his commentary on the *Parāshara smriti*, one of the *Dharma-shāstras*, supported the notion that the king was an incarnate deity, but this was not a universal opinion. He also held that the functions of government should be exercised by the Kshatriya, or military caste, alone. In this view he was to be upheld by Nīlakantha, a writer on legal questions of the sixteenth or seventeenth centuries, but Mitramishra, Nīlakantha's contemporary, contended that government was not a monopoly of the Kshatriya caste and that all who ruled were bound by the responsibilities appertaining to kingship.

In general, Hindu political theory accepted the Brahmanical concept of *dharma* (duty, virtue, creed, law, or way of life) as prior and fundamental to government. Monarchy was the accepted form of political organization, and kingship was looked upon as a necessary institution, whether divine or human, for the maintenance of the *dharma*. The fundamental duties of the monarch were to enforce the *dharma* of the various classes and castes, to punish those who violated it, and to protest his subjects in return for his right to tax them. Rulers should normally come from the Kshatriya, whose duty was to rule, but they should appoint Brahmans as religious advisers, be consecrated by Brahmans, and accept Brahman interpretations of the *dharma*. To maintain his legitimate position the king might resort to any sort of device; yet he was also bound by the *dharma*, and writers often laid great emphasis on his duty to promote the well-being of his subjects. Subjects were supposed to be submissive, but some writers emphasized the duty of subjects to resist a king who violated the *dharma* and sanctioned the deposition of bad rulers.

International relations were generally looked upon as a ceaseless struggle between states. The ruler was justified in using any method—alliances, balance of power, conquest, deception, spies, assassination—to protect and promote the interests of his state. Practical manuals on the art of politics, like that of Kautilya, were as cold-blooded as anything in Machiavelli or the writings of the Chinese Legalists. In contrast to the theory of *Realpolitik* in international relations, however, stood the ancient Hindu-Buddhist conception of the *cakravartin*, or divine world-empire—a peaceful, prosperous, and well-ordered universal empire ruled by a god-king. This ideal, while not entirely forgotten in India, was stronger in Buddhist-dominated areas, where the ruler was often conceived as the secular counterpart of the Buddha. The theory of *cakravartin* rule was generally accepted in Burma, Siam, Cambodia, and Majapahit, despite the fact that those kingdoms were neither peaceful and well-ordered nor universal.

*   *   *

Neo-Confucian Political Ideas

In China thought turned much more often to political affairs than in India, although in neither country was political philosophy sharply distinguished from general thought. Since Confucianism was primarily a social and political philosophy, despite the interest of the Neo-Confucians in metaphysics there was no dearth of political commentary in their writings. Nothing essentially new, however, appeared in their political remarks, and no individual writer of the period stands out. Confucian political theory remained authoritarian, patriarchal, and ethical, with vaguely democratic overtones. The state was the family writ large and was to be governed and held together by the same moral, ethical, and cultural ties. The accepted form of government was monarchy, but the monarch was expected to govern the state as a father would his family—through kindness, guidance, virtue, and moral force, backed when necessary with punishment.

The power of the emperor as the agent of Heaven was absolute, but he was expected to exercise it in accordance with Confucian principles. He was to be assisted and guided by a bureaucracy of scholars who knew the Confucian code and whose duty it was to admonish him when he violated it. This duty was specifically assigned to a censorate, which was responsible for denouncing misuse of power and funds by officials in general. In theory, the emperor ruled by virtue of a mandate from Heaven, which might be withdrawn if he did not rule in an enlightened and benevolent way. Plagues, famines, natural disasters, and popular discontent were evidence that the will of Heaven was being violated and were warnings to the ruler that he must mend his ways. Flouting his advisers' words was further indication on the part of a ruler that he was violating the will of Heaven.[11] In the last analysis, however, the will of Heaven was expressed through the acquiescence or non-acquiesence of the ruled, and the right of revolution was recognized.

As indicated in Chapter VI, Neo-Confucian writers, in conformity with their metaphysical concepts, insisted that governments too had a cosmic li, or principle, and would prosper if they adhered to it or decline if they departed from it. Consequently traditional Confucian principles of government came to be regarded as expressions of the cosmic principle (li). Rulers and many other officials took advantage of this tendency to insist that their acts, however arbitrary, were in conformity with the li of government. As a result, the absolutism of the ruler and the authoritarianism of officialdom were strengthened and a static rather than a dynamic concept of government came to dominate. Yet none of the really great Confucian writers sanctioned the growing absolutism, and a number of Confucian scholar-officials were punished, sometimes with death, because they protested against what they considered violations of the proper principles of government.

In China, during this period, no theory of international relations envisaging an association of equal but contending states gained prominence. Confucian theory conceived of the world as a natural unity along patriarchal lines in which China, the Middle Kingdom, was the centre of culture, enlightenment, stability, and authority. Outside peoples were looked upon as younger brothers who naturally wished to emulate China. The emperor was held to be the patriarch of a family of nations to whom the less important rulers looked for guidance and enlightenment. This theory, in essence, denied the inevitable conflict of interest between China and other people and posited a suzerain-vassal relationship in which differences were to be harmonized and sublimated as in a family. The vassals owed to their suzerain respect and homage in the form of tributary missions and were expected to co-operate with China in maintaining peace and order. In return, they received a certain amount of protection and were permitted to trade with and learn from China. The rulers of vassal states were confirmed in their offices by the emperor, and matrimonial alliances sometimes cemented the relationships between suzerain and vassal.

China tended to keep her interference in the internal affairs of vassal states to a minimum, but at times she did not hesitate to intervene when such action seemed to suit her best interests. New peoples were welcomed as vassals, but China never thought of dealing with outside peoples on a basis of equality. During the Yüan and the early Ming period the vassal-state system was greatly expanded in the central Asian, East Indian, and Indian Ocean areas, but after 1435 China made no effort to expand or even maintain the system except with immediately adjacent peoples. Although this scheme held up the ideal of a universal, if hieratic, system of world organization directed toward peace and order, in practice it was a device for protecting China by maintaining peaceful and docile vassals on her borders.

Other countries of the Far East more or less accepted the Confucian political theories. Korea and Vietnam modelled their governments on that of China and fitted themselves into her vassal-state system. In Japan political theories were an amalgam of Confucian ideas, Buddhist cosmic conceptions, and native tribalism. The important political thinkers of the period were the Shinto writers Kitebatake and Ichijō (see Chapter III), who began laying the foundations for the theocratic and absolutistic monarchy of later times. No writer undertook a theoretical justification of Japan's feudal system of the time.

LEGAL THOUGHT AND PRACTICE

Varying Systems of Law in Europe

In Chapter I and elsewhere we have referred to the growth of the ruler's legal and judicial authority in Europe at the expense of the nobility and the church. Concomitant with that growth, and sometimes in close relationship with it, went several other developments in the field of law.

Before the fourteenth century, in accordance with the then prevailing tradition of co-operation between empire and papacy, law was treated as a basically uniform element of all Christian civilization. The natural law of the Roman Empire was thought to have passed, according to Divine Will, to the popes and the emperors. The Respublica Christiana was founded on both the canon and the civil law. During the fourteenth and fifteenth centuries legalists in Europe rivalled theologians in grappling with the debatable issues of ecclesiastical and temporal government. The conclusions of the Thomists were analysed and reinterpreted not only by the Ockhamists with their 'new' logic but also by the canonists and especially by the 'civilians' (as the experts in Roman civil law were called) with highly developed legal techniques. The basic principle, however, of the thirteenth-century theorists remained unchanged; the law of a state was still regarded as the expression of the customs and will of its people and, therefore, binding on all, even the ruler,

This view was considered justifiable on the grounds that positive municipal law was but the earthly counterpart of natural divine law.

For all that, after 1300 and the era marked by Dante's grand plea for politico-religious unity, western Europe grew both more and more diversified and more and more secularized. Civil law eventually eclipsed canon law; national systems of law replaced imperial papal law; pluralism of law as well as of sovereignty became increasingly evident. To be sure, the assumption of a single divine, natural law persisted, and that law was respected as ubiquitous, but whatever authoritative forms it acquired were likely to be different in different states. The people still might on occasion be considered the final arbiter of law, but the people actually operated in diverse ways in England, France, Spain, Germany, Italy, and elsewhere. Through representatives in parliaments, estates general, cortes, diets, and even church councils, they exercised their prerogatives jointly with, or subordinated to, their respective rulers, and the variant customary law of their various regions received varying formal expression and recognition in such representative bodies. In Italy, where no single political head could lead in a single direction, diversification was still more confounding; each city state had its own autonomous system of law. Similar diversification prevailed in the German regions despite the leadership, often only theoretical, of the Holy Roman emperor. And Spain was not one but three 'Spains'.

England was more advanced toward a unified system of law than the continental countries. She had a well developed 'common' law, which was based on practical experience with English institutions of long standing and was unified in a royally controlled legal organization. That is, it was both traditional and royal. Even in England, however, ecclesiastical courts were originally independent of royal control and operated under the regulations of canon law.

During the Middle Ages in all regions of Europe laws were—in theory—made and enforced by the rulers with the tacit or express consent of the people or 'the stronger part' thereof. A growing number of lawyers contributed to the efficiency and prestige of royal governments. After the eleventh-century revival of Roman law in Italy, civil law was studied at the law schools of Bologna, Padua, Pavia, and other cities in Italy, and later in other countries as well, although canon law continued to be stressed, especially at great theological centres such as Paris. From the start of the new trend in legal studies the legalists turned out by the faculties of law at English, French, Spanish, and especially Italian universities readily found employment. Some obtained positions in the governments of their own or foreign countries; some worked at compiling and improving the several systems of national law.

Under the increasing influence of Roman law a new legal philosophy appeared in the fourteenth century, especially in the works of Italian civil lawyers. Since Roman law was contained in books, it was fit for study in universities, and since the arrangement of those books was very disorderly and hard to understand, the jurists who studied them were forced to develop a systematic juristic method. That method was used to systematize the growing body of canon law, too, and later even the treatment of the various customs (i.e. systems of customary law).

Roman law also came to affect the crystallizing rules of law in a number of countries. It had a far-reaching influence—a process known as the 'Reception' —everywhere except in England, the Scandinavian lands, and Switzerland, and even in those countries the law was not entirely unaffected by it. The Reception of Roman law varied greatly in method and in content. In northern France, for instance, the Roman law infiltrated the supposedly German *coutumes*, or unwritten law, steadily from the twelfth to the seventeenth century; Germany on the whole held it off until late in the fifteenth century but then received it suddenly; in the Low Countries an initial infiltration seems to have been succeeded by something in the nature of a catastrophic Reception. Everywhere the Reception was most pronounced in the law of property and obligations (contracts and torts) and in matters of legal technique; hardly anywhere were the rules of family law or the less technical parts of the law of succession altered by Roman law. Indeed, most of the feudal elements in the law survived until the French Revolution and even afterward.

Roman imperial law placed a strong emphasis on the authority of the ruler. The people were still recognized as the ultimate source of law, but they were thought to have delegated authority permanently and irrevocably to the ruler. Thus, in the minds of theorist no less than in actual government, almost everywhere the ruler tended to supplant the people as the supreme lawgiver. Only among a few theologians and political theorists were the ideals of natural law and popular sovereignty upheld with the old vigour.

A great age of legal compilations had passed with the thirteenth-century *partidas* and *specula* and Bracton's summary of English common law; yet in the fourteenth and fifteenth centuries written law took some notable steps in advance. In Italy the school of civil lawyers known as the 'glossators' had by 1300 begun to decline, but their method had led to the *Glossa* of Franciscus Accursius (d. 1263), which was generally regarded as the standard interpretation of the Roman codes. To rival them, there now arose a school of 'commentators', who tried to harmonize Roman law with local customs, applying to their study the methods of the Schoolmen and developing a traditional analytical method of legal exegesis that became known as the *mos italicus*. Since Bartolus de Sassoferato (d. 1357), whom we encountered above as a tempered monarchist, was the outstanding teacher of this method, its practitioners were frequently called 'Bartolists'. Commentaries on Roman law multiplied, as Bartolus, his student Baldus de Ubaldis (1327 ?–1400), and later Italian 'civilians' continued an already venerable tradition of commentaries on civil and canon law. One of the most notable of the Italian commentaries on Roman law was that of Cino de Pistoia (1270–1336), a friend of Dante and Petrarch. Dictionaries of canon and civil law also appeared. Before the sixteenth century nowhere else in Europe did legalists record achievements comparable to those of the Italian 'civilians'.

*   *   *

Codifications of National Laws

The concept of a single fundamental law, of a divine law of nature, that dominated legal theory before 1300 was based upon the assumption that Christians, being uniformly subject to divine will and having the same concept of God and nature, were bound by and ready to submit to the same standards and regulations of human behaviour. The existence side by side of multiform codes—feudal law, commercial law, common law, canon law, and Roman civil law—contributed, even in the church-dominated centuries, to the weakening of the monolithic principle implicit in a divine law of nature. After 1300 the gradual breakdown of imperial and papal prestige in western Europe, and the resulting increase of independence for city states and national states, roused recurrent doubt regarding the possibility or acceptability of a uniform interpretation of God's will. This doubt was reflected in further pluralization of law. National monarchs and town councils disregarded or even defied papal and imperial authority with increasing impunity, while legal theorists, both ecclesiastical and civil, explained and justified such actions by reinterpreting natural law.[12]

The heightening competition of the day between rising dynasts and feudal nobility hastened the movement, for it provided nationalizing authorities with an impetus toward separate, centralized codes of law for their separate peoples written in their separate vernaculars. The first such code in Europe appears to have been the *Siete Partidas* formulated by Alfonso X, the learned ruler of Castile, in the thirteenth century. In the mid-fourteenth century the Spanish cardinal Albornoz, while in the service of the Avignon popes (see Chapter III), after restoring papal rule in central Italy, organized it under an effective government code, the *Constitutiones Aegidianae*. In France private compilations of local *coutumes* appeared, and in 1453 Charles VII formally encouraged the systematic preparation of local codes in northern France, the land of the *droit coutumier*. Such codes tended to incorporate principles of Roman law and royal ordinances with local juridical practices and concepts. The process went on until the eighteenth century, eventually providing one of the sources for Napoleon Bonaparte's national system of codes.

Several rulers of eastern Europe also took a lead in this regard. Along with the royal bulls, charters, statutes, constitutions, and other administrative regulations which they more or less willingly conceded, they also tried to systematize the local practices, feudal customs, and royal decrees of their several lands, but they did not hesitate to introduce innovations where they thought desirable—which was usually to court popular support against aristocratic rivals. Under King Wenceslas (Vaclav) II (1289–1306) the codification of the mining law of Bohemia (known thereafter as the *Ius Regale Montanorum* or the *Constitutiones Iuris Metallici*) began. It fortified the royal claims upon the natural resources against the claims of the feudal aristocracy and so was comparatively more favourable to the workers in the mines than was usual in contemporary practice. Around 1346 Casimir III (the Great) codified separately the laws of Great and Little Poland; he revealed a favourable attitude toward burghers and peasants, but it was successfully counteracted by the gentry (*szlachta*) of Poland. In Serbia Stephan Dushan issued his *Zakonik* (*Book of Law*) in 1349. Emperor Charles IV, who was also king of Bohemia (1346–78), promulgated the *Majestas Carolina* in 1350; it remained ineffective, however, because of the opposition of the Bohemian nobles. The enlightened son of Hunyadi, King Matthias Corvinus, crystalized Hungarian law in a famous code of 1486, but after the suppression of a bitter peasant uprising, led by György Dozsa, it was overridden by the considerably less humane code of 1514, never formally promulgated, and the *Tripartitum Opus Juris Consuetudinarii* (1517), a manual of Hungary's customary law. Both of these codes were prepared by István Verböczy. They not only gave the Hungarian nobles special privileges *vis-à-vis* their sovereign but also tightened their hold upon the peasantry. A Russian code of laws (*Sudebnik*), issued in 1497 by the government of Ivan III, was augmented in 1550 by that of Ivan IV. It reflected the Muscovite policy of building up autocratic administrative power in order to counteract feudal decentralization, but at the same time it improved the economic status of the aristocracy by greatly restricting the peasants' right to move away to the towns or to freer and newer lands, thus attaching them still more firmly to their lords.

*   *   *

Laws Merchant and Town-Laws

The commercial interests of the burgeoning middle class urged them on to take a leading part in the struggle for more systematic codes of law. Traders tended to band together against unfair practices among themselves and against undue exploitation by both the rulers and the nobles of the countries in which they found themselves. As a general rule, they supported the kings against the centrifugal tendencies of feudalism. They preferred, however, to regulate their own commercial affairs by their own common standards, settling their disputes in courts and by laws that they themselves controlled rather than submitting to the laws of foreign sovereigns or to codes that might contain no provision directly applicable to the dispute in hand. Roman law had embodied some commercial provisions, and despite the decline of trade during the Middle Ages actual practice had given rise to compilations of 'the custom of merchants' in several Italian cities, Rhodes, Oléron, Catalonia, and other maritime centres. With the increase of trade came new commercial codes, often named after a mercantile town or region. Such were the *Sea Laws of Flanders* (essentially the same as the famous twelfth-century *Roles of Oléron*), the *Sea Laws of Visby* (later elaborated as the *Sea Laws of Lübeck*, which finally became the laws of the Hanseatic League), and Barcelona's *Consulate of the Sea*. By the choice of the litigants themselves suits concerning contracts, partnerships, 'international' payments, and certain other commercial matters were often adjudged in accordance with these 'laws merchant'.

Somewhat similar developments occurred in some of the landlocked cities of Europe. Often for commercial reasons but also because of political conflicts with a feudal lord, a city could attempt to formulate a coherent town-law. Usually this sort of event (occurring since the earlier Middle Age) resulted in a code peculiarly applicable to that city, but the best codes sometimes became models to be adopted or adapted by other cities.

*   *   *

The Dawn of International Law

During the fourteenth century the incidence of war mounted, and legalists, During the fourteenth century the incidence of war mounted, and legalists, no less distressed than others by the carnage, began to wonder how to regulate the conduct of war along some lines resembling international law. A work entitled *De Bello*, dedicated to Cardinal Albornoz, achieved some fame, and an earlier essay by the French legalist Pierre Dubois, *De Recuperatione Terrae Sanctae* (1306), seems to have been better known. Dubois argued that if the Holy Lands were ever to be recovered, the European rulers would first have to create peace among themselves, and he thought they could best do so by joining together under the leadership of the French king. He proposed a series of needed reforms to that end, but his appeal—quite understandably—elicited no enthusiastic response among Europe's rulers.

As politically sovereign units proliferated, economic and political philosophies became more secularized, realistic, and dynastic. Increasingly complicated practices called for a mercantilist reinterpretation of the Aristotelian-Christian generalizations on economics. Abstract moral principles were blunted by the concrete realities of prevailing mercantile, diplomatic, and military methods. In governmental administration, law and lawyers were taken farther away from theories in books and brought nearer to earth. Autocratic dynasties, as the actual forces behind law, became masters rather than subjects of it. They and their staffs of middle-class lawyers made or moulded it to serve their own political ends. Finally, at the dawn of the sixteenth century, Machiavelli's frank pen metamorphosed the abstract, theocratic unity of medieval law into the pragmatic, diversified legalism of the sovereign authoritarian state. He was not, however, creating a new system; he was merely giving explicit literary expression to what was by that time fairly common practice. The principle of *raison d'etat* (national self-interest) rather than of international justice was to dominate international affairs in the centuries that followed.

*   *   *

The Sharī'a and Its Supplements

Outside Europe the ancient legal codes were likewise highly respected, both at local and wider levels. After 1300 they were interpreted most often in accordance with the views of famous commentators. Hindu law, for instance, was contained in the ancient *Dharma-shāstras*, consisting of many detailed instructions, often based on religious precepts, for the conduct of public as well as personal affairs. The commentaries on these *Dharma-shāstras* served as the basis of Hindu law throughout our period. In the Islamic world the *sharī'a*, the all-embracing legal system established by the Muslim religion, provided a common set of presuppositions which held together the most diverse communities, but it was almost everywhere supplemented by administrative regulations as well as by local custom, both of which were sometimes codified. The great codes of the Ottoman Empire were essentially elaborations of the *sunna* (traditions allegedly documented by the Prophet's sayings) adapted to special conditions. One was promulgated in the fifteenth century by Mehmet II and was called the 'Pearl', the other in the sixteenth by Sulaimān the Magnificent and was called the 'Confluence of the Seas' (*Multaqa-al-abhar*). In China the T'ang code provided a model for the codes of later dynasties.

Islam is a civilization of highly sophisticated legal concepts, and various schools of interpretation of the law existed (see Chapter II). Before 1500 the Hanbalite school seems already to have lost ground to the other schools, especially to the Hanafites and the Shāfi'ites. The Malakites meanwhile consolidated their hold on the Maghrib. Nevertheless, the legal writings of Ibn Taimiyya (see Chapter VI) gave the Hanbalite school new life, and his insistence upon freedom from *taqlid* (the unquestioning acceptance of the teachings of the schools) eventually found great favour with the Wahhābis.

The Muslims permitted other legal systems to survive in the areas under their control. In India the Hindu system operated side by side with that of the Muslims, who were subject to Muslim law, while Hindus were left largely free to apply their own laws to themselves. In many areas in the north a mixed system grew up among Muslim converts in which Hindu customary law and caste rules survived to a large extent. Islamic rulers in the north, guided by the *'ulamā'* and assisted by various law officers, followed the orthodox Sunnī law as set forth by the Hanafī school, while non-orthodox Muslims followed so far as possible their own religious law. The Islamic rulers issued various decrees applicable often to Hindus as well as Muslims, but these were not codified before 1500, and no systematic statute law appeared. Generally speaking, the various religious, social, and tribal groups were largely self-governing communities with their own religious and customary law, and royal decrees did not basically affect the system under which they lived.

* * *

Dharma and Its Supplements

Law (as distinct from religious duty and social convention) did not commonly occupy so important a place in the social structure of other eastern lands as in that of Islam or of the western countries. In the non-Islamic East, law did not become a distinctive subject of study or develop a clearly defined philosophy. Civil law (torts, contracts, and other matters having to do with private rights in the West) in particular was left undeveloped, either remaining within the realm of custom and common ethics or being regarded as acts subject to defined penalties. On the other hand, some acts that were considered punishable crimes in the West remained religious or social offences not subject to legal penalties.

Since law in the non-Islamic East did not develop the same specialized characteristics as in Islam or in the West, highly specialized groups of legal officials did not evolve. Although judicial officials generally came from those learned in the lore of their culture—for example, Brahmans in Hindu areas and Confucian literati in China—they usually combined other administrative functions with their judicial activities. Judges frequently acted as both prosecutor and judge, and no distinct group of lawyers developed. As a rule, the judges exercised a great deal of freedom in interpreting and applying laws and custom to individual cases, and the law itself might differ from individual to individual, depending, among other things, upon his religion, profession, caste or class, or tribe. The principle of impersonal law applicable to all alike had at one time found advocates in China but had long since been discredited.

Judicial procedure in the non-Islamic East was likely to be summary and arbitrary, although, in theory, appeals to the sovereign were permitted. It was not codified, and rules of evidence were not highly developed. Both oral and written testimony were permitted, and, as in the West, torture was likely to be used not only upon the accused but also upon witnesses. In general, the accused was considered guilty until proved innocent. The doctrine of collective responsibility, by which a family or clan might be held responsible for acts of a relative, and neighbours, whole villages, or the local headman for the acts of fellow villagers, was widely applied. As elsewhere, punishments were generally harsh, and although sentences of fines, imprisonment, and banishment were also pronounced, corporal punishment of some kind, like whipping, maiming, strangulation, or beheading, was general. Cruel forms of execution were not uncommon, although burning seems not to have been so frequent as in the West. At the local level, tradition and customary law dominated and were administered by village headmen and elders, sometimes assisted, as in Japan, by a representative of a higher authority.

Hindu religious and civil law was generally set forth in the writings relating to *dharma*. Since *dharma* embraced the whole range of life's duties and responsibilities, it cannot be defined as law in any narrow Western sense. The oldest of the writings on *dharma* were the *Dharma-sūtras*, but the later metrical *Dharma-shāstras*, being more detailed and systematic, became the basic law books. Of these many *shāstras* the *Code of Manu*, the *Yājñavalkya-smriti*, and possibly the *Parāshara-smriti* were the most respected. Vijñaneshvara's *Mitāksharā*, an eleventh-century commentary on the *Yājñavalkya*, was in reality an independent juridical treatise, extremely important in north India and the Deccan. The great *shāstras* had all been written before our period, but several distinguished commentaries on the earlier ones appeared. In addition, law digests increased in significance after the twelfth century, and several appeared after 1300.

The *Dharma-shāstras*, although claiming validity for all castes, were written primarily in the interests of the Brahmans. Their extensive sections on the rights and duties of kings contained the most distinctly legal material. They included sections on the duties and responsibilities of the four great classes of Indian society, on principles of government, on domestic law (encompassing legal procedure and what would be civil and criminal law in the West), on rules of caste, and on morality. Under procedural matters, written and verbal evidence and ordeals were discussed. Other sections dealt with such matters as debts, pledges, sales, partnerships, wages, contracts, disputes over boundaries, defamation, assault, theft, adultery, and inheritance. The most widely known commentary of this period on the *shāstras* was that of Kullūka on the *Code of Manu*. It was written in Benares in the fifteenth century but was largely a recapitulation of the twelfth-century commentary of Govindarāja. Bālambhatta Vaidyanāth and his wife Laksmidevi commented on the *Mitāksharā* and emphasized the property rights of women. Mādhava's fourteenth-century commentary on the *Parāshara* contained a good deal of legal material. Among the law digests, the *Dāyabhāga* of Jīmūta-vāhana, variously placed between 1090 and 1400, came to dominate the law of inheritance in Bengal.

In Siam, Burma, Cambodia, Malaya, and the East Indies the *Code of Manu* became widely known and influential. Siam had a code that was based on the *Manu*, although its most ancient legal canons, dating from the time of Rāma Thibodi (1350–69), presented Thai legal principles before Siam was much affected by Hindu ideas. The *Wagaru Dhammathat*, the oldest extant Burmese law book, compiled at the end of the thirteenth century in Pegu, was essentially a digest of *Manu*. Cambodia also had a code based on the *Manu*. Geja Mada (d. 1364), chief minister of Majapahit, had a law book compiled which replaced an earlier adaptation of the *Manu*, the *Kutaramanava*, used in Java. As Islam invaded Malaya and Indonesia, Islamic law began to compete with Hindu *dharma* and local customary law. Generally speaking, however, local customary law dominated the area, although it differed from country to country, from tribe to tribe, and from locality to locality.

*   *   *

I, Li, Lü, *and Their Supplements*

The Chinese, because of their great political unity and administrative stability, possessed a highly unified legal system, Conduct, however, was supposed to be guided by the Confucian principle of righteousness and proper behaviour (the *i* and the *li*); law was looked upon only as an adjunct to the application of these principles. The public and officials alike tried to avoid resort to law, because its use was a humiliating reminder that the higher principles had been violated. Civil suits were largely avoided, and no codes of civil law developed beyond customary practices administered by local elders. Even when the law came into operation, the magistrates considered the *li* and *i* involved when judging the evidence and applying the penalties prescribed by law. Chinese and all non-Chinese who lived outside the few tribal administrative areas were potentially subject, of course, to the laws of the empire, but tribal peoples and non-Chinese, such as the Muslims and the small Jewish communities, were generally allowed to live in accordance with their own customs and laws.

China's laws fell into three main categories. One of them comprised imperial decrees and decisions, generally issued in response to proposals made by officials, and local orders arising from the discretionary authority of provincial and local officials. Many of these decrees were applicable only to specific areas or particular problems and, once the need which had given rise to them had passed, fell into disuse, unless they were incorporated into the codes or were revived to meet a new situation. A number of the decrees were of an instructive and exhortative nature, and only some of them carried penalties. A second category of laws comprised the decrees relating to administrative organization and procedure, which were periodically collected into administrative codes known as *Hui-tien*, or *Collected Statutes*. Many of the *Collected Statutes* were merely descriptive or procedural in nature, but others carried penalties. The third category of laws was the legal code proper, or *Lü*.

The *Lü*, also organized along administrative lines, set forth the fundamental laws that had arisen out of the experience of the past. The code issued during the reign of the first Ming emperor was based directly on that of the T'ang dynasty. It began with a general section on principles and definitions (including a description of ordinary punishments), treasonable offences, and the conduct of officials. Then came six sections of matters that normally fell respectively within the purview of the six administrative boards of the central government—civil offices, revenue, ritual, military affairs, public works, and punishments. The section relating to punishments was the largest and contained much of what would be considered criminal law in the West.

The code, in fact, made no distinction between administrative, civil, and criminal law, and thus various kinds of actions that in the West would have fallen under the headings of social custom or civil law became penal matters in China. The section on punishments dealt with abusive language, disobedience to parents, quarrelling, slander, treason, homicide, bribery, corruption, forgery, fraud, incest, and adultery. The section on revenue dealt with succession, inheritance, certain aspects of marriage, smuggling, and usury, along with other matters. The code was highly patriarchal, at every turn buttressing the status of the emperor, the officials and literati, those in senior or superior status, and the father as head of the family. Abusive language to a father might, for example, be punished by strangulation, and fathers under certain circumstances had authority of life and death over children. Although severe in many regards, the code was systematic, self-consistent, and consistent with contemporary mores. Penalties were carefully graded according to the seriousness of the offences; they included slicing, decapitation, strangulation, exile, imprisonment, the cangue, beating with large or small bamboo, castration, and fines; in certain cases self-execution was permitted.

Court procedure was based on the assumption that the emperor was the source of justice. Most cases were reviewed by higher tribunals before sentence was carried out. Appeal usually was permissible and, theoretically, in serious cases could be made to the emperor. No execution, except in times of crisis, could be carried out without imperial approval. Trial took into account both facts and circumstances and considered a host of circumstances that might mitigate or compound a crime. They included motive, intent, type of weapon used, status, age, sex, mental condition, religion, and the relationship of the defendant to the injured party. By the doctrine of collective responsibility whole families might suffer from the treason of a single member, a father or a superior might be punished for the acts of a child or a subordinate, and if a woman's paramour killed her father or husband, she was strangled along with her paramour. Confession was necessary for conviction, and this requirement inevitably led to the use of torture to extort confessions.

The *Lü* was supplemented and interpreted from time to time by the *li*, or supplementary statutes, prepared by the Board of Punishment and issued by imperial decree. They arose largely out of judicial experience, since detailed reports on cases went to the Board of Punishments for study and review. Case books were also compiled and circulated for the use and guidance of magistrates and review officials, who invariably considered precedents in their decision of cases.

In other Far Eastern countries Chinese ideas of ethics and law combined with local custom to form the legal system. Korea and Vietnam promulgated codes derived from those of the Chinese. Japan at one time had the *Taiho* code, based on codes of the T'ang dynasty, but, as a result of the rise of feudalism, the old code fell into disuse and was largely replaced by the house laws of the various feudal families. While influenced by Chinese ideas and the older code, these feudal codes also reflected local custom and experience. They were a compound of ethical principles (both Chinese and Buddhist) and administrative, civil, and penal law. They dealt with the duties and responsibilities of members of the feudal hierarchy, the conditions under which land was held and inherited, and the punishments for rebellion, murder, adultery, forgery, removal of land markers, and other offences. The house law of the Hōjō family, issued under the title of *Jōei Shikimoku* in 1232, was widely imitated by other feudal houses and became the basis of feudal law in medieval Japan. Feudal law continued to grow during our period through the precedents and interpretations established by the courts of the shoguns and of the various feudal houses.

ECONOMIC THOUGHT AND PRACTICE

From Aquinas to Oresme

Aquinas had condemned some contemporary commercial practices, which, however, were already helping to transform Christendom from a rural to an urban civilization. In his opinion (and that of the Catholic Church generally) the increasing of a debt by the addition of interest (called 'usury') and certain other financial operations were un-Christian. On the other hand, he defended slavery and serfdom, and the servile status of the worker of the soil tended to harden as Roman law more and more replaced customary law. The writings of Dante, a citizen and official of Florence, the outstanding financial centre of Italy, testify to the general approval of Aquinas' economic views at the beginning of the fourteenth century; the *Inferno* reserved a special horrible place for 'usurers'. Oresme who, among his many claims to distinction, was an outstanding economic theorist, pronounced no serious strictures upon traditional principles. His *De Origine et Natura, Jure et Mutationibus Monetarum* (c. 1356), although it offered some penetrating analyses of monetary fluctuation (see below), generally summarized prevailing economic theory with approval. In the succeeding century Gerson maintained that it was contrary to nature for money to breed money.

Yet, despite public contempt and ecclesiastical pronouncements, the times favoured a practical realism in economic affairs. In fact, Scholastic theologians generally approved the *commenda* ('sleeping' partnership) and other true partnerships (and thus endorsed a most important factor in the future development of capitalism), but they quite consistently condemned fictitious partnerships, monopolies, and conspiracies in restraint of trade. Although the church's disapproval of usury gave general direction to medieval economic theory, in actual practice its animus was directed chiefly against 'manifest' usury—that is, against those who were notorious as userers because in their money-lending, pawnbroking, or other transactions they openly increased the principal of their loans. Bankers were seldom regarded as 'manifest' usurers since they did not openly lend money at interest, being careful to operate by forms that had not incurred theological reproach. For instance, the *cambium* (exchange contract) was regarded as a permissible business transaction, since it was thought to involve not a loan but a transfer of money and so to earn a charge for service rather than to extort usury as strictly defined—that is, as an increment in the principal of a loan. In fact, at the close of the fifteenth century the Franciscans of Italy were allowed to collect fees on loans for the overhead expenses of their *monti di pieta* (pawnshops), though they customarily charged the poorest little or almost nothing. Shortly afterward, Pope Leo X formally approved pawnshops, and Cardinal Cajetan, a Dominican and commentator *par excellence* on Aquinas, went along with the other churchmen who regarded taking advantage of the fertility of money as pardonable.

Jews and other non-Christian financiers often assumed the role of unlicensed usurers and pawnbrokers, thus increasing their risks and, therefore, their interest rates and their unpopularity, but most of the European moneylenders of the Middle Ages were Christians and most of the great bankers were Italian. The names of two great money centres, Cohors in southern France and Lombardy in northern Italy, gave to the words *Cahorsin* and *Lombard* a connotation of moneylender or pawnbroker, frequently in a pejorative sense. Even though the outstanding theorists of the fourteenth and fifteenth centuries hesitated to defend interest, conspiracies in restraint of trade, and other profit-making practices of businessmen, it is extremely debatable whether church scruples impeded the march of capitalism (see Chapter I).

The thirteenth century and the first half of the fourteenth were a boom period for financial enterprise. In Italy mercantile operations, like contemporary political organisms, tended to merge into ever larger units; and the largest strove to monopolize business in their respective spheres or regions of operations. Family business firms grew bigger and more daring, took on more costly enterprises, required greater capital, and so evolved into partnerships, with several owners pooling their resources and sharing the profits and losses. Greater capital meant greater enterprise and more efficient organization. With agents in various parts of the world, with systematic and constantly improving methods of accounting, with carefully audited balance sheets, with accumulating statistical data, with newly devised or better administered methods of transporting funds and credit, such companies expanded into distant regions, attempting to monopolize markets, competing for transport facilities, and amassing fabulous profits for eager partners.

Setbacks and bankruptcy nevertheless occurred. In the mid-fourteenth century economic conditions in the West took such a decidedly bad turn (partly a result of the Black Death and the Hundred Years' War) that the next century (1348–1453) has been referred to as a 'depression', and even after that recovery was slow.[13] The labourers of the industrial towns, the peasants, and the lesser nobles, by contrast with the mercantile plutocracy, were truly hard hit, and their discontent was reflected in the vernacular literature of the day. The *Vision of Piers Plowman* (at least partly attributable to William Langland) made a plea for economic justice based on Christian idealism. 'He who commits the sin of usury', cynics said, 'goes to Hell; he who does not, goes to the poor house.' And in England John Ball, released from prison after leading the Peasants' Revolt, preached a sermon on the popular text: 'When Adam delved and Eve span, who was then the gentleman'?[14] But the fourteenth-and-fifteenth-century theorists did little to probe the social discontent of the lower classes, nor did they expound, or in fact seem to realize, the widely prevailing shifts in population, markets, and agricultural production.

The constantly shifting economy, however, did attract the attention of theorists to serious problems of a financial nature—money, credit, and trade, for instance. In fourteenth-century Italy, the Perugian jurist Baldus wrote a number of *consilia* (*consultations*), in which he made detailed comments on the legal aspects of bills of exchange and other such business transactions. Contemporary mathematicians (notably Jacopo of Florence and Paolo Dagomari) wrote treatises in the Italian vernacular concerning interest, exchange, partnerships, and weights and measures. France rivalled Italy in producing specialized financial writings. About 1300 Pierre Dubois commented on the problem of monetary depreciation and inflation. A half-century later, Oresme produced his *De . . . Mutationibus Monetarum* (mentioned above), one of the first comprehensive treatments of monetary theory.

In this work the author re-examined earlier ideas (with special reliance on his older contemporary Buridan) and analysed them dispassionately. Commenting in detail on usury, monetary stability, the ratio of gold to silver, and similar problems of economics, he came to some basic but at that time relatively uncommon conclusions. In the midst of the Hundred Years' War and the fourteenth-century depression, when the value of the *livre tournois* was being changed several times a year to suit the preference of France's ruler, Charles V, Oresme insisted that for a system of coinage to be sound it must be not a set of mere tokens of a value arbitrarily fixed by those in authority but, rather, a popularly acceptable medium of exchange, each piece with a mercantile value of its own and fluctuating in purchasing power with its intrinsic value. His importance lies less in the partial truth of this view than in the fact that, as a theorist, he approached economic problems as subjects of objective study. His treatise was a notable victory for empiricism in economic thought and deserves to rank with Etienne Marcel's contemporaneous political protests as a denial of arbitrary royal authority. It brought, or at least helped to bring, about an ordinance of Charles V that for a generation assured monetary stability.

*   *   *

Banking in Europe

Meanwhile practical business affairs had wrought some radical changes in economic thought and practice. One of these was the amplification of banking. By the beginning of the fourteenth century the importance of the fairs as trading and financial systems was diminishing, and more or less stationary banks were replacing the peripatetic moneylender (see Chapter I). In Germany and wherever banking was inadequate, the fairs still provided the necessary centres of trade and finance, but in the fourteenth and the fifteenth centuries at least eleven cities in Italy, three in France, three in Spain, one in Flanders, and one in England became banking cities. Sometimes, as for the needs of the papal court, they also furnished itinerant banking facilities.

A rich and important merchant-banker might have branch offices or correspondents in several cities. Francesco Datini of Tuscany (c. 1335–1410) established branches in Florence, Pisa, Avignon, Barcelona, Valencia, and Palma de Mallorca; he had correspondents in Bruges, London, and other places; and he had close associations with other banking houses. Branch banking was at first managed by employees called 'factors', who worked for fixed salaries and were given power of attorney, but in the hard times of the fourteenth century a series of bank failures induced Datini, the Medici, and other Florentine banks to adopt an organization by partnerships. Branches abroad were then managed by partners who received no salary but shared in the profits of the branch. Upon his death Datini willed most of his fortune to a charitable foundation, the Ceppo di Poveri, which he had initiated and which still carries on its philanthropic work from the palace in which its founder once lived. Datini thus was a significant pioneer both in international banking and in private philanthropy.

In the course of time banking became a highly diversified activity. The Medici bank invested its moneys in other enterprises like silk and wool manufacturing and so pioneered in commercial and investment banking. Bankers were now regularly charging interest though still concealing their charges—on exchange operations, for example, by manipulating the rate of price of exchange. In the fourteenth and fifteenth centuries exchange banks existed in the major trading centres of Flanders, Spain, and Italy and even in some of the smaller towns of Germany, but in England private money-changing was severely prohibited, foreign coin being under the control of the royal exchanger in the Tower of London (with branches in other ports). Public banks began with the municipal *taula* of Barcelona in 1401 (which in 1853 was absorbed by the Bank of Spain). Double-entry book-keeping and other improvements in accounting made possible the ready transfer of credit; bills of exchange and certain forms of bank money were beginning to be common; and checks, first used in the fourteenth century, were also becoming familiar. Continued depression brought on repeated bank failures in the fifteenth century, but the private transfer banks were the chief victims of the consequent public displeasure, and public banks grew more numerous in the sixteenth century.[15]

*   *   *

Mercantilism and Free Enterprise

As explained in Chapter I, the prevailing theory of governmental economics in Europe during this period, was that which eventually came to be known as mercantilism. From the economic point of view, it was a programme to allocate a country's resources so as to make it prosperous in time of peace and strong in time of war. From the political point of view, it envisaged a way of putting control of a country's economy in the hands of its ruler and was a fitting economic corollary of political autocracy. It was expressed in practise by the strict regulation of markets, guilds, exports, and imports, by royal monopoly or subsidization of certain industries, and by the grants of monopolies and patents to favourites.

Mercantilism, coupled with canon law and guild regulations, had rendered enterprise considerably less than free in the period before 1300. The development of the non-guild middle man in commerce who bought wholesale from the manufacturer (usually a member of the local guild) and sold retail to the consumer, and the emergence of the 'domestic' or 'putting-out' system of manufacture (see Chapter I) tended to intrude upon the established guild monopolies and royal controls. Guilds and mercantilist theories did not succumb rapidly, however, to these intruders, and before 1500 their intrusions did not make a deep impression.

*   *   *

The Muslim World and Asia

From 1300 to 1500 the countries outside western Europe produced little that was new in the field of economic thought and practically nothing that could be called substantive economic theory, independent of moral or political philosophy. Scattered ideas relating to India's economic affairs were to be found in the commentaries on the *Dharma-shāstras* and *Artha-shāstras*, in the legal digests of the period, and in decrees issued by rulers. In China the writings of various Confucians and numerous administrative decrees dealt with economic matters, but strictly in accordance with traditional precepts. In Japan economic ideas were represented in the land regulations of feudal lords, in rules governing the guilds (the *za*), and in the efforts of the *za* either to break down customs barriers or gain monopolistic control for themselves. In general, Asia's economic theories and practices, though autochthonous, were much like Europe's—a combination of communal tradition with partly physiocratic and partly mercantilistic concepts.

The most important theoretical discussion of economics in Muslim literature was that of Ibn-Khaldūn. He analysed the nature of money and the

R*

effects of government spending and of taxation under varying historical circumstances. He explained how an abundant government revenue under some social conditions might lay no burden on a society while under others the same society might be overwhelmed though the expenses of its government seemed to require far less revenue. Among other things he opposed governmental commercial ventures. Other Muslim writers on economic matters were divided chiefly into two groups. One wrote fiscal manuals for rulers, commonly stressing the importance of fostering agriculture; the other wrote handbooks for merchants. The law and practice of the fisc were highly complex and produced some controversy, varying greatly from area to area.

The Ṣūfī writer Badr-al-Dīn (1358–1416) became enmeshed in a tangle of economic, religious, and political impulses. He himself preached a doctrine of community of property and attracted a large following among the impoverished in the days when Timur was ravaging Anatolia. Upon the death of that conqueror, Sultan Mehmet I undertook to reunite the Ottoman Empire but encountered considerable opposition. In the area around Aidin a serious dervish revolt broke out, led by Bürklüdje Mustafa among others (1416), but it was repressed. Despite grave doubt of Badr-al-Dīn's complicity, he was hanged along with the known leaders of the revolt.

The Islamic land-tenure system in the Middle East had grown increasingly complex over the centuries, reflecting the accumulative effect of ancient tradition, the *sharī'a*, and a number of experiments in high politics. The arrival of the Mongols had caused a major confusion in the system, and when it was again straightened out in this period, important traces of Mongol law (*yāsā*) had been added to the earlier elements. In most areas the net result was to discourage independent peasant effort. Far-sighted attempts on the part of some enlightened viziers in the early-fourteenth century failed to improve the situation basically, and in the fifteenth century unstable political life and a declining economic level seemed to preclude any further serious effort.

In Asia as in Europe and elsewhere agriculture was the basic support of society and state and was run very largely by communal practices. Private ownership of land had evolved more clearly in China than elsewhere. Government regulations and other controls beyond local practices were dictated more by fiscal needs and political ambitions than by economic or social theories. Governments promoted agriculture, their main source of revenue, through water control, irrigation systems, and reclamation projects. In China and the countries under its influence the farmer occupied a high place in the social scale; he was lauded as the foundation of society and was encouraged to be thrifty and hard working.

In Asia (as elsewhere) commerce and industry were not ordinarily favoured as much as agriculture. In India the attitude toward merchants and artisans seems generally to have been one of laissez-faire, although some rulers, especially those in seacoast areas, encouraged merchants and skilled craftsmen. In Malacca and other trading states of the Indies merchants and artisans were encouraged by the rulers and the mercantile aristocracy. Even in feudal Japan the shoguns and some feudal lords engaged in trade and encouraged mercantile activity. In China the artisans, long organized into guilds, were encouraged but to a somewhat lesser degree than farmers. The moralistic Confucian scholar-officials, like the clergy of the West, looked down upon the merchant as a kind of pariah who produced nothing new or useful and made profit at the expense of the rest of society. Merchants were therefore considered fair game for the exactions of officials. The Mongol rulers tended to encourage foreign trade, but the Ming rulers, especially after the Yung-lo emperor (1403–24), tended to discourage it except as a part of the tributary system, in which it could be controlled and milked to the advantage of the government; they even forbade Chinese to go abroad. Many of the gentry and officials from the south-coast provinces of China defied this policy, and illegal trading grew up between the Chinese and the Japanese and, later, the Portuguese. Eventually it developed into piracy, which seriously infested the south coast and weakened the government, particularly during the sixteenth century. The Chinese government also maintained monopolistic control over salt, certain metals, and some other products. Most Asian governments seem to have been, like Western governments, concerned to prevent the outflow and to promote the inflow of precious metals. Japan in particular was anxious to import coins from China.

HISTORICAL THOUGHT

Europe's Historians

European scholarship in the fourteenth century revealed considerably less change in historiography than in economic theory. The typical historiography of the Middle Ages (i.e. annals and chronicles) continued, usually restricted to events in the author's region but sometimes unrestricted in time or place (often covering all the known world from the beginnings to the author's present). As formerly, most chronicles were written by clergymen in the language used by their church and were dominated by religious interest. Generally those of this period were inferior in quality to their predecessors, especially to those of the English-Norman school. The fourteenth-century Latin *Polychronicon* of the English chronicler Ranulf Higdom was a noteworthy example of a clerical history of the world. It was an impersonal chronicle that began with Adam and came down to his own day; it was continued after his death by others. The chronicle (1377) compiled by the monk Lavrientyi of the Suzdal-Niznegorod principality mirrors the contrasting literary tendencies of contemporary Russia. It reflected the continuing cultural influence of Kiev along with the local pride that emerged with the successful outcome of the struggle with the Tatars and the hopeful beginning of the struggle with Moscow. This *Lavrientski Chronicle* opens with the oldest extant text of the Old-Slavonic *Story of the Times*, compiled by the twelfth-century Kievan monk Nestor and his followers. The Nestorian account began with the Deluge and included episodes probably borrowed from the *byliny* (*epic songs*) and the hagiography of Russia. Lavrientyi and his continuators kept Nestor almost up to date until well into the seventeenth century.

Another heritage from preceding centuries was the layman's history in the vernacular, which generally reflected secular interests. In western Europe it had to vie with the Latin chronicles, usually written from a more pious point of view. Inspired by his own crusading experiences, a French nobleman, Jean de Joinville, produced (*c.* 1309) a spirited account of Louis IX's crusading exploits that is generally regarded as a worthy successor to Villehardouin's thirteenth-century account of the Fourth Crusade. Jean le Bel (*c.* 1300–*c.* 1370) and Jean Froissart (*c.* 1337–*c.* 1405) continued the tradition of history in the vernacular. Their work dealt chiefly with the society they knew, that of the French aristocracy. Froissart's *Chronique de France, d'Angleterre, d'Écosse et d'Espagne* dealt largely with countries he had seen and events he had witnessed. In the fifteenth century Georges Chastellain, Jean Molmet, and Olivier de la Marche wrote works that similarly reflected the persistence of feudal aristocratic ideals in France. The same trend in historiography can be found contemporaneously in other regions but to a lesser degree.

In Italy burgher influences were especially strong. The type of history written in the vernacular by a burgher from a burgher point of view is well exemplified in the *Florentine Chronicle* of Giovanni Villani, a friend of Dante. This work was a chronicle of, by, and for townsfolk. Although medieval in its sweep through the centuries from earliest Biblical times to his own day and in its emphasis on religious events, it is a mine of information on everyday urban affairs. It gives statistics on prices, imports, revenues, and school population and other quantitative data that are invaluable to the modern historian.

With the vogue of humanism, vernacular urban historiography in Italy was temporarily eclipsed by Latin classicism. For a long time after Villani, Italian historians tended to follow Roman models and to stress Latin style. This counter-vernacular trend can be traced to Tuscany as clearly as the trend toward the vernacular to thirteenth-century France. The Tuscan Aeneas Sylvius Piccolomini (later Pope Pius II) wrote several works of a historical nature. Although he himself was the author of a history of Bohemia, he regarded 'such a subject as the history of Bohemia or . . . Hungary' as 'wasting time', and held up (1450) Livy and Sallust as historians of 'the first rank',[16] more because of their literary merit than their subject-matter. He spent a good part of his pre-papal career in Germany and Bohemia, and his *Historia Bohemica* is a leading source of our knowledge of the Hussite wars, despite its biases, rhetorical flourishes, and legends. Among his numerous literary productions were his memoirs (*Commentarii Rerum Memorabilium*), a *Cosmographia*, giving his interpretation of universal history, and a series of short biographies of illustrious contemporaries (*De Viris Claris*). Though not printed until the sixteenth century, his writings had a marked influence on humanist historians in Italy, Hungary, and elsewhere in central Europe.

Leonardo Bruni (1370–1444) wrote the history of his native Florence in classical Latin and from a point of view very different from that of Villani. Bruni's history, like Villani's, swept through the centuries but with Roman rather than Biblical history as the underlying theme. His critical handling of sources and his literary ability have led some modern commentators to give him the somewhat debatable title of 'the first modern historian'. Whether he deserves that title or not, Bruni marks a change for the better in European historiography. He exhibited a scholarly scepticism regarding long-accepted documents and insisted upon testing them for authenticity.

Bruni was followed in this scholarly direction by Flavius Biondus and other savants. These men applied the techniques of humanist philology and archaeology as well as common-sense detection of literary and historical anachronism to their documents. Lorenzo Valla (*c.* 1407–47) did not hesitate to criticize even holy scripture. He combined a biting rhetoric with keen critical analysis in several iconoclastic attacks, not only disproving the validity of the so-called Donation of Constantine and of the apostolic authorship of the Apostles' Creed but also ridiculing medieval moral standards and the faulty linguistics of his contemporaries. Nicolas of Cusa, by a strict historical reasoning cast doubt upon the authenticity of some of the so-called Isidoran documents (ninth century), showing that parts of them (now known as the False Decretals) contained anachronisms.

With this new critical spirit, European historiography became something more than a mere chronicling of events or an unquestioning restatement or paraphasing of literary sources. Esteemed as masters of the historical method, Italian humanist historians were employed abroad by kings seeking to glorify their lineage and to justify their own careers. Paulus Aemilius of Verona served as royal historian in France under Charles VIII and Louis XII, and before his death (1529) wrote ten books *De Rebus Gestis Francorum*, and Polydorus Vergilius of Urbino wrote in twenty-six books his *Anglicae Historiae* for King Henry VII. If the purposes of the royal patrons was far from disinterested, nevertheless these writers used a critical method. Vergilius went so far as to raise suspicion regarding the Arthurian legends.

A return to the vernacular language came in the late-fifteenth and early-sixteenth centuries with the works of Guicciardini and Machiavelli. These Florentines wrote detailed factual histories of Florence and Italy, stressing the importance of contemporary politics (see above). Their historical works, displaying the same realistic secularism that characterized their political philosophy, were written in Italian. Speaking of events of their own day and often of their own experience, they applied to the task an analytical keenness and a tough-minded scepticism that has made their writings sometimes disconcerting to modern readers. Guicciardini was perhaps the less gullible and sentimental of the two, but both were far removed from the uncritical readiness of medieval chroniclers to record whatever they heard. Their disillusioned, amoral spirit fortified the dispassionate, unrhetorical impartiality they tried to convey and so moved in the direction of the judicious detachment so highly prized by some of today's historians.

Works of history comparable to the two Florentines' were rare elsewhere in Europe. Philippe de Commines' *Mémoires* portrayed, with clarity and a commendable degree of disinterestedness, the despotic régime of the 'Spider King', Louis XI, and his successor, Charles VIII. Perhaps because he came a generation before Guicciardini and Machiavelli set the tone, he was less disillusioned than they, but he was nevertheless a keen and honest political analyst. North of the Alps and east of the Rhine few European writers of this period can be classified as scholarly historians. Of these several were Poles, and foremost among them was Jan Długosz, known in Latin as Longinus (1415–80). His thirteen-volume study of the geography, ethnology, and history of his country, his *Historia Polonica* (printed in 1614), was completed in 1479, shortly before his death. Drawing on his experience as tutor of King Casimir IV's children, as ambassador, and as archbishop of Lvov for the recent years, he also exploited the archival and literary sources in the several foreign languages at his command (Czech, Hungarian, and German among them) as well as in Polish and Latin. His aim was to make the Polish people proud of their heritage; his heroes were the church and the Polish nobility. Though partisan, he was not uncritical. Długosz corresponded with Aeneas Sylvius, whose eloquent Latin style he greatly admired.

An intriguing work, which may be classified as history but was at the same time something more and less than that, was Afanasiĭ Nikitin's *Journey beyond the Three Seas*. Between 1466 and 1472 the author, a merchant of Tver, had travelled, primarily for commercial and diplomatic purposes, across the Black, Caspian, and Arabian Seas, visiting the lands washed by their waters, including Abyssinia, Anatolia, Persia, and India. He was a sort of latter-day Russian Marco Polo. A quarter of a century before Vasco de Gama would reach India by sailing around Africa, Nikitin, though by a different route, had already been there and had recorded the things he found, giving particular attention to India's commercial products and religious faiths. While convinced of the truth of his own creed, he made a genuine effort to record faithfully what he believed, though occasionally credulously, to be correct.

At the close of the fifteenth century historiography appeared about to enter a distinctly modern state—critical in method, disinterested in spirit, straightforward in style, and secular in purpose. The Reformation, however, was to convert European historiography once more to religious ends and to make it a vehicle of rhetoric and polemic (see Chapter IX).

★   ★   ★

Hindu and Islamic Historians of India

Among India's historians a distinction must be drawn between those of Hindu and those of Islamic heritage. All during our period Hindu writers remained preoccupied with other-wordly, religious, moral, and metaphysical ideas and rarely found time for mundane historical matters. As a consequence, they left little historical literature worthy of mention. Some of the later *purānas* and *tantras* provided a historical theory involving endless cycles of creation and destruction, of which the Kali age (supposed to last for 432,000 years of progressive deterioration beginning with the death of Krishna in 3102 BC) was the last stage of the current cycle. Known historical events thus paled into insignificance, hardly worthy of systematic notice. A few Sanskrit epic poems (*kāvya*), most of them intended to instruct the reader in moral principles and the power of the gods rather than to give a sober account of historical events, and a few vernacular works were about the only historical literature left by the Hindus of these centuries. Kalhana's twelfth-century *kāvya*, *Rājatarangiṇī* (River of Kings [of Kashmir]), which stands up well in comparison with other great historical epics of the world, was continued by Jonaraja, who died in 1459; his pupil Shrīvara, in *Jaina-Rājatarangiṇī* covered the period from 1459 to 1486. Later, Prājya Bhatta and his pupil Shuka carried the epic of the Kashmirian kings slightly beyond the annexation of Kashmir by Akbar. In the fourteenth century Sarvānanda's *Jagadū-carita* sang the praises of a Jain merchant who had helped his fellow Gujaratis during a thirteenth-century famine. Several bardic chronicles of the Rajput clans were written in Hindi. The most important were the fourteenth-century *Hammir-rāsā* and *Hammir-kāvya* of Shārang Dhar, which dealt with the house of Ranthambor.

In Islam generally historical scholarship maintained its high position as a record of the prophetically founded community—its rulers, its scholars, and its saints. In contrast to the Hindu writers, the Persian writers at the courts of the Islamic kings of Delhi produced, like Muslim scholars everywhere, numerous chronicles and histories of the world and of the Afghan and Delhi rulers. Most of these works, however, were narrowly conceived accounts of the sultans, marred by sectarian moralizing and by flattery of their royal patrons. Among the more important were the *Ta'rīkh-i Fīrūz-shāhī*, written during the reign of Firūz Shāh (1351–88) by Ẓīa-ud-dīn Baranī. The author recommended his own work as a record of great kings and conquerors, as a source for the rules of administration, as a fount of admonitions to kings and rulers, and as 'right and true, and worthy of all confidence'.[17] It gave an account of the Delhi kings from Balban (1266–86) to Firūz Shāh, making an eloquent plea for a strong monarchy. The reign of Firūz Shāh was covered also in a work by a contemporary writer, Shams-i-Sirāj 'Afīf, who went into considerable detail regarding administrative matters and social conditions among the common people. The *Ta'rīkh-i Mubārak-shāhī* of Yaḥyā Aḥmad 'Abdullāh Sirhindī, although it dealt also with earlier periods, was especially important for the Tughlaq sultans from Firūz Shāh on and for their Sayyid successors (1414–50), of whom the author was a contemporary.

*   *   *

Islamic Historians Elsewhere

With the spread of Islam went also a certain consciousness of the desirability of objectivity in the writing of history. Numerous areas, such as the Sudan, for the first time began to produce written chronicles, which normally, however, reflected care for dates and facts more than for imaginative interpretation.

In the centres of Islam several new tendencies enriched historical writing. Local history, after a long development, perhaps reached its peak in the Egyptian studies of al-Maqrīzī (fifteenth century), greatest of a remarkable school of historians of the Mamlūks. The Mongol invasions had broadened the historical vision, especially of Persian Muslims. At the beginning of the fourteenth century Rashīd-al-Din Faḍl-Allāh produced the first history that can truly be called universal so far as the northern half of the eastern hemisphere was concerned. Making accurate use of good informants from as far away as Europe and China, his monumental work is at the same time a singular example of breadth of coverage and cautious fair-mindedness. He fostered and inspired a school of historians dedicated to exact work and a broad viewpoint.

In an age of thorough but often uninspired historical work, Ibn-Khaldūn stands out. As in so many other fields, he developed in history, too, the possibilities that Islamic scholarship had ripened. His chronicles are characterized by a consistent interest in illustrating the social forces that lie behind dynastic events. The introduction to his famous universal history does at least three especially noteworthy things: it presents a systematic and enlightening survey of a total civilization as a working unity, including its crafts and sciences; it gives a sociological analysis of the historical dynamics of politics and culture; and it attempts to make a place for the study of history in the Aristotelian philosophical framework. Ibn-Khaldūn's well-known plea for an internal criticism of historical reports, alongside the external criticism which Islamic historiography had long highly cultivated, is merely incidental to his philosophical thesis.

*   *   *

Historiography in China and Its Neighbours

In the countries of southeast Asia historical writing was represented only by some chronicles and poems, which made little effort to distinguish fact from fiction. Of these, the *Pararaton*, or *Book of Kings*, a fourteenth-century Javanese chronicle, and the *Nagarakertagama*, a poem composed about 1365 by Prapanca, head of the Buddhist clergy at Majapahit, were perhaps the most important.

Although the period 1300–1500 was not the most productive in Chinese historiography, the technique of Chinese historians was perhaps at that time more highly developed than any other in the world. A profound knowledge of the past was held to be an essential part of Confucianism, and historical information was considered indispensable for the proper functioning of government and society. The government, therefore, took precautions to see that significant records were preserved and that appropriate historical works and manuals were written. A Historical Bureau maintained the daily records of each reign (known as the *Diaries of Activity and Repose*), and after the death of a monarch a group of historians was designated to prepare from these and other records the *Shih lu*, or *Veritable Records*, of his reign. Together with other available materials, these records were used by an especially appointed historical commission to write the standard history of a dynasty upon its close.

These elaborate dynastic histories had come by the fourteenth century to follow a regular pattern. They were made up of (1) annals of the various reigns; (2) tables of the imperial family and important officials; (3) treatises on the history of subjects important to the administration of government such as astronomy, the calendar, ritual, music, elemental influences, geography, rivers and canals, food and commodities, law and punishment, civil offices, the examination system, chariots and costume, imperial guards, the army, the militia and colonization, and literature; and (4) biographies, which formed the largest single section of each work. Aside from the official dynastic histories, about twenty-five other types of historical works, some of them official but most of them private, were produced. They included general histories of an annalistic or topical nature, accounts of special periods, collections of biographies and documents, treatises on government, historical geography and chronology, historical criticism and historiography, bibliographies, and histories or gazetteers dealing with provinces, prefectures, districts, and cities.

The Chinese historians aiming at high standards of scholarship, emphasized accuracy, objectivity, and the wide use of original materials and developed to a high level the art of textual criticism. In order to maintain objectivity they generally tended to quote extensively from the sources; judgments were usually confined to concluding remarks or summaries (although they entered, of course, into the selection of the material used). When two conflicting sources could not be harmonized, some writers quoted from both, although a tendency prevailed, particularly in general and dynastic histories, to decide which was right and to quote only from the preferred source. A direct and sober style was cultivated, flights of literary imagination being deemed improper in historical writing. Works on historical criticism from Liu Chih-chi's *Historical Perspectives* (*Shih-t'ung*) of 710 to Lu Shen's *Essentials of Historical Perspectives* (*Shih-t'ung hui-yao*), completed about 1515, emphasized the desirability of the widest possible range of sources, of a questioning spirit, of independent, critical judgment, and of support of conclusions by evidence. Historical works, official and other, were systematically reviewed by later scholars, and a large literature accumulated supplementing, correcting, and criticizing earlier works.

Notwithstanding these merits, judged by modern standards traditional Chinese historiography had patent weaknesses. The rather rigid chronological manner of presentation and the practice of quoting extensively discouraged genuine historical synthesis. Conventional conciseness of style and other literary usages helped to create obscurities, and the resulting stylistic conventions led to the omission of illustrative details. Certain types of economic, social, and even literary information were considered unimportant and so were recorded only inadvertently. Events connected with the emperor or the court were emphasized to the exclusion of information about humbler affairs in the provinces. Ethnocentrism was always evident in passages relating to foreign peoples.

Perhaps the greatest weakness of the Chinese historian, despite his tradition of objectivity, was his penchant to regard history as the working-out of certain Confucian moral principles. This moralistic interpretation was tied up with the idea that dynasties ruled by virtue of a mandate from Heaven and, if they abused their position and ruled badly, the mandate would be withdrawn. Thus, the end of a dynasty automatically implied Heaven's disfavour. Almost inevitably subsequent historians would accentuate the shortcomings and wickedness of the terminal rulers and officials of a dynasty, while the defects of its founders were lightly touched upon or entirely passed over. Likewise, since loyalty to superiors and the ruler was a cardinal virtue, unsuccessful rebels were castigated, while those who succeeded in establishing new dynasties were praised for having expressed the will of Heaven. Thus dynasties were made to rise and decline in a fairly uniform cycle. The last ruler of a dynasty was almost bound to be viewed as a 'bad' emperor, and the first one as a 'good' emperor. This tendency was most pronounced in certain general histories produced under the influence of Chu Hsi and the Rationalistic school of Neo-Confucianism. The school's belief that if the proper principles (*li*) were not followed, disaster was bound to result easily led it toward bias. It selected for emphasis those facts of history which showed that the difficulty or failure of particular rulers or dynasties were the result of their having failed to follow the proper *li*.

Such historiographical weaknesses were prominent in several supplements and abridgements of Chu Hsi's *Mirror* and in some shorter general histories published during the Yüan and Ming dynasties. Of these works perhaps the most important was the supplement of Shang Lu (1414–86) and others, covering the Sung and Yüan periods. The dynastic histories for the Sung, Liao, and Chin dynasties, prepared during the 1340's by a commission under the direction of the Mongol T'o T'o, and the *Yüan shih* (*Yüan History*), prepared under the direction of Sung Lien about 1370, suffered from hasty preparation as well as from the effort to trace in history the workings of moral and philosophical ideas. In addition, though based in part on the Mongol *Tobciyan* (see Chapter X), the *Yüan History* reflected the Chinese bias against the Mongol rulers. The omissions, distortions, and discrepancies of these works were not allowed to go unchallenged, and a number of elaborate critical and corrective histories (by Wang K'o-k'uan, Wang Yu-hsüeh, Hsü Chao-wan, and others) also appeared in the fourteenth and fifteenth centuries.

The encyclopedic study was another significant type of Chinese historical literature, and an important work illustrative of this type was produced at the very beginning of our period. It was the *Wen-hsien t'ung-k'ao* of Ma Tuan-li (*c.* 1250–1319), an elaborate encyclopedia of the history of Chinese civilization. It was arranged under twenty-four topics, including taxation, population, currencies, markets, schools, examinations, offices and their functions, ritual, military matters, punishment, geography, astronomy, literature, and frontier regions.

Chinese standards influenced the historiography of neighbouring countries. Koreans and Annamese in general imitated Chinese historiography but succeeded in producing only annalistic compilations of indifferent merit. Historiography was not highly developed in Japan, where most historical writings were the products of Buddhist monks. If one leaves aside various historical novels of the war-romance type and a few indifferent chronicles, perhaps the two most important works were the *Genko-shakusho*, a history of Buddhism, written about 1322, and Kitabatake's *History of the True Succession of the Divine Emperors* (already noted in Chapter III). Kitabatake's aim was to enhance the position of the imperial family. While he expounded history in accordance with current Chinese leanings toward moral and philosophical principles, he failed to measure up to Chinese standards of accuracy and critical judgment.

NOTES TO CHAPTER VIII

1. Explicitly expounded by Gregory the Great, the theory of Divine Right remained very foreign to the thought of the Middle Ages except, indeed, in the case of Wycliffe, where it appeared in the fourteenth century, as also in Spain with the meeting of the Cortes of Olmedo (1445). Thomas Aquinas, to whom it was unknown, justified the right to resist an unjust government. (Raymond Polin.)

2. Professor R. Polin feels that this statement should be amplified since, in his opinion, Machiavelli cannot be said to have propounded or defended an autocratic ideology. Firstly, his whole work runs counter to what would today be called an ideology. He is indeed the first philosopher to make political reality the subject of truly scientific analysis. What he tries to bring to light are the principles of an effective political technique, whether in the service of a prince or of a republican form of government. Moreover, his prince is in no way an autocrat, trying to justify his power by reasons transcending his

person. His is merely a man who has learned the means of achieving power, as well as how and at what price to use these means effectively. He is also a man knowing how to govern, and lucid and courageous enough to apply this knowledge. He seeks justification neither within nor above himself, but in his works alone. And as is rightly said here, the ends accomplished by his works may very well be moral ends, in the sense of conformity with one or other accepted moral code.

The physical violence of his time and his experience as secretary of the Florentine republic, and sometimes as its ambassador, no doubt helped him to discover that politics are calculations, the rational mean of the forces in human groups. Rising superior to the contingencies of his time, he reached the level of universal premises.

Machiavelli is the founder of modern political philosophy; he does not seek to justify a political system. He seeks to study the conditions and means of political action in order to educate and train good 'politicians'. For him, the quality of those who govern is certainly more important than the legitimacy of the regime—more important too, no doubt, than the nature of such regimes.

3. Professor R. Polin stresses that in the fifteenth century Nicholas of Cusa was to defend in his *Concordantia Catholica* the supremacy of law over the prince and to regard the community as the source of law, since law must be made by those whom it constrains. Therefore he does not hesitate to proclaim that all authority stems from a choice determined by an agreement based on free consent. Such choice is, moreover, in conformity with the law of nature and with the order willed by God. If it opts for a monarchical form of government, the monarchy it chooses will be elective. On this condition only can it be held divine in character.

4. Marsilius of Padua often appears a very modern writer. On many points his theory of sovereignty anticipates that of Hobbes. But his theory of sovereignty as issuing from the people by the will of God and his theory of government by the *valentior pars* should not be interpreted as already democratic in perspective. In reality, his whole thought is dominated by the struggle between pope and emperor, church and state. One of the best means of weakening the power of the pope was, of course, to oppose to his authority that of the councils, that is to say of collective organisms involving systems of representation, of election, of voting, which reappeared in the democracies of the future. It so happens that in striving for the pre-eminence of emperor and state, Marsilius opened up modern lines of thought. (Raymond Polin.)

5. William of Ockham, who, for his part, places the origin of authority in God but regards it as transmitted by the people, declares that while the prince is free in regard to laws, he is nonetheless subject to the law of natural equity. His power remains subject to the pursuit of the common good; he makes law, but with the common good in view, and laws made in his own interest would not be valid. Ockham even goes so far as to allow that a prince violating natural law should be deposed by force. (Raymond Polin.)

6. To Professor R. Polin the argument of Machiavelli is the following: 'Since man is capable of wickedness and evil, he who governs must be in a position to assure respect for law. He must therefore dispose of a sufficient force to impose obedience by constraint on those not reasonable enough to obey in response to persuasion. This is a universal argument and valid not only for a despotic government. As the highly liberal Locke will later entirely agree with Machiavelli, the availability of an adequate public force conditions the very existence of a public authority. This means in effect that political constraint is workable only if it includes the possibility of sanction, which does not necessarily rule out the implication of moral components.

Professor Gottschalk sees small difference in essentials between the comments of Professor Raymond Polin and of the late Professor MacKinney except in regard to their respective emphases upon the ideas of authoritarianism and morality in Machiavelli's writings; MacKinney emphasized Machiavelli's authoritarianism, leaving a little room for morality, while Polin leaves a little room for authoritarianism, emphasizing morality in Machiavelli's thought.

7. Professor R. Polin feels that it is indeed remarkable that medieval political thought had quite systematically sought limits to the power of those who govern in divine will, either

in the presence of the church and the authority of the hierarchy in the feudal system or again in the structure of existing firmly established political communities. After the break with medieval tradition, and while the theory and practice of absolute sovereignty were in process of development, those philosophers concerned with liberties were obliged to start afresh from new premises.

8. See F. G. Heymann, 'The Role of the Towns in the Bohemia of the Later Middle Ages', *Journal of World History*, II (1954), 338.

9. F. G. Heymann, *John Žižka and the Hussite Revolution* (Princeton, 1955), p. 233.

10. *Ibid.*, p. 477.

11. Professor R. Polin points out that it may perhaps be useful to remember here that when Confucius was born, in the sixth century before Jesus Christ, the astonishingly stable political traditions on which Chinese life was based were already almost two thousand years old. These traditions being transmitted by learning, it is easy to understand what a source of strength they were for men of letters, that aristocratic élite which assured the administration of the country and, to all intents and purposes, its government.

12. Professor R. Polin believes that it should not be forgotten that a philosopher as important as Thomas Aquinas differentiated very clearly between various sorts of law: the eternal law of divine providence, that is of God himself, and the natural law which specifically governs reasonable beings and which is revealed to them by natural enlightenment. On the other hand, there exists also a divine law expressed in the Scriptures and positive human laws applicable to reputedly immaterial domains. The plurality of positive laws was thus perfectly well understood and accepted. All laws, however, expressed reason and aimed at justice, a unique justice in conformity with the unity of Christian morality. (See also p. 499 and n. 1.)

13. Robert S. Lopez in M. Postan and E. E. Rich (eds.), *The Cambridge Economic History of Europe*, Vol. II (Cambridge, 1952), p. 338 and n., and Robert S. Lopez and H. A. Miskimin, 'The Economic Depression of the Renaissance', *Economic History Review*, 2nd Series, XIV (1962), 408–26.

14. Both English and German versions of this couplet are quoted in Edward P. Cheyney, *The Dawn of a New Era* (New York, 1936), p. 131 and n. 39.

15. For a detailed bibliography, see Raymond de Roover, 'New Interpretations of the History of Banking', *Journal of World History*, II (1954), 38–76.

16. *De Librorum Educatione*, trans. in W. H. Woodward, *Vittorino da Feltre and Other Humanist Educators* (Cambridge, 1921), p. 152.

17. Quoted in E. M. Elliott and John Dowson, *History of India as Told by its own Historians* (London, 1871), III, 94.

CHAPTER IX

POLITICAL AND SOCIAL THOUGHT AND PRACTICE
(1500–1775)

POLITICAL THEORY

Theories of Absolutism in Europe

I N the sixteenth century, as the number and power of Europe's absolute dynasties grew, the tendency toward a theological justification of autocracy kept pace. While Machiavelli's *Prince* remained the best-known literary plea for strong political leadership, writers like Luther and Calvin also supported autocracy. The reformers pleaded for strong governmental leadership on religious ground, finding divine sanction for absolutism in several Biblical texts, such as Jesus' mandate to his followers to render unto Caesar the things that are Caesar's. Luther vigorously advocated the autocracy of German princes (see Chapter IV), thereby providing a religious sanction for the later principle of territorialism—*cuius regio eius religio* (that is, a territory's religion is that of its ruler). In fact, Luther and Calvin went no further than the Scholastics in circumscribing the power of Christian princes.[1] They limited it only by an injunction to respect natural law, which to them was the will of God, leaving somewhat vague what was to be done if a prince transgressed natural law or differed with his subjects regarding the will of God.

Because Calvin held forth in the free Swiss city-state of Geneva and because his strict doctrine of predestination paid no heed to class distinctions, he is sometimes lauded as an exponent of Christian democracy. We shall see below that in Holland and England as well as Switzerland Calvinism indeed tended in that direction. Whereas Luther came to rely on the Christian prince as the instrument of temporal authority, Calvin relied on republican magistrates. But even though he, like Luther, believed that the state was divinely ordained, he held that the church was independent within the sphere of religious activity, and in actual practice he and his fellow clergymen actually came closer to dominating the Genevan city-state than to being dominated by or completely independent of it. Geneva, ruled by an oligarchy even before Calvin, became still more oligarchic under his auspices. Its General Assembly consisted of all the heads of families, the Assembly met infrequently, and real power lay with the Consistory, which Calvin controlled.

To most sixteenth-century minds democratic republicanism seemed in fact a form of government attractive only to the malcontent and subversive.

The persuasion was prevalent that for most of the countries of Europe geographical and historical circumstances made some form of monarchy inevitable. For Machiavelli, historical change rather than fixed religious precepts or prevailing institutions provided the principles of political action. The hereditary, paternalistic monarch of the Bible as exemplified in Italy's despots and the elective head of the Catholic Church both seemed to him obstacles to the unity and expansion of his beloved Italy. Hence he preferred a monarch (or a republican leader) who would rise to power by his own efforts, probably including force and fraud, who would retain it by preserving the confidence of his people (blaming others, if need be, for unpopular measures), and who would use it to defend the life and liberty of his state: 'For where the only safety of the country depends upon the resolution to be taken, no consideration of justice, humanity or cruelty, glory or shame, should be allowed to prevail'.[2] Machiavelli's prince was guided principally if not exclusively by *raison d'état* and *Realpolitik*. Even when elective (as Machiavelli considered desirable), the ruler's power to achieve a programme was limited only by political realities—that is, what his subjects and his fellow-rulers could be made to tolerate.[3]

Machiavelli's *Prince* had little influence during his lifetime. Yet his view of sovereign power was not essentially different from the more prevalent view of divine-right monarchy. In fact, he pointed to the French monarch as the model of the king trusted and unquestioned by his people. The sources and the rationale of the divine-right philosophers, however, were different from Machiavelli's. They leaned on the Biblical precedent of the anointment of Saul by Samuel and on Paul's injunction of obedience to 'the powers that be' because they are 'ordained by God', and their philosophy had little in common with the unabashed philosophy of force and guile which he had derived from his study of history and from his revulsion against the lip-service to morality prevalent in the Italy of his day. The paternalistic responsibility that devolved upon crowned heads from being the anointed of God— a responsibility upheld in western Europe during the Middle Ages and to be maintained by James I of England, Filmer, Louis XIV, Bossuet, and Fénelon in the seventeenth century—was a far cry from the Machiavellian indifference to humane considerations where the safety of the state was involved. Nevertheless, both schools of western European thought believed in a sovereign ruler limited very little, if at all, by other temporal forces, and a Russian monk, Joseph Volotzki (d. 1515), upheld a similar theory for the tsars. The essential difference between the Machiavellians and the divine-right school was that whereas resistance to a Machiavellian prince was political error (his error if rebellion succeeded, the rebels' if it failed), resistance to a divine-right monarch was religious sin (for God alone could rightly rebuke his anointed). The Third Estate in the last Estates General to meet before the French Revolution, that of 1614, went so far as to signify—in opposition to Suàrez and other advocates of popular or papal supremacy—that no power on earth, whether temporal or spiritual, could absolve the king's subjects from their obligation to obey him faithfully, and thus it gave endorsement to the nascent absolutism of the Bourbons.

While this theory of royal absolutism was rounding out, a partly supplementary, partly conflicting theory arose—that of the enlightened royal patriarch, the father of his people. Andrzej Frycz Modrzewski's *De Republica Emendanda* (Cracow, 1551) advocated a concentration of governmental power in the hands of a sovereign king, who, however, should use it to protect the peasantry from abuse occasioned by the nobles' privileges. Later in the same century Jean Bodin wrote *Les six livres de la république* (1576). In this and other works he presented lessons from his study of history that differed from Machiavelli's. To be sure, he still found that legality rested on power: he defined sovereignty as 'supreme power over citizens and subjects, unrestrained by laws',[4] and he found it generally vested in kings; monarchy had originated, he believed, in the primitive family and, after passing through various complicated forms of association and corporation, had matured into the modern state, to which all the other forms had become subordinated. Yet he distinguished between the tyrant and the just king, though both were sovereign. A tyrant made law of his own arbitrary will; a just king felt bound by the laws of God and nature, treaties with other sovereigns, the customs of his people, and the contracts which his predecessors or he himself had made. Hence a royal sovereign who was not a tyrant was bound by many restrictions, but they were moral and not legal restrictions, since by definition he himself made the laws.

Bodin's prince, if he chose, might be no less absolute than Machiavelli's. Although Bodin, too, thought of sovereignty as the prospect of a historical process rather than of divine will, his prince nevertheless was the 'image of almighty God': 'The laws of the prince should bear the stamp of divine laws.'[5] Thus, unlike Machiavelli's prince, who was not bound by moral considerations, or Bossuet's, who was answerable only to God, or Hobbes's, who was subject to no social contract (see below), Bodin's prince was bound all at once by morality (the laws of nature), God (the laws of God), and social contractual obligations (treaties, contracts, customs), though if he wished to act tyrannically, he would also be free from all legal restraint. Bodin's sovereign had the power to be a despot, but he preferred to be enlightened, and not alone out of the fear of God.

A Russian contemporary of Modrzewski and Bodin, Tsar Ivan the Terrible, argued the same way in self-justification. Prince Andrey Mikhaylovich Kurbsky, having first sought safety in flight to Lithuania, engaged in a famous controversy with the tsar, contending that royal whim must be checked by a senate (i.e. an aristocracy) of 'virtuous men'. In prose that has been since regarded as a masterpiece of Old Russian, Ivan replied somewhat along the lines of Volotzki's argument—that the tsar's power should not be limited—and he cited examples from history and his own experience to show that a ruler's sharing power with nobles brought on division, disorder, and bad government, all of which it was the tsar's duty to avoid.

When, in the seventeenth century, rebels succeeded temporarily in destroying the British monarchy, advocates of royal sovereignty were obliged to inquire whether any rebellion, even a successful one, against a royal sovereign might be justified. Thomas Hobbes, while in exile with the defeated Stuarts, argued (1651) that almost never[6] was a rebellion against a sovereign lord rationally or morally justifiable. He resorted neither to Biblical text, or revelation of God's will, nor to 'right reason', or intuition, to make his point but, re-examining the classical idea of social contract, appealed rather to persuasive reasoning from basic premises about the nature of man. As befitted a mechanistic contemporary of the seventeenth-century 'scientific revolution', he meant to be empirical and inductive in conning the laws of nature.

For Hobbes, man in the state of nature was a competitive and violent creature whose life was 'solitary, poor, nasty, brutish, and short'.[7] Guided by self-interest, natural man seeks peace and security, and so slowly reaches a set of understandings with his fellowmen that in the course of time acquire the force of a social contract, by which each gives up his freedom of action in order to create a state, the 'Leviathan', and to establish order where anarchy prevailed before. This contract binds the individual to the community, but the government that results is not bound by it; the subject is thus pledged to irrevocable obedience, while the king, an instrument of the contract but not a part of it, is pledged to nothing. Hence rebellion was ruled out as a method of resolving social disputes and political ills.

Only in a few paragraphs of Hobbes' book did his rational exposition, while still premised upon a hypothetical notion of the origins of society, make concessions to contemporary reality: if a reigning monarch cannot provide that protection against anarchy which was the original purpose of the contract, his subjects have the right to seek another government that can. In fact, Hobbes himself returned to England and made his peace with Cromwell's Commonwealth. Hobbes, in essence, bolstered the old theological argument in favour of absolute monarchy[8] with an additional secular argument, insisting upon the subject's personal inadequacy and moral obligations (the contract) as the justification of royal sovereignty[9] rather than counting, like Machiavelli, upon the ruler's skilfull manipulation of human interests or, like Bodin, upon the ruler's enlightenment.

*   *   *

Opposition to Absolutism

Starting from the same premise as the divine-right monarchists—namely, the will of God, another school of thought was meanwhile coming to a far different conclusion. Among the Protestant sects of the Reformation era the

Anabaptists may perhaps alone be cited as proponents of democracy. The Zwickau 'Prophets', especially Münzer, preaching a mystic doctrine of guidance by 'inner light', questioned the validity of man-made laws, private property, and social organizations, and eventually took up the sword against the 'godless'. Münzer's disciples turned to Anabaptism, but the chiliasm of the Anabaptists was ambivalent in its political implications. They were theocratic and in some ways anti-republican, particularly in the tenet that the good Christian did not participate in government. Yet their communist economy, their devotion to popular leaders, and their political equalitarianism sometimes caused them to be identified as republicans, and their fanaticism and defeat in Europe brought discredit to the republican ideal (although their survival as Mennonites in the Netherlands and America eventually aided it).

The bloody religious conflicts of the sixteenth century led some of the bolder Calvinists to press the premise of the will of God to a more drastic conclusion than Calvin ever had done. They vindicated revolt and even tyrannicide—if it succeeded (for otherwise it could not be the will of God)—as a last resort against rulers who persisted in violating their 'contractual' obligations to God on the one hand and to their peoples on the other. Particularly after the shock of the St Bartholomew Massacre, Huguenot 'monarchomachs' presented arguments of this sort. No king must force his subjects to transgress the law of God, they contended, sometimes appealing to Classical history as well as the Bible for precedents of revolt and tyrannicide. Theodore Beza (1519–1605) in *The Rights of Magistrates over their Subjects*, François Hotman (1524–90) in *Franco-Gallia*, and an anonymous author in *Vindiciae contra Tyrannos* (*Vengeance against Tyrants*, 1579), usually attributed to either Hubert Languet or Philippe du Plessis-Mornay, spoke up against growing royal absolutism and in favour of some sort of limitation on arbitrary power. The idea of a contractual bond between the ruler and his subjects was further elaborated during the Dutch revolt by Johannes Althusius (1557–1638), a German Calvinist. Assuming that states are made up by the federation of communities of sovereign peoples, he argued that a breach of the social contract by the ruler justified secession of parts of the realm or resistance by the 'ephors' (the internal magistrates and assemblies).

About the same time Spanish jurists were seeking to justify Spain's interference in the affairs of England, France, and other countries on behalf of Catholic resistance. Suàrez and the historian Juan de Mariana (1536–1624), both Jesuits, argued in the same vein as the monarchomachs: a tyrant, even when the legitimate ruler, may be resisted to the point of assassination if he violates the law of God, and it is lawful for a neighbouring prince to aid in his overthrow.

The idea of a social contract legally binding a prince was made fairly familiar in England by Bodin's contemporary Richard Hooker. In *The Laws of Ecclesiastical Polity* (of which the first books were published only in 1594) Hooker was primarily concerned with defending the established Anglican

Church against the attack of Presbyterians, and he maintained that the same principles that justified secular government justified ecclesiastical government as well. Essentially those principles were based upon the consent of the governed, expressed in a social contract that could be broken only by consent of the governed: 'Unto me it seemeth almost out of doubt and controversy, that every independent multitude, before any certain form of regiment established, hath, under God's supreme authority, full dominion over itself.' Hooker's contract was mutable. Whether in the religious or in the secular sphere, the contract issued from a mankind endowed by God 'with full power to guide itself, in what kind of societies soever it should choose to live'.[10] Hooker thus raised doubts about royal absolutism even as the Tudors were building it up in England.

The effort of their successors, the Stuart monarchs, to control both state and church and to dominate Parliament were among the factors that led to the Great Rebellion (1642–52) and the Glorious Revolution of 1688. By acts of force the British people showed that the divinity that 'doth hedge a king' was not sacred enough to keep one of their kings from execution, another from exile, and two others from the obligation to accept explicit conditions if they were to be allowed to sit upon their thrones. More or less contemporaneously estates and *Stände* in the United Provinces, France, Sweden, Spain, and elsewhere tried, with more limited success, to acquire a share of the government and to restrict the growing power of their hereditary dynasties.

The Social Contract and 'Enlightened Despotism'

Out of these conflicts, directly or indirectly, came at least three classic discussions of the social contract—Hobbes's, Spinoza's, and Locke's. Hobbes's view has been set forth above as a ratiocination of absolute monarchy: the compact between natural man and society bound the society but not the government. Spinoza gave the controversy lengthy consideration in his *Tractatus Theologico-politicus* (1670). The state, he claimed, like Hobbes, is formed by a social contract and rules by power. Yet the very bases of power work against its abuse, for one base is reason, another the desire to avoid unrest and revolution, and a third the wisdom not to command the impossible. Unlike Bodin and Hobbes, he counted on *both* the enlightenment *and* the self-interest of the ruler for good government. He concluded that representative government within a monarchy was best, since it was the most likely to preserve the natural rights of man.[11] Locke's *Two Treatises of Government*, written before but published after the Glorious Revolution of 1688, attempted to show that the governed shared sovereignty with the king. Controverting Hobbes, he expounded the theory that the government was party to the social contract and thus removable when it failed to perform its contractual obligations to the satisfaction of the other party, the people. He set forth also a theory of division of powers between the legislature, controlled by the people, and the executive and federative, controlled by the king.[12]

These three classic models of the social contract underwent modification in other men's writings in a variety of ways. As early as 1625 Grotius had equated natural law with human reason (see below). In Germany Samuel Pufendorf (1632–94) developed a concept of the social contract that wedded Hobbes' cynical view of man with Grotius' hopeful view of sovereignty— political power limited by rules of reason that would be substantially valid 'even if we should grant . . . that there is no God' (prolegomena to *De Jure*, ¶ 11). Hence Pufendorf's society rested on two contracts, one which the individual made with the community and another which the community made with the government, the community promising obedience and the government promising regard for the general welfare. Some of the German philosophers of the eighteenth century, like Wolff, accepted this view. Borrowing Locke's theory of the division of governmental powers, though without particular attention to the social contract, Montesquieu in the *Esprit des Lois* (1748) set forth a theory of 'mixed governments'. Analysing the British constitution somewhat inaccurately, he found that its strength lay in a tripartite division of government—the distribution of political authority among the king, who had executive power, the aristocracy, who controlled the legislature, and the people, who were defended by the courts from the abuse of power by king or aristocracy.[13] Rousseau gave to the social contract the finishing touch of popular sovereignty (see below).

By the eighteenth century the idea of absolute monarchy, embodied in the Continental rulers, thus was offset by the idea of limited monarchy. The *philosophes* pleaded for enlightened monarchy and praised its exponents, Frederick of Prussia, Catherine of Russia, Joseph of Austria, Charles of Spain, and others. Frederick himself, before becoming king of Prussia, had joined the chorus in a work entitled *Anti-Machiavel* (1739), in which he rejected the idea that states were the property of their rulers and advocated instead that rulers regard themselves as merely the first servants of the state. The theory of 'enlightened despotism' was perhaps best set forth by the Physiocrats, particularly in Mercier de la Rivière's *L'Ordre naturel et essentiel des sociétés politiques*. As we shall note shortly, the Physiocrats were interested more in economic than political justice. Their political argument ran: Since land was the source of wealth (their major premise) and since a landlord would naturally want his income to be as great as possible, the king as the state's chief landlord would inevitably be concerned that his realm should be as productive as possible; hence he would be 'enlightened'—that is, he would rule according to the laws of nature, attempting to discover what they were in fact rather than exercising his own arbitrary whim or misinformed judgment. With the Physiocrats the idea of absolutism came full circle—'divine right' had become a 'natural order' based upon autonomy of the market.

*   *   *

Political Theory and Behaviour in Islam and Hindu India

Elsewhere similar political problems were giving rise to responses that were in some ways similar to those advanced in Europe. Islam is the social, even the political, religion *par excellence*. Although since the time of the Medina Caliphate it had been unable to fulfil its goal of a social order in which religious and political aspects would be one, the aspiration could not be laid aside by seriously pious Muslims. The '*ulamā*' never ceased to think of the ideal unity of Islam in terms of a *khalīfa*, a caliph ruling a human empire. The Ṣūfīs made much of a very different sort of *khalīfa*—the Quṭb, the human being who as perfected microcosm is the final end of, and holds limitless sway over, the world of nature and of men together. He is a Muslim and exercises his power largely upon and through Muslims (particularly through the *Abdāl*, lesser figures in the saintly hierarchy), but a recognized place under his care is available for the believers in every faith however crude—not only for peoples of the Book as in the historical caliphate but also for outright pagans. The kings who come and go are but the servants of such a saint, as many beloved anecdotes make clear; no caliph had such power over his governors as the Ṣūfī *shaykhs*, and especially the supreme *shaykh*, the Quṭb of any given time, had over the earth's rulers. That no one really knew who were the Quṭb and the *Abdāl* in his own day only served to make their power the more awesome.

The motion of the Quṭb who, with all the *shaykhs* as his assistants, continuously kept order in the world, is more than a piece of popular superstition; it is also more than a deduction from a subtle cosmology. The stories told of 'Abd al-Qādir—whose foot was on the neck of every other saint—are no doubt in part the result of the ardent loyalty to their *ṭarīqa* of the Qādiriyya *shaykhs*. That the leader of the Suhrawardiyya in India should be called Makhdūm-i Jahāniyān—'he whom all worldlings serve'—no doubt in part reflects the imperious personality of the man. When the mild and saintly Niẓām al-Dīn Awliyā' told the story of the saint who, flying over a greater saint's *khaniqah*, failed to show respect and so was thrown to the ground by that saint's power, he wanted in part to teach his listeners humility, but the notion that these and similar stories embody—the notion of the invisible hierarchy of the *shaykhs* of the *ṭarīqas* and their invisible government of the world—is inescapably political. It is as if the Ṣūfī *ṭarīqas*, in an age when it was no longer feasible for a single conventional government to give unity to the whole of Islam, were able to offer not only a flexible element of social order but also a correspondingly elastic sense of all-Islamic political unity.

Nevertheless, concrete political reality put a major claim on Muslim thought everywhere. After the extreme attenuation of political life in the late Middle Ages, the development of the great empires of early modern times offered a new and more hopeful climate for political thinking. The response was vigorous and varied. In Iran the chief political concern of theologians tended to be the confirmation of the Shī'ite character of the state, whose monarch was held to be essentially the representative of the Hidden Imām, the Shī'ite eschatological figure, who also spoke through the *mujtahids*. Majlisī was able to assert the effective control of the Shī'ite *mujtahids*— perhaps weakening the state through the bigoted way he exploited his success. The responses in India and in the Ottoman Empire, perhaps more interesting as theory, have been dealt with elsewhere (see Chapters VII and below).

Islamic authors in India, generally speaking, upheld the ideal of an absolute monarch ruling over a theocratic state and enforcing the Islamic law as interpreted by the *'ulamā'*. But Akbar in practice, and Abu'l-Faḍl in the preface to his *Ā'īn-i-Akbarī* (*Institutes of Akbar*), developed the ideal of the benevolent, non-sectarian despot. Akbar conceived his function as the promotion of the well-being of all his subjects, Muslim and Hindu alike, and he further considered himself as both political head (sultan) and religious head (caliph) of Islam in India (see Chapter V). Abu'l Faḍl, a contemporary of Jean Bodin, distinguished between the 'true king' and the 'selfish ruler'. The true king is possessed of a divine light communicated directly by God; he endeavours to remove oppression and promote the general welfare, bringing security, health, chastity, justice, good manners, faithfulness, truth, and growing sincerity. He is characterized by paternal love of his subjects without sectarian blemish and by a daily increasing trust in God. He is 'continually attentive to the health of the body politic, and applies remedies to the several diseases thereof'; by 'the warmth of the ray of unanimity and concord, a multitude of people become fused into one body'.[14] This enlightened, non-sectarian concept of kingship was not favoured by the more orthodox Muslims, but it was generally followed by Akbar's immediate successors. Then a more narrow, orthodox, sectarian view was adopted by Aurangzīb, and it contributed to the decline of the Mogul Empire.

Hindu India contributed nothing of importance to formal political theory during this period, but, as elsewhere, religious disputes had political consequences. The reinvigoration of Hinduism in the *bhakti* religious movement stimulated the rise of the Sikhs and the Marathas, contributing to the growth of Hindu nationalism and to democratic and equalitarian ideas in Hindu society generally. In a work entitled *Dashabodh*, the seventeenth-century Maratha writer Rāmdās denounced the Muslims and encouraged political activity, particularly the formation of secret political associations upon a basis of equality among Hindus, and his religious order practised complete equality. The Marathas developed a confederacy rather than a highly centralized monarchical form of government. The Sikhs became complete equalitarians and, under Islamic pressure, developed military communism as a political system.

*   *   *

Political Theory and Behaviour in China

In China of the late Ming period, the growing despotism of government and the Rationalistic philosophy which had, perhaps unintentionally, contributed to it were challenged. A number of writers insisted on a return to 'true' Confucian principles, which, although generally authoritarian, placed certain limitations upon the ruler and his officials and advocated a dynamic benevolent despotism. The Idealistic philosopher and statesman Wang Yang-ming (Chapter VII) in both his writings and his actions resisted despotism and insisted on government for social betterment.[15] His emphasis upon moral intuition, incumbent upon and available to all alike, implied liberation from certain traditional bonds and a moral equality for all. One of his sixteenth-century followers, Wang Ken, in his *Wang tao lun* (*Treatise on the Kingly Way*) discussed the means of improving government and promoting universal peace. Many of the later Idealistic philosophers, however, gave but passing attention to improvement in government, and only with the rise of the Tung-lin movement (Chapter VII) at the end of the century did significant protests appear. Imperial indifference to governmental affairs, growing official arbitrariness, and popular moral laxness then became the targets of severe criticism.

The fall of the Ming dynasty encouraged a minority group of scholars to attack the abstract and static political thought that had developed along with Neo-Confucian philosophy and to insist upon the more dynamic and practical ideas of government that they thought they found in the original Confucian writings. Most of these critical scholars opposed the Manchu (Ch'ing) dynasty. They denounced autocratic government and insisted that the ruler should be limited and guided by enlightened officials who, heeding the rules established by the sage emperors of antiquity, would be motivated by a true Confucian esteem for the value and worth of every individual. An official, they held, should not be an impractical theorist acting arbitrarily or in accordance with some abstruse philosophy but rather a morally enlightened man of wide learning and practical knowledge of the country's needs. They considered government a sacred trust, reflecting the interests of the people and administered for the people's benefit. Lamenting the inequalities of wealth and power, they proposed the redistribution of land. None of them, however, seems ever to have conceived of any form of government other than patriarchal monarchy. Their ideas were continued into the eighteenth century by the School of Han Learning.

Huang Tsung-hsi, Ku Yen-wu, Fei Mi (1625–1701) and his son, Yen Yüan, Li Kung, and Tai Chen, most of whom have been discussed in Chapter VII, contributed to this critical point of view. In essays on 'Kingship' and 'Law' in his *Ming-i tai-fang lu* (1662), Huang Tsung-hsi developed a theory of the degeneration of kingship into despotism that in some particulars suggests the later theories of Montesquieu. The early sage-kings, he argued, laboured without selfish ambitions, and they established a rule of law that protected and benefited the people. With the establishment of hereditary rule, however, degeneration set in because the ruler came to regard the empire as a personal patrimony and devised laws to promote his own personal interests and his family's at the expense of the people:

'Anciently the people loved and supported the ruler, looking upon him as a father, considered him to be like Heaven, and in fact he was. Nowadays the people resent and hate their ruler, regarding him as a thieving enemy, calling him a 'mere fellow' without any rightful claim to their allegiance, and in fact he is'.[16]

Deterioration, Huang continued, had been especially marked under alien dynasties and had reached new depths with the decay and abolition of the premiership under the first Ming ruler (for the prime minister had previously served as a check upon the autocracy of the ruler); Neo-Confucianism, with its devotion to metaphysical abstractions and its unquestioning loyalty to the ruler, had contributed to the degeneration of government; rulers no longer served as model examples, and officials sought only to please the tyrant and promote their own interests, without regard to the welfare of the people; as a result, the people, taking their cue from those above them, had likewise become selfish and indifferent to the general interest.

Tai Chen was fundamentally more realistic in his ideas, which vaguely anticipate those of Helvétius and Holbach. While he, too, denounced the bad effects of Neo-Confucianism, the tyranny of rulers and officials, and the evils of self-seeking, he recognized that the drives for self-protection and gratification were basic, and he insisted that such drives, if properly channelled, could be turned into virtues rather than vices. The problem of good government was to institutionalize the basic desires and impulses of people into activities that, while satisfying the individual's needs for security, recognition, and satisfaction, would, at the same time, be beneficial to society as a whole.

The views of this group of critics were not widely disseminated and seem to have had little effect. In some ways, to be sure, the K'ang-hsi emperor was a good example of a benevolent despot; Leibniz in the *Latest News from China* (1697) called him 'the Louis XIV of the East'. But in the eighteenth century the Ch'ien-lung emperor turned his back on tolerance, repressed freedom of expression, sought out and destroyed or expurgated the writings of authors who criticized the Manchus, desecrated their physical remains, and persecuted their descendants. Most officials under the Ch'ing dynasty remained loyal to the customary abstract and static Neo-Confucian political philosophy.

*   *   *

Political Theory in Japan

We have already discussed (Chapters V and VII) some of the Confucian writers and Shinto nationalists of this period who made important contributions to Japanese political thought. Practically all the Confucian writers showed nationalistic leanings, advocated strong paternalistic government, and tended to identify native Shinto with Confucianism. The followers of Chu Hsi, such as Hayashi and Arai, generally supported the authority of the shogun and called for unquestioning loyalty to superiors. While they laid stress upon the ceremonial and institutional aspects of government, they also insisted that government should serve the people. The Kogakuha, or Classical, school tended to emphasize the practical and ethical aspects of early Confucian political thought. Ogyū Sorai was more cynical. Arguing (shortly after Hobbes but without knowing about him) that human nature was essentially evil and could be controlled only by an authoritarian enforcement of the ethical and ceremonial regulations established by the ancient sage-kings, he provided a philosophical justification for enlightened absolutism. The Ōyōmei school, to be sure, were followers of the equalitarian tendencies in the moral philosophy of Wang Yang-ming and were critical of the shogunate's failure to look after the well-being of the people, but by emphasizing rigorous self-discipline and devotion to duty, they appealed to the military and encouraged authoritarian ideas.

Kumazawa Banzan, of the Ōyōmei school, was perhaps the most interesting and influential (in long-range terms) of all the Japanese Confucian writers. His *Dai Gaku Wakumon* (*Certain Questions Respecting the Great Learning*), written between 1686 and 1691, was a treatise on government and economics which was highly critical of the shogunate and its policies, insisting that the shogun was only the viceregent of the emperor. He appealed for *jinsei*, or benevolent government: the ruler's first duty was to promote the welfare of the people; he should employ only just and upright officials; he should exploit the resources and products of the land for the people and not as a monopoly for himself or a privileged group. The people, in turn, should assist the lord in securing benevolent government, obey him, and make up for his shortcomings. Kumazawa advocated a lengthy programme of social, economic, political, and religious reforms—among other things, fusing the samurai and the farmers, training the younger sons of nobles as teachers and otherwise reforming and extending education, rebuilding forests, constructing flood-basins, increasing the storage of rice to prevent famine, making rice legal tender, re-opening foreign trade, improving defences, reforming Buddhism, and ending the inquisitorial methods used against Christians. He was also intensely nationalistic.

The ideas of the Confucian writers buttressed the philosophy of the Shinto nationalists. Such theorists as Mabuchi and Motoori (see Chapters V and VII) now came forward with a doctrine that was farther advanced toward nationalism than any in the West or elsewhere: the Japanese were a chosen people, ruled over by a divine emperor, who should be restored to full power in order to bring to Japan, and ultimately to the world, the benefits of the unique Japanese polity, which combined people and ruler in one body devoted to carrying out the divine will. The foundations were thus laid for the theocratic, absolutistic monarchy of the next century.

★   ★   ★

Concepts of Self-Government and Revolution in Europe

In Europe the prevalent and most commonly acceptable form of government during this period, we have noted, also was monarchy—whether despotic or enlightened. Montesquieu advocated monarchy for countries like France, where the king's power should be limited by aristocratic defenders of the fundamental law through their power in the courts. Nevertheless, he believed that despotism was natural in huge countries like Russia, Turkey, and China, where vast expanses and extremes of climate were encountered. Almost no writer of the sixteenth, seventeenth, and eighteenth centuries believed that a country as large and exposed as France (let alone China) could long survive as a republic. The ideal commonwealths of More's *Utopia*, Campanella's *Civitas Solis*, Bacon's *New Atlantis*, and numerous other utopias imagined between 1500 and 1800 were islands or otherwise limited and strategically isolated communities. The history of republics led writers to believe as a general rule that the republican form of government was adaptable only to such communities and that a republic collapsed, as had the Roman Republic according to Montesquieu, when it became a vast and heterogeneous empire. If they were to survive and flourish, republics either must be commercial aristocracies, like Venice and Genoa (both of which, in Montesquieu's day, were conspicuously declining) or, if bourgeois oligarchies, must be bound together into federations, like the Swiss cantons, Dutch provinces, or Hansa cities.

Outside of some parts of Switzerland, democratic government—i.e. by officials chosen by a liberally enfranchised male electorate—though tried several times, endured nowhere but in the small and sparsely settled American colonies of Rhode Island and Connecticut. By special royal charter those colonies elected their own governors and legislative assemblies and did so by a fairly wide franchise. In 1775 the other eleven Anglo-American colonies on the North American mainland were either proprietary colonies, whose governors were named by the proprietor (Maryland, Pennsylvania, and Delaware), or royal colonies, whose governors were named by the crown (Georgia, the two Carolinas, New Jersey, New York, New Hampshire, Massachusetts, and Virginia). Although each of these eleven proprietary or crown colonies had a representative assembly, a property qualification and usually also a religious qualification restricted the number who could vote for its members. Of the eleven only Massachusetts had a property qualification low enough to permit most of the adult male inhabitants to vote, and apparently about half of them actually did. Thus, although experience with representative government was universal in the Anglo-American continental colonies, participation in government was as a rule a prerogative of the propertied conformist and not of the people at large. From these colonies, nevertheless, was to come a great experiment in democracy after 1775.

Other experiments with representative government were made during our period. Calvinist emphasis upon lay participation in the government of the church, acceptance of the electoral principle in both secular and church affairs, and at least theoretical insistence on the independence of the church from the state, all pointed in a democratic direction and (as we have seen) helped to suggest a social-contract theory. Following the pattern of Calvin's Geneva, Reformed consistories tried to exercise political pressure and often exerted a genuine political influence in the name of their congregations. The Brownists (Separatists) of seventeenth-century England went so far as to maintain a strict theory of congregationalism—that is, the complete independence of each congregation from all other forms of control.

Another effort in a democratic direction was that of Oldenbarneveldt as chief civil official (land's advocate) of the province of Holland. Abetted by Hugo Grotius as chief civil official (pensionary) of the city of Rotterdam, he endeavoured to establish the freedom of action of the province of Holland from domination by the Dutch union's stadholder, Maurice of Nassau, William of Orange's son. Maurice was backed by the States-General, whose members were resentful of the predominance of Holland's bourgeoisie. This conflict for political power became merged with a dispute between the mild Calvinists (Arminians), whom Oldenbarneveldt supported, and the believers in a rigid doctrine of predestination (Gomarists), who looked to Maurice for support (see Chapter IV). It ended in the execution of Oldenbarneveldt and the imprisonment and subsequent flight of Grotius. A victory for the Arminians of Holland probably would have advanced the republican cause in the United Provinces, thus making the final outcome of the Dutch War of Independence a decisive republican triumph. Largely in consequence of the Arminian defeat, the Dutch republicans fought a sometimes successful but usually a losing battle against the Orange cause until ultimate failure in the nineteenth century.

The English Civil War and Interregnum, likewise in some of its phases featured by disputes among Calvinist factions, was also ultimately a defeat for republicanism, but it naturally gave rise to several anti-monarchical views. The ideas of the Levellers, as expressed by John Lilburne and his sympathizers, were definitely republican, advocating the sovereignty of at least the propertied people and the responsibility of Parliament to the nation. The Diggers, a more radical wing, of which Gerard Winstanley was the spokesman, insisted also upon economic equality. The Fifth Monarchy Men, an unorganized group of millenarians who read in the Book of Revelation that the Second Coming would take place in 1666, recalled the political and economic views of the Anabaptists.

Cromwell's army, largely Independents in religion, was more of Lilburne's opinion than of the Diggers' or the Fifth Monarchy Men's. Its proposed Agreement of the People was, along with the Dutch Union of Utrecht (1579), one of the earliest written constitutional documents of a republican tinge. It implicitly abolished kingship and the House of Lords by placing in the hands of a unicameral parliament, elected by universal manhood suffrage, a limited political power—limited by a bill of the rights of Englishmen that not even Parliament was permitted to set aside. 'I thinke that the poorest hee that is in England hath a life to live as the greatest hee', one of the Levellers said.[17] Cromwell, less radical than his New Model Army, tried in vain to save the monarchy, but when Charles I was tried and beheaded, a republic called the Commonwealth was created informally, along the lines laid down in the Agreement of the People. With the overthrow of the Commonwealth and the establishment of the Cromwellian Protectorate the instability of the republican form of government seemed once more demonstrated. Yet the Agreement of the People remained a model for Americans and Frenchmen to contemplate in 1776 and 1789. Moreover, the sentencing of a king to death by a commission appointed by a House of Commons that arrogated to itself the power of the people was a brutal fact and no mere metaphysical theory. The world now had a concrete example of the principle that kings could not maintain themselves if they did not have enough support from the governed.

Thus Europe's tradition of social-contract philosophy, going back at least to the Stoics, was time and again reaffirmed during the religious controversies of the sixteenth and seventeenth centuries. Through Voltaire, Montesquieu, and the Anglomania of the eighteenth century, the lesson of the mutual responsibility of governors and governed was impressed deeply into the consciousness of the *philosophes* and their readers. In that century the parlements of France in their intermittent contest with the kings for judicial power issued cogent remonstrances that articulated and gave wide currency to ancient, deep-seated convictions concerning the fundamental laws of the French. The parlements, representing the aristocratic classes, appealed, along with Montesquieu, to custom and historical documents to bolster their case, but most of the other *philosophes* looked rather to 'higher reason' and an intuitional concept of the laws of nature.

Among the *philosophes* the most explicit presentation of higher justice as resting upon a social compact was Rousseau's. His *Contrat Social* (1762) presented a version of the compact that borrowed from both Hobbes and Locke but agreed with neither. Rousseau's natural man, a pre-moral being, was, like Locke's and unlike Hobbes', capable of good (though also of evil). If he surrendered his pristine liberty to form a society, it was only in order to make his natural rights still more secure. He reached that objective by making a social compact that bound him as an individual to the 'general will' of his society. Rousseau, unlike Locke, did not make the government a party to the compact, nor was the government, as in Hobbes' view, above and beyond the compact. On the contrary, the people were sovereign, their general will (which Rousseau somewhat mystically differentiated from majority will) was law, and they could at any time change the form of government or their rulers.[18]

By the end of our period, the right of revolution, the idea that governments might be changed by the will of the people, was rife in many quarters of the Western world.[19] This idea was eventually assumed to mean that 'governments derive their just powers from consent of the governed'. That thought, defiantly proclaimed in the American Declaration of Independence of 1776, had long been maturing as part of the Americans' political credo. It was a credo that had come to them not only by way of the Calvinist doctrine of congregational responsibility, the monarchomachs, the Great Rebellion and the Levellers, the Glorious Revolution and Locke, the contract theory, the popular libertarian *Cato's Letters* (1720–23), and the *philosophes* but also by way of their own experience with representative government.

LEGAL THOUGHT AND PRACTICE

Natural Law and International Law

Natural law has been variously defined. To the Greeks it consisted of the principles of justice to be found in nature itself as divined by reason. During the European Middle Ages the *lex naturalis* was equated with the law of God. The accumulating knowledge about primitive peoples during the Age of Discovery intensified the Europeans' tendency to think of natural law also as the law of men in some 'state of nature', whether 'nature' was the Garden of Eden, Arcadia, or an exotic land. The development of the physical sciences made some construe the law of nature as a set of automatic, mechanistic principles of human conduct and institutions completely independent of supernatural guidance and empirically discernible.[20]

The distinction between municipal law and the principles of divine justice, between decrees enforced by a civil power and axioms of universal reason, was often obscured where positive law was considered merely an effort to attain the truths of eternal nature. When writers like Bodin and Grotius defined sovereignty as supreme political power beyond the veto of other human forces, they not only clarified the actual source of human law, they also reflected the political actuality of their day; in the sixteenth and seventeenth centuries, when national dynasties were maturing into absolute monarchies, a common saying had it that 'as the king wishes, so the law wishes'. But what if sovereign wills were not clear or were in conflict?

For Grotius, author of the work (*De Jure Belli et Pacis*, 1625) that along with Vitoria's *Relectiones* (1557; see Chapter VII) is still regarded as the starting point of international law, natural law was the unalterable, universal, substantive code of reason, sanctioned by the usages of nations (*jus gentium*); it would be valid even if God had no concern for the affairs of men; it might be called upon to fill the gaps left by royal decrees and legislative enactments.

Grotius found more room for natural law in international than in municipal affairs. Among equal sovereigns, he reasoned, mutually binding treaties and commonly accepted practices could be regarded as an indication of their respective wills, and if such treaties and practices were lacking, reason might be applied to discover the relevant laws of nature. Hence sovereigns were, he concluded, as much bound by the *jus gentium* as by their own decrees. His *De Jure Belli et Pacis* attempted to derive from treaties and international practices, as well as from natural law, a set not only of rights but also of duties to guide and control what he called 'the family of nations'.

Subsequent writers on the subject of 'civilized warfare' might disagree with his view that international law was binding in the same sense as municipal law, but their writings likewise advanced the notion of a family of nations modelling their conduct toward one another upon some accepted or acceptable rational bases. Hobbes, Spinoza, and Pufendorf qualified their adherence to this principle somewhat by maintaining that in the *jus gentium* agreements were not binding, since sovereigns could not be bound even by their own treaties and still remain sovereign. But they recognized no fundamental difference between the *jus gentium* and the *jus naturae*, for both were based upon reason, and only reason dictated how sovereigns should act toward one another. Although the analyses of the problems of war and peace by the great legal minds of the seventeenth century became classic, the efforts to prove that international peace and order, no less than domestic peace and order, depended on a basic, substantive law of nature did not have noticeable immediate results.

On the contrary, sovereign states were often conceived of as existing in a state of nature approaching anarchy, warfare being the *ultima ratio regum*. Indeed, the frequent wars of the period made pacifists of some of the most influential writers from Erasmus to Voltaire. The ideal communities of More, Campanella, Bacon, and other utopians engaged in war only for defensive purposes. A few daring men—Sully, minister of Henry IV, the French abbés Eméric Crucé and Saint-Pierre, and the *philosophe* Rousseau—elaborated schemes to assure peace through the creation of greater solidarity and cooperation among the nations. In general, the prevailing atmosphere of rationalism and humanitarianism during the Enlightenment tended to relegate war and conquest to the realm of barbarism or abuse of monarchical sovereignty—an attitude which was old and widespread in China and India no less than Christendom. Everywhere it was equally ineffectual.

*   *   *

The Increase of Law Codes in Europe

In the sixteenth century, leadership in the study of Roman law passed from Italy to France. The *mos italicus* of the Bartolists, who had displaced the glossators (see Chapter VIII), was displaced in turn, by the *mos gallicus*. In lieu of the analytic method by Scholastic exegesis of the Bartolists, French civilians emphasized a philological and historical approach. The new emphasis was taught by Guillaume Budé (1468–1540), French archaeologist, humanist, and jurist, and by Andrea Alciati (1492–1550), who wandered back and forth between Italian and French chairs of law, and it reached its highest point with Jaques Cujas (1522–90). It led not only to the establishment of more authentic texts of the Roman codes, now at last freed from accretions by the glossators and others, but also to a better understanding of their meaning in their own rather than in a Scholastic literary context and historical setting. Hugues Doneau (1527–91), who, like a number of other French jurists, fled from France after the Massacre of St Bartholomew, wrote abroad much of his twenty-eight books of *Commentarii Juris Civilis* and was largely responsible, along with other French and local civilians, for the influence of the *mos gallicus* in Germany, Holland, and elsewhere.

The nascent power of the absolute monarchies had meanwhile led to the crystallization of positive national legal systems. Royal judges brought local seigniorial courts and feudal justice more fully under the control of a royal bureaucracy and made court practices more uniform. The increasing sway of royal justice and of national law was reflected in the large number of codes drawn up during these centuries. Foremost perhaps of the continental criminal codes of the sixteenth century was the imperial *Constitutio Criminalis Carolina* (1532), but during that century came several other legal codes as well. We have already mentioned the Hungarian code of 1514 (see Chapter VIII). Still others were the Spanish *Nueva Recopilación* (1567), the Portuguese *Manuelinas* (1514), the so-called Lithuanian Statutes (1529, 1566, and 1588), the Czech Statute of King Vladislav (first published in 1500 and expanded in several later editions), and the Polish *Correctura Jurium* (1532–34). The Muscovite *Sudebnik* (see Chapter VIII), when revised and extended in 1550, diminished the power of the gentry by giving greater authority in fiscal and civil as well as criminal matters to district (*zemskye*) administrative bodies.

In the seventeenth century, the Cartesian vogue of geometric clarity was added to the political and social pressures for legal uniformity. Among other codes came the Portuguese *Fillippinas* (1603), the Bavarian code (1616), and the Russian *Ulozhenie Tsarya Alexya Mikhailovicha* (1649). In 1683 Denmark received the completed version of the *Danske Løv* from the hands of its absolute monarch Christian V, who in 1687 also replaced the late-medieval Norwegian *Landsløv* with the *Norske Løv*. Sweden waited for her *Sveriges Rikes Lag* until 1734, during a period of parliamentary government. All these Scandinavian codes were intended to cover the whole field of law (except ecclesiastical relations). In contrast, a series of French ordinances (1667–85), including Louis XIV's *Ordonnance civile*, or Code Louis, inspired by Colbert and Guillaume de Lamoignon (1617–77), dealt only with commercial law, criminal law, and civil and criminal procedure. They did not touch civil law, in some ways the very heart of the law. And since the Scandinavian codes were partly casuistical in method and purported mainly to sum up existing practice, they did not resemble modern civil codes either.

Before modern codes could be compiled, a school of national lawyers had to come into existence. They were needed to foster the growth of enlightened absolute monarchies, to convince the enlightened monarchs that codification was in their interest, then to undertake the arduous task of codification, and finally to force their codes through against the opposition of a conservative profession. There were few such lawyers in our period. The only civil code to come into existence before 1775 was the Bavarian Code of 1756, but it was incomplete and designed merely as a supplement to the Roman law in force. Successive drafts of law codes were produced in the reigns of Frederick the Great and Maria Theresa, but the completed Prussian Code dates only from 1794 and the Austrian Civil Code from 1811. In France, efforts at partial codification petered out towards the middle of the eighteenth century, and it needed the cataclysm of the Revolution and the driving force of Napoleon Bonaparte to produce a uniform Civil Code in 1804. Nevertheless, despite their inadequacy, the eighteenth-century measures suffice to show that enlightened rulers sought to place law on a more equitable basis. In addition to the Swedish Code of 1734 and the Bavarian Code of 1756, there came the ordinances (1731–47) of Louis XV, inspired by Chancellor d'Aguesseau (1668–1751) and supplementing those of Louis XIV, the Bohemian criminal code of Emperor Joseph I (1707), the Austrian *Constitutio Criminalis Theresiana* (1768), the Prussian *Codex Fridericianus* (1747), and the beginnings of Frederick's *Allgemeines preussisches Landrecht*.

Royal codes for the most part were based upon the *Corpus Juris Civilis* of the Roman Empire (which in eastern Europe lasted until 1453). Yet each incorporated local differences and national preferences, thus reducing Roman law to a common link among them without creating uniformity of legal practice or institutions. Uniformity was further hindered by the prevalence, in certain areas, of customary law, stemming from the mores of the Teutonic invaders of the Roman Empire, and, in certain others, of common law, based upon the study of precedents. The French *coutumes*, the German *Landrecht*, and the Spanish *fueros* were examples of customary law; English law was the example *par excellence* of the common law. Royal codification, once it included practices sanctioned theretofore only by customary or common law, automatically made them part of the written law. Moreover, some of the customary law of France had been codified as such—that of Paris, for example, in 1510 (thus becoming a model for the French colonies to imitate), that of Orléans in 1560, that of Moulins in 1566, and that of Blois in 1579.

Parts of the customary law stayed outside the written codes, and common law, strictly speaking, never was codified. Besides, it constantly grew as precedents increased. Nevertheless, the tendency toward national uniformity made itself felt even in these uncodified legal systems in the forms of commentaries that acquired at least a semi-official standing by winning the approval of the legal profession and the courts. Beginning with Charles Dumoulin's commentaries on the *coutumes* of Paris (1539) French jurists had tried to build a code based on common usage until Lamoignon and Aguesseau finally attempted, in the ordinances attributed to their influence above, to incorporate the Roman law that prevailed in southern France with the customary law that prevailed in the north. But they had only limited success, and a single code for all of France had to await Napoleon. In English-speaking countries codification was resisted by some legal minds that preferred the elasticity of uncodified practice, but commentaries on English law appeared. Next to Bracton's the most influential has been the *Commentaries on the Laws of England* (1765-69) by William Blackstone, which came in time to serve as a source not only of study for English precedent but of inspiration to codifiers of new state laws in the United States.

Religious law was widely considered outside royal jurisdiction, though its privileged standing was slowly being undermined in Christian states as the power of the churches waned. Canon law gradually became codified in the centuries after Gratian's *Decretum* (c. 1140) had first systematized it, and it reached a definite form in 1563, just about the time the Reformation and the growth of national churches weakened the jurisdiction of clerical courts over laymen and even clerics. The decretals, constitutions, and codices approved by various popes and previously available in various forms were published in an edition of 1671 along with the texts of certain decisions of the Council of Trent under the title *Corpus Juris Canonici.*

The Sephardic refugee Joseph Caro (see Chapter V) completed (1555) a similar undertaking for Jewish law. His *Shulhan 'Arukh (Prepared Table)* set forth the duties and obligations, religious and other, of the Jews, derived mostly from the Talmud. When criticized and expanded by the Polish rabbi Moses Isserles (1530-72), the *Shulhan 'Arukh* shortly became acceptable to Ashkenazi (German) Jews as well. It has served ever since as the basis of Jewish laws in ghettoes and other communities where Jews follow orthodox practice. Before the Jewish 'emancipation' of the nineteenth century, this code held good for nearly all but 'baptized' Jews.

*   *   *

Cruel But Usual Punishments

On the whole, the new law codes breathed the growing spirit of enlightenment. They attempted, for instance, to reduce the number of crimes punishable by death and the special privileges of certain kinds of individuals (mostly clerics and nobles) in the courts. Nevertheless, torture of wilfully mute prisoners was not unknown, the *peine forte et dure* being abolished in England only in the reign of George III. In other countries torture even of witnesses, whether or not prisoners, was permitted in the courts. The *ordonnances* of Louis XIV gave the practice royal sanction, and it underwent no serious change until the *question préparatoire* (torture to elicit information not

S*

essential to the continuation of a trial) was abolished (1780), although the *question préalable* (torture to elicit essential information) continued until the Revolution. The *Constitutio Theresiana* permitted torture, but it was abolished in the Empire in 1776 and all but eliminated in Prussia by the code of Frederick the Great. It disappeared in Denmark under the enlightened minister Struensee in 1771 and in Sweden under Gustavus III in 1772. It was disapproved by Catherine the Great, though not formally forbidden in Russia until her successor's reign.

Severe penalties after conviction remained common, and prisons were usually unspeakable dens, financed at least in part not by the state but by the fees of the prisoners. When John Howard was sheriff of Bedfordshire (1773), he found that a number of prisoners, although innocent or eligible for release, could not get out of filthy, disease-ridden cells, where they had nothing to do all day long, merely because they could not pay the necessary fees to the jailer. Except for such fees, jailers were unpaid, until the House of Commons in 1774 abolished the fee system and provided salaries. Howard's *State of the Prisons in England and Wales* (where the prisons were not the worst) did a great deal to make the world aware of the problem.

Howard was not the first or the foremost in the field of prison and law reform. As early as the 1500's houses of correction or 'bridewells' had been built in England to allow sturdy minor offenders the opportunity to work for pay. Amsterdam opened in 1593 a reformatory for women. Pope Clement XI separated young prisoners from old in the prison of St Michel in Rome. Yet Casanova's description of 'the Leads' in Venice and Latude's of the Bastille in Paris, though they probably exaggerated, did not baselessly malign the jails of the eighteenth century. The continental writer who did the most to awaken the conscience of European rulers to the barbarity of their penal codes and institutions was the Marchese di Beccaria, who in his *Dei delitti e delle pene* (1764) attacked the prevailing system of secret indictments, torture of innocent witnesses, indiscriminate sentences of capital punishment, mutilation, branding, and inhumane prisons.

Enlightenment on criminological matters was a painfully slow process. How unenlightened in some regards one could be who was a beacon in other regards was shown by Blackstone. In his *Commentaries* he wrote:

'To deny the possibility, nay, the actual existence of witchcraft and sorcery, is at once flatly to contradict the revealed Word of God in various passages both of the Old and New Testament; and the thing itself is a truth to which every nation in the world hath in its turn borne testimony'.[21]

This was written over 130 years after the heroic Jesuit poet Friedrich von Spee, who had confessed hundreds of witches condemned to die at the stake had pleaded for an enlightened reconsideration of the subject in his anonymous *Cautio criminalis* (1631). It came about 30 years after the English and Scottish laws against witchcraft were repealed (1738), and almost contemporaneously with Voltaire's, Goldsmith's, and others' ridicule of witch-craft and demonology. Obviously, official cruelty and private superstition did not wholly vanish as enlightenment grew. In the seventeen years (1726–43) alone that Cardinal de Fleury dominated Louis XV's court tens of thousands of *lettres de cachet* were issued, arbitrarily imprisoning those who had incurred official displeasure; in Lisbon the last victim of an auto-da-fe was burned in 1761; in 1771 a Moscow archbishop was lynched when he tried to aid the government during a plague to keep crowds from gathering around an image of the Virgin; a witch was burned in Switzerland as late as 1782, and two in Poland as late as 1793.

★　　　★　　　★

Muslim, Hindu, and Southeast Asian Law

As already indicated (Chapter VII), a noteworthy shift took place in Muslim legal preferences with the rise of the new Islamic empires. The lands under control of the Ṣafavī dynasty followed the Shī'ite version of the *sharī'a*, dividing into two major schools, the Usūlīs and the Akhbārīs, while the Ottoman Empire incorporated the Sunnī version into its constitution. The shift in Iran from Shāfi'ī and Ḥanafī law to Twelver Shī'ite law, however, entailed for the most part only minor changes, and the same was true of the extension of Ḥanafī law in the Ottoman Empire (where, in fact, for disputes that did not need to come before a regular court, the parties continued to apply the law ancestorially used in their families). The development of an imperially centralized system in the Ottoman Empire was more important, for it brought with it extensive legal reformulation. Many local legal principles were integrated with the *sharī'a* system, and both *sharī'a* and non-*sharī'a* (*qānūn*) law were subjected to codification of a sort. As indicated in Chapter VII, Majlisī was the outstanding Shī'ite legist of the seventeenth century, and Abū-l-Su'ūd Khoja Chelebī was the greatest legal mind of the Ottoman Empire.

Under Sulaimān Qānūnī (the Lawgiver) Abū-l-Su'ūd was *shaykh-al-Islām* (that is, the highest authority in matters relating to religion and sacred law). He went far toward establishing an elevated but realistically organized position for the *sharī'a* in the Ottoman Empire, coming nearer than perhaps any other Muslim thinker to establishing effective constitutional principles for a state in harmony with *fiqh* (the recorded fundamentals of traditional Islamic jurisprudence). At the same time, he was a central figure in the process of adjusting Islam to the new conditions that had developed since the time of the Mongols. Heretical groups such as the Yazēdīs and the extreme Ṣūfī *ṭarīqas* by his day had become widespread. Chelebī extended the Ottoman policy of adjustment toward them as well as toward such social innovations as the drinking of coffee.

In India under the Moguls, justice was generally speedy and often arbitrary. The emperors devoted part of at least one day a week to hearing cases directly. Akbar and his immediate successors adjusted the administration of justice so as to allow for the interests of their Hindu subjects. In judging cases involving Hindus Mogul law officers were expected to give attention to Hindu law and custom, though the basic law they administered was, of course, Islamic. Akbar asserted his superiority over the *'ulamā'* in the interpretation of the law, but under Aurangzīb the dominance of the *'ulamā'* was reestablished and Hindu interests tended to be disregarded. At the local level the village elders continued to administer justice by traditional procedures, attempting to settle disputes by arbitration and agreement without appeal to law. Civil disputes that went to trial and criminal cases were often heard by traditional *panchāyats*, or village juries, whose findings and recommendations were passed on to higher authorities for final decision. The Moguls developed a more systematic and uniform system of law and legal procedure than had existed under their predecessors. Under Aurangzīb the Ḥanafī legal decisions were compiled into the *Fatāwa-i 'Ālamgīrī*, which became the first standard legal code of Islam in India.

Several Sanskrit digests of Hindu law were produced during this period. The outstanding ones were by Raghunandana (sixteenth century)—twenty-eight treatises (*tattvas*) relating to procedure (including ordeals) and inheritance. Of the seventeenth-century digests Kamalākara's *Nirnayasindhu* was used particularly in the Maratha area, and Nīlakantha's *Bhagavantabhāskara* and Mitramishra's *Viramitrodaya* were widely consulted. Mitramishra also commented on the old juridical treatise, the *Mitākshāra*.

In southeast Asia, few changes took place during this period in the traditional legal ways and codes. In Burma, under King Thalun (d. 1648), the first law book in the Burmese language, the *Manusarashwemin*, was compiled, and under King Alaungpaya (1752–60), founder of a new dynasty, and his immediate successors a good deal of other legal literature appeared. In Malaya and Indonesia, Islamic law of the Shāfi'ite school more completely replaced Hindu law. In areas like the Spanish Philippines and Portuguese Goa, which came under direct European administration, Western systems of law secured a footing.

Legal Codes and Practice in China and Japan

In China, the Manchus rarely made original contributions to Chinese legal institutions. In 1647 the emperor issued the *Ta-Ch'ing lü-li*, the Chinese code best known to the West. It followed with only minor changes the Ming code, which, in turn, had been largely based on that of the T'ang dynasty, but also incorporated modifications made during the Sung and Ming periods. From time to time, later editions were issued which incorporated supplementary statutes and interpretations drawn up by the Board of Punishments. Several compilations of cases were also issued for the guidance of magistrates.

In the philosophy of law Huang Tsung-hsi was the outstanding figure of the period. In a brief essay entitled 'Law', he underlined the principle that law was superior to the will of the monarch, but his concept of law was more that of *li* (traditional behaviour) than that of law in a Western sense. He believed that the only 'laws' of enduring value had come from the sage rulers of great antiquity and characterized the welter issued by later rulers to strengthen their position as the 'rule of illegality'. Ideally, he reasoned, laws should neither hamper officials in fulfilling their responsibilities nor interfere with the people in the proper pursuit of their welfare. Clearly upholding the superiority of Confucian ideas of conduct (*li* and *i*) over laws (*fa*, *lü*, *li*) in a narrow legal sense, he maintained that the fewer the laws the better for everyone.

The feudal law of Japan was considerably developed and systematized under the Tokugawas. *The Law of the Military Houses* (*Buke sho-hatto*), issued by Ieyasu in 1615, and the *Code of a Hundred Articles* (*O-sadame-gaki hyakkajō*), like earlier house laws, were combinations of ethical injunctions and legal prohibitions supported by extracts from Chinese and Japanese classics. Aimed at preserving the supremacy of the overlord, basically they merely put into writing certain feudal principles underlying thitherto customary practices. Feudal law was further elaborated by various official pronouncements upon subjects not covered by these codes and by precedents established in the decisions of law officers. Commentaries on basic legislation and case-books setting forth the precedents were issued for the guidance of law officers. Punishments were harsh, and sharp class distinctions made them harsher for commoners than for samurai. Since other feudal houses tended to follow the house law of the Tokugawas, in the end a comparatively unified system emerged. It was not guided, however, by any theory of jurisprudence but developed along empiric lines as specific problems arose. The rationalistic element in the system was furnished by certain ethical principles, the chief of which was the reciprocal loyalty and obligation of superiors and inferiors.

ECONOMIC THOUGHT AND PRACTICE

The Precept of Thrift in Europe

In Europe, Protestant theologians generally did not depart widely from the thirteenth-century Scholastics in their attitude toward economic problems such as just price and usury. Luther, like Aquinas, condemned the taking of interest and inveighed against wicked merchants, and while Calvin permitted the taking of interest, he did not approve taking it from the poor. He also agreed with Luther in emphasizing the 'calling' of every Christian to his particular work as a member of a godly society, thus giving even to menial labour a Christian quality. Calvin's acceptance of the validity, even righteousness, of worldly activities and virtues—and especially, of worldly thrift—has been regarded by some as an inspiration and a mainspring of the capitalistic spirit.[22] Others have seen in the lower-class origin of the Calvinists (especially of the English Puritans) a better explanation of modern preoccupation with business. While the Calvinistic concept of the intramundane ascetic life often seems to have led to thrift, and thrift to a concept of worldly accumulation as a result and visible sign of virtue, this point of view was neither originally nor exclusively Calvinist. Economic activities both in Italian and in Northern towns reveal capitalistic zeal in the period before Luther and Calvin; precepts of thrift appear in pre-Reformation books such as the *Trattato della cura della famiglia* (1431) of Leon Battista Alberti (1404–72). Protestant influence, however, took a prominent place among the new factors favourable to secular endeavour along economic as well as other worldly lines. Discount, for example, developed first in England at the close of the seventeenth century—earlier than in Catholic countries—apparently because of a more lenient Protestant attitude toward 'usury'.

Mercantilism and Its Opponents

Another of the newer economic and political developments was the deliberate policy of governments to promote middle-class enterprise along with the landowners' agriculture. Mercantilism became the prevailing economic theory as changes in certain political and economic conditions became pronounced—as feudalism and barter diminished and political centralization and money increased, as trade with the East sucked Europe's bullion away, as cities rose, as the laws against usury became less stringent, as national dynasties assumed absolute power, and as a rising commercial middle class importuned to be heard. We have already seen (Chapter I) how 'the mercantilist system' issued from the effort to create economic self-sufficiency or superiority in agriculture, manufacture, and trade during an era when markets and raw materials were accessible only by slow means of transportation such as sailing vessels and wagons and when neighbouring realms might frequently be expected to be hostile. The objectives of the system were a confusion of political with economic purposes: it sought both common welfare and royal power; it proposed to achieve an independent and prosperous realm in times of peace and a strong, self-sufficient, well-prepared economy in case of war. Essentially, however, it was a policy for increasing domestic revenue rather than international power. Its results were, on the one hand, government interference in the form of regulation of guilds, supervision of markets, tariff duties, excise taxes, navigation systems, and colonial restrictions and, on the other hand, government aid in the form of paternalism, subsidies, public works, royal industries, monopolies, patents, and charters.

The mercantilists did not form a school and so at times disagreed with one another, and some of them contradicted themselves. Bodin was the unintentional progenitor of the French mercantilists. While he propounded a modern-sounding quantity theory of money, recognizing that money fluctuates in purchasing power and that increase in the amount of money may mean only higher prices rather than greater wealth, in his two *Réponses aux paradoxes de M. Malestroit* (1566 and 1578) and in his better known *République* he advocated an orthodox mercantilist programme of high import duties on manufactured articles and explicit restrictions on the export of raw materials. Bodin's ideas were elaborated by Henry IV's Calvinist controller-general of commerce, Barthélemy de Laffemas, who, in an effort to build up native industry, not only advocated a policy of protection and austerity but also of subsidy for manufactures and inventions, in opposition to the influential minister Sully's agrarian preferences. The French poet Antoine de Mont-chrétien in a *Traité de l'oecomonie politique* (1615), without indulging in monetary theorizing, advocated a thoroughgoing regulatory and protective system for French industry.

An absolute monarch could not easily distinguish between his personal economy and the economy of his realm, and so mercantilism won approval in the era of absolutism as good for the crown and therefore good for the subjects. When, in the 1630's, Thomas Wentworth, later Earl of Strafford, was Charles I's lord-deputy of Ireland, he applied the policy of 'Thorough', a new name for the old policy of high-handed autocracy, which in its economic aspects was mercantilism. He regulated the food trade, encouraged the linen industry, raised the tariffs, suppressed piracy, and developed the country's resources at the same time that, in the interests of the English wool industry, he prohibited trade in Irish wool. Under Louis XIV, Minister Colbert developed mercantilism to so thorough a system that its more advanced application came to be known as Colbertism. He regulated the size and quality of textiles—so much so that a certain kind of lace came to be known as Colbertine. He had roads built, rivers dredged, and canals dug. He policed markets. He manipulated tariffs to the point where, somewhat inaccurately,[23] France's war with the Dutch (1672–78) has sometimes been considered primarily a war over tariff and trade rather than religion and politics. He attempted to unite the domestic markets of France, separated by local *péages* (*tolls*), provincial *douanes* (*customs*), and town *octrois* (*gate taxes*), into a single tariff union, but he succeeded in uniting only twelve of the central provinces, those which profited most by free trade with Paris, into a tariff union (*Les Cinq Grosses Fermes*), within which provincial *douanes* were no longer collected. Even so, inside this union other kinds of duties, and outside it provincial *douanes* as well, were still collected. The mercantilists' anxiety to assure free trade *within* the realm, their hostility to interference by foreign countries, their willingness to promote free exportation, their opposition to the clergy's business scruples, and their other efforts to promote industry and commerce often prompted them to talk of 'freer trade', but they rarely meant freedom from regulation by their own monarchs.[24]

More or less contemporary with the French mercantilists were several from other countries. Antonio Serra, in *Breve trattato ... d'oro et d'argento* (1613), advocated an industrial as opposed to an agricultural economy and advanced a theory of favourable balance of trade. Gerard de Malynes, in *Maintenance of Free Trade* (1622) and *Consuetudo vel Lex Mercatoria* (1622), attacked dealers in foreign exchange but advocated a favourable balance in bullion. Thomas Mun's subtitle (*Or The Balance of our Forraign Trade is the Rule of our Treasure*) for his *England's Treasure by Forraign Trade* (written c. 1630) disclosed its major thesis, and he argued further that a favourable balance was measured by bullion alone. Edward Misselden in *Free Trade or the Means to Make Trade Flourish* (1622) at first recommended regulated rather than joint-stock companies such as the East India Company, which exported bullion in return for Indian goods, even though in *The Circle of Commerce* (1623), in which the term 'balance of trade' seems first to have been used,[25] he reversed this position.

In the states of the Holy Roman Empire, where decentralization tended to retard the development of absolutism, mercantilist thought crystalized only at the end of the seventeenth century. Several Austrian 'cameralists' (i.e. university-trained government officials, administrative experts, and political theorists of an absolutist, mercantilist bent) then wrote extensively on the subject. Wilhelm von Schroeder, who twice visited England, accepted and imported some of Mun's ideas. Philipp Wilhelm von Hornigk's *Oestereich über Alles, wann es nur will* (1684) propounded a policy of strict economic regulation that would, he thought, make Austria not only self-sufficient but also superior to all other countries. Johann Joachim Becher (1625–85) in a *Politischer Discurs* (1688) on the 'real causes' of profit and loss among the states indicated in his very subtitle that he was concerned with the question 'how to make a country populous and prosperous'; his answer was essentially to advocate a monarchical paternalism directed toward the stabilization of economic conditions and, thereby, the increase of population. The economic importance of population growth was given added emphasis in the eighteenth century. J. H. G. von Justi and Joseph von Sonnenfels laid special stress upon demographic factors such as employment, immigration, food supply, and housing as well as exports, imports, and trade balances.

Under the growing absolutism of the Romanovs, mercantilism came to dominate the economic literature of Russia also. The Croatian pan-Slavist Jurij Krizanic (1617–83) preached in Tsar Alexis' Moscow the mercantilist doctrine of enlightened absolutism, stressing, however, the need for state control and support of agriculture no less than of trade. Ivan Tikhonovich Pososhkov's *Kniga o skudosti i bogatstve* (*Book on poverty and wealth*) (1721–24) urged upon Peter the Great a revision of the tax system, combined with a programme of austerity and other reforms calculated to accumulate wealth and improve the peasants' lot. Enlightened officials like the seventeenth-century diplomat Ordyn-Nashchokin and the eighteenth-century historian V. N. Tatishchev not only tried to apply mercantilist principles but also advanced them in their writings. So did the greatest Russian scholar of this period, M. V. Lomonosov (1711–65).

Several of these Austrian and Russian writers, while reflecting a mercantilist preference for royal control of the national economy, are not exclusively classifiable as mercantilists, for they gave attention to government finance, agriculture, industry, labour, and other economic activities as well as or rather than commerce. Some theorists of western Europe similarly mark a deviation from orthodox mercantilism, as the realization dawned that money's purchasing power may fluctuate, regardless of its intrinsic value, with changes in production. William Petty's *Treatise of Taxes and Contributions* (1662) and *Political Arithmetick* (1690) departed from mercantilism sufficiently to consider land and labour as sources of wealth and to advocate that royal tax power be used as a means of securing a more equitable distribution of wealth. Marshal de Vauban, Louis XIV's leading military engineer, in a *Projet d'une dixme royale* (1707), incurred the royal displeasure by arguing even more explicitly for such a distribution, suggesting that the royal tax power be used to collect a tithe on land and alleviate the distress of the poor. Sieur de Boisguilbert in *Le Factum de la France* (1706) advocated an income tax for the same purpose. Without being a genuine free trader, Boisguilbert moved from mercantilism in the direction of *laisser faire*. He contended that wealth consisted of goods and not of money and that hence the interests of an economy were best served not by amassing bullion but by allowing nature and free enterprise to work their own way (*laisser faire la nature et la liberté*).[26]

The growing plea for political liberty which we examined above was being paralleled by, and probably was interrelated with, demands for *laisser faire* in commerce. Such demands took hold best where economic growth made a good domestic market appear more desirable than a favourable balance of trade and made tariffs appear more justified as a way of protecting home industry than of securing an advantage in trade abroad. Early in the seventeenth century, Grotius as an advocate of the Dutch East India Company argued in *De jure praedae* for the freedom of the high seas for all nations against Portuguese (and by implication Spanish, English, and other) claims of commercial and naval control. All during the eighteenth century the Physiocrats of France (Gournay, Cantillon, Quesnay, the elder Mirabeau, Mercier de la Rivière, Turgot, Dupont de Nemours, *et al.*), basing their economic theory on their premise of the exclusive productivity of land, taught the doctrine of *laisser faire*. They maintained that the king as chief landlord should be concerned to achieve the largest possible *produit net* for the entire country (and hence the highest possible revenue from taxes) rather than a favourable balance of trade; he would therefore be best advised not to tax commerce or industry.

In Hume's *Political Discourses* (1752) the mercantilist theory was both summarized and criticized. Hume advanced a quantity theory of money; he considered the stock of money within a country a determinant of prices and of consequent economic behaviour in the short run, even if it might be negligible in its long-run effect. He also pointed out the inconsistency between depending on foreign trade for a favourable balance and hoping thereby to achieve national self-sufficiency.

In 1776, as the steam engine began to speed up England's already partly industrialized economy and as the revolt of her American colonies shed doubt upon the wisdom of a programme of tight colonial mercantilism, Adam Smith published his *Wealth of Nations*. Although he conceded that the quest for opulence should take second place to considerations of national defence, he reasoned that a nation's resources were otherwise best exploited by a policy of autonomy in industry and markets: and although he recognized the importance of natural resources (land) in the production of wealth, he insisted upon labour and capital as component factors. He thus laid the foundation of classical economic theory while undermining the hold of old-style mercantilism. The last important work to champion the mercantilist system proved to be James Steward's *An Inquiry into the Principles of Political Oeconomy* (1767).

★   ★   ★

Trade and Economic Theories of Asia

The steady eastward flow of gold and silver, one of the major reasons for European economic speculation, was a cause for concern to the countries that received it, for the influx of bullion and the Western demands for certain Asian products brought higher prices to the Asians. No full-fledged theory of *laisser faire*, however, appeared outside of Europe during this period, for Asian theorists continued to look to government for correction of public evils. On the whole, they looked in vain. Each of the European trading powers attempted to monopolize as much of the trade of the East as it could, and the eager competition among the Western merchants encouraged local rulers to pursue their traditional policy of attracting precious metals into their domains. In general, the Western countries had little else to exchange that the Eastern peoples wanted, and so in return for spices, silks, and other Eastern commodities an uninterrupted stream of precious metal poured from Europe into India, China, and other countries of Asia. The ruling dynasties there found it profitable to continue much in the old ways to promote agriculture and the native crafts and to pursue traditional fiscal and tax policies.

Trade practices changed somewhat, however, as the Westerners acquired influence. The arrival of the Portuguese broke the Arab control of the spice trade, destroyed the Islamic commercial empire of Malacca, and did some damage to the trading activities of other mercantile peoples in the area. The Portuguese tried unsuccessfully to monopolize the spice trade, but the Dutch, after replacing them in the East Indies, succeeded in doing so. Yet Europeans did not completely dominate the foreign trade of southern and southeastern Asia until the nineteenth century, after the British and the French as well as the Portuguese and Dutch became entrenched there. The Spanish from the beginning of their control of the Philippines managed trade as a royal monopoly, but they encouraged Chinese traders and settlers from Fukien, who supplied them with silks and other Far Eastern products in return for

Spanish dollars. Thus the Mexican dollar was introduced into the Pacific area and came ultimately to be the chief medium of foreign trade in China and southeast Asia.

Some Eastern governments made an effort to assure what in the West was called 'a favourable balance of trade'. Perhaps Japan alone of the Eastern countries, because of her demand for Chinese silks, was a steady loser of precious metals. Besides the Chinese and the Japanese themselves, first the Portuguese and then the Dutch supplied Japan with these wares. In 1637—but not for bullion losses alone (see Chapter V)—Japan began a policy of national isolation and accordingly forbade its own shipping to go abroad and most foreign shipping to come to Japan. The strict limitation of Dutch and Chinese trade thereafter reduced the outflow of precious metals to a trickle. Ming China made similar efforts to forbid Chinese to trade abroad but could not keep them from dealing with Japan, the Philippines, Batavia, and Vietnam. It also tried to restrict 'barbarian' traders to tributary relations but did not prevent the Portuguese from establishing themselves in Macao (near Canton) or the Dutch in Formosa. The Dutch were driven from Formosa in 1661 by a Ming adherent, the famous Koxinga (Cheng Ch'eng-kung), during his struggle to resist the Manchus. Once entrenched in China, the Manchus pursued a somewhat more liberal policy toward foreign trade, although they succeeded in confining it to specified areas under quite rigid controls.

The eighteenth century was a period of peace and prosperity in China. Prosperity increased as the planting of two crops per season became common in south and central China and as new crops such as the sweet potato and maize were introduced from the West. In consequence, a rapid growth of population took place. Commenting on this phenomenon in a brief essay on the 'Reign of Peace', Hung Liang-chi (1746–1809) produced a theory of population somewhat similar to that of Malthus (see Volume V). Hung noted that during times of peace population increased much more rapidly than the food supply and that natural checks such as floods, famines, and epidemics did not eliminate the surplus population. As population grew, wages and the average rate of income declined while prices rose, unemployment increased, and the condition of the masses deteriorated. He saw no fundamental solution to this unhappy situation, but instead of leaving the outcome to the chances of an autonomous market, he recommended that government do all that it could to alleviate the problem by encouraging the cultivation of new lands, the better use of old lands, and the improvement of crops, by collecting taxes more equitably, and by enacting legislation to discourage waste and extravagance. In other essays he denounced the belief in fate and speculated on the respective roles of heredity and environment in the ceaseless struggle for existence.

In Japan, despite isolation and the feudal regime of the Tokugawas, a town-centred mercantile economy grew up. As in the West, the increase of commerce was accompanied by an increase in the use of money as a medium of exchange and by price fluctuations, which were damaging especially to the peasants and the samurai. These economic phenomena encouraged the period's most original speculations in the field of economic thought outside Europe. They were in the main a combination of ancient Chinese economic ideas, Confucian moral principles, and practical administrative measures aimed at solving a pressing economic problem.

Shortly after 1710 Arai Hakuseki, as Confucian adviser to the shogun, came forward with a series of proposals for dealing with high prices. In his view rising costs were caused by successive debasements of the coinage, and he proposed as a solution a sound coinage and a great reduction of the amount of money in circulation. He demonstrated a grasp of the quantity theory of money not inferior to that of its exponents in France and England about the same time. His philosophy, dominated by Confucian moral values, did not lead to *laisser faire*. Opposed to luxurious living, he favoured sumptuary legislation and the rigid control of foreign trade in order to limit the importation of luxury items, thereby also restricting the outflow of precious metals.

In 1725, in his *Siden (Political Discourses)*, Ogyū Sorai, of the Classical School of Confucianism, provided a different analysis of the economic problem. By this time, although some prices had fallen. others still were high. Ogyū argued that the fundamental cause of the rise in prices was not the degradation of gold and silver or the increase in their quantity but the increase of demand for commodities created by the luxurious living habits of the samurai who had deserted the rural area for the cities, of the merchants, and even of the peasantry.[27] The programme he proposed included a return of the samurai to the rural areas, enforcement of simpler modes of life by tightened sumptuary legislation, the cancellation of debts, the restriction of future credits, the limitation of interest charges, some managed inflation, and an increase in the velocity of money circulation by the extensive coinage of copper.

In 1729 Dazai Shun's *Treatise on Political Economy* (*Keizai roku*) reviewed the whole field of economic activity. He gave separate chapters to food and wealth, government, social institutions, defence, music, and religion among other matters. His work was a composite of Chinese economic and moral maxims with Chinese and Japanese economic experience. Though it presented no really coherent economic theory, it compares in some ways with the philosophy of the French Physiocrats, who, in fact, also evinced interest in Chinese institutions. In general, while it fulminated against merchants, extravagance, and luxurious living, it advocated hard work, devotion to agriculture, and a simple natural economy in which great value would be placed on food and the necessities of life rather than on money. An ideal government could conduct a well regulated economy, Dazai felt, but for decadent times like his own he seemed to favour an essentially *laisser faire* policy.

Miura Baien (1723–89), about 1775, wrote a short treatise, *The Origin of Value*. He attributed real value to goods and held that economic trouble arose because of desire for money rather than for goods. He developed a quantity theory of money; its only use was as a medium of exchange, and if it increased without a corresponding increase in production, prices would rise, and idleness and wastefulness would result. He advocated the saving of commodities but not of money, the raising of wages to encourage efficiency, taxation of the rich to discourage idleness, and the use of public works and technical education to increase the production of essential goods. During the eighteenth century, along with these more scholarly works a considerable number of popular writings also appeared dealing with such matters as trade, agriculture, and money.

HISTORICAL THOUGHT

The Development of Historical Method in Europe

Whereas European historiography, it is sometimes said, was the servant of religion and eschatological during the Middle Ages, during the Renaissance it was the servant of classical literature and secularistic. While this generalization is only relatively correct, it is true that Renaissance historical techniques centred considerably more than those of the Middle Ages in the accurate textual criticism of Hebrew, Greek, and Latin classics. Outstanding examples of this pursuit were the application of philological techniques to the authentication and analysis of the False Decretals, particularly the so-called Donation of Constantine (see Chapter VIII).

The religious polemics of the sixteenth century, while re-emphasizing the providential interpretation that characterized medieval historiography, brought out more clearly than ever the necessity for careful textual criticism of venerated documents. The humanists' zeal in the study of Classical manuscripts was diverted by northern scholars to Biblical sources, in which they sought not only religious inspiration but also scholarly assurance. Erasmus cast doubt upon the textual accuracy of the Vulgate, the generally used and only church-approved Latin version of the Bible. Luther, in his search for salvation and for factual knowledge concerning the church, turned to the Bible, the Catholic Church fathers, and early church history. What such searchers believed they found was not always in keeping with what the Catholic Church taught, and Roman Catholic scholars, in turn, combed their church archives for evidence in favour of their side. Thus humanists, Protestant reformers, and Catholic apologists all contributed to a trend back to the original sources in the quest for historical truth.

The history of the Christian church which eventually came to be known as *The Magdeburg Centuries* (so-called because it was prepared at Magdeburg and organized by centuries) constituted a strategic weapon in this battle of the history books. Subsidized by several German Protestant princes and originally published (1559-74) as a seven-volume *Historia Ecclesiae Christianae*, it was a collaborative work by Lutheran scholars, the first church history from the Protestant point of view. Using ancient documentary materials, these Lutheran theologians, headed by Matthias Flacius, questioned the historical justification of some Catholic practices and institutions and vigorously attacked the dogmas and rituals, the persecutions and disciplinary measures of the medieval church, claiming that they were anti-Christian deviations from the pristine church to which the Protestants sought to return.

To counteract the impression *The Magdeburg Centuries* made, Filippo Neri requested one of the members of his Oratory, the learned Cardinal Caesar Baronius (1538-1607), to produce a work worthy of rivalling the Protestant account. The result was Baronius' *Ecclesiastical Annals (Annales Ecclesiastici a Christo nato ad annum* 1198), twelve volumes (1588-1607) containing many documents drawn from ecclesiastical archives. Despite numerous and sometimes justifiable criticism, the high level of competence of these two opposing works stands out in contrast to the unrelieved partisanship that characterized most of the polemics in the pamphlet war between Catholics and Protestants. *The Magdeburg Centuries* was the first great collection of original sources for the history of the Christian church, even if not a work of impartial scholarship. Baronius' *Annals* was no more impartial, but it, too, contained a formidable array of rare and useful documents.

The sharpening of history as a weapon in religious controversy led also to improvements in the knowledge of chronology. Joseph Justus Scaliger (1540-1609) found the study of chronology chiefly a listing of events in Greek and Roman history and made it a comparative discipline. A son of the famous philologist Julius Caesar Scaliger, he mistakenly supposed himself a descendant of the ancient Scala family of Verona, a mistake that was to cost him dear. He lived most of his life in France and Holland, recognized as the foremost classicist and critical historian of his day. He edited Classical texts, studied Ancient history, and dated every bit of historical information he could locate in time. By carefully collating Persian, Babylonian, Egyptian, and Jewish chronologies with the Greek and Roman, he provided a *Thesaurus Temporum* (1606), the basis of modern historical chronology. Converted to Protestantism, he ended his career at the University of Leyden, applying his critical abilities to the analysis of many documents that otherwise might have been used in support of Catholic interpretations of history.

Scaliger's most damaging attack was directed at Baronius. He published a twelve-volume work—about equal in size to Baronius' *Annals*—which was not a compilation of competing documents but a devastating analysis of Baronius' use of sources. Although Baronius had made a genuine effort to avoid error, Catholic scholars were never able successfully to refute the major points in Scaliger's case, especially after Isaac Casaubon fortified Scaliger's critique. The Jesuits in particular attempted to defend Baronius, even resorting to a successful refutation of Scaliger's claim of descent from the Scalas. This personal attack perhaps did something to hasten Scaliger's death but little to bolster the reliability of Baronius' conclusions.

Despite rival scholars' doubts regarding each other's methods, a large body of old source materials entered the common domain, encouraging the quest for and preservation of new ones. The preservation of the books and papers of the English monasteries after their dissolution by Henry VIII dictated the establishment (1578) of the State Paper Office (which about three centuries later became the Public Record Office). Similar central state archives were afterward created elsewhere (e.g. Stockholm in 1618). Great libraries were searched for historical records, not least of them the Vatican Library, of which Baronius was director, and assiduous scholars studied the authenticity of the records thus unearthed. Claims of venerability, divine inspiration, or Christian zeal were no longer regarded as sufficient tests, for always the hair-splitting criticism of dubious historians in the opposite camp had to be anticipated.

The Congregation of St Maur won for Catholic scholarship the leading role in establishing tests for the authenticity of historical source materials. The Maurists were a congregation of French Benedictines. Their principal monastery was at St Germain-des-Près in Paris, where they had established a school of historical studies. The writers of this school frequently made use of both unpublished material and printed collections of sources. By the mid-seventeenth century, a good historical library could assemble, in addition to the printed works mentioned above, a compilation of French and Norman writers by André Duchesne and the first volumes of the *Acta Sanctorum* of some Jesuit scholars working under Father John Bolland in Antwerp. With such a library at his disposal the Maurist Jean Mabillon embarked (1668) upon a set of *Acta Sanctorum* limited to Benedictine saints. The authors of this Benedictine work generally applied careful principles of dating, testing, textual comparison, emendation, and editing. When they were criticized by a Bollandist editor for improper exploitation of their sources, Mabillon explicitly expounded their method in *De Re Diplomatica* (1681). He thereby laid the foundations of the disciplines known as 'diplomatics' (the testing of the authenticity of medieval Latin manuscripts) and 'palaeography' (the reading of such manuscripts).

Perhaps the capstone in the scholarly study of medieval documents was the publication of Charles Du Fresne du Cange's *Glossarium ad Scriptores Mediae et Infimae Latinitatis* (Paris, 1678), a dictionary of medieval Latin. In 1688 Du Cange followed this work with a similar dictionary of medieval Greek. Although much medieval literature has been found and published since his day, these glossaries (supplemented from time to time by other scholars) remain the leading guides to the understanding of medieval Latin and Greek as well as early monuments of scholarly lexicography. Shortly thereafter (1708), Bernard de Montfaucon published a *Palaeographica*

Graeca. With the new methods and tools well-trained investigators could detect the general patterns of style, form, idiom, orthography, abbreviation, handwriting, and other characteristics of particular regions at particular times, and so eliminate all but the more clever forgeries and locate the genuine documents in time and place.

By the beginning of the eighteenth century the scholarly application of a series of sciences that historians ethnocentrically call 'auxiliaries to history' had come into being. The sciences of chronology, diplomatics, and palaeography made possible the careful editing of authentic medieval source materials. Epigraphy and archaeology, confined more closely to the field of Classical history, followed the same general lines of evolution. The humanists in their search for Classical manuscripts, coins, sculpture, and other relics of Greece and Rome, laid the foundations of the study of Ancient artifacts (archaeology) and of Ancient inscriptions (epigraphy). When the Roman architect and archaeologist Andrea Palladio (1518–80) published a scholarly study of the Ancient basilicas and other monuments of his city, religious history gained access to Ancient remains as a source of knowledge. By the end of the eighteenth century, national source collections were taking shape —Thomas Rymer's *Foedera*, etc. (1704–35), Dom Bouquet's *Recueil des Historiens de la Gaule et de la France* (1738–1833), L. A. Muratori's *Rerum Italicarum Scriptores* (1723–51), Leibniz's *Scriptores Rerum Brunvicensium* (1707–11), among others.

Parallel with the testing and compiling of original source materials went the progress of bibliographical techniques. In 1492 the learned Benedictine Johann Trithemius compiled a catalogue of church writers (*De Scriptoribus Ecclesiasticis*), a work which was continued about a half-century later by Cardinal Bellarmin. In 1545 Konrad von Gesner (1516–65) began to publish his *Bibliotheca Universalis*, containing bibliographical data on both sacred and secular works in Latin, Greek, and Hebrew. Thenceforth series after series of bibliographical works, especially concerning clerical writers, appeared, usually under the title *Bibliotheca.*

*   *   *

New Subjects of Historical Investigation

Meanwhile, the major themes of historical writing had undergone considerable change. The increasing availability of national collections of historical documents heightened the concentration upon a national and regional historiography imbued with a secular philosophy that assigned a primary role to human designs and character. In addition to his history of Florence, Guicciardini produced a *Storia d'Italia*, the first noteworthy Italian national history. While restricted to events of his own day (1492–1532), it attempted in ten volumes of great—even wearisome—detail to cover the political history of Italy as a whole rather than as a congeries of principalities. Though less famous and less influential than Machiavelli, Guicciardini was (as indicated in Chapter VIII) the more reliable historian; while he had had a hand in many of the events he narrated, his tone was dispassionate and his explanation fair. The Spanish historians Gerónimo de Zurita (1512–80) and Juan de Mariana (1536–1624) told the story of their country—Zurita that of Aragon to the death of Ferdinand, and Mariana that of Spain to the accession of Charles V in 1519. While Mariana was perhaps more patriotic than scholarly, Zurita was a careful student of the original records. The French historians Jacques August de Thou (1553–1617) and Theodore Agrippa d'Aubigné (1552–1630) each wrote a history of his own times, the times of the religious wars in France—de Thou as a moderate Catholic and d'Aubigné as a Protestant. De Thou's excellence lay in his effort to be judicious and to document his statements carefully; d'Aubigné's in his to be circumstantial and lively. Of a scholarly excellence comparable to de Thou's were the historical studies produced by Pufendorf, who was a professor at the University of Lund for a time and at Berlin during his later years. In addition to detailed histories of Sweden from the era of Gustavus Adolphus onward, he wrote scholarly biographies of the rulers of Sweden and Brandenburg.

A rising national spirit was discernible also in the historiography of Russia. Early in the sixteenth century Father Filofei, in epistles addressed to Prince Vasily III, Tsar Ivan III, and others, maintained that after Rome and Constantinople, Moscow was the 'third Rome' and there would never be a fourth. The chronicles of that century (foremost among them the *Chronicle of Nikon*) supplemented the older ones with numerous new official documents, lives of saints, legends, and other kinds of sources. About this time the connected narrative began to supersede the mere chronicle. The *Stepennaya Kniga (Book of Generations)*, instead of recording events year by year, organized them by generations of tsars, narrating the lives of the metropolitans as well. The *Chronograph* (1512) was an early attempt at universal history from Creation to the fall of Constantinople in 1453 centring on Russia; later additions took it to the election of Michael Romanov as tsar. The *Synopsis* (1674) was the first printed textbook of Russia's history (from the founding of Kiev to the times of Tsar Alexis); it eventually went to thirty editions. Thus when Tatishchev prepared his five-volume *History of Russia* (to 1533), which he presented to the St Petersburg Academy in 1739, he had a considerable quantity of sources to draw upon in addition to the documents that he had himself discovered. Gerhard Friedrich Müller (1705–83), a German member of the St Petersburg Academy, who had been with Behring's expedition, compiled a voluminous collection of documents on Siberian history and prepared other extensive works, either in Russian or in German, on Siberia and Russia. The uncritical methods of these predecessors induced Lomonosov to undertake an *Ancient Russian History*, insisting that an indication of interconnections in the historical process was at least as important as the collection of mere facts, but he never finished his task. By this time Russian historiography was not only nationalist in theme but also secular in outlook.

The renewed interest in church history tended to encourage still another method of historical presentation, namely biography. In the effort to rebut the historical arguments of rival churches, ecclesiastical writers composed biographical works in goodly number. Stage by stage Roman Catholic patrology, hagiology, and martyrology led toward an enormous undertaking that should deal with every Christian saint. A forerunner of this enterprise was Bishop Aloysius Lipomanus's *Sanctorum Priscorum Patrum Vitae* (1551–60), but a Flemish Jesuit, Heribert Rosweyde, author of a *Vitae Patrum* (1615), actually laid out a plan for a more formidable series. Finally, in 1643 Father Bolland began the above-mentioned *Acta Sanctorum Quotquot Toto Orbe Coluntur*, which is still in progress. Some years later (1668) Mabillon began the Maurist *Acta* of Benedictine saints, and rivalry between the two Catholic groups of hagiologists resulted in the criticism that, as earlier indicated, led to his *De Re Diplomatica*.

Even before the Catholic *Acta Sanctorum* had taken shape, John Foxe (1516–87) produced a work that was a Protestant analogue. While in exile at Strasbourg during Mary Tudor's reign, Foxe wrote—in Latin—a *History of Christian Persecutions* (to the year 1500), with special emphasis on Wycliffe and Huss. Eventually (in 1563) this work emerged in English as the famous *Book of Martyrs* under a lengthy title that indicates the book's polemical purpose and its method: *Actes and Monuments of these latter and Perillous Dayes, touching matters of the Church, wherein are comprehended and described the great Persecution and horrible Troubles that have been wrought and practised by Romishe Prelates, speciallye in this Realme of England and Scotland, from the yeare of our Lorde a thousande to the time now present. Gathered and collected according to the true Copies and Wrytinges certificatorie as well as the Parties themselves that suffered as also out of the Bishop's Registers, which were the Doers thereof.* Immensely popular in post-Marian England, Foxe's *Martyrs* was refuted in certain details by Roman Catholic writers and so was corrected and republished. A frankly propagandist work, it was inferior to the *Acta Sanctorum* in scholarly accuracy but nonetheless exerted wide influence during and after the author's lifetime, serving as an ever-ready handbook for zealous Protestants.

Meanwhile the widening geographical horizons brought a new concept of world history, which we have already examined in Chapter VII in connection with its impact on theological thought. The common medieval interpretation of history had been based on Biblical prophesy: after the fall from Paradise man would move through a succession of four terrestrial empires, three of which were already past, until he regained Paradise. In 1566 Bodin in his *Methodus ad Facilem Historiarum Cognitionem* departed from prophesy and sought to explain history rather as a progressive succession of racial cultures. Bishop Bossuet's (1679) was the last significant effort to write a world history based upon Christian teleology. In the next generation Vico suggested substituting the sense of human development and recapitulative experience (a view since sometimes called *historicism*) for providential design as the key to the understanding of history, and though Vico was relatively neglected in his own day, Montesquieu, who independently had arrived at much the same philosophy, was not. Furthermore, as the knowledge of the non-Christian world and the awareness of empires unknown to the prophet Daniel accumulated, Europe's historians were required to take account of empires and cultures they could not help but esteem in the Islamic lands, India, the Far East, and America. Voltaire's *Essais sur les moeurs et l'esprit des nations* (1756) spoke of Japan and Peru as well as of Europe, and Montesquieu sought illustrations for his *Esprit des Lois* (1748) in all parts of the world. From Bodin through Vico and Montesquieu to Burke and Justus Möser interest in law, the arts, literature, science, and other cultural manifestations as genetic and organic institutions and in peoples rather than rulers as the carriers of 'civilization' (a new word in the eighteenth century) deepened, and the co-existence of several peoples with different national spirits and regional cultures became more acceptable as a historical thesis, taking precedence over that of an inevitable succession of universal empires leading toward the ultimate triumph of Christianity.

Thus, in the eighteenth-century Enlightenment the Catholic ideal of a world united into one triumphant Christian empire gave way to the view of history as the common adventure of humanity. At the same time, the decline of the ideal of a 'catholic' empire was reflected in a growing number of national histories. The Earl of Clarendon's *True Historical Narrative of the Rebellion and Civil Wars in England* (1702–04), Ludvig Holberg's *History of the Realm of Denmark* (1732–35), Tatishchev's *History of Russia* (1739), Voltaire's *Siècle de Louis XIV* (1751), Hume's *History of England* (1754–61), and William Robertson's *History of Scotland during the Reigns of Queen Mary and of King James VI* (1759) are among the outstanding examples of histories centred upon a national theme. The number of biographies of the heroes of great nations also grew—among them Pufendorf's of the Great Elector (1695), Voltaire's of Charles XII (1731) and Peter the Great (1759), Robertson's of Charles V (1769).

The contemporary vogue of Neoclassicism in literature (see Chapter XI) and art (see Chapter XII) brought with it a broadened, secularized interpretation of the history of Antiquity. Edward Gibbon in *The Decline and Fall of the Roman Empire*, which began to appear in 1776, gave an account of that empire from Trajan's time through the Middle Ages which focused upon Byzantine affairs and the Islamic cultures rather than upon Rome and the papacy, and was none too friendly to the triumph of Christianity in the West. Johann Joachin Winckelmann in his *Geschichte der Kunst des Altertums* (1764), relying on the recent finds in Herculaneum and Pompeii, emphasized the importance of artifacts along with written sources in an appraisal of ancient cultures, and dealt with Egyptian and Persian as well as Greek and Roman culture. He conceived of art as capable of substantive development independent of the lives or persuasions of artists, and Grecian art was for him far superior to the Christian art of the Middle Ages and the Renaissance. Thus, along with their contemporary Voltaire, Gibbon and Winckelmann in different ways made of history a weapon with which to attack traditional Christian preferences, a spyglass with which to sweep an ever widening theatre of human affairs, and a source of a philosophy of progress unlike any that the concepts of original sin and redemption and of the plenitude of God could have permitted.

*   *   *

Islamic, Hindu, and Southeast Asian Historiography

Throughout the Dār al-Islām historical writing continued abundant, usually dealing with the local or regional Muslim community, its learned men, and its rulers. Significant work was done by a series of perceptive Turkish historians, the most celebrated being 'Ālī Chelebi of the late-sixteenth century, who like many other scholars could write prose without over-affectation despite the heritage of floridity from the waning Middle Ages. Late in this period several Turkish historians attempted to analyse the causes of the gradual decline of the Ottoman administrative and military structure.

The Islamic historians at the Mogul court were particularly prolific, producing several works of first-rate importance, which, however, suffered from the defects noted in the previous chapter—narrowness of conception, sectarian moralizing, and flattery of patrons. The memoirs of the emperors Bābur and Jahāngīr, *Bābar-nāma* and *Tūzak-i Jahāngīrī*, had genuine historical merit, but probably the best contemporary history of the period was Abu'l Faḍl's *Akbar-nāma*. It included the *A'īn-i-Akbarī* (*Institutes of Akbar*), with invaluable information on economic and institutional matters; its purely historical parts covered the Moguls from Timur's time to 1602. With breadth of view and eloquence of style, it sang the praise of Akbar. By way of counterbalance, the orthodox writer al-Badā'uni, who also served at Akbar's court, left a rather critical account of the reign in his *Muntakhab-al-Tawārīkh*. Probably the best general history of Moslem India was the *Ta'rīkhi-i Firishta* of Muḥammad Kāsim Hindu-Shāh Firishta, completed about 1620 at the court of Bijapur. In addition to an introduction dealing with Hindu India, it contained histories of all the Islamic kingdoms of India and concluded with an account of India's Muslim saints, its climate, and its geography. Among the histories of the reign of Aurangzīb was the *Muntakhab-al-Lubāb* of Muḥammad Hāshim (Khāfi Khān).

During this period Hindu India's most notable historical works were epic poems. Though not purely Hindu, probably the outstanding one was the *Padumāvatī* (*c.* 1540) of Malik Muḥammad Jāyasi, a Persian scholar at a Rajput court. It dealt in a general way with the siege of Chitor by Emperor Alā-ud-din in 1303. The poet, though a Muslim, had been profoundly influenced by Kabīr and wrote his poem in Hindi, generously embroidering it with details borrowed from Hindu mythology and ending with an allegorical religious interpretation. Many other bardic chronicles were produced in Hindi at the courts of the Rajputs; the *Chhatra Prakāsh* of Lāl Kavi, dealing with the history of the rajas of Bundelkhand to about 1730, was one of the most distinguished of them. The Vijayanāgar emperor Krishnadeva wrote in Telegu a notable epic, the *Āmuktamālyada*, which throws light upon the society and institutions of his reign (1509–29). In the seventeenth century several historical poems on Mysore appeared in Karanese.

The historiography of Southeast Asia consisted of little more than the chronicles and annals of the several kingdoms. Many of them were works of imagination rather than of sober history, and the best of them tended to mix fact with folklore and legend. They were usually defective in chronology, laudatory of their royal patrons, and confined to events connected with the royal courts. The oldest surviving Burmese chronicle, a late-fifteenth-century work by monk Shin Thilawuntha, has a mythological approach that renders it of little historical value. Benna Dala wrote in Talaing (*c.* 1570) a chronicle of Razadarit, king of Pegu (1385–1423). A chronicle written by Mg Kala about 1724 dealt with the Toungoo dynasty, which began in 1486. The *Shwemawdaw Thamaing* was a record kept at the Shwemawdaw pagoda in Pegu over a long period of time. For Siam, the *P'ongsawadan* (or *Chronicles of Ayut'ia*) was compiled about 1680; it is generally more reliable than later accounts. A Pali religious work, the *Jinakalamalini*, put together at Chiengmai about 1516 by the priest Rat'ana Panyayana, dealt with the rulers of the northern Thai area. The oldest extant Cambodian chronicle, completed sometime before 1796, survives in a Siamese edition; it covers about a century beginning in 1346. Laos had its annals, and the *Sejarah Melayu* (*Malay Annals*) dealt with Malacca and the Malay Islamic world. The *Badah Tanah Djawi*, written in Javanese prose, was the principal chronicle for Java. Accounts of Islamic kingdoms in the Philippines were recorded in Moro *Tarsilas* (*Chronicles*).

*   *   *

Historiography in the Far East

Vietnam and Korea compiled annals of a somewhat superior quality, modelled on the *Shih-lu*, the dynastic annals, of China. The *Dai Viêt sur ky* (*Annals of Great Viet*), produced in Vietnam between 1672 and 1675, covered that country's history from the beginning to the seventeenth century. The *Tongkuk Tongham* (*Mirror of the East Country*), which was prepared shortly before 1500, covered Korea's whole history, and the *Yijo Sillok* (*Annals of the Yi Dynasty*, which began in 1392) were regularly prolonged by an account of each reign after its close.

Chinese historical scholarship was probably at its best in the seventeenth and eighteenth centuries Although none of it would rival the historical classics in literary worth, a large body of historical literature of scholarly and critical quality was produced. This quality stood out especially after the critical scholars of the seventeenth century and of the School of Han Learning freed historical scholarship from the biases of Sung Neo-Confucian philosophy. The government continued to patronize the traditional official histories. The *Ming History* (*Ming shih*), compiled between 1678 and 1739 by a group of able historians, was completed under the supervision of Chang T'ing-yü. It was, generally speaking, superior to the Sung and Yüan dynastic histories. The *Shih-lu* of each of the Ch'ing (Manchu) emperors was regularly prepared after his death. Various supplements brought the famous *Comprehensive Mirror* of Ssu-ma Kuang (eleventh century) up to date, those by Hsü Ch'ien-hsüeh (1631–94) and by Pi Yüan (1730–97) being perhaps the best. The *Abridged Comprehensive Mirror* of Chu Hsi was also brought up to date. So were the several encyclopaedic treatises on history and institutions such as the *T'ung-tien* and *T'ung-chih*; Wang Ch'i provided (*c.* 1586) the most important individual effort of this sort. The encyclopaedia was in a sense a Chinese invention, although the Chinese encyclopaedia was more like an anthology than a collection of original essays. The great encyclopaedia of the Ch'ing period, the *Ku-chin t'u-shu chi-ch'eng*, in 10,000 chapters (*chüan*), was compiled during the K'ang-hsi period and published with moveable copper type in 1726.

The most important Chinese historiographical works of the period probably were the shorter monographs by the great critical scholars. These studies challenged the authenticity of early texts, commented upon, supplemented or corrected prior works, or dealt with particular questions within a wide range of subjects such as historical geography, philosophy, government, education, literature, jurisprudence, religion, art, music, politics, agriculture, crafts, currency, folkways, and medicine. Among the writers of such monographs were Huang Tsung-hsi, Ku Yen-wu, and Yen Jo-chü (who have already been considered in Chapter VII or earlier in this chapter). Yao Chi-heng (1647–1715) and Ku Tung-kao (1679–1759) challenged the authenticity of early works. Ts'ui Shu (1740–1816) in *K'ao-hsin lu* (*A Record of Beliefs Investigated*) exposed the 'stratified fabrications of ancient history', showing how the myths of certain ancient rulers had been built up by later writers. Chao I (1727–1814) produced critical notes on the twenty-two dynastic histories. Ch'en Ching-yün (1670–1747) discussed mistakes in the 'fundamental elements' of the *Comprehensive Mirror*. And Hang Shih-chün (1696–1773) attempted to distinguish the verified from the doubtful in the dynastic histories.

Chang Hsüeh-ch'eng (1738–1801), a younger contemporary of Gibbon and Voltaire and perhaps the best of China's critical historians of the period, deserves to be ranked with the world's most prominent historiographical theorists, although he was not so recognized during his lifetime. The chief author of several local histories or gazetteers, he also laid down principles intended to improve historical scholarship. He strongly favoured general cultural historiography as affording the best opportunity to show the genetic aspect of history and the manifoldness of the factors that influenced historical development. His ideas on this subject were set forth in his *Fundamental Principles of Cultural History* (*Wen-shih t'ung-i*), while his *Fundamental Principles of Historical Criticism* (*Chiao-ch'ou t'ung-i*) discussed historical method, especially textual criticism. He believed that 'history is normative in that it provides fundamental principles governing humanity and is not merely a collection of records or reports of events'.[28] The historian, he held, must be more than a compiler, must have broad learning, creative ability, insight, and critical judgment and should be free to shape his history as the material dictated. Chang maintained that too great attention to formal patterns of historical writing had led to a decline in the quality of Chinese historiography. He criticized some historians for having insight without learning, others for having learning without method, and still others for having method without insight. He himself never wrote a general history of the type he so firmly upheld, thus in a sense violating his belief that 'knowledge' and 'action' should be inseparable.

In Japan during the Tokugawa period, as a result of the influence of Confucian scholarship, historiography attained a respectable position. Hayashi Razan, exponent of the official Chu Hsi school of philosophy, began a history of Japan, which was finished by his son, Harukatsu, about 1675 under the title *Honchō Tsūgan*. Modelled on the *Abridged Comprehensive Mirror* of Chu Hsi, it became Japan's official history. It betrayed the faults but lacked the general factual accuracy of its Chinese prototype. Arai Hakuseki wrote an autobiography, entitled *Burning Faggots*, and two historical works—*Hankampu* (1701), a history of the *daimyos* from 1600 to 1680, and *Tokushi Yoron* (1712), a general history of Japan. The Shinto nationalists also were active in ferreting out the details of early Japanese history, but they were interested less in accuracy and understanding than in praising what was native and damning what was borrowed from China.

Japan's most important historiographical enterprise was associated with the Historical (or Mito) School of Confucian studies sponsored by Tokugawa Mitsykuni (1628–1700) and his successors as head of the Mito branch of the Tokugawa family. This school of historians was greatly aided, and their scholarship probably rendered more thorough and sound, by Chu Chih-yü and other refugee critical scholars from China. They were, nevertheless, motivated by a nationalistic bias, which caused them to search for things uniquely Japanese and to exalt the imperial institution. Under Mitsukuni's leadership, a chain of scholars, eventually including Kuriyama Sempo (1671–1706), Azaka (1656–1737), and Miyaka Kwanran (1675–1712), began about 1657 the compilation of the *Dai Nihonshi* (*History of Great Japan*). The first part, the imperial chronicles, was completed about 1709, but the whole not until the early twentieth century. It centred attention upon the throne, providing support for the eventually triumphant conviction that the shogunate should be abolished and the emperor restored to his true position.

THE ENLIGHTENMENT AND SOCIAL THOUGHT

For some historians the period of the Enlightenment in Europe began when La Bruyère wrote *Les Caractères* at the close of the seventeenth century.[29] His indignant reproach of the self-satisfied members of society who either themselves oppressed the wretched or were indifferent to oppression by others and his heart-rending descriptions of the misery of the poor may not have initiated but certainly gave eloquent reinforcement to a nascent trend in secular letters—social consciousness. In France a succession of writers took up the plea for greater social justice. It will suffice here to recall a few of those considered elsewhere in other chapters in other contexts. Vauban sought a new system of revenue that would tax the rich in order to alleviate the poor. Fénelon endeavoured to teach pacifism and paternalism to his royal pupil. Meslier's *Testament* combined an exposition of materialism with an attack on the clergy, urging the distribution of church property so as to give land to those who were the recipients of charity. Rousseau lamented that the prying of tax officials obliged the peasants to hide even the little that they had. Mably and Morelly advocated a system of society in which property would be held in common for the mutual benefit of all. In addition, a score or more of hopeful authors from Tyssot de Payot at the close of the seventeenth century to Louis Sebastian Mercier and Restif de la Bretonne at the end of the eighteenth century set forth utopias that steadily progressed from imaginative descriptions of a never-never-land in the direction of blueprints for a planned society.

The age-old hope that society might be so organized as to provide justice for all rather than privilege for the few seemed more than an idle dream or a devout prayer to men like these. For in the eighteenth century it drew not only on the ancient sources of righteous indignation at social injustice and of pious wishes for a nobler world but on the course of modern science as well. Until the middle of the eighteenth century social betterment was counted upon to come not merely through the beneficence of the ruling classes but rather through the accumulation of knowledge and the improvement of human institutions. Francis Bacon at the beginning of the seventeenth century had claimed that the growing accumulation of scientific knowledge would, among other things, lead to the amelioration of society, and at the beginning of the next century the Abbé de Sainte-Pierre wrote several books propagating the conviction that, by the application not only of science but also of reason to human problems, man could perfect his institutions, whether local postal services or councils for collective international action.

Some of the bolder spirits of the eighteenth century went even further along these lines. The growing awareness that outside of Europe there existed societies that were happy and peaceful, while lending support to an older persuasion—that the fundamental nature of man, 'man in the state of nature', is essentially good—pointed to a newer persuasion—that he is also capable of continuous achievement by his own unaided efforts. Some travellers like the Baron La Hontan in America and Louis Antoine de Bougainville in Tahiti, and some, like Raynal, who had never travelled outside of Europe but had picked up hither and yon consoling notions about exotic cultures, made current an exoticism that was perhaps too roseate and sanguine. Certainly the *bon sauvage* rarely seemed to those who knew him personally quite so attractive as he appeared to the devotees of the current vogue in Europe. Yet the Chinese sage seemed astonishingly wise even to those who had seen him in China. Jesuit reports made literate Europeans familiar with the high level of Chinese culture, and the strife over Chinese theological beliefs between Dominicans and Jesuits in the notorious Rites Controversy at the close of the seventeenth century (see Chapter V) drew the attention of the learned world of the West to several striking similarities between the Chinese creeds and Christianity. Deists in England, *philosophes* in France, and philosophers like Leibniz and Wolff in Germany wondered whether truth, goodness, and justice were indeed a European monopoly and whether the answers to questions of ethical conduct, if valid at all, were not valid for humanity as a whole. No matter how the *philosophes* might disagree about European man, they believed that humanity's lowest common denominator was high indeed. Furthermore, although Defoe's Moll Flanders and Prévost's Manon Lescaut did not find the new Americans entirely beyond reproach, American Quakers, Pilgrims, and frontiersmen were often considered object lessons in the beneficial effects of a 'return to nature'.

This sort of speculation on the comparative nature of humanity was but one manifestation of the current interest in what are now called the social sciences. Man's growing curiosity about his inner nature, about human psychology, was betrayed likewise in a flood of searching, introspective memoirs and autobiographies (of which those of St Simon, Rousseau, Boswell, Franklin, and Casanova are perhaps the most famous), written with candour and lengthy detail for all to scan. The concern with the workings of the human mind combined with philosophical, scientific, and educational factors examined elsewhere (see Chapters VIII, XV, and XVI, for example) to send authors in quest of a better understanding of human institutions. Descartes' and Rousseau's indifference[30] to history was counterbalanced by Vico's, Montesquieu's, Burke's, and Justus Möser's insistence that man could best be understood by his place in history, and his institutions by an examination of how they had come to be what they were. This emphasis upon man as a historically determined being, with institutions that were, so to speak, organically derived from their historical context, gave rise, as seen above, to the philosophical attitude later known as 'historicism'. Where the great historians of the sixteenth century had written religious polemic (e.g.

Flacius and Baronius) and those of the seventeenth and early-eighteenth had engaged in accumulating and editing collections of sources (e.g. Mabillon and Muratori), those of the late-eighteenth sought to explain what caused the growth and decline of cultures (Montesquieu, Gibbon, Voltaire). In general, history taught them as historians the same lesson (*vide* Condorcet) that 'natural philosophy' taught them as *philosophes*—the lesson that man was capable of self-propelled progress and was destined to indefinite perfectibility.

The growing middle class of Europe looked upon the *philosophes* as allies. It believed, for the most part, that enlightened monarchy was the best form of government and usually, as we have instanced several times, was on the side of the monarch in his disputes with the privileged classes. Middle-class spokesmen tended to regard with particular favour those *philosophes* who came after Montesquieu but did not support his plea in the *Esprit des Lois* for a *monarchie nobiliaire*—that is, for checking royal authority through an honoured and privileged social class. Even the views of *philosophes* like Bayle and Voltaire on freedom from an established church—views generally unacceptable to other segments of society—were welcome to many of the middle class—not merely to Protestants, Jansenists, and other dissident groups but frequently also to the Catholic bourgeoisie. Indeed, some Catholic churchmen, while favouring a state church and certainly disapproving of Voltaire's campaign against the *infame*, did not oppose toleration of Protestants and objected to the privileges of the upper clergy. Thus, the *philosophes* found a ready audience for their incisive observations upon the favoured position of the nobility, whether it was in the military services, government, church, taxes, society, local economic organization, landholding, or other profitable and honorific institutions and influential posts. In fact, the *philosophes* rarely originated—more often, rather, they only reflected and articulated—the views of the bourgeoisie on the privileged classes. The levelling of privileges was the common and major objective of middle class and *philosophes*; the feudal abuses and social injustices that weighed down the overwhelming majority of Europe's population was for them an important but a subordinate target.

*   *   *

The Artist as Social Critic

The artists joined in the battle for 'enlightenment' to a much more limited extent than the men of letters. Although the art of Poussin and the writings of Félibien in seventeenth-century France upheld the moral purpose of art and were concerned with showing noble figures and actions and, in a sense, a rational, ethical world, they were not greatly concerned with social thought. Jacques Callot's 'Miseries of the War' (1633) depicted pillaging, fires, fighting, and hangings but in a manner that passed no judgment on war or violence; and his series ended with the distribution of rewards by the ruler at his court, making war appear to have been glorious and worth-while. Satires in the form of prints were directed against rulers and popes by various Germans in the early-sixteenth century, and against Louis XIV by the Dutch in the seventeenth, but few of them can be classified as art. Leonardo da Vinci and, in the seventeenth century, Bernini, LeBrun, and others did caricature-like studies of men with animal features revealing their innate temperament and appear to have prepared the tool of caricature for the service of enlightenment, but William Hogarth, who began engraving on copper around 1720, is the only major figure explicitly associated with caricature before 1775. He, too, revealed the temperaments of men through animal-like features. While his 'Marriage à la Mode' and 'The Rake's Progress' seem mere commentaries on human nature with little expectation that loveless marriages and rakes would disappear (Pl. 23), his series on cruelty to animals and against drinking and his 'Gin Lane' appear to be clearly directed toward the improvement of society. To be sure, scenes from contemporary and particularly carnival life were painted or etched with wit and documentary detail by the Tiepolo family and Pietro Longhi in Venice, and in Genoa Alessandro Magnasco, with much greater fantasy and decorative intent, depicted grandiloquent scenes of monastic life, synagogues, and everyday events of the city. In the art of the Italians, however, Hogarth's moral purpose is absent.

Several painters of the eighteenth century revealed the sympathy for human suffering, the *sensibilité*, characteristic of Rousseau and other *philosophes*. Jean-Baptiste Chardin's paintings, usually dealt with everyday, touching, intimate human relations, and Jean-Baptiste Greuze gained fame for the moral messages of his paintings, dealing with subjects like 'A Father's Curse' or 'The Paralytic Tended by his Children', but apparently they fell short of explicit concern for 'social thought'. Portraits in which nobles were depicted as shepherds or gypsies seem to have been conceived in a completely playful spirit. In Spain the imitation of the *majos* and *majas* ('gypsies') by leading members of the court reached an extreme not paralleled elsewhere in Europe, but this fad can only with some straining be interpreted as expressive of democratic leanings on the part of the nobility. In the tapestry series done by Maella, Bayeau, and Goya in the second half of the eighteenth century various scenes from the life of common people are depicted, but they do not seem to have been intended to convey a social message.

The studied use of art as an instrument for the spread of social ideas was just beginning as our period ends. Jacques-Louis David's expositions on civic duty and loyalty came closer to such concerns than the work of his predecessors, but his paintings began at the point where our period ends. When Goya produced the original sketches of his 'Caprichos' (1794), he made clear his purpose—to comment on the foibles of society—as if he had had no predecessors in that regard.

★   ★   ★

The 'Enlightened Despots' and the philosophes

The so-called 'enlightened despots' fo the eighteenth century, of course, knew or, at least, knew of the *philosophes* and their writings. Frederick of Prussia, when he was not annoyed by Voltaire as a neighbour, considered him a personal friend. Catherine of Russia invited Diderot, Mercier de la Rivière, and other *philosophes* to visit her court, treated them handsomely, permitted their works to be translated into Russian, and had the libraries of Voltaire and Diderot transported to Russia. German princelings corresponded with Rousseau. And yet, great though the interest of the 'enlightened despots' usually was in French social and political philosophy, they were not exclusively dependent on the French *philosophes* for theoretical formulae. They were usually quite capable of deriving their own formulae from their own traditions and situations, and they had other good minds close at hand. The German Aufklärung had such intellectual lights as Leibniz, Thomasius, Wolff, Lessing, and the Cameralists; the Russians had Tatishchev, Lomonosov, Prince A. D. Kantemir, translator and satirist, Nikolai Ivanovitch Novikov, editor and principal author of two courageous serial publications and publisher of numerous books, and T. A. Tretyakov and S. E. Desnitsky, public-spirited professors at the new (1755) University of Moscow; and the list could well be prolonged for these and other 'enlightened' countries. Nearly all contemporary intellectuals, however, whether crowned heads or middle-class critics, tended at least to pay lip service to and sometimes actually to follow the lead of the French *philosophes*.

Anyway, the 'enlightened despots' did not really need intellectuals and formulae to guide them. Opportunism generally was enough to persuade them to be paternalistic, and it was not necessary for their purpose to subscribe to any rationalist theory of human perfectibility or of natural rights. They usually were induced to undertake their programmes of reform not by theories but by practical considerations—by such arguments as that ecclesiastical and aristocratic privileges were a menace to royal power as well as to national welfare and that hopeful and prosperous subjects made better soldiers, producers, and taxpayers than did the downtrodden. None of these rulers more earnestly attempted paternalistic reform than Emperor Joseph II, who took steps in his Habsburg lands in the direction of emancipation of serfs, redistribution of tax loads, confiscation of church lands, toleration of dissidents and Jews, promotion of commerce, uniformity of justice, and other objectives approved by the *philosophes*; yet Joseph made no secret of the fact that he looked upon kingship as a hard-headed business, and once he deliberately slighted Voltaire. Frederick could not get along with Voltaire in person. Catherine enjoyed talking to Diderot but seems to have considered him somewhat academic, and in her later years, frightened by the Pugachev rebellion and the French Revolution, she sent critics of her regime like Novikov and young Alexander Nikolaevich Radishchev to jail.

If the reforms of the absolute monarchs did not spring full-fledged from the brains of the intellectuals, the 'enlightened despots' nevertheless helped to spread the *philosophes*' ideas. Not only did some of the monarchs befriend the *philosophes* and express admiration for their philosophy but they also gave currency to the *philosophes*' writings, patronized their plays, and promoted the academies, clubs, salons, and *sociétés de pensées* in which their latest views were aired. Most of the *philosophes*, in their turn, were believers in enlightened monarchy. The time was not far off, however, when enlightened monarchy would prove manifestly inadequate to meet the rising demands for reform, and then the more radical ideas of the *philosophes* like popular sovereignty, the abolition of aristocratic privileges, and church disestablishment would come to have an almost irresistible power (see Volume V).

NOTES TO CHAPTER IX

1. In Professor R Polin's opinion Calvin, like Luther, participated in a stronger affirmation of the individual and of individual liberties by developing the doctrine of free right of criticism while at the same time contributing to a reinforcement of the powers of the sovereign by freeing them from the bounds which medieval philosophy had often sought to impose on them. Their influence thus tended both toward individualism and toward a self-critical form of absolutism.

2. *Discourses on Livy*, Book III, ch. xli.

3. While the expression *raison d'état* does not appear in Machiavelli, it is clear that a rational political system such as he elaborated must order the means at its disposal in relation to its aims. Moral considerations and forces are, however, included in such a calculation. 'Human actions are judged by their results.'

   While faith in the divine right of established kings may constitute one such moral force, his theory of power based on understanding of natural necessities and rational calculation of the use of force have no common measure. The 'moralism' of this appeal to divine right may, in his view, be no more than a means of 'propaganda'.

   But nothing in Machiavelli's viewpoint prevents the aim of a policy from being a moral value as, indeed, appears to be the case with his own political concept. (Raymond Polin.)

4. *La République*, Book I, ch. viii.

5. *Ibid.*, ch. x.

6. Professor R. Polin indicates an important exception: when life is threatened by the sovereign the contract is broken and each citizen regains the right to revolt. Not the least paradoxical aspect of the work of Hobbes is the fact that the justification of absolute sovereignty is also the basis of claims to the inalienable rights of the individual.

7. *Leviathan*, Part I, ch. xiii.

8. Professor R. Polin argues that whereas Machiavelli calculates rationally the technical conditions of effective political action, whatever its object, Hobbes, on the other hand, calculates rationally the organization of institutions designed to lead infallibly to peace. For Hobbes, political necessity is based neither on religious bond nor on moral obligation, but on the necessity for rational calculation. For him, too, absolute rationalism leads to the justification of absolute sovereignty. The logical outcome of the system should normally be a reasonable sovereign.

9. Professor R. Polin notes that by this theory of law as by his theory of consent, Hobbes was one of the first to help direct the political thought of the Reformation into the path of liberalism. His influence on Locke is marked.

10. *The Works of That Learned and Judicious Divine, Mr Richard Hooker* (ed. John Keble, Oxford, 1845), III, pp. 343–44.

11. In Professor R. Polin's opinion, starting from the principles of Hobbes Spinoza arrived at very different conclusions, setting limits to the power of the sovereign in order to safeguard the freedom of the citizen. He counts heavily on liberty of expression and the resulting education of both citizens and governments to direct the state into reasonable and liberal paths.

12. Professor R. Polin thinks the following points should be stressed: the *Two Treatises*, written in about 1680–82, were directed at least as much against Filmer as against Hobbes. If not actually designed to justify the revolution of 1688, they at least tended in this direction by insisting on the limits to be imposed on the power of governments, whether these were limits inherent in the nature of human affairs (the law of nature, certain inalienable natural laws, particularly the right to judge for oneself) or limits established by contracts based on free consent. Locke, in fact, distinguished three sorts of power, but he did not consider them as truly separate and is therefore very far removed from a theory of check and balance of power, an idea essentially attributable to Montesquieu. It is the concept of trust and trusteeship which determines the relations between the government and the governed; and in case of breach of contract this trust can be challenged on behalf of the people. In fact, the people, the nation taken as a whole, is considered to be the source of all sovereignty, because, as such, it is reasonable. Thus we find expressed here a liberal and individualist doctrine and a theory of the sovereignty of the people both of which were destined to exert a great influence on the development of ideas and of political regimes in Europe for more than two hundred years.

13. Professor R. Polin points out in addition that Montesquieu above all proposes a theory of political government by demonstrating that the successful functioning of a regime of any kind depends, on the one hand, on the compatibility between the nature of that regime and the sum of natural and social conditions in which it is placed and, on the other hand, on the compatibility, the cohesion, between existing institutions and laws and the nature of the regime and the principle which inspires and sustains it. On this descriptive, quasi-sociological analysis is superimposed an option in favour of the liberal regime most rationally adapted to conditions of political life in Europe. Montesquieu opts for a moderate monarchy and finds in the separation of powers and in their reciprocal balance the means of preserving liberties and of checking the abuses and the arbitrary nature of uncontrolled and unlimited power. (See also above, pp. 514 and 539.)

14. Abu'l Fazl 'Allāmī, *The Ā'īn-i Akbarī* (2nd ed., Calcutta, 1927), Vol. I (tr. H. F. Blockman), pp. 2–9, especially p. 4.

15. Professor R. Polin warns that the greatest circumspection must be exercised in applying western political concepts to the description and interpretation of the political thought of other civilizations. The West itself finds it difficult to attribute to such concepts a well-defined, unequivocal meaning. To use them in relation to other civilizations may well lead to a great deal of approximation and misunderstanding. While reasonably legitimate equivalencies to the political and moral concept of the individual can, for instance, be found in Chinese thought, we meet with scarcely any corresponding concept in any other Asian civilization. (See above, pp. 98–99, n. 2.)

16. Huang, 'Monarchy', in Creel, *Chinese Thought*, p. 223. See also L. K. Tao, 'A Chinese Political Theorist of the Seventeenth Century', *Chinese Social and Political Science Review*, II (1917), pp. 71–82.

17. Quoted in Godfrey Davies, *The Early Stuarts 1603–60* (Oxford, 1945), pp. 149–50.

18. The text here is concerned with Rousseau's idea of social compact. Professor Polin expands on Rousseau as follows:

> Rousseau is the century's great originator of ideas and emotions. Natural man, the subject of his study, is man reduced to his absolute essence, to that which makes him human. By nature, man is innocent, this side of good and evil; he is free, each man being in essence the equal of all others; his liberty takes the form of perfectibility, endowing him with the capacity of transforming his nature and of progressing in the course of history.

History is something to which he submits. Induced by penury to associate with other men, he becomes dependent on them and, losing both his liberty and his equality with others, becomes alienated and corrupted.

History is also something he can actively create; by constructing an artificial state on the basis of a contract drawn up as a last free and natural unanimous act by all citizens, conferring on each civil and moral liberty and equality, he can transform the nature of man and deliver him from corruption and alienation, by forging for him a new and artificial nature.

This new man enjoys a new liberty, since by obeying laws he also participates in sovereignty, invested in the people as such, expressing itself in their will, a will which is general both in object—the common weal—and in form—the universal form of reason itself. If each individual decision is taken on the basis of a simple majority by 'the will of all', which is the algebraic sum of the votes of the citizens, it is because the general will, always unanimous and universal, has chosen and established once for all the criterion of the majority.

Thus the sovereignty of the people is founded on the universality of reason and with it, the democracy chosen by Rousseau, for which we would opt with less misgiving were modern man less corrupted and were it possible to establish democratic states in which a limited number of citizens might learn to find happiness and the guarantee of their liberties in a frugal way of life.

19. Professor R. Polin maintains that the philosophers of the seventeenth and eighteenth centuries, Hobbes among them, occasionally advanced the theory of the individual right to rebellion (see above). The greatest of them never advanced a theory of the 'right to revolution' though they sometimes studied revolution as a fact, as 'an appeal to Heaven' as Locke put it, in case of a breach of contract between sovereign and people. They avoided postulating a regime in which revolution would appear as a right. They were generally content to consider various forms of resistance capable of insertion in the legal framework. Only one constitution, moreover, was to inscribe among its principles the right to revolution: the French Constitution of 1793, which was never put into force.

   The text defines 'the right of revolution' as 'the idea that governments might be changed by the will of the people'. That idea the authors find not only in Locke but also in the American Declaration of Independence and (if they were to go beyond 1776) in the French Declaration of Rights of 1789, which included 'resistance to oppression' as one of the four 'natural and inalienable rights of men'.

20. The theory of the law of nature, barely outlined in certain rare texts of Plato and Aristotle, was developed by the Stoics, in particular in Rome, as the law expressing the nature of man and constituting an obligation, both in respect of the individual and in relations between men. For them, this law, perceived by reason, was the voice of reason itself. Christian thought was on occasion also to consider it somewhat as the voice of God. And these two traditions continued to mingle with or confront one another right down to the modern era, the rationalist interpretation tending during the seventeenth and eighteenth centuries to dominate the religious interpretation, which, however, remained almost always present in the background. At all events it never ceased to form the basis of an obligation, essentially moral in character. (Raymond Polin.)

21. Quoted in Preserved Smith, *A History of Modern Culture*, Vol. II: *The Enlightenment 1687–1776* (New York, 1934), p. 530.

22. E.g. Max Weber, *Die protestantische Ethik und der Geist des Kapitalismus* in *Gesammelte Aufsätze zur Religionssoziologie* (3 vols.; 1922–23), Vol. I, part 1, translated by Talcott Parsons as *The Protestant Ethic and the Spirit of Capitalism* (New York, 1950); R. H. Tawney, *Religion and the Rise of Capitalism* (London, 1926); and Ernst Troeltsch, *Die Soziallehren der christlichen Kirchen und Gruppen* in *Gesammelte Schriften* (4 vols.; Tübingen, 1912–25), Vol. I, translated by Olive Wyon as *The Social Teaching of the Christian Churches* (2 vols.; London, 1931). For a discussion of the literature on this subject see M. M. Knappen, *Tudor Puritanism, A Chapter in the History of Idealism* (Chicago, 1939), especially pp. 341–53 and 513–14; Robert W. Green (ed.), *Protestantism and Capitalism: the Weber Thesis and Its Critics* (Boston, 1959); and Raymond

de Roover, *L'Evolution de la lettre de change, XIV–XVIIIe siècles* (Paris, 1953), pp. 144–46. See also above, p. 321 n. 61.

23. See Herbert H. Rowen, 'John DeWitt and the Triple Alliance', *Journal of Modern History*, XXVI (1954), p. 14, n. 75.

24. See E. A. J. Johnson, *Predecessors of Adam Smith, the Growth of British Economic Thought* (New York, 1937), pp. 61–69 and 142–57.

25. *Ibid.*, p. 62.

26. Quoted in E. R. A. Seligman, 'Boisguillebert', *Encyclopedia of the Social Sciences* (New York, 1937), II, p. 620.

27. See N. S. Smith, 'An Introduction to Some Japanese Economic Writings of the 18th Century', *Transactions of the Asiatic Society of Japan*, XI (1934), p. 72.

28. Han Yu-shan, *Elements of Chinese Historiography* (Hollywood, 1955), pp. 165–66; see also David S. Nivison, 'The Problem of "Knowledge" and "Action" in Chinese Thought since Wang Yang-ming' in Arthur F. Wright (ed.), *Studies in Chinese Thought* (Chicago, 1953), pp. 126–34.

29. See Philippe Sagnac, *La Formation de la société française moderne* (Paris, 1945), I, pp. 152–53.

30. Professor R. Polin points out that while Rousseau indeed devoted no work to historical science, he was, however, a great reader of history and laid much insistence on the role of history in education. Moreover, his *Discourse on the origin of inequality* is entirely devoted to speculation on the history of humanity. It can even be said to constitute a philosophy of history which is one of the vital sources of the philosophy of history of Kant and Hegel.

   The authors agree, on the whole, with this remark. The implication that Rousseau was indifferent to history is based upon his attitude that where historical experience conflicted with a logical construction, historical experience could be disregarded. This attitude is to be found in the Discourse on Inequality ('Let us begin by getting rid of facts, for they do not touch our question') and the Social Contract ('How has this change [from freedom at birth to chains] come about. I do not know. What can render it legitimate? I believe I can settle this question'.) Rousseau keeps Emile away from history books until his later teens and then (Book IV) finds little good to teach him in the historians (except for Plutarch).